Cauldron of the Gods

Frontispiece: Fragment from the sandstone pillar from Pfalzfeld, c. 400 BCE. Up to the 17th century the pillar had a height of c. 2,20 m and may have stood on top of an unknown burial mound. Today, after being moved several times, it has a height of 1,48m

Cauldron of the Gods

A Manual of Celtic Magick

Jan Fries

Mandrake of Oxford

Copyright © Year III (2003)
by Jan Fries and Mandrake of Oxford
First English Edition
ISBN 1869928 61x (paperback)
ISBN 1869928 709 (hardback)

Published by
Mandrake of Oxford
PO Box 250
OXFORD
OX1 1AP (UK)

A CIP catalogue record for this book is available from the British Library and the US Library of Congress.

A note of caution

The study of prehistory has made so much progress over the last decades that many of the generalizations of the sixties and seventies are seriously outdated today. As this development continues, some of my remarks will inevitably be invalidated by the time this book reaches you. Let me ask you not to trust my words but to do your own research

Contents

Note on spelling: Names in Medieval manuscripts do not have a standard form. There are many variations, sometimes even within a single text. As the sources vary, so does my use of the names in this book. When consulting the index look out for alternatives

Nemetona, goddess of the sacred grove.

0. Introduction: Welcome to the Nemeton.

Let me introduce you to three words of the Gaulish language: brixtia, *nerto and *nemetos.

Brixtia or brictia is *magic*. We find a later version of it in the old Irish bricht, *magical formula, spell, enchantment*. Brixtia can refer to a great deal of different activities. Many of them are related to speech, sound and poetry. Among the Celts we have evidence for spell craft, invocations, prayer, biting satire, curses and prophecies that come true. People enjoyed blessings, protective formulae, riddles and storytelling. Now Crowley defined Magick 'as the science and art of causing change to occur in conformity with will'. To do so, true will has to be focused and expressed in some way. We have to rely on images and symbols to communicate will. The magician communicates will, and will can be expressed in many ways. The Celtic mages and sorcerers used words for much of their brixtia, but when we look closely into their

art much more can be discovered. A word is a stimulant for imagination, and imagination, especially when it is trained and inspired, is the mainspring of all magic. There is the language of gestures for example. Dancers (occasionally nude) and ritual celebrants appear in pre-Roman Celtic art and masked or half-human figures, often with animal attributes, are a common theme of Celtic coins. Song and music had their part in ritual, cult and ceremony; think of rattles, jingling metal pieces, pan pipes, bronze trumpets and simple harps. Sacred architecture is another such language. The symbolism of natural spaces of worship and even more so the images and symbolism inherent in temple buildings, mounds, ditches, pillars, sacrificial pits, wells, ceremonial avenues and square enclosures. Then there is the language of sacrifices and offerings. Our prehistoric Celts were highly systematic about what they sacrificed and how they did it. The same goes for burial customs, the rites that ensured the safe passage of the deceased to the otherworld,

---

* For those not familiar with it, the star in front of a word means that it is reconstructed.

and protected the community from the return of the 'dangerous dead'. And the language of symbolic acts. To bless a talisman, to stab an enemy effigy, to bury a message to the gods of the underworld, to cut a plant with special rites, to go on a field procession… all of these are parts of a language.

*Nerto is power and strength. It is related to *narito - *magically strengthened*, and goes back to the Indo-European *ner- meaning *creative force*, or *magical energy*. Nerto is force, the energy and power that makes the ritual work. This power can be understood on many levels. On the physical level, it appears as life energy, vitality and joy. It also informs and inspires special places, natural or man-made, which invite ritual, such as the cliffs and pinnacles preferred by Hallstatt time Celts for open air sacrifices, or the holes, pits, wells and cult-shafts favoured in the La Tène period. Sacred spaces, temple architecture, images, symbols and the like have the purpose of making the neirto more intense. The same goes for costume, masks, ritual tools and sacred objects. Nerto infuses brixtia with life, nerto feeds the gods, nerto connects us with all living beings. When you communicate with the gods, a certain amount of nerto keeps the contact clear and the visions steady. In the old days, this was done by sacrifices of animals, foodstuff, drink, valuables and occasionally humans. Such sacrifices produced emotion, and emotion is what the gods and spirits require for manifestation. Nowadays, other formula have proved far more efficient. In ritual, nerto can be raised by passionate dancing, wild music, prolonged prayer, chanting, rhythmic breathing, shaking and swaying,

exhaustion, intense lust and any other activity that produces strong emotion, lucid awareness, joy, rapture and ecstasy. These forces are channeled using imagination and focused according to belief. Nerto can also be produced using less pleasant emotions, such as fear, horror and revulsion, or through hunger, longing and doing-without. Remember that different approaches tend to produce different qualities of nerto. In ritual and magic, the important issue is that the emotional energy should be congruent with the spirit, deity or force invoked. If you call on a love deity you need an entirely different state of mind than during a rite that raises the war gods. If you work the rite on your own, you need imagination, identification and play-acting. Done for the community, masks, costumes and symbolic acts may be of use to stimulate emotion.

When nerto and brixtia combine, we get a powerful ritual that spells a message to the otherworld. Who receives the message? Who works the change? Who responds to the call and makes the spell come true?

*Nemetos - means *of sacred nature* and refers to any experience or consciousness of the divine.

Before we set out to explore the notion of sacredness, you may like to consider just what seems sacred to you. How do you recognize the holy, the sacred, the transcendental? When do you sense the quality of the divine? When have you had the experience of something sacred? Was it combined with a deity, a place, a setting, a time, season, were other persons or life-forms involved? Are there sites, seasons, days or times that are holy to you? To the Celts, as far as we know, much of the

Nantosuelta

quality of sacredness was manifest in sacred groves, or so the Roman authors tell us. Apart from the poet Lucan, whom you'll meet later on, they did not bother to record what such a grove looks like, and how you can tell its difference from any other bit of woodland. Archaeology can likewise contribute very little insight, as groves tend to leave very little evidence behind, unless there is some small shrine or building in them, or a barrier that divides the sacred space from the everyday world. This was occasionally the case, especially in Gaul of the middle and late La Tène period. Worship in earlier times is much harder to explore. However, the real question is not what Celtic groves looked like. It may be much more interesting to explore what they look like to you.

How would you imagine a sacred grove? This is a chance to do some dreaming. Settle down, take a few deep breaths, calm down, relax, close your eyes and imagine how you would like your grove. Take your time and enjoy. Would the place be in the mountains, hills, valleys or plains? Is there water nearby-a spring, a stream, a lake or swamp? And what is it like inside the grove? Are there stones, rocks or caves? Aged trees and swaying bushes, thickets, shelters, open places? Is the grove cultivated in any way? Can you see trophies, sacrifices, statues of wood or stone? Are there paths? What about sacred plants or animals?

There is a lot you can discover as you build up your nemeton. This is a Gaulish term deriving from *nemetos- of sacred nature. To the numerous Celtic tribes, nemetons could mean a number of different things. Some of them were sacred groves, others were meeting spaces, had religious buildings and temples and so on. One in central Turkey was called drunemeton, which might mean *oak-sacred grove*. However not all nemetons were oak groves. There is good evidence that many sorts of trees were held sacred by one Celtic tribe or another. Lucan gives a gripping account of a sacred grove some distance from Massilia (Marseilles), which Caesar cut down to use the wood for a siege. The grove, so Lucan rhymed, was a darksome shady place of fearful silence where no birds sang or beasts roamed. Here the tree-trunks stood smeared with gore, black against the sky. At glaring noon and darkest midnight the deity of the grove was known to make its rounds, and at these times, neither worshippers nor priests dared to visit the place.

No wanton breezes toss the dancing leaves,
But shivering horror in the branches heaves.
Black springs with pitchy streams divide the ground,
And bubbling tumble with a sullen sound.
Old images of forms misshapen stand,
Rude and unknowing of the artists hand;
With hoary filth begrimed each ghastly head
Strikes the astonished gazer's soul with dread…
Oft, as fame tells, the earth in sounds of woe
Is heard to groan from hollow depths below,
The baleful yew, though dead, has oft been seen
To rise from earth, and spring from dusty green;
With sparkling flames the trees unburning shine,
And round their boles prodigious serpents twine.

Pharsalia, 3, 605, translation Rowe.

This gloomy atmosphere did not detain Caesar from having the trees cut. Seeing his soldiers, many of them recruited in Gaul and familiar with sacred groves from their own worship, afraid of the task he spoke: 'Cut you the wood and let the guilt be mine' and attacked a mighty oak with an axe. Soon his soldiers were busy cutting ash, holly, alder and cypress, much to the dismay of the locals.

Trees and plants could be sacred, so many Celtic people thought, and the same applied to animals. Again, abstraction is part of this belief. Species of beasts and plants, as you will read further one, were not sacred as such. More often, a given beast or plant could manifest the energies and sentience of a deity. Here we are dealing with gods who appear in many guises. Who were the gods of the early Celts? We don't know much about the religions of the Hallstatt time, but the later La Tène Celts left us a number of religious statues. This was quite a development. The early Hallstatt time Celts were remarkably shy about naturalistic representations of humans or animals, let along deities in human form. They were aware that such things could be done (as they imported decorated Greek pottery goods and pieces of art) but rarely made a try. This tendency is so surprising, considering how good the artists and craftsmen of the time were, that we are possibly dealing with a religious taboo. When these people worshipped, they often made do with something basic, such as a simple wooden statue or a standing stone with a crude face carved into it. So crude that it seems primitive. But what motivated these people to make a crude image of a

deity when they could have easily produced a magnificent piece of bronzework or finely sculptured sandstone? Some Celts did this. Others, and they are in the majority-did not. It was only well into the La Tène period that most gods came to acquire a cultivated shape. After all, a lot of Celts had been traveling, and while they first laughed about the simple-mindedness of the Greeks to worship their gods in human form (this happened when Delphi was sacked) sooner or later they acquired the taste. After the Romans had occupied Gaul and put the Druids out of business, the surviving religions picked up the Mediterranean fashion and began to produce local variations of Roman prototypes. This started the so called Gallo-Roman Style, and more statues, altars and inscriptions of Celtic gods than ever. All of this goes to show that the representation of the divine change. If you think of a deity, you require a certain amount of imagination to form a link. The deity needs a form (or many) to communicate. When you have a religion that makes little use of anthropomorphic idols, or keeps them so simple that they cannot be mistaken for human beings except when one is really spaced out in the middle of the night, you have to offer and perceive your gods in other forms. Here nature shakes a welcoming branch and offers entrance to the wildwood consciousness. When you are out in the living world, preferably on your own or with understanding, silent friends, you may find that lots of special things are happening all the time. Chatter hides them, swiftness hides them, but when you slow down and open up everything is here. Nature is full of insights and initiations. That's why the Druids taught in hidden places deep in the forest, that's why the bards and poets went for walks in the wilderness. To understand the earlier Celtic gods, you have to seek them everywhere. This gives us a concept of deities that is partly abstract and based on non-definition. In another sense, manifestation is possible in a multitude of ways. If the world is a language, the gods express themselves in some nouns, some adjectives and a lot of verbs. Celtic gods are often accompanied by animals. Some of them are partly animal, and some completely so. Arduinna, goddess of the Ardennes forest, rides a boar. Artio and Andarta are bear-goddesses, Matunus and Artaios are bear gods. Cernunnos bears the horns of a stag and holds a horned serpent. Ravens and crows are generally associated with deities of war and death. Nantosuelta is often accompanied by crows, maybe a hint that her name, Winding River, refers to the path of the dead, the milky way. Her spouse Sucellus, the Good Striker, appears holding a hammer/club and a vessel. He is in the company of a dog or wolf. Verbeia holds serpents, Epona rides horses and donkeys, Tarvos Trigaranus is the Bull with the three Cranes. Cocidius comes with stag and dog, another dog-deity is Cunomaglus, the Lord of Hounds. Damona is a cattle goddess, Sirona of the stars bears a serpent and three eggs. And think of the many animal statuettes, fibula and ornaments that came up in Celtic tombs! When you find a large bronze boar in a tomb, you may be certain that the animal was probably not revered for its boarishness but as a symbol for a divine sentience and energy. When a god can look like a beast, that beast, encountered

in the wild, may be an incarnation of divine sentience. Did any of the Celts believe in sacred animals? We are happy to have some data on Celtic diet, thanks to archaeological analysis of bones and foodstuff. From what we know they hunted anything. No species as such were spared by the community (though possibly by individuals, as later Irish myths hints) and so we have to consider whether any animal was thought sacred, or whether it was only particular animals, under particular circumstances, that had a divine quality. The ones sensed in trances, in visions, in dreams, encountered under ritual circumstances and so on. The same may apply to plants and trees. While oak was certainly a sacred wood to some Celts, this did not stop them from cutting large amounts of it in order to fortify their ring walls.

What is sacred to you? Is a given animal species sacred to you, or is it only animals imbued with the divine that come under this category? If some tree is sacred - does this apply to all members of the species or is it a special quality acquired by a select specimen?

What if we leave the idea of sacred THINGS and move to a quality of sacredness that reveals itself in an open mind? Nemetos. A consciousness of sacredness, a truly awakened mind delighting in the wonder of the world. Something you do in your mind to recognize that there are marvels and miracles in the world, in yourself and everywhere. An activity that changes your mind so intensely that it shakes, shatters, exalts, confirms and creates anew. The sacred is often very new, just as each ritual is not a repetition of an earlier event, but the original event itself. There are no copies, only originals. Nemetos means that you sense this, in every ritual, every experience, every chance you have to perceive and wake up and come to yourself. What takes you beyond yourself? How much do you need to realize? This quality of awareness is one of the hidden elements in Celtic religion. How do you recognize when a particular tree is sacred? How do you know if an event is an omen or simple coincidence? When is the flight of birds, the shape of a cloud or the weaving of a spider of significance? The answer, of course, is your own. Just as you craft the dream of life in your mind and travel your circuit, you also equip it with gates and passages leading beyond. How can you cultivate the joy of holiness, of wholeness, in your life? As the Celts declared certain sites a nemeton, they also named a goddess Nemetona. Hardly anything is known of her, apart from a couple of inscriptions from occupied Gaul, Germany and Britain. They show that she was important and widely known, just as the nemetons were, but with regard to her iconography, mythology and ritual, nothing survived. Was the goddess worshipped in an anthropomorphic shape? Or did she appear laughing in the screech of the crows, the flapping of dark wings, the gentle touch of somber evergreens, the gurgling of a brook or the gusts of the ghostwind in the shaking, trembling trees? Imagine eyes that glare like amberfire rowan berries, the pupils tiny, focused, opening up, glowing dark and shiny with deadly nightshade sweetness, then pale, the sightless gaze of a dead fish turning slowly in a pool, unblinking, the steady gaze of the viper in morningmoist heather, then lighting up in chiming starlight, a song returning to its source. Imagine skin of roots and bark, tangle and lichens, fur and scales, feathers and raw earth. Imagine teeth like gleaming quartz, like sharpened flint, bent cruelly like bramble thorns to grasp and hold and tear. Imagine faces, glaring, wild, a-swoon, delirious with lust that appear and disappear, materializing out of whatever is handy in the scenery. And remember the quality of awareness that makes all this possible. Some of the joy and passion of these experiences has gone into the drawings of this book. Many of the more fantastic pictures were inspired by evocations and obsession trances with Nemetona, who proved a very elusive and enchanting ancient deity. But perhaps the concept deity is misleading here. Nemetona personifies the quality of sacredness itself, the matrix of consciousness which permits the gods and spirits to manifest. Not an easy entity - the concept of sacredness can verge on sheer horror, shock or madness on occasion - but one that may be worth encountering if you really wish to dream your way into Celtic magick, and bring back something new and worthwhile from the foaming cauldron. Nemetona opened the way for other deities. Artio of the mountains of the beginning appeared, breaking open the gates of the deep realm. Cernunnos dancing in the moonbright, darknight forest. Nantosuelta leading the souls along the long, flowing river of stars to the four cornered fortress in the center of the sky. Sucellos brewing the ingredients of enchantment in his cauldron, striking the earth to make the

seasons change. The Celts had many gods as their concept of the divine had many faces.

Celtic art is one of the keys to this book. While the priests, Druids and sorceresses left no sacred texts for later generations, they did produce works of art that can act as dream keys to their secret lore. To understand what these items are able to tell you, use them as a focus for a trance. Gaze into the image, empty your mind, calm down, allow the silence to surround you, listen to the voidness as you gaze and feel…when you are empty, silent and absent, you come very close to the secret self of all awareness…and before long you will find the lines moving, colours appearing, things shifting, simplifying, transforming…and as you sense this you can delight in the awareness that the images are speaking with the deep mind and that before long - an instant, a day or a month - the communion will stimulate your mind, your being, your reality, like the moon breaking out of the clouds, like the sun after the rainstorm, like the thundering surge of the ninth wave. This is a gentle and subtle form of magick much like the consecration of sigils. It works best when you enjoy it, relax and go with the flow.

The abstract - remember how we started out with abstraction? - is more than obvious in Celtic art. Celtic art is mainly religious, it is also deeply concerned with perception and the mysteries of awareness. Many pieces of art can be interpreted in several ways, this may well be the original intent of the artists. You discern a face, then an entire figure, then a scene in what a moment earlier had been a senseless array of bubbles, leaves, blossoms and tubes. This is another hidden quality in Celtic art and magick: multiple points of view. The god who transforms into a beast explores the world in several shapes. The worshipper who realizes her/his identity with the gods leaves the confinement of a single personality. The priest, shaman or sorcerer who becomes obsessed by a god or beast partakes of the qualities of either, and manifests them for some end, such as a healing rite, a seasonal ritual or the banishing of a malignant influence. Gods can be human and humans can be gods. If the god is also a beast, our shapeshifter may get both sorts of awareness at once. If you have read *Visual Magick* (and done the exercises) you may be aware that obsession by a spirit animal can transform awareness and abilities. Shapeshifting is such an important part of Celtic myth and sorcery that we may speak of shamanic trance techniques (though not necessarily of shamanic healing rituals).

Be that as it may, what seems initially confusing tends to reveal meaning as you go along. We follow a crooked path through the forest of shadows when we seek the vision of the ever old, ever young, always

---

Overleaf: Cult wagon of Strettweg, Steiermark, Austria. Ha C, 7th century BCE, bronze. Height of central goddess 22.6 cm. The item seems to show some sort of ceremonial procession involving nude male and female figures, some armed, riders and deer. The central figure is probably a goddess holding a dish on top of which an ornamental cauldron (not illustrated) was placed. Seen from above, the wagon is rectangular, but in its center the goddess is standing on a wheel. The combination of cauldron and chariot was developed in the bronze age, and remained a popular religious image well into the Hallstatt period.

here and never been. This book, I'm sorry to say, is full of highly confusing material. Our cheerful Celtic artists and poets delighted in leaving things half revealed and half concealed. As a result, there is no easy way to comprehend the lot in one go. However, there are ways in which you can make things easy for yourself. To soak your mind in Celtic thought, you could do as follows. Are you comfortable? Lets do something new. Close the book. Calm down and relax. When you think of nothing specific your mind begins to produce alpha brain waves. It feels like dozing. The good thing about alpha waves is that they set in naturally when you close your eyes, think of nothing specific and cultivate not-doing. And as you enjoy the sensation of half sleep you can press the book against your brow and tell your deep mind in a slow, clear voice that you want it to read this book and to select and store all information that is really important for you, so you may recall it whenever you will. Use simple phrases, positive terms, and repeat it a few times. Not too often though, if you have an intelligent deep mind it may resent overbearing orders. Be kind and friendly and your deep mind will cooperate. Then open the book and leaf through it once. Keep your eyes open wide, so you can take in both pages in one glance. Look at each page for a second or two, without reading. This can be a temptation, it can also be fun. How often do you do weird rituals with new books? Go through the whole book. Then close it, and your eyes, press it against the brow again, ask your deep mind to select what is useful and to store it for easy recall. Say thank you! And do something else.

After a pause sit down again. Go through the book once more. This time, look at all the pictures and read their captions. Then ask your deep mind once more to select, store and recall what is good for you. Make another pause. The third circuit through the book starts very similar. Tell your deep mind what you want. Then go through the book and read all the poetry. This may be even more confusing than what you did earlier, basically as the best poets and bards of the British Isles tended to be quite beside themselves, over the top, round the bend, over the hills and far, far away, while they composed, sang and prophesied. Their songs are not only full of allusion and abstraction, they also show all signs of scatterbrained trance rambling. It takes a while to get used to this, so you may as well start now. After going through the book a few times in this fashion, leave it to rest for a day or two. Then pick it up and read systematically. You will find that the earlier fits of deep-mind-reading have provided a background structure, a web to sort and arrange information. As the computer people warn: system overload equals pattern recognition. For a programmer, this may be a dangerously deceptive tendency, for the mage, the visionary, the bard and poet it provides a blessed source-spring of fresh inspiration. Who creates the patterns out of the raw and chaotic jumble of sensory perception? While we will never be sure what the old Celtic visionaries were getting excited about, we can use some of their gifts to cultivate a new consciousness, and a new quality of sacredness, in our world, in our flesh, in living truth, now.

Regarding the poetry in this book, much

Sucellos

of it comes from the classic translation *The Four Ancient Books of Wales* edited and published by William F. Skene in 1868. This translation was made on Skene's request by two eminent linguistic experts, Reverend D. Silas Evans of Llanymawddwy, who dealt with *The Black Book of Carmarthen*, *The Book of Aneurin* and *The Red Book of Hergest,* while Reverend Robert Williams of Rhydycroesau worked on *The Book of Taliesin.* Substantial quotations from these translations were unavoidable, you will find them scattered all through this book. It might be asked why no more recent translation was used. Occasionally this has been done, as the Skene texts, though the first reliable treatment of the manuscripts, do contain a measure of inaccuracy. Readers acquainted with earlier renderings of this material may observe that the Skene version is less mystical and romantic than what they are used to. In all fairness I would add that Skene, unlike all earlier translators, was not interested in reviving fantastic Druidry, and did not bend the texts to suit his fancies. His texts are not exactly easy reading and contain many enigmatic and incomprehensible passages. Personally I much prefer an honest riddle to a wonderfully mystic translation that only

Brass boar; height 39 cm, originally top of a standard, Soulac-sur-Mer, Dép, Gironde, 1st century BCE

Torque-end with several faces, bronze, Courtisots, Marne, France. c. late fourth century BCE.

makes sense as its translator chose to inflict his own fancies and prejudices on the subject.

Finally, let me express my thanks to all who supported the writing of this book. I had the pleasure of discussing its topics with many friends and acquaintances. Then there were those daring souls who actually set out to explore Celtic magick practically, who tranced, travelled in the wildwood and developed their own vision of pagan magick for the future. Among those whose enchantment, inspiration and originality supported this project, my thanks are especially due to Anad and Julia. Others who helped, laughed and supplied their own ideas, and to whom I am very thankful, are Astrid & Gavin, Mike & Maggie (Nema), Mogg & Kym (Mandrake of Oxford), Kenneth Grant, Paul, Ronald Hutton, Ruth, Sally and her home community and Volkert. Thanks are also due to the many researchers, scholars, spell-crafters, poets, storytellers and artists whose work has contributed to this book. I wish to thank the spirits of the wildwood everywhere, the Celts who settled in the Taunus mountains and all the gods and muses who breathe into the cauldron.

And I wish to thank You for using the magick of the past to invent something new and worthwhile for the future. Ipsos

Artio. The long way out of Andumnos

1. People of the Mounds

Imagine the forest. As darkness falls, the somber beeches disappear in misty twilight and shadows seem to gather under their branches. Far away, the blackbird's call tells of the coming of the night. The birds cease their singing, silence descends, soon the beasts of the night will make their appearance. Between tangled roots, hidden by nettles and brambles, the earth seems to ripple. A few humps of earth seem to emerge from the ground. They are the last traces of burial mounds, of mounds, which were tall and high 2500 years ago. Many of them have disappeared, hidden by tangled roots of beech and oak, ploughed flat by careless farmers, others again show caved-in tops where grave robbers have looted the central chamber. The locals shun these hills. There are tales that strange fires can be seen glowing on the mounds, and that on spooky nights, great armed warriors arise from their resting places. Then the doors to the deep are thrown open and unwary travelers have to beware of being invited into the halls of the dead and unborn.

Here the kings of the deep feast and celebrate, time passes differently and strange treasures may be found. Who knows the nights when the gates are open? Who carries the primrose, the wish-flower, the strange blossom that opens the doors to the hollow hills?

Pre-Roman Celtic cultures are usually classed in two periods. These have the names of the places where the cultures were first studied, that is, the Hallstatt culture is named after an Austrian village where an extensive cemetery was discovered, and the La Tène culture is named after a site in Switzerland. Roughly speaking, the distinctive Celtic culture can first be observed in the Hallstatt period, which lasts from c.750 BCE to 450 BCE when the La Tène period begins. If you study books on Celtic art you will soon finds out that Hallstatt and La Tène are not just periods of cultural evolution. The Hallstatt period has its distinct art form, and the La Tène period shows its own original developments.

There is more to these phases than styles in art and fashion. Within the Hallstatt phase, a great cultural transformation took place, and at the beginning of the La Tène period an even more important upheaval occurred. At these times of transition, social organization, religion and funeral customs underwent great changes. To study what these people did in terms of magic and religion is a rather difficult task. We could take the easy way, that is, we could project a lot of stuff from medieval bardic poetry and romance into the dim and unknown past and pretend that this is what ancient Celtic magic must have looked like. Well, there are plenty of books of this sort on the market, so you'll forgive me if I'll use these pages to take a look at the archaeological record instead.

Before we get to the magick, however, it may be useful to form some idea of the cultural context. First, a short look at Hallstatt society may be in order. Scholars roughly divide the Hallstatt period into two phases. Early Hallstatt is called Ha C, late Hallstatt, the time of the so called 'princely burials' is called Ha D.

Now you may wonder just what constitutes Hallstatt A and B, if the Hallstatt period began with Ha C. The answer is simple. The terms Ha A and B were originally used to designate the early and late Urnfield culture, in a time when scholars believed that the Hallstatt culture was the direct descendant of the Urnfield people.

Nowadays this assumption has gone out of fashion, and so have the terms Ha A and B. In the Hallstatt period we observe the appearance of early but distinctive Celtic culture. Our first references to people who

may be loosely described as Celts come from the Hallstatt period. Hekataios of Milet (c. 560-480 BCE) informs us that the Celts live behind Massilia (Marseille) beyond the land of the Liguri. In his time, Greek traders had established a flourishing colony at Marseille, from where they supplied the locals with a number of Mediterranean luxuries, such as wine, glass, pottery goods and the like. Such items soon became fashionable and very much sought after by the nobility, which may have resulted in considerable economic problems. What the Greek traders received in turn is not that easy to determine. Furs, slaves, honey and beeswax may have been valuable export products, but so far there is no evidence to support this assumption.

Be that as it may, to the Greeks, who were mainly interested in the coastal trade, the land of the Celts was somewhere inland, beyond Massilia and the land of the Liguri. As in Hekataios's account, the Iberi live west of Massilia, this leaves us with the country north of the Provence as a candidate for early Celtic settlements.

Next, Appolonius of Rhodos recorded in his *Argonautica* that the Celts can be reached if one travels up the Rhodanus (the Rhone) and crosses a number of stormy lakes. While Appolonius lived in the 3rd C. BCE, he made use of sources going back to the 5th C. BCE, which corresponds with the late Hallstatt phase. The lakes in our source may well be the lake of Geneve or the Swiss lakes, maybe even the Bodensee.

Our third and last source for the early Celts is in the *Histories* of Herodotus (c. 484 -430 BCE), who has been called 'the father of history', though 'father of sensational journalism' would have been closer to the mark. In the works of Herodotus, the Celts are mentioned twice. Herodotus freely admits that he has never traveled in their lands, so a certain amount of confusion can only be expected. He vaguely defines Celtic country as lying beyond the Pillars of Hercules (Gibraltar, i.e. somewhere outside of the Mediterranean) to the north, where, apart from the Celts, only a fantastic race called the Kyneti manage to survive. Approached from overland, the Celts can be found at the source of the Danube near a city called Pyrene.

Now the 'source of the Danube' admirably fits with our Hallstatt people. What does not fit is the city Pyrene. It is possible, so many scholars speculate that Herodotus was referring to the Pyrenees. These mountains, however, are a long way from the Danube. The coastal traders, from whom Herodotus may have received some of his data, may have inferred that the Pyrenees extend inland to join the Alps. Mind you, Herodotus didn't know about the Alps or Carpathian mountains. Instead he referred to two rivers called Alpis and Karpis, to the left and right of the Danube,

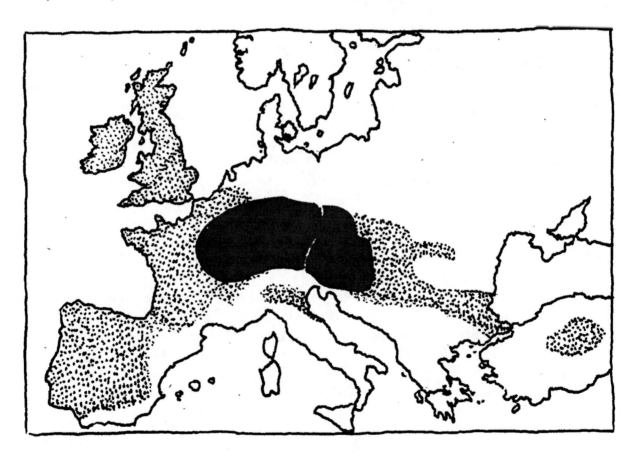

Map of the Hallstatt culture, east and west (black) and the La Tène culture (dotted) after the great Celtic expansion of the 3ʳᵈ and 2ⁿᵈ century BCE.

so we should be a little careful with his geography. Maybe he got completely confused about the location of the Pyrenees and the Danube. On the other hand, it is possible that there was once a city called Pyrene which we simply don't know about. Regarding the Celts, Herodotus got his data from earlier sources, as in his time, Greek trading was prohibited in the western Mediterranean.

So there you have it, these three references are the oldest regarding Celtic people. What we have is two items. One is a culture loosely called Celts (Celtoi) by a number of classical writers. The other is evidence for a nameless culture unearthed by excavations north of the Alps. If you add the two together, you arrive at what is called the early Celts. This is a bit of scholarly guesswork, as after all, we have no idea what the people of the Hallstatt culture called themselves. The name 'Celts', though convenient, may be misleading. The early Hallstatt culture was limited to a much smaller territory than the later La Tène culture. You can find Hallstatt type settlements in the region north of the Alps, that is, in Switzerland, Austria, southern and middle Germany, parts of France and in the east, towards Bohemia, Czech, Slovenia and Hungary.

Scholars make a distinction between the eastern and western Hallstatt culture. Eastern Hallstatt tombs favour heavily armed males with battle axes. You find them in the eastern parts of Austria, in south east Germany and further to the east.

Western Hallstatt culture underwent two distinct phases (Ha C and Ha D). In the first phase, there is a marked emphasis on long iron swords, in the second, weapons as grave goods went largely out of fashion. With regard to art, the early western Hallstatt people were remarkably shy of using naturalistic images of animals and people. This is amazing, as they bought and enjoyed plenty of pots and vases showing naturalistic paintings from the Mediterranean. For some mysterious reason they did not attempt to copy them. You can find some abstract pictures of people or beasts in a very few western Hallstatt period tombs, plus a number of semi human stone-figures which graced the top of burial mounds. Then there are a number of beautiful small monstrous heads and entities which grace fibulae and drinking equipment. These images, for all their excellent execution, avoid naturalism. Human faces - provided they are human and not divine or demonic - are either completely abstract or distorted while beasts are often a blend of several species.

The eastern Hallstatt culture was slightly more liberal in this respect-images include people who box or fight (or dance?), musicians, figures in skirts (or robes?) raising their hands in adoration, hunting scenes, work on the fields, deer, horses and waterfowl, but these are all highly abstract and rare. Celtic art could have been naturalistic at this early stage but wasn't, and indeed it took the Celts a long time (well into the La Tène period) before they dared to portray people realistically. Could this be evidence for some religious prohibition? Or did the artists of the time chose to be naturalistic only in perishable material, such as wooden carvings or embroidered textiles?

To begin with, it might be useful to consider the sort of society the Hallstatt people lived in. Let's take a look at the excellent studies of Konrad Spindler. In Ha C, the early Hallstatt phase, our Celts lived in villages and hilltop settlements. Most people worked as farmers, but it is quite uncertain whether these people had a free status or functioned as slaves. Grains were cultivated (at least nine varieties, including modern rye, oats and wheat), people ate peas, lentils, beans and wild grapes. The basic source of meat were domestic animals, mainly pig, cattle and sheep, but hunting added to the diet. A wide range of animal bones has come up in excavations, so we know that the people of the Hallstatt time hunted just about anything including bear, wolf, boar, deer, European bison, aurox, eagle, raven, vulture. So far there is no evidence for hunting taboos.

The range of clothing materials and textiles was much greater than is usually assumed. Sheep wool sometimes survives to our age, and so the first reconstructions favoured pictures of Celtic chieftains clad in Scottish jumpers. Linen and linseed oil however, was probably a lot more popular (sheep were kept, but not in very large numbers).

The Hochdorf burial supplies many fascinating insights. The noble on his amazing metal couch was resting on at least thirteen different layers of textiles. We know about them, as luckily the bronze has preserved small amounts of the material. These include fine cloth spun from tree-bark fibres, imported silk from China, furs, wool, linen and blankets spun out of horse - and, a lot more difficult, badger hair. The Hallstatt people kept cattle and pigs, as well as dogs, sheep, goats and horses. Horses were rare and probably amazingly expensive. It is not even certain whether horses were ridden, all evidence points to four wheel wagons, many of which made it into the burial mounds.

The domestic animals were smaller than today's. The same went for people. The average height of males was 1,72 m, of females 1,59 m. This is taller than most people in the classical world, and explains why the Celts seemed like giants to the Greek and Roman authors. Nobles, as found in the wealthiest tombs, were often taller, which goes to show what a protein rich diet can do.

The average life expectation for males was 35-40 years, for females 30-35 years. Infant mortality cannot be estimated, as there are very few child burials. A life expectation of 35 years, by the way, is not bad for the time. In the medieval period, with its lack of general hygiene, the average life expectation went down another jolly ten years, which goes to show that Christianity can damage your health. Some Celtic people were fond of washing and practically invented soap while the Christian missionaries believed that washing was sinful and ought to be avoided. The nobility of Hallstatt times regularly shaved, and several tombs include tools for personal hygiene, such as pincers and equipment to cut fingernails and clean ears. They also liked to dye their hair using red ochre. The question of hygiene is one of those tricky issues. While the nobility definitely liked to wash and shave, we have no way of estimating the standard of health and sanitary conditions among poorer people, most of whom never had a proper burial. The pieces of clothing found in the salt mines of the Dürrnberg are full of lice eggs. Likewise, the amount of women who died giving birth is so high that we can be certain that the midwives, or whoever did the job, did not bother to keep their hands overly clean.

With a modern life expectation of eighty years it can be hard to imagine a world where people of 40 years were considered elderly. In 1881, the average life expectation in Germany was 35.5 years for males and 38.5 years for females. Seen by such standards, the Hallstatt people must have lived a rather healthy life. On the other hand, it was still a lot of toil for a hazardous and often altogether too short life.

Most farmers worked the fields or herded cattle. There was a small section of society which had specific professions, such as traders, smiths, gold smiths, bronze workers, carpenters and the like. Also, there must have been some people specialized in medicine and religion. There were skilled doctors in the Hallstatt period. The noble of Talhau 4 met with a violent accident. He suffered major injuries on the right arm and shinbone, and had his skull cracked with some utensil. The healers of his time patched him up so well that he continued through life with a large coin-sized hole in his skull.

Whether such services were available for simple folk is another question. What attracts most attention is, of course, the so called nobility with their rich tombs. It is very easy at this point to fantasize what this nobility may have been like. There were privileged individuals in early Celtic society, but there is no evidence whether these were nobility in the medieval sense of the word, whether they attained their status by inheritance, oracle, election and whether the job was limited to worldly power or involved religious duties. They could have been aristocrats, they could also have presided in some priestly function. There are no priestly tombs as such on record, so who do you think performed that office? It's a shame that so little is known about the way the early Celts lived. Most of what we know is the legacy of tombs.

Everybody knows that the Celts buried their dead in mounds. So much for common knowledge, in reality things are a lot more complicated. There were barrow graves of various types in the earliest central European cultures. The first Neolithic farmers had barrows, they seem more rare in the early bronze age time. In the high bronze period they were almost obligatory. The early Hallstatt period supplies plenty of barrows, and favours burial by fire. In the late Hallstatt period (Ha D) the fire funerals almost disappear with regard to the nobility, but survive amongst common people. With the beginning of the La Tène period, the balance swings towards fire funerals and flat tombs again.

The vast majority of European barrows come from the Hallstatt period, some scholars estimate 90%. This does not mean that they stopped at the beginning of the La Tène period. For all the violent changes, La Tène did not completely discontinue the habit. Some mounds come from La Tène times, some are even from the Roman occupation and a small number of early medieval mounds have also been discovered. Hallstatt mounds, for all their popularity, show a lot of variety. There are basically two sizes, that is, mounds for common people of better income, which have a diameter of 6-20m, and the famous mounds of the higher nobility, which begin around 30m diameter and may go all the way to the Magdalenenberg mound with its diameter of 102m. Some tiny mounds of 3m diameter have also been found, these were barely big enough to cover the corpse.

Before we look at the giant mounds, most of which are a specific element of the late Hallstatt time, we should think about the mounds in general. As a rule, a mound is erected over a central tomb which may or may not have been a central wooden chamber with stone walls and ceiling. Mounds come in round and ovoid form, recent research has shown that there were also square mounds (pyramids?), and that these may be more common than is generally acknowledged. The square form may be related to the square shape of the religious sites of the later La Tène time, but this is a bit on the speculative side. Exposed to the elements, to rain and snow, heat and wind, a square and a round barrow look pretty much the same after a couple of decades.

To erect a barrow, the local earth was used. Wooden shovels and wickerwork baskets were used to transport the earth, sometimes horses and cows pulled wagons full of earth. To protect the newly made mound from erosion, it was turfed over with grass. The central chamber of a barrow was often made of oak. This gave rise to a lot of speculation regarding the sacred nature of the oak. Perhaps the oak was used

Early Hallstatt period pottery
Top: ceramic rattle in bird shape, found in a grave, Waldbuch, Bavaria, Germany, 7-8th century BCE.
Middle: ceramic horse with bowl, Kirchensittenbach, Bavaria.
Bottom: Vessel showing human figures with vastly enlarged hands, Staufersbuch, Bavaria.

for its sanctity, but definitely it was used as it is such trusty and enduring wood for building. The Hallstatt Celts preferred oak, when they ran out of it, they made do with fir. This happened quite frequently in Ha D, as the ringwalls of the time required an immense amount of great old oak trees. Ringwalls have to be repaired every so often, as the timber inside tends to rot and disintegrate after 15 or 20 years.

As a result some Hallstatt settlements seem to have stood on pretty barren and windswept hilltops. Ringwall repairs, by the way, are one of those riddles. If sections of your fortification can only be relied on for a dozen years, this means that some part of the wall was always under repair. This may have posed some interesting military problems. The people of the Heuneburg got so fed up with repairs that they had a large section of their fortress protected by a wall made from burned bricks, a style of fortification popular in Greece. In all likeliness they invited a number of experts from the sunny Mediterranean to the dark forests of the Danube. The white plastered wall looked out of the place but lasted much longer than the local equivalent. Greek bricks or local timber and stone - who happened to labour at such monuments? It takes a large work force to maintain a Hallstatt fortress/settlement, so there must have been some surplus labourers, apart from the ones needed to work the fields and herd cattle. It's easy to produce monumental architecture in a friendly climate. In the Hallstatt period the weather was not very favourable and there was very little surplus wealth. The question of the work force remains an unsolved riddle.

Some barrows had a small wall or a stony fringe around the bottom, most of them were plain and natural. The thing that few people know about barrows is that they often housed many corpses. This custom started very early. Even the early Hallstatt people occasionally inhumed corpses in mounds belonging to the earlier Urn-field culture, and if possible, they liked to put their dead in the central spot. This continued in the Hallstatt mounds. As an estimate, the smaller mounds contain an average of 4-10 corpses, the large mounds of Ha D could contain up to 120 individuals. So, if you read of fairies celebrating under a hollow hill, that hill may well come from Hallstatt D, which was a good period for mass gatherings.

Should you want to build your own mound in your backgarden, leave plenty of space in the sides for your family and friends. Mounds are not an isolated phenomena either. Often they turn up in clusters. Small clusters of around ten mounds, those with 40 are pretty substantial and if you find more than 60 mounds in one location, this may mark a place of considerable importance.

Archaeologists have done their best to figure out whether there were any religious rules to mound building. So far, each rule has been shattered by countless exceptions. You can find mounds in valleys, on fields, close to rivers, in forests, on mountainsides, in clusters or all by themselves.

Mounds were not the only form of burial. Sometimes one discovers flat tombs between mounds, and by the time La Tène culture begins, flat tombs become the fashion. What we know best are the impressive mounds of the late Hallstatt period. This time (Ha D) is characterized by a number of changes. For one thing, the trusty bronze sword went completely out of fashion. For another, trade with the Mediterranean became so important that a lot of chieftains may have impoverished their dependents. Rural Celtic society generally had little surplus wealth, with bad harvests and cattle plagues it must have been hard to make ends meet at the best of times. Some Celtic tribes profited from salt, or close proximity to trade routes. Others were much poorer, and could not afford to bury so much wealth with their deceased.

It remains uncertain where the nobles of Ha D made the wealth they spent on luxury goods from the sun drenched south. In this period the burials become extremely costly and each generation 'wasted' valued goods by putting them into the mounds. It may be an interesting question whether the nobles of Ha D exploited their subjects until social stability was threatened. Never in the Celtic world was there such a strong contrast between rich and poor folk. On the other hand a number of new technologies developed. The potter of Ha D used a spinning pottery wheel, the woodworker became adept at turning wooden cups and bowls. Ha D tombs offer the richest treasures of Celtic history.

One typical element of the time is the so called 'princely tomb'. This name is not a very happy choice, as it projects the existence of a medieval feudal system into a period about which we know very little. 'Princely tombs' are an archaeological category, they are defined by closeness to a large settlement, a certain amount of wealth, gold and Mediterranean import goods. Such a definition is misleading as it evaluates only in terms of unperishable grave goods. Take for example the Pazyryk tombs in the Altai mountains in Siberia. These tombs contain an amazingly rich treasure-fine textiles, carpets, silk, musical instruments, horse harnesses and a four wheel wagon, all perfectly preserved as the ground became frozen after the burial. The same tombs, if they had existed in middle Europe, would have yielded only a metal mouthpiece for horses and an earthenware bottle, everything else rotted away. Excavators would have classed them as extremely poor.

Similar problems come up in Celtic excavations. In most tombs horn, leather, wood and textiles can only be traced if they are close enough to bronze that the toxins preserve the organic materials. In some cases, this can lead to interesting errors. A Celtic grave field at Mühlacker yielded two types of burials, one of them with some wealth, the other rather poor. Consequently, the first excavators proposed that there was a two-class society with distinct funeral rites. Nowadays, the two 'classes' of the Mühlacker cemetery are known to be simply men and women, the women, having more treasure on them, being the 'upper class'. In the 'princely tombs' of Ha D this situation is reversed. The vast majority of burials are male, and this goes not only for the central tomb but also for the countless people inhumed later. A 'Princely Tomb' was usually a grand affair. There are not many of them around, and most were robbed at one time or another. In most cases, they were giant mounds with an oaken central chamber surrounded by stone walls. Occasionally these grave chambers were lavishly decorated with textiles. Grave goods are impressive and go beyond the deceased personal needs.

Here we get a glimpse at the life after death conceptions of the Ha D nobility. To begin with, the deceased is usually clad in fine costume and adorned with all sorts of status symbols. Gold ranks very high on this list. As most Celts had no direct access to gold, they obviously had to import it. Golden bowls were an especially popular acquisition, as these could be cut into slices, each of which could be turned into a golden neckring (torque). Many nobles wore golden torques in their tombs, whether they did so in daily life is another question, as many of these golden items were too thin to survive daily use.

The noble of Hochdorf, for instance, had not only a golden torque but also gold plated shoes and ornaments. True, the shoes would have come apart after two steps and the golden fibulae (safety pins) could never have held his cloak together. This was a triumph of the goldsmiths art: to make ornamental gold foil as thin as a tenth of a millimeter! In Hochdorf, the goldsmiths built their workshop right next to the mound, and produced objects specifically for the deceased. Even items like the ceremonial dagger were wrapped in paper thin goldfoil and after the work was done, the workshops were burned to the ground.

Thanks to such customs, we know that the deceased was expected to have an afterlife of some sort which involved representation. The deceased was to appear even more golden, glorious and shining than in real life. Another item in the Hochdorf tomb is a massive cauldron of Greek origin containing some 300 litres of honey mead, nine drinking horns (one of iron, eight from the savage wild aurox) and nine bronze plates. Drinking equipment is a regular feature in 'princely tombs', as is a large amount of food. Pigs or parts of them are so popular as tomb-provisions that it seems interesting that later Island Celtic traditions (see the *Mabinogi*, fourth branch) connect pigs with the otherworld. The amount of feasting equipment goes beyond personal needs, it suggests that there were important social occasions and mind-bending carousal in the realm of the dead. Fishing and hunting was also possible in the otherworld, the Hochdorf noble had utensils for both.

The Hochdorf tomb, however, is an exception in that it was not plundered. In

Anthropomorphic figures (deities?) of the western Hallstatt culture.
Top left: Stele of Ebrach, Bavaria, height 1.03m. Is the figure wearing a hood or a death mask?
Top right: Stele of Breuberg, Hessen, height of fragment 0.45 m. Another death mask?
center: quartzite plate showing figure and axe, Sietschen, Graubünden, height 1.8m.
Bottom left: statue of Hirschlanden, Baden-Württemberg, height 1.5m. The warrior has a sword and what may be a birch-bark hat. The crude penis could be a later addition. Bottom center: Stele of Tübingen-Kilchberg, fragment, Baden-Württemberg. Found standing on top of a burial mound. Bottom right: Statue of Holzgerlingen, Baden-Württemberg, height including 'horns' 2.3m, here shown with horns attached. The statue is janus-headed, i.e. one face and one arm to front and reverse.

most other Celtic giant mounds, the central chambers were badly violated. What remains are the countless tombs in the sides of the mound. It is possible that entire dynasties went into these mounds. A mound that is to contain, say, a hundred corpses is necessarily a large affair. The erection of the huge Magdalenenberg mound can be dated, thanks to dendrochronology. The Magdalenenberg mound is approximately 45 000 cubic meters of earth erected over a period of c.18 years. Using these estimates, it is possible to surmise that the Hohmichele mound with its 30,000 cubic meters of earth took around 12 years to complete and so on. Of course such estimates are rather speculative. At the Black Forest edge (Magdalenenberg) the climate only permits c.7 months of digging each year. Closer to the Danube the temperature is kinder and some poor sods could toil almost throughout the year. Smaller mounds were probably completed in one or two years.

On top of the 'princely burials' a stone pillar may have been set. These only survived in a few cases - such as the figure of Hirschlanden, the Stele of Breuberg, the statues of the Glauberg, but there are older records mentioning the existance of anthropomorphic stone pillars. The figures and stelae, as far as we know, often show what may be a death mask and strangely shaped hands. Usually the arms are folded over the chest in a specific position and sometimes there are strong and oversized legs supporting the torso. That a very similar statue has been unearthed in the Piceni culture of northern Italy may well say something about trade routes and contact with various north Italian cultures.

Female tombs can also be found in the giant hills. As a rule, these look less wealthy, but then, it may well be that the wealth in them was simply left to rot over the years. Gold is pretty rare and so are import goods from the Mediterranean, apart from glass beads and elaborate coral necklaces. Four exceptionally rich female tombs have been found, two of them contained chariots, a third the remnants of a horse-harness, so maybe there was a chariot. About a hundred chariots (or remnants of them) have been found in Hallstatt period burials, some of them were completely built without metal. There may have been more of them around, but obviously, few traces can be found. As these chariots are built for use, and often seem to include a throne seat of some sort, we arrive at the interesting question whether such chariots were used for ceremonial occasions, or whether the deceased were taken for a ceremonial ride before inhumation.

A sign of high status seems to have been thick barrel-bracelets. These were made in one piece: the woman who wore them put them on in late childhood and then lived without ever taking them off again (the same seems to go for some Hallstatt times neck-rings). Being of impressive size, they would have made menial work a difficult matter, so possibly the ladies who wore such items were not expected to get their hands dirty. Two of those ladies were so fat that their bones did not remain in the straight position you find in normal funerals, one had a circumference of 1.20m, as could be seen from her girdle (a posh item 9 cm broad adorned with approximately 7000 tiny bronze ornaments). This tomb is interesting as it is one of the rare cases of a mutual funeral: above the chamber of the leading lady, the much thinner corpse of a woman was found who had only a few items of cheap jewelry. Could this be the maid or slave of the wealthy lady below?

In the Hallstatt period, the most impressive and wealthiest burials tend to be male. This refers to wealth which survives the ages. We have no idea whether female tombs may not have contained wealth in a more perishable form, such as costly clothes, wooden carvings and the like. Some wealth is of spiritual and not of material value, and if a sacred object happens to consist of wood it is unlikely to survive the centuries. Keep in mind that it is extremely hard to guess about daily life when you can only look at grave goods. It is, for instance, by no means certain that the wealth inside of a tomb actually belonged to the person during life or was worn on everyday occasions.

The few children's tombs of the Hallstatt period include jewelry which was too big for them, and which could only have been of use in adult life. This yields another interesting idea: in the otherworld, children can grow up. Please think about this for a moment. Children, if they received a regular burial, often had talismanic items on themselves. Perhaps it was believed that they needed special protection on the way.

The same goes for young women, who occasionally lie on their sides or on their bellies, some of them have bones missing or strangely arranged. This looks like the many cases of giving dangerous folk a bizarre burial in order to prevent them from rising. Candidates for such inhumation rites were criminals, suicides, but above all,

persons who died an untimely or messy death. Possibly these women died in childbirth or at some dangerous or unlucky occasion, became a threat to the living and had to have an unusual funeral. While it is uncommon to find young women in a tomb, it is a lot more rare to discover the burial of a youth or an adolescent. Were these unimportant, or not full members of society? It gets even harder when we look for child burials. Some children were buried in the settlements, a few select ones were even admitted into the great burial mounds. These often carry numerous amulets. For what purpose? Could they expect danger on the way to the under- or otherworld? On the other hand, we could ask whether the adults carried amulets or magical objects as well?

The answer is not easy. Amulets as such are rare in adult tombs, but then it is distinctly possible that some of the ornaments had a similar function. Many fibulae have that special look which invites the question whether they had a sacred or symbolic meaning. The same goes for amber, which was occasionally made into ornaments right on the spot where the burial took place. Was amber worn by the living or was it exclusively used for funeral rites? More on talismanic items and odd burials in the next chapter.

The noble lady mentioned above and the thinner woman who accompanied her on the way to the otherworld brings us to the topic of shared burials. A number of them appears in the Hallstatt period and gives rise to the question why a person might accompany another into the hollow hills. It would be deceptively easy to point at Indian

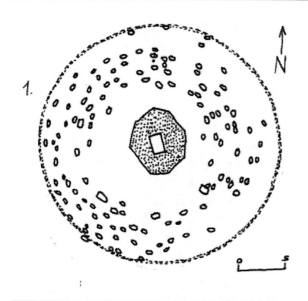

Great barrows with multiple burials of the Hallstatt period.

1. Magdalenenberg, Villingen-Schwenningen, Baden-Württemberg, Germany, diameter 102 meters, central chamber set in a polygonal stone tumulus plus 102 later burials, after Spindler.

2. Dautmergen, Baden-Württemberg, the central chamber contained the burial of a man and a woman, seven later burials in the periphery, 6th century BCE. The mound was surrounded with a ring of poles and a ditch, after Reim.

3. Breisach-Oberrimsingen, Baden-Württemberg, central chamber plus 21 later burials, ranging from Ha D to LA 1. Black dots show ceramic goods, the nail shaped symbols show corpses and give the direction of their heads. The mound was originally crowned by a stone stele or figure which was removed violently and destroyed in 1930. After Wamser and Bittel.

4. Glauberg, Hessen, Germany, late Hallstatt or early La Tène mound with two burials and a square pit in the center, set in a complicated system of deep ditches. A 'ceremonial avenue', 350 meters long, between ditches approaches the mound from the valley below. Next to the mound was a small square building (a shrine?). Dots mark large poles, x the place where the statue was found in a ditch, I in the left ditch the location of the corpses of an old woman and a child. Partly excavated, after Schmid.

traditions, such as the Sati custom of widow sacrifice, or the messy ritual which Ibn Rustah claimed to have seen among some 10th C. Vikings. Caesar, writing about the late La Tène period in Gaul, claims that the deceased were often burned in the company of relations and servants. With the Hallstatt time Celts, this sort of thing was definitely not the rule.

There are a few tombs which were made for couples. It might be interesting to discuss Magdalenenberg tomb 100 here. It contained two adults, male and female, in a stone-walled tomb. Unlike most other burials, the dead were not resting on their backs but lay back to back on their sides. Maybe they were unusual people - the woman wore the only toe-ring of the entire Hallstatt period. The back-to-back position may have a magical or symbolic meaning. It calls to mind the tomb of a young woman in Esslingen-Sirnau. Her grave goods include 18 golden earrings, bracelets, coral beads, nine bronze-rings worn at the hips, a ring with a moon-shaped pendant, and a unique

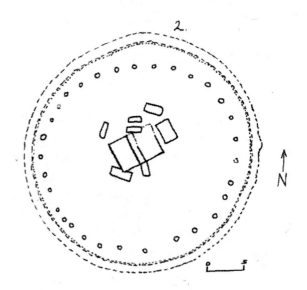

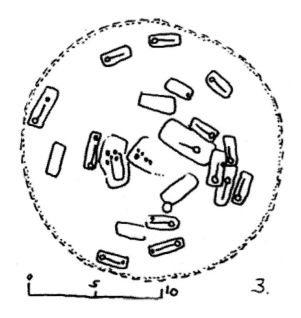

3.

bronze amulet, showing a nude couple lying back to back. The passion for the number nine is worth considering, quite a few dead people of the Hallstatt time were inhumed with articles numbering 3, 9 and 18. This tradition continued over a long time, you can find it in the La Tène period and even later in the writings of the medieval bards. Arguably one person in the Magdalenenberg tomb chose to follow the other, or maybe the matter was not entirely voluntary. It is also possible that the two died at the same time, perhaps due to a plague or through enemy action.

There are roughly forty shared burials in the western Hallstatt region, which amounts to 1 or 2 percent of the known burials. Some of them look like couples, such as side tomb 6 of Hohmichele (two corpses resting side by side on a cow skin), some possibly imply a master/servant relationship (mound *Croix Du Gros Murger*, two corpses and a horse skeleton. One of the corpses

wears ornaments, the other doesn't), and still others are simply enigmatic, such as tomb 93 of Magdalenenberg, containing a grown warrior with a child in his arms.

In several cases it is possible, even likely that the people who share a tomb did not die at the same time. This implies storage of a corpse, possibly for years, and points to phazed burial.

Before we leave the mounds I would like to mention some other matters of interest. One of them is the possibility that the corpses may occasionally have been embalmed. Some hair found in the central tomb of the Magdalenenberg mound was exceptionally rich in arsenic. Likewise, the noble of Hochdorf had his golden torque removed violently after death, it was repaired and replaced before the burial, so possibly the corpse was treated in some way in the meantime. An embalmed corpse may tell us something about the beliefs of the period. Are we dealing with a personality cult or a belief in bodily resurrection?

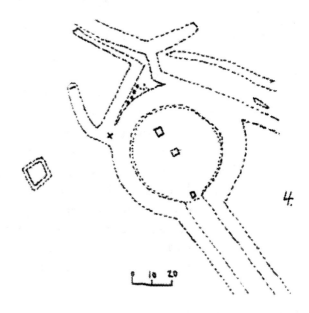

4.

Another fascinating matter is the way the Hallstatt people thought about their future life after death. In the early Hallstatt phase, both east and west, most men carried heavy weapons. Many corpses bear swords, axes, spears, a helmet, chest armour, leg protection, shield and so on. When these folk travelled into death, they expected some fighting, and armed accordingly.

Then the western Hallstatt realm underwent massive changes. The immensely rich 'princely tombs' and giant burial mounds started a new religious trend. Body burial became the fashion of the day, starting among the nobles and later being copied by most of the population. Even more striking is the new ideology.

The nobles of Ha D bore very few weapons in their tombs. Only 10-20% of the men are armed for combat. The others tend to wear ceremonial daggers with grips too short for proper handling, there are just a few light lances for hunting or the odd assortment of hunting arrows. Instead of armour you find costly textiles with embroidery, instead of heavy duty helmets light hats sewn out of birch bark.

Life in Ha D was just as violent as in the centuries before and after. Nevertheless the burial customs indicate that at this time, the nobles believed in a peaceful otherlife where no real fighting was required. This attitude changed at the end of the period and most of the old dynasties were extinguished. In La Tène A fire burials were suddenly popular and the ashes went into flat tombs with heaps of weapons.

So far we have looked at a few customs and traditions with regard to burials. There are few binding rules in this matter, the grave goods and the condition of the tomb varying enormously. What is common to the wealthier sort of funeral is simply that some sort of mound was erected. What is the meaning of a mound? Is it a replica of a pregnant belly, a vehicle of transition from one world to another? A bit of meditation may be useful now. Welcome to the wide world of subjective dreaming! If you want to learn something original, let me ask you to do a stimulating exercise.

Exercise: The Mound Journey

First, take a few deep breaths and move your body around for a minute or two. A little exercise is just the thing to get tension out of your limbs, you will find that this makes relaxation and good trance-traveling much easier.

Sit down somewhere nice and quiet. Place a dark piece of cloth over your eyes. Close your eyes, relax, calm down and go into a gentle trance state. You can do this the active way, say, by using suggestions or visualization, or you can slow down and watch your breathing for a while. If you simply close your eyes and think of nothing specific, alpha brain-wave activity will increase automatically. It happens by not-doing. Go deeper into your trance. Allow your inner voice/s to become slow and slower, calm the fast images, allow your muscles to unknot, relax, enjoy, you are on the way. When your body rests comfortably, your mind is free to work without distraction.

Build up a nice mound in your imagination, and walk around it until the image stabilizes. Look at it, feel it, build up an atmosphere, involve your senses as much as you can. Take your time. Even if you are experienced in creative visualization, it may take a while before the vision becomes steady. Some dreamers need to build up the mound a few times before they are satisfied that 'it is real'.

The next step is to enter the mound and to learn the secrets of the deep. One method of entering the tomb is recommended by folk tales, that is, you could imagine that your soul goes traveling in the form of some small animal, such as a mouse or a serpent. Imagine that you lay your body down next to the mound. How you leave it resting on the ground, how your dream body slips out of the flesh and goes traveling. You can enter the mound in human shape if you dare, but you could also become some suitable animal or even an abstract form. Sometimes this is safer - you never know who you are going to meet inside. Make the image of the mound so impressive that it straight-away produces the proper sort of atmosphere. What images turn you on? Would you prefer a cluster of mounds rising from a windswept hillside under a bleak sky, or a group hidden under shady trees in the late twilight? How can you make the image really impressive? How big should the mound be? From where do you approach it? What is your first impression?

Too many budding Magicians make things hard for themselves by playing around with weak or half-hearted images. If you wish to imagine something that impresses you, make it impressive! Use colour, texture, structure, contrast and fine detail. Add shade, setting, time of day...this is your imagination and it can be used to make images really strong. Do you prefer sharp outlines, as seen on a clear day, or gloomy, half-defined impressions fitting a hazy evening all alone with darkness approaching fast? Add the other senses...feel the air, and the temperature, touch the ground, listen to the wind and the sounds of small animals, add the smell of damp soil and the aroma of the wildwood if you like... I can't tell you what you need to get going, but you can. What gives an emotional impact? If you do this a couple of times you will find that the imagination becomes more defined with each repetition.

It is a good sign if the mound begins to be so real that you become uneasy about going in. A sense of spookiness can guide you to the proper vision; sometimes fear can be like a beacon leading to hidden treasure. What you want is an imaginary mound that is really alive in the magickal sense. A mound with a mood and a mind of its own. You will soon learn that a mound needs not only be a tomb, it can also have a sentience of its own. Sooner or later you will encounter ideas and images which you did not consciously invent. If you find them totally unrelated, maybe you have begun to drift off.

If you think about what happened at work the other day you have plainly lost your track. You can solve this trouble by associating more closely with the mound-representation, by banishing and invocation (see *Visual Magick* for an introduction to creative imagination). Some of the ideas you encounter may be more valuable. It could be that your deep mind is telling you something, or maybe you have caught a strand of dreaming from the mound builders themselves.

Even memories from other lifetimes (real or imaginary) may come up. If you are wise, you will refrain from insisting on objective truth. In magick, art and science, many different forms of truth appear. No matter whether you have discovered a subjective or an objective truth, you will certainly emerge from your trance journey with a lot of new ideas and possibly with a transformed personality.

It is wise to act as if the mound is real, but it is also wise to suspend judgement on the validity of what you discover. The mound you explore is a representation which you made up in your mind. The more convincing you represent the mound, the more impressive may your experience be. This is a statement about perception, not about reality.

A good and detailed vision can yield more valuable information than a sloppy and hasty effort. Nevertheless both of them are equally real or unreal. The good visualization is easier to handle and more convenient, but it is not necessarily more true. What is a real vision for you? No matter how good your insights are, they are still subjective and may include any amount of errors. Even if they were totally accurate, you still couldn't be certain. And you don't have to be. Certainty is for people who have stopped learning and wondering. Your visions are magick, in that they transform you from within. The mound you visit is, after all, your own mound, which exists right there in your mind. When you have explored for a while, give your thanks and return the way you came. Close all doors and gates properly, and when you are back in your body, wake up, take a few deep breaths and get up slowly. Record your experiences in your diary. Should you feel upset by your visions, do a banishing ritual, take a cold shower and go for a walk.

Raising the Dead

There is plenty of hidden lore in the realm of the dead, or in that part of your mind which your living personality considers dead (i.e. beyond ego). This is what necromancy is all about. When you explore a mound, you are effectively working a necromantic rite. This sounds really wild and dramatic, so perhaps you ought to recall that every time you are reading something by a dead author, the same applies. At which point I would like to add that necromantic rites had a respectable place in the enchantments of the medieval bards. The famed Irish work *Dindsenchas* is based on precisely these ideas. The word means literally 'hill-tales', or more exactly, tales from the mounds and hilltop settlements. The tales were collected between the 9th and 11th C., and consist mainly of place-anecdotes. The Irish poets believed in the importance of keeping the lore of the land alive. Their repertoire of tales included hundreds relating to local traditions, hills, roads, mounds, villages, rivers and pools. When such knowledge, or any other old piece of lore happened to be forgotten, the poets assembled for a necromantic rite. Using the mound attributed to some dead hero they did their best to raise him and to get the true story from one who had participated in it. (See *The Tain* for an example) In a similar way, Taliesin (well, one of them) was asked by prince Elphin to name the heroes resting under the mounds of Britain (*Black Book* 19).

The graves which the rain bedews?
Men that were not accustomed to afflict me:-
Cerwyd, and Cyrwyd, and Caw.
The graves which the thicket covers?
They would not succumb without avenging themselves:
Gwryen, Morien and Morial.
The graves which the shower bedews?
Men that would not succumb stealthily:-
Gwen, and Gwrien, and Gwriad.
The grave of Tydain, father of the Muse, in the region of Bron Aren:
Where the waves make a sullen sound
The grave of Dylan in Llan Beuno....

Truly did Elffin bring me
To try my primitive bardic lore
Over a chieftain-
The grave of Rwvawn with the imperious aspect.
Truly did Elffin bring me
To try my bardic lore
Over an early chieftain-
The grave of Rwvawn, too early gone to the grave.
The grave of March, the grave of Gwythur,
The grave of Gwgawn Gleddyvrudd;
A mystery to the world, the grave of Arthur...

This is just a short selection, the full poem has 73 verses and names more slain heroes than anyone has ever use for. Taliesin, having been everywhere and having experienced everything, is expected to know the names and deeds of the dead

Who owns this grave? This grave?
And this?

Ask me, I know it;

In a later verse it is the Awen itself, the spirit of inspiration, which declares the hidden mysteries.

If you set out to discover the secrets of the buried by having a bit of a trance ritual near a cluster of mounds, the Awen may reveal similar insights to you. If you have some convenient barrows in your neighbourhood, you may like to learn who went into the hollow hills. It can be helpful to approach this ritual with a measure of reverence. For one thing, it can be pretty bad manners to walk over a mound (unless you know it's inhabitants very closely). A bit of prayer and invocation can be useful. Let me suggest that you forget about set formula and simply speak from the heart. Emotion, channeled by means of prayer, offerings, ritual and music may well be the force to get your imagination and the spirits going.

I like to use shaking and trembling for out-of-doors evocations, for one thing it increases the lucidity of the visions and for another it keeps me warm. Excitement gets the tremors going. If you would like to master this approach properly, you can find a practical introduction in *Seidways*. Again, a useful attitude is to keep a really open mind. This means that no matter whether your visions are vague or overwhelming, you should consider them as a truth, but not as the only one. A bardic truth is not the same sort of truth that satisfies a scientist. It is not better or worse, it is simply on an entirely different level of understanding. The bards and poets who used necromancy to learn about the past used their imagination as a legitimate means to explore the unknown. Thus, if you go trancing into a mound, your insights may or may not accord with the scholarly consensus of your time. Nevertheless, you can be sure that you are engaged in a typical activity of the Celtic seers.

Worship of the Height

Before we leave the Hallstatt period I would like to mention some interesting changes in ritual. The change from fire burial to body burial, as it occurred between Ha C and D, needs not imply a complete reform of the existing religion. It started among the nobles and was eventually accepted by the commoners, but it was never the only method of burial. Even in the high time of body inhumations you can find the odd fire funeral here and there, so we can be sure the new cult did not entirely suppress the older tradition. The Hallstatt people also left evidence for a number of sites where generations offered to their deities. The places in question (seven of them are known, so far) are all exposed to the elements, usually on rocky pinnacles, steep slopes and elevated hillsides. High are the tops of the rocks, wide is the bright sky, the wind blows, tree tops are swaying, the gods partake of the passionate gift. In Eggli there is evidence for the offering of sheep and goat by fire, as well as approximately 1500kg of pottery shards. The vessels probably contained food. Such offerings were already popular with the Urn-field people, the later Hallstatt time Celts often continued the sacrifices, as well as the use of the sacred location. Dellingen, only 15 km from the Magdalenenberg produced shards from

around 1000 pottery vessels, as well as the cinders and ashes of sacrificial goats, sheep and cattle. Osterstein yielded some 70 000 shards and evidence for burned animals. Here the ritual activity started even earlier, in the late bronze age, continued all through the Urn-field and later the Hallstatt period was marked by violent transitions. All of the old noble seats disappeared in a rather short time, some of them due to warfare. Within 50 years or so, the major Hallstatt time fortifications went out of use. Strangely, however, the local villages near the seats of power continued as they were. This issue is still unresolved, as excavations of ordinary settlements are neither popular nor paid for by the government. The few villages that were unearthed all show signs of continuity in the period when the grand noble fortresses of Ha D are burned down or de-popularized. Who destroyed the seats of power? The La Tène people, would be a simple answer, but just who were they? Should we imagine invaders? Or did the change come from within the culture, maybe in form of a new religion or a violent uprising?

After the fall of the Hallstatt dynasties, you can find evidence of tomb robbers. As far as we know tomb robbery did not occur in the Hallstatt period, and graves were only opened when another corpse went to join the others. The Hallstatt people did not steal from the dead, and if they unearthed some older object while building a mound (such as a flint arrowhead or stone tool) they tended to return it to the ground by burying it together with the grave goods.

The La Tène people, whoever they were, had a different attitude. Usually they took out only the central tomb, which was often rich in treasure, ignoring the numerous tombs in the sides of the mound, many of them containing valuable goods. It seems as if the grave robbers did not know about the burials in the periphery of the mound. They focused on the center, which was often difficult to open with its stone walls; the tombs in the periphery would have been much easier to loot.

Were the La Tène Celts foreigners? Were they aware of the many side-burials? Did they take out the central tomb for profit or did they have a religious reason? At the same time, the custom of open-air-offerings abruptly discontinues. The sky-exposed ritual sites are shunned. Instead, we find at the very end of the Hallstatt time, the very first subterranean offering place. The site is close to Tournus not far from the Saone, at the southern limit of the Hallstatt region. The item is a small shaft. At the top, it is 5m across. Narrowing continuously, it reaches a diameter of 1m at a depth of 2.5m, and continues to the bottom, which is 4.5m deep. The entire shaft was filled with animal bones (some of them burned) and pottery shards, the same sort of stuff that earlier went to the rocky pinnacles.

Here we have the first step into an entirely new direction. Instead of deities residing in the height, the offerings now reach the otherworld by going into the depths. This is the start of a new tradition typical for the Celts of the La Tène time, which finds its most extreme form in cult shafts of up to 35m depth. The gods of the deep have replaced the deities of the height.

Coins: These coins are not a representative selection of the wide scope of Celtic coins. If this were the case, the vast majority would show faces in profile and horses, riders, charioteers on the reverse. What I have drawn is mainly the more magical images, a range of animals and symbolic or abstract forms. Most of the coins are not to scale nor completely precise. Too many books on Celtic coins give images in size 1:1, and as most Celtic coins are less than 2 cm in diameter, this is certainly a strain on the eyes. In some cases I have made the lines clearer than they appear on the original coins, many of which are somewhat worn. The attribution of coins to Celtic tribes are often hypothetical and based on major distribution centers and scholarly guesswork. This does not matter much, as the maps showing territories of Celtic tribes are likewise hopeful reconstructions. As coins circulate and many tribes moved around a lot, errors in attribution are likely. For my sources, consult the bibliography.

Overleaf: Coins 1, Deities, seers, visionaries!
top left: Sequani, Gaul, note centipede (!) top right: Coriosolites, Gaul, disintegrating head
center: Remi, Gaul, right side very worn, compare with horned god (Gundestrup cauldron)
bottom left: Tincommius coin, Britain, woman with hat!
bottom right: Namnetti, Gaul, bard or prophet! Note vision to star and breath (!) words (!) coming from mouth.

2 Mysteries of La Tène

Hallstatt culture, east and west, ended when the old 'noble seats' fell into disuse- a process that was often (but not always) accompanied by violent changes. This did not happen all at once. As the territory settled by Hallstatt type Celts was rather large already, and had no centralized authority, the change to the early La Tène culture took several decades. In some outlying districts, such as Central Germany north of the Main river, people were still following the customs of the Hallstatt time when the alpine Celts had long changed to the burial customs and new religious practises of the La Tène period. Thus, when you read that the La Tène time began 450 BCE, this date is as rough an estimate as they come, and needs not be taken very seriously. With the La Tène period came a lot of distinct changes in art and religion. To begin with, in most places, the fabulously wealthy mound burials were abruptly discontinued, instead, you find evidence that many of Hallstatt mounds were being plundered.

Then, the arts developed in thoroughly new directions. Hallstatt time art was always shy about naturalistic renderings of living beings, and left rather few of them (at least in lasting materials), it also enjoyed rather angular and straight forms in abstract ornamentation. La Tène developed wildly into curves, fish-bladder ornaments, ovoids and anything resembling the lush growth of vegetation. It also began to introduce lots of living creatures into its aesthetic range, human faces, demonic monstrosities and any conceivable creature a mead besotten visionary can dream up. In the Hallstatt time, such images - usually grotesque faces or masks, appear only in relatively few mounds, and may well have functioned as talismans, intended to ward off evil.

When we look at early Celtic art we have to keep in mind that the cultures which evolved it were deeply religious. Celtic art is religious art. The change from Hallstatt to La Tène is a religious and social change, but it won't get us very far to generalize about the exact nature of this change when so little can be known for certain. This book, being concerned with the nature of Celtic religion, magic and enchantment, is not the place to discuss the many changes in history that took place between Hallstatt D and the coming of the Romans. The topic is simply too overwhelming, and luckily there are plenty of books where you can read up how settlements were organized, how Mediterranean influences transformed technology and life, what happened when the Celtic tribes expanded into new countries and so on. All I can offer here is a brief look into the more occult side of La Tène culture. I hope that you are the daring sort of mind explorer who doesn't feel satisfied with my commentaries and goes out to read up the cultural context in scientific literature. This may not sound like a great achievement, but strange as it may sound, the world of popular Celtic literature is so narrow-mindedly self-contained that you rarely, if ever, find a proper archaeological study in use. Instead, plenty of modern Neo-Celticists seem to prefer a literature that has been out of date for decades, if not centuries. I will highlight a few aspects of La Tène culture in these pages on the understanding that research is never finished and that new evidence is being unearthed every day. Also, I have to point out that I do not like to use the term 'Celt' at all. It's such a misleadingly modern term, coined by a handful of not-too-well informed authors of antiquity, and used in a sloppy fashion by almost all popular writers. You get books that generalize on 'Celtic Magic', 'Celtic Society' and 'Celtic Religion' with a simple-minded carelessness that makes serious researchers shudder.

Imagine 2500 years hence, an author writing on 'European Magic' or 'European Religion'. You would be delighted to learn that 'The Europeans' had bullfights, a slanting tower, wore tartan, made music on long wooden trumpets, ate lutefisk with spaghetti, kicked balls into goals (probably a fertility cult though it does sound much like the opposite), traveled in balloons, had talismanic cuckoo clocks and worshipped a wide range of deities, such as a nude man on a cross, a lamb, a pigeon, a hare, a box full of moving pictures, rectangular pieces of paper, noisy metal vehicles and small plastic boxes that were held to the ear in an obvious gesture of adoration. When you read about what 'The Celts' did or didn't do, remember those mysterious Europeans.

Well, you recall that it was already difficult to generalize about the western Hallstatt culture, which was still confined to a relatively small part of central Europe. La Tène culture is a lot more complex, especially as it involves the great Celtic expansion, when you find Celtic people occupying land all over France, in Britain, Ireland, Spain, Portugal, North Italy, Czech, Slovakia, Rumania, the Balkan, and even central Turkey. It would be an easy matter to assume that the invading Celts inflicted their culture on the original population of these lands, but in the real world each conquest is accompanied by a blend of populations. Thus, you get a lot of different countries speaking in various Celtic tongues, each of them with a Celtic aristocracy, but strongly influenced by the native cultures. The result is a wide range of cultural and religious differences. But even in the Celtic homelands in Central Europe things are amazingly complicated. The people so easily called 'Celts' in our times were never a single or unified culture, and for each similarity you can find a dozen odd divergences thanks to the patient shoveling of the excavators. Let me offer examples from the wonderful world of burial customs.

As you recall, with the beginning of the La Tène culture, the burial customs underwent several important changes. The large mounds went out of fashion and single tombs became the rule. In some places, the corpses were burned, in others the corpse was laid out on its back. Compared to the wealth of Hallstatt D, La Tène burials are almost cheap, and unlike Ha D, most of the men were armed. Now one thing that the people of La Tène A and B cared for was the orientation of the grave. This had not been an issue when the large mounds were built - if you bury up to a hundred people in a single mound, you have the corpses facing in all sorts of directions. With single burials, and the new religions (whatever they may have been), proper alignment of the corpse became a must. In the Champagne and the middle Rhine region, the majority of burials have the head to the north-west (45%) and west (30%). At the same time, burials in Switzerland and Baden-Württemberg favour placing the head to the south (45%) to the north (18%) and to the east (19%). This may seem complicated, but is partly due to the social status of the buried. The richer warriors had their heads to the east. Austrian and Transdanubian burials have the heads to the south (57%) and south-east (28%). In Slovakia, 50% of the heads are aligned to the south, 35% to the south-east. Bavaria, Mähren, Schlesien and Bohemia have almost 80% of the heads to the north and c. 5% to the north-west.

These percentages are rough estimates based on H. Lorenz in *Die Kelten in Mitteleuropa*, 1980. As you can see, in each of these districts people were highly systematical when it came to burial. Now burial customs have a lot to do with religion and beliefs in some sort of otherlife. The La Tène Celts definitely believed in sacred directions, they just couldn't agree on one. If you look at these alignments you can't help noticing that the early La Tène folk already had several distinct religions and/or cosmologies. Also, consider the corpses which were not buried in the fashionable direction of their district. Occasionally such differences may have been due to chance or carelessness, but on the whole, they may remind you of the 'dangerous dead'. Often enough such graves have the deceased in an odd posture, with crossed legs, raised arms, folded (bound?), with dislocated limbs, on the belly and so on. There is no common formula for burial of dangerous people, the main thing is that you treat them differently. We'll get to them later on.

The early La Tène still had lots of body burials in flat graves, then it became a religious necessity to burn corpses, and this fashion continued till the Roman occupation. Mind you, it was never exclusively followed and we have no idea just who adhered to it.

Also, the practise of corpse burning never followed a single rule. You get people who carefully pick the bone pieces out of the ashes for burial, and others who throw the whole heap of ashes, bones and bits of wood into a grave. Some bury all of the burned bones in a body-sized tomb, others collect them in some container - a bag or an urn - or simply inhume a few bits to represent the whole. Still others tried to lay out the burned bones in the form of a skeleton. Grave goods were sometimes burned or buried intact, some corpses were burned nude, others in costume. There are even graves that show a mix of customs. As a result we may say that cremation becomes the rule by the middle La Tène, but that there is no standard rule that was followed, not even in relatively small districts.

Then there is the problem of cemeteries. Most Celts preferred to have their dead some distance from their settlements, which may or may not point at a certain fear of them. Whether the cemeteries had a boundary is unknown. Nor is it certain who was actually buried. Apart from the cemetery of Nebringen (Baden-Württemberg), a layout in family groups cannot be assumed. The theory that men, women and children were buried separately has likewise been shattered by the evidence. Fire or body burial, the percentages of corpses do not reflect the population. Child burials should make up almost half of all burials but are extremely rare. Female burials are completely absent in some districts, not so in the Pfalz (SW Germany) where women and children make up almost half of all graves. Many places simply defy investigation as the dead are so thoroughly burned that the different sexes cannot be estimated. Again, the treatment of women and children points at extremely different social systems. Whatever the case, you should keep in mind that it was always only a small minority who received a proper burial at all.

What happened to the rest of the population, and what sort of faith these people had, remains anyone's guess. It gets even more enigmatic when we consider burials in the late second and first century BCE, when the so called oppida-cultures built ever larger ringwalls housing whole tribes. We can see the eroded walls of these great hilltop cities, and estimate that thousands of people inhabited them, but strangely, their form of burial completely eludes the excavator. Whatever most the Celts of the oppida-period did with their dead, they did it without leaving traces. No graves, no grave goods, nothing. Of course there are plenty of colourful theories, ranging from ashes scattered in the wind, cast into rivers, buried without trace, to sky-burials, where birds or wild beasts devoured the corpses. Anything could have happened. And again, this sort of thing is not the rule either, whatever you find or don't, there are always exceptions.

Before we continue with our study, I would ask you to pause a moment and imagine the wide range of possible burial customs. Modern people often think that burials are boring. Well, to a culture that believes in a very vivid otherlife, a good burial is just as important as a good life. Considering how tough life was in those days, it may well be that the otherworld was even more important. These people took death and the journey to the otherworld very seriously. Imagine you had to bury your spouse, a friend or companion. Imagine yourself being buried. What would it mean to you if you knew that one day you would join a lot of others under a hollow hill? Or inhabit a single grave in a cemetery? What would you think if you cast an offering into a fire, if you knew that a very similar fire would one day consume you? What goods would you like to have in your grave? In what direction would you like to face? What difference does it make when a body is buried intact, or burned, or has no specific grave at all? All of this may tell us something about the nature of soul and identity. Think about it if you want to understand the Celts.

Talismans

The people of the late Hallstatt time and the early La Tène period were extremely fond of placing talismanic objects in graves. With the word talisman I am simply referring to any unusual objects that have no function in costume nor in the otherworld. We know very little about talismans worn in daily life, but we have plenty of evidence for talismans in tombs. To begin with, it may be useful to consider that the items found in graves are not necessarily the items owned and worn in daily life. Some of them may have been, but as many grave goods show no sign of wear, or are non-functional, we have to be careful when we visualize proud Celts strutting around wearing their burial costumes.

Now you may wonder how anyone can be certain whether a given object, such as a glass bead, a piece of amber or an unusual bronze pendant functioned as a talisman or as a simple piece of popular jewelry. If you examine just one or two burials, this would indeed pose a difficult question. Things get easier when lots of burials are examined. In many cases, talismans do not appear on their own but come in heaps and collections. Some harmless looking items reveal a talismanic significance when you keep finding them in burials of specific population groups and in company with items that are more obviously magical.

For this section I shall make use of the fascinating study by Ludwig Pauli, who in 1975 listed all known (and reliable) excavations of Celtic talismans . Talismans come in several categories. So do the people who wear them. As an oversimplification, we can state that most talismanic objects come from the burials of women and children. Males rarely have talismans on them (at least talismans that can be recognized as such), and among these there is a large proportion that seems to belong to the group of 'dangerous dead'. A talisman can be thought of in several ways. You could think of it as a sacred object that protects its bearer, be it in life or the journey to the otherworld. You could also propose that a number of dead people were such a threat that their society gave them talismans to make sure the spirit of the deceased stays safely underground. Of course when we look for talismans we are confined to the items that happen to survive. We also have to expect talismans made from wood, leather, horn, feathers, plants and organic materials that didn't make it to our time. Let's take a look at what we can find.

Rattles. Clay rattles, filled with small clay balls, appear in several tombs of the Hallstatt period. Often they are shaped like waterbirds. Early excavators assumed that they were children's toys or musical instruments. As they show very little (if any) signs of use, it seems that they were specially made for the burial. Ladies of the Hallstatt period often had metal rattles - tinkling bronze pieces and the like - in their tombs. In the early La Tène these items became smaller and gradually went out of fashion. You wouldn't think of them as talismans if they didn't come together with a number of unusual objects. Sometimes only one of these bronze plates was buried, good evidence that the object was not intended as a musical instrument.

Bronze objects. Here we have a wide range of items. Pendants in the shape of wheels, triangles, squares, axes, shoes, feet, deer and naked humans can be found in plenty of graves, often several of them at once, strung up on a throng or a bronze wire or placed beside the corpse. Small bronze clubs are also in evidence. These are unusual as they are almost never found in the company of other amulets. As the location of such goods in the graves varies a lot, we can assume that they were not usually worn as part of the clothes. The triangles can also be found in northern Germany, quite a distance from the La Tène Celts.

Unfinished items. Here we come upon a number of objects which were specifically made for the burial. You get bronze rings and bracelets in their unpolished state, with jagged edges, making them impossible to wear. Some of them are unlucky casts, others are plain rubbish or were destroyed on purpose. There are scores of such items in evidence, showing that this was not just a single incident but a regular custom.

Pieces of metal. Plenty of young women and some suspect males had odd bits of metal in their graves. This could be a folded piece of bronze foil, broken parts of swords or lances, a handful of bronze rubbish, a piece of iron, bits of wire and so on. In many cases old and broken metal items were consigned to the graves. Pieces of iron are especially common in children's graves. It would be tempting to explain such gifts with the well known medieval belief that the fairies, the evil spirits and all their kin are afraid of iron, or that you can bind an evil person in the grave with it. It is a distinct possibility that similar beliefs were entertained in the middle of the first millenium BCE. However, in our early Celtic tombs, not all such items are iron. Special attention should be given to tiny bronze ringlets, such as you get when a necklace breaks. These were a popular item in unusual graves, in some of them, you find such ringlets scattered over the entire corpse.

Fat, hollow bronze rings with no discernible function are known from some young women's graves and a few children's. Several of them were filled with unusual substances, such as tree resin or pitch, one child had such a ring filled with jet, another two rings where the inside was made or iron. In each case, the substance inside was not visible from the outside and the item had no functional value.

Minerals of unusual sort are also a popular addition. Four children and one young woman (?) of the Dürrnberg had small quartz crystals near the jaw, possibly they had been placed inside the mouth prior to the burial. Pebbles, quartz, jet, jasper, mica and iron ore have all been found in amulet collections, all of them

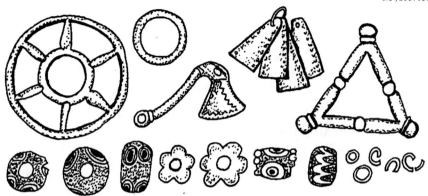

DURRNBERG, GRAVE 71/2 SMALL SELECTION OF TALISMANS
TOP ROW BRONZE, BOTTOM ROW GLASS BEADS & METAL RUBBISH

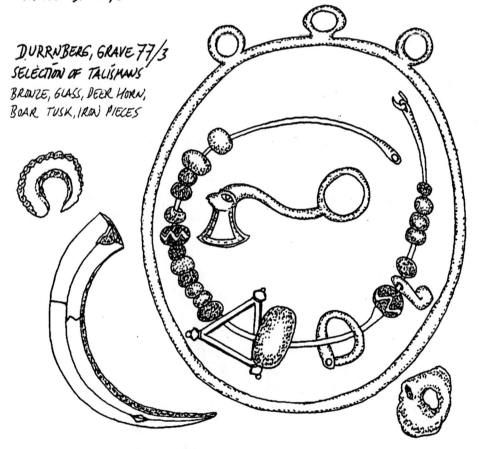

DURRNBERG, GRAVE 77/3
SELECTION OF TALISMANS
BRONZE, GLASS, DEER HORN,
BOAR TUSK, IRON PIECES

Amulets. Dürrnberg, after Pauli.

unpolished and obviously not intended as jewelry. Even large pieces of stone were buried - substantial pebbles, chunks of sandstone or naturally perforated stones. Half a dozen graves contained stone-age flint tools such as axe heads or arrowheads, while graves containing small fragments of flint are too numerous to be counted. Petrified snails, sea urchins and shells also appear.

Shells just as important. There are only three Cowrie (Cyprea) shells known from our period, unusual, as Pauli notes, as they were really popular import goods in the Neolithic, the early bronze and the early medieval period. River shells appear in several talismanic collections. The cemetery of Dreitzsch contained lots of them, several showing traces of red pigments.

Snail shells also had talismanic virtues. At least 14 burials included them. In most cases it was obvious that they had never been part of the costume. You find them scattered over the corpse, resting between the legs, near hands and feet, in a heap above the head or even three burials in a circle of helicidae snail houses. In two cases (snails and river mussels) the shells were in a layer below the actual funeral.

Boar tusks are probably the most popular amulets made from animals, more than twenty of them have been unearthed. Some of them were found in warrior tombs but the large majority comes from the tombs of women and children. A few of them are set in bronze and evidently made for wearing, most of them were simply placed in the freshly excavated tomb.

Deer horn is another favourite. You find antler fragments in several graves, often

without the least purpose, and the unusual women's coffin of Dannstatt was entirely covered with antlers. She also had one of those odd earthenware rings lying within her hips which have excited so many scholars - did they seal the womb or are we dealing, as some naïve enthusiasts proposed, with some really crude pessary? Similar rings or hole stones have been found in the pelvic region of several women. When it comes to animal amulets, boar and deer are the absolute favorites.

Here is a bit of speculation. several scholars have noted that pigs and boars were considered otherworldly beasts by several Celtic cultures. This was reflected in the early burials but also in medieval Island Celtic literature, such as the *Mabinogi*, which explicitly states that pigs were a gift from Arawn, lord of the otherworld. There is also a scene where the divine enchanter Gwydyon hunts for the soul of his assassinated foster-son Llew with the help of a black sow. The archaeological evidence shows that when it comes to grave gifts, stags horns and teeth were almost as popular as boar tusks. The stag as an otherworldly creature has been overlooked by researchers, however, even though the *Mabinogi* begins with King Pwyll hunting an enchanted stag that has been sent as a lure by the very same Arawn. Riding after the stag into the depths of a shady glen, Pwyll inadvertedly enters the otherworld. Similar stags abound in European and oriental folklore, in fact, it seems that whenever the otherworldly ones seek to catch a prince or king, they bait their trap with a deer. This brings us to a mysterious line by one of the Taliesins: *What pigs, or what wanderings of stags.* (BoT7). Could it be that the wanderings of pigs and stags are to the otherworld? Whatever may be the truth, we can be certain that the people of early La Tène sought to derive a measure of protection from the spirits of these animals.

Animal pieces. Bear teeth were used as talismans in at least eleven burials. Less common are other beasts, such as burials with horse teeth or bones(9), with cattle teeth(4), with wolf teeth(2), dog teeth(2), rodent teeth(2), bone fragments from the aurox(3), cat jaw-bones(2), and a large number of astragali from various species.

Human teeth as talismans are known from four burials.

Amber poses the problem that it could have served an ornamental purpose. However, we regularly find it in the odd burials which are rich in talismans. The same goes for

Glass beads. Here the evidence is fairly simple. Most amber and glass beads come from the burials of young women and children. The Dürrnberg for instance provided 359 glass beads from 331 burials. Of these, 314 burials were young women under the age of 25 and children. Similar statistics can be cited from other central European cemeteries. Whatever the reason, women over the age of 20 very rarely had glass in their tombs. This doesn't look like fashion. We can also recall that Pliny the Elder pointed out the talismanic virtues of amber in the classical world.

Now that we have examined some of the talismanic items you may wonder how come so many children and young women were equipped with them. Keep in mind that the burial of young women and children

happened fairly rarely. We cannot know what children were so distinguished, especially as there are cases when children did not get talismans at all. The child with most amulets in the early Celtic world (Dürrnberg 71/2) was of retarded growth, and possibly its parents believed that it required more protection. Now to this day many cultures think that children are threatened by evil spirits or influences, and attach convenient talismans to them. That this was the case in the early La Tène seems likely, even though it cannot explain everything (one burial with talismans was for a foetus, good evidence that not all amulets were worn in daily life). In Turkish Kurdistan I saw many children wearing a single polished stone on a throng around the neck; protection against the evil eye. It wasn't a simple stone, of course. To achieve its protective power, it had first to be taken to Mecca. Such stones, looking not unlike many beads of the Celtic tombs, are generally worn to get children and adolescents through the dangerous period before adulthood begins. This brings us to the young women. It is a possibility that to our early Celts, a woman was considered a child until she married. In this case, she would wear a talisman if she chanced to die earlier. We need not only think of Kurdish traditions here, all over the classical world very similar customs were en vogue. Even Roman kids wore talismans till they entered adult status. In these cases, we are thinking of talismans as a means of protection for the deceased. However from the way many young women were buried, we have to infer that these were also often believed to be a threat to society.

Dangerous Dead and Unusual Burials.

Most cultures on this planet know people who are feared and shunned, be it in life or death. The dangerously insane are one such category, so are victims of accidents, suicides, shamans, witches, untimely deaths and above all women who die in childbed. You can recognize the dangerous dead by the odd way they are buried. In places where the majority of corpses rests on the back, you find the dangerous ones lying on the side, possibly bound up, squatting, lying on the belly, legs crossed , with raised arms and in especially severe cases, with dislocated limbs. All of these and more can be found in the early La Tène period. Many talismanic items come from such burials. Missing limbs appear in several graves, most prominently in the cemetery of Manre (Monte-Trote) where 32 of 89 skeletons were headless. This was taken as evidence for human sacrifice by some excavators. The placement of the bones, however, shows that the dead must have been kept on some sort of platform where they decayed, before falling bit by bit to the ground.

Here we are dealing with a two phase burial. Two phase burials can also be inferred from a corpse with dislocated limbs. The male skeleton of Ilvesheim was left to rot until his limbs could easily be rearranged. The lower leg bones were then placed between the thighs, the feet remaining were they were. The hands also remained in position, but the arms were separated from the torso and placed at a safe distance to the sides. Numerous iron goods made sure that the dead would never rise and haunt the living. Such manipulations are made easier

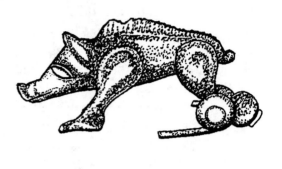

Fibula: expensive brooches or talismanic jewelery?
Top: boar fibula, Hallein-Dürrnberg, Austria, 4-3rd century BCE.
Center: black cockerel fibula with ornaments in red coral, mound of the 'Lady of Reinheim', Germany, 370-320 BCE.
Bottom: fibula combining the image of a shoe (a popular talisman) with a bird of prey. Dürrnberg, Austria, 380-350 BCE.

when the corpse is thoroughly decayed. They were frequent and can easily be proven. Five burials are known where the corpse was completely taken to pieces.

However, it may be a mistake to believe that a two phase burial was only used for unpopular corpses. The evidence from the oppidum of Manching could also show that the usual form of burial involved leaving the dead to rot for a while. A Hallstatt grave from Kappel revealed a girdle containing the eggs of carrion flies (thus proving the exposure of the corpse for some time before burial), and indeed the double burials in Hallstatt mounds raise the question whether occasionally a corpse was kept above ground until it could be buried with another, for whatever reason it may be. If you visualize Celtic funeral fields, it may well be that there were plenty of rotting corpses waiting for a decent burial.

Of course the simplest way to prevent the dead from walking is to turn the legs or feet around, to cut them off or to tie them up, there is evidence for each of these methods. Dislocation of the head was another solution. A warrior from Chouilly had the bottom of a quiver in place of his head. Marson provided a woman with a dark bowl in place of her head (this might remind you of the much later Irish belief that the head is the cauldron of inspiration and knowledge). The patina in the grave of a girl from Villeneuve-Renneville reveals that her head and neck ring were removed some time after she had died. The Dürrnberg provides a skeleton whose head was placed 50 cm to the right of the corpse, Kamenin

a skull resting on the pelvis and weirdest of the lot, Wohlen, the corpse of an old man whose deformed head was moved 50cm to the side. In its place was a bowl containing the skulls of several shrews. Can you explain this? It might be fun to try. We could continue in this way for a while. Then there is a Dürrnberg grave containing a person who had been burned, except for the lower jaw. Or Vevey, a young man who would not rise from the deep, as his feet had been burned on the spot. There are at least a dozen cases of partial burning on record. And while we have lots of skeletons without heads, there are also several burials of skulls without body, not to mention cases where a single corpse went into the deep with several skulls.

That some insane people were treated to such burials is evident from tombs containing badly deformed skulls, from warriors who had been knocked on the head too often or from some cases where trepanation did not make anybody happier. Likewise we can surmise that magical people, witches and sorcerers were feared by their communities. I would guess that the woman from Dannstadt, with her antler covered coffin may have been such a case. Then there are suicides, well, yes, each suicide can be understood as a not very pleasant statement about the validity of life in a given community. But just what is so dangerous about women dying in childbirth? Personally, I cannot understand this at all. However, there are lots of cultures that indulge in exactly this belief. The Catholic church has a special rite for women on their first visit to church after giving birth (showing that she is unclean), and Heinrich

Heine recorded an Austrian myth stating that women who die before marriage become air spirits who haunt young men and dance them to death.

What our La Tène Celts believed is open to speculation, but the fact that so many young women were treated like dangerous demons remains glaringly obvious. The double burial of two such women, aged twenty, from Grafenbühl offers an excellent example. Besides a wide range of amulets (including a triangle, bronze foil, amber, glass, bone beads, boar tusks, a small flint axe, and a pendant made from a horse's hoof bone) the two were securely fastened to the ground by a large stone slab placed across their breasts. That some Scots bards used to meditate with a big stone on the chest may or may not be related. Be that as it may, not every young woman was treated to such a burial or was inhumed with amulets. Elder women very rarely had amulets on them (though the Hallstatt time cemetery of Tauberbischofsheim-Impfingen shows that in this community, the mature women all wore a specific girdle), indicating that their position in life was somehow more secure. Then there are the young men, who were buried very rarely at all. Older men often had weapons in their graves, and maybe these were also deemed a protection from whatever dangers may await a traveler to the otherworld. It seems to be distinctly possible that some fibula (ornamental safety pins) also had a talismanic function.

And while we are dealing with unusual burials it might be interesting to mention the Dietersberg-cave near Egloffstein in southern Germany. There is a deep pit within the cave. Excavators found it to contain the remains of 35 individuals, all ages and both sexes being represented, even small children and babies. Starting in Ha C, some religiously minded folk ritually cleansed the shaft with a fire burning in a bowl and began to throw corpses in. This continued till La Tène A. Together with the dead a number of the usual amulets were unearthed, as well as the remains of numerous animals. In Linz, Austria, excavators unearthed the remains of nine people, mainly females and children who had been impaled with a burning pole and buried at the bottom of a three metre shaft. Whether we consider these shafts as evidence for human sacrifice or as convenient spots to get rid of the dangerous dead is open to speculation. Finally, here is a case that really defies interpretation. In Beilngries, excavators discovered an artificial skeleton. It consisted of human and animal bones (horse or cattle) which had been carefully laid into a grave to form a fictional skeleton in the typical south/north orientation of the district. It's a one of a kind riddle showing all too clearly how little we know about the beliefs and customs of the La Tène Celts.

Offerings to the Deep

With the coming of the La Tène period, the world beneath the surface acquired more importance. In the late Urnfield and Hallstatt time, numerous sacrifices had been made from lofty pinnacles, rocky cliffs and towering mountainsides. With the beginning of the La Tène period, the emphasis turns downward. Let us begin with the square enclosures or *Viereckschanzen* as they ar

technically called in Germany. The
excavators who first came upon the specific
arrangement of walls and ditches took them
as fortifications. Today we are aware that
most of the square enclosures are a way to
mark a sacred precinct and that they served
no military purpose. There are several
hundred of these enclosures in evidence.
Most of them have a wall and a ditch, and
most of them are moderately square. They
can be found in a wide belt between Brittany
and Bohemia. In Britain only a few sacred
enclosures or shrines have been identified
so far. This is understandable, as you can
only class such buildings as religious which
have no certain purpose or functional use.
Or yield votive offerings to the excavators.
This means that the vast majority of sacred
buildings and locations cannot be traced.

Mind you, of the two dozen sites
identified in Britain, 70% were rectangular
or square (Hutton). Most of the square
enclosures were discovered in southern
Germany. Often, a square enclosure was
located near a spring, a rivulet or stream,
which may be of religious importance or
simply convenient. The square enclosures
are often in unremarkable settings, few of
them were at exposed places or have a view
worth mentioning. On the whole, the sites
had a single gate. The direction of this
entrance varies a lot, with the remarkable
exception that none of them faces north.

In several square enclosures, traces of
small buildings have been unearthed. We
know small roofed shrines from the Gallo-
Roman period, so possibly the buildings
were of a similar nature. True, Pomponius
Mela and Lucan inform us that the Celts of
Gaul venerated their deities in secluded

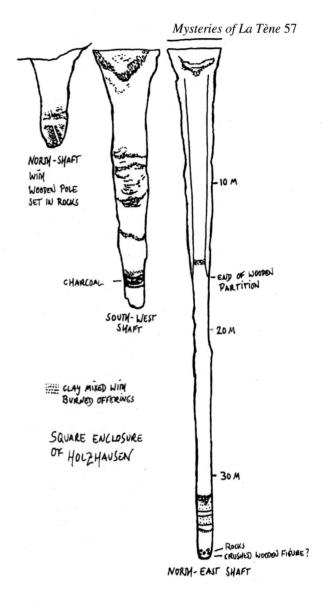

The Cult-shafts of Holzhausen (after K. Schwarz

woodland groves, and Tacitus and Dio Cassius claim the same for the British Celts. This may have been the general rule. Nevertheless, archaeology has uncovered evidence for the many small temple buildings or shrines. It would be tempting to speculate on square enclosures, square Hallstatt mounds and relate them to the otherworldly four-square grail castle of early British poetry. Be that as it may, the square enclosures occasionally had cult shafts, deep holes to receive all sorts of offerings. Such shafts have been found in several Celtic cultures. Some shafts were part of square enclosures, in other cases we just know about the shaft but have no idea whether it was located in a sacred site.

The enclosure of Holzhausen, Bavaria, had three such shafts. The north shaft had a depth of 6 m and contained a wooden pole (2 m long) that had been carefully erected using clay and rocks. The s/w shaft with its 18 m depth contained layers of burned sacrificial offerings. The deepest of the three is the n/w shaft with its depth of 35 m. The pole-pillar-tree trunk in the short shaft is worth contemplating. Why would anyone erect a single pillar really deep in the earth and, as careful analysis reveals, treat it so that traces of flesh and blood remain on it? To point at the veneration of sacred trees by Celto-Germanic people (and a lot of other Indo-European cultures for that matter) is not enough. It does not explain why the tree was venerated underground. What would you propose? Take a look at the shafts of Vendee in France. The deeper one, 12 m, was carefully divided into four sections. The bottom of the hole held a small statue and was filled with earth full of deer antlers, branches and shells. This section was closed by a layer of rock. Then followed the next section, basically earth packed with animal bones and items of pottery. Another layer of rocks closed this part. Above it, the excavators discovered an impressive layer of charcoal, topped by more rocks. Above this part, the shaft was full of stone and bones, some of them human. The top of the shaft was done in masonry and stone smiths closed it carefully with a lid. The other shaft at Vendee with its 8 m depth contained another standing tree, crudely hacked so that several of its branches stand out. Next to it a hollow tree trunk. Around them, earth, pottery, jugs, human and animal bones. The top closed by masonry.

What is the religious background of this ritual? A British example is the shaft at Swanwick, Hampshire, 24 ft deep and 14 ft in diameter. At its bottom stood a 5 ft wooden post, set in clay. The shaft had a layer of charcoal, above it 20 loom weights (clay) and fragments of a saddle quern were buried. As in the other cases, the tree trunk showed traces of dried flesh and blood. Now the loom weights date roughly between 1200 and 1000 BCE, making the whole structure a lot older than the Hallstatt Celts.

Cult shafts were not an invention of the La Tène time Celts, though they certainly made a high art of them. There is one in Vledder, Netherlands, that dates in the late bronze age. Another one, two miles from Stonehenge, is a shaft cut through the chalk to the depth of 110 ft. Most of it was empty, apart of a bit of rubbish left by the bronze age builders and some fragments of pottery. It is by no means certain whether this was originally a cult-shaft, a well, or perhaps a mixture of both. Its close neighbourhood to Stonehenge makes it a sacred site. So there were some shaft builders in the late bronze age, the custom does not appear prominently in the Hallstatt period, but we find it becoming a great fad with the coming of the La Tène period.

The custom even continued for a while into the Roman occupation, just as some square enclosures remained in some sort of use (not necessarily their original use) once the Romans came and conquered. Mind you, the practise of burying offerings in holes and shafts was also popular in ancient Greece and Rome, so there was no reason for the Romans to object.

Cult shafts contain all sorts of items. The shaft (or well?) at Biddenham contained a human skeleton, fragments of an altar slab, a damaged statue, shards from c. 50 Roman urns, bones of horse, fox, ox, dogs and pebbles. The shaft/well of Wolfhamcote contained a large square rock with a hole in the center as well as 24 urns, 12 of them intact. Most remarkable is the well or shaft of Ashill, Norfolk, where the top section contained pieces of painted wall plaster, pottery, bones (including toad, as Anne Ross remarks in her excellent study), remnants of a bucket, a wickerwork basket and an iron knife. In the layer below there were perfect urns packed in hazel leaves and nuts. Between the urns were the odd bits of bone, some iron utensils (talismans?) and fibulae. Below them, at the very bottom of the shaft, a layer of flint.

The under- and otherworldly virtue of hazel is a subject of the chapter on tree lore. On the whole, you can observe that our La Tène Celts happily inhumed all sorts of goods, sacred, profane or plain rubbish, in deep holes. This was not their only approach to the otherworld. Many cult shafts look pretty similar to wells, in some cases scholars are by no means certain what they are dealing with. A well is a gate to the deep, as many central and north European cultures believed. Now the la Tène people were exceedingly fond of making sacrifices to the gods of the netherworld. Plenty of offerings were thrown into wells. There is a well dedicated to the goddess Coventina in Carrawbrough. It contained pins, more than 14.000 coins, glass, ornaments, pottery, a bronze dog and horse and a human skull. It also contained several large altars, some dedicated to the goddess of the well herself. While it is possible to make offerings by throwing valued items into wells, it is also possible to communicate through this gate.

At Chamalières, a sacred site near a warm spring yielded some exceptional treasures. The remnants of thousands of wooden tablets, once cast into the sacred well were unearthed in 1971, together with a leaden tablet. The latter had retained its inscription, making it one of the very few documents in the Gaulish language:

> *By the magic tablet, I honour the divine Maponos Arvernatis, in whom a god dwells. Quicken us (in the attack) and the following (men) by the magic of the Anderoi (*Brixtia Anderon, possibly: magic of the underworld gods*): the invoker C. Lucios Floros Nigrinos, Aemilios Paterin(os), Claudios Legitumos, Caelios Pelign(os), Claudios Pelign(os), Marcios Victorin(os), Asiati(os), the son of Addedillos and the Segovii, who will swear the oath. The small thing will become great, when*

he has sown it. I straighten the bent one. Though blind, I will see so by means of the song tablet. He will strike that one (the enemy). I prepare them for Lugus. Luxe (?). (Trans. By Karl Horst Schmidt, 1981).

Whatever the occult purpose of this rite was, some of the names are familiar. There is Maponus (of the Arverni) and there is Lugus. You'll read about them later on. In the version by Schmidt, the tablet has a distinctly aggressive mood, involving such ideas as striking, an attack and so on. This is certainly suitable for a medium of sorcery that often involves curses. What is your interpretation of the enigmatic text? Are its authors planning a revolt or cursing some mutual enemy? An interpretation by Wolfgang Meid, 1992, proposes that we are dealing with a group of elderly men asking Maponos, the youthful god, to cure them of such ailments as impotence (*small... shall become big*) rheumatism (*I stretch (what is) crooked*), and failing eyesight (*as one deprived of eyesight I shall see*). As spell magick this makes a lot of sense, though we should keep in mind that the original meaning was, is and will remain uncertain. The text contains some interesting terms, such as *risu naritu* (with magically powerful inscription), from Celtic **nerto*-power, strength, Celtic **narito*- magically strengthened, deriving from the Indo-European root **ner*- creative force, hence

magic power. Think about it. Not quite as certain is the expression *brixtia anderon* (magick of the subterraneans, magic of the underworldly gods), from *anderos*- under, *infernus*. This is the usual interpretation and probably the most likely one. Nevertheless, while *brixtia* is definitely magic, the *anderon* could also come from Celtic **andera*- (young woman) as proposed by P.L.Henry. It may seem a bit frivolous if our spell-writers thought of combating the effects of aging by the charms of young women, but this is also a possibility, and given how shaky translations of Gaulish tend to be, we cannot discount it out of hand.

Regarding the *brixtia* of women, see the passage on the lead tablet of Larzac in the chapter on classical Druidry. Maybe it would be worth thinking and dreaming about the nature of the underworldly ones. Who are the gods of the underworld? Who are they today, and who were they in Celtic times? Irish mythology tells us that the sons of Mil drove the earlier gods, the Tuatha de Danann, under the hollow hills, into the deep beneath the crust of the earth. How many generations of early gods were forced underground by the gods of younger and more aggressive cults? Whom will you meet should you go trance traveling into the hidden realm? It is no easy matter to explore the magic of the deep ones, the spells and

---

Top left: small bronze items from the Heidetränk-oppidum, Taunus, Hessen, Germany, late La Tène.
Top right: horse head with long neck, unknown location, Taunus mountains.
Bottom: La Tène grave goods from the Wetterau, Hessen, Germany. Ram skull from Bad Nauheim, cremation urn from Rockenberg, spiky cups from Heldenbergen and Bad Nauheim. Cult objects, punk art or practical jokes!

glamours of gods who were forced from the bright heavens and the colourful face of the earth when their cults underwent massive changes and the feeble minds of mortals turned to new ideals. Many Celtic gods who were strong and powerful in their prime are resting, dead but dreaming, half defined and half forgotten, in a realm of shadows and distorted memories. To wake them is no game but a dangerous initiation requiring imagination, responsibility, patience and care. It also helps if you like to laugh about yourself and are prepared to learn a lot of unexpected things. Forgotten gods tend to come as a surprise and a shock, they need a lot of adjustment to come to terms with a period that is so utterly different from the times when they were worshipped with blood and bones. How will the Celtic deities transform to become gateways to a better future? If you wish to find out for yourself, how about using the term *brixtia anderon* as a mantra while you go traveling?

Tablets of metal or wood were a popular mode of conveying messages to the otherworld. Thousands of people left inscriptions at, near or in the well of Chamalières, each of them a plea for help and support. In an age when very few people could read and write, even a simple inscription such as the above has a highly magical character. Compare the act of casting a message into the deep with modern sigil magic. What do you observe?

The Sanctity of Water

Water worship took several forms. You find sacred wells venerated in most Celtic countries. The locals believed in the healing powers of the waters, they also believed in the deities associated with the place. Often there were goddesses associated with specific wells and sources. The La Tène time people of the Continent, Britain and Ireland often identified their rivers and streams with specific goddesses. Examples for this custom abound - think of the river Wharfe (Verbeia), river Boyne (Boand), Shannon (Sinann), the Seine (Sequana), Yonne (Icauna), Saonne (Souconna), the Marne (Matrona), river Reuss (Rigusia), River Main (Mogons) and so on. This means that the river is the deity, in all her joyous and terrifying aspects. The river goddess could have a friendly face, but she could also cause devastating floods, sink boats and drown fishers. It is no coincidence that many of the Celtic people believed that their river required a sacrifice each year to keep the river goddess in a good mood. Should the sacrifice be forgotten, the river was wont to take one. There is a curious folk tale. Fishers at the side of the stream hear a strange voice proclaiming 'The time is here, the man is not'. Then they see some poor fool walking along in a stupefied daze. In some versions, the victim falls in and drowns instantly, in some the fishers try to hold and save him, alas, to no avail, as he hurls himself into the floods at the first opportunity. I've found variations of this tale in Scottish lore, Vorarlberg legends (Austria) and at the Kinzig river in Hessen. For our research, it may be useful to keep in mind that for the Celts we know of, rivers were usually goddesses. Traces for pagan Celtic shrines have been found close to the sources of several such rivers, showing that it was good policy to approach the goddess in her friendly mood, when she is still young, fresh and playful.

Other aquatic places of importance were confluences of streams, you find them feature prominently in some of the later folk traditions. It is likely that water itself was thought of as a sacred substance. Think of dew, the mysterious water that appears out of nowhere, and was venerated by central and north European pagans. To this day, rural Scots seal a contract by shaking hands across running water and this is held to be more binding than a written contract. Spitting into the palm before shaking hands seems to come from a similar tradition. And what of the healing virtues of spring water collected at sunrise on Easter morn in total silence, a tradition that appears in Germano-Celtic countries on the Continent? Many Celts traveled considerable distances to visit sacred sources and springs to take the water. Under Roman occupation, this custom continued. In their veneration of wells, the Romans met Celts and Germans on a similar religious foundation, and their cults could easily blend. So when you study the sacred wells of the Rhineland, you find that the coming of the Romans increased the popularity of these sites. Where earlier periods made do with one or two small shrines, under Roman rule you can find clusters of buildings, many of them guest houses, arising at the blessed spring. Most of the sacred wells of Britain yield very little evidence for pagan Celtic activity. Not because they weren't popular, but simply as subsequent generations - Roman and medieval-overbuilt and innovated these sites so thoroughly. Under Roman rule, we find plenty of dedications to 'the nymphs' of a given place. These were originally goddesses of wells and springs; the Romans, for all their respect, did not bother to call them by name.

It is not only at sacred wells that the doors between worlds are open and the other side can be reached. You can observe a very similar form of thinking when you explore the countless items thrown into rivers, lakes and swamps. From Switzerland to Scotland, various people took items of great value, some old, some new, and cast them into the deep. Some were purposely destroyed or damaged, as if to make little of their worldly value, or to show more clearly that they were not to be used by human hands. Rings, bracelets, torques, swords, shields, armour, helmets, cauldrons, trumpets, coins... all were cast into the hungry waters. This sort of thing is evident from many Celtic people, but again, the custom seems to have an elder ancestry, when you consider that in some districts, Neolithic farmers cast flint tools into rivers, and bronze age folk eagerly sacrificed weapons and similar goods.

In Britain, most of the rivers that contained such offerings flow eastward. Ronald Hutton writes about a strange pattern discernible for British offerings dating between 1200 and 400 BCE. In this period, *Shields and vessels were almost always left in bogs and pools, while swords went into rivers. Neck ornaments were not found in either.* In the middle iron age, the water hoards of Britain become less popular, while in the late iron age (starting c. 100 BCE in Britain) swords were replaced by cauldrons as the most popular offerings, and destruction of offerings prior to immersion became the common fashion. The offering was part of a sharing, a gesture of thanks for the wealth or victory provided by the gods.

Of course the question remains, just who made what sacrifices and to what purpose. Why do we find so many amazingly valuable weapons in rivers, when by comparison many a warrior chieftain went into a grave carrying inferior equipment? What do we make of the words of Strabo and Diodorus Siculus, who noted that the Gaulish people used to cast treasure and plunder won in war into pools as an offering to their deities? What of the golden torqued wooden statues found in the Swiss lakes (Geneva, Villeneuve)? Or, as one of the more disgusting offerings, what meaning had the face masks, cut out of hairy male leg-skin, which were found, with some regularity, in north German swamps, but also in southern (Celtic) Germany and Switzerland (Rosenheim, Singen and the Chiemsee)? And, as a final but thoroughly speculative idea, what do you think of the tale of King Arthur, who, when dying, ordered that his sacred sword be cast into a lake? While it would be deceptively easy to generalize on river and lake offerings, this may well be misleading. Though the custom seems widespread, it may have had a different interpretation in many countries. In some cases the items cast into rivers and pools are very similar to those found in tombs. Could the river have functioned as a burial place? In that case the ashes of the dead would have been washed away, leaving any offerings.

All we can be sure of is that the places where the underworld was near were used for a number of rituals involving offerings of some sort. In each of these location, the veil between worlds is very thin. This is the case physically - you don't have to dig a hole but can throw stuff in and plop! It's gone. It is also the case when you consider states of mind.

Few natural phenomena can be so hypnotic as watching small, gentle ripples on a sheltered lake. Look into the waves as they wash against the shore. Allow your eyes to unfocus and calm your thinking. If you like you may allow your body or head to sway gently, this is useful to amplify the trance. Try different speeds, slow swaying makes for a deep and restful consciousness while fast swaying can easily lead to shaking, trembling and a wild, excited trance state. With water, and the soothing sparkle of light on the surface, a slow trance may be more fitting. Slow down inner speech and let it fade away. Breathe gently. Soon enough the gentle rhythm of the water will induce a state of dreamlike reverie. Observe the reflection of branches and trees in the water, look down and see the clouds float by. Or watch the surface of water when a soft rain turns it into a mandala of ever renewing circles. What about sparkle and sunshine? Simply empty your mind, embrace the silence and see.

Trance needs not be made by effort, under some conditions, it happens naturally. The seers of antiquity knew quite as much about 'mind machines' as modern researchers, they knew that certain phenomena in nature can induce trance when approached with patience and an open mind. As you'll read later on, some seers divined by looking into the swirling eddies and whirlpools of streams to find an oracle. Irish poets used to visit the realm where

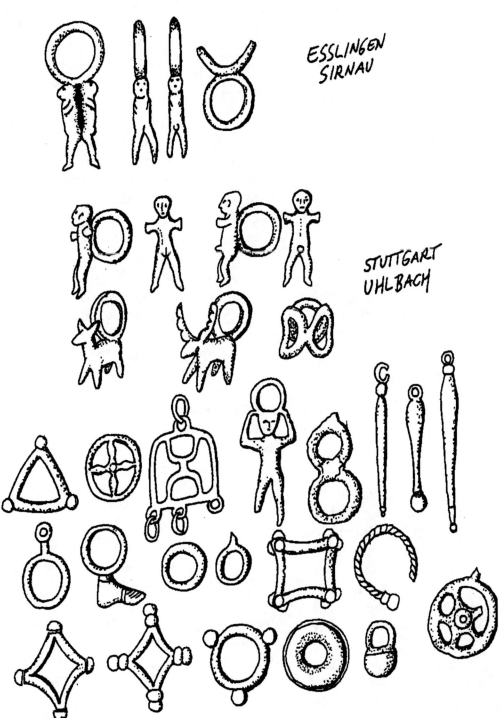

ESSLINGEN
SIRNAU

STUTTGART
UHLBACH

Bronze amulets from various graves, after Pauli.

land and water meet to divine and prophecy. Whoever approached a sacred well, spring, lake or stream stood a good chance of experiencing a massive change of consciousness, provided the mind was receptive and silent. You can do the same. What deities are asleep in the rivers of your neighbourhood? What were these rivers like in earlier times? Who will respond to your dreaming? What gifts will you make, and what message will you write for the dwellers below the surface? What will you write it on? Lead is not a very elegant solution and most wood floats. You could take some earth, smooth it, write your message or sigils, dry it for a while and then cast it into the bottomless deep. What is below the well, the shaft, the cave hole or the glittering waters of the stream? What is below the surface of the mind?

Exercise: Into the Deep

Remember the exercise of the last chapter? Here is a chance for some active day-dreaming. Find a peaceful spot, lie down, put a dark cloth over your eyes, relax thoroughly, ease your breathing, slow down and enter a gentle trance. Imagine you see yourself resting peacefully. Imagine you leave your body. Look at it from above. Go through a gate - invent one. The main thing is that you dissociate from consciousness of your physical body and its resting place. If you go through several gates, tunnels and passages before you approach your destination, you give your imagination more time to stabilize and the deep mind opportunity to prepare an experience of value. Explore till you find an attractive hole, cave, well, spring, lake or swamp hole.

Here is a chance to enter a Celtic otherworld, the hidden realm beneath the surface. Stay there and build up the imagination. This may take a bit of patience. Many beginners in astral projection or dreaming-true complain that the visions seem hazy, unfocussed, fleeting, translucent or otherwise unsatisfactory. It's always this way when you begin to build up something worthwhile in the imagination, be it a new deity, a spirit or a place of mind. Use all senses, see and feel and hear and taste and smell your scenery. Allow it to become more defined, more 'real' (what exactly means real to you?

How can you tell whether something appears real or not?). When it seems real enough, pray a while, invoke the gods of the deep and if you are up to it, go in and find out. Do this repeatedly, practise will make the imagination more stable and the visions congruent. If you expect instant results you may as well forget about such trances and settle down in front of the TV. It takes a while before the astral world (the realm of imagination) becomes properly defined. It is not going to become as solid and stable as the material world, but it can develop to a point where you can go traveling, exploring and discovering. The astral realm is quite as real (or unreal) as the physical world, but it does not follow the same laws and conventions. If you explore the astral, you are exploring what is usually unconscious to you. You are traveling deep within your mind, but in another sense, all dreams and minds are connected, and the realm you explore may have been shaped earlier by dreamers and visionaries of the Celts, the Urnfield people, the Megalith folk, the first Neolithic farmers, the Paleolithic travelers or whoever began the dreaming. Each visitor, each poet and each dreamer contributes to the enchantment. With each visit, each invocation and each trance journey, the visions will improve. That's why shamans, Druids, bards, poets and similar folk invest so much time in their training. A good contact to the otherworld has to be built up, it has to be developed and refined. Then you will find that it takes on a life of its own. The deity you imagine so patiently will become a living sentience with a mind of its own, the astral world you explore will surprise you with events and insights you had never consciously expected. This is the point where the real magick begins and you can learn something new and worthwhile. What will you meet, learn and realize as you explore the hidden realm?

Places of Worship

As mentioned earlier, it is by no means easy to decide whether a given cult shaft in a square enclosure happens to be a pit to receive offerings or was a functional well. Excavation at the square enclosure Fellbach-Schmiden near Stuttgart show a 'cult shaft' which was definitely a well with wood-covered walls. It had a depth of 20 m and even a crude ladder ascending one corner. This does not invalidate the sacred character of the site. To the Celts, the Germans and indeed the bronze age cultures that preceded them, there was always something sacred to water and wells - and this one contained a number of offerings, including pottery, animal bones and three wooden sculptures, showing a magnificent deer and two beasts with rather long and pointy horns - goats or capricorns come to mind. The latter used to flank the statue of a deity, now sadly lost. High concentrations of phosphate in certain levels of the sacred well show that at some point of history unfriendly folk dumped a lot of manure into the hole, a popular method of poisoning the water. Manure poisoning also appears in a well at Pforzheim, where a wooden statue of the goddess Sirona was found.

We have no way of knowing how many cult shafts were originally full of water. On the other hand, there are a lot of square enclosures which have no cult shafts or pits whatsoever, and there is even one that has recently turned out to be a fortified farm with no sacred purpose whatsoever. This poses a lot of problems. It used to be fashionable to class any moderately square enclosure as sacred. Modern researchers have grown more cautious, when a square enclosure yields no evidence for sacrifices they don't know what to do with it. This is the case with plenty of square enclosures. In fact it turns out to be one of the most important differences between the sacred districts in Gaul and those in southern Germany and the east. Gaulish square enclosures, especially in northern France, tend to yield lots of evidence for sacrifices of beasts, they are full of destroyed weapons, war trophies and often human bones. Many of them underwent several centuries of transformation, involving repeated innovation of temple. Although the rituals underwent considerable changes, the sacred location itself remained popular. There are sacred spaces in Gaul that were popular in the middle La Tène and remained so well into the Roman occupation, sometimes up to the fourth century CE. By contrast, the square enclosures of Germany occasionally have fascinating cult shafts or wells. Apart from this they tend to yield few sacrificial offerings, if any and these are often crude, cheap or plain rubbish. When buildings are part of the enclosure, they usually appear in the corners. Also, they often cease to be visited once the Romans came and conquered. Whatever this may mean, it certainly gives the impression that there was a massive religious difference between these sites. Last, here is a perplexing question posed by Ludwig Pauli regarding the south German square enclosures. If the Celts of middle and southern Germany made use of square enclosures for ritual and congregation, how come those south German Celts who moved to settle in Switzerland in the late La Tène period did not introduce this important custom to their new homeland? Was the migration accompanied by a religious reform?

Sacred Groves

Now you may wonder what happened to our nature-loving Celts worshipping trees and such in sacred groves. What is the nature of the Nemeton? Our Roman sources repeatedly claimed that Celtic (or Druidic) ritual happened in sacred groves, secluded forest dales or even in caves. This may or may not have been the case, but it certainly produced the misleading idea that for the Celts the natural and the sacred were more or less identical, much as was claimed for the so called Germans. Perhaps this was the case with worship in Hallstatt times. Where are the sacred places of the Hallstatt people? Apart from the mounds and some suspicious

arrangements of ditches and 'ceremonial avenues', there are only a few towering cliffs where regular worship and sacrifice can be attested. This is very little hard evidence, and poses the question whether the Hallstatt folks indeed performed some of their ritual in wild natural spaces where few traces of activity remained. Mind you, we have no archaeological evidence for any sacred grove as such, as sacred trees and the like tend to leave no trace that can be unearthed by later generations. More so, a grove may be well and good for small scale rituals, such as initiations and rites of passage, but was it really the place where the public rituals were celebrated?

Scholars of the last centuries had a certain bias towards the romantic vision. They believed in the Roman account, which is based on the idea that Gaulish barbarians perform primitive rites in the seclusion of hidden forest glades. This vision has its enchantment, especially for people of our age, to whom urban life has become almost inevitable. The more the concrete spreads, the more we long for the peace and enchantment of the green world. We are the ones who clothe Nemetona in a mask of leaves, berries, hair and feathers. It is a doubtful question whether most Celts saw the forest as peaceful and thought its enchantment attractive. In those days, people did not generally go for walks, and those who did, only with great caution.

Excavations of the last decades have shown that, for all the sacred groves that may or may not have been, there was quite a range of sacred buildings or temples in the middle and late La Tène period. The sacred grove, birth place of the awaking

Male head with dish for offerings, Corbridge, Northumberland, Britain. Sometimes called 'Maponus-head'
though there is no evidence for this identification. A good example for the head as a cauldron.

consciousness, became a place set apart, marked with a wall, a ditch, later with palisades and buildings. It was still a Nemeton, in the sense of a sacred space, but the ideas regarding holiness underwent a number of drastic changes. Here we come to the cults of ancient Gaul. While the square enclosures of Germany offer few insights into ritual activity, and many of them show little evidence for sacrifices, the excavation of fifty or more Gaulish temples have produced material that may be revolting to the faint hearted. Do you believe in romantic Celts? This is an excellent opportunity to keep an open mind. If you feel disgusted by what a number of Celtic people did for the sake of religion, victory and a good harvest, I suggest you study your reaction while you are reading and learn what you, personally, believe to be fitting for sacred activity. Next, how about giving those Celts an equal chance and imagining a world where revolting sacrifices make sense?

Temples of Gaul

For a start, here are some generalizations regarding the Gaulish temples excavated over the last decades. In most cases, there was a sacred district defined by a square or rectangular shape, surrounded by a wall, one or two ditches and possibly a palisade. As mentioned earlier, the walls and ditches provided some sort of privacy, they were definitely not used as fortifications. In most cases, the entrance was somewhere towards the east. Mind you, the temples were rarely precisely oriented towards any specific direction.

Likewise, the interior structures were not precisely measured. In the center of the square enclosure we usually encounter one deep circular pit, sometimes surrounded by a cluster of smaller holes. The central pit has a function not unlike that of an altar: it gives a focus to ritual and receives offerings. In the early La Tène period, the pit is simply a round hole. Later generations improved on it by putting a roof over it to keep the rain out, and before long we find small and simple shrine buildings above the central pit. Often enough, these buildings started out with a round or ovoid shape, just like the pit did.

Seen from above, such a temple space consists of a square enclosure with a round pit and/or building in the center. From the middle to the late La Tène time, many of these buildings underwent considerable elaboration. By the middle of the 2nd C. BCE we may speak of temple buildings. In several cases the building above the pit had become rectangular, and judging from the timbers that held the roof, some of them must have been quite high. Simultaneously the function of the pit changed. Before, it had been a place where slaughtered animals could decompose in their own good time. In the late La Tène period it was replaced with a site for burnt offerings.

It would be tempting to speculate whether the burial customs of the period influenced this custom. Some Gaulish temples were used to make food offerings, such as in Mirebeau, where a large number of miniature food vessels, all executed in careful detail, presumably with food and drink in them, were discovered. Food offerings had their place in the rites of burial, the same goes for items of jewelry, torques, fibula, bracelets etc. all of which appear in Gaulish sanctuaries as offerings to the gods. Some enclosures seem to have been specialized for certain offerings, perhaps the best known case is Snettisham in Norfolk, where 75 more or less intact torques of the finest quality plus fragments of another 100, as well as 100 bracelets and 234 coins were unearthed so far.

Coins were popular offerings in the Gaulish temples of the late La Tène period. This may sound bizarre, but when the Romans occupied Gaul and began to complain about what seemed like cruel human sacrifices to them, the high time of violent Gaulish sacrifices was already past. Starting at the end of the second century BCE, symbolic offerings became a strong fashion. Instead of the usual assortment of skulls, bones, decaying beasts and weapons we encounter numerous wheel shaped amulets (rouelles) made of gold, silver, bronze or lead and an ever increasing amount of coin offerings.

A good example is Villeneuve-au-Châtelot, starting with sacrificed weapons in the fourth century BCE, changing to rouelles and coins in the first century BCE and continuing well into the Roman occupation, more than 70 000 have been discovered so far. The coins were sometimes buried in holes, in other cases they were carelessly scattered around. Three coins, hidden in a hole, were discovered in the wood of one of the statues found in Lake Geneve near Villeneuve. It has been claimed that the coins were offered as they represent wealth. I suspect that this was not the only reason. Celtic coins are among the most beautiful works of art ever produced in

Europe. The images work a strong enchantment on the mind, a good enough reason to associate them with religion and involve them in ritual.

However all of these were fairly late developments. Let us return to the earlier period when slaughtered bulls went to rot in sacred pits and war trophies were considered stylish temple furniture.

In many sacred enclosures, the ditches (or a system of pits) were filled with offerings. These include animals, human bones and in several cases, weapons, shields, armour, chariots and assorted war trophies. These trophies are often the same sort of valuable material that tends to turn up in warrior graves. Sacrifice of animals appears in all known Gaulish temples. There are considerable differences regarding species and the actual mode of sacrificing.

Another element that often comes up in sacred enclosures is towering cult pillars. We have no idea what they looked like, whether they were plain, carved or decorated. The wood decomposed ages ago, but the deep sockets that held the poles are still visible. This may be one of the elder elements in Celtic temple equipment. A series of cult pillars has been traced next to a complicated system of ditches and barrows of the late Hallstatt/early La Tène time at Glauburg in Hessen.

So much for a general view on Gaulish temple enclosures. Such structures are not confined to Gaul herself. Archaeologists found one lovely example for the Gaulish style of temple buildings on Hayling Island off the south British coast; good evidence for the numerous Celts of Gaul and Belgium who sailed across the channel to win a new homeland.

To liven up this account of sacred architecture, I would like to discuss a few of the most impressive sites of Gaul.

Exploring Gournay

Let us first take a look at Gournay-sur-Aronde in northern France where the Bellovaci had their oppidum. We will explore this place in some detail, using the extensive research of Brunaux, as it shows a lot of fascinating evidence for the changing trends in Gaulish religion. Also, it may offer a dream-key to La Tène time religion for readers who enjoy to do something practical (I hope this means you!). To begin with, the enclosure of Gournay has an almost square shape of 45 x 38 m with an entrance towards the north-east, where the sun rose over a river and a marshy, swampy terrain. Building at Gournay began early in the 4th C. BCE, not with the square enclosure but with the excavation of a square pit of 2 by 2 meters. Along the edges of this pit approximately 20 earthenware vessels of various sizes were placed while its center remained empty. The vessels may have held sacrifices of drink and foodstuff. This pit remained open for a time. Then it was covered with earth and a small mound, with a diameter of c. 10m was raised over it. At this time the building of the square enclosure began, which was situated roughly to the east of the mound. The square enclosure began as a humble affair. Imagine an open space surrounded by a ditch 2m deep and across. This is phase 1 of the sanctuary (see illustration), we have a square open space surrounded by a ditch and an embankment inside of the ditch. Several tall poles were set up within this space, and the main ritual focus was a deep, round pit, somewhat west of the center.

There is no evidence for buildings, trophies or sacrifices in this period, and what happened in this space remains anyone's guess. It could have been feasts, assemblies, communal worship, rituals or folk dancing for that matter. Whatever it was, it left no traces. The second phase, between the fourth and third century BCE has the ditch fortified with wooden planks and surrounded with a tall wooden palisade, thereby marking the boundaries between the inside and outside in a more emphatic manner. Perhaps the rites became more secretive or there was a stronger need to make a distinction between the sacred space and the surroundings. The palisade, though looking a bit like a fortification, was more like a symbolic boundary. Measuring carefully, the priesthood of Gournay set up a ring of nine smaller pits around the central one. It says something that these smaller pits are all equidistant from the center (so much for precision) but also somewhat irregularly shaped, giving a general impression of symmetry without the need to be obsessive. Another addition of this period is a mysterious pit outside the entrance. Phase three, dated between the third and second century BCE, shows further changes. The nine pits around the deep central pit are filled up, now lost. Instead, we find a primitive building over the central pit - a couple of wooden pillars supporting a roof. The 'building' has no walls, maybe its sole purpose was to keep the rain out of the pit. The ground-plan of the structure is round. At this stage most of

Monster from Noves, Bouche-du-Rhone, so called 'Tarasque' after a monster of local folk legend, late La Tène period, height 1.12m. Originally the monster was shown devouring a human, of whom only a fragmentary arm and one foot remain.

the standing poles of the square enclosure disappear. We also witness the excavation of another ditch, this one surrounding the enclosure outside of the palisade.

In phase four, in the second century BCE, the round building is replaced by a rectangular one. The new one has wattled walls on three sides, but the side towards the entrance remains completely open. In this period there are several tall poles standing within the enclosure. The entrance is shifted slightly to the north, thereby putting it in line with the direction of the rectangular building. As a result, the light of the rising midsummer sun could enter through the gate and shine into the building and its sacred pit. The inner ditch is enlarged to hold more trophies. The outer ditch surrounds the entire enclosure, entrance is in all likeliness over a short wooden bridge. Above the entrance we may imagine a towering portal on six pillars, a massive and impressive structure where an assortment of trophies and human skulls were exhibited. They are the only human skulls found at Gournay. Next to them the skulls of bulls and cows were found, doubtlessly another vital part of the decoration. In this period most sacrifices were made.

Now let us reconstruct the gory details. On certain occasions, a elderly bull or cow was led into the enclosure and tied to one of the poles close to the pit. During some unknown ceremony it was killed with an axe blow, a swordthrust or a spearstab (all of these methods can be traced), and thrown into the pit in one piece. Then it was left to rot for six to eight months. The bones were then collected and the pit was cleaned. The skull was carefully detached and placed near the entrance, the rest of the bones were thrown into the ditch. The inner ditch contained the carrion of some 40 bulls and cows. It might be worth contemplating whether the massive bull rising from the bottom of the Gundestrup cauldron may symbolize a slaughtered bovine in its pit (see illustration). The cauldron and the sacrifical pit have a lot in common, both are the focus of ritual, vessels to receive, to hold and to transform the offering, gateways into the deep, entrances to the world beneath the surface.

Bulls and cows were not the only animals slaughtered. There is good evidence for sacrifices of domestic animals (pigs, sheep and dogs). The way these were offered underwent several changes. In the third to second century BCE cattle and pigs were killed, but not cut up or eaten. In the second to first century BCE they appear in ceremonial meals, as do sheep and dogs. Horses were sacrificed in all Gaulish temples, but they were never part of a sacrificial banquet. This is unusual, as Haffner (1995) points out, horses appear in everyday diet. The sacrifical animals were thrown into the inner ditch, not carelessly but following a regular and symmetrical pattern (see illustration).

The inner ditches of Gournay contained a lot more than animal parts. Starting in the early third century BCE the priesthood of Gournay began to collect trophies. A surprising amount of weapons, pieces of armour and shields were found, all in all some 3000 weapons and at least 300 complete suits of armour. Most of them were exhibited in the open for years. Then, on some important occasion, they were

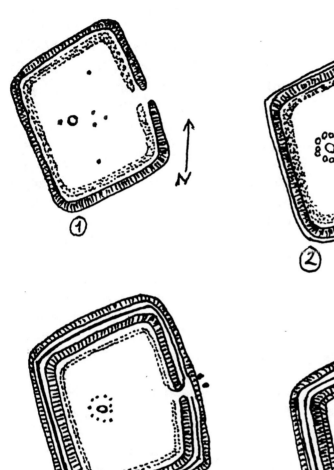

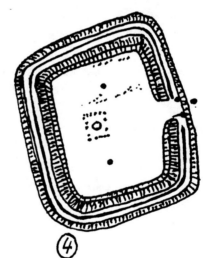

Rough sketch of
the development
of Gournay-sur-
Aronde, dep.
Oise, N. France,
based on Brunaux.

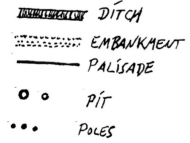

DITCH

EMBANKMENT

PALISADE

○ ○ PIT

• • • POLES

ritually destroyed: bent, broken, smashed, and thrown into the ditches. A selection of weapons seem to have been exhibited on a platform above the gate. This ritual pattern (exhibition followed by ritual destruction) can be traced at several Gaulish sanctuaries. It may well be an important element in La Tène time thought, a similar idea is expressed when a priceless sword is bent or broken before offering it to the deity of a river, lake or swamp. Perhaps a statement of Polybios may be of interest here, who recorded that after an important battle, the victorious Gauls destroyed the collected plunder, the arms of their opponents and some of their own arms as well. To Polybios, this looked like a bunch of drunk barbarians having a fit of brainless destruction. Drunk or not, there may well have been a religious background to the event. Apart from this, the ditches revealed the bones of a dozen adult people of both sexes, whose limbs had been cut off with a knife (for what purpose?), not to mention six (or more) skulls, all carefully prepared by extracting the brains, that seem to have had a place above the massive portal.

It may be worth going on a journey in the imagination to learn about the cosmology favoured by the people of Gournay. Even regarding Gournay our reconstruction is hypothetical and limited to a certain time span. The original entrance was to the east-north east, and not in line with the sacrifical pit or its first building. Generally speaking, the east can be seen as the direction where all heavenly bodies, sun, moon and stars, emerge from the otherworld. Its counterweight is the west, where they all disappear into the deep, and hence, the underworld. While the enclosure itself contained nothing unusual, to the west of the pit was the hidden quarter, the space directly behind the rectangular temple. More so, outside of the enclosure, and to the west of it was the mound containing the vessels with their offerings, all of them set in a square pit, and given to the dwellers of the underworld. We cannot be sure that the priesthood of the second c. BCE knew what was within a mound built two centuries earlier. Maybe they thought it was a grave of earlier times. This would not be unusual, there are quite a few square enclosures in Gaul and Germany that were close to elder mounds. Consider that to enter Gournay, you had to walk roughly westward (i.e. towards the direction of disappearance, the gate of death and the underworld) while to leave the enclosure was to go to the east, the direction of birth and re-emergence. In the south of the enclosure was an open space which was used, as the experts hypothesize, for ceremonial feasting.

This activity was an important ritual of the second and first century BCE. I wonder how they developed a healthy appetite in a place like this. Outside of the square enclosure and c.100 metres south of it was a fortification which was inhabited in the early and late La Tène period, so we might speculate whether the south symbolized communal gatherings, settlements or human activity in general. With regard to the north, the northern section within the enclosure offers a mystery. In the clay rich ground the traces of branches and pieces of wood were discovered. These were not only scattered over the ground but also carefully collected and buried in special pits. One hypothesis

The contents of the inner ditch of Gournay, based on
Brunaux, 1986

HUMANS
HORSES
CATTLE SKULLS
SHEEP, SOME PORK

regarding these finds is that there was a
paddock within the northern quarter where
maybe sacrificial animals were kept prior to
slaughter. This would explain branches, but
not why such branches were carefully
collected and buried. Another theory, which
I find more convincing, is that there was a
group of sacred trees in the north, maybe a
tiny 'grove', symbolic of the sacred groves
which are so often associated with Celto-
Germanic ritual. If we imagine sacred trees
we could speculate that their falling
branches and twigs were not treated
carelessly like any other rubbish but
carefully buried. The association of trees
and towering poles with the north also
makes sense as north is usually associated
with the world tree or the pillar of heaven,
rising high above the earth and supporting
the skies, a notion very common in Eurasian
cosmology.

    This, of course, is not all there is to
Gournay, as the sacred district was
continually rebuilt and re-decorated over

the centuries, and may well have seen many vital changes in religious belief. Just as we know little about the beliefs entertained by the priests of Gournay we cannot be sure just who constituted the priesthood. There may have been Druids in Gournay in the late La Tène period, but regarding the earlier worshippers the only way of finding out is to go time-traveling keeping an open mind and suspending belief. If you are good at trance journeys and undaunted by the odd corpse you are invited to go into the inbetween-space of the foursquare enclosure, to embrace its mysteries and to understand the hidden meaning it may have for you. This is not going to produce any facts in the historical sense but may result in a subjective, but magically valid initiation.

Going below the surface is only recommended for those with a lot of experience in dealing with half forgotten deities, the wisdom to care for what awakes and the tact to leave asleep what wants to remain so. You could also assign the various directions of Gournay and the meaning they may have had to the six sides of a dice and invent a new system of divination. With four points for the ground, three for the sky and six for the gateway you may even build up a system of numerology. Not an ancient Celtic one but a new one suited for a new interpretation. Try to define each direction with a few nouns, adjectives and verbs. In the process, the cosmology will become more vivid in your imagination. This is not an act of reconstruction but one of creative re-interpretation. In this sense, Gournay was not only a focus for many religious world-views but may well become so again, if in a new shape that is suited to

another age and its beliefs.

The end of the strictly Gaulish period came around the year 125 BCE when the sacred enclosure was systematically dismantled for unknown reasons. The pit and the ditches were filled, palisade and buildings were burned to cinders and the site was carefully cleaned. Then followed a period of inactivity. During the first century CE and under the Roman occupation a new temple building was erected on the very spot where earlier the pit had been (phase five). Instead of a pit, our 'temple' contained a place for fire offerings. Around 100 CE the site was destroyed again, but rebuilt during the next century (phase six). It functioned as a Gallo-Roman temple up to the fourth century, showing that while rites and religion transformed, localities remained sacred.

A Hoard of Trophies

Things get even more extreme when we take a brief look at the sacred enclosure of Ribemont-sur-Ancre, some 50 km north of Gournay. By the mid-nineties, only a third of Ribemont had been excavated, but what came up makes it one of the richest and most macabre cult places ever found. Unlike Gournay, Ribemont is not very typical of Gaulish enclosures. Some experts do not even consider it a temple but as a war memorial celebrating a number of victories of the later third century BCE. As Ribemont had a complex history and was in use (or some use) well into the Roman occupation, I shall not bother to unravel all the details of its evolution. Suffice it to say that the square enclosure of Ribemont was surrounded by a palisade towering 3m from the ground and that the open ditches, so characteristic for Gournay are missing here. Instead, Ribemont may be the only cult place where parts of the sacred structures were actually outside the enclosure. Two of these structures have been studied so far. One is the portal above the entrance, where the only skulls of the site were kept. The other is a tall building outside the wall. It seems that there was a roofed platform erected at some height where a large amount of gory trophies were kept. Here things become extremely complicated.

I cannot give the whole background to the deductions that will follow, and can only hope that the interested reader bothers to read up on the topic (see Brunaux 1995). Where the building stood, the archaeologists uncovered more than 10 000 human bones and several hundred weapons on a space of only 60 square meters. These items were not scattered at random. Most bones were in the place where anatomy places them, and likewise, swords were in sheaths, sheaths attached to belts and so on. However, the corpses had certainly been tampered with. To begin with, none of them had a head. Stranger still, each body was cut apart at the waist. The priesthood of Ribemont carefully set up the corpses so that each top half was attached to a different bottom half! What emerges is a rather weird image. There is a roofed platform several meters up, at the very outside of the square enclosure, right next to the wall. On it are a number of mutilated corpses, sitting or standing upright in very little space. They wear weapons, shields and armor, but they lack heads and their bodies are put together from two separate carcasses. These corpses

rot. But as they are high above ground, well aired and protected by a roof, they do not completely disintegrate. The muscles and soft organs decompose, while the sinews and skin mummify. During this process the limbs seem to move in grotesque and unnatural ways. When at some unknown event the whole platform collapsed (or was cut down), the mummified corpses dropped several meters but remained pretty much in their earlier state. The whole affair brings to mind a remark by Diodor, who claimed that, after combat, the victor cuts off the head of the fallen opponent and binds it to the reins of his horse. While he rides home, to exhibit the gory trophy above the front door, the servants collect the rest of the corpse and the weapons. Could it be that these parts ended in such temple spaces?

Ribemont had more to offer than this. All around the palisade, human bones abound. Again, we encounter headless bodies put together from different tops and bottoms, and again, these corpses are equipped with full armour and weapons. Judging from their state, it seems that these morbid works of art stood upright, leaning against the wall, and rotted leisurely for years. Within the sacred enclosure and close to the corners things get more bony still. Here we encounter tiny open enclosures looking like a square with a wall length of 2 m. These walls were entirely built from long bones laid carefully across each other. Some 2000 of them (almost 600 people) went into the northern building, most of them human, some from two dozen horses. These produced a wall that may have been 70-100 cm tall. Probably these early 'bone-houses' were roofless. The bone walls simply marked a small and sacred space where unknown rites were performed. Inside, the ground was paved with human hip bones. At the center was a small pit, 25 cm in diameter but almost a meter deep, filled with the crushed and burned remnants of hundreds of human long bones. The south eastern bone house also supplied a number of human long bones. In addition, there were fragments of bone that looked suspiciously as if the marrow had been extracted. Cannibalism? Or just cleaning? Think about it. Go through all possibilities. As the bones had been through a period of decomposition before being cracked, it seems likely the marrow was inedible. All in all, the excavation of Ribemont has yielded more than 15,000 human bones so far. Several thousand metal objects appeared, among these some 500 lance points. Keep in mind that the site is only partly excavated. There may be plenty of surprises waiting for us. The exhibition of trophies, corpses and bones came to an end around the beginning of the first century BCE. From that point, religion in Ribemont became a more symbolic and less revolting matter. The change in belief must have been thorough, as when the Romans came to occupy the land, they saw no reason to object to anything (apart from Druids). A large settlement developed around the complex, the temple was rebuilt and everything remained fully functional well into the third century.

To sum up the situation, it may be said that the Gaulish temples, especially in northern France, were intensely dedicated to the collection and veneration of morbid trophies. Of course it would be an easy matter to take all the human bones as evidence for human sacrifice. This could be the case, but is not necessarily so. The warrior figures at Ribemont may have been sacrifices, but they could also be an exhibition of noble enemies who died on the battlefield, a mass execution of prisoners of war or even a number of local warriors honoured with the task of protecting the temple. Who knows whether the burned bones in the pits belonged to friends or foes? Who knows whether it was a privilege or an insult to have one's bones built into the walls? Whose bones formed the ground of the bone houses and whose were crushed and burned? Be that as it may, I would like to point out that, regardless who ended up in these temples, they were certainly places of sheer decay. It is one thing to exhibit bones, for example, lots of people all over the world did and do so. The question is just how they detach them from the flesh. Boiling a corpse is a lot cleaner than allowing it to rot at leisure. When the bull decayed in its pit at Gournay, it must have been quite a sight. Can you imagine the stench, the writhing maggots, can you hear the buzz of a myriad of carrion flies? All of these had their place in the world of La Tène time Gaulish religion. These people, regardless whether we believe them to be Druids or some unknown priesthood, made their sacred places temples of rot and putrefaction. What is sacred to decomposition? Can you look at a dead beast at the wayside and appreciate its aesthetics, just like Baudelaire used to? This

Magic of the Anderoi.

is not just a cult of the dead, it is a cult of decomposition. I would argue that this does not imply that the Gaulish priests were necessarily morbid or obsessed with death.

To modern people, the sight of a corpse is a terrifying spectre, but this is due to the fact that Western cultures seem terribly afraid of death in all its forms, and attempt to banish it from daily life. May I ask how many of my readers have ever seen a person dying? And how many of those who eat meat have ever attempted to kill an animal? Yes, it is easier to leave the dirty work to others. I wonder whether it is such a healthy attitude. The Celts lived closer to death, every child was used to seeing animals being slaughtered, not to mention things that happen when criminals are executed or when spring brings war, cattle stealing and night time attacks to settle old scores. Now if you look at a decaying animal you will probably find it hard to appreciate that death and decay do have their own aesthetic beauty. Many Buddhists and some obscure Tantric sects meditate on decaying corpses or visit the places of death and burial to habituate themselves to such experiences. It may well be that the priesthood used such sites of horror to conquer their own fears and qualms, and to come to a mature understanding of the fact that matter always disintegrates. With such a background, a temple of stench and rot may be the very place to overcome fears and worries. Horrid aesthetics can produce catharsis, leading to habituation and eventually peace of mind.

So, instead of leaping to conclusions, may I ask you to use this opportunity? Close your eyes, build up a sacred enclosure in your imagination, and explore. Can you watch warrior corpses mummify or a bull rotting in its pit and see these unique sights without getting emotionally upset?

Roquepertuse

Last, let's take a look at Roquepertuse. This sacred district has been paraded as an example for Celtic temples ever since its careless excavation in the twenties. The museum in Marseilles has proudly exhibited the would-be reconstruction, basically a few stone pillars with niches for skulls, parts of statues showing unknown deities and a sitting bird that has undergone too many interpretations for its own good. The result, though impressive (see illustration) left a lot of questions open. Excavations in the early nineties by B. Lescure show that Roquepertuse was a great deal more mysterious. To begin with, the sacred enclosure was not a secluded and isolated affair but located right next to a settlement. It was also much larger than previously assumed. In fact, where early excavators saw only a small sacred district, modern research envisions such a large site that the question comes up whether all of it was religious. Next, the stone pillars, set in the museum at 70 cm distance, were more than 2 m apart. There were quite a lot of them, as well as top pieces connecting them, and a roof on top of that. Apart from evidence for a platform in a second floor, and for a massive flight of stone steps leading up, we have to imagine the stones painted in vivid colours. These are invisible to the eye by now, but using the fluorescence method, we can see horses, a snake, a horse with a fish tail and a wide range of geometrical symbols.

These images produce more problems than they solve, the green colour for instance was an import from Verona in northern Italy. The same goes for the images: the fish-tailed horse is not part of Celtic or Greek iconography but appears prominently among the Etruscans. This raises the question whether Roquepertuse was a typical Celtic temple at all. Remarkably few purely Celtic items have been found at the location. The evidence points not only to massive imports from northern Italy. We have to wonder whether the people of Roquepertuse were one of those Celtic tribes who settled in northern Italy in the fourth century BCE and underwent considerable cultural changes thanks to the influence of their Etruscan and Ligurian neighbours. Ah yes, and with regard to the skulls in their niches, now turns out that these faced into the sacred building. This may be worth thinking about. When you have skulls above the front door or on the outside of a wall, it may be reasonably certain that these had an apotropaic function and were used to scare enemies, evil spirits and door-to-door salesmen. It might also be assumed that such skulls were not necessarily of friendly or honoured people. In Roquepertuse the skulls were to be seen inside the temple, they were protected by a roof and in all likeliness they were treasured and respected. A good example that skull-worship took many forms within the Celtic world. The settlement and sanctuary of Roquepertuse were destroyed by unknown persons around the year 200 BCE, good evidence for the fact that life in Celtic Gaul was not as peaceful as some would have it.

To sum things up, I would like to propose that the sacred spaces of the La Tène time Celts were not only places as such but also sites of transcendence, passages to other realms and realities. Just as the slaughtered bull transformed into a swarm of buzzing and creeping flies and worms, leaving only the bare bones behind. Were carrion eating beasts, such as crows, ravens, wolves, dogs, pigs, flies, insects etc. sacred to the Celts? You'll meet most of them in Celtic myth. Speaking of carrion, can you imagine what a health hazard such a sacred enclosure was? Someone cared for these places. Someone arranged the corpses, someone cleaned the pit after the bull had gone to pieces. Was it Druids or some unknown priesthood? And just how did they deal with infection, carrion poison and an impressive mortality rate? Was this the price paid for the ability to scare the whole population, to control the nobles and the keep the rulers in submission? Just think about it. If the Druids of Gaul had such absolute power as the Roman authors claim, how did they secure this power in a society full of quarrelsome hotheads? Was the purpose of Ribemont and Gournay to scare the population out of their wits?

And what shall we make of the square shape of the enclosure? Isn't it tempting to relate it to the four-square grail castle, to the four-cornered, revolving castle of the otherworld or to the human body with its four main posts (two shoulders, two hips) of medieval bardic lore? What, indeed, makes a square or slightly rectangular shape sacred? And why is there not a single *perfectly* square enclosure? What makes trapezoids so special?

Perhaps you would like to meditate on this idea for a while. To begin with, you might assume that a square or rectangular groundplan must have been familiar, just like the walls, ditches and palisades, from fortifications. This, however, is not the case. The Celts built fortifications and ringwalls around hill-or mountaintops. Sometimes they improved on nature by making slopes steeper or flattening the living space on top. Nevertheless they adapted their defenses to the natural terrain. Celtic fortresses tend to have irregular shapes and rounded corners. It was the Romans who introduced rectangular forts, and showed how superior they were to all the earlier earthworks.

So we can forget about the military background. Where else can the Celts have found a model for their temples? Consider where squarish shapes appear in nature. You'll soon find that they are rare. What is so eminently useful as a ground plan for human buildings, settlements or roads turns out to be amazingly rare in the natural world. So where is the prototype of the square enclosure? Was the shape selected as it is indeed so 'un-natural'? Or should we seek our answer while contemplating the skies? For the sake of creative speculation I would like to draw your attention to the constellation Ursa Minor in the northern sky. I have to thank Anad for this remarkable idea. Here we have a moderately square enclosure, though perhaps I ought to add that two of the four stars that define its 'square' are difficult to see in our modern polluted nightskies. Ursa Minor, the small bear, is of importance as it is so close to the north axis, to the place where earlier cultures

believed the pillar of heaven to uphold the sky. Nowadays north is almost exactly at the star Polaris, itself part of the tail of Ursa Minor. The north point, defined by the angle of the earth axis, keeps moving. In the La Tène period it was closer to the 'square' or 'rectangular' enclosure of Ursa Minor than to Polaris. For speculation's sake you could call it a foursquare, revolving, spinning castle and compare it with Taliesin's song 'I will praise the sovereign' BoT 30, (see chapter 'Cauldron of the Otherworld'), Cu Roi's castle in Irish myth, the ground plan of such sacred Celto-Germanic board games as Gwyddbwll, Tawlbwrdd, Tablud, Tafl, Fithcheall, Brandubh, or with the enchanted foursquare castles that abound in early Grail literature.

Be that as it may, it is possibly useful to think of Celtic sacred places in terms of sites of transition, of transcendence and of transubstantiation. Whatever seemed holy to them was also a gateway to another consciousness. Sacred groves, square enclosures, wells, swamps, lakes, cliff-tops, caves and so on make lots of sense when you think of them not as places but as points of transition. Holiness implies experience of the numinous, what is sacred is not necessarily a thing or place but a quality of experience. This goes for artificial structures just as it goes for hallowed woods or sacred rivers. Look for the gateways!

Tracing Shadows Through a Maze

It is simply bad luck that we know so little about the deities of Celtic prehistory. That there were lots of gods and that there may have been dozens of religions is moderately certain, but what these were all about is a

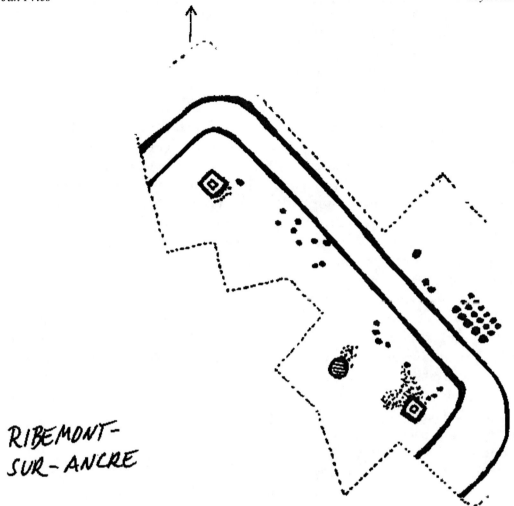

RIBEMONT-
SUR-ANCRE

 HUMAN CORPSES
• BONE SPLINTERS
▣ BONE ARRANGEMENTS
◉ FIRE PLACE

Map of the excavation of Ribemont, after Brunaux.

question that you can hear answered by the gurgling waters, the dancing flames of the camp fire, the howling winds and find written across the star-sparkling skies. Whatever early Celtic religion may have been like, we simply cannot know. This situation improves a little when we come to the last phases of the La Tène period, when Greek and Roman authors began to record the odd items on the faith of the Celts of Gaul. Now Gaul, for all we know, is not representative for the many cultures of the so-called Celtic world. Nevertheless, these tiny bits and pieces, many of them of doubtful validity, are all we can lay our hands on. What were the Celtic dcities like?

Next to nothing survives with regard to most. Let's take a look at a few of them. Take the famous passage by Lucan (*Bellum Civile/Pharsalia*). Lucan tells his readers that the three major deities of Gaul were Teutates, Esus and Taranis. Well, to know the names of three Gaulish gods wasn't bad for a Roman poet who had probably never been to Gaul. His brief note, however, was heavily abused by scholars and popular writers, most of whom copied it without a trace of doubt. The scholars of the 19th century in particular tended to view 'the Celts' as if they were a single nation, or even worse, something like a badly organized empire. In tune with the prejudice of their own time, they assumed a unified religion, and Lucan's statement was the very thing to support their delusion. You find the fable of the three major gods pronounced as plain fact in plenty of the older studies, nowadays, scholars are more cautious, not so countless adherents of Neo-Celtic cults.

The religious inscriptions of Gaul name 375 gods, of which 305 are only named once (Hutton 1991). This does not mean that the latter were unimportant, it simply means that we have very little evidence. Most of the inscriptions come from altars, statues and sacred buildings of Romanized Gaul. Prior to the occupation, most deities were not venerated as statues of stone, nor was their name recorded. The people of occupied Gaul, Germany and Britain learned how to make statues and inscribed altars from the Romans. They did have the odd stone statue or wooden figure earlier on, but it was only upon contact with Roman religion that such items became really popular. We have to assume that the people of the late La Tène time often had abstract notions of the appearance of their deities. Well, once occupied, the stonesmiths began to produce statues for the legions, and soon enough statues of local deities followed, most of them shaped very much like the Roman prototypes. There are plenty of Gaulish deities in evidence that look almost exactly like Roman gods, except for a Gaulish name or some small attributes.

Teutates, Esus and Taranis

Here we run headlong into the 'Roman Interpretation'. The Romans tended to give the names of the gods of their own country to the deities of occupied provinces. In some cases this is helpful, as it provides a hint regarding the function of a given (unknown) deity. More often, the interpretation misleads, as when we have different Roman gods attributed to a single Celtic deity, or when the deity was so unusual that the Romans had no proper equivalent. Well, when we consider the archaeological evidence for Lucan's three gods, things become very obscure. Teutates (or Toutates) can possibly come from *Teuto-Tatis, meaning 'Father of the Tribe'. This makes him the major tribal deity, but does not tell us who this major deity happens to be. Father of the tribe points at ancestral worship, possibly at deified ancestors, but of course each tribe traced its origin to a different ancestry, and had little tolerance for the tribal father of its neighbours or enemies (the terms were often interchangeable).

There are a few inscriptions to him, found in Britain, the Steiermark and even in Rome. The former ones equate him with the Roman war-god Mars, the latter with Mercury, god of traders, travelers, thieves and journalists. None of this tells us much of his character, let alone of the rites and myths of his cult. Esus is even more difficult to trace. His name (etymologically an unsolved riddle) appears on a single inscription from Paris. The name stands under the picture of a man cutting branches from a leafy tree. In their usual enthusiasm, experts have identified this tree as a willow, an oak and even a gigantic mistletoe. A fairly similar picture of a Celtic deity (identified as Mercury) has come up in Trier. Maybe it shows Esus and maybe it doesn't. Taranis, a word derived from 'thunder' appears on no altar at all. There is no deity of such a name in evidence. We have inscriptions for gods named Taranucus, Taranucnus and Tanarus, all of them identified as Iovi (Iupiter), which would suit sky gods and wielders of thunder and lightning.

All in all, this is very little hard evidence for the supposedly most important three gods of Gaul. Now things became even worse as Lucan's passage was elaborated by later writers. Unknown scribes of the 4th and 9th C. added the details that the three gods used to receive peculiar human sacrifices: Those to Teutates were drowned in a vat, those to Esus hung in trees (till the limbs fell off) and those to Taranis burned in a wooden vat. That various forms of human sacrifice were practised by the pre-historic cultures of trans-Alpine Europe is fairly certain, but whether they were actually performed in this fashion for these three specific deities remains an open question. How much did Lucan, writing in the 1st C. CE, know about Gaul a hundred years earlier? And how much could the anonymous scribblers who added the gory details 300 and 800 years later know? Instead of offering the passage with several well-deserved question marks, a host of academic and popular writers published it as a self-evident fact and added a fantastic tangle of theories regarding elemental attributions, the sacred triple death and trinities in general.

A Deity of Horses

Well, Lucan's three cronies are not the only deities who were assumed to be pan-Celtic gods by modern researchers. Take Epona for instance. Unlike the gods we examined earlier, the cult of the horse goddess Epona (or Equona) is well documented. Her name comes from the Gaulish word *epos- or *equos-, a horse, and thereby amply demonstrates her function as a goddess of horses, riders, cavalry and travelers. There are about 60 inscriptions of her name and some 250 images of her. These come from many parts of Europe: Eponas have been found from Spain to Scotland, from the Balkan to Gaul, even a few from Italy and Rome herself. Usually her icons show a woman riding a horse or mule, or driving a chariot. This mass of material has made some early researchers propose that Epona was an all-Celtic deity, known and worshipped by Celtic people all over Europe. Sad to say, but things are not as simple as they seem. While the cult of Epona may have been native to the Rhineland (this is open to debate), it was made popular by Gaulish mercenaries serving in the Roman legions. Keep in mind that the legions were not simply Italians at arms but a multi-national force recruited from all parts of the empire. Caesar made much of his 'German' riders when he conquered Gaul. Gaulish legionaries and Rhineland Celts were employed to conquer the Celts of Britain. Legionaries from Gaul left dedications and altars to their god Mercurius Avernicus at Miltenberg, south Germany. British Celts seem to have been employed to build the Limes, the Roman frontier wall stretching for hundreds of miles across Germany. People who joined the legions certainly got around during the 25 years of their service. Wherever they went, they took along the deities of their homeland. In times of danger, they vowed to dedicate a new altar to their gods, and when the deities turned out to help, such an altar was ordered from a local stone-smith.

Epona became a special patroness of the cavalry, and wherever cavalry was employed, inscriptions to her abound. Strange as it sounds, Epona was a Celtic deity who made a career thanks to the Roman army. She certainly had more followers in the legions than in her original homeland, wherever that may be.

Rhiannon and the Morrigan

Some researchers have identified the medieval Welsh horse-woman/goddess Rhiannon (*Mabinogi*) as a late form of Epona. As we know so very little regarding Epona's cult, rituals and mythology, and even less of Rhiannon, this identification may or may not be true. You will notice that the names of the two sound very dissimilar. Rhiannon possibly comes from the Gaulish Rigani, meaning Great Queen. There is a deity of that name mentioned together with the goddess Rosmerta in the inscription of Lezoux. Sadly, Great Queen is such an abstract title that it may have been applied to quite a few Celtic goddesses.

The Irish trio of war goddesses appears as a single figure with the name Morrigan (or Morrigu), be it as a wrathful woman, a carrion crow, a raven, a wolf or an eel. The name Morrigan probably had a very similar meaning as Rigani, Mo meaning Great and Rigan Regent or Queen (another option is Queen of Nightmares). For all we know, Rigani, Rhiannon and the Morrigan may have very little in common except their grand titles. This sad state of disinformation goes for most of the Celtic deities. Belenus, for example, is often described as a solar god by sloppy researchers. Plenty of deities have similar names. This could mean that they are all local variations of a common deity, but on the other hand the suffix bel- means shining, bright, and such a term could have graced the titles of many other

The bone house. Ribemont dreaming.

divinities. It says less about the deity in question than about the human mind. Most people find bright and shiny things more attractive than dull and dark ones. If you take a given idea, vision or memory and make it bright and shiny, in most cases you will find it becoming more attractive. You can use this to build up a stronger vision of your deities, to motivate yourself, or to make certain ideas more attractive.

Lugus

Then there is the Gaulish god *Lugus-, whose cult can be traced in a variety of town names, such as Luguvalium (Carlisle) and Lugudunum (the root of Lyon, Laon and perhaps Leyden). A Celto Iberian inscription, engraved on rock and discovered at Penalba de Villastar, Teruel, Spain in 1908, offers an enigmatic insight into the cult of Lugus. A rough and somewhat disputed translation of the lines by Rolf Ködderitzsch, 1985, (translated from the German) runs:

> Unto Eniorsis and Tiato of the Tiginos we dedicate the furrows and unto Lugus the arable land. Unto Enorsis and the Equaesos provides Ogris the protection of the arable land, and unto Lugus the protection of the land cleared for cultivation.

This is not very helpful. More readable is the translation by Wolfgang Meid, 1994, which clears up several uncertain points, and yields an altogether different meaning:

> To the mountain-dweller as well as to

…, to the Lugus of the Araians, we have gone on a field procession (or 'we have come together through the fields'). For the mountain-dweller and horse-god, for Lugus, the head of the community has put up a covering.

This points at ceremonial processions, a common religious practise in many pagan cultures, and fits the nature of Lugus as a deity associated with harvest time and riding. The covering is more enigmatic-was a statue or idol covered, clothed, or was the temple roof renewed? The differences in the two renderings are all too understandable when you consider that this is the third-longest inscription in the Gallo-Iberian tongue, a language that is still very much under reconstruction. Lugus was a popular god with a number of Celtic people, and possibly, as some hypothesize, the deity whom Caesar referred to as Mercury. Sadly, we know nothing about the cult, religion, rites and mythology of Lugus. To fill this embarrassing vacuum, it has been popular to abuse the myths of medieval Ireland and Wales. In Ireland we come upon the radiant Lug Mac Ethen, son of Cian and grandson of the divine healer Dian Cecht. In the battle between the Tuatha de Danann and the monstrous Fomors from under the sea, it is Lug, bright and shining, who appears like the rising sun, spell binds the Fomorian hosts by dancing around on one leg, keeping an eye closed, and who finally wins the day when he hurls a magic missile (a ball made from chalk, poisons and the brains of slain enemies) through the single eye of the Fomorian leader (who happens to be his other grandfather). The Irish Lug is called

Samildanach (Skilled in all Arts) and Lamfada (With the Long Arm). In Irish myth he is the model for a perfect regent. He is also a multi-skilled trickster, the inventor of horse riding, horse whips, the Lughnasad feast and the sacred board game fidchell, not to mention the divine father of Ireland's greatest hero, Cu Chulain. Lug's reflection in British medieval myth is a less impressive character. You find him in the 4th branch of the *Mabinogi* and in the songs of Taliesin, under the name Lleu Llaw Gyffes. Lleu can be translated as Light or Lion, Llaw Gyffes as Skillful Hand or Certain Aim. If it weren't for this title, we wouldn't be aware of the relation between Lug and him at all.

Unlike the Irish Lug, Lleu is a very human figure who is born prematurely to his mother Arianrhod under bizarre ritual circumstances and much against her will. He is reared in an incubator (a wooden chest) by his uncle Gwydyon, the famed enchanter and spell-caster. His only claim to divinity is the fact that, after his assassination, he does not die but ascends the sky in the shape of an eagle. This eagle laboriously flutters to the otherworld where it perches on a mighty oak and begins to rot. Eventually he is found by his uncle Gwydyon and returned to human shape. In this state he confronts his assassin Goronwy and kills him with a spear cast that penetrates a rock behind which Goronwy was vainly hiding. This is not bad for a mortal but hardly enough to suffice for a god. We also know Lleu was one of *the three red reapers of Britain* (Triad 20) and that *his grave is under the sea flood, where his shame was: he was a man who gave right to no-one* (BBC 66). Good

evidence that the *Mabinogi* only recorded a small segment of his original mythology, which happens to be lost. Where the Irish Lug inaugurates high kings, the British Lleu remains a pale mirage, a figure of the story-tellers art. Now it has been a common fashion to take the medieval Irish and Welsh tales as distorted evidence for the cult of the earlier deity Lugus. The trouble is that the Welsh and Irish traditions show numerous differences, and that both of them were recorded almost a thousand years after the original deity was worshipped. Worse yet, the Indo European root *leuk- means to shine, to glow, and can be found in such words as light, lux, lumen, lucid etc. Light is not a name, it is an attribute that has been related to lots of deities. You could as well try to reconstruct Lugus by examining the myths of the Norse god Loki. Mind you, Loki is blood-brother of Odin, and Odin in turn has a lot in common with the Irish Lug. Both are associated with sacred spears, ravens, riding, and both are known to have inaugurated kings. What a mess!

Such subjects could do with detailed study. It's a sad but true story that most modern Celtic enthusiasts subscribe to the fable that the so called Celtic and Germanic people were arch-enemies. You get books on Celtic myth that compare the Celts with the native American plain dwellers, for what it's worth (actually a lot, In terms of money), but you get very few authors who bother to point out that in central Europe, the mix of so-called Celtic and Germanic tribes was so complicated that their Roman contemporaries could hardly tell them apart, and to this day scholars are squabbling about which tribe belonged to what cultural or linguistic group.

Telling the difference between German and Celtic tribes is very easy provided one accepts Caesar's definition and doesn't bother to look into recent research. The closest counterpart to the Gaulish Taranis is the German Donar, the Anglo Saxon Thunor and the Norse god Thor. Gwydyon may well be related with Wodan/Odin; the winter goddess Cailleagh be a reflection of Hel, Helja, Hella, Huldra; Brig and Frigg may share more than similar names; Njörd, Nodons, Nehallenia and Nydd arise from the same oceanic source and whether Lugus came after Lug, Lleu, Loki or the terrible Lukiferus is anyone's guess.

It might be useful to disgress a little in this place. One of the problems of modern research is that so many earlier researchers treated the material in such a crude fashion. Just as the first archaeologists did their job by blowing up tombs with explosives, the first prehistorians had a reckless attitude and explained a good many things they didn't understand by half. In the 19th and early 20th century a lot of European nations were hungry for the religion and culture of their would-be ancestors, and scholars were paid to get results, no matter how. This was the time when 'national identities' were the fashion of the day, when there was a demand for ancestors one could be proud of. It was the time of some great forgeries. It was also a time when scholars who preferred question marks to certainties found themselves without a job. Worst of the lot, there was politics. It's hard to imagine, but people believed in politics in those days. French prehistorians did a remarkable job in convincing their country people that the origin of all Celtic culture is Gaul. German historians proposed an ancient conflict between proud, noble-minded Germans and degenerate Celts who had too much access to heady southern wines. English scholars went one step further, and proposed that there is a fantastic gap between the Celtic and the Anglo-Saxon inhabitants of their islands. The Anglo-Saxons, so they proposed, were straight, logical thinkers, very sober minded, a bit dull, but really good at administration. By contrasts the Celts thought in fuzzy circles, believed in a million superstitions, were highly intuitive and made good poets. Using such theories, it became an easy matter to explain why government belonged to the English, and why the Welsh, Scots and Irish could count themselves lucky that such capable thinkers were ruling and exploiting them.

This sort of thing was proposed by scholars and eagerly gobbled up by common opinion. As there was so much political tension behind it, a fundamental difference

---

Early reconstruction of the portico of the temple of Roquepertuse, 15 km from Aix-en-Provence, France. Recent research shows that the space between pillars was wider, the skulls did not face outwards but inwards into a hall and the location of the bird (shown more fully reconstructed at the bottom of the page) was probably not on top of the structure. Middle La Tène period, Celto-Liguarian.

was made between British and Anglo-Saxon (Celt and German). Using such theories it could be proved scientifically that the Irish were not fit to govern themselves. Some scholars went beyond this point and proposed that the whole matter was one of Aryan supremacy. In their opinion, the Irish were not even Indo-Europeans. To avoid the deplorable fact that Irish is an Indo-European language they made up a number of vague new terms, and invented a dark 'Hibernian' or 'Atlantic' race from which the Irish were to have originated. If you come upon small, dark Celts and tall, fair Germans in literature you can be sure they were invented in the 19th century.

While modern scholars have long dismissed such theories, common opinion has not. To this day the Celts are believed to be a romantic culture with plenty of magic, while the Germanic and Anglo-Saxon people are often portrayed as down-to-earth and no funny business. This is in spite of the evidence. We have plenty of Celtic myths, of course, but very little actual ritual has survived. The spells and sorceries of the Anglo Saxons, let alone the North Germanic cultures are much better documented. And while we are at it, did you notice that the way the so-called Celts and Germans were defined a hundred years ago corresponds pretty closely to the hogwash that people utter when asked to define the differences in male and female thinking? Or the silly superstitions pronounced in the seventies regarding the brain hemispheres?

Gods of the Land

Let us continue with the deities of the late La Tène period. As you may recall, a good many goddesses were associated with water, and worshipped as sources, springs, lakes and rivers. Other goddesses were in charge of the land. The goddess Abnoba was associated with a mountain range of the same name, it corresponds with the Black Forest. The goddess Arduinna was in charge of the Ardennen mountains between Maas and Rhine. A similar relationship exists between the goddess Boand and the river Boyne, the god Condatis and the city of Condate, the goddess Eriu and Ireland and so on. Plenty of deities are known who were in charge of local scenery. These deities were of great importance to the locals, but obviously the tribes living a couple of hundred miles away hardly knew or cared for them. This may have posed some problems when the tribes migrated, as happened already in the Hallstatt period (some evidence for Hallstatt type settlers appears in Britain around 600 BCE, thereby starting the British iron age), but with more frequency between 350 and 200 BCE when you had Celtic tribes swarming all over Europe and Asia Minor. What happened to the local deities when their worshippers moved? What is your answer?

In many cases (but not all) the land was personified as one or several goddesses. This lead to the Irish custom of wedding the king to the tutelary deity of the land. You have probably heard of this ceremony. A pretty savage version of it was recorded by Gerald of Wales in the late 12th century: the potential king of Donegal copulated with a mare. After intercourse, the horse was killed and cooked in a cauldron. The subjects ate the flesh while the king bathed in the broth. Then he was dressed in white, had to stand barefoot in a footprint carved in a rock and finally received a wand of office. The mare of this story is to represent the tutelary goddess of the land, which, given the evidence, is not unlikely. However, I should add that this story, apart from a few ancient elements, is as questionable as it comes. Writers generally quote it as if Gerald had seen it in person, and comment on it in the light of ancient Hindu horse cults and sacrifices, which is always sound fun. They hardly ever mention that Gerald had never been to Donegal, Donegal had been Christian for at least six centuries, and the folk who told this tall tale were not at all sympathetic with the royal house in question.

Whether the Gaulish Celts believed in tutelary goddesses to whom a king ought to be wedded is a moot point, when Caesar came to Gaul, the institution of kingship had long been replaced by a quarreling aristocracy. The British Celts differ from the Irish in that they seem to have had a number of queens. This casts doubt on the question of whether the regent was married to a goddess of the land. Did such queens marry a male diety or was the symbolism of less importance? In other Celtic countries evidence is totally absent. We could continue with our studies for a while, no one being any wiser.

Cernunnos

While it is impossible to map out all Celtic deities, we might as well take short look at some of the better known ones. First the enchanting Cernunnos, the horned god, whose name appears on a single altar from Paris, as 'ernunnos'. The neo pagan and the Wicca movement are very fond of this deity, whom they consider a god of hunting, a lord of the wildwood and, in the most extreme cases, 'the eldest type of male divinity', whatever that may mean. Like them, I find 'the horned god' a fascinating figure, but would argue that this is not one god but a blend of many. In plain reality, there is just one horned god with a name. It is supposed to mean 'the Horned One', or so the enthusiasts claim, while linguists point out that anything with horns in it ought to be spelled Carnunnos. Be that as it may, horned gods abound in Celtic religions. While all of them wear horns of some sort, their actual function and appearance rarely fits the wiccan interpretation perfectly. Why is the horned god from the Gundestrup cauldron clean shaved, surely an unusual state for a god of wild places and wild beasts? What about the black Lord of the Beasts, who appears so prominently in the *Mabinogi*, who has only one eye, one leg, but no horns? What of the armed horned gods associated with warrior cults in Britain? Why do most of the horned deities, in spite of their supposedly 'male' symbolism, show no genitals? And how can the horned goddesses be explained? How come they are not even mentioned in most popular books? Whoever 'ernunnos' may have been, I doubt that he is identical with the other horned gods.

Matrones

Another favourite are the Matrones. Here things become really tricky. So many scholars of the 19th century have proclaimed the worship of a hypothetical great mother goddess in ancient times…you know, the sort of deity you get in one package with fertility cults and worship of genitalia. That was a mouth watering subject among last centuries academia, it still is among badly informed neo pagans. The Great Goddess, worshipped by countless neo pagans all over the world, has very little hard evidence behind her. She was invented by scholars who sought a counterpart to the usual male monotheistic patriarchal god of Judao-Christian origin. These scholars thought that monotheism is the natural state of things, which is a very modern assumption, and comes fist in eye with such ideas as centralized government, one single faith and so on. Too many modern authors follow this trend. They propose a single Celtic mother goddess and have the cheek to pretend that all other female deities of the Celts are simply partial aspects of one great big mum. When you read that even blood-crazed, unmarried and childless war-goddesses are supposed to be aspects of the Great Mother Goddess you may come to ask if the term has any meaning at all. Have women no right to exist unless they happen to be mothers? Can women be anything apart from the dreary virgin-mother-crone merry-go-round? Is procreation the only thing that matters? How come not all male gods are dumped in the cardboard box labeled 'Father God'? Can't we think about divinity without involving human sexual mechanics? And what shall we do about sex changing deities, beast like deities, deities who assume beast form to couple or the gods who have no sexuality at all? If the ancient Celts believed that all female deities were aspects of a single all-inclusive mother goddess, why should they have bothered to invent hundreds of them?

As it turns out, we know next to nothing about the family- and sex-life of most Celtic deities. When we look for mother-goddesses, we find the Matrona, who did the job professionally, and even these do not accord with popular prejudice. The word Matrones means Mothers. The Matrones are three women, usually seated, who were popular in the last days of La Tène and even more so during the Roman occupation. In Britain, there are almost 60 dedications and inscriptions to them, 49 of them in Roman forts or made by members of the army, many of whom came originally from the Rhineland. In the wake of the legions their cult spread far and wide. Some 11,000 dedications, icons and altars to the Matrona survive, most of them from the 2nd to 4th century. As you can tell from the names, they are mother goddesses. Its a lot harder to tell from their iconography, as most of them show no sign of pregnancy, nor are they accompanied by children. Sometimes they hold a basket of fruit, but then, so do numerous deities in the Gallo-Roman imagery. Unlike popular opinion, which was strongly influenced by Robert Graves' vision of a triple goddess of his own invention, the Matrona do not follow the pattern of virgin, mother and crone. In most cases, all three women look pretty much the same, of the same age, social status and appearance. There is a lot of difference between the various renderings of the three, sometimes you see them robed, nude, with hats, hoods, free hair etc, but usually, in each group of three there are no individual distinctions. That they are three aspects of a single goddess, as Graves and his followers claim,

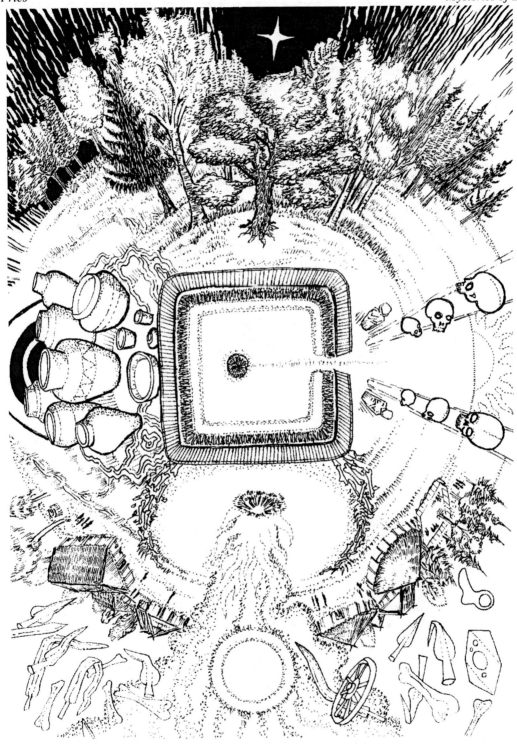

Speculative cosmology. Dreaming a square enclosure.

is nowhere evident. Instead, we owe our thanks to the Roman army for inventing such a lot of Matrones. There were Matrones 'of all nations', 'from overseas', 'of Italy, Germania, Gaul, Britain', of small provinces, such as the Matrona of the Suebians, the Frisians, 'of the household', and even Matrones 'of the parade ground'. This hardly sounds like a single trio, its more like a popular concept that was adapted to individual needs.

A trace of them may survive in the medieval British myths, where you can find one Madron (Mother) whose sole known characteristic is the fact that she had a son called Mabon (Boy) who was mysteriously taken from her directly after birth and kept on a desolate island as one of the three famous prisoners of Britain. Mabon may go back to a Gaulish deity called Maponus (Divine Youth) whom the Romans identified with Apollon, patron of arts and healing. There is a statue of him with a lyre, you may also remember his name from the lead tablet of Chamalieres. An altar found at Hexham calls him Apollo Cithareodus, i.e. The Harper, a dedication from Ribchester associates him with hunting, and shows an image of a hunter goddess. In the tale of Culhwch (*Mabinogi*) he briefly appears as an expert hunter who is required by King Arthur to hunt a monstrous wild boar. Another Mabon, called Vab Mellt, is the son of lightning in bardic poetry. How much he and his old mum have in common with their pagan prototypes is another of those questions.

The Matrones, by the way, offer good evidence for the problems inherent in finding the origin of Celtic cults. In the 19th century scholars often proclaimed that when you find an altar or an inscription, you can be sure the deity was adored in that place. The difficult question is by whom. Were the Matrona ever worshipped by the British? The icons that survive were mostly made for high ranking officers from the Rhineland. You find a wealth of inscriptions and altars at the very places where the fighting was hardest, such as Hadrian's wall in Britain or near the Limes across Germany. The legionaries stationed in these places had good reason to pray and sacrifice to the deities of their homelands for a much needed victory. Nothing like a bit of sheer terror to make people turn religious. Well, if Roman officers commissioned altars where they were stationed, these deities are usually the very deities who are not worshipped by the locals. It is only when the locals pick up the custom and decide to have their own deities portrayed in Roman fashion that we come upon something genuinely home grown.

In discussing the issue of imported deities, I am obliged to Ronald Hutton who kindly suggested I should look for inscriptions that do not come from combat areas (or veteran retirement places, such as the Cotswolds) but from out-of-the-way-places. Dog-Latin or a non-Roman style of iconography may also be good evidence for worship by the natives. Speaking of unusual cults, I should mention a matter that is rarely found in popular literature. I am referring to the inscription of Botorrita, written in Celt-Ibernian script on a bronze plate. The plate comes from a settlement which met destruction during the first century BCE. It has approximately 200 words, about two thirds of which are legible.

This text, based on the German translation by Karl Horst Schmidt 1976, slightly amended to suit English grammar, seems to refer to temple regulations.

The three (sacred) buildings …of Togoites and Sarnikios, not is it allowed… neither is it permitted to damage (them) with fire nor to burn (them), nor is it permitted to cut (them) to pieces, and who wants to win these (buildings), shall set apart silver to take, 100 ritual donations for the…Togoites, and who (protects) the cattle stable or that (stable) of Coros, or the walls or protects another (building), they shall cut out a path above (?)…shall they cut out while he is protecting those (buildings), outside (and) inside three bears shall suckle. In the hall of Neitos they shall be sent. As he to whom they shall send those who have suckled, has female bears, as (he) (has) the female bears of Custaix, as he slays those who belong to him either outside or inside, they shall sacrifice every tenth of them for this strong (?), may they be large or small, (?)…, for Sarnikos (and) Akainakoi they shall not be killed; for Togoites, Urantios or Arandis they shall/will be allowed to thrive, they shall sacrifice (every) tenth (female bear). These…

What do you make of this mysterious text? Some details may be worth commenting on. Several bear cults used to exist in the La Tène period, dedicated to such goddesses and gods as Artio, Matunus or the Gaulish Mercurius Artaios. That bears were sacrificed on occasion seems possible, but not too likely, as most of the sacrifical animals favoured by the Celts were domestic. When the above translation was published, it caused a lot of excitement. The bears were simply too good. In the meantime, the tablet was thoroughly cleaned and restored. A more recent translation, by W. Meid (1994), who transcribed the text after a new study of the original, shatters the romance. In his rendering, the bear-sacrifice disappears. What remains is a straightforward text regarding the ordinance of sacred land for agricultural purposes.

Concerning the 'hilly' region of Tocoit- and Sarnicios it has been decreed as not-permitted: Neither is it permitted to put (things) upon nor is it permitted to perform work, nor is it permitted to cause damage by destruction.

And whoever wishes to perform such things, should take…cut up (coined) silver, that is 100 units, to deposit it at (the temple of) Tocoit.

The text begins with prohibitions and with the fees for transgression. It goes on to tell us that those who construct cow-sheds, paddocks, walled enclosures or small huts are obliged to cut out a path. Those who cut out paths are bound to remove all materials within three days (?) and take them to the territory of Neitos. Next follow obligations and fees for sowing and harvesting, a rule that neither enclosed nor open land in the inner area nor next to Sarnicios may be harvested and finally the declaration that using the land for agriculture and pastoral purposes costs a tithe.

This at the cult feast of Tocoit- and Sarnicios, we proclaim, truly and holily, (namely I), Ablu Ubocum, the regens of the council (and the following persons).

On the reverse of the plate these people are named. Each person is addressed with the term *pintis* possibly from IE *bhendh-* , meaning bound or committed. What we learn from this inscription is that the gods Tocoit- and Sarnicios 'owned' a sacred space, enclosure or larger area, and interestingly, this land was divine property and did not belong to any community. The space, when not in use for sacred purposes, was rented to members of five communities. Our text is a list of regulations in one sense. In another, it went beyond being a simple contract. The occasion was sacred, the pledge was engraved for durability and proclaimed at the cult feast of the deities involved. The feast is called *aiuisas*, a word closely connected to the OhG. *eh-* (sacred law), *ehwa-* (right, law, eternity, forever), *e(o)haft* (just, holy), and *ehwart* was a high priest, a guardian of law, holyness and tradition. The word has a fascinating ancestry and goes back to the IE * *aiw-* (life-force, life-span). What else do we learn about society, religion and economy among the Celt-Iberians? Think about it.

Divine Beasts

Two more points might be discussed before we leave this chapter. One of them is the fact that a good many Celtic deities are associated with animals, such as horses, wolves, boars, bears, serpents and so on. The beasts can be thought of as representatives for certain divine qualities, but it is just as possible that a given deity appears as the beast itself. We find some of this in iconography. In the statue of the young man with deer feet, in the unknown god with the boar on his flanks, in the bear goddess Artio, in Verbeia's statue (she holds two serpents) and of course in the many animals associated with gods on the sides of the magnificent Gundestrup cauldron. When we find animals on their own, it is just as possible that they represent deities. Plenty of animal statues have come to us from Gaul and other countries with a Celtic population. But even more important, I believe, is the rendering of beasts on Celtic coins. As you noticed, I have used the opportunity to draw some of my favourite coins. You find them scattered thorough this book, not as they happen to fit the pages they appear in but as I simply find them too beautiful to ignore them. In these unique coins we can see the vision and imagination of many artists at work. Coins were something the Celts developed during the La Tène time. During the great migration period, many warriors, in some cases even entire tribes, left their rainy homelands to seek treasure in the sun kissed lands around the Mediterranean. Many went touring down the Balkan, where they plundered and ravaged until the armies of Phillip II of Macedonia or his son Alexander the Great provided a career with a future. Those who returned years later were laden with unheard of treasures. Among these treasures was something unique. Tiny disks of gold, very small but all the same very well made. One side showed a head in profile (generally old Phillip or young Alex with his semi-divine ram-horn haircut), the other side a horse-riding warrior. The first coins made by Celtic craftsmen were styled pretty much like the originals. This means that you had to have one head, one rider or charioteer with horse and some silly squiggles (the inscription). Of course these coins were not meant to pay for anything. If you wanted to make a deal, you paid in cattle, foodstuff or in the currency of cast iron bars. The latter was easiest, as you could cut iron to make up the precise price. The first coins of Gaul and southern Germany were more like talismans, valuable gifts made by great chieftains to keep their warriors happy, or useful sacrifices, many of which were buried or scattered in temple districts. Think of them as something that could be offered to the gods. Thus, we find Celtic coin manufacture making a slow start around the 4th C. BCE and becoming a flourishing fashion by the second. By then, most designs had become extremely original and totally Celtic. I suggest you look very closely at the images. Turn them around: Celtic art is ambiguous and has many layers of meaning. Some things only appear when you look upside down. Or if you shut up your thoughts and stare into the pulsing lines in total silence. There is plenty of magic in these tiny images. They can be used for so much that I can't understand why we don't see them in pagan jewelry, painted drum skins, meditation mandalas, trendy tattoos or divination cards. Look at them with your soul. They are like pantacles of evocation. You can wake the spirits with these images.

Deity with damaged face from Euffigneix, dep. Haut-Marne, France, sand stone, height 26 cm. The center shows a boar, the left flank (not shown) instead of an arm a large eye. Dated between late La Tène and early Roman occupation.

Head Cults

The other matter we should mention in passing is the so called cult of the head. Whether it was really a specific cult, or whether the heads were simply a basic element of various religions is very much open to debate. Many Celtic people were ardent head hunters. The classical authors made much of this point, mainly as they couldn't understand it. Now head hunting is not the same all over the globe, and we should refrain from looking at ancient Europe through the eyes of an Amazon head shrinker. What exactly lay behind Celtic headhunting is hard to say. Greek traders, so Diodorus and Strabo report, were astonished to see that Gaulish warrior aristocrats kept embalmed heads in wooden boxes, and when they offered good pay for these gruesome souvenirs, were even more amazed that their owners would for no prize part with them. The archaeological evidence supports this point of view. Most famous are the temples of Roquepertuse and Entremont. In the former was a portico surmounted by a bird of prey although some auhtorities consider it a water bird. Beneath it were a series of niches housing human crania. According to Ann Ross, they were all from males, none over 40 years of age. In the latter, the heads are sculptured crudely on stone. Both traditions can be traced in many instances. Images of heads graced plenty of cult-places, shrines, walls and even the occasional early medieval church. You find heads on religious objects, on dagger handles, on cauldrons and drinking jugs. Heads are so popular with the Celts that Ann Ross declares them to be *the most typical Celtic religious symbol.* Often

such heads looked extremely crude. It is hard to believe that the fantastic craftspeople of the La Tène time couldn't have made a better job of it. When the heads are crude, coarse or totally distorted this was done on purpose. A head was a head, and it was known to work. Whether such heads had an apotropaic purpose or whether they represented ancestors, slain enemies or even deities is something that can't be decided. The Celts left no guidebook on how to get ahead. When we look at the evidence for real heads, things become even more tricky. Imagine how battle weary warriors return to their communities, bloody faces dangling from the saddle, fly covered carrion sticking to the ends of their lances. Many an Irish myth makes head hunting a fine art and a past time for real men. Mind you, real men seem to have amazingly few friends. As Conall so proudly proclaims when demanding the hero's right to cut up a pig (*The Tale of Macc Da Tho's Pig*, trans. J. Gantz):

> 'I swear by what my people swear by: since I first took spear in hand, there has not been a single day when I have not killed a Connachta warrior, not a single night when I have not destroyed with fire, and I have never slept without a Connachta head under my knee.'
>
> 'You are a better warrior than I , it is true,' said Cet. 'If Anluan were here, he would give you another kind of contest. It is our misfortune that he is not in the house.'
>
> 'Oh, but he is,' said Conall, and taking Anluan's head from his wallet he threw it at Cet's breast so that a mouthful of blood splattered over the lips.

If you ever thought of the Celts as romantic, keep that head in mind. It's hardly surprising that Joyce reacted to such tales of brainless heroism by writing an epic novel on normal people having an utterly unheroic day. While I doubt that all Celts indulged in such feats of simple-minded slaughter, the fact remains that heads were special. Heads of enemies, so Irish tales report, could end up being smoked on a spit or stuck on a stake in a dungheap. On the other hand, lots of heads were venerated. As Livy tells us, the head of a promising Roman statesman was made into a cherished drinking vessel and kept in a shrine by the Boii around the year 216 BCE. An altar from Apt, graced with the name of Mars and those of a number of Celtic dedicants, stood over a collection of eight or nine human skulls. Now the easiest explanation is that the heads of enemies were being

Epona accompanied by horses and donkeys, found in the Roman fortress Kapersburg, Taunus mountains, Hessen, Germany.

honoured as trophies in these temples. Of course it is just as possible to assume that the heads of the priesthood were kept in such fashion, or that it was a selection of special heroes on exhibition. If the head is the seat of the soul, as some Celts seem to have believed, then having your head under an altar may even be accounted an honour. It gets harder to understand when we look at the Roman authors who proposed that the people of Gaul believed in reincarnation. What sort of otherlife or rebirth can you expect when your head rests in a place of honour, or happens to disintegrate in someone's privy? This takes us to the next stage of our journey. Who were the priests behind Celtic religion?

3. Druidic Dreams

The good thing about Druids is that we know everything about them. So did the romantic historians of the last centuries, so did the medieval bards and of course the Romans knew more about them than anybody else. Everybody knows about the Druidy Druids, and this is the main reason why nobody really understands what Druidry was all about. It is also the main reason why Druids are so popular in fantasy literature and New Age cults. A topic that everybody knows about has great commercial virtues. In an obscure and much debated way, the Druids seem to be related with the British bards and the Irish filid. While very little of original Druidic magic can be traced, we do have material on the magic of bards and poets. This situation has tempted a number of researchers to define the bards and poets as Druids-in-disguise, and to write massive works on Druidic arts that are simply medieval bardic material attributed to a much earlier period. Personally, I find the bards and poets much more interesting than the Druids. However,

we can't just go along with this book unless we include them in our research. This is rather regrettable, as, unlike everybody else, I do not know everything about the historical Druids and would much prefer to ignore them. The mythical ones are much more fun.

In the songs of the medieval bards, the occasional reference to the Druids appears. Usually, these references are brief and not very informative, as if the bards who composed the songs assumed that the audience know all about Druids anyway. Maybe they did maybe they didn't. Perhaps the bards themselves didn't feel entirely sure about the topic, and as we'll see later on, perhaps the notion of the Druids that the bards alluded to does not entirely accord with the actual activities of the Druids of the pre-Roman period. This may seem confusing, and it jolly well is. The *Book of Taliesin* is particularly full of such items. Let us ponder some of them before we rush into the unknown and attempt to work out what Druidry may have been originally.

Here are some of those snippets from the word-hoard of the Taliesins. I give them out of context as basically there is very little context to them. Most of the songs attributed to Taliesin seem to be garbled, confused or badly copied. You'll get used to it. As a result there are plenty of mysterious persons, incidents and phenomena that happen to pop up from time to time without having much to do with the rest of the song. This goes especially for Druids.

The worlds profit (is) small,
The heat of the sun is lost.
The Druid will prophecy
What has been will be.
Sky of Geirionydd,
I would go with thee
Gloomy like the evening,
In the recesses of the mountain…
There will be to me a judge unprejudiced, void of guile;
The astrologers (or diviners) prophecy,
In the land of the lost ones.
Druids prophecy
Beyond the sea, beyond the Brython.
(Book of Taliesin 52,
The Praise of Lludd the Great)

Ye intelligent Druids,
Declare to Arthur,
What is there more early
Than I that they sing of.
(BoT 8, *Battle of Goddeu*)

Talkative is the privileged orator
Of kings in the luxuriant circle of the good mead.
Like the sun, the warm animator of summer, let him sound the greatest song.
I will sing the wise song, the song of the host of harmony,
They will be, thou wilt be a Druid in summertime, the aspect of the son
Of Leenawg, with a flowing manly robe.
Light, a robe of heat; vapour of heat, heat of vapour.
Whilst it rose it was contained without disgrace. (BoT 38)

Druids foretell what great things will happen (BoT 6, *The Omen of Prydain the Great*)

Glorious the protection of the dragon to the people of the Brython.
Chief of armies, a respecter of breastplated men.
Deep, the prophecy divine of the Druids.
(BoT 53)

I am a harmonious one; I am a clear singer.
I am steel; I am a Druid.
I am an artificer; I am a scientific one.
I am a serpent; I am love; I will indulge in feasting.
(BoT 3, *The Fold of the Bards*)

Let the brewer give a heat,
Over a cauldron of five trees,
And the river of Gwiawn,
And the influence of fine weather,
And honey and trefoil,
And mead-horns intoxicating
Pleasing to a sovereign,
The gift of the Druids.
(BoT 13)

The evolver of every elevation before Druids.
Nudris they knew not, a gentle sight to see Mabon.
(BoT 24, *The Rod of Moses*)

As you can see, there are plenty of

obscure references to Druids scattered in the *Book of Taliesin*. They don't exactly tell us much about Druidry, but then again we can hardly expect the bards around the eleventh century to be well-informed about a priesthood that was violently suppressed a thousand years earlier. Nevertheless, the fact that Druids are referred to with such frequency does indicate that their reputation lingered on. In Taliesin's songs, as far as can be told from such lines, the Druids function basically as prophets, diviners and custodians of old and obscure knowledge. They are also the brewers of the golden mead that intoxicates the king and the noble warriors, that is, those who could afford such expensive beverages.

What do you make of the lines that link the Druids to the robe of heat? It would be inviting to speculate about certain forms of heat-generating yoga in this place. The Tibetan rite of gTummo shows that even in our time, there are people who manage to endure extreme cold in trance states that generate massive heat through finely focussed breathing and a lucid imagination. Some tantalizing hints from the medieval literature of Wales show that such an idea existed in Britain, if not a similar practise. May I mention King Arthur's old foster-brother Cei who could be so hot that the rain evaporated above him? How about this one? *And I set myself to swim the sea till I came to the Island of the Naked Monks; and there the Knight of the Lantern learned his druidry at first. And rough stark naked people were they, for neither wind nor cold, sun or rain troubles them.* This piece of information comes from the romance *The Story of the Crop-Eared Dog.* As you can see, some people in the wild Gaelic

west could evidently use a robe of heat. Do you think that heat generation was part of Druidic magic? Probably we'll never know for certain. Finally, another brief reference from *The Four Ancient Books of Wales*:

At All-Saints it is habitual for the heath-tops to be dun;
High foaming is the sea-wave, short the day:-
Druid, your advice!
(*Black Book of Carmarthen* 30)

Such items have given rise to a lot of speculation. A number of romantically minded authors, such as Lewis Morris, William Owen Pugh, Edward Williams, Rev. Edward Davies and Algernon Herbert proposed that the bardic poetry of Northern Britain and Wales contains-in a somewhat veiled form - some of the lost wisdom of the Druids. This was a charming and stimulating idea, if somewhat hard to prove, as so very little was actually known of Druidic wisdom. Lack of evidence, however, is nothing to a romantic fantasy. When people are hungry for some venerable item of ancient knowledge they usually find one, even if they have to make it up.

The nineteenth century was a great period for making up ancient wisdom. In addition to those who re-invented Druidry by doing strange things with medieval poetry there were plenty of others who proved that Druidry was really an early form of Hinduism, Buddhism, Christianity, Odin worship and the like. Many writers were involved in this movement, and some of them, like Williams, Davies, and Herbert, rearranged and mistranslated the ancient bardic songs of the *Book of Taliesin* to make their point more clearly. Williams and Pugh even introduced their own lines (with the best of intentions) which can only be classed as plain forgery. As Lady Guest innocently included some of these flawed items in her classic translation of the *Mabinogi,* considerable damage was done. Such an outburst of creative history could not arise without producing an equally drastic reaction. When Nash published the first reliable translation of the Taliesin songs (1858) he made a point of being totally skeptical regarding any Druidic mysteries supposedly hidden in the text. Skene, in 1868, published an even more cautious rendering of the *Four Ancient Books of Wales* which did not really make any romantic happy as it raised more questions than it solved. In this book, I have often made use of the Skene translation. While such a sober examination was direly needed, it did not stop the romantic movement from inventing the Druids it desired.

At this point we leave the question who the Druids really were and enter the field of politics. During the nineteenth century the historical sciences were not very developed. When scholars attempted to work out what the ancient people of northern Europe were like, they generally did this by reading what the Greek and Roman authors of antiquity had written on the topic. While this was better than total ignorance it certainly produced a very biased attitude. Few classical authors had actually been north of the Alps, and of those who had, several did not care much about ethnology but had an interest in deceiving their readers for reasons of their own. The primary source for conditions in pre-Roman Gaul was Julius Caesar, a brilliant strategist but a questionable ethnographer, who had considerable interest in bending the facts to legitimize the conquest of Gaul in the eyes of the senate and the tax-payers.

The scholars of the nineteenth century were aware that they couldn't trust all that had been set down in the distant past, but lacking a functional archeology they could not develop independent verification for the old tales. Facing such difficulties they did their best. People who ask questions want answers, preferably simple ones, and those scholars tried their best to answer them. Some of the fables they made up are still around today. Not so much among historians or archaeologists but in the popular books, in the movies, the TV programs, and certainly in the new Pagan religions and the New Age movement. If we wish to learn about the nature of Druidry and the Celtic religions, we have to ignore the various myths that were evolved in the past two centuries.

Druids in the Classical Period.

How Druidry began, where and how it evolved and what it was good for are questions we can happily ignore, as nobody knows the answers. Our first reference to Druids comes from the pens of a number of Greek and Roman writers. A few of them lived in a period when Druidry was declining, in fact the majority lived after the Roman empire had prohibited the cult. Nevertheless they are the only sources roughly contemporary with the Druids themselves. This does not mean that we can trust them. The Romans in particular were not very sympathetic with the Druids and

Multiple points of view. Dual deities.
Top left: coin of the Mediomatrici. Coins
with Janus heads were first imported from
Rome, some Gaulish tribes made their own,
as the idea corresponds with their beliefs.
Top right: golden finger ring from
Rodenbach with double face. Bottom:
Double head with water-bird-beak (?) or rest
of a floral crown, originally set on a pillar,
temple of Roquepertuse

had good reasons to say nasty things about them. The Druids, on the other hand, may have said a lot of nasty things about the Romans, but as they were on the losing side and did not write books, their protests have faded into oblivion. While the Roman authors are not trustworthy witnesses, at least they did write some passages on the subject. Without their evidence we would hardly be aware that the Druids existed at all.

According to **Diogenes Laertius,** the famous authors Aristotle and Sotion mentioned Druids in books which have not survived. Refering to them, Diogenes wrote in his *Lives of the Philosophers* that the Celts and the Galatae had seers whom they called Druids and Semnotheoi (an uncertain word that may possibly mean 'Reverend Gods'). These seers made pronouncements in riddles and dark sayings and taught that *the gods must be worshipped, and no evil done, and manly behaviour be maintained.*

Though Diogenes wrote in the third century CE, his sources came from the second century BCE, which makes his homely remark the oldest reference to Druids that we know of.

Next in chronological order we come to the writings of **Gaius Julius Caesar**, which include the longest passages on Druids that have survived. His description is too long to be given in full, so let me recommend that you get yourself a copy of his *De Bello Gallico* and read it. Most of the remarks on Druids and the religions of Gaul are in the sixth book, but it is useful to read the others as well, to get an idea of the cultural context and the sort of person who wrote it. In spite of its homicidal atrocities, its

author cultivated a charming and entertaining style. To understand Julius Caesar, you should keep in mind that he was a member of a noble, but impoverished family, that he was too clever by half and that his political ambitions were practically unlimited. By various intrigues he managed to become the statesman in charge of Gallia Minor, a Roman province including parts of northern Italy and the Alps. This province was hardly sufficient for Gaius Julius's financial requirements, so he soon managed to find a good and ethical reason to invade Gaul itself, which had hitherto been a free country. In the following years, he gradually invaded and occupied all of Gaul, as well as southern Britain, gathering immense wealth from plundered towns and a thriving slave trade, until he had enough financial and armed support to return to Rome, to overthrow the republic and to make himself the first of the Caesars. To do so, he had to deal with a lot of opposition in Gaul, but even more so among the Roman senate, which was not very happy with the way Gaius Julius was wasting taxes to occupy a country which seemed barbarian and of little value to the people of Rome.

Caesar saw the Druids as a political problem. In the middle of the first century BCE, if we can trust his account, the Druids of Gaul were a caste. Caesar wrote that the society of Gaul was divided into three castes. While the common people, as he put it, were treated almost like slaves, the Druids enjoyed such power and privilege that they were not required to pay taxes or to participate in warfare. These Druids may have been philosophers and priests, but what really concerned Caesar was their function as law-givers, judges, physicians and scholars. They performed the public and private sacrifices, educated the noble young men, decided judicial cases and advised the rulers. This makes it likely that the Gaul of Caesar's day was a theocratic society, and that the Druids were its unofficial regents. People who wanted to make a sacrifice did so through the office of a Druid, who acted as an intermediary between the gods and the population.

Caesar tells us that the Druids of Gaul were under the control of a chief Druid, and that all those Gaullish Druids used to assemble once a year in the center of Gaul, in the land of the Carnutes, in a consecrated conclave (some modern researchers believe that this may have been at Chartres). Perhaps we should examine this idea critically.

When Caesar came to conquer Gaul (59-49 BCE) he found the country not as a single nation but as a conglomerate of distinct tribes, most of them not friendly with their neighbours. This is very typical for the Celtic people, in that they never managed to evolve a centralized government or religion. These tribes had similar languages (at least some of them did) and apparently they did look somewhat similar (to the Roman conquerors) but they did not worship the same deities. Making things easy for the Roman audience, Caesar claimed that the Gaulish people descended from a mysterious ancestral deity called Dis (this is a Roman term for the god of death and the underworld) and that they worshipped the usual Roman pantheon - Mercury, Apollo, Mars, Jupiter and Minerva. Of course these are not the names by which the people of Gaul worshipped their deities.

Caesar in his arrogance did not bother to portray the local deities properly but simply gave their Roman equivalent. He was not the only author to do so. Who cared about the barbarian deities of a foreign culture anyway?

Archaeological research has found evidence for almost four-hundred distinct deities in ancient Gaul, showing clearly that Caesar's account, for all its readability, is somewhat too simple to be true. Some were tribal deities, or gods associated with specific functions, others were closely associated with specific rivers, mountains, forests or tribal lands, thus of little concern to tribes settling in other parts of the country. Religion in Gaul, not to mention all the other countries loosely called 'the Celtic world' nowadays, was a highly complicated matter. Likewise, Gaul was not simply divided into three parts, as Caesar claimed to make the political situation more comprehensible. Josephus, the historian who wrote about the Jewish revolt in the first century CE, called Gaul the milk-cow of the Roman empire, consisting of more than three-hundred tribes which were being controlled by a single legion. That this control was possible, and indeed that Caesar with his original force of one legion could successfully begin the conquest of Gaul, is good evidence that the Gaul of his time had no political unity worth mentioning. As he describes in such touching words, Caesar was repeatedly asked to give Roman support to one Gaulish tribe against another. Of course the future emperor was always glad to do so, basically as each tribe who appealed to him had to supply plenty of soldiers and provisions, while each tribe who sought to oppose the Roman army was soon on its way to the slave market. This, and the generous amount of gold that was lying around openly in the temples (Diodor exaggerates - Gaulish gold looked good but was often only wafer thin) was sufficient profit to finance Caesar's future career.

It turned out to be a highly efficient strategy to use Celts to fight other Celts. Now consider the control that the Druids had over the population, and think of the claim that the Druids were all under the control of some Arch-Druid. Would such a policy of 'play one enemy against the other' be possible if there had been a centralized council of Druids? How would such a council think of tribes which invited the Roman conqueror into the land just to get rid of their own neighbours? If this council existed, and if it actually enjoyed the power Caesar attributed to it, just why did it allow the conquest to happen at all? But let us continue with this strange story.

Caesar claims that before the conquest, several Gaulish lords were attempting to win supremacy over all tribes. The brother of one such lord, a certain Diviciacus (or Divitciacus), became a close friend of Caesar and did much to strengthen Roman rule in Gaul. He may be of interest to us, as possibly Caesar derived his knowledge of Druidry and the Gaulish religions from him. Caesar did not approve of Druids. For one thing they were a political nuisance. For another, so he wrote, the Druids had a number of revolting methods of sacrificing humans in the name of religion. The Rome of Caesar's time did not approve of human sacrifice any more, so the bloodthirsty Druid sacrifices had good propaganda value and proved once and for all just how barbarous those Druids were. Mind you, Caesar had no scruples about selling entire tribes into slavery and the civilized Roman citizens, while disgusted by human sacrifice, were highly enchanted by violent circus games that tended to cost hundreds to thousands of lives on each festival day.

Anyway, Caesar wrote that the Druids did disgusting things for religious reasons (unlike the Romans, who did them for civilized reasons, such as profit and entertainment). He never mentioned that the noble Diviciacus, his good friend, was a Druid himself. This little detail was recorded by Cicero, who met Diviciacus in Rome. Apparently the Druid, for so did Cicero call him, could make predictions based on augury and conjecture. By inviting Caesar and the Roman army into his country, Diviciacus had not only destroyed the career of his brother Dumnorix but was also responsible for the unification of Gaul under Roman control. This does not look like a Druid who acts under the command of an All-Gaulish council of Druids. It raises the question if such a council existed at all. It also makes me wonder about the ethics that Diviciacus believed in, as the conquest of Gaul cost the lives of some 60000 Gaulish people.

Be that as it may, Caesar provided some insights into the spiritual ideas of the Druids. He claimed that training for a Druid took up to twenty years, most of the time being devoted to the memorization of knowledge which was kept in verse. As he wrote, the Druids did not approve of setting down important knowledge in writing, though for minor matters, the people of Gaul made

Mnas Brictas: Women endowed with magic

Top left: Silver figure from the crater of Vix, late Hallstatt time.

Top right: image from a bronze bucket, Váce, Yugoslavia.

Bottom left: Celto Iberian bronze figure, a popular import from Spain, found in Aust-on-Severn, Glos., England.

Bottom center: dancer, bronze figure from a series of nine nude dancers of both sexes (as well as a deer, a horse and three wild boars), found buried on the banks of the Loire in Neuvy-en-Sullias, near Orléans, France, close to the sacred site of Fleury. Uncertain age.

Bottom right: mysterious statue of a woman with serpent (her genitals being the serpent's egg), Oo valley, France. The dating is disputed, late Hallstatt and early medieval period (Eve and serpent!) are equally possible.

use of what seemed like the Greek alphabet to Caesar. He recorded that the Druids of Gaul often journeyed to Britain to get a good education. Apart from having discussions on the stars, the calendar and the nature of the universe, the Druids believed *that souls do not die, but after death pass from one to another*. In his opinion, this belief constituted a useful motivation strategy to make warriors fearless. For all its flaws, Caesar's account is the most detailed description of the Druids that exists. It emphasizes the political function of the Gaulish Druids and keeps their religious function in the background. The Gaulish Druids, with their monopoly on knowledge, religion, law, science, medicine and education, were clearly a problem when it came to controlling the land.

A number of scholars of the eighteenth and nineteenth century assumed that Caesar's account is an objective description as it suited the colonialist and imperialist attitudes of their time. While several contemporaries of Caesar were highly skeptical about the strange tales from Gaul, a good many academics of the 19th century admired the victorious strategist and took his account for gospel. Many generalized what Caesar had said about the situation in Gaul, and proposed that all the Celtic people, not just the Celts of Gaul, were ruled by a Druidic theocracy. Though this theory is still popular in our days, it stands on somewhat shaky ground. There were Celtic people in several European countries at the time. No Druids appear in the account of the North Italian Celts. To enter Gaul, Caesar had to deal with Alpine Celts, but he never bothered to mention any Druids

among them. Nor did he mention Druids when he crossed the Channel and invaded Britain. This does seem a bit odd if we consider that he had written earlier that the Gaulish Druids preferred to travel to Britain for training. If Britain was such a hot spot for Druidry, just why didn't he mention any Druids when recounting his battles and conferences with the natives? Middle and southern Germany were as Celtic as Gaul, but the Roman historians did not write about any Druids in these lands. Caesar glibly claimed that the 'Germans' (anybody living east of the Rhine) had no Druids, no proper deities nor zeal for sacrifices. Given what the archaeologists have unearthed over the last decades, the remark on deities and sacrifices is completely wrong.

To understand such comments you should keep in mind that Caesar practically invented the concepts of 'Gaul' and 'Germany' and had a strong interest in showing that the former was a wealthy country well worth conquering while the latter was a dreary bog peopled by savages best left alone. Plenty of important people in Rome considered anybody north of the Alps as a crude barbarian and seriously questioned if Caesar's ten years campaign was worth the taxpayers money. They were also worried that Gaius Julius was using unethical methods in his conquest, and after one particularly messy massacre the senate seriously discussed whether the future Caesar ought to be handed over to the barbarians (who were to punish him at leisure). It was argued that Gaius Julius' success, being based on broken vows, mistreated messengers and a number of violent atrocities could enrage the deities of the Roman state and bring divine revenge. The massacre, however, had been a great financial success to Gaius Julius, who bribed a number of senators and barely escaped capital punishment. Be that as it may, there are no references to Druids from the 'German' parts of the empire. Though several Roman writers recorded that there were priests and priestesses of some sort in central Europe, none attached the label 'Druids' to them. Neither are there references to them in the eastern Celtic countries, such as Czech and Romania, or in the south, among the Celts of Spain or Portugal. Poseidonios, from whom Strabo and Caesar got some of their data on Druids, visited some Celtic people in Spain and Gaul. Strabon quotes him on a number of revolting methods of divination (such as reading entrails) performed by the Celto-Iberians on humans, but though these appear fairly similar to what he relates of Gaulish Druids, the Celto-Iberian priests, whoever they may have been, are not called Druids. In fact it may sound doubtful that such a tight theocratic and supposedly centralized institution as Gaulish Druidry could have functioned in rural Iberia (see F. Simon, 1998), where things were a lot rougher. Likewise, we do not hear a word of any Druidic reincarnation theory from Spain. Instead, Silius Italicus informs us that:

> *The Celt-Iberians consider death in battle an honour and the cremation of the corpse of the fallen a crime; as they believe that his soul ascends to the gods of the sky, when the vulture devours the body of the slain.*

This statement is fully supported by Claudius Aelianus who adds that the bodies of those who die shamefully of a disease are mutilated before cremation. As Simon adds, maybe an event from the Celtic invasion of Greece (280 BCE) is relevant here. As the Greeks observed to their disgust, the Celts under Brennius did not bother to collect or bury their warriors on the battlefield, leaving them as food for ravens, crows and carrion eaters. A warrior's heaven for the bravely slain sounds much like the stuff familiar from old Norse religion, and miles away from Druidic reincarnation or from traveling to a subterranean otherworld. Good evidence that the 'Celtic world' was not as uniform a culture as is generally claimed, but contained plenty of room for highly individual developments and a lot of originality.

Or think of the Celts living in the extreme east, as their mercenaries had been swept there in the wave of Alexander's armies. The Galatians of central Turkey had a sacred place called Drunemeton (Strabo), this is supposed to mean sacred oak grove. Other writers take the word dru- as evidence for the presence of Druids in this place, but this is linguistically improbable and Druids do not necessarily grow on oaks. Many Indo-European cultures venerated oaks as symbols of the gods of the sky but most of them did this without Druids. While Nemeton means sacred space or sacred grove, the nature of this site, and the trees which grew there (if any) is far from clear. Too many authors have hypothesized oaks wherever Celtic rites were celebrated. We cannot even be sure it was a sacred grove at all. A nemeton can be a grove, but the term was also used for sacred spaces and in some cases even for temples and suchlike buildings. Strabons remark only tells us that the Galatians used to have assemblies there, he never said anything about rituals.

Though Britain and Ireland had their Druids, as can be seen from their appearance in later medieval literature, Caesar did not feel it necessary to mention them, so maybe they were of less importance. It is highly unlikely that the Druids of the British enjoyed such political power as the Druids of Gaul. In the other Celtic countries, while there most certainly existed some sort of priesthood and a lot of free-style enchanters, it is unlikely that these people called themselves Druids or had similar political functions. While the scholars of the last century took Gaul as a model for all Celtic countries, and saw Druids everywhere, modern historians are beginning to wonder whether Gaul may have been an exception to the rule.

Our next source is **Diodorus Siculus**, who wrote c. 8 BCE that among the Gauls the Pythagorean doctrine prevails *that the souls of men are immortal and live again for a fixed number of years inhabiting another body.* This theory had a number of adherents. To the Greek and Roman authors, the best known reincarnation-guru was the venerable Pythagoras of Samos (570-500 BCE) who formed a cult at Croton, Italy, in 530 BCE. Pythagoras, apart from being a sober mathematican, proposed a number of bizarre theories. Many of these were concerned with maths, with the relation of numbers, measure, music, intervals and the hidden order of the universe. He sought divinity in the regularity of nature and formed a society of those who believed in beauty, goodness, measure, order, harmony

and absolute obedience to the chief clown. As a result, once the old philosopher had died, his students feared to introduce innovations, and eventually the order died of sheer stagnation.

One of Pythagoras beliefs claimed that every soul reincarnates in accordance to prior virtues or sins, until the pure souls attain to all-harmony. His faith implied a hierarchy of souls. Ovid (43 BCE -17 CE) dedicated a large section of his *Metamorphoses* to Pythagoras and his teachings. He wrote that the lips of Pythagoras were moved by a deity, and emphasized that the Pythagoreans were strict vegetarians who did not soil their body by eating meat. In the Pythagorean doctrine, all souls keep changing continuously, so that humans may be animals in their next lives or vice versa. In fact, anything can become anything else in the Pythagorean gospel. How far this theory accords with the unknown Druidic theory of reincarnation remains a tricky question. The well-educated intellectuals of Rome and Greece did not know of any other sort of reincarnation, and so it may have seemed natural to them that all reincarnation faiths had their roots in the familiar Pythagorean belief. It may be interesting that Caesar did not derive the Druids from the Pythagoreans, nor is there evidence for vegetarism or advanced mathematics in ancient Gaul. There are some hints at vegetarian seers in medieval Britain (such as Merlin in Geoffrey's *Vita Merlini* or the Irish Suibhne) but it is questionable whether these inspired prophets considered themselves Druids.

Diodorus described the Druids as *philosophers and theologians* and made much of

Female head with hood (a goddess or priestess?) from the temple of Entremont, height 29 cm, 2nd century BCE. The damaged throat section shows that unfriendly folk removed the head violently.

their skill at divining the future, be it from birds, entrails, or the death-cramps of a sacrificial victim. He wrote that no one in Gaul makes a sacrifice without the assistance of a Druid (a point that may have been copied from Caesar) and adds that the Druids occasionally function as peace-makers, stepping between combatants or hostile armies.

In **Strabo**'s *Geographica* the Druids are briefly mentioned. This is typical, most of the classical authors devoted only a few lines to what they considered the priesthood of a primitive country. Strabo claimed that the Druids were diviners, natural philosophers and judges. He also commented on their human sacrifices and informed his readers that the Druids preferred to sacrifice criminals. In years with a big yield of criminals they believed there would also be a big yield from the land. This sort of attitude may imply that the Druids, who judged the criminal cases, may have been especially severe when not enough sacrifices were available or the weather promised a bad harvest. Not very nice, but that's the sort of thing you get in theocracies. Strabo added:

> However, not only the Druids, but others as well, say that men's souls, and also the universe, are indestructible, although both fire and water will at some time or other prevail over them.

This reference may be of interest as it is an early remark on the various catastrophes which are so important in the myths and beliefs of so many pagan cultures. In Strabo's work you can also find an attempt to connect the Druids with the bards and the vates. Only a few classical authors referred to these distinct functions (without

coming to a consensus as to who is who and who does what), but as this matter is a bit complicated I shall deal with it as we come to the bards. Knowing what sort of stuff his readers were after, Strabo also detailed several gory ways in which the Druids practised human sacrifice for divination and religious worship.

Our next informer is **Pomponius Mela**, who wrote c. 40-50CE, in a time when Gaul had been thoroughly Romanized. He notes that the atrocious customs of the Druids are no longer practised, that is, they had reformed their cult to the extent that they no longer slaughtered their victims but only drew some blood. In his account, which leans heavily on Caesar, we learn that the Druids used to meet in secret caves and secluded dales. His version of Druidic reincarnation introduces the novel idea *that souls are eternal and that there is another life in the infernal regions* - quite a difference to the earlier accounts, as it introduces a subterranean otherworld. He also came up with the unlikely story that people used to borrow money, promising to repay it in the next lifetime.

The poet **Lucan** (*Pharsalia*) also had to mention Druids in his works. Writing during the reign of Nero (54-68CE) he basically repeats what others reported before him, if in finer poetic language. What is new in his account is the notion that the Druids used to worship simulacrums (Idols? Statues? Fetishes?) in their sacred groves. Mind you, Lucan's groves are romantic wonderlands. They are so darksome and scary that even the Druids were afraid of going there, lest they encounter the gods whom they worshipped. Another goodie is his cheerful, but perplexing comment:

> And you, O Druids, now that the clash of battle is stilled, once more have you returned to your barbarous ceremonies and to the savage usage of your holy rites. To you alone it is given to know the truth about the gods and deities of the sky, or else you alone are ignorant of the truth.

Once again reincarnation was alluded to:

> you tell us that the same spirit has a body again elsewhere, and that death, if what you sing is true, is but the mid-point of long life.

That the idea of reincarnation had such fascination for the Roman authors becomes understandable when one considers that there are few otherworlds as miserable, gloomy and dull as the one deceased Romans went to.

Our next source seems a lot more reliable. This is **Pliny the Elder**, the author of the famous *Natural History*, a writer with a keen interest in other people's superstitions. Better still, Pliny had actually been to the Roman provinces of Germany and Gaul. Writing around 77 CE he gives the fullest account of Druid rituals that has survived. In his writings the Druids are referred to as magicians, which is understandable as they had lost most of their political functions a hundred years earlier when Julius Caesar came, saw and conquered. Pliny's account is so well known that you can find parts of it in many books on Celtic religion. Commenting on the mistletoe, Pliny

recorded:

> The Druids - for so their magicians are called - held nothing more sacred than the mistletoe and the tree that bears it, always supposing that tree to be the oak. But they choose groves formed of oaks for the sake of the tree alone, and they never perform any of their rites except in the presence of a branch of it; so that it seems probable that the priests themselves derive their name from the Greek word for that tree. In fact they think that everything that grows on it has been sent from heaven and is a proof that the tree was chosen by the god himself. The mistletoe, however, is found but rarely upon the oak; and when found, is gathered with due religious ceremony, if possible on the sixth day of the moon (for it is by the moon that they measure their months and years, and also their ages of thirty years). They chose this day because the moon, though not yet in the middle of her course, has already considerable influence. They call the mistletoe by a name meaning, in their language, the all-healing. Having made preparation for sacrifice and a banquet beneath the trees, they bring thither two white bulls, whose horns are bound then for the first time. Clad in a white robe, the priest ascends the tree and cuts the mistletoe with a golden sickle, and it is received by others in a white cloak. Then they kill the victims, praying that god will render this gift of his propitious to those to whom he has granted it. They believe that the mistletoe, taken in drink, imparts fecundity to barren animals, and

that it is an antidote for all poisons. (XVI, 249)

There are four other references to Druid rituals in Pliny's *Natural History*. One of them refers to the Serpent Stone, a topic which I have discussed in the first chapter of *Seidways*. The other two references are not often quoted in books on Celtic religion.

Similar to savin is the plant called selago. It is gathered without using iron and by passing the right hand through the left sleeve of the tunic, as though in the act of committing a theft. The clothing must be white, the feet washed and bare, and an offering of wine and bread be made before the gathering. The Druids of Gaul say that the plant should be carried as a charm against every kind of evil, and that the smoke of it is good for diseases of the eyes. (XXIV,103)

The Druids, also, use a certain marsh-plant that they call samolus, this must be gathered with the left hand, when fasting, and it is a charm against the diseases of cattle. But the gatherer must not look behind him, nor lay the plant anywhere except in the drinking-troughs. (XXIV, 104)

Sadly, the identity of these plants is unknown to us. To confuse things a bit, Pliny also mentioned a complicated ritual used by the magi of Gaul to cut vervain, a plant that they believed to be another heal-all, bringing good health, fortune, friendship and the like. This could be a Druid ritual, but it is just as possible that the magi he referred to were simply hedge-wizards with no relation to the Druidic caste. A fourth reference to Druids (XXX,13) informs us that Druidry flourished in the province of Gaul up to the time of the emperor Tiberius, and that in Pliny's day, Britain was still fascinated by magic and ceremony. He concluded his remarks with praise for the Romans:

for having put a stop to this monstrous cult, whereby to murder a man was an act of greatest devoutness, and to eat his flesh most beneficial.

These few paragraphs did more to produce the romantic fable of Druid mystery than anything else. During the eighteenth and nineteenth century the mistletoe ritual was treated as if it were the height of the Druidic religion, while it was obviously only a rare and rather minor event. Mistletoe itself was classed as the most sacred plant of the Gaulish Celts, though according to Pliny the only mistletoe worth using grew on oaks. In nature, one rarely finds an oak mistletoe, as the plant is much more common on apple or poplar, and these, apparently, were not used. It might be argued that the mistletoe itself was only of minor importance, as its special qualities came from the oak it grew on. Then there was the faulty etymology that related Druids with oaks. Pliny thought that the word Druid came from the Greek druz, the oak. Most alluring, of course, was the image of the venerable Druid, clad in his sort-of-white robe, climbing a tree and cutting mistletoe using an expensive but rather useless tool. I wonder how well you can climb in a robe.

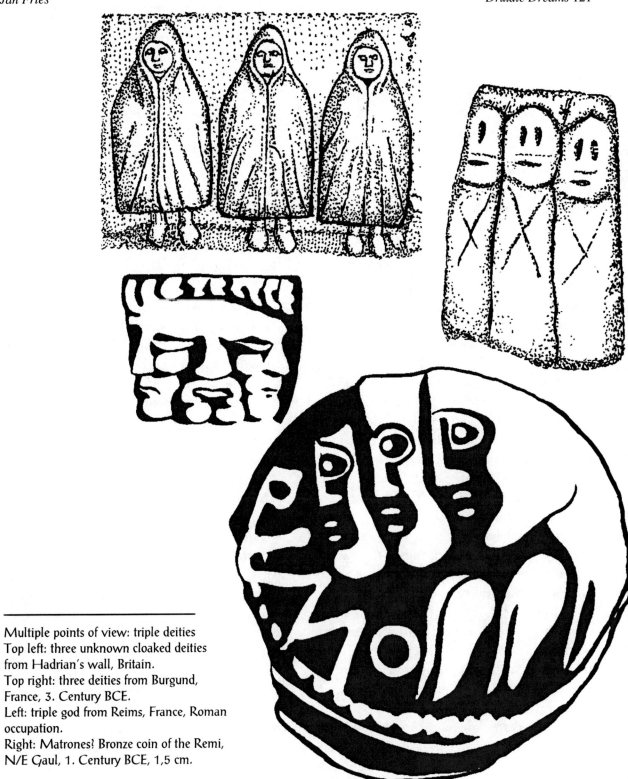

Multiple points of view: triple deities
Top left: three unknown cloaked deities
from Hadrian's wall, Britain.
Top right: three deities from Burgund,
France, 3. Century BCE.
Left: triple god from Reims, France, Roman
occupation.
Right: Matrones! Bronze coin of the Remi,
N/E Gaul, 1. Century BCE, 1,5 cm.

Or do you fancy Druids climbing in underwear? Generalizing from this account, nowadays everybody believes that all Druids wore white, all of the time, and that a ritual that may or may not have been performed in some part of Gaul was fashionable in the entire Celtic world. Stranger yet, while countless Druid-revivalists took the mistletoe rite as the utter truth, one rarely finds them praising those lines that mention religious cannibalism.

Tacitus, the famous Roman historian, describes the destruction of some Welsh Druids in his *Annals*, XIV, 30. In 60 CE, the Roman commander Suetonius Paulinus personally raided a Druidic enclave on the island of Mona (Anglesey) off the coast of north Wales. Apparently the Druids stood on the beach, with uplifted hands, chanting dreadful curses against the intruding legionaries. Meanwhile a number of women in black robes ran between the warriors of Mona, waving firebrands, to incite them to battle madness. This singular scene spellbound the Roman soldiers for a while, but soon enough Suetonius appealed to them not to be scared by frenzied women. This broke the spell, the legions advanced and the slaughter began. Next, the sacred groves of the island were cut down. Tacitus mentions that there were altars covered with the blood of captives as the Druids used to consult their deities by examining human entrails. This massacre proved to be the end of organized Druidry in Britain. By the time Agricola assumed command in Britain (78 CE) the Druids were not worth mentioning any more. This episode has caused a lot of speculation. That there existed a Druidic enclave on Mona is not

unlikely, as Mona, with its flat countryside, was a lot more fertile, and consequently more wealthy than the rest of Wales. Gerald of Wales, writing around 1190, called it the corn-chamber of Wales and claimed that its harvests were so rich that Mona could feed all the inhabitants of Wales. The most difficult question with regard to the passage is the function of those black-garbed ladies who behaved like furies. Were they Druidesses, as has been claimed so often, or simply cheerleaders? What's your guess? Whatever your answer may be, it says more about your beliefs than about the actual truth.

Valerius Maximus, writing in the first century has few words about Druids. He relates their faith to the Pythagorean doctrine and repeats the tale of debts being repaid in the next life.

Dion Chrysostom, c.100 CE, briefly mentions that the Gaulish Celts had Druids and compares them to the Persian Magi, the Egyptian priests and the Brahmins of India. He informs us that their kings were so dependent on their council that it was in truth the Druids who ruled while the kings *on golden thrones* and *in their palaces, became mere ministers of the Druids' will*. This is not exactly reliable, as Dion probably never journeyed to Gaul. More so, Gaulish chieftains may have been mightily proud of their drinking halls, but no sober minded Roman would have ever called them 'palaces'. The 'golden thrones' are even less likely.

Suetonius, around 120 CE remarks that the religion of the Druids of Gaul was forbidden to all Roman citizens, due to its barbarous and inhuman practises, and that the emperor Claudius (41-54) went beyond this prohibition and suppressed it thoroughly.

Lampridius, writing c.300 CE tells us that Alexander Severus, while attempting to drive some German tribes out of Gaul in 235, encountered a prophetic Druidess.

> While he was on his way, a Druidess cried out to him in the Gallic tongue, 'Go forward, but hope not for victory, nor put trust in thy soldiers'.

This is not unlike a number of hostile prophetesses encountered by Roman commanders while conquering the provinces of Germany.

A Druidess also appears in a tale recorded by **Vopiscus**. It seems that the future emperor Diocletian, when he was but a humble soldier serving in Gaul, had a quarrel with his landlady regarding the payment of rent. As he did not want to pay up, the dear lady told him that he was far too greedy and mean. As a joke, he replied that he would be more generous if he became emperor. The landlady, who happened to be a Druidess, replied:

> Laugh not, Diocletian, for when you have killed The Boar, you will indeed be emperor.

After hearing this prophecy, Diocletian became so obsessed with boar-hunts that he went to great lengths not to miss any. For years he kept killing boars, but he did not receive the imperial purple until he had slain the Praefect Arrius, who had the surname The Boar. Vopiscus also informs us that the emperor Aurelian, who reigned 270-275,

> consulted the Gaulish Druidesses to find out whether his descendants would remain in possession of the imperial crown. These women told him that no name would become more illustrious in the state annals than that of the line of Claudius.

These episodes, from the third century, are fairly good evidence that there were Druidesses in Gaul at the time. The problem is the late age of the stories. By then, the institution of Druidry had long been demolished and its political function had disappeared. Third century Gaul was under Roman rule, its citizens spoke Latin, wrote in Latin script, built their houses, roads and cities in the Roman fashion, were judged according to Roman law, and where it came to politics, the nobles generally did as the Roman senate told them. The intellectual, cultural and religious monopoly of the Druids had been broken more than two centuries earlier. This raises several questions. Had there been Druidesses in the old days before the conquest? Caesar speaks only of male Druids, and mentions young men who were taught by them. This is not necessarily a sexistic observation. To the Romans, the idea of priestesses was nothing unusual, as there were priestesses in Rome and the Mediterranean world. All references to Druidesses as such come from a later period. Sadly, the writings of the medieval bards and filid, let alone the Christian monks, are not exactly the most reliable source with regard to prehistory

DEAE·ARTIONI
LICINIA·SABINILLA

and have to be treated with great caution. Then there were several inspired seeresses, such as the famed prophetess Veleda, who got in the way of the Roman conquest of Germany. She supplied the very prophecies needed by the Brukteri tribe and its leader to start an armed rebellion. Not too successfully, as in the end her own tribe sold her into Roman slavery, where she was employed to clean the temple lamps and to provide oracles on a strictly commercial basis.

While these inspired priestesses seem to be authentic enough, none of them is called a Druidess nor can we be sure if they were part of an organized and centralized religion. Or think of the British Queen Boudicca who certainly performed the office of a sacrificial priestess in the sanctuary of (war-goddess?) Andraste during the revolt against the Romans in 61 CE (Cassius Dio). She is nowhere called a Druidess, though an inscription from an altar in Bordeaux, dedicated by a British trader in 237, calls her a deity. Was Boudicca deified after her death or did she derive her name from an earlier deity? And just what had the Druidesses of occupied Gaul in common with the Druids of earlier periods? It seems

Goddesses in Gallo-Roman style
Left: star Goddess Sirona (Dirona) with serpent, bowl and three eggs, from Hochscheid, Germany, where she appears as companion of the god 'Apollon' Grannus, (associated with healing). The statue is based on images of the goddess Hygieia (in charge of health), daughter of Asklepios (god of healing).
Right: horned goddess with deer antlers, London, England.
Bottom: bear goddess Artio, statue dedicated by Licinia Sabinilla, from Muri, Bern, Swiss.

likely that we will never know for certain.

Another third century author, a certain **Hippolytus**, remarked that the Druids had received the Pythagorean faith from one Zamolxis. He had been a former slave of Pythagoras, and just the sort of person a Celtic priest would accept a new religion from.

Ammianus Marcellinus, writing in the fourth century about things he didn't really understand, likewise called the Druids men of great talent and members of the intimate fellowship of the Pythagorean faith. We are at the bottom of the barrel here, the Druids have faded into legend, and the sources simply repeat what had been related earlier.

Before leaving the subject of classical Druids here is some fascinating stuff on the role of women as priestesses and enchantresses in Celtic countries. We have several images of women who seem to be engaged in ritual activities. A magnificent bronze bucket from Vace shows a woman clad in a finely worked ceremonial robe or mantle, holding one hand open to the sky, the other bears a vessel. In all likeliness she is not a goddess but an acting priestess, testifying that among the Celts of the Balkan, women did hold sacral offices.

Another fascinating find are a series of figures found buried in Neuvy-en-Sullias, close to the sacred site of Fleury. The figures show nude dancers, male and female, in what was evidently a religious ceremony. Possibly the finely wrought figures were buried to save them from some enemies. It says a lot about the individual religions of the Gaulish tribes that generally a tribe that happened to sack the settlement of another did not bother to spare the sacred site of its enemy. The statues of its gods were carelessly demolished, good evidence that the Gaulish tribes did not share a common pantheon in the middle La Tene period, nor did they believe in religious tolerance. Caesar's account of centralized Druidry hardly fits this behaviour, unless we propose that the Gaulish Druids are a phenomena of the second and first century BCE, as is a distinct (but not very popular) possibility.

Often considered a priestess is the 'Lady of Vix' who had such magnificent grave equipment including a Greek bronze vessel adorned with leering Medusa faces that happens to be the biggest vessel known from the entire classical world. It was topped by the figure of a woman or priestess crafted in silver, remarkable as silver is a lot rarer than gold in the western Hallstatt realm and was probably much more expensive. What the vessel was good for remains one of those riddles, as the bronze shell is so thin that filling it with fluids would have made the whole thing burst apart. Regarding the 'Lady of Vix' the sexual identification is not as certain as most authors would have it. The skeleton was in a rather bad state when the tomb was excavated, and the main reason the excavators decided on calling it a lady was the absence of weapons and the presence of ornaments. As we know today, most males or the late western Hallstatt period did not wear weapons in their tombs anyway, and there are several cases of definitely male burials in the time which happened to have supposedly 'feminine' jewelery such as arm- and earrings. Such cases are not frequent, but they exist. Spindler, discussing the case, points at another option, which is likewise generally ignored by simple minded researchers: the possibility of transvestites or sex changers, often an element in shamanic activity. When we class a badly preserved corpse as male or female simply on account of jewelery or weapons we may be inflicting modern sexistic attitudes on cultures about which we happen to know very little.

When we come to the account of the classical authors, we encounter one of those weird tales that Poseidonios recorded when he traveled along the coast of southern Gaul, and which Strabon copied and preserved. At the estuary of the Liger, and not far into the ocean, so Poseidonios was told, lies an island where women of the Samnites live in a sanctuary of 'Dionysos' (i.e. some Gaulish deity associated with ecstatic frenzy and intoxication). The island is forbidden to all men, though the women are free to sail to the mainland should they fancy to do so. These priestesses have a curious annual ritual. Once every year they renew the roof of their temple, a task that has to be completed before sunset, and every one of them has to carry her load of building materials. A woman who drops her load is torn to pieces by her colleagues, who carry the bloody shreds around the sanctuary in rapture, shouting with joy, until the ecstasy leaves them. This event is not exactly an accident, as some pre-selected women is knocked over on purpose. What do you make of this tale? While it does contain a measure of detail, we have to keep in mind that Poseidonios never saw any of its participants but was told his tale by a (presumably) male informer or a sailor, by definition the very sort of person who could not be present anyway. More so, his account is the only one regarding the matter, none of the Romans fighting or settling in Gaul at later times mentions any of it. Caesar, who copied a lot from Poseidonios (including the Druidic story of burning human sacrifices in wickerwork men) did not bother to include it in his books. The only shred of supporting evidence is the much later medieval Irish story of the Island of Women, an otherworldly paradise somewhere far away beyond the western horizon. If we take it as evidence for a female priesthood of some ecstatic cult, we should keep in mind that most of its activities sound rather unlikely.

However, there is a bit of evidence for wild women which comes from Gaul and has not been distorted by gossip and foreign storytelling. A tomb in Larzac, some 15 km south of La Graufesenque, dept. Aveyron, dated c. 100 CE, contained an urn with the cremated remnants of what was probably a woman. The urn was closed with a lead tablet. This tablet turned out to be inscribed with more than 160 words in Gaulish language (and Roman script), making it the longest Gaulish inscription available. As you will read later on, there was a popular sorcerous custom in the late La Tene time and during the Roman occupation to write spells and curses on lead tablets, which were cast into wells or buried in tombs to transmit their message to the gods of the underworld. Diodor informs us that the people of Gaul throw letters into the crematory fire, supposedly in the belief that the dead would read them. While letters of paper or parchment sound unlikely, or are simply undetectable using archaeological methods, tablets of metal may fit. The text

poses several fascinating riddles. It seems to deal with the magical battle between two groups of women who are called *mnas brictas* (women endowed with magic). The first group is represented by the women Severa and Tertionicna, leaders of indigenous and non-indigenous followers. Let me quote Wolfgang Meid 1992:

This group had apparently practised harmful magic upon another group, and it is this other group, which, with the help of a 'wise woman' udluia, tries to counter this attack, reduce its effects, render Severa and Tertionicna innocuous, and even proposes some kind of non-aggression pact.

So much about the general meaning of the tablet. The actual details, however, are rather problematic. For one thing, Gaulish is a language that is not very well known, leading to plenty of scholarly debate. For another, the original text was partly erased by another writer who added some lines at the cost of the earlier text. We can be certain that the text refers to groups of women who work magic, words like *brictas* and *brixtia* are earlier forms of the old Irish *bricht* (magical formula). Severa and Tertionicna are accused of practising *ni - tig*, harmful magic (literally to stick, to stab, to prick into) and they are to be rendered *lissata* or *liciata*, meaning spellbound or fettered with bonds. In the short passage by the second scribe occurs the word *antumnos* (for *andumnos*), meaning the underworld, the term may come from **ande - dubnos* : very deep. This is the prototype for the much later Welsh word Anwfn. Other

interesting words are *anatia* (soul) related to the later Wesh *eneid*, and in the final section, the terms *barnauno* (standing trial, being judged) from **barna-* to judge, related to the old Irish *brehon* (judge), and finally *ratet* (a pledge, promise, guarantee) suggesting that the two rival groups came to an agreement. I would propose that this tablet, unlike the ones that contain curses or request the gods of the underworld to bring someone to a sticky end, may have been a document testifying that both groups had settled their differences. This 'contract' may have been given to the deep ones to make sure all concerned keep the peace. And while none of the participants is called a Druidess, the text is good evidence that in occupied Gaul organized groups of women, possibly priestesses, worked devastating spells on each other.

Riddles from Antiquity

So much for a brief summary of the writings of the classical authors. While we can count ourselves lucky that so many writers referred to Druids, it is in the fine details that their accounts are lacking. Most of our sources devoted only a few short lines to the subject, and these are full of repetitions. The authors of ancient Rome rarely bothered to give their sources, and so we cannot be certain whether an author was well-informed or just repeating what Caesar had written earlier. Most of these authors wrote in a period when Druids had become extinct and this does not make their account more reliable. Indeed the entire amount of classical references to Druids can easily be printed on less than ten small pages, as was done by T. Kendrick, whose remarkable and sober-minded study is still among the best books on the subject. Quite obviously it is not an easy task to reconstruct an ancient religion given so little trustworthy evidence. The other big problem arises when we consider the validity of the sources. This has become a big issue among the Neo-Celticists, many of whom make money by peddling a perfect past, a golden age of peace and plenty. One of the tricky issues is human sacrifice.

There have been plenty of authors who have dismissed the entire issue as a nasty Roman propaganda story, as a cruel myth to legitimize the equally cruel conquest of Gaul. If you listen to these authors you might get the impression that the Druids were a bunch of venerable, ecological-minded, friendly old men, doing good, helping the poor and sick and abhorring all sorts of violence. Probably they also sang pop-songs, smoked dope, loitered on the

Gods in Gallo-Roman style.
Left: God with deer hooves, made from four pieces of sheet bronze, one eye made of white glass and blue enamel (the other is missing), height 45 cm, Bouray, Seine-et-Oise, France. Attempts to date this statue vary enormously, the average estimate being between the 1st century BCE and the 1 century CE.
top r. Horned god, bronze, Magerides, dep. Corrèze, France. The god is holding a torque and wears Gaulish trousers with a tartan pattern combined with a Roman mantle, the sort that is usually found on statues of Mercury.
bottom r. Image of Esus, found on a pillar, together with the Roman deities Iovis (Iupiter), Volcanus (god of smiths) and the Gaulish deity Tarvos Trigaranos (a bull deity accompanied by three cranes). Esus is shown cutting a tree. Paris, blueish sandstone, height 107cm.

beach and wished the Roman army to have a nice day. On the other hand, quite as many authors have proposed that all the horror stories are true, that ancient Gaul was a tough place full of cruelty and early death and that the Roman historians didn't need to make up unfriendly propaganda stories as the plain reality was usually much worse. Considering how little can actually be known, the crucial issue seems to be what sort of past one would like to believe in. Of course both factions have a number of good arguments for their point of view, but the evidence is so shaky that neither can prove anything. This makes the whole debate (which has been going on for more than two centuries) a clash of faiths. Personally, I find it most interesting to listen to the arguments proposed by the various factions. If you have a number of tales and no way of investigating which of them is reliable (apart from such subjective arts as time-travel), just which items would you consider likely? This is the moment to learn something about your own beliefs. It is also a chance to do something practical. Do yourself a favour and examine what your own opinion is. I shall now write a couple of words and I would like you to examine how you understand them. The phrase is: ...*the Druids assembled in a sacred grove.*

Please stop here and recall how you represent this idea in your head. When you read that the Druids assembled in a sacred grove, you require a representation to make sense of the words. There will be images you made of this event, as well as sound and feeling. Observe what you imagined as you read the words. It may be that your representation was so fast that you hardly noticed what you imagined. In this case, slow down and go back so you can watch your mind at work. Now let me proceed by asking some more questions. Were the Druids you imagined all male? What age group? What costume did they wear? Did they have talismans, or wands, or a specific haircut? What mood were they in? What were the trees of that grove? What time of day, what season of the year? And just what were they doing? You will find that you have to hallucinate to make sense of my harmless words. Nobody knows what the Druids usually wore, let alone whether there were Druidesses in the pre Roman period when the cult was still flourishing, nor how they usually conducted their ceremonies. It gets even better when we come to the Druids private life. Can you imagine a Druid on a holiday trip, or one who comes home after a long day at the altar? Do you imagine the Druids were married? What did they eat? What did they do for relaxation?

Anything which you imagined which cannot be found in the classical texts is plainly your own imagination. This can't be helped. If you imagine people about whom so little is known for certain, you will have to invent a lot of details. All people who read about Druids do so. The point is, that most people remain unaware of their own contribution: they do not examine how they think, and consequently take ideas for granted which are definitely not self evident. I have asked a number of persons to make sense of this harmless and fairly content-free phrase. Some had Druids at a fire in the night, others saw an oak forest in summer, many visualized Druids in white (though one person hallucinated bear skins) and all invented a ceremony, be it serene or ecstatic, as it suited their own world-view. Even when you visualize the more or less detailed accounts given by Pliny (do this now) there are plenty of items which you'll have to make up to make the events come to life. You may find that you are taking plenty of ideas for granted that cannot be traced to any sort of historical evidence. This, incidentally, can hardly be avoided. Speculation on so little data always requires a bit of creative hallucination. Usually, the hallucinated bits remain unconscious to you, but they still exist in your mind and form your impression of the subject. Here you can also find a good clue why Druids have been such an exciting topic during the last centuries. The less one knows the more one has to invent. Thus, Druids do more to stimulate the imagination than the more prosaic cults where more data is available.

Next, imagine a dodgy topic which has excited a lot of scholars over the past two centuries. The issue is human sacrifice. As you may recall, most classical authors had a lot to say about this practise, and delighted in describing how it was performed. This matter has brought about much quarreling among historians, many of whom went to considerable lengths to prove its reality or to argue it away. To begin with, you can learn something about your own beliefs. Please imagine one of those human sacrifice rites now. Then imagine a Druidic rite that is friendly, peaceful, and involves the offering of flowers and grains. Are both visions equally convincing? Do you prefer one to the other? Pause now and examine them again. Is one of them larger, brighter,

closer, better developed, more detailed, more colourful, more lifelike? What is the difference between the two visions, apart from their contents? Which vision seems more 'real' to you? For the fun of it, turn it the other way around. Imagine the more convincing vision in the less convincing form and vice versa. What happens? How can you convince yourself to something you doubted earlier, and how can you find doubt in something that seemed self evident and natural previously?

Now for the next bit of fun. First assume a pro-Druid point of view and propose that the Druids were indeed custodians of some ancient and highly refined wisdom, and that there were extremely few, if any human sacrifices being committed by them. True, there have been archaeologists who unearthed evidence that looks remarkably like violent death for the sake of religion, but then, a lot of it can be explained away as executions of criminals or prisoners of war, odd burial customs or unusual accidents on the way to work.

Then assume a pro-Roman point of view and propose that the Druids, at least the ones of Gaul, were basically a power-hungry elite that had no qualms about killing a lot of people for the sake of a good harvest and general holiness.

Or pretend that you are a Druid who goes in for human sacrifice and argue that it isn't such a bad custom, as after all, reincarnation makes up for it. It could be claimed that the victims of those sacrifices were actually honoured and happy to be slain, as they may have gained advantages in some sort of after-life.

Then there is the question of frequency.

Caesar and others gave the impression that the sacrifices were often large affairs involving multiple victims. Criminals (and the odd innocents) who burn to death in great wickerwork figures, however, leave very little evidence for the archaeologist to uncover. Thus, the relative scarcity of sacrifices who make it to the shovel of the excavator can be interpreted in several ways. You could argue that such sacrifices were rare and in-between, or that we just can't find them.

What other points of view could you assume? The interesting issue, as you argue each point of view, is to observe whether you find it convincing, or at least probable. How do you do this? What do you imagine to form an opinion? What sort of images seem more convincing? How do you convince yourself?

What makes the exercise so funny is that regardless of whether you convince yourself or not, you still cannot be certain. All of these things happened more than two-thousand years ago and there is no way of being sure. Thus, what you can learn when you argue each position is not what really happened but how you convince yourself, and how you shape your own belief by hallucination. This is a lot more useful than finding out what the Druids really did. It may show the shape of the fables you would like to take for reality and teach the skill of keeping a really open mind.

Turning from the nasty topic of cruelty and sacrifice we could examine the equally questionable positive fantasies connected with the Druids. Caesar and others mentioned the deep interest Druids had in such matters as astronomy, cosmology, the calendrical sciences, medicine and the like. While all of them hinted at some sort of wisdom, none of them bothered to give examples. Consequently, many modern writers have proudly cited the sciences supposedly perfected by Druids, but failed to give evidence for them. Again, Druidic wisdom has become a glorious opportunity to invent all sorts of bizarre ideas. When you read that Druids believed in reincarnation, your mind has to imagine (or hallucinate) something to make sense of these words. it is very hard to imagine what reincarnation means without involving concepts we are familiar with, such as the reincarnation-models favoured by Pythagoreans, Hindus, Buddhists or Theosophists. Sadly, these models do not agree with each other, and the Druid version may differ from all of them. We cannot know, but given the invitation to imagine, it is extremely difficult to avoid hallucination.

Or take the supposed Druidic interest in calculating the length of the year. For quite a while, this has been paraded as one of the few issues that can be proved. The item in question is the Coligny calendar. Bronze fragments of an ancient calendar were discovered near Coligny in France, and enthusiastically described as Druidic. Sadly, the calendar is very open to debate. For a start, the inscriptions are in Roman letters, though they seem to be in some Celtic language. More difficult yet, the calendar was found near a Roman road, together with a statue of Apollo, and shows a calendrical arrangement that was en vogue before Julius Caesar reformed the calendar. This points at a curious Gallo-Roman tradition, which is not the same thing as a

Druidic one. The Coligny calendar shows a five year cycle of sixty months plus two intercalary months at the beginning and middle of the cycle, thus dividing it into two sections of 2.5 years. So much for the good news, as Diodorus had written that the people of Gaul held quinquennial sacrifices. The first half of the year began with a month called Samon, the second half with one called Giamon. Various scholars have guessed that these unknown words mean mid-summer and mid-winter, or the beginning of summer and winter, with no proof worth mentioning. Old Irish Sam means summer, but the beginning of winter was called Samhain. Thus, Samon could be summer or winter, and no-one knows for certain. The months were sorted into those with 30 days, called Mat (possibly 'good') and those with 29, called Anm, which can conceivably mean An Mat, i.e. 'not good', provided Mat really means good and Anm is an abbreviation. The terms could also mean complete and incomplete. Not even the start of the month can be fixed with certainty. Did a dark fortnight precede the bright, or did the month begin on the sixth day as Pliny recorded? The Coligny calendar does not accord with what is so carelessly called 'the Celtic year' nowadays. This is really the year of the Celtic Gaels of Scotland and Ireland as the Brythonic Celts of Wales and Cornwall did not subscribe to it, and what the various Continental Celts calculated is anyone's guess. What makes the whole thing really problematic is that the Coligny calendar, previously assumed to come from the first century of our era, is nowadays dated as coming from the second. This is not a time when any form of Druidry

was tolerated in occupied Gaul. Stranger still, why would anybody in the Roman empire make use of a calendar that was so inaccurate that it required an extra month every 2.5 years when the rest of the empire had been using the much more accurate Julian calendar for more than a century?

The Decline of the Druids

With the Roman occupation, many local cults and religions changed considerably. The Druid order, as a form of organized religion, seems to have disappeared quite thoroughly. This was partly due to violent suppression, but even more so due to the changes in the social structures that occurred when Gaul and Britain became parts of the empire. Once the local policy was being decided by the senate in Rome, the Druids lost their function as political counselors. Roman law replaced the local Druid courts and education ceased to be a Druidic office. As soon as Gaul was occupied, a considerable amount of nobles embraced whatever blessings the empire had to offer. To begin with there were wine and luxury goods, but this was only the first and most attractive feature in the program. More important were Roman fashions, architecture, education, a language that could be understood in large parts of Europe, a wide network of trade routes, the famed Roman peace and an attitude that transformed nobles from members of some minor tribes into citizens of the empire.

It is an interesting phenomenon that so many modern pagans believe that their ancestors hated the innovations that came in the wake of the conquest. In prosaic reality, the slaughter was soon forgotten and people embraced the new ideas, fashions and opportunities. Many nobles sent their young men to Rome for a good education, and when these returned, they had transformed quite thoroughly and thought along lines that would have been impossible for their ancestors. In his *Agricola*, Tacitus mentions that the nobles of Britain soon adopted Roman dress and customs, and were eager to learn Latin. Many young men joined the legions and marched through the empire as there is nothing more attractive than being on the winning side. These changes also affected religious life. On the whole, the Romans permitted the local cults to continue with their ways, provided they adhered to the laws of the empire, honoured the guardian angel of the emperor, paid taxes and kept the population docile.

For several centuries, the Celtic deities were worshipped as before the conquest, though in a somewhat softer form. Some of them even gained more worshippers. Each province of the empire supplied soldiers for the legions, and the legionaries carried their deities across Europe. Some gods, such as the Persian Mithras or the Celtic horse goddess Epona were a lot more popular in the legions than they had been prior to the conquest. One of the innovations introduced by the occupation was the fashion of setting memorial stones. Considering the archaeological evidence, few deities in the Celtic world were worshipped with statues before the Roman army started the fashion. Once the new trend had begun, however, it became immensely popular. Many Celtic people in Gaul, Germany and Britain had images made of their favourite gods. At first, these were closely modeled on the Roman originals, but soon enough a distinct Gallo-Roman style developed and Celtic stone-smiths produced statues and altars that were sought after in wide parts of the empire.

We owe to this fashion most of our knowledge of most Celtic gods. For the surviving Druids (provided there were any), things had developed badly. Some aspects of their religion had survived, but their own function as a powerful elite had disintegrated. They were no organized religion any more, their secret wisdom was no longer sought after, and of the many offices they fulfilled, only a bit of magic and prophecy remained. When in 312 the emperor Constantine officially embraced Christianity, so did much of the empire, and before long a lot of pagan religions disappeared. Mind you, the transformation was neither easy nor violent at first, and the Christianity of those days was a far cry from what we are used to nowadays. Few people had sympathy for the sort of Christ who preached poverty and asked people to turn the other cheek. Christ became popular as his cult promised, first of all, success in war and a jolly good afterlife. This seemed agreeable to a lot of nobles in an age when the Roman empire was beginning to fall apart. As an exclusively monotheistic religion, Christianity put an end to the pluralism of the older pagan cults. This conversion had a more severe effect on the pagan religions than the Roman conquest itself and put the last nail in the Druid's coffin.

Not so in Ireland. The Roman army never conquered Ireland, though no doubt some

Coins 2, Shapeshifting. Humans or Gods in
animal form. top r: Boii, Bohemia, silver, 25mm,
bird-woman! FARIARIX.
center l: Osismi, gold, 20mm, horse-human,
note thumb gesture and stylized "harp"
center r: Osismii, gold, 20 mm, human profile
with "bear" headdress
bottom: Petrocori, silver, 14 mm, human-boar.

traders must have journeyed there on occasion, and so the Irish Druids survived until the green island assumed Christianity. These Druids were not the same sort of folk that seems to have existed in Gaul. When Caesar invaded Gaul, the local society was a moribund aristocracy with plenty of influential chieftains struggling for control of their own and allied tribes. By contrast the British and the Irish seem to have favoured sacred monarchies. There seem to have been kings who were wedded to the goddess of the land, and such kings were basically sacred figures burdened by countless rituals and taboos. These kings were advised by Druids, but these Druids do not seem to have enjoyed such absolute power as the ones in Gaul. While the British Druids disappeared thanks to Roman persecution, the Irish Druids held their function up to the fifth century when Christianity made their function redundant.

Possibly another Druidic enclave existed in the north of Britain and Scotland, realms avoided by the Romans and christianized much later than the rest of the island. As a note of caution I would like to add that it is rather hard to be certain about the island Celtic Druids. To study them, we have to rely on medieval manuscripts which were generally written by unsympathetic Christian monks several centuries after the Druidic decline. While the scholars of the 19th century (and well into this one) were eager to class the medieval literature of Ireland as an objective expression of ancient Celtic beliefs, archaeological research has revealed plenty of cases where this was not the case. Many of the medieval legends are based on traditions which the monkish literati did not understand or imported from other parts of Europe. Some of those monks were unsympathetic regarding pagan beliefs, but an even greater majority was totally ignorant of them. Consequently, the literature dealing with Irish Druids has to be examined with great caution.

When Druids are described, they are often cast into a Christian form. The *Tripartite Life of St. Patrick* (8-10th century) claims that the Irish Druids wore white robes, a tonsure and baptized children with water. As this work was written at least 350 years after the disappearance of the Irish Druids we have no way of verifying these details. Neither had its author. Such similarities led some researchers to the optimistic theory that maybe the Druids and the early Christians existed side by side for a while, in a form of peaceful coexistence, and that a lot of Druid lore flew into the teachings of 'Celtic Christianity'. In the last century, this fashionable fable attracted Christians who were bored by their creed and wanted a bit of Celtic romance to feel special. From the historical point of view, the evidence for this theory is more than shaky. When St. Patrick was roaming Ireland, banishing serpents and spreading the good word, those Druids who got into the way of the saintly man came to a messy end. There are several medieval accounts detailing how St. Patrick battled Druids in miracle-working contests. These are pretty similar to certain legends found in the Bible, and just like those Biblical contests, they end in the destruction of the false prophets.

Generally, Druids in Christian gospel are a bit of a disappointment. Most of them are not members of an organized religion but seem to function as heathenish magicians, and all of them are in league with the devil. Often enough they are dashed to pieces, swallowed by the earth or burned to cinders by fire from heaven, which goes to show just how wicked they were. This does not really sound like peaceful coexistence. When St. Patrick composed his hymn a*gainst incantations of false prophets, against black laws of hereticians, against surroundings of idolism, against spells of women, and of smiths, and of Druids (The Guardsman's Cry of St. Patrick)* he certainly proved that he meant business. This was very much in accord with the decrees of the emperor Theodosius, who had ordered in 394 that pagan temples, rites and ceremonies were to be completely abolished, and enforced it thoroughly.

Druids in Legend.

Seven years your right, under a flagstone in a quagmire,
Without food, without taste, but the thirst you ever torturing,
The law of the judges your lesson, and prayer your language;
And if you like to return
You will be, for a time, a Druid, perhaps.

Runs an old Irish poem, quoted by Bonwick. You'll find out about the quagmire as we go along. While the classical authors were generally concerned with what they considered fact, the medieval authors who mention Druids usually included them in fantastic legends. You can find plenty of Druids in the writings of medieval Irish scribes. The problem with these Druids is that they appear in legends which often contain elements of folk tale, and that many of the miracles worked by these Druids are closely paralleled by Christian hagiographies or simple fairy tales. Now the easiest approach to this topic, and probably the most popular one, is to take the Irish legends as genuine expressions of ancient Celtic traditions. Many authors, especially in the last century, saw Irish myth as a storehouse for prehistorical wisdom, coming from a culture which had not been shaped by Roman occupation. While some of this may be true, so is the fact that the Irish scribes who set down the legends were strongly influenced by the Christian faith, and consequently neither familiar nor friendly with pagan ideas. Also, they wrote long after the Druids of Ireland had been abolished, which raises the question of how much they could have known about the topic anyway. Last, the Irish scribes, be they monks or filid, had considerable learning with regard to the classical authors of ancient Rome and Greece. When we encounter some old Celtic element in Irish myth which has a close parallel in the works of the classical authors, we could take this as evidence that the Irish legends support data from Roman times, and that both sources confirm each other. We could also ask if the Irish scribes happened to know the Roman text, and copied from it. Both explanations are possible. Archaeological excavations have shown that not all items paraded as genuine old Celtic lore in legend are trustworthy. Indeed, it often appeared that the medieval scribes had some vague and partial information regarding a person, an event or a place, and made up the missing details as they went along. So let us now consider what the Irish Druids of legend supposedly did. I trust that you are skeptical enough to realize that we are dealing with complicated myths here, and that these often say more about the beliefs of the medieval filid than about the actual Druids. This does not imply that we are dealing exclusively with fantasy. When you hear of a Druidess turning a rival into a pool of water, such a notion is not supposed to be considered in the ordinary sense as true or false. We may as well be dealing with a magickal reality, so that the unlikely event becomes an accurate expression of a psychological truth.

Another interesting issue is the meaning of the word Druid in Irish literature. While the classical authors had a specific cult and priesthood in mind, the Druids of Irish literature are not associated with specific forms of organized religion. Quite a few are simply independent sorcerers and prophets. The word Drui, as it is used in medieval Irish literature signifies a wizard or sorcerer, and Druidry is often simply sorcery and spell-craft. Maybe this sorcerer was a priest and maybe s/he wasn't. If you find a Druid in these texts, you cannot be certain if the term was used in the religious sense that it had for the Roman literati, or whether it simply referred to a powerful enchanter. To assume that all Irish Druids were organized in a cult, as the Druids of Gaul may have been, may be rather naive.

In the early legends, several Druids are portrayed. As these tales take place before Christianity was introduced to Ireland, we find Druids holding important positions in the royal courts. These Druids are unlike the evil devil worshipping Druids that were fought by St. Patrick with God on his side, they also differ from the Druids that the classical authors wrote about. For a start, the Irish Druids were neither judges nor law makers. They were not as strictly organized as the Druids of Gaul. The Druids of medieval Irish legend held honourable positions as prophets, seers and advisors, and generally they frequented the courts of minor and major kings. If they had a centralized organization, the Irish myths give no evidence for it. In fact, you can find Druids of different provinces engaged in magical war with each other.

To begin with, we may cast a swift look at the legendary history of Ireland. Several medieval texts claim that Ireland was not settled once and for all but that there was a series of invasions, and that one wave of conquerors followed the next. Several early Celtic scholars assumed that there is a historical background to these invasions, no matter the numerous mythical elements and semi-divine entities. Modern researchers have become more cautious about attributing each social and cultural change to a violent invasion. Some massive cultural changes come in the shape of fashions and are introduced not by raging warriors but by traveling artisans and enterprising merchants.

According to legend, when the people of Partholon invaded Ireland sometime in very early proto-history, they were accompanied by three Druids. These had the names Fios (intelligence), Eolus (knowledge) and Fochmarc (inquiry). Such a trinity sound less like historical people than like one of the many triads popular among the Island

Celts. If they did anything noteworthy, the legend fails to record it. Later, the Tuatha De Danann, who may have been deities, extraterrestrials or simply another wave of Celtic immigrants, invaded Ireland. Their origin is obscure, as various accounts claim that they came from Spain, from Denmark, or directly from the stars. These also had Druids, but as many of the people of Danann had divine powers anyway, the Druidry among them is nothing really special. Several of the Tuatha De Danann are called Druids, first of all Brian, Inchar and Iucharba, and the two Druidesses Beonill and Danann, plus a number of persons skilled in the Druidic arts. The Tuatha De Danann (Tribes of the Goddess Danann) spent much of their time fighting a cruel war against the Fomorians ('from under the sea'), most of whom appeared like terrifying zoomorphic monstrosities. In this war, the people of Danann used magic against their enemies. Now many of the Tuatha were at least of semi-divine nature, and, as you will read in the chapter on Bride, it appears that some of them were once worshipped as deities. In this function, they could perform spell-craft and miracle working of the type which was blamed on human Druids in other legends. In preparing for the battle, the Druid Figol son of Mamos announced: *I will cause three showers of fire to pour on the faces of the Fomorian host, and I will take out of them two thirds of their valour and their bravery and their strength, and I will bind their urine in their own bodies and in the bodies of their horses. Every breath that the men of Ireland shall exhale will be an increase of valour and their bravery and their strength to them. Though they bide in the battle till the end of seven years, they will not be weary in any*

wise. The suggestion that links exhalation with an increase of battle-power is of especial importance here. Such suggestions show skill in hypnotherapy, and indicate that at least some people among the island Celts were aware that certain forms of breathing can increase vitality. This insight will seem natural to every advanced student of East Asian martial arts, in Europe such wisdom is seldom recorded. Another interesting aspect of the tale may be that, though the Druid Figol contributes spell-craft to the outcome of the battle, he is not in charge of other activities which were associated with the classical Druids. Figol is not a healer, this task is performed by the wonder working physician Diancecht, he is not a poet, as the task of satirizing and cursing the enemy is performed by the fili Cairbre son of Etain. Neither is he alone in spell craft. The legend mentions sorcerers among the Tuatha De who reduce the courage of the Fomorians and bind their urine, just like the Druid Figol promised, and two witches, Be-Culle and O Dianann, who promised: *We will enchant the trees and the stones and the sods of the earth, so that they shall become a host under arms against them, and shall rout them in flight with horror and trembling.* Likewise, the divine smith Goibniu contributed his wizardly skills in weapon making, the sorcerer Mathgen promised to hurl the mountains of Ireland on top of the Fomorians and the Dagda ('Good God') joined in the *mutual smiting, the destruction and the wizardry.* Thus, there was plenty of magic in the second battle of Mag Tured, but most of it was not directly attributed to Druidry.

The Tuatha De Danann did not only fight the Fomorians but also a number of invading tribes called the Fir Bolg (whose name may possibly be related to the Celtic tribe of the Belgae). In the inevitable war, three Druidesses of the Tuatha De, Bodhbh, Macha and Mor Rigan caused black clouds and dark mists to envelop the Fir Bolg army and made showers of fire and blood pour from the skies. For three days they terrified their enemies, until the Druids of the Fir Bolg, Cesarn, Gnathach and Ingnathach broke the spell. By then, the Tuatha De had used the opportunity to withdraw to a better strategic position. The Druid Cesarn, by the way, was not only a caster of spells but also an interpreter of dreams. When the battle finally took place, both sides had their Druids and sorcerers on the battle field, working enchantments and spell craft against their foes. This is very much in keeping with the usual Celto-Germanic approach to battle strategy. The people of middle and Northern Europe generally believed that success in war was not so much a matter of planning and organization but depended on the favour of the gods. Thus, a king who embodied the truth of the land could expect to win, provided the rites were followed, sacrifices were offered and no taboos were violated. If this didn't work, one could easily blame the failure on some hidden sin of the nobility, or on the unreliable temperament of the war gods. To use sorcery in battle was simply common sense, whereas a detailed and extended strategy, as used by the Roman army, was frowned upon. As a result, the Celtic and Germanic tribes organized their armies in kinship groups and knew one battle formation (the wedge), they were able to throw fantastic fits of obsessive battle rage

but failed miserably when it came to sustained effort. In later periods, the spellcraft on the battlefield seems to have become part of the office of poets and bards.

Druidic sorceries are a popular topic in Irish legend. It would be too much to cite all instances in these pages, but an example or two might be useful to give you an idea of the supernatural skills associated with Druidry. When Mider (possibly a deity in prehistorical times) brought his new wife Etain home to the Tuatha De, his first wife Fuamnach had a terrible fit of jealousy. Other women may have made a scene, but Fuamnach had been trained by the Druid Bresal Etarlam. Taking her hated rival to the central chair of the house, she bade Etain sit down in this seat of honour, and struck her with a staff of red rowan. While the Druids of Pliny's account were compulsive about oaks, the Irish Druids were more interested in rowan and yew. The blow of the rowan staff turned Etain into a pool of water. Then Fuamnach fled to the Druid Bresal, who had been her foster-father in the first place, and Mider also left the house, as living with a pool of water was not quite the way he wished to pass his time. This was not the end of the rivalry, however. *The heat of the fire and the air and the seething of the ground combined to turn the pool of water that was in the center of the house into a worm, and they then turned the worm into a scarlet fly. This fly was the size of the head of the handsomest man in the land, and the sound of its voice and the beating of its wings were sweeter than pipes and harps and horns. Its eyes shone like precious stones in the dark, and its colour and fragrance could sate hunger and thirst in any man;*

<u>Coins 3</u>
top l & r (front &
reverse): Helveti,
gold, 16 mm
center l:
Lingones, triskel
center r: Helveti?
"Freiburg type",
gold, 18 mm, for
all its abstraction,
this was a popular
motif which was
produced in
several variations
bottom l:
Catuvellauni,
Britain, minted in
Camulodunum
(Colchester),
barley. During the
reign of
Cunobelin, the
Catuvellauni
exported large
amounts of grain
to Gaul
bottom r:
unknown, called
"German silver
type, bushel"

moreover, a sprinkling of its drops could cure every sickness and affliction and disease. This fly accompanied Mider through his land... (The Wooing of Etain, Yellow Book of Lecan, translation J. Gantz). Being of superhuman character, Mider was aware that the fly was Etain, and refused to take a new wife. The fly buzzed him to sleep every night and woke him when enemies approached, and made sweet music, so Mider refused to eat and drink unless he had the fly in his company. This galled Fuamnach so much that she used her Druidic skills to conjure a violent storm wind which blew the fly right off the island and into the tempests and waves of the wide ocean. For seven years, Etain in fly form buzzed through the air until finally the wind ceased and she returned to Ireland, rain-drenched and quite beside herself. There she was caught by the Macc Oc, Mider's foster son, who immediately recognized Etain, and took her home to nurse her back to health in a crystal bower full of fragrant herbs. Fuamnach soon heard of this, so she asked Mider to invite Macc Oc for a drink, and when Macc Oc had gone out, she raised another tempestuous wind that blew the fly right out of the bower and into the upperworld, where it flew restlessly for another seven years. Finally it managed to alight on a rooftop in Ulaid, fluttered dazedly indoors, and collapsed into the winecup of Etar's wife, who innocently swallowed it.

Soon enough the dear lady found herself pregnant, and Etain was reborn in human shape in the human world. Later in life she was married to king Echu Airem of Temair, but did not remain his wife for very long, as

Midir came from the hidden world under the hollow hills and won her by trickery and carried her away. Like two swans the two rose from the royal hall. Then king Echu had a fit of rage and sent his Druid Dallan to seek out the hiding place of Etain and Mider. The Druid traveled across Ireland for a whole year without success. Finally he cut four wands of yew and inscribed them with ogham letters. Then he made a divination with the staffs (I wish I knew how), and discovered that the two were living under a mound at Bri Leith. The Druid told his tidings to king Echu, who instantly gathered a large force and proceeded to dig up the fairy hill. This upset the Tuatha De Danann, who were by then living underneath the hollow hills, and before long Mider had to appear before the enraged monarch. In his company, however, were fifty women, all of whom looked exactly like Etain, and Mider challenged the perplexed king to take his choice and find his former wife. King Echu had them pour a liquid into a vessel (serving guests of honour was part of the queen's obligations), and finally decided on one woman who seemed much like his former wife to him, though he wasn't quite convinced. Mider gave her to the king and asked him to pledge himself content. Once Echu had done so, Mider smiled and confessed that Etain had been pregnant when he had spirited her away to the otherworld. Time passes differently in the otherworld of the Sidhe, so Etain's daughter was born and grew up in the country beneath the surface while only a short time had passed in the mortal realm. To his disgust, the king had to realize that he had chosen his own daughter for his wife, and Mider disappeared with a laugh and was never seen again.

Later the Sons of Mil invaded Ireland, as a Druid of theirs, one Caicher, had foretold that they would do so. On arrival, they were met by the People of Danann, who declared that a battle at this time would be jolly unfair, as they had been caught unprepared. Consequently, they made a treaty that the Sons of Mil had to return to their ships and sail beyond the ninth wave. Then they were permitted to come back and have a fight. When the Sons of Mil had sailed beyond the ninth wave, they found their return to Ireland thwarted. The Druids of the Tuatha De Danann were standing at the shore conjuring a mighty storm in the hope of drowning the invaders. So fierce was the uproar of the winds that the very bottom of the ocean was raised to the surface, and the proud warriors were mightily sick of the sea. The Sons of Mil also had Druids and enchanters among their number, who now proceeded to counter the magic of the storm with enchantments of their own. One of them, the famed poet Amergin White Knee, stilled the churning waves and howling winds with a song that invoked the blessing of the Island. Several songs are attributed to Amergin. As they are full of inspiration, I would like to quote two of them here. They are both from the *Leabhar Gabhala*, the *Book of Invasions*, and their language is so archaic that they may well have been recorded in the eighth century. To begin with here is the invocation of Ireland herself, in the translation of R. A. S. Macalister and Eoin MacNeill. This enchantment broke the spell of the Druidic storm and calmed the waters.

I invoke the land of Ireland.
Much coursed be the fertile sea;
Fertile be the fruit-strewn mountain;
Fruit-strewn be the showery wood;
Showery be the river of waterfalls;
Of waterfalls be the lake of deep pools;
Deep-pooled be the hill-top well;
A well of tribes be the assembly;
An assembly of kings be Temair; (Tara)
Temair be a hill of tribes,
The tribes of the sons of Mil,
Of Mil of the ships, the barks.
Let the lofty bark be Ireland,
Lofty Ireland, darkly sung:
An incantation of great cunning,
The great cunning of the wives of Bres,
The wives of Bres, of Buaigne.
The great lady Ireland,
Eremon hath conquered her,
Ir, Eber have invoked for her.
I invoke the land of Ireland.

Next the song that the poet sang when he first set his foot on Irish soil. It is not a song of conquest but a statement of magical identity.
I am the wind which breathes upon the sea,
I am the wave of the ocean,
I am the murmur of the billows,
I am the ox of the seven combats,
I am the vulture upon the rocks,
I am the beam of the sun,
I am the fairest of plants,
I am a wild boar in valour,
I am a salmon in the water,
I am a lake in the plain,
I am a word of science,
I am the point of the lance of battle,
I am the god who created in the head the fire.
Who is it who throws light into the meeting on the mountain?
Who announces the ages of the moon?
Who teaches the place where couches the

sun?

(If not I)

(Translation by Douglas Hyde.)

To this poem several glosses were later added later, which you can occasionally find in other renderings of the song. Mr. Hyde incorporated them in the last three lines. D'Arbois de Jubainville renders them as: *Who will enlighten each question, if not I? Who telleth the ages of the moon? Who telleth the ages of the moon, if not I? Who showeth the place where the sun goes to rest? If not the file?*

Also, the word vulture may be a bit questionable. Some translators give it as hawk. There are several European species of vultures, mostly inhabiting the high mountain ranges, but whether there were any around in prehistoric Ireland is a question I shall gladly leave to an ornithologist.

It would be tempting to comment on the various lines of these wonderful samples of magical spell-craft, but for the time being it may be more useful if you read them aloud and simply sense the skill and inspiration that went into them. We shall examine similar poems like the second one later, as the 'I am' formula is a matter that frequently comes up in the songs of shamans and of the British Taliesins. Such poetry contains many elements and formula that can be used like hypnotic inductions to change perception and transform belief. Regarding the first poem, it is in a metre called rosc, which is typified by alliteration, fast utterance, and the repetition of elements from one line in the next. These songs were not recited by calm and dignified priests but by an excited and ecstatic mind in a state of poetic frenzy. Now the interesting thing about these songs is that in the second one, Amergin works himself into a state of rapture in which he transcends his human identity by becoming a number of other beings.

To invade the island, the Sons of Mil take care to first come to terms with its spiritual nature. After the singing of the enchanting verses, the storm died down and the invaders returned to the shore. From there they proceeded to move inland. On their way they were approached by the goddess of the island in three forms. These were the deities Eriu, Banba and Fodla, all three of them belonging to the People of Danann. Each of them greeted the invaders and threatened to halt their progress, claiming that their cause was an unjust one. To each of the three, Amergin promised that her name would remain the name of the island forever, which satisfied the divinities. Equipped with the blessing of the island itself, the warriors of the invading force soon hurled themselves against the troops of the people of Danann and won a bloody victory. Eriu, the goddess who gave her name to Ireland, was slain at the battle of Tailtiu. Little is known of her, save that she is associated with circles and rings, her name means *regular traveler*, and Smyth (1988) speculates that she may have been a solar goddess. Her sister Banba was slain in the same battle, by Caicher the druid, and so was Fodla. For all their respect for the three goddesses of the land, the Sons of Mil did not shrink from killing them.

It might be assumed that Amergin White-Knee is a fitting representative of the Druidic profession, if it were not for the fact that he is specifically called a fili, not a Druid. Some researchers have chosen to pretend that the filid were simply a branch of the Druids, as this cunning identification supplies them with plenty of source material on 'Druidic' matters. If you pretend that each fili and bard of medieval literature is a Druid in disguise you can gather an amazing amount of 'Druidical' lore, and sell it to the New Age market with no-one any wiser. This type of misinformation is quite fashionable, it has produced countless vapid works on what the authors assumed to be the secret lore of Druidry, or the forgotten religion of the ancient Celts. Neither the bards nor the filid called themselves Druids. The one exception to this rule is one of the Taliesins, who claimed that he would be a Druid. Of course he was, but as the Taliesins claimed to be just about everything, they may be a bit unreliable for historical data. I would argue in all fairness that we leave it to the filid themselves to sort out who was a Druid and who a poet. Who says that Druids had a monopoly on magic? The filid of legend often behave a lot more magical than the classical Druids.

In the *Ulster Cycle* of legends, the Druid Cathbad appears prominently. His function is basically that of prophet. In one instance, he informs the Lady Nes that the day and hour are suitable to conceive a king or queen. As no other male is available, Lady Nes chooses Cathbad to father the child. The pregnancy lasts for three years and three months and ends in the birth of King Conchobar. According to the *Tain Bo Cuailnge*, King Conchobar spoke before anybody else at his court. Before Conchobar, however, his three Druids were

expected to utter their opinion. This little snippet of information can occasionally be found in popular literature as proof that generally, 'the Druids spoke before the kings'. Tough luck that it refers to one specific king of Irish myth. It says more about the beliefs of the medieval poets (who recorded or made up the tale) than about Druidry in history. At Conchobar's court, Cathbad had a Druidic academy where he taught a hundred young men. His lessons, as far as they are recorded, are basically concerned with the art of choosing the right moment to begin specific enterprises. He bestows names and foresees what fate is in store for a young warrior who would ask for his arms on certain days.

The warrior in question is young Cuchulainn, of course, who is so fascinated by the seer's prediction that he immediately goes out for his weapons, in spite (or because) of the heroic but extremely short life in store for him. In the well known tale of *The Exile of the Sons of Uisliu*, Cathbad hears the scream of a babe in the womb. He prophecies the fate of the child, thereby fixing its tragic life. It is the very prophecy that makes the tragedy happen. These tales give some indication that there was a measure of fatalism in Irish thought. They also show that prophecies can be self-fulfilling, and that the very act of uttering a prediction can produce the reality which it foretells. One version of the *Tain* has Fergus remark that Cathbad is *the source of knowledge, he who commands the elements, he who rises into the sky, who blinds the eyes and who steals the valour of strangers with his Druidic power*...In one episode, Druids delay the progress of queen Medb's army for a fortnight as they are waiting for a sign. A poem in the *Tain* mentions *Two hundred Druids to lead us*, but gives no further details. Could this mean that Druids were in charge of battle strategy? Cuchullain himself killed three Druids in the epic, who are named *Foot, Fist and Palm*, as well as their wives, who are called *Lust, Shame and Nothingness*. Imagine for a moment that these names refer to functions. What would it be like if they were your names, and what does it signify, o wise one? Another episode has a number of *magical sweet mouthed harpers* come out of a red cataract to charm Queen Medb's army. Their spell work failing, the army turns against them, and the harpers escape in the shape of deer. The *Tain* explains this case of shape shifting by stating that they are *Druids of great knowledge*. When Cuchulllain fell in love with a woman of the otherworld he became so mad that his health wasted away. King Conchobar sent healers, filid, musicians and Druids to bring Cu to Emain Macha. Seeing them approach, Cuchulainn had a fit of rage and tried to kill the lot of them. The healers sang Druidical chants to soothe him, and held his hands and feet until he came to his senses. To heal him, he was given an elixir of forgetfulness, and a similar broth was offered to Cu's wife Emer, so that she could forget her jealousy.

Even more important as a source on Druids is the *Forbhais Droma Damhghaire*, the tale of the siege of Knocklong. This important manuscript, recorded in the 15th century *Book of Lismore*, gives the story how high king Cormac Mac Airt, accompanied by his five Druids and his warriors, sets out to enforce unjust taxes on Fiacha, the king of Munster. It appears in the list of tales

given in the *Book of Leinster*. This means that some version, not necessarily the one we have, was well known in the 12th century. The Druids in this legend come in several varieties. Some of them are human beings living at Cormac's court in Tara, working there as professional seers and counsellors. They have foresight and skill in sorcery, and in the end they curse Cormac so that he chokes on a fish-bone and dies. To wage his war, Cormac receives the support of the otherworldly folk of the Sidh. From a fairy hill emerge three daughters of Maol. They are Druidesses, but as they come from a distinctly non-human reality, they appear as death dealing sheep with heads of bone and beaks of iron. In their company appear two male Druids in human shape who are invulnerable fighters. Such Druids are hardly samples for any surviving Celtic priesthood. They bear the name 'Druid' as they are sorcerers, and apart from that, the text makes it clear that they are not even supposed to be human.

Through the spell craft of Cormac's Druids, the Munstermen suffer one terrible defeat after the other. Their land is laid waste, their crops are blasted, their wells dry up and finally their very courage falters. To repel Cormac's forces, they finally enlist the help of the blind Munster Druid, Mogh Ruith. It would be too much trouble to retell this story in full detail here, especially as an excellent translation by Sean O Duinn exists, which is highly recommended. You will find references to the spells of Mogh Ruith scattered through this book. In this place, it should suffice to describe Mogh Ruith himself. His name can be translated as *Servant (or Slave) of the Wheel*. Some researchers made him a priest of a solar cult, more daring visionaries have identified him as a solar deity. Mainly on the assumption that anyone who works miracles in an old legend must have been a deity originally. Yet another interpretation, found in the *Coir Anmann (Origin of Names)* proposes that Mogh Ruith is a distorted version of *Magus Rotarum*, as he used to work his divination with wheels.

Mogh Ruith, for all his sorcery, does not appear very much like a deity. He is an old blind man living a secluded life far from the realm of humans. In his youth, he has been trained by the Druidess Banbhuana and learned all magick arts, even the ones that come from the Si, the people living under the hollow hills. Other sources claim that he was the son of an Irish scholar and a slave girl from Britain. This account also credits Mogh with having been taught by Simon Magus himself. There is even a tradition claiming he personally beheaded John the Baptist, and that this awful misdeed brought evil weather, hunger and disease over the people of Ireland.

For all his seclusion Mogh has five students; good evidence that Magicians have an obligation to pass on the essence of their craft. When the Munstermen ask him for support, he immediately requests an exceptionally high fee. This tells us that, for all his isolation, Mogh Ruith has a sound head for business. It also shows that he is not in the least concerned for the well being of his countrymen. It is only after his demands are met that he decides to aid the troops of king Fiacha. Much of the story is concerned with these matters, and with the way the blind Druid chooses which territory

he wants as a wage for his sorcery. On the other hand the tale is full of wonder-working, of magical battles between shapeshifters, of enchanted stones, rains of blood, giant serpents, water magic, Druidic firestorms and the like. Plenty of useful insights can be found in this legend, but very little of it has historical value. We could continue in this style, by giving further samples of Druidic enchantment, but where these are of interest for magickal practise, I have placed them in various other chapters. Finally, I would like to ask you to consider the validity of these ancient accounts. How many different interpretations can you invent? Which Druidic activities would you relate to a specific priesthood of a forgotten religion and when do you think the term Druid was simply used for a sorcerer?

Druidic Revival

The return of the Druids into popular knowledge began at a fairly late time. Most of the medieval authors in Britain did not even know the word Druid. There are no Druids in the works of Nennius, Bede, the *Saxon Chronicles*, the Arthurian Romances, the *Mabinogi*, or the popular bestsellers of Geoffrey of Monmoth. In all of these works, anybody who may have been a Druid originally was classed as a magi, a term derived from the *Bible*. Interest in Druids resumed with the rediscovery of the classical authors. All of a sudden Europe remembered (or invented) its early history, and historians began to wonder if Druids were responsible for stone circles or flint arrowheads. In the 17th century King James I became interested in the magnificent megaliths of Stonehenge and ordered the architect general, Inigo Jones, to examine them. Jones was the first writer to propose that Stonehenge may have been a Druidic temple. He discarded the idea, however, in favour of a Roman origin of the monument. Other historians attributed the structure to the Phoenicians, the Danes and Saxons, great fun, given that no dating was possible anyway.

The first serious proponent of the Druidic theory was John Aubrey (1626-1697). William Stuckley, writing about Stonehenge and Avebury (1740 and 1743) passionately favoured the Druidic origin of these monuments and began a popular fashion. He also erected his very own Druidic temple in his garden in Grantham and had himself called by a Druidic nickname. Up to this point, nobody had associated the megalith monuments with the Druids, in fact, nobody had cared much about Druids anyway. In a similar fashion, it wasn't until 1805 when Cambry published his *Monumens Celtiques* that the French megaliths became Druidic. When such works entered popular opinion, all of a sudden Europe was full of Druidic temples. Any prominent rock was called a Druid altar. Romantics wanted Druids, and discovered them wherever they went. To this day there are countless Druid temples around which became such at the beginning of the 19th century. Modern archaeologists argue strongly against this idea. No matter what public opinion postulates, there is no trace for any Druidic activity at any of the megalith sites. Mass gatherings, fires and sacrifices all leave traces, and such traces are nowhere evident. This, again, poses the interesting question why those magnificent

megalith buildings were not used for ritual or ceremony. Modern pagans like to do things at dolmen or stone circles, and if you've ever spent a night on your own at such a site you may come to wonder why they weren't popular with the Celts, the Saxons, the Vikings and whoever else came across them. Strange as it seems, the megaliths were apparently ignored by a good many later cultures. Or is it possible that they were actually feared? Popular folk-lore, as recorded by enthusiasts in the last centuries, often associates megalith structures with giants, dwarves or the fairy folk. Neither of these were really popular with the pagan people of the past, and so it is distinctly possible that the megalithic monuments were shunned on purpose. Or would you prefer to imagine rituals at megalith sites that left no traces for later excavators? This may be possible, but it is not very likely. However, given the countless exceptions to each rule that have been discovered by archaeologists in recent years, I hope that one or two megalithic monuments may have been involved in the rituals of the Celts. They are simply too good to be ignored.

The romantic movement re-discovered the songs of the Welsh bards around the middle of the 18th century, when Lewis Morris (1700-1765) and Evan Evans brought the topic into the public interest. Not much later, in1792, the bardic revival began, started by Owen Pugh and greatly accelerated by the amazing Iolo Morgannwg (Edward Williams, 1747-1826). Iolo became interested in ancient British lore when in 1784 he met Evan Evans, who claimed to be a bard. In debtors prison he began to busy himself with the study of ancient manuscripts, and, once released, became an enthusiastic collector of eldritch material. What he found, however, was a disappointment to him. The old texts were fragmentary and generally did not contain the data he was looking for.

Now this did not stop Iolo, who was out to revive the wisdom of the bards and Druids no matter what. As a young man he had already shown his talent as a poet, and passed off some of his works as unknown poems by the famous medieval bard Dafydd ap Gwilym. Some might call this forgery, but to Iolo, who was frequently in dire need of money, it was simply business. Thus, he soon went beyond collecting and began to make up the material he needed, creating hundreds of ancient manuscripts by the simple expedient of mixing his own inventions with bits and pieces gained from elder texts. As a surrealistic work of art his achievement can only be admired. As could have been expected, his contemporaries were easily deceived, and Iolo became the main authority on Druidic and bardic mysteries. The big problem with his writing is that Iolo made use of genuine material which he cunningly blended with his own visions. As a collector, he acquired plenty of old texts. Sadly, most of his manuscripts are today lost and so it becomes a tricky question to determine just when he was quoting or making it up. With the aid of that lucid vision that comes out of the depths of a laudanum bottle (the muse of many a poet of his age) he revived, or invented, a most complex system of Druidic and bardic masonry, including cosmology, costume, hierarchy, rituals, regalia,

ceremony and theology which has exerted a spell of fascination on many followers of the neo-Celtic faith. That there are some genuine old Welsh, or possibly even Druidic items in his system is fairly certain, but it is highly unlikely that anyone, let alone romantic Iolo, could have told you which. Some of the works he collected or wrote were published under the name *Barddas*. This volume was published by the Welsh Manuscript Society in 1862, after having been edited by Rev. Williams ab Ithel. It appeared to be *a collection of original documents illustrative of the theology, wisdom and usage of the Bardo-Druidic system of the isle of Britain.* The preface informs us that the participants of the National Eisteddfod of 1858 had offered a price for the fullest documentation of the Bardo-Druidic system. Only one contribution appeared, which was signed Plennydd. It came from the collection of the late Iolo and was in his handwriting. The judges were convinced that the material was utterly authentic and proclaimed that Iolo was incapable of perpetrating literary forgery. The texts collected in *Barddas* came from several authors, some of them anonymous, and purported to come from the period before the Continental Celts migrated to Britain. They were preserved, so the authors boast, with *unfailing memory.* In spite of this, the cosmology given in *Barddas* is not polytheistic and pagan but features a monotheistic god plus angels, and leans heavily on Christian concepts. This would be fitting for texts coming from medieval bards, who were Christians, but it is certainly not the sort of lore the pre-Roman bards or Druids believed in. To make up for such trifling problems, *Barddas* states that after the conversion to Christ, the bards received *a more clear awen (inspiration) from god, and knowledge about all things divine beyond what had been seen before, and they prophesied improving awen and knowledge.*

In *Barddas*, Iolo or his sources postulated an interesting cosmology. In his gospel, souls have their beginning in Annwn (the otherworld), then traverse the circle of Abred (the middle world) where they are reborn countless times to experience all sorts of lifetimes and to attain purity and saintliness. When they have become sufficiently pure they leave Abred after death and attain Gwynvyd, the upper world, or heaven. This simple system is complicated by the circle of Creugant, which seems to resemble some sort of purgatory and which can only be endured and traversed by god. While most of these ideas cannot be traced to any old Welsh tradition, the concept of Annwn, or Annwfn appears in the lore of the bards. Several bards referred to an under-, or otherworld with this name, but their descriptions do not accord with Iolo's version. We shall discuss the topic of Annwn in the cauldron chapter. In this place it should suffice to point out that that the Annwn of the medieval bards, as it is mentioned in some Taliesin poems and in the first branch of the Mabinogi, is a term for one or several otherworlds that have no moral value. These worlds exist as exotic and dangerous places, but they are not bad or evil. In the first branch of the *Mabinogi* you can learn that Annwn is a place pretty much like the human world: you find splendid kings who hold court and fight each other for supremacy, if need be with the help of human heroes. Iolo's Annwn is

where there is the least possible of animation and life, and the greatest of death. While it might be argued that the Annwn of the song I *shall praise the Sovereign (BoT30)* is a fairly deadly place it still remains that of Arthur's warriors, seven returned from the place. Thus, we are dealing with an otherworld, not with a land of the dead or some vision of hell.

According to the three principal qualities of man shall be his migration in Abred: from indolence and mental blindness he shall fall to Annwn; from dissolute wantonness he shall traverse the circle of Abred, according to his necessity; and from his love for goodness he shall ascend to the circle of Gwynvyd.

To reach the circle of Gwynvyd, reincarnation was required.

Gwynvyd cannot be obtained without seeing and knowing everything, but it is not possible to see and know everything without suffering everything…And this knowledge cannot be obtained without experience in every form of life, in every incident, in every suffering, in every evil and in every good, so that they may be respectively known one from the other. All this is necessary before there can be Gwynvyd, and there is need of them all before there can be perfect love of God, and there must be perfect love of God before there can be Gwynvyd…and there shall be no migrating through every form of existence after that.

Be that as it may, I do not wish to blame

all of the odd bits in Iolo's teachings on that inventive enthusiast. *Barddas* is supposed to be the work of several authors. Some of these ideas seem to come from Llywelin Sion while other teachings may have been provided by the Welsh bards of the medieval period themselves. Other items in the text are a mysterious system of sacred letters, a complicated doctrine of the elements, a guide to the cycle of the year, the regulations of Bardism and an amazing amount of triads. Another interesting document is the so-called *Book of Llanwrst*, said to come from one of the Taliesins. This document claims that there are eight parts of man:

The first is the earth, which is inert and heavy, and from it proceeds the flesh; the second are the stones, which are hard, and are the substance of the bones; the third is the water, which is moist and cold, and is the substance of the blood; the fourth is the salt, which is briny and sharp, and from it are the nerves, and the temperament of feeling, as regards bodily sense and faculty; the fifth is the firmament, or wind, out of which proceeds the breathing; the sixth is the sun, which is clear and fair, and from it proceeds the fire, or bodily heat, the light and colour; the seventh is the Holy Ghost, from Whom issue the soul and the life; and the eight is Christ, that is intellect, wisdom, and the light of soul and life.

The parts of the body itself are identified with various faculties, they may remind you of various systems of occult anatomy from Asia. There is an ancient urge of human dreamers to identify the parts of the body with states of mind:

1. In the forehead are the sense and intellect;
2. In the nape is the memory;
3. In the pate are discretion and reason;
4. In the breast is lust,
5. In the heart is love;
6. In the bile are anger and wrath;
7. In the lungs is the breath;
8. In the spleen is joyousness;
9. In the body is the blood;
10. In the liver is the heat;
11. In the spirit is the mind;
12. In the soul is faith.

While modern researchers are well aware that many of the items in *Barddas* are forgeries, it is by no means certain which items these would be. Reincarnation, for instance, was not a well known theory in 18th Century Europe. Iolo may have found the idea suggested by the classical authors, and he may possibly have known of the Pythagorean doctrine, if only from Ovid's treatment of the subject. Neither was occult anatomy such a well known topic. Perhaps these ideas were part of the bardic doctrine, perhaps Iolo reconstructed them and perhaps he was so visionary that he invented an entirely original magical system. This could be called forgery, it could also be called inspiration, and this is pretty much in accord with the bardic tradition.

Far from being strict traditionalists, the gogynfeirdd bards invented a lot of material. Bardism, if we may call it so, is an art that depends on the inspiring breath of the Awen, and this element of creativity is the primary spring that keeps the tradition from becoming rigid and obsolete. The medieval bards do not seem to have understood all of the elder tales that had been passed to them. R. Hutton cites research that seems to show that the bards of the 13th century already had problems understanding language of the 9th, and that those of the 9th had only vague notions of the language and culture a couple of hundred years before. Language and custom, after all, are always in a state of flux. This goes for our own culture, but even more so for cultures that did not commit knowledge to writing but relied on such highly creative mediums as songs committed to memory. When *Barddas* claims to offer material preserved with *unfailing memory* this proves a splendid opportunity to become suspicious. When the medieval bards did not understand the songs and teachings of their ancestors, they also chose to invent anything they required. Regarding Iolo, I would in all fairness argue that the tradition of making things up has always been part of the bardic vocation. This is not the historians approach, but it does constitute genuine innovative magic which enchants, spellbinds and creates something new and worthwhile. The only regrettable aspect of such projects is that they inevitably pretend to be genuine, old and true. Personally I have much more admiration for a magician who can honestly admit that the new system is indeed new, rather than attempt to make it more credible by faking its history. Who says that the elder faiths are any better than the ones you'll come to invent tomorrow? The test of each magical system is its efficiency, and its ability to transform and inspire those who work and play with it. This does not necessitate old age, in fact there are plenty of old faiths which are totally useless and obsolete in our day and age. Would you care to climb oak trees in a night shirt? Nowadays the mistletoe is protected in several European countries, there are strict regulations with regard to cattle slaughter and no passing policeman will look aside should you try to burn people in your front garden to make the flowers thrive. Many ancient rites (if they were ever performed the way we read) had their use and are no longer meaningful. If you wish to do something Druidic, imagine what a modern Druid would like to do. Better still, what would a Druid of the future be up to?

4. Evolution of the Bards

As with the Druids, there is little surviving data on the activity of the bards of the pre-classical period. With the appearance of Greek and Roman historians, this situation improved a bit and provides us with a couple of insights into the professional activities of the bards of ancient Gaul. Athenaeus, writing in the second century BCE gives a tale which he had from the (sadly lost) writings of the famous geographer Poseidonios. In order to become really popular with his subjects, the Arvernian lord Louernious held a great feast. In those days, festivities were as popular as today, perhaps even more so, as there was less entertainment available for the population and life was short anyway. Lords and chieftains were expected to be generous and often enough great treasures were spent to win sympathy and support. Those nobles who had access to mineral wealth, to gold, silver or salt, who controlled the trade routes or the rivers often became extremely rich in the process and were required to show their standing by handing out treasure and gifts as if their value did not matter to them. This was part of the function of each ruler, but it was even more important when a noble desired to become ruler and tried to sway the public opinion by wasting treasure in a splendid and careless way. The feast of Louernious seems to have been such an occasion. To celebrate properly, a square enclosure was set apart for the merrymaking, and it may say something about the size of the congregation that this territory stretched a full 1.5 miles in every direction. Free food and drink was supplied to keep all guests happy, and of course a considerable number of hungry mouths came traveling to join the celebration. For several days, Louernious demonstrated his wealth and generosity. Then, on the final day he topped this show by having himself driven in a chariot across the plain, throwing hands full of gold and silver to the 'tens of thousands' of Celts who followed him. It was at this moment that a poet arrived. He was the first bard who made it into the history books, but regarding the feast he was almost too late. The bard had been delayed on the way to the feast, and now that he arrived, no doubt a bit worn and weary from the journey. He saw Louernious passing in his splendid chariot, surrounded by a cluster of people who fought for the treasure that was showered on them. Our bard gave a start and ran after the chariot. Elbowing his way through the mob he caught up with the vehicle. Running at its side, and possibly panting mightily, he began chanting a praise song for Louernious, celebrating the incomparable generosity of the host and his own ill-luck of arriving so late. Louernious, well pleased with the poets effort, hurled a bag of gold at him. This immediately prompted a creative fit in our bard, who improvised that the very tracks of Louernious chariot were a source of gold and generosity to mankind.

Here we have the first appearance of a bard in classical literature. As you can see, the poet showed behaviour that was typical for most of the bards that came after him. He knew where to obtain a good profit, how to flatter nobility and was capable of improvising under decidedly difficult circumstances.

Our next source is Appian's *Gallic History*,12, which describes an event that took place in 121 BCE, when an ambassador of the Allobroges (or possibly the Arverni) had a conference with Consul Domitius, who represented the Roman army. The Gaulish ambassador was obviously a man of some importance and wealth. He traveled in the company of attendants, servants and dogs and even had a bard in his company. On encountering Consul Domitius, the bard boldly stepped forward and chanted in barbaric fashion a praise song celebrating the noble birth of their wonderful King Bituitus, his bravery, his success in battle and his immense wealth, the great virtues of the ambassador and of course himself. Appian noted that it is for such eulogies that all ambassadors of distinction travel in the company of bards. While a bard seem to have been important in the political encounters of Gaulish statesmen, his boasting did not impress the Roman consul at all.

Such tales give good evidence that persons with a bardic function held a vital position in the diplomacy of ancient Gaul in the second century BCE. Though they were not diplomats, they served to support the role of the diplomats, to provide a good reputation for the nobility and a bit of entertainment as well. To modern minds, such a job may seem somewhat strange. The early bards, much like the later ones, were adepts in the art of boasting. It was expected from them, a noble who was not praised in the wildest terms obviously did not amount to much. People who listened to the genealogies and heroic deeds, as proclaimed by bards, often knew that matters were not quite as glorious as they were made to appear, but this was no reason to tone down the superlatives. One of the crucial issues in many Celtic cultures was the reputation a given person enjoyed.

If you read the heroic literature of Ireland and Wales you will soon get used to a world where prestige was essential to survival, and boasting an acceptable part of social exchange. A ruler without praise or a warrior without tall tales was simply unthinkable.

Not only that the most amazing anecdotes were made up, it also appears that politeness required the audience to listen to each wondrous tale and to pretend that it was but a sober-minded, realistic account. If you wanted to triumph over a loudmouth you could invent a better story, or engage a professional, a bard, to do the job for you.

Such behaviour may seem tasteless in modern society, but it had a useful function in the societies of the past. Each long dark winter through, the kings and nobles feasted with their warriors. As they drank deeply of the sweet ensnaring mead they told each other of their own great deeds, and the bards of the hall proclaimed the praise songs celebrating the even greater deeds of the ancestors. Then, with the coming of springtime, the king's coffers were empty and the time for war had arrived. A good king was expected to make war at least once a year, to invade the country of another regent, to burn, loot, raid and steal cattle. When the warm season arrived, pledges of alliance were given or broken and the noble warriors had to prove the validity of their boasting in combat.

In those days, warfare was a highly ritualized activity. Often enough, the armies assembled in an open space. Then a warrior of good family would step forward and boast about his prowess with arms and what he intended to do with them in the very near future. From the other side, a similar-minded hero would appear, and bellow his own great lineage and bloodthirsty intentions. Word led to word, insults followed, and before long there were bits of anatomy flying hither and yon. Then the next couple of heroes stepped forward

and repeated the procedure. In some accounts the nobles spoke for themselves, in others they had a professional bard or their own charioteer do the boasting for them.

Then there were group combats, or even the odd duel among kings or chieftains, but all in all this sort of warfare was a slow affair as everybody wanted to be seen and admired. Warriors were not so much afraid of dying as of gaining a bad reputation. Death, after all, was something that happened to everyone, and had to be expected. Nor did it matter much, provided the fight was heroic and the bards made a good poem out of it, a praise song that would live on through the generations and inspire those who came after to equal deeds of bravery. In this fashion the boasting, whether self-proclaimed or performed by a professional, set a standard for behaviour and incited warriors and regents to live up to their own reputation.

The function of the bards was to keep the memory of past heroism alive and to incite the living to similar deeds of bravery. When noble warriors required praise to feel self-respect, the same went in an even stricter fashion for chieftains and kings. From what the classical authors reported, it appears that the primary function of the bards was a political one. In our modern jargon, we could compare the bards to public relation specialists or to official spokesmen. This, however, is not all that was to their profession. It would be nice if some of my readers had the good taste to complain that praise for the mighty is not exactly the sort of bardism they would like to explore. Agreed. There are several sorts of magical functions that were part of the bards trade, but before we get to them it might be useful to get the more prosaic parts of the job done.

Praising kings may not be a very spiritual affair in our eyes, but it provided a good wage for the poets and a lot of luxuries. Also, the praise of monarchs and rulers was a distinctly spiritual activity in those days. To understand this, I shall have to devote a few lines on the subject of sacred monarchies. For a start, it has to be remarked that the Celtic cultures were not all organized in the same way. The regents of Caesar's Gaul were often aristocrats who became chieftains when they became popular enough to win the support of the nobility of their tribe. This involved plenty of intrigue, bribery and lavish entertainment of important people. In ancient Britain and Ireland, a kingship system was en vogue which appears as a sacred monarchy. This may seem simple enough - if we can trust the few shreds of evidence - but it certainly wasn't. Generalizations are lies. Truth to tell, the mechanisms of government are next to unknown in most parts of ancient Europe. How far a king was born, or chosen, or elected is a moot point with regard to the countries we have evidence for, as this evidence is generally fragmentary. In most Celtic lands, not even fragmentary evidence is available, and who got the job of regent remains anyone's guess. There may have been kings, or ruling queens, or a semi-democratic form of election by vote or divine blessing, but as it is none of these can really be verified.

Even with the better documented systems of the Island Celts the evidence is often contradictory and can be interpreted, or argued away, in several ingenious ways. It seems a distinct possibility that the Celtic cultures developed several systems of rule and that the customs of one tribe were not necessarily shared by its neighbours. Anyway, the island Celts who have made it into history and literature seem to have favoured some sort of sacred monarchies. They had kings (and among the British queens) who were not so much regents as religious potentates. A king was married to the land, to the goddess of the land, and represented its virility and virtue. As husband of the kingdom, the king was obliged to accept a number of religious offices. He had to participate in certain rituals, had to behave in a time-honoured fashion and had to refrain from a number of bizarre activities. Especially the Irish tales give interesting accounts of kings who were burdened by a series of taboos that spirits, ancestors or Druids had inflicted on them at the time of the coronation. The tale *The Destruction of Da Derga's Hostel* gives an excellent example for this tradition. Right now, it suffices to say that the bards, with their knowledge of history and their praise songs exerted a subtle control over the regents. As the intellectuals of their day, with their vast store of ancient tales and traditional rituals, they kept the kings in line. Praise by the bards affirmed that the king was doing his job as expected. In those days, a king or ruler was held responsible for many matters that hardly concern the rulers of today. Here is a verse which the chief poet is said to have chanted to the Irish kings on the day of their inauguration, translated by Douglas Hyde:

Seven witnesses there be
Of the broken faith of kings.
First - to trample on the free,
Next - to sully sacred things,
Next - to strain the law divine,
(this defeat in battle brings).
Famine, slaughter, milkless kine,
And disease on flying wings.
These the seven-fold vivid lights
That light the perjury of kings!

A just king caused good harvests and fair weather, victory in war and general prosperity. A false prince, so Tadhg Mac Daire sang, is accompanied by dearth, servitude, want of provisions, plagues, wars, conflicts, defeat in battle, rough weather and rapine. When the usurper Cairbre ruled, so the 'Four Masters' recorded, *evil was the state of Ireland during his reign, fruitless her corn, for there used to be but one grain on the stalk; fishless her rivers; milkless her cattle; unplenty her fruit, for there used to be but one acorn on the oak.*

A just king was not necessarily a good ruler or a cunning strategist. Victory was seen as a gift of the gods, consequently a king who followed the religious and social obligations could be expected to be successful. Irish manuscripts tell us quite a lot about the requirements of a king. King Cormac is said to be the author of an Irish manuscript entitled *Instruction of a Prince* (*Book of Ballymote,* quoted after Hyde). He tells us that a king is elected *from the goodness of his shape and family, from his experience and wisdom, from his prudence and magnanimity, from his eloquence and bravery in battle, and from the number of his friends.*

Asked how a king should conduct himself among the wise and foolish, among friends and strangers, among old and young, Cormac replies: *be not too knowing nor too simple; be not proud, be not inactive, be not too humble nor yet haughty; be not talkative but be not too silent; be not timid neither be severe. For if thou shouldst appear too knowing thou wouldst be satirized and abused; if too simple thou wouldst be imposed upon; if too proud thou wouldst be shunned; if too humble thy dignity would suffer; if talkative thou wouldst not be deemed learned; if too severe thy character would be defamed; if too timid thy rights would be encroached upon.*

The important thing is that the king leads a blameless life: *let him enforce fear, let him perfect peace, much metheglin and wine, let him pronounce just judgements of light, let him speak all truth, for it is through the truth of a king that God gives favourable seasons.*

When asked what is good for the country, Cormac states: *frequent convocations of sapient and good men to investigate its affairs, to abolish each evil and retain each wholesome institution, to attend to the percepts of the elders; let every assembly be convened according to law...*Who do you guess were these sapient and good men? Who investigated the affairs of the country, if not its intellectual elite?

Strange as it may seem, a good many regents did not actually decide policies. How could they, when their counsellors were so much better informed? It was the king's job to be a religious focus, and this office limited their freedom of choice to a considerable extent, unless they were crafty enough to make some secret deals with their bards and Druids to ensure that their obligations and taboos were not too restrictive. The bards praised and celebrated their kings when these were behaving properly. If not, a bard was entitled to use satire, and this act was greatly dreaded by the nobility. A regent who had been satirized had few chances of ever being taken seriously again, his realm lost all divine blessings, his neighbours conspired to invade the land and otherwise ill harvests, poverty and plague could be expected. Thus, the power of satire came pretty close to what might be termed cursing, as you will read in the chapter on spell-craft. With regard to the Celts of Central Europe and Britain, the role and function of the kings transformed during the Roman occupation. This changed some of the aspects of government, but it did not affect the bards much.

Bards and Druids.

Several classical authors hinted that the bards and the Druids, at least those of Gaul, were closely related. Diodorus Siculus, writing his *Histories* (see vol. V, 31, 2-5) around 8 BCE, informs us about the Gauls: *And there are among them composers of verses whom they call bards; these singing to instruments similar to a lyre, applaud some, while they vituperate others.* Strabo, in his *Geographica*, noted that among the Gallic people there are three groups of men who are held in great honour: the bards, the vates and the Druids. *The bards are singers and poets; the vates, diviners and natural philosophers; while the Druids, in addition to natural philosophy, study also moral philosophy.* He goes on to explain that the Druids, whom he calls *the most just of men*, are therefore entitled to function as judges in public and private disputes. Occasionally his Druids *even arbitrated cases of war and made the opponents stop*, they also decided the murder cases, the guilty party being

sacrificed. Sadly, he did not bother to elaborate on the functions of the bards and vates, as the bloody rituals attributed to the Druids were no doubt better entertainment in the eyes of his audience. The reference to the vates may be of interest here. Vates is not a Celtic but a Roman term, but it has related expressions in several Indo-European tongues. Latin vates means a prophet or seer, the word is close to the English vaticination (prophecy). A related term of Old Irish is *fath, faith,* likewise meaning prophecy and prophet. Welsh has *gwawd,* meaning poetry, while the Anglo Saxons had *woth* meaning melody, voice and sound. Gothic *wods* is obsessed or inspired, depending on how you think about these issues. An older Germanic root of this term can be found in the name of Wodan. Germanic *wuot* means madness, rage, frenzy, fury and similar phenomena. These were not only applied to anger or aggression but also to the inspired frenzy of the seer, the ecstatic madness of the shaman, to song and prophecy and enchantment (see *Helrunar* for more details). The source of this complex of words is an even older Indo European root, *(a)ue- refering to breath and blowing winds, also related is the Indian storm god Vata (see *Seidways*) and the Old Indian *vayati, vati* = to blow. It might be worth considering that all of these words had their beginning in the idea of breath, the breath that changes consciousness, that manifests prophecy and enchantment, that is the mainspring of inspiration. As a guess, I would propose that the Welsh Gwydion, the great enchanter of the Britons, may also be related to this word-root. Or consider the following. One

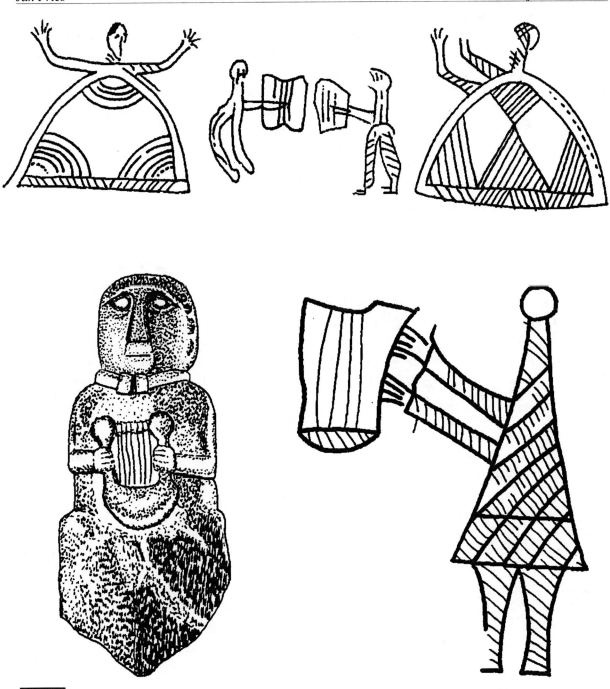

Harpers.
Top: early Hallstatt time ceremony showing ritualists in costume and harpers, incised pot, Sopron-Burgstall, Hungary.
Bottom right: Another harper from an incised pot, Sopron-Burgstall.
Bottom left: Statue of deity with lyre, Paule, Brittany, France, c. 100 BCE, height 42 cm.

possible interpretation of the word Druid is based on the assumption that its Welsh counterpart Derwydd is related to the Latin *videre* = to see. This is the root of Latin *vates*, a seer or prophet.(Tolstoy 1985). This is not the only explanation. A fashionable, but unreliable etymology follows Pliny's idea that the term Druid may be related to the oak and proposes 'oak-seer'. Another etymology proposes that Druid comes from dru-wid, meaning full of wisdom, once again this claim rests on shaky foundations.

A much later account was written in the 4th century CE by Ammianus Marcellinus (XV,9,8) who proposed that the gentler arts were introduced into Gaul by the bards, the euhages and the Druids. *It was the custom of the bards to celebrate the brave deeds of their famous men in epic verse accompanied by the sweet strains of the lyre, while the euhages strove to explain the high mysteries of nature. Between them came the Druids, men of greater talent, members of the intimate fellowship of the Pythagorean faith; they were uplifted by searchings into secret and sublime things, and with grand contempt for mortal lot they professed the immortality of the soul.* Sounds good, doesn't it? Nevertheless there are a number of trifling difficulties attached to this account. For one thing, by the fourth century, the earlier priestly function of the Druids had long been abolished and the religions of Gaul had undergone considerable changes. The Pythagorean reference is likewise a bit unreliable, and the euhages cannot be found in other accounts. That bards existed in the fourth century is likely, they seem to have made it almost into the modern era, but no doubt their function and style of performance

underwent a couple of changes as language, religion and culture keep transforming. While the bards were related to the Druids in some way, they don't seem to have sacrificed humans, and consequently the persecution that crushed the Druid order was not applied to them. But just what is the relation of the bards and Druids? Several authors have oversimplified the issue by claiming that the caste of Gaulish Druids was composed of three distinct branches. In their opinion, the bards constituted the lowest class, the vates the middle of the hierarchy and the Druids with their political and judicial office ordered everybody around. Such a structure has its charm, especially as the threefold division was a popular feature in many Indo European societies, but when it comes to working out who did what, the evidence contradicts itself. At the risk of boring all Celtic enthusiasts to tears let me name some of these incongruencies. As you read earlier, Strabo had bards, vates and Druids, while Marcellinus, ignoring the vates, introduces the euhages. What was expected of the Irish poets, i.e. the memorization of a fantastic amount of verses over a period of up to twenty years, was attributed to the Druids by Caesar. However, there are no bards, vates or euhages in Caesar's account, and indeed the prophetic function of the vates is a Druidic office in his book. Strabo claimed that the Druids performed the sacrifices, Diodorus attributed this function to the diviners. Tacitus has the Druids as prophets and sacrificial priests but no bards or vates, Lucan adresses the bards as vates. Caesars old crony Diviciacus, according to Cicero, was both a Druid and a diviner while Pliny the Elder only referred to Druids and magi in Gaul, which may or may not amount to the same thing, and did not refer to bards or vates at all. Gaulish Druids seem to have been judges, in Ireland this function became part of the office of the poets. By contrast, Welsh poets did not judge. This has led to a lot of scholarly confusion. Some authorities proposed the threefold system described earlier. Others claimed that bards, euhages, vates and anybody with a prophetic strain was really a Druid. It might just as well be argued that all Druids were really bards, and that anybody was somebody else, this nicely sounds like transmigration of offices but doesn't get us any further. Yet another theory claims that the various groups were really distinct and separate and not governed by a central authority or hierarchy. It is amazing what can be proved when one arbitrarily excludes some testimonies and takes the rest as the undiluted truth. As a further complication, our oldest source, the work quoted by Diogenes Laertius couples the term Druid with the mysterious *semnotheoi*. Kendrick relates that this word is not found elsewhere. He translates it 'reverend gods' and adds that this makes no sense. It might, so he proposes, be conceivably be rendered as 'reverencers of the gods' but admits that this rendering is scarcely admissible. Just for speculations sake, may I propose that a reverend god might be an incarnate divinity, a deity in a human body, as happens in so many cults that invite their gods to enter and obsess their worshippers? This sort of phenomenon may not have been familiar to Mr. Kendrick, as in his day shamanism was not yet a

scholarly topic. Thus, we finally come to the insight that the old testimonies regarding the functions of Druids, bards, vates, euhages and semnotheoi are pretty confused and that there is no way of determining who was who and who did what. Even if we knew who (if any) of the classical authors actually reported the truth it would still be limited to a specific period and a specific place. A century earlier or later, or only a hundred miles elsewhere things may have been completely different.

Finally, it might be interesting to consider the term bard. This word, as we know it, derives from the Latin *bardus* which comes from the hypothetical Celtic word *bardo. Maier (1994) proposes that the term originally meant one who 'raises his voice', i.e. sings or chants poetry. Tacitus in his *Germania* mentions an interesting custom called barditus. This was a special sort of war-chant which was raised by the assembled host prior to battle. Apparently the 'Germans' (the people living in the Roman province Germania, at least half of whom were Celts) held their shields close to their mouths and chanted in a deep, rough and droning voice. The shields amplified the sound and the resulting vibration raised their courage. It seems that they also divined the outcome of the battle from this war-chant, and believed that it was not so much a union of voices as a union of battle power. The word barditus remains an enigma. It could be related to the Celtic *bardo, but it might also come from the Old Norse barth, which means a shield. Another even more obscure hypothesis translates it as 'beard-chant'. This is based on a mysterious reference to the thunder god Thor, who blew into his beard to raise a 'beard-call', whatever that may be (Golther quoting *Fornmanna Sögur* and *Olafssaga Tryggvasonar*). Tough luck that the Old Norse form of 'beard call' is skeggrodd or skeggraust and doesn't sound like barditus at all, though its nice to observe to what lengths some scholars may go. With the exception of ancient Gaul, Britain and Ireland, the term bard was unknown in most parts of Europe. It became fashionable in the 17th century when it was introduced into several European languages from the French *barde* and the Latin *bardus*. As a good old-fashioned word like this was just the thing to inspire the romantics, a lot of writers made use of it and applied it to anyone who happened to sing, no matter the language, century or culture.

5. A Confusion of Faiths

When the alarm came, the men of Gododdin were anything but prepared. For a long year they had been feasting in the brightly lit hall of their king, for a year they had laughed and played and trained at arms. Three hundred nobles were they, ravens in their delight of slaughter, wolves of the warrior bands, proud and mighty under the bright eye of the sun. That fatal night, as in so many nights before, they had been feasting at the tables of their king, feeding on the juicy flesh of oak-fattened pigs which they drew from steaming cauldrons, each with his own flesh hook, and in due order of precedence. Deep into the night they had guzzled the golden mead, gift of the bees and brewers, and when the carousal was greatest, and the minds delirious, the call to weapons came. Guardsmen gave the cry of alarm, an army of invaders had appeared, drawing closer with fierce speed and reckless courage. With a shout of wrath and anger, the warriors of Gododdin made for their horses, brandishing their trusty weapons, ready to repel the pale faced invaders, the dogs from beyond the sea. Riding as fast as they could they made for their foes, strong in battle valour, but many of them sitting all too uneasily on their steeds. At Catraeth in the fresh light of the early morning they encountered their enemies. Like a surging flood-tide of steel and madness they hurled themselves against the invaders, like the wings of dawn the spears flew, and like the thundering rage of the great ocean itself they smashed into the armed multitudes that opposed them. Three hundred noble warriors of the pure speech of the Brython against a thousand foes from beyond the sea. Sword blades screamed as they bit deeply into mail and flesh, faces blanched as riders tumbled to the ground. The men who went to Catraeth, three hundred fighting men, fierce and merciless, attacked without pity, hacked without hesitation, cruelly laughing drew blood from the enemy. Limbs were severed, heads were chopped, under the new light of the bright dawn the slaughter was committed. Three hundred nobles who had sat peacefully under the light of rushes, listening to the songs of bards and the timeless tunes of the musicians became as wolves on the battlefield, as boars in the trackway, like raging bulls they cut and dismembered and suffered terrible defeat. They fought like the white crested waves hurling themselves against the shore, outnumbered and hopeless, yet before they were slain they slew. And after the clash had calmed, only one man of the three hundred remained alive. Neirin survived the crimson battle mist. Standing between his slaughtered friends and relations, he was taken prisoner and put in chains. Burdened by the cold iron he stood, his face turned to the skies, and when night fell, he composed an elegy for the slain. This was the bright Song of Gododdin, and Neirin sang it, perforce, as he was no bard, with the inspiration granted by god, and with the deep grief of having seen his countrymen become food for the ravens and crows. One by one he recalled his friends and comrades, the nobles who had been gentle and generous at the court of their king, and pitiless slayers on the day of their doom. Then, deep in the night he was rescued, his song was remembered, then recorded, and today the *Y Gododdin* is the oldest piece of surviving British literature.

So much for a brief summary of a short, bloody and futile incident which became one of the most famous tales of slaughter and hopeless defeat. I hope you'll forgive the language I have used, as it comes close to the sort of poetry favoured by the bards of the sixth century when the battle occurred. What makes the tale of the battle of Catterick, Yorkshire, so important for

our research into the world of the bards, is the fact that it gives such early evidence of a warrior society of which so very little trustworthy evidence has survived. The *Y Gododdin* is not only a remarkable portrait of the early medieval 'heroic society' with its proud and easily enraged, mead guzzling warrior-aristocrats but also remarkable as it describes, in the most glorious fashion, a total defeat! The later bards who sang the song of Neirin, who added to it or who composed their own versions perpetuated a tale of greatest valour and thereby provided a model for total heroism in the face of overwhelming doom which was highly popular in later centuries. The book of Neirin was not only well known, it was famous. When the scholars of the past centuries attempted to reconstruct what life may have been like in this early period, they assumed that the song of Neirin was an almost untainted picture of a society deeply influenced by pagan beliefs. Though no pagan deities appear in the elegy, the very descriptions of the ruthless and destructive character of the slain heroes seemed to come from a pagan, if not entirely barbarian culture. It is not common for us to find warriors praised for cruelty, for reckless battle frenzy and for merciless violence, and consequently, most researchers decided that these were characteristic attitudes of a pagan society. Moreover, as the bloody elegy contained very few supernatural elements, it was rightly considered useful source-material of historical value. That Neirin was a real person emerges from the 9th century writings of Nennius:

Ida, the son of Eoppa, possessed

countries on the left-hand side of Britain, i.e. of the Humbrian sea, and reigned twelve years, and united Dinguayth Guarth-Berneich. Then Dutigern, at that time, fought bravely against the nation of the Angles. At that time Talhaiarn Cataguen was famed for poetry, and Neirin, and Taliesin, and Bluchbard, and Cian, who is also called Guenith Guant, were all famous at the same time in British poetry.

This entry can be dated, as Ida died around 560. All poets mentioned lived in the sixth century, and several of them are mentioned briefly in the *Book of Taliesin*. Talhaiarn is also mentioned in the somewhat questionable *Iolo mss.*, where he is said to have presided at the bardic chair of Urien Rheged at Caer Gwyroswydd. After his death, this office was held by Taliesin, who also held the same office in three other bardic chairs. This story, for what it's worth, comes from Llewelyn Sion, who recorded it in the late 16th century. It may be of interest that Neirin refers to Taliesin. I'll give that reference in three versions to give you an idea how much translations of early British poetry can vary:

> I Aneirin will sing / what is known to Taliesin / who communicates to me his thoughts / or a strain of Gododin / before the dawn of the bright day. (Nash)
> I, Aneurin will compose / as Taliesin knows / an elaborate song / or a strain to Gododin, / before the dawn of the brightest day. (Skene)
> I , Aneirin / (yet not I: / Taliesin, whose poetry / is powerful, knows this), / sang the Gododdin / before the golden dawn. (Short)

How would you interprete the meaning of these lines? Then again, the earliest poetry composed by Taliesin, in the sixth century for his patron, Urien Rheged, refers to Neirin:

> Do I know his name - Aneurin the poet with the flowing song, /
> I being Taliesin, from the borders of the lake of Geirionnydd?
> (*Red Book of Hergest*, after Skene)

It comes as no surprise, that those scholars who studied the *Y Gododdin* in the past centuries saw it as a valuable source of pagan poetry, to which a couple of Christian elements had been added by later scribes. Many scholars assumed this point of view, and thought that it might be possible to reconstruct pagan, if not Druidic beliefs, by the simple method of kicking Christian material out of the bardic poetry of Britain. Nowadays things seem to be a lot more complicated. A recent study by Professor Griffen offers an unexpected interpretation, which I would like to acquaint you with. To begin with, the early name Neirin (you find it written as Aneirin after 850) was not popular. This may seem surprising, as Neirin was certainly famous and his eulogy was quite well known in Britain. For some mysterious reasons, people disliked to give his name to their sons. Now (A) N-eir-in, so Professor Griffen suggests, can be translated as 'the non-combatant', which is basically a title, not a name. Who could be a non-combatant? In an age when pacifism was definitly unpopular, a non-combatant could be a coward, and who would call a son a coward? On the other hand, cowards were despised (there is some evidence for this in bardic poetry). Cowards did not become famous, they were not praised and they were definitely not rescued, as happened to Neirin when Cenau son of Llywarch released him. Why was Neirin spared in a battle where all his companions were slaughtered, why was he permitted to sing an elegy to the slain in the middle of the night? A simple but misleading answer would be that Neirin was a bard, not a warrior. Neirin, however, points out that he was no bard.

Also, the bards of that period participated in battle, singing, cursing and fighting with sword and spear. Neirin tells us that he is no bard, did not fight and was not expected to. The likeliest explanation is that he himself was a priest. A Christian priest could honourably abstain from fighting and would be worth rescuing after the battle. This assumption is strengthened by the fact that the language of the Christian elements in his song is just as old as the rest of the material. If the theory is true, Neirin was not a bard singing an elegy for the fallen but a priest singing mass for his companions and fellow Christians. In this sense it becomes understandable why Neirin stated that the song was by him, yet not by him: we are dealing with an inspired utterance.

A parallel case occurred a year after the battle of Catraeth, c. 601, when 1100 monks accompanied a British army to a battle against Germanic invaders at Bangor-Y-Coed. Instead of fighting, the monks knelt and prayed for victory, and when their army

lost, they were all executed. While the actual numbers of slain monks seem to be a bit overdone, the tale is evidence for a non-combatant attitude of the clergy.

This brings us to the tricky question just what is supposedly pagan in early British literature. The scholars of the last centuries had assumed that the praise of warriors for being cruel, merciless and savage would constitute a pagan attitude, mainly as it did not accord with the gentler forms of Christian virtue praised in modern times. I had similar problems when I began research of this literature. Having grown up in a culture which is still dominated by Christian ethics, I assumed that I would know what constitutes Christian thought and consequently took a lot for granted which evidently wasn't. The Christianity of today is a far cry from the Christianity of the sixth century, which was considerably more violent. Let's take a brief look at early Christianity. No, we don't have to go back to the Qumran texts now, even though they offer plenty of evidence for fanatic savagery and merciless hatred right at the beginning of the Christian tradition. Let us set our dream machine to the beginning of the 4th century. At this time, the Roman empire, the 'mother of all nations', had ceased to expand.

The formerly aggressive policy had long been abandoned, the legions stood defensively against the barbarians who hurled their warriors against the frontiers, and internal feuds prevented effective action against the invaders. While decadence and corruption weakened the power of the emperors, morals decayed and several outlying parts of the empire had broken from the main structure and declared an uneasy independence. At this time, the Christian cult was considered a dangerous and subversive underground movement. Minucius Felix (*Octavius*, early 3rd C.) accuses them of child sacrifice and cannibalism. Tertullain (late 2nd C) relates a tale according to which the early Christians ended their worship by extinguishing the lights and having a mass-sex orgy. It's strange how often cannibalism, group sex and incest come in one package. Several early Christians stoutly denied such accusations, and in turn accused the Jews, the witches and any convenient pagan of pretty similar crimes.

Unlike the many religions of and in Rome, Christianity was special and elitist. The cult had a special appeal to the poor, as it accepted anyone as a member, even slaves. It also appealed strongly to women (don't ask me why) who made up the largest part of the early congregations. If you became a Christian, you were bound to a single deity and prohibited from participation in any other cult. This was a novelty and in strong contrast to the countless cults en vogue throughout the empire. The Roman empire, while not especially friendly towards rebellious priests, tolerated any religion within its boundaries which adhered to Roman law and adored the holy guardian angel of the emperor, i.e. the guardian angel of the empire itself. Many religions accepted this condition, and continued to thrive side by side as the empire expanded. It was only intolerant fanatics, such as the Zealots of Palestine or the Druids of Gaul and Britain, who were put out of business as they would not stick to the rules. There was a multiplicity of faiths, hundreds of deities were available, and many citizens of the Empire belonged to several cults. It was an easy matter to invent and worship new gods, you only needed permission of the senate, and if you stuck to the basic rules, the new cult was granted official recognition. This went to such extremes that many functions of daily life were in the charge of dozens of extremely similar, but nevertheless different deities. The Roman empire, for all its advantages and drawbacks, was the only known period in European history when all religions existed side by side in peaceful tolerance.

When the Christians proposed that only their god was the one true deity, most people in the empire feared that such an intolerant attitude would enrage all other deities and attract divine retribution. Now the early Christians, for all their appeal to the exploited and downtrodden, were also cunning enough to realize that political power could be attained by converting persons of high standing. Thus, they appealed to the rich and mighty by proclaiming that their god was a giver of success in battle. In this function, they found themselves rivaled by the religion of the victory giving Mithras, which was especially popular among the legions and functioned almost like a secret society.

The emperors were not that happy about the Mithras followers, who were trained and armed and sworn to obedience to higher hierarchical ranks of whose hidden interests few were certain. Consequently, once the Christians had become influential enough, they made a deal with the aristocracies which resulted in a persecution of the Mithras

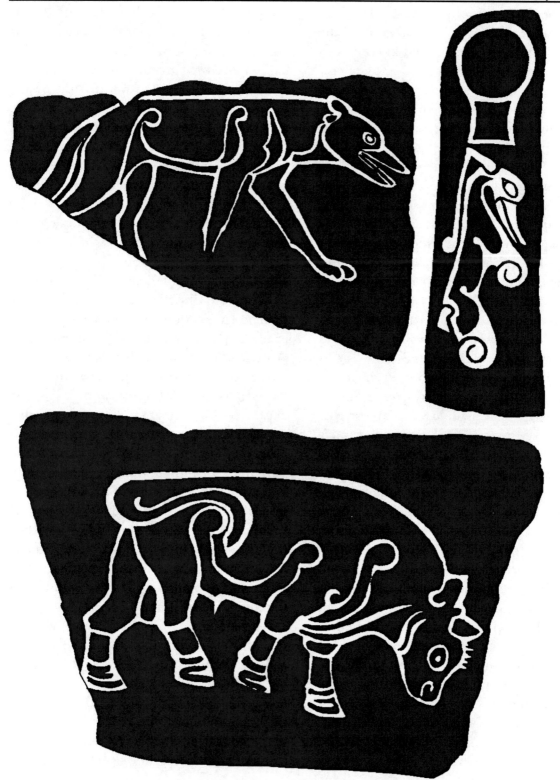

followers. Their greatest success, however, was when they promised Christ's blessings to the young emperor Constantine. At a decisive battle in 312, so legend claims, Constantine saw the symbol of Christ appear in the air and heard a voice proclaiming 'in this sign you will be victorious'. As his victory was almost a miracle, he decided to become a Christian himself. Not because he fancied the religious inheritance of the near-East but because Christ was simply and foremost a war god and a giver of victory.

With the emperor a Christian (of sorts) the cult could finally emerge out of the darkness of the catacombs. Mind you, Constantine was still a cautious character and took care not to offend the other religions. He favoured the new religion, but he did not set out to persecute the others. This changed gradually. Around 331, land and treasures of pagan cults were beginning to be confiscated, in 337 pagan sacrifices were officially prohibited while in 357 a universal closure of pagan temples and sanctuaries was ordered. When I say 'pagan' in this context, I would like to remind you that to the Christian mentality, all pre-Christian faiths were pagan. This applies to the countless religions of the conquered countries as well as the very religions of Rome itself. Then in 361, the tables turned and the last heir of Constantine, one Julian, abolished Christianity and reintroduced the polytheistic faiths of old. Sadly, he died only two years later, and the legions chose a Christian successor for the throne.

In 363 Christianity was restored, but the pagan cults were tolerated for a while. In 391, Eugenius usurped the western part of the empire and reinstalled paganism, but in 394 Theodosius beat him soundly and ordered a complete prohibition of pagan temples and sacrifices. It is only after this time that we can speak of Christianity as strong enough to outlaw all other religions. A few years of violent persecution followed, then the empire itself collapsed and each former part had to cope as well as it could. Though the nobility considered itself as citizens of the Roman empire, and continued to use Latin, the next generations were already developing a new culture which had to make do without the protection of the former empire.

For many Romanized countries, the decline of the empire came as a shock. The last emperors had depleted the former provinces of all useful legionaries to fight out their wars for the throne. In Britain this was especially problematic, as the legions chose one Maximilian as their emperor, and marched to Rome with him, hoping to install him on the throne. This project failed badly, and the island was left virtually defenseless against the assault of Germanic tribes. For the bishops of the early church, these times were far from easy. To retain their power, they had to make a number of concessions to the cultures where they preached, thereby

Medieval Pictish animal art
Wolf: stone from Ardross, Inverness-shire, Scotland, 7th century CE.
Bull: Burghead, Morayshire, Scotland, 7-8th century CE.
So called 'Pictish beast' and mirror symbol (?), Meigle, Scotland, 8-9th century CE.

developing various different forms of Christianity. In Germany, the priests told their flock that Christ had died on a gallows, as this sort of death penalty was much closer to the legal system than the Roman practise of crucification. In Britain, zealous missionaries preached about the warlord Iessu Grist, who rode with his invincible army of saints into the very depths of Uffern (a cold hell) where he overcame Satan and rescued the souls of the unbelievers.

Another question which could be argued is just how Christian these kings and their bards happened to be. When the bards praised their monarchs as Christian, one of the reasons they did so was to contrast them to the invading Angles and Saxons who were not, at least as far as the sixth century was concerned. This made a political conflict a religious matter. This changed somewhat once the Anglo-Saxons were converted, but the conflicts continued.

On the other hand, those early Christian monarchs were only Christian to a limited extent. The venerable Gildas, who wrote an enraged book called *The Ruin of Britain* around 540, devoted a lot of energy to show how unchristian the monarchs of his age were, and predicted in no uncertain terms what fate would be waiting for them on judgment day. In his book, all the British kings are condemned as unjust tyrants who swear false oaths, protect the evil, keep many wives, wage unjust wars etc etc - the list is long and you can find any imaginable misdeed in it. Now Gildas wrote as he still retained a vague hope that those monarchs would realize the evil of their ways and revert to true Christianity. Like many of the saints of his age, he was a passionate

believer, if not a total fanatic. This is another matter which shows a marked contrast to modern Christianity. The works of Bede, for example, are full of praise for the first Christians missionaries in Britain. I was amazed to read to what extremes of devoutness and self-sacrifice these early fanatics went in order to impress the public. You will find no fat-bellied corrupt priests in these pages, but a lot of miracle working holy men who gave everything for their belief. It is only such lunatics who can convert a country, and once it has been converted, the zealous pioneers seem to die out and are replaced by scheming power-merchants.

Holy wells and the rituals associated with them had been an essential item of the Roman and pre-Roman faiths in Celtic and Germanic countries. As they were so popular, the churchmen did not dare to prohibit their use. Instead, they merely cast out the evil pagan influence, invented a couple of new myths about their origin and redefined them as Christian sanctuaries. The so called 'Celtic' church was especially fond of this practise and was criticized by the church of Rome for its over-veneration of wells, sacred waters and rites of baptism. This influence can be found in plenty of items of bardic poetry. A poem attributed to Taliesin, which survives in the *Hanes Taliesin*, gives an interesting example of this practise, as well as of the curious blend of Christian and pagan ideas common to bardism.

In water there is a quality endowed with a blessing;
On God it is most just to meditate aright;

To God it is proper to supplicate with
seriousness,
Since no obstacle can there be to obtain a
reward from Him.
Three times have I been born, I know by
meditation;
It were miserable for a person not to come
and obtain
All the sciences of the world, collected
together in my breast,
For I know what has been, what in future
will occur...

What do you think about these lines?
The sanctity of water was common in many
pagan religions, as well as in Christianity.
Thus the first line could be Christian, Celtic
or Roman, and everybody satisfied. The
second, third and fourth lines imply
monotheism, and thus seem Christian. Line
five introduces rebirth, which may be a
pagan element or a poetic metaphor. That
Taliesin has all the sciences in the world
collected in his breast and happens to know
all past and future, however, comes close to
blasphemy, as omniscience is a quality of
God, who may grant some of it to his
prophets. That God would have given the
lot to a warrior poet is definitely not a
Christian idea, but may tell us something
about the way the bards thought about
themselves. The medieval bards themselves
did consider themselves Christians, but they
also considered themselves equal, if not
superior to kings, and the very flower of
creation.

In Ireland, Christianity developed
differently. As the emerald Isle was never
part of the empire, it did not acquire its
religion by decree of state but through early
missionary effort. Unlike Romanized Gaul,
which had large Christian communities in
the 2nd century, and Britain whose first
congregations are dated around the year
200, the first recorded evidence for
Christianity in Ireland comes from the 5th
century. With the coming of St. Patrick,
whose father and grandfather were Christian
already, the cult received a much needed
boost. While there are plenty of saintly
legends on how the wonder working saint
toured the country, and how he took such a
hard policy against Druids and snakes (there
is some vague evidence claiming that some
Welsh Druids were known as Adders, so
who knows whether he was banishing
reptiles or humans?), there is little factual
evidence how the conversion occurred. It
has been proposed that the conversion was
peaceful, as no martyr's deaths are recorded,
and one school of thought persistently
claims that Druidry and Christianity
practically blended, but I find it hard to
accept this belief, considering the fanatic
attitude of the saint and the way his various
battles against Druids and unbelievers are
recorded.

The full conversion of the island,
however, was not effected till the death of
the last semi-pagan king, Diarmait Mac
Cerbail (565) who was the last monarch to
hold the pagan *feis temro* (feast of Tara).
After the conversion, however, Ireland
supplied plenty of religious fanatics who
roamed the Continent doing missionary
work. Many of these were close friends of
the aristocracy (it pays to have a god of
victory) and so they could count on armed
support when they toured the countryside
baptizing wells and cutting down sacred
trees.

The latter activity brings Saint Boniface to mind, who was born c. 650 in Kirton, Devonshire, and who was authorized by Pope Gregor II to do missionary work in Germany in 719. In the process he toured Bavaria, Thuringa, Hessen, converting 'thousands' of pagans (so he said), if need be using force. In 743 he held the council of Leptinä where he did much to define the newly invented 'devil' and published a list of 27 pagan customs he was very much against. (See Wolf 1989) Keep in mind that in this period, pagan did not so much refer to anything 'purely' Celtic, Germanic or Latin (if there ever was such a thing), but to a blend of these, distorted and confused over the chaotic centuries following the collapse of the Roman empire. My commentaries are in brackets.

1. Shameful customs at the burial places. (plenty of activities fall under this heading, including unchristian ceremonies and the use of parts of dead bodies for various purposes)
2. Shameful customs among the dead. (This could refer to sacrifices for the ancestors)
3. The Sporkel-feasts. (Sporkel is an old Germanic name for February, when ceremonies for the return of the sun and the beginning of spring were being performed)
4. The huts of the gods. (Presumably shrines containing images)
5. Pagan ceremonies in church. (This includes feasting and dancing in church, animal sacrifices, divination etc.)
6. Customs on rocks. (sacrifices, fires and worship)
7. The Nimidae. (Worship and sacrifices in sacred groves and forests)
8. Sacrifices to the saints. (Worship was allowed, sacrifice wasn't)
9. Service of Jupiter and Mercurius. (This may refer to the Roman deities, to the Germanic Donar and Wodan, or to a number of Celtic deities identified loosely with these concepts, such as Taranis/Tanaros and Lugus)
10. The attachment of stripes and ribbons. (Basically amulets of parchment, textiles or metal worn around the neck or concealed under clothes)
11. The sacrificial wells. (This includes all sorts of offerings to the deep, but also making vows at sacred wells, a custom that Boniface punished with five years of penance)
12. Incantations. (this may mean spells, enchantments and the like)
13. Divination from birds and the dung of oxen. (The former is augury, popular in all classical cultures of ancient Europe. The latter refers to Roman ideas regarding oxen shitting on ceremonial occasions and what this portends)
14. Divination and fortune telling.
15. The fires lit by friction. (Need fires, ceremonial fires and fires of purification)
16. The brain of beasts (another sort of divination?)
17. Pagan observations at the hearth. (Omina)
18. The uncertain places. (Read 'unseen'. Probably a reference to sacred sites)
19. The straw bundles. (Possibly the last sheaves of corn, cut ceremonially at the end of the harvest. Also a reference to bundles of plants hidden in the house or carried close to the body as amulets)

20. The disappearance of the moon. (The Roman custom to aid the moon during an eclipse by shouting 'Vince luna!')

21. The furrows round settlements. (possibly a continuation of the custom of having ditches around sacred sites, as can be found in the early Neolithic, megalith culture, the bronze age and Celtic times. In earlier periods all sorts of sacrifices and bones went into the ditches, in Boniface's day it was usually bundles of sacred plants)

22. Pagan congregations. (This includes seasonal festivals, but also the February fun - season of mummery and ridicule, that was later turned into carnival as it couldn't be abolished)

23. The feast of the dead when a saint is introduced. (Uncertain. Possibly ancestral worship, or the seasonal customs that were turned into the Christian festivals of all-saints and all-hallows in 835)

24. The idol of flour. (It was a popular custom to make images of certain deities which were baked, worshipped or eaten. To participate in such activities or to eat of the figures was strictly forbidden to Christians. See the chapter on Bride, or your baker, and have a bite of gingerbread man)

25. Idols made of cloth. (Good evidence that when people are poor, but strong in belief, images of deities can be made out of just about anything)

26. Carrying idols over the fields. (Ceremonial processions with images of deities were widely popular in Germanic and Celtic countries, and usually an occasion of much festivity)

27. Wooden feet and hands. (Votive offerings. Probably a reference to the custom of making images of diseased limbs which were involved in healing rituals or offered to the gods of healing. Very popular during the Roman occupation)

Now if we want to understand what is pagan about the mythology of the island Celts, it may be useful to recall that not every unchristian item is necessarily Celtic. Between the destruction of the Druids in the first century and the early fourth century when Christianity became acceptable there is an interval during which religion underwent plenty of changes. The religions of the Roman occupation were a mixture of three influences. One was native Celtic belief, which had lost a lot of its deeper meaning once the Druids had ceased to function as its priesthood. The second was the state religion of Rome itself, and the third the countless cults which were spread through the empire by the legions. Lacking a functional priesthood, the British must have been in an interesting religious dilemma, and no doubt their faith transformed a lot to adapt to new circumstances. Also, thanks to the legions, a lot of religion got around. Many people still believe that 'the Romans' were a lot of dark haired Italians. This may have been so very early in the history of Rome, but once Rome expanded, new lands were conquered and their inhabitants contributed to the legions. The term Roman is not an ethnic but a cultural one. In Central Europe there was a surplus of young men who could not expect to inherit. What could they hope for if they stayed at home? To join the legion was a sure way of getting around and maybe the chance to come home with some wealth. Thus, there were plenty of non-Italian people in the legions. Some of the Celts of the Continent did service in Northern Britain, and left many inscriptions to their deities. A lot of British legionaries served in mainland Europe, and wherever they went, the deities of their homeland accompanied them. If these deities fulfilled useful functions, legionaries of other cultures could become involved in their worship. This changed the character of the deities, as gods transform to suit their worshippers (and vice versa), which does not make research any easier. Then, with the flowering of Christianity, we observe a weird mixture of all creeds. While the church gradually became the dominant force, Christian dogma transformed repeatedly. There are a couple of items which you can find in the very lives of Christian saints which have an amazingly pagan flavour.

A Christian Buried Alive

Let me tell you a bizarre tale. St. Columba, an Irishmen busy converting the Scots found that his newly built monastery in Iona kept falling apart. The cause of the trouble was an apparition looking like a blend of a woman and a fish, for whenever this being shook itself, so did the island, and down tumbled the walls and buildings. The dear saint was mightily enraged abut this dismal state, but alas, found that he could do nothing to prevent it. The fish-woman, however, had a solution. In her opinion the buildings lacked a human sacrifice. One of the monks, so she suggested, should have himself buried under the foundations in a hole seven times as deep as the man's height. If this were done, the tremors would cease and the buildings stand intact. While St.

Columban was not too happy about this proposition, one of his monks, (or possibly his brother) with the name Dobhran (or Odhran) volunteered to be the sacrifice. Eventually he convinced the saint, a pit was dug and the volunteer was buried alive. The tremors ceased and the building commenced. After twenty days, however, St. Columban became really worried about what had happened to Dobhran. He had the stone lid lifted from the shaft and looked into the deep. As soon as this occurred, Dobhran, who was still alive but somewhat bored, made a frantical leap to the surface and managed to look out of his hole. His gaze was so fierce that the reeds of Iona instantly turned red. Terrified by the apparition, St. Columba screamed for help. 'Clay!' shouted the saintly man 'Clay on the eyes of Dobhran before he sees more of the world and its sins!' So Dobhran was swiftly buried again, and it is not recorded that anyone dared to lift that lid again.

In another version of this tale, poor Odhran manages to exclaim 'hell is not as bad as is reported...' but St. Columban has him buried before he gets a chance to utter further blasphemies. Behind this legend lies the very unchristian idea that important buildings require a living sacrifice, who acts as a guardian spirit of the place. A parallel to this notion can be found in the tale of Merlin Ambrosius, who narrowly escaped the fate of being slaughtered to keep King Vortigern's tower from tumbling. Such sacrifices occured with some frewquency in the old days. The earthwalls of Maiden Castle covered the grave of a man between 20 and 30 years of age who was killed and buried in the 2nd century BCE before the walls were raised. Foundation burials occured in several Roman fortresses, mainly of animals but occasionally children. There is even a reference to such customs in the first book of *Kings*, relating how the rebuilding of Jericho cost the lives of the sons of the architect. Remnants of this tradition are not unusual in medieval times. I know one minor castle where excavators found an egg which had been mortared into a wall. Several early medieval castles received foundation burials of dogs, sheep, horses or cattle. There is a chapel dedicated to Odhran in Iona. The sacrifice has become a spirit of the place, and is regularly approached by the locals with prayers and petitions. In fact he is their link to the otherworld. It would not surprise me if a good many barrow graves served a similar function in the pre-Christian period.

Bardic Christianity

Some of this confusion found its way into the poetry of the Island Celtic bards and filid. For example when you study a poem of Taliesin, you may find that its religious background is far from easy to comprehend. Many adherents of the modern Neo-Celticist gospel solve these difficulties by claiming that the poetic material is mainly pagan Celtic, and that the Christian scribes of later ages censored it, kicking out unwanted beliefs and adding their own pious lines. That there may be a Roman influence in old British poetry is a matter that is very rarely acknowledged. Now it may well be possible that the songs were censored, but then, lacking any originals, this proposition is remarkably hard to prove. Also, the proposition implies that the Christian

scribes were actually aware of what constitutes pagan material. If a poem mentions a Roman deity, a well educated scribe might have guessed that this was a pre-Christian idea, but when it came to Celtic deities, of whom an amazing amount were in existence, chances are that a scribe would have failed to recognize them as deities at all. Paganism was no topic of study in those days and monks were not expected to show interest in such matters. On the other hand a considerable number of bards, filid and monks did have an interest in preserving the folklore and traditions of their countries. In many cases they seem to have preserved material which they did not fully understand.

When we come to the Gogynfeirdd period between the 11th and 13th century, mythological issues changed even more. The bards of this time had a renaissance, mainly as the English were too troubled with the Normans to bother about the British. Plenty of the finest mystical songs of the book of Taliesin were composed in this late period. The problem about the Gogynfeirdd is that they had already forgotten the meaning of many elder traditions of their culture. Modern Neo-Celticists like to pretend that the bards were all strict traditionalists who venerated their ancient secret Celtic lore and would not have dreamed of changing it. The Gogynfeirdd not only changed but innovated lots of it. Much of the material paraded as Celtic in books on Druidry was not preserved but made up in the period. To do so, a number of old elements were used, but many of these were interpreted in radically new ways, as their elder meaning had been lost centuries earlier. The mythology of the Gogynfeirdd, such as you can find it in the *Mabinogi*, is not simply a distorted rendering of elder tales but contains items which were invented then and there, by poets who were not only Christian but who were well acquainted with all sorts of European legends and myths. These poets were creative, they believed themselves imbued with the very spirit of inspiration and the gift of prophecy. Where it comes to visionary realization they seem to have considered themselves superior in understanding to churchmen and scholars. This implies that they may well have invented their own spiritual tradition, their own ideas of salvation, and they certainly venerated a freshly created goddess called Ceridwen whom they saw as the patroness of all poetic learning. Of course their lore was not a popular religion but a store of teachings limited to the bardic profession itself, just like Ceridwen, mentioned by several bards of the period, was never worshipped by the common people. To round all this fascinating and confusing stuff off, I would like to quote one of the poems attributed to a Taliesin of the Gogynfeirdd period. Please examine it carefully and attempt to reconstruct just where you can find pagan and Christian elements. As information overload equals pattern recognition, I am sure that you will discover a lot of interesting ideas in it. Who knows, maybe some of them might be true!

Book of Taliesin 9

I will address my Lord,
To consider the Awen.
What brought necessity
Before the time of Ceridwen.
Primarily through my life
Poverty has been.
The wealthy monks
Why will they not speak to me?
Why will they not cause me to tremble?
One hour that I was not followed,
What disappearance of smoke?
Why sang he evil?
What fountain breaks out
Above the covert of darkness?
When the reed is white,
When it is a moonlight night.
Another was not sung,
It was shaken out,
When is apt to be forward
The noise of waves on the shore.
In the vengeance of the ocean,
A day will reach to them.
When a stone is so heavy,
When a thorn is so sharp.
Knowest thou which is best?
Its base or its point,
Who caused a partition
Between man and frigidity?
Whose is the most wholesome sore?
The young or the old?
Knowest thou what thou art
When thou art sleeping?
Whether a body or a soul,

Or a secresy of perception?
The ingenious minstrel,
Why does he not inform me?
Knowest thou where should be
The night waiting the passing of the day?
Knowest thou a sign,
How many leaves there are?
Who uplifted the mountain,
Before the elements fell?
Who supports the structure
Of the earth for a habitation?
The soul of whom is complained of?
Who has seen it, who knows?
I wonder in books
That they know not truly
The soul, what is its seat.
What form its limbs,
Through what part it pours out,
What air it respires?
A war petulant,
A sinner endangered.
A wonder in mockery,
What were its dregs.
Which is the best intoxication,
Of mead or of bragget?
When their happiness
Was protected by the God of Trinity
Why should I utter a treatise,
Except of thee?
Who caused coin
Of current silver?
When is so current
A car so prickly;
Death having a foundation,

In every country is shared.
Death above our head,
Wide is its covering,
High above the canopy of heaven.
Man is oldest when he is born.
And is younger (and) younger continually.
What is there to be anxious about,
Of the present attainment?
After a want of property,
Does it not make to us a shortness of life?
Enough of sadness,
The visitation of the grave.
And the One that made us,
From the supreme country,
Be he our God, and bring us
To him at the end!
Believed through the will of the Lord.
As many as are on wrath through the circles,
Have mercy, God, on thy kindred.
May I be meek, the turbulent Ruler,
May I not endure, before I am without
motion.
Grievously complaineth every lost one,
Hastily claimeth every needy one.
An exceedingly displeased mind will not run
From (its) present course, when I am angry.
I will declare when I am in the gravel,
From the maintenance of gifts,
From being numbered, from going to be a
martyr
In the reckoning of Saint Segerno.
From a word when sin may be to me,
Let there be no sigh from those that hear
me.

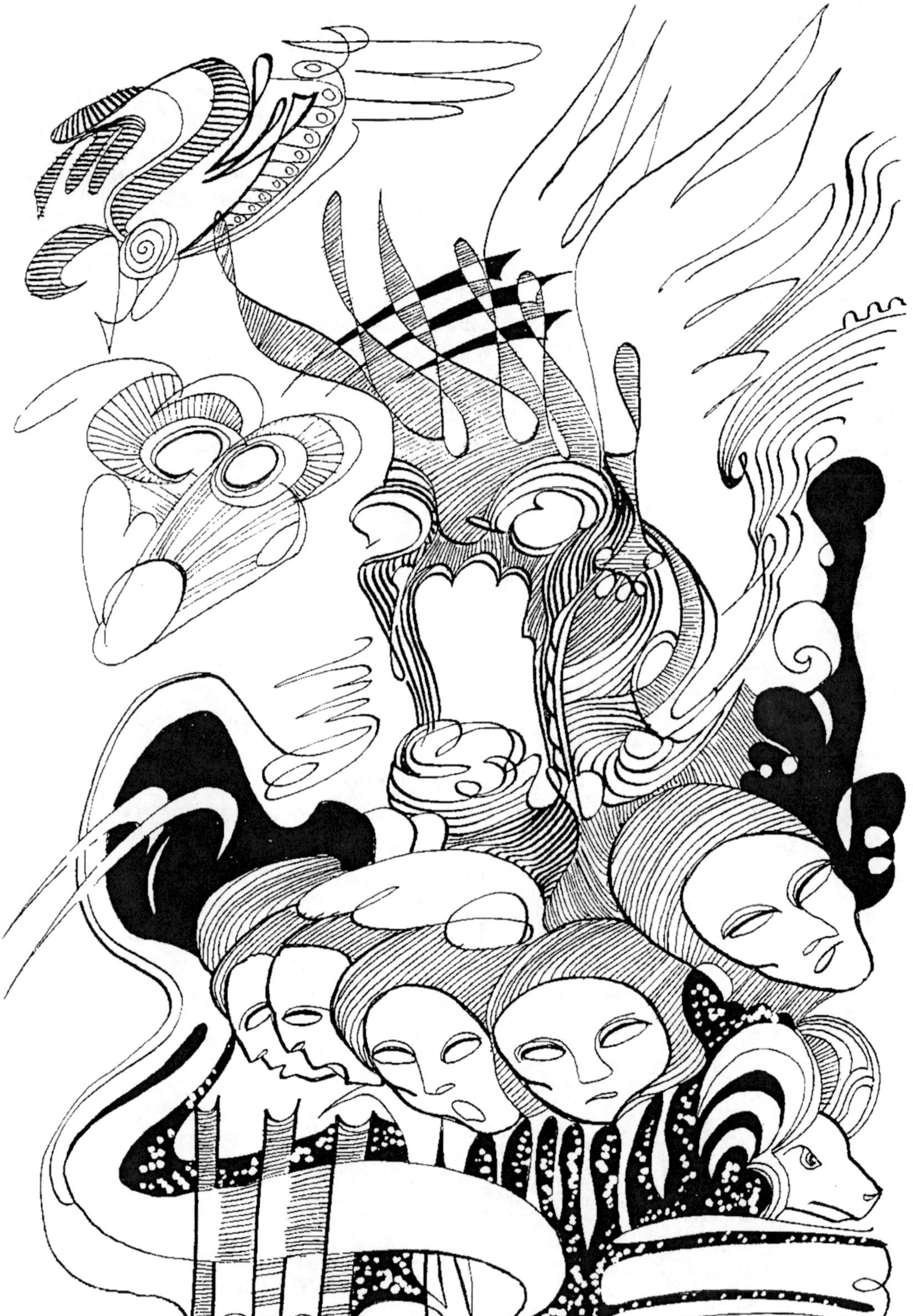

6. The Filid of Ireland

By the medieval period, our sources regarding bardic activities become more voluminous. This literature comes basically from two related but distinct cultures: the Gaelic speaking Celts of Ireland and Scotland and the British Celts of Wales, Northern Britain, Cornwall and Brittany. In both branches of Island Celtic culture, the term 'bard' was in common usage. However, there was a massive difference in regard of status, function and training. Are you ready for a bit of confusion? In post-Roman Britain, the word bard remained an honorable title, as it had been in earlier periods in Gaul and elsewhere. The British bards were a well-trained professional association and enjoyed a legal status that often equaled or surpassed that of nobles. Their profession was based on song and story telling, but often their activities went far beyond the task of refined entertainment, and involved political functions, diplomacy, magic, spell-casting, prophecy and more.

In Ireland, things developed differently. There were bards in Ireland, but they enjoyed a very low social status and were regarded as little better than vulgar minstrels, touring the countryside entertaining commoners. The status enjoyed by the British bards was paralleled in Ireland by the professional association of the poets. These called themselves filid and their art filidecht. The word filid (singular *Fili* or *File)* meant 'seers' and seems related to the earlier term vates, which you may recall from the chapter on Druids and bards. Filidecht was a noble art and the filid functioned much like a professional guild, if not a secret society. They had their own ethics, their own law-codes, regulations, an extensive training program and a number of secret languages and ciphers which were completely unintelligible to the population. Much of what Caesar observed about the Druids sounds as if he were speaking about the Irish filid. Like the Druids, the filid had at least a dozen years of training to attain the first rank of their art, and like the Druids, the filid acquired much of their knowledge by memorizing verses.

Caesar speculated that the Druids disliked the written word, as memorization is better training for the mind, and used the Greek alphabet if a bit of writing could not be avoided. This is not quite accurate. Many Celtic coins show curious letters in a distinct blend of alphabets - the influence of Greek can be observed side by side with runic letters coming from those strange Alpine alphabets, and Caesar, as a cultivated aristocrat, was acquainted with the Greek alphabet and the fact that the few bits of writing used in Gaul were not a simple copy of Greek writing. However, he chose to simplify things, which does not make him a very reliable witness.

Now the Irish filid were not very fond of the written word either, but they did develop their own alphabet, the Ogham script, and several dozen methods to encode it so that not even another poet found it easy to read. Another close similarity between the Gaulish Druids and the filid is that both groups functioned as law givers, an office which was definitely not shared by the British bards. As a result, the filid often enjoyed as much, if not more political power than the kings.

One of the results of this monopoly on law were strict regulations which limited the freedom of the common bards of the countryside. The laws passed by the filid saw to it that bards were not permitted to receive proper training in poetry, that they were not allowed to sing for royal or noble patrons, and that a number of poetic metres were taboo to them. As a result, Irish bards remained poorly trained, impoverished and had few chances of achieving a better status, even if they showed talent or genius, and the filid treated them with contempt.

According to Douglas Hyde's invaluable study, the bards, just like the filid, were organized in strict hierarchies. They were divided into two classes, the patrician (saor) and plebeian (daor) bards, and had a number of wonderful titles, such as Anshruth-bairdne (great stream of poetry?), Sruth di aill (stream down two cliffs?), Bo-bhard (cow-bard), Tuath-bhard (lay bard) Cul-bhard (black bard) and so on. Like the filid, each bardic rank, no matter how low in social status, was associated with a specific metre and not permitted to use the metres of the higher ranks.

This situation eventually changed. Over the centuries, the filid became thoroughly unpopular, they lost a number of their privileges and with them the right to pass laws. By the time of the Danish occupation of Ireland (the first assaults seem to have occurred around 795), their influence was much reduced. When the Danes left (after more than two centuries of carnage and devastation), the filid found that their original power and reputation had become a thing of the past. In late medieval literature, the words bard and filid are almost interchangeable and of equal value. In that period, it was possible to write about respectable and honoured bards, which would not have been permitted when the filid jealously guarded their secrets.

As the bardic schools of Ireland functioned well into the 17th Century, there is a lot of literature using the term 'bard' as an honourable title. Likewise, a considerable number of poems and tales were eventually recorded in written form. The modern notion that bards and poets chanted everything from memory is a bit misleading. While books were certainly rare and immensely valuable, whenever they were available, the bards were expected to read from them to their employers. That many of these manuscripts come from a relatively late period is not necessarily a sign that they are of recent composition. It can also be seen as an indication that the Irish oral tradition survived in strength for longer than in other parts of Europe. If you have plenty of reliable story tellers on the road you don't think of recording their tales in a book.

The Scholar's Primer

Now if we want to explore the trade and secrets of the filid, we are exceptionally lucky that not only literature but an entire book on poetic training has survived. There are two versions of the *Auraicept Na N-Eces ('the Scholar's Primer')*, one of them having found its way into the *Book of Ballymote*, (c. 1400) the other into the *Yellow Book of Lecan*, (c. 1350) while the *Trefhocul* with their comments on poetic training and regulations can be found in the *Book of Leinster*.

The *Auraicept* was among the objects of study which the filid were supposed to master in the first year of their training. Having read the good book, I can only comment that such a task seems hardly possible, at least not with the version of the primer which has come to us. The *Auraicept* is basically a grammar. As such it may not seem overly exciting to students of romantic island Celtic lore. However, a grammar was not just a grammar in those days. (note the way the word 'just' decreases the value of the item...another magical word caught in

the act of shaping our awareness!) That a grammar may be magical can be seen from the many medieval grimoires, the spell books of sorcerers. A grimoire is simply a grammar. As the grimoires gave the basics of congress with extraterrestrial entities such as angels and demons, a grammar is primarily a spell-book giving the regulations that make the magic of language work.

The *Auraicept* is a grammar, and a mightily confused one. Most of the text is in middle Irish, but there are sections which retain the speech forms of old Irish. At least four authors were said to have contributed to the text. The first of these was the celebrated Cenn Faelad of the clan of Ui Neill who died in 679. To begin with, Cenn was a promising poet until he participated in the famous battle of Moira. This bloody incident was not only the occasion when the gifted seer Suibhne Geillt became mad and prophetic, grew feathers and began to hop from mountaintop to mountaintop, it also almost marked the end of Cenn's life. In the middle of the slaughter, Cenn received a heavy blow to his head which, as the text puts it, dashed out his brains. In spite of this serious wound, medical experts managed to patch him up and heal him, which is quite an achievement if you consider the state of medical science in those days.

Cenn survived and resumed his poetic work. In fact, he became immensely enthusiastic about poetry, metres, word roots and the like, the blow having equipped him with *a brain of oblivion*. This term, as the primer tells us, means that he could not forget anything. It would be tempting to point out that early Irish grammar was designed by a poet with a hole in his head, but on closer inspection, most grammars seem to have started thus. Also, it appears that Cenn was not the earliest poet to struggle with Irish grammar; he may have used some earlier books which do not survive. After Cenn Faelad, a number of other poets contributed to the text. Among them are the semi-legendary Ferchertne, Fenius and even Amergen White-knee, the latter being a leader of the Milesian Celts when they invaded Ireland approximately nine centuries earlier. That he managed to contribute to a book composed much later shows that he invented a time machine and was cheated out of his royalties. Beside these and a number of anonymous authors, the *Auraicept* clearly shows the strong influence of the *Etymologia* or *Origines* of Isidore of Sevilla (died 636) whose twenty volumes had considerable effect on early medieval thought, and especially on the bards. His cosmology can be found in some of the songs of the Taliesins and in the words ascribed to Taliesin by Geoffrey of Monmouth in his *Vita Merlini*. When Taliesin chants that the world is divided into five zones, (two cold, one hot and two temperate), this item of cosmology can be traced to Isidore and from Isidore all the way to Ovid, who probably didn't invent it either.

In our age, there are plenty of enthusiasts who are ready to identify every unusual idea in bardic literature as the genuine wisdom of the pagan Celts. While some items of bardic lore are arguably pagan, Roman and pre-Roman, we should bear in mind that the medieval bards were not only influenced by biblical thought but also by the scholars and philosophers of Europe. Britain was not that far from the Continent, bards travelled frequently to the courts of Brittany and elsewhere, and the Irish filid in particular had close ties with the intellectuals of various European kingdoms. Plenty of Irish scholars, many of them trained as filid, were found at European courts where they taught classical languages, religion, history and the finer arts. Zimmer, quoted by Carter, mentions Clemens, who taught at the court of Charlemagne, Dicuil at St. Denis, Dungal in Paris, Sedulius in Lüttich and Metz, Moengall in St. Gall and Johannes Scotus at the court of Karl the Bald. As an example for a well trained fili, he cites the famous Cormac, who had *quite passable knowledge of Latin, Greek, Hebrew, Old Norse, Anglo-Saxon and Cymric*, besides the extremely detailed knowledge of Irish which was expected of a poet.

Indeed medieval Ireland was not an isolated outpost at the western rim of Europe, as it may have been in the time of the Roman Empire. The Green Island was thoroughly Christianized long before most other countries in northern Europe. It had some of the earliest universities and incidentally supplied a lot of those zealous minded missionaries who made life so unpleasant for the last pagan cultures. Some of these churchmen had poetic training, so we should be careful when we research the lore of the filid for the odd bit of pagan Celtic wisdom. Even in the so-called dark ages, literature got around. Though books were rare and extremely valuable, they were

Coins 4: top l & r (front & reverse) Carnuti, central Gaul. center l & r (front & reverse) Carnuti, central Gaul. bottom l: Coriosolites. bottom r: uncertain.

appreciated and studied in depth, and maybe with more attention than people give to books in our age. The same applied to meetings with unusual people - in a time when communication was slow, and people often remained in relative isolation during the winter months, the chance to meet a stranger, and to learn some new knowledge, was an important opportunity. Maybe the filid and bards listened and observed more carefully than people in our age.

Exercise: The Unique

Perhaps we should play around with our minds at this opportunity. It has a lot to do with the consciousness of the fili or bard, in that it is the art of the poet to appreciate and refine an experience, and to distill three blessed drops of insight out of the raw materials that went into the cauldron. If the three drops are well distilled, their magick will enchant the minds of all who partake of them.

Would you like to learn something about uniqueness? For the fun of it, I suggest you try an experiment. Take one of your favourite books and imagine that it is the only book you have, and that you can count yourself lucky to own such a treasure. Go into this mind-frame deeply. Then open the book and read a chapter, in the awareness that it is unique and intensely valuable.

What happens? How intense is the reading experience? How much important data can you discover? Is the experience different to the everyday reading which you usually practise? When I do this, I find myself regarding and remembering the text with a lot of attention, more attention, in

fact, than I usually give to the written word. I also recall the contents easier, and often discover ideas in the text which I had not noticed while reading in a sloppier fashion. By making the book and the reading experience a unique event, you can get a lot more insight from a book than you usually do.

The same applies to other activities in life - if you treat what happens to you as a unique experience, you will sense it more deeply, and appreciate it more fully. Try this mind game. Imagine you are an alien. Imagine you have travelled a million light-years to study this amazing planet and its inhabitants. Its your first visit to earth and you only have one day to delight in all the new experiences. If this were your sole chance to experience anything from this planet, what would you chose? What would interest you? What would you appreciate? What will you find enjoyable that seems ordinary and commonplace when you are in your usual human personality? What else do you find boring and dull? Try to be an alien and discover the pleasure in it. There is so much pleasure everywhere around. Colours and sounds, feelings, scents and tastes, the miraculous spider web of the senses. It's amazing how easy it can be to forget the sense of wonder and astonishment in life. Grown up people do that. They get used to all sorts of events, decide that there are important and unimportant matters, become dead serious, and before long they need to go to great lengths to find entertainment and pleasure in life. This is habituation. It's getting used to the world and limiting it for the sake of convenience and security, until finally everything is normal, dull and meaningless. If you get to that point, remember. Be the alien. Find out what everybody else has forgotten. Enjoy.

Or try the drastic treatment prescribed by Castaneda. Have Death at your side as you go out, and imagine it is your last day on earth, and your last chance to appreciate the fullness of life. This is a useful frame, especially for people who tend to waste opportunities or who float through life with little concern or attention. On the other hand, some people become so over-stimulated by the presence of death that they tense up and hurry. Such a state may reduce the pleasure of experience. It all depends. Death as a guest is one useful dream, the traveler and the alien are more neutral. What they all have in common is a mind-frame that makes life special and precious. Or think of a good holiday you had, maybe a time when you went traveling in foreign places. Journeys are always under a time limit, and a time limit is sometimes useful to make people appreciate their experience more fully. Each experience in life is unique, but usually people do not bother to enjoy this fact. They treat events as if they were commonplace and routine. While they do one thing they already plan the next, and after a long day they look back and discover that they have done a lot, and enjoyed very little. This says more about shallow observation and lack of awareness than about the actual events.

And before we continue with our study of filid lore, I would like to ask you to give yourself a treat. Think of what you are doing now. Think of what you intend to do later on. Think of what this day may have in store for you. All of it is unique, one of a kind, and will never happen exactly the same way again. Take this thought and carry it through the day with you. It's your chance to discover something new. Life is never dull or routine, it is only our awareness which can make an event dull. If you make the world a dull place, it will appear dull to you. Dullness or excitement are all in the mind. If you realize the wonder, the joy and the wealth of possible experiences that each moment could hold for you, you may understand that the miracle of the world is always there. Each moment, and each activity, each event and each book is unique and will never happen like this again. This is part of the magick of the poets: it is awareness of the uniqueness of each moment which can turn events into miracles and a lifetime into a legend. What legend will your life make?

Poets and Philosophers

But let us take a closer look at the *Auraicept* and the way the filid used to think about their profession. To begin with, the *Auraicept* claims that the word fili comes from *generous seeking*. Another explanation claims that the word is derived from fi = *that which satirizes*, and li = *that which praises*. A third theory explains a fili as a philosophus, *owing to the duty of the poet to be a philosopher*. While the etymology behind these explanations is more than questionable, it does reveal how the filid thought about themselves. Also, you may have noticed that there are three explanations given for this term, and the use of triple interpretations is typical for the Celtic/Germanic love of trinities. You'll see plenty more of them as we go along.

The filid, so the *Auraicept* states, were also known as *the men without doubt*. This idea is something which I find a bit hard to stomach. Sure, such a title could imply that the filid were not to be doubted, but if the filid themselves aimed at transcending doubt, this is regrettably stupid. Any spiritually minded person or philosopher who seriously believes they know everything, or who becomes too certain, is bound for one of the worst traps the human mind can produce. Doubt, after all, is a blessing. If you are absolutely certain about something, this does not mean that the issue in question is certain. It simply means that your mind's representation of the matter is so extreme that it leaves no space for questions, and that you have stopped learning. When doubt is completely abolished, belief becomes conviction and imprisons the mind. It is amazing how many spiritually minded people hunger just for this state: they wish to abolish doubt, and believe that should they be rid of it, they will have certainty, and hence, be happier. Of course they will also inhabit a narrow little fanatic's reality, a closed system in which surprises, riddles and unexpected developments are plain impossible. Doubt can be the very solvent that gets people out of too narrow belief structures - and frankly, any belief structure becomes too narrow unless it is critically examined and innovated from time to time.

However, the issue of being without doubt can also refer to the fact that the master filid were indeed expected to know everything. Irish literature is full of really bizarre etymology. The filid were expected to know what each word of their language meant, and how it originated. To live up to expectations, a lot of dodgy explanations were invented, which became gospel as soon as they were uttered. Considering how strained some of these explanations are, it seems obvious that their authors were under great pressure. It's a tough job to be all-knowing.

Heritage of Babel

For the filid, an important matter was the question how their craft originated. They had a legend to explain this, a legend that was so important to them that it is repeated twice in the *Auraicept*. It is not a typically Celtic legend, however, but a strangely transformed biblical tale. Once upon a time there was a nobleman called Nimrod in the lands of the near East. He was a valiant fighter, a great champion, and a man possessed by the need to go hunting. Nimrod was a hunter of stags, a courser of hares, a trapper of wild boars and a snarer of birds. Wherever he went, no animal managed to escape his skill, and soon there was a multitude of like-minded men following him across hills and dales, who chose him as their leader. Finally Nimrod could resign from his function as a counselor: the men of his entourage made him the first king to rule mankind after the flood. Nimrod the hunter became Nimrod the first among kings and regents, and greater ambitions than hunting expeditions enflamed his simple little mind.

Nimrod and his 71 (the number 72 seems to have had a lot of importance for the filid) fellow regents decided to build the mightiest tower that the world had ever seen. There were three reasons for the building of the tower. First, all people feared that the flood might return, and they hoped to escape the roaring waters in the tower. Second, Nimrod and his fellows wanted to ascend to heaven while still incarnate and alive. Third, they desired that their names should be famous for generations to come. For the building, Nimrod and the 71 regents united all the tribes of mankind. They made use of nine materials to build the tower: 1. Clay, 2. Water, 3. Wool, 4. Blood, 5. Wood, 6. Lime, 7. Acacias, 8. Flax-thread, 9. Bitumen. Soon enough the mighty tower of Babel began to rise towards the height of heaven.

If you know the *Bible*, you have probably come across the tale how the tower was built, it's in *Genesis* 11. The account given in the *Auraicept*, however, is much more detailed. The *Bible* postulates that before the building of the tower, all human beings shared a common language, so everybody understood each other, which may or may not have been a good thing. The Biblical account claims that the tower was built as humans wanted to reach heaven to make a name for themselves, and that they feared to be scattered through all countries. After they had built a couple of floors, however, the Lord in his wrath decided to put a stop to this bunch of upstarts. He confused the languages, so that none was able to talk with his neighbour any more. Soon enough, the builders were quarreling with each other, then violence broke out, and finally the assembled multitudes scattered and sought a more peaceful living elsewhere. Thus the *Bible* showed that the multitude of languages were a punishment for the sin of wanting to go to heaven. God-fearing folk see it as a tale of sinful ambitions duly thwarted by a wrathful deity.

For the filid, the story was a different one. To begin with, the nine materials that went into the building of the tower corresponded with the nine materials out of which language is composed. The Primer says that it is nine materials, but only lists eight: 1. Noun, 2. Pronoun, 3. Verb, 4. Adverb, 5. Participle, 6. Conjunction, 7. Preposition and 8. Interjection. Do yourself a favour and think about this. The tower of Nimrod, as far as the filid were concerned, was created out of the elements of the primal language: language was to save humanity from the next flood, to take humans to heaven, and to make their names immortal. So much for the good intentions.

The tale, as given by Moses, ended in the ruin of the tower. Mankind, no longer capable of free communication, had a lot of frightful rows until they all split up and went their own ways, complaining mightily. For the filid, however, the ruin of the tower was but the midpoint of a longer story. After the confusion of languages, 75 poets came to Babel from far-off-Scythia. In medieval history and myth, it was often assumed that the Scoti (the Irish and the Scots) had originated among the fierce horse riding Scythian cultures of the Black Sea which had been described in such colourful detail by Heredotus. From the ethnological point of view, this is not very likely. For the medieval historian, it formed an attractive if unprovable tale and equipped a branch of the Island Celts with a charming proto-history. The primer tells us that the 75 poets came to the ruins of the tower as they believed that they would *remain in perfection* in this unusual place. Please think about

Coins 5, canine images.
top: Redoni, gold, 22 mm. Note horse goddess
(Equona!) and aquatic dog
center: Petrocori, bronze, 14 mm, dog and bull head
bottom: unknown tribe, Melden, bronze 17mm,
winged dog

this. We are not dealing with a biblical story of sin and punishment any more. The filid believed that Babel was the place of origin, the source from which all languages appeared, and the fountain of their own art. The poets consisted of three sages, who spoke the principal languages, and 72 poets speaking 72 languages of the world. The three principal languages, according to the *Primer*, are Hebrew, Greek and Latin. There are three reasons for this selection, namely as

1. There were more compositions in these three languages than in any other language,

2. They influenced all other tongues and

3. The inscription on the cross was in them.

This may come as a surprise to many neo-Celtic enthusiasts, but the filid were not as blindly patriotic as some modern writers would like to have them. The *Primer* explicitly states that the holiest language is Hebrew (for three reasons, as usual): the language of heaven, the tongue spoken before the flood, and the speech that will be used after the day of judgement. Likewise, the *Primer* acquaints the budding fili with the Hebrew, Greek and Roman alphabets before it details the native Irish ogham alphabet.

Chief of the Poets at the ruin of Babel was one Fennius Farsaidh whose ancestry was Scythian and Goth. He directed the assembled poets to study, but soon enough they realized that Babel held no *perfection of languages*. Therefore, the 72 minor poets went traveling, while the three sages remained at the tower and waited patiently. After seven years, the poets returned, each of them having mastered one of the 72 languages on earth. 72, called *the number of the tower*, was immensely popular in the Primer. You find 72 counselors of Nimrod, 72 workers, 72 building materials, a foundation 72 paces wide, the tower rose to a height of 72 paces, 72 students of Fennius, 72 races of mankind, 72 languages, and 72 people to whom the languages originally belonged. Such a passion for the number 72 implies that the fili may have had some numerological system. Though this system has not survived, there is evidence that once there was such a thing. The *Primer* has an interesting but brief reference which informs the attentive reader that there are perfect, quite perfect and imperfect numbers. You may recall perfect numbers from Euclid, whose *Elements* gives the following definition: *A number n is called 'perfect' if it is equal to the sum of its divisors including 1 but excluding n.* In Euclid, the smallest perfect number is 6 (1+2+3=6), the next one being 28 (1+2+4+7+14= 28).

Imperfect numbers are the primes, *for they are not multiplied by factors.* Examples for imperfect numbers are 3, 5, 7, 11, 13, 17, 19, 23, 29, 31, 37, 41, 43, 47, 53, 59, 61 etc.

Now the filid went beyond Euclid in that they invented quite perfect numbers. Quite perfect numbers can also be divided by factors, and when these are added up, yield sums which are larger than themselves. The number 12 is quite perfect, for example, as it can be divided by 1, 2, 3, 4 and 6. If you add 1+2+3+4+6= 16. As 16 is larger than 12, 12 is a quite perfect number.

Examples for the filid's quite perfect

numbers : 12 (16), 18 (21), 20 (22), 24 (36), 30 (42), 36 (55), 40 (50), 42 (54), 48 (76), 54 (66), 56 (64), 60 (108), 66 (78), 70 (74), 72 (123), 78 (90), 80 (106), 84 (140), 90 (97), 96 (156), 100 (117), 102 (114), 104 (106) 108 (172) and so on. As you can see, the number 72 is quite perfect, and so are several other numbers which keep appearing in island Celtic mythology. The problem is that the *Primer* only gives a tantalizing short reference to this peculiar system. We have no idea what the filid used the quite perfect numbers for, apart from demanding quite perfect wages. Nevertheless, the fact that some system once existed ought to be enough to stimulate the more qabalistical minded readers to do some independent creative thinking. I have no idea if old Irish numerology can be resurrected, but maybe it can be replaced by something even better. Just consider the possibilities. Could it be that this numerology is based on the idea of sharing, in that numbers which can be justly divided are more perfect than the ones which cannot?

Now the 72 poets returned from their journeys and assembled at the blasted tower. Of these, 25 poets were the noblest, and as the Primer states, it is from their names that the 25 letters of the ogham alphabet were formed: *Babel, Lot, Pharaoh, Saliath, Nebuchadnezzar; Herod, David, Talamon, Cae, Kaliap; Muiriath, Gotli, Gomers, Stru, Ruben; Achab, Oise, Urith, Essu, Iachim; Ethrocius, Uimelicus, Iudonius, Affrim, Ordines.* Well, this is just one of the theories proposed regarding the origin of ogham, the *Primer* offers several, and as the text is such a jumble of badly organized ideas you'll have to get used to the occasional contradiction.

Be that as it may, there were five poets among the 25 who were more noble than the rest, and these are the ones who gave their names to the vowels. After the 72 poets had demonstrated the languages they had mastered, they humbly asked Fennius to select one of these tongues, *so that speech might not be in anyone's possession save themselves.*

Fennius chose the language of Gaedel, son of Angen (or Ether) whose language was Gaelic. Recognizing the desire of the poets to have secret languages which the uninitiated could not comprehend, he also created:

1. The additional language,
2. The language parted among the trees (the letters were called trees or woods by the poets),
3. The language of the poets,
4. The common language that serves everyone.

What these special languages consisted of is not certain, but they worked admirably in keeping a monopoly on knowledge. The dark speech of the poets occasionally appears in Irish legend. It has been proposed that the Irish poets retained an older type of Gaelic as their own private language, but this enchanting idea cannot be proved. Nor would it be necessary. The poets and seers saw themselves as a spiritual order, and much of their art depended on vision, insight and inspiration. As most of you will be aware, there are plenty of mind shaking revelations which are really hard to communicate, as ordinary language tends to debase intimate experience. Some words (just think of love, as a typical example) have been so thoroughly abused by shallow minded ego-trippers that many an adept shrinks from using them. Consequently, Magickians tend to create new languages for their own use and to communicate experience among like minded friends. This happens all the time, it happens among all specialist groups, and it especially occurs to those who experience more than they can express. When you find that you can't come to terms with a word that has been abused, invent a better one.

The poet's dark speech did not require eldritch proto-Celtic to remain incomprehensible to outsiders. The filid Ferchertne and Nede held their famous dispute to win the office of the chief poet and came to an admirable agreement, as they understood each other too well. Tough luck nobody else did. The *Book of Ballymote* states: *Obscure to everyone seemed the speech which the poets uttered in that discussion, and the legal decision which they delivered was not clear to the king and the other poets.* This proved to be a problem, as King Conor Mac Nessa did not like being let out of an argument. He angrily proclaimed that in future, the poets were not to hold the post of the judges any more. This proved to be a considerable reduction of their status, as the filid had been the official judges since the sons of Mil invaded Ireland.

It may seem surprising that the filid honoured Hebrew, Greek and Latin more than the language of their homeland. Yet while the classical languages were considered older and more perfect than Gaelic, their own language was thought more beautiful. It was also believed to be more comprehensive, as it included *every obscure sound of every language.* Of course this was plainly wrong, otherwise the filid would not have needed to invent additional letters for their alphabet to deal with Greek and Roman words. The value of Gaelic is one of those matters which may have troubled the filid. The *Auraicept* calls it a young and worldly tongue and seriously inquires whether its use is rude before god. The answer is a grudging yes, but then we learn that before God, all philosophy, grammar, dialect, metrics, learning and literature are rude: *small their avail in heaven above.*

The Poet's Path

We may now proceed to consider the actual activities of the filid. The Irish poets were a well organized guild. Caesar's comments on the strict organization of the Gaulish Druids (which may or may not be true) seems to fit what we know of the Irish filid. It does not fit what the medieval authors wrote about the Irish Druids, who appear as a bunch of independent sorcerers and prophets. The filid were not only poets in our sense of the word. The art of filidecht includes the mastery of literature, science, history, law, grammar, custom, tradition, genealogy, song and satire, as well as profound skill in divination. Up to King Conor's intervention, the filid had a monopoly on justice, so that their political power often exceeded that of nobles and kings. Neither the bards of Britain nor those on the continent had so much influence.

Not every fili was a law-giver, of course. There was a special group of filid known as brehons, a term that comes from breitheamh, meaning law-giver or judge. What is so unusual about the brehon laws is that they were not passed by aristocrats, kings or any other form of government.

The brehons made the laws, and they also tried the cases, but they were personally responsible for their verdicts. If their judgement proved unjust, they had to return their fee for that specific case to the offended party and pay for damages and the like. Brehon laws covered all aspects of Irish life. They defined the five main classes of society and their value, they established what customs were to be followed by each class, how children were to be brought up, how treaties had to be fulfilled, the wages and privileges of each professional group, the proper conduct of kings and so on.

Brehon laws defined the hierarchy in family and society. They also ensured, that for most offenses, financial compensation was possible. In some respects, the brehon laws were fairly liberal. Divorce was available for men and women, this is extremely unusual for the jolly world of medieval Christianity. Polygamy was also permitted under specific circumstances; when a wife became chronically ill, her husband was entitled to marry another wife. This second wife had a tough start of her marriage, as during the first three nights, the chief wife was permitted to abuse her any way she liked, short of killing her rival. Also, the chief wife received the bride-price which had been paid to the secondary wife. This shows that women could have considerable private property in ancient Ireland, which was not the case in many other parts of the Christian world.

However, it may be well to keep in mind that official laws are one thing, but that the way people act is another. Just as with our modern laws, the brehon laws were a confused tangle of regulations, so that a cunning judge could easily find precedents for any verdict he desired to pass.

Considering the high status and authority of the filid, it comes as no surprise that their training was hard. To reach the higher ranks of poetry, at least a dozen years of training were required. In the first year, the entire *Auraicept* had to be mastered, as well as 50 ogham alphabets, 20 stories and six poetic metres. After mastering this first unit (which could take much longer than a year), the student became a fucluc (word maker?) and was entitled to a retinue of one person. For a praise song, a fucluc charged the price of a three year old heifer. After a minimum of another year of study, the fucluc became a macfuirmid. To do so, another 50 ogham alphabets had to be mastered, 30 tales, lessons in philosophy, grammar and several poems. A macfuirmid travelled with a retinue of three retainers at feasts, one on a circuit or at everyday occasions, and his price for a praise song was a cow in calf. After a minimum of six years, i.e. after reaching the sixth grade, the fili travelled with five retainers for ordinary needs, and with twelve when it came to feasting. His price was five cows for a praise song, plus expenses.

This wage was only exceeded by the ollam (pronounced ollav). The ollam knew more than 350 types of versification, 250 prime stories, 100 secondary stories, divination by trance-vision and dreaming true, as well as everything taught in the lower grades. His training required a minimum of seven years, but it did not end then. An ollam of the top grade was required to study a minimum of twelve years. Such a distinguished personage travelled with eight retainers on the circuit, had twelve for ordinary needs, ten at poetic contests and twenty-four at feasts. If he composed a praise song for a noble, that noble had to be immensely wealthy, as he had to feed the entire company, bestow gifts on them and pay treasure worth a chariot or a bond-maid.

Being cunning by nature, the filid made laws which protected them on journeys and at home. In ancient Ireland and Britain, many crimes could be absolved when the guilty paid damages for their deeds, this was called the honour-price (eric in Irish, galanas in Cymric). This was a useful idea, as it absolved the families and clans from the obligation to commit revenge (unless they wanted to). While it may seem cruel to accept a fee for an insulted or slain relation, it kept society more peaceful than you will find it in countries were revenge is the only possible road of conduct. After all, not every killing, especially when committed after heavy drinking or provocation or by accident, is worth starting a blood feud or a clan war. In the Semitic religions, with their eye-for-an-eye-policy, only a killing could revenge a killing, and of course each killing led to the next. The so called Celtic and Germanic people invented the option that a financial penalty could do the job as well, an admirable idea which reduced violence between clans to a considerable extent. As the official law-makers and judges, the filid had fixed a specific honour price for each

Fragment of a staff, 70 cm, gilded wood with bronze leaves, buds and berries, found with imprinted gold-foil disks showing a triskel, c. 250 BCE, oppidum of Manching, Bavaria, Germany. A poets branch or a symbolic tree! The leaves closely resemble woodbine.

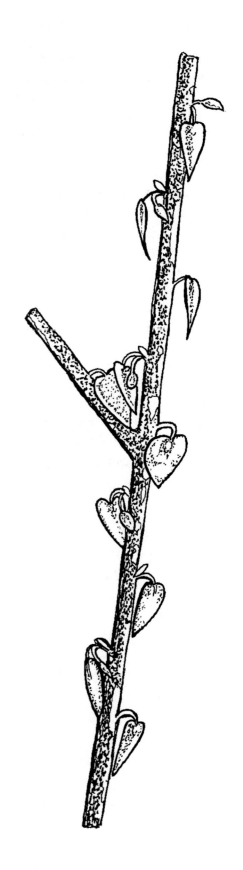

person in society. Slaying an ollam was as expensive as killing a king, and enough to ruin a clan. This allowed the poets to travel in great security.

It may come as a surprise that these amazing wages and privileges were already greatly reduced by law. While the British bards charged a lot for their eulogies, the Irish filid charged so much more that they were occasionally persecuted because of their exceptionally high demands. Unlike popular belief, a good many poets and bards were not venerated as they were simply too greedy. Take the following example. In ancient Ireland, the poetic schools were only rarely fixed to specific locations. More common, a chief poet travelled in the company of a retinue of lesser poets. When Samhain came and the dark season began, the time for traveling was largely over. Soon the weather turned the roads into a muddy morass, rains came pouring from the slate grey sky and snow was soon to follow. You would not expect a cultivated poet to go out of doors in such a disagreeable climate. The traditional way to pass the six dark months till the coming of May was to find a rich patron. While the host could expect six months of tales and songs from his guest, the fili and his entourage expected unlimited generosity.

According to the *Leabhar Breac*, groups of nine poets used to tour the countryside. Between them they carried a silver pot (another sacred cauldron?) which was attached to nine spears by means of bronze chains and golden hooks. When they chanced upon a wealthy looking settlement they made a grandiose entrance. Singing a eulogy praising the virtue of their host, they entered the hall, and expected to be paid lavishly for their efforts. The host was probably not that happy to receive such costly visitors, but the rigid codes of honourable behaviour demanded that he could not simply kick them out. Instead he had to pretend that he was mightily pleased with the song, and had to throw rich offerings of gold and silver into the poet's pot. Often enough, the host had to pay more than he could afford, if only to prove a wealth and generosity which wasn't that genuine. Anything less could result in terrible consequences.

If the poets thought themselves underpaid, they were entitled to use satire. To our modern minds, a couple of nasty remarks in rhyme do not amount to much. To a society as deeply obsessed by honour and pride as the Island Celtic, a satire was not just a friendly jest but a lethal curse. A satirized ruler could just as well resign and jump off a cliff, as his subjects, let alone other regents, simply would not respect him any more. We'll go into this topic in the chapter on enchantment, as the making of satire involved a remarkable cursing ritual. If a fili was wronged, the poet's guild saw to it that the satire got around. Likewise, if a poet demanded a gift, the host was not permitted to withhold it, no matter the consequences. From time to time, this situation became unbearable.

Many filid were famous for their greed and insolence, a topic which comes up in several old manuscripts but which is ignored by romantically minded researchers. There was a public revolt against the filid at Drumketta in 590. At that time, they numbered c. 15 000 and were an unbearable nuisance. It took all the diplomatic efforts of St. Columba, himself a former fili, to prevent their abolition. Instead, they had to accept a massive reduction of their number and wages.

At the end of the seventh century, high king Aed Mac Ainmirech likewise regarded them a burden on society and attempted to outlaw their profession for good. He was not successful in this matter, but he achieved a further reduction of their numbers and restrictions of their political and financial power. His laws settled that henceforth, only one ollam had to be retained by each king. Each of these ollams had a clearly defined status, received a specific amount of land and a specific wage for his songs. These laws associated master poets with specific locations, which in turn did much for the development of poetic academies. The regulation of fixed wages for poetic effort was such an important issue that it was included in the *Trefhocul* poem, recorded in the *Book of Leinster*. Essentially, the *Trefhocul* is a lengthy bit of poesy giving remedies for faulty poems. *Trefhocul* means three words, that is, three words to repair poems. In it you can learn that there are 12 basic errors that keep occurring in song and poetry, and as no doubt you are as enchanted by the neat lists of the filid as I am, here are the full twelve: 1. Wrongness, 2. Too many rhymes, 3. Overlong, 4. Overshort, 5. Want of emphasis, 6. Overemphasis, 7. Absent to a present, 8. Singular to plural, 9. False gender, 10. False alliteration, 11. False rhyme, 12. Error. Each of these flaws is listed together with two ways of repairing the matter, this yields the three words (one wrong word and two right ones) out of

which the *Trefhocul* are composed. The poem is not exactly easy reading, containing, as it does, 365 measures of poetry. Presumably these correspond with the 365 days of the year, the 365 joints and sinews of the body, the 365 diseases and the 365 healing herbs. This connects the art of the poets with the art of medicine and the great work of making humans whole and complete. We may speculate whether the filid saw their art as a form of healing or whole-making. That the regulations regarding the status, wage and amount of retainers were part of this important poem shows quite clearly that the filid, after having been almost outlawed by the outraged population, took great care to stay in line.

Under a Golden Branch

Another interesting question is how the filid appeared in public. Most people have their bias towards Druids in white, regarding the costume of bards and filid they are usually less specific. The tale of Ferchertne and Nede records that minor poets traveled under a branch of copper. Such branches were carried by the retainers of poets, who held them high above their lords. Poets of medium experience travelled under a branch of silver, while the highest ranks of ollam sported a branch of gold. We can only speculate what these branches may have looked like, provided they existed at all and were not a later medieval invention. So far the archaeologists have not unearthed a poet's branch in Ireland. In 1984 excavators at the oppidum of Manching, Bavaria unearthed a forked wand, 70cm in length, dated c250 BCE, which had been carefully decorated with bronze woodbine leaves, buds and berries, plus gold foil showing triskeles . The entire wand was covered with gold. Whether this 'golden bough' was a poet's wand of office or a piece of religious equipment remains an open question. However, there are several otherworldly entities in Irish myth who appeared carrying magical branches. Also, there is a distinct link between the bards and filid and the magic of the wildwood. Taliesin, for instance, not only expresses his love for the high trees, but hints at a subtle link between bards, trees, blossoms and bushes. We will look into this topic later on. Thus, we cannot be sure if these poet's branches ever existed on the physical plane. What is reasonably certain is that they existed as an archetypal form, as a dream image, and as a magickal reality. Maybe one day you will find yourself walking leisurely through the forest, carrying a branch of enchantment in your hand, and learn the meaning of the wildwood-wand as you go along.

Another fascinating item is the feather cloak. Ferchertne and Nede contested for the feather cloak of the chief poet. The blind Druid Mog Ruith put on a similar feather cloak, or possibly a feather mask with long wings, when he rose into the skies to work his spells and enchantments against the invasion of the Munstermen under high king Cormac Mac Airt. The feather cloak of the chief poets, if we can trust the myths, was of three colours. At the top it was radiant gold, the middle was made out of bright feathers and the bottom feathers speckled. Of course we cannot be certain if all filid, or even the ollams all wore feather cloaks. It would be inviting to hallucinate

them all in this attire, just like Druids are usually hallucinated in white, but I trust your critical faculties and hope that you'll resist the temptation of generalizing given such lack of evidence. Anyway, counterparts to such feather costumes can be found elsewhere. Some feather cloaks were simply insignia of rank and status, but in several cases, they had a distinctly shamanistic function. There were shamans in Siberia, for instance, who donned feather cloaks when they set out to fly into the otherworlds. Of course they did not fly in their physical bodies but in their imagination, pretty much like Mog Ruith did when he sent his Druidic fire against the Druids of Tara. The cloak can be understood as a symbol of an ability, as a sign of office, and as a tool that makes it easier for the shaman to produce a specific consciousness.

When a costume is closely associated with a specific trance state, wearing it will make the trance easier. In Nepal, the shamans of the northern Magar have a headdress consisting of bundles of bird feathers and leaves from their tree of life. Again, it is the ability to fly into the otherworlds which these items signify. Feather cloaks were also popular among the Wu, the early shamans of China. The Wu had a strong influence on the development of early Taoism, and to this day, a *feather clad one* can be a term signifying a Taoist sorcerer. I suspect that the feather cloak of the Irish filid may well be related to these Eurasian Shamanic traditions, but wouldn't dream of arguing about it. In the last years, a growing fashion to label any bit of Island Celtic trance practise as 'shamanic' has collided with an opposing dogma that will only accept serene priests of the no-funny-business-school as genuine. People argue passionately about the existence or non-existence of Celtic shamanism, but what they are really getting excited about is the question, whether their own tradition (real or imaginary) ought to include wild and shamanic elements or whether it should all be done in a dull, dignified and churchy fashion. Well, if you need a tradition to legitimize your activities, your magick won't amount to much. Perhaps all Irish ollams went around wearing feathers, and perhaps only a crazed handful of daring individualists did so. Who knows? And who cares? More important, as far as the actual practise is concerned, is what you need to get going.

Another sign of the poetic vocation may have been a distinct haircut. The *Fate of the Sons of Tuirenn*, a well known medieval Irish tale, hints that the poets used to tie their hair in a special knot. Again, no further evidence appears. Last, the Brehon laws permitted certain professional castes to carry moderately harmless weapons to defend themselves against mad dogs. Priests for instance were allowed their crook. Poets were allowed to carry a tabhall-lorg (tablet staff) inscribed with ogham. When St. Patrick was touring Ireland, he was met by some men carrying inscribed staffs (or tablets), according to a MS. from 807.

Celtic Harps

Now if you were asked to imagine a poet, you would probably imagine him carrying a harp. This instrument, though closely connected with the art of the poets, needs not be as self evident as many would have it. For a start, the Celtic harp of today is a refined late medieval instrument. The oldest surviving Celtic harp is the so called Brian Boru harp (Trinity college, Dublin) and comes from the 15th century. Illustrated manuscripts give evidence that there were harps in earlier centuries, but these were not traditional Celtic instruments but copied from harps that had come from the Continent. The early harps, favoured by the bards and filid of prehistory and the early medieval period, were much smaller instruments. Usually they had a rectangular shape and five or six strings, which were probably tuned in a pentatonic scale and played with fingers and plectrum.

Similar items were favoured by the skalds and skops of the Germanic cultures, a magnificent specimen has been unearthed in the Sutton Hoo burial. Such instruments were not very refined, but they were robust and could be carried on a journey. In ancient Gaul, a type of harp was known that closely resembled the Greek lyre. The statue of the god of Paule, Britanny, shows such an instrument. Unlike many Greek lyres, the one from Paule had seven strings, which makes me wonder if it was really tuned to a pentatomic scale. Nowadays everybody assumes that the bards of Britain and the filid of Ireland harped while they sang and recited. Some of them evidently did. One of the Taliesins chanted that he is a harper and a musician, as well as lots of other things. However, there is also evidence that musicians enjoyed a low status in Ireland. Harpers were higher on the social scale than the other musicians, in fact they were the only musicians who had any legal rights, and an honour price protecting their lives.

The Brehon laws established that the honour price of a harper was four cows. This proves that harpers were counted as nobility, if very low nobility, as only the members of the higher classes were valued in cattle. The other musicians had no honour price worth mentioning, and probably led a pretty unpleasant life. On the whole, most musicians abroad in Europe during the medieval period had a very low social and legal status, unless they happened to be employed by some mighty aristocrat. Many countries treated them like actors, vagabonds or beggars, meaning that almost anybody could abuse, cheat or exploit them. Female musicians were in a worse position, many were expected to work as prostitutes when off stage, and there were no laws to protect them from rape. The Irish harpers may have had a really privileged position in society, compared to what their counterparts in other European countries had to live with, nevertheless, they were still considered as rude labourers and entertainers. Many bards and filid, just like the Continental troubadours, wouldn't have dreamed of doing something as vulgar as making music with their own hands. When they sang, chanted or prophesied, they had a skilled servant who accompanied the song on a harp or some other instrument.

Before leaving the subject of harps, it might be interesting to wonder about the way they were played. Gerald of Wales wrote quite a bit about this subject, and recorded that the Welsh and Irish harpers used to tune their instruments in B flat. This scale, and the very similar one of E flat, are very popular in Bretonic folk music. Gerald wrote that in Wales, harping was popular among the nobility, especially among noble ladies, who were ever ready to assault guests with their playing. All tunes, so we hear, used to begin and end with the sound of B flat. Its really sad that we have no idea what B flat sounded like in the late 12th C. Strange as it is, we know more of the scales of the late bronze time, when plenty of tuned trumpets, always in pairs, were made in C, E flat and E, than about harping in medieval Britain.

Gerald also recorded that to his amazement, the Welsh harpers play fast and that their music is nevertheless soothing. I suspect that we are dealing with a trance phenomena here. As I mentioned in *Seidways*, monotonous drumming at a speed between 3,5 and 4,5 beats per second tends to increase theta brain wave activity in passive listeners after approximately 10-15 minutes. Theta brain waves are typical for deep trance states and highly lucid visions. If you play harp you will know from experience that 4,5 beats per second is an easy matter, and that indeed harping, especially when you play without thinking, can be a wonderful trance induction. It also has healing virtues - Geoffrey recorded in his *Vita Merlini* that the mad mountain seer was brought to his senses by a harper who sought him out in the wild forest and played till the poor madman recalled his human past and began to weep uncontrollably, well, who could blame him. The harper took Merlin/Myrddin to the castle of King Rhydderch Hael, where civilized court life soon made him go crazy again. You could call this an amusing anecdote regarding early British psychotherapy. Had the harper used a drum, everyone would be falling

Coins 6
top l: Remi, wolf. top r: cisalpine Gaul, silver, wolf or fox? center: Silvanekten, 17 mm, wolf devours human (or frog-faced alien)
bottom l: Vindelici, gold, 16 mm, red deer
bottom r: Viromandui, bronze, 14 mm, multi-horned deer

over themselves in an effort to prove British shamanism. Well, it certainly is, there were plenty of shamans in Siberia, Eurasia and Scandinavia who didn't drum but induced trances and conjured spirits using very simple string instruments. So did Orpheus, why don't we find him in the books of the neo-shamanistic fringe? In medieval Irish myth, one of the gods, the Tuatha de Danann, the Dagda (Good God) was a skilled harper. The Dagda invented the three basic tunes of early Irish music. This were the sad tune that made everyone weep with grief, the happy tune that made folks dance on the tables and the soothing tune, sending the audience to sleep and dream. If you make music, it might be worth developing three such tunes for everyday needs. Need I add that simple, portable harps and lyres, ranging from say, 5-12 strings are rather easy to make using a suitable piece of wood, some zither pegs and nylon strings?

From a Dark Cell

When it comes to the training of the poets we are very much in the dark. It is one thing to say that the filid learned an enormous amount of tales, songs and verses, and quite another to explain how they managed to achieve this feat. Luckily, there is one fascinating snippet of information that may answer this question.

John Matthews, in his *Taliesin* (1991) offers an unexpected gem from '*The Memories of the Marquis of Clanricarde*'. If we can trust this account, as late as 1722 Irish poets used to train their students under very special conditions. The budding poets received their education in a secluded low house far from human settlements. Special care was taken that the scenery afforded few distractions, and that the setting was as quiet as possible. The house was divided into a series of cells, each of them containing a young poet on his bed, plus a minimum of furniture. The building had no windows, care was taken that neither sound nor light could get in and I wouldn't dream of commenting on the air quality in there. When the students were memorizing their lore, they were allowed to leave the house only during the hours of darkness. By day they rested in their dark little cells. From time to time a tutor entered the premises, carrying a small candle. For the students, who doubtlessly suffered from sensory-withdrawal, the small flickering flame must have been stunning. By its light, they were told tales and songs and made to repeat them. They also had to write down what they recalled from yesterday's lesson. Then the teacher left and the students returned into the dark womb/tomb where they repeated their lines and experienced the legendary events in wonderfully lucid visions. When they told their tales in later life, these poets knew from direct experience what they were talking about.

While this account is certainly late, it does show that the master poets knew about trance states and how to make use of them in training. Of course we cannot be certain that this is really an old custom, merely that it is a highly efficient one. Mind you, we are not simply dealing with an unusual way of education here. Prolonged periods in darkness, silence and comparative isolation feature prominently in the initiation rites of many cultures. They are meant to shatter the former personality of the initiate, to produce crisis, to induce a consciousness that comes close to death or insanity. Out of the shambles of the former identity, the initiate is reborn. The filid who made it through such a period of training in darkness had been through a lot. They had seen visions denied to ordinary people, and of course they were so transformed that they hardly comprehended their earlier life any more. This is the second birth, a state of awareness that forms the foundation for the training of many shamans, sorcerers and healers world-wide.

If you wish to explore such techniques, I suggest you spend plenty of time in total darkness. Some people get depressive under such circumstances, others get excited. Close the door and windows, put a piece of cloth over your eyes, lie down on the hard floor and tell a long and convoluted tale to yourself. Martin, quoted by Matthews, informs us that in the 18th C. the bards of the western Highlands used to retire to a secluded place for a day, where they shut all doors and windows, wrapped a plaid around their heads and laid on the floor with a stone on the belly in order to find poetic inspiration. The stone is a fascinating element in this formula, as it places the bard in a position closely resembling burial. It is often from a state closely resembling death, when the human ego has been thoroughly suspended, that the greatest visions arise. Part of this may be achieved by play acting.

When we look at the custom of covering the head or eyes with cloth, we find some parallels in the classical world. A large icon of Epona, from Beihingen, shows the goddess seated between seven horses.

Beneath her you can see a man riding a chariot with three horses and a man standing in front of an altar. He has an amphora (of wine) and a cloth over his head. Beside him, another man is dragging a sacrificial pig. The cloth on the head of the sacrificant is of importance. To cover your head with a cloth is to veil yourself from worldly things, to go into the dark and to encounter the goddess on her own plane, that of the inspired imagination.

Such a cloth may come in handy should you wish to trance or meditate under difficult circumstances. Rowlands (1985) refers to the *Memories of the Marquis of Clanricarde* and proposes that a similar style of training may have been favoured by the bards of Britain. As you will read in a later chapter, Mona, the island Anglesey, was called *the dark island, cell of song*, by Iolo Goch in the 14th century. Now Mona is by no means darker than any other part of Wales. If bards were being trained in Mona, as Druids presumably were prior to the year 60, then the reference is to their training habits. Though the reference is hardly proof of anything, it does hint at darkness and cells of song. We can keep this in mind as we go along. Numerous seers and visionaries embraced darkness in order to come to the pure and flowing stream of original, undefined selfhood. The darkness and silence of the enchanter's secret cells, however, is not just a useful training tool. In another sense it creates a consciousness that goes beyond the limits of ordinary human thinking. Most people simply disintegrate when they are left in darkness and silence for too long - it's a common tactic to 'brainwash' someone. I once read about some experiments when well trained soldiers were put into a water tank where they floated comfortably in total silence and absolute darkness. After a while, they forgot their bodies and began to experience wonderfully lucid visions. These hallucinations became so 'real' that the soldiers began to doubt their sanity (actually they should have done so before they joined the army) and began to struggle against the hallucinations. A more experienced mind-explorer would have accepted the visions, instead of fighting them, and may have come to some rewarding new insights by following the way of no-resistance. In some trances, the more you struggle against unpleasant thoughts, the stronger they become. It's much easier to deal with such material by allowing it to float by and fade away without making a scene. The soldiers tried to fight the visions and to keep their sanity - and of course they simply went nuts under the strain. We can only speculate what happened to the poets under these circumstances. Those who made it may have had more insights than they would ever dare to utter.

Land of the Living

And here we come to the point where the known world and the otherworlds interface. A good many poets hinted that they had been born or raised in the otherworld. Nede chanted that he came from a colourful land without falsehood, where the nine hazels of the poet's art grow and truth is measured by excellence. These are common euphemisms for the Irish otherworlds, you can finds them in several manuscripts. The Irish god of the sea, Manannan, sang of Moy Mell (The Pleasant Plain) under the ocean:

Unknown is wailing or treachery
In the familiar cultivated land,
There is nothing rough or harsh,
But sweet music striking on the ear.
Without grief, without sorrow, without death,
Without any sickness, without debility,
That is the sign of Emain,
Uncommon, an equal marvel.
A beauty of a wondrous land
Whose aspects are lovely,
Whose view is a fair country,
Incomparable in its haze....
Wealth, treasure of every hue,
Are in the gentle land, a beauty of freshness,
Listening to sweet music,
Drinking the best of wine...
A beautiful game, most delightful
They play (sitting) at the luxurious wine,
Men and gentle women under a bush
Without sin, without crime...

These lines from *The Voyage of Bran*, translated by Kuno Meyer, are pretty typical for several sorts of Irish otherworlds. When Mider invited Etain to come with him to the otherworld, he chanted of a wondrous land where the hair is the colour of the primrose, where the body is as fair as snow, where teeth are white and cheeks are foxglove red, where grief and sorrow are unknown, abundant streams of wine and mead flow through the gentle hills, and youth never grows into old age. Here all people are handsome, conception is without sin and stain, and everyone feeds on as much pork as possible. This otherworld, so we learn, is under the hollow hills, but it is also here on earth. As Mider puts it, it is the sin of Adam which prevents humans from

Coins 7, ophidian images
top l, r, center: snakes of the Boii
bottom: unknown, found in the treasure of Jersey

seeing the people of the Sidhe and their wonderful, bright and many-coloured land. I very much agree - as soon as the Christians turned the best things of life into sins, the land of joy and refreshment indeed became invisible to most of the population.

A fairy lady from an otherworld sang:
I have come from the lands of the living in which there is neither death, nor sin, nor strife, we enjoy perpetual feasts without anxiety, and benevolence without contention. A large Sidh (Shee, 'fairy-mound') is where we dwell, so that it is hence we are called the Sidh (Shee) people.

She asked young Connla to accompany her to the otherworld, far beyond the western horizon, to embark with her in a boat of glass and to sail to the lands of hope, promise and eternal pleasure. A similar boat (coracle) of glass, in the hands of a pilgrim, is briefly alluded to in a Taliesin song - a vehicle to the Elysium far beyond the misery of the mortal realm. In spite of Druidic counter-spells, Connla gave in to the fairy lady's chanting. Together, the two set sail and disappeared into the sunset.

To this day there is a well in the otherworld called Connla's Well, deep below the green blue sea, where the nine hazels of poetic excellence are growing. From the well spring the streams of the senses. Each year the salmon of knowledge come traveling up these rivers until they reach the very source of all senses, the well of poetry itself. In one enchanted hour, the nine hazels simultaneously sprout leaves, blossoms, nuts and all of these cascade into the well. The waters turn purple, the salmon

eat of the nuts of wisdom, and carry the new wisdom into the world. You find references to this well in *The Adventures of Cormac in the Land of Promise*, the *Dindshenchas* describe a very similar well out of which the river Boyne is said to spring. The river Shannon is likewise connected with such a well. This one is called the well of Segais. Both the well of Segais and the well of the Boyne are associated with women (or goddesses?) who died when they approached the underwater-fountain too closely. From Connla's Well five rivers flow, they are identified with the senses and as Manannan reveals, the folk of many arts (the filid) are those who drink both from the streams and the well itself. The well of the Boyne has seven streams, you might wonder whether there are seven senses, luckily Taliesin tells us that this is the case. The extra senses are speech (to call) and instinct. The filid knew of this well, and went to visit it. So can you, with a bit of experience in trance magick, dreaming or astral projection, and return from the otherworld as one who has learned much, and transformed the entire world in the process. Remember how you dreamed or imagined your way into a mound? You can use the same technique to imagine yourself traveling to the otherworlds deep below the waves. The bards, poets and filid did the same. If you wish to share their initiation, go to the source of the senses, the secret well beneath the bottomless sea, the colourful land beyond the western horizon, the splendid halls beneath the hollow hills. You can find them in your dreaming, in your astral voyages, but you can also open your mind, wake up, and find the otherworld is here.

7. Three Rays of the Awen

Bardic Frenzy

In the 6th century, the venerable Gildas composed a bitter sermon against the evils of his time. His work, entitled *The Ruin of Britain* is a vitriolic castigation of the British kings. Gildas was probably acquainted with several of them, and knew what he was talking about when he accused them for their tyrannical ways, their vicious vices and unchristian conduct. One king in particular attracted his wrath. We will meet him with some frequency in the following chapters, so you may as well get used to him now. This was Maelgwn Hir (the Tall), king of Gwynedd in northern Wales, whose name may loosely be translated as 'Great Hound'. Maelgwn (latinized Maglocunos), the Dragon of the Island, great-grandson of the legendary Cunedda, had begun a most promising and pious churchly career when he abandoned his throne and became a monk. Possibly Gildas knew Maelgwn personally at this time, which would explain why he gave so much special attention to this distinguished character. Well, the cloisterly retreat of Maelgwn was not to last for very long. Soon enough the monarch decided to abandon the spiritual life. He returned to the throne and established his power with such violence that eventually he became the most powerful king of the British. In the process he murdered his own wife, and later a nephew, so he could marry the widow of the deceased. Gildas frowned on such behaviour, just like he deplored the fact that a former child of the church could have resumed the worldly life with such enthusiasm.

A legend given in the *Anomalous Laws* explains the Traeth Maelgwn (Beach of Maelgwn) in the Dovey estuary. At the time, Maelgwn had not yet achieved supremacy over the other rulers of Wales. In order to determine the high king, all contestants had their thrones set on the beach, and vowed that whoever would remain on his throne longer than the others would receive the title Brenin Pennaf (chief king) and authority over all other rulers. All regents took their seats and composed themselves in patience. After a little while, the waters began to creep towards the strand. The ever hungry tide was returning. White crested surges came rolling over the beach, hissing and foaming, and one after the other, the thrones were submerged by the fury of the waves. Only Maelgwn remained seated, composed in due serenity, and watched the brine-soaked regents struggling for the land. His counselor Maeldaf had cunningly attached great waxen wings to Maelgwn's throne, and with the aid of this contraption, Maelgwn and his royal seat floated on the waves.

When we return to Gildas, we find one matter that attracted the sage's scorn was vanity. To Gildas disgust, Maelgwn had little interest in listening to the praises of god but was more fascinated by hearing his own praise sung by the courtly bards. In Ifor Williams translation, Maelgwn cared only for …*your own praises (which are nothing); the voice of the rascally crew yelling forth, like Bacchanalian revellers, full of lies and foaming phlegm, so as to besmear everyone near them.*

These words contain several ideas which may be worth considering. Every king of 6th century Britain employed a number of bards at his court whose functions included the chanting of praise songs, be it for their employers and their royal family, be it for noble guests who were visiting the court. Such compositions were a matter of status, and it is unlikely that any king of the age could have done without them. Gildas tells us something about the style of the performance which may come as a surprise to all who expect dignity from a bard. The frenzied outbursts of Maelgwn's bards are in strong contrast to the terms Gildas uses for the praise of god. When he states that

Maelgwn cared no more for the gentle voices of Christ's soldiers nor the melodious chanting of the church, he gives testimony that bardic chanting was often neither melodious nor gentle.

Anyone acquainted with obsession trances will recognize that the bardic performance contained a wildly shamanic element. The Bacchanalian revellers remind us of the ecstatic cult of Bacchus, whose followers were in a frenzy of rage, ecstasy and intoxication. Nowadays Bacchus is well known as a deity associated with wine. Wine, however, needs not be the substance you can buy in a shop today. Modern wine is the outcome of countless generations of selective breeding. A lot of selection was not applied for reasons of taste or effect but to make the plant more resistant against environmental conditions and had economical reasons. There are around 250 chemical substances in wine, and the relations between them vary. Some varieties which were well known in the ancient world have long disappeared, and with them the effect they had on the mind. Some sorts of wine had such drastic effects on consciousness that they were outlawed.

The cult of Bacchus was not only related to wine. In ancient Greece, a number of psychedelic substances were added to initiation-wines, such as belladonna, henbane, mandrake, and poppy. The same practise is attested from ancient Egypt. An Egyptian myth claims that the goddess Isis conceived her child, the falcon headed Horus, after eating grapes (Rätsch 1988). It is hardly surprising when such a sorcerous

---

Celtic Iberian script.

CELTIC IBERIAN SCRIPT, 3 C. BCE

Sound	Glyphs	Sound	Glyphs	Sound	Glyphs
A	ᑭ ᑭ ◁ D	N	/\	PU BU	□
G	⟨ V C G	O	○ ⊙ □	TA DA	X
D	X	P	Γ Γ Γ	TE DE	⊖ ⊕ ⊘ ⊟ ◇
E	⊭ Ⴈ ⊨ ⊨	S	Ƨ Ч Ƨ	TI DI LI	Ψ Ψ ¥ ¥
U	↑ ↑ ↑	Q	⊠ ⊠ X	TO DO	⊔ ⊔ ⊔
Z	T	R	◁ ◁ ⍴ ◊ Я	TU DU	⊗ ⊕ △ △
H	H H H	Š	M	CA GA	⋀ ⋀ ⋀ ⋔ Я
TH	⊕ ⊘ ◇	T	Ψ Ψ Ψ Ψ	CE KE	⟨ ⟩ ⟨ ◁ D E G C
IJ	Ⴎ /\ N	PA BA	I	CI GI	⟋⟍ ⟋⟍ 丩
K	K ✳ ⋮	PE BE	Я Я Я Я 25 25 W	CO GO	⊠ ⊠ X ⊠
L	Ⲅ ∧ ∧ ∧	PI BI	Γ Γ	CU GU	∪ ◇ ○
M	⋎ ⋎ ⋓ ⋓	PO BO HO	✳ ✳ ✳ ✳		

broth confers amazing visions and unusual states of mind, and may explain why the wine of antiquity was venerated as a sacred substance.

Nevertheless the cult of Bacchus, with its ecstatic dances, its furious music and its inspired madness, is not simply a matter that can be explained away as a drug-crazed orgy. The revellers may have been intoxicated by one or more psychoactive substances, but then, no drug, however powerful, is a guarantee of religious frenzy or genius. For one thing, to use a drug for a specific means requires a trained mind. We have all seen people who handled alcohol wisely, and others who simply became vulgar and disgusting. That the Celts used alcohol for festivities is well known, and Celtic beer was occasionally refined with psychoactive substances, such as belladonna, henbane, broom etc. Hemp and sleeping poppy are also possible. The former was cultivated early in the Hallstatt period, while stylized buds of the latter appear on fibula and ornaments of the La Tène period. This practise survived up to the late middle ages, when a number of laws were passed to prohibit additives. The famed German purity laws, first passed in Thuringa and Bavaria, permitting only the use of hops, malt and water. These laws were enforced by church and king, neither of whom approved of hallucinogenic experiences. Hops, with their characteristic bitter taste, were unknown in earlier times. The plant has a sedative effect and preserves the beer, so it could be stored. Before it became known in Europe, beer had to be freshly brewed for each occasion. Also, the store was drunk to the last drop, as it couldn't be kept.

The same psychoactive substances that went into beer were doubtlessly added to honey mead to fortify it, and must have been known to the bards and the members of the nobility who could afford such expensive beverages. One of the Taliesins composed a *Song of Ale* which contains several allusions to the brewers art, such as:

…He shall steep it in the Llyn,
Until it shall sprout.
He shall steep it another time
Until it is sodden.
Not for a long time will be finished
What the elements produce.
Let his vessels be washed,
Let his wort be clear.
And when there shall be an exciter of song,
Let it be brought from the cell,
Let it be brought before kings.
In splendid festivals… (BoT 20)

This strange alchemy might refer to brewing, but it could also refer to the refinement the budding bard undergoes while ripening to perfection in his shady cell. Another song by a Taliesin gives a couple of dark hints regarding the brewing of a magical elixir. This procedure is associated with the Druids, so perhaps we are not simply dealing with the production of alcohol. As the poem is highly inspiring, and as I know that you love riddles, let me quote it here.

The Chair of Taliessin

Book of Taliessin 13

I am the agitator
Of the praise of God the Ruler.
With respect to the concerns of song,
The requisites of a profound speaker,
A bard, with the breast of an astrologer.
When he recites
The Awen at the setting in of the evening.
On the fine night of a fine day.
Bards loquacious the light will separate.
Their praise will not bring me to associate,
In the strath, on the course,
With aspect of great cunning.
I am not a mute artist,
Conspicuous among the bards of the people.
I animate the bold,
I influence the heedless;
I wake up the looker on,
The enlightener of bold kings.
I am not a shallow artist,
Conspicuous among kindred bards,
The likeness of a subtle portion,
The deep ocean (is) suitable.
Who has filled me with hatred?
A price in every unveiling.
When the dew is undisturbed,
And the wheat is reaped,
And the bees are gentle,
And myrrh and frankincense,
And transmarine aloes.
And the golden pipes of Lleu,
And a curtain of excellent silver,
And a ruddy gem, and berries.
And the foam of the sea.
Why will the fountain hasten
Water-cresses of purifying juicy quality?
What will join together the common people?
Wort, the nobility of liquor.
And a load that the moon separates,
The placid gentleness of Merlyn. (Verlyn)
And philosophers of intelligence

Will study about the moon.
And the influence of an order of men,
Exposed to the breeze of the sky.
And a soddening and effusion,
And a portion after effusion,
And the coracle of glass,
In the hand of the pilgrim,
And the valiant one and pitch,
And the honoured Segyrffyg,
And medical plants.
A place of complete benefit,
And bards and blossoms.
And gloomy bushes,
And primroses and small herbs,
And the points of the tree-shrubs.
And deficiency and possession,
And frequent pledging.
And wine overflowing the brim,
From Rome to Rossed.
And deep still water,
Its stream the gift of God.
Or if it will be wood the purifier,
Fruitful its increase.
Let the brewer give a heat,
Over a cauldron of five trees,
And the river of Gwiawn,
And the influence of fine weather,
And honey and trefoil,
And mead horns intoxicating
Pleasing to a sovereign,
The gift of the Druids.

Of course the easiest approach for this song is to take it as a praise of drugs and the states that can be attained with them. We could use it to speculate how much drug-lore the bards had, and whether they made use of strange toxins to find vision and inspiration. On the other hand there are plenty of shamanic cultures worldwide which achieve states of inspiration and ecstasis without the use of drugs. I would not argue that the bards were necessarily drunk or otherwise drugged when it is quite as possible that they achieved their states of divine inspiration without such tools. The human brain is able to produce an amazing variety of consciousness states. Some of them may have a chemical background, as every drug effect that changes awareness corresponds to an effect the brain can and does produce on its own, given a bit of stimulation. Each psychoactive substance that can be found in nature is similar to neurotransmitters and hormones which are produced in the brain. Indeed the so called placebo effect is good evidence that the effects of all sorts of drugs can be produced by the mind itself, given a bit of proper suggestion, stimulation and belief.

This, however, is not all there is to an ecstatic consciousness. The brain can also produce radical shifts of awareness when different parts of it are activated, when its rhythms change, when unusual neural pathways are activated and so on. Motion and dance can change awareness, confusing sensual stimulation, swaying, shuddering and shaking - the history of all cultures is full of methods to produce specific states of mind. One could even claim that culture is a set of behaviour forms and sensual stimulants which are established to produce specific forms of consciousness. Whatever people in any given culture do or avoid defines their group consciousness.

In this sense it might be useful to propose the idea of closed and open cultures. A culture that permits experiment with unusual forms of awareness lives and evolves, a culture that prohibits deviation from the norm is a closed system and will eventually suffer from entropy, inertia and bad taste. Another possibility which has not been sufficiently explored is the changes of consciousness which result when the Ch'i, the life energy (or the kundalini-fire serpent) moves around within the body. Last, there may well exist changes of awareness which are not produced by body or form but come from the formless self that creates the world and all its forms each second anew. All of these, and more, provide a wide field of new and unusual states of mind.

If the bards shrieked and foamed, and had so little control over themselves that they besmeared everyone around them with their foaming saliva, this points at a form of shamanic obsession. If they were capable of composing and remembering poetry at the same time there must have been an element of control and inspiration to the procedure. Between madness and genius, the bards performed their office. To explain this with simple intoxication won't do.

The Spirit of Prophecy

It might be observed by the critical reader (I hope this means you) that a single reference written by an angry priest may not be enough to confirm that the bardic vocation involved states of ecstatic madness. Luckily, we have the evidence of Giraldus Cambrensis (Gerald of Wales). Gerald toured Wales in the company of Baldwin, Archbishop of Canterbury in 1188 to recruit volunteers for a crusade. At the time, Wales was one of the last strongholds of Celtic culture and a wild place that few cultured people knew anything about. As Gerald was not just an ambitious churchman

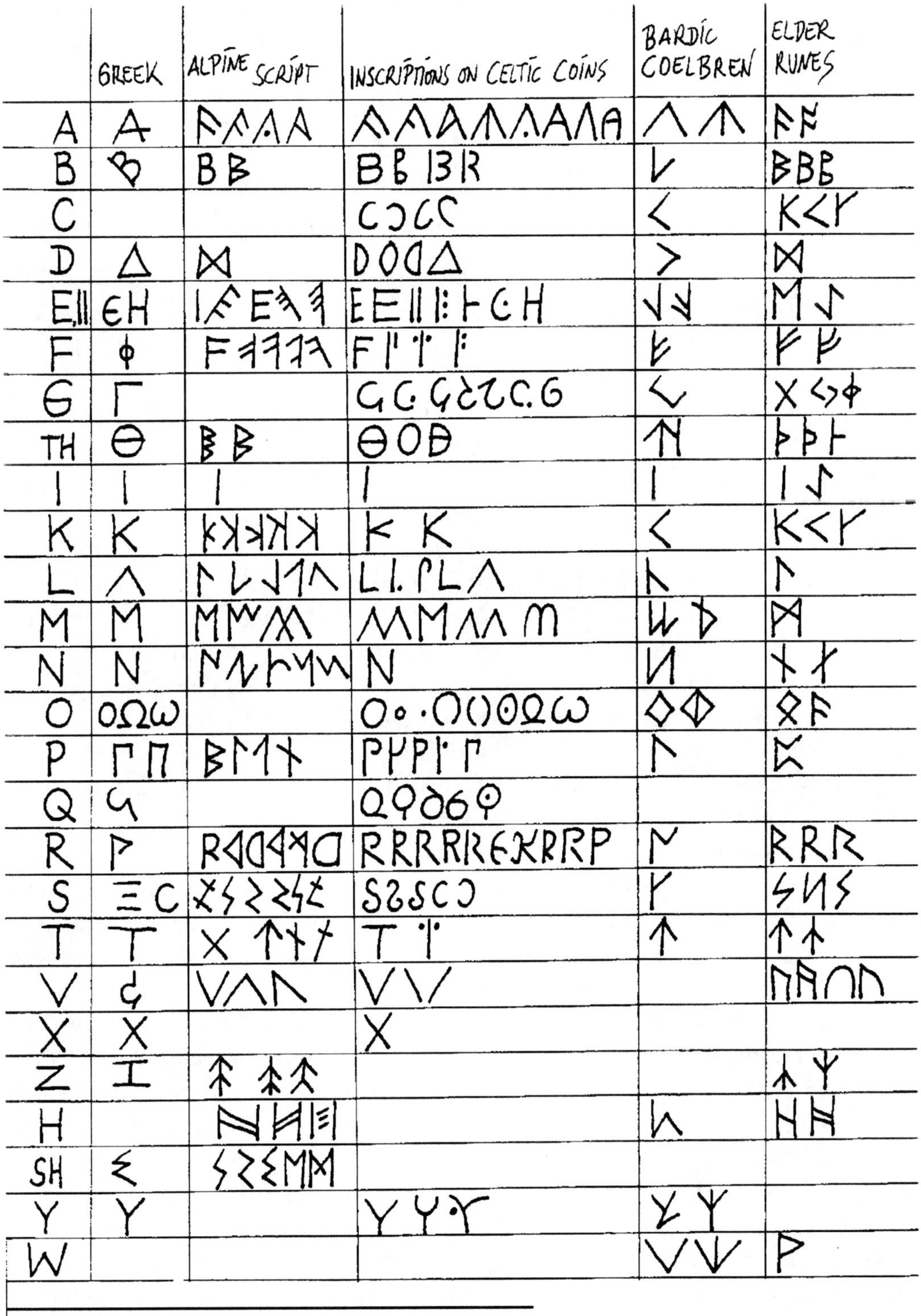

	GREEK	ALPINE SCRIPT	INSCRIPTIONS ON CELTIC COINS	BARDIC COELBREN	ELDER RUNES
A	A	⊦ΛΛΛ	ΛΛΛΛΛΛΛΛ	Λ Λ	⊦⊦
B	ß	BB	Bß ß R	V	BBB
C	C		CϽCϹ	<	KᐸↃ
D	Δ	Ⴑ	DOʘΔ	>	Ⴑ
E,II	ЄH	IƐEᘓ	EEIIⴌ⊦CH	√√	MↃ
F	φ	Fᐢᐡᐢ	FIᐟ᛫	⻌	⊦⊦
G	Γ		CᏟᏟᏃᏃᏟᏟᏀ	⅃	XↃφ
TH	θ	ßß	θOθ	Λ	⊦⊦⊦
I	I	I	I	I	I S
K	K	⊬⊬⊁⊁K	⊬ K	<	KᐸↃ
L	Λ	ᒥᒪᒍᐱ	LI᛫ᒉᒪΛ	Ⴑ	⅃
M	M	MMᴟ	ΛΛMΛΛ m	⊔⊅	Ⴑ
N	N	ᴎⴌⴓⵑ	N	Ⴈ	⊬⊬
O	OΩω		Oo᛫ꓳꓳOΩω	◊φ	⊗⊦
P	ΓΠ	ßⴌↃ	PↄPᛁᐧᒥ	Γ	Ⴑ
Q	ϙ		QϙϘΟϙφ		
R	ᚱ	RᑕᑕᐢⴌↃ	RRRRↃↄKRRP	Ⴈ	RRR
S	ΞC	ⵋᛏᛦᛦ⵷	SⵦSCↃ	ⵑ	ⵑⴎⵑ
T	T	X⊹⊹⊹	T᛫ᛁ	⊹	⊹⊹
V	ᘛ	VΛΛ	V\/		ΠᐱΛΠ
X	X		X		
Z	Ⅰ	ⵝ ⵝⵝ			⊹⊬
H	H	ⴼⴼⵀⵌ		Ⴈ	Hⴼ
SH	Ⴒ	ⵌⵌⵀⵀ			
Y	Y		�74⵲⵲	�⵲	�⵲
W	W			ⵠⵠ	⊦

Letters on Celtic coins in comparison with Old Alphabets

but also a prolific author, he was interested in anything that seemed unusual to him and wrote a lively and highly entertaining account about his experiences. This account is full of odd items and amazingly tall tales, but in between the crazy stuff (which Gerald in all likeliness did not believe, but told for its entertainment value) there are surprisingly accurate accounts of customs and local beliefs. One of the chapters in his *Description of Wales* supports the evidence given by Gildas. Let me quote parts of Lewis Thorpe's translation:

Welsh soothsayers, who behave as if they are possessed

Among the Welsh there are certain individuals called 'awenyddion' who behave as if they are possessed by devils. You will not find them anywhere else. When you consult them about some problem, they immediately go into a trance and lose control of their senses, as if they are possessed. They do not answer the question put to them in any logical way. Words stream from their mouths, incoherently and apparently meaningless and without any sense at all, but all the same well expressed: and if you listen carefully to what they say you will receive the solution to your problem. When it is all over, they will recover from their trance, as if they were ordinary people waking from a heavy sleep, but you have to give them a good shake before they regain control of themselves. There are two odd things about this: when they have given their answer, they do not recover from their paroxysm unless they are shaken violently and forced to come round again; and when they return to their senses they can remember nothing of what they have said in the interval. If by chance they are questioned a second or a third time on the same matter, they will give completely different answers...

Before we continue with Gerald's account, it may be useful to remark on a couple of points. To begin with, the awenyddion are not an obscure sect or association of mediums. The word awenyddion means poets and is unquestionably a term conferring a certain status. The awenyddion were poets, but they were not necessarily bards, nor were they employed by kings or nobles to compose praise songs. The term comes from the word awen, which means 'muse' in modern Welsh, but which denoted the spirit of inspiration in earlier times. The bards and the awenyddion were those who could call upon the awen to inspire their utterances. As Lewis Thorpe notes in his translation, the word awen originally meant oracular frenzy. The trance of the awenyddion, as Gerald has it, was not induced by any external means or rituals. He notes that: *When they are going into a trance they invoke the true and living God, and the Holy Trinity, and they pray that may not be prevented by their sins from revealing the truth.* This places the event in a religious context, sadly, it does not inform us how much prayer they used, and whether the prayer was part of the trance-formation or whether it was simply for the benefit of the audience.

Next, these seers must have acted in some unusual and undignified way, otherwise Gerald would not have compared their act with possession by devils. In shamanism, different deities and spirits produce different sorts of obsession. Possession by a gentle spirit is hardly detectable to the uninformed observer while wilder spirits generally delight in wild motions and behaviour. This is one of the keys to obsession magick: to develop the trance strongly, it is useful to become as congruent with the obsessive entity as possible. Each spirit or deity has its own characteristic moods, postures and idiosyncrasies, and if you cultivate these, obsession is easy and natural. For the same reason, Magicians generally tend to be attracted to those deities who are pretty much like themselves anyway. If you are obsessed by a deity who shares many characteristics with your personality, you will find contact easy, but the rite will not make such a large difference to your awareness. This sort of thing is basically a difference in degree and refinement. If you go out to unite with a deity who shows a different attitude, the rite of communion may be a bit more difficult, but the change will be much stronger and you may discover all sorts of sensations which had been unknown to you before. Budding Magicians usually start out with a couple of gods who are similar to them in some way, and at this stage, the danger of falling into monotheism is strong. Later, when they develop a circle of, say, eight or twelve deities to represent their entire magical universe, they may find that the circle is out of balance unless they include a wide variety of deities representing all sorts of possible approaches to reality.

A good circle includes representatives for all kinds of functions. In the case of the awenyddion, it seems obvious that the entities in charge of oracular utterance are wild and frenzied. Now it might be observed that rites of obsession generally begin with a bit of madness, shaking and swaying. This is often the case, as swaying, shuddering and frenzied behaviour are useful means to dissociate everyday perception and to induce a trance. In Voodoo, for example, obsession may begin with the wild stuff, but may calm down if a calm deity enters the body of the devotee. The awenyddion, however, did not show any signs of becoming calmer while the trance developed. This is supported by the remark that the oracular bout continued until stopped by outside interference. The seers obviously went into their trance and let go of all control, bodily as well as in their utterances, and left it to the audience to decide when it had enough. It makes me wonder what happened if the audience was not satisfied, and did not give the shaking which signaled the end of the fit. Did the awenyddion have a confederate who saw to it that the prophetic utterances were not unduly extended?

Next let us consider the question of forgetfulness. In some cultures, obsession is expected to involve a total black-out of the human personality. We find this phenomenon in certain types of Voodoo. Here, the devotee is 'mounted' by a deity, which may involve plenty of wild and crazed behaviour. Some of this is useful to develop the trance in the devotee, some of it is useful for the audience, as it appears impressive and convincing. Voodoo devotees, however, are supposed to be totally absent while their deity is present within them. When the deity leaves, the devotee generally collapses in exhaustion and recalls nothing, or very little of what went on during the trance. Such behaviour typifies what may be called religious obsession. The important point of it is that the devotee is not interested in achieving conscious contact with the deity. Such matters may be of interest to the priesthood, they are not interesting to the devotee who channels a god for the service of the community. You could also compare it to schizophrenia, as the devotee is either human or divine, but has few experiences in between these extremes. To simplify the situation somewhat, a person who identifies completely with the human consciousness cannot recall what it is like to function in divine awareness as there is no *solution of continuity* (Kenneth Grant's expression) between the states.

In magical obsession, the situation is different. Magicians may like to shift into divine awareness, just like shamans enjoy incarnating all sorts of spirits, but when they do, they retain a measure of awareness and influence, and when they leave their trance they take as much of the memory with them as is possible. It is the frame of experience which makes the difference. A Voodoo devotee is a servant of her/his deities, who run the show as they like in the service of a religious community. Obsession happens under control, i.e., when there are people around who take care that the trance develops properly, the gods are satisfied and their mediums are protected. Magicians and shamans often experience obsession on their own and consequently have to look after themselves to avoid injury. Also, they

want to know who obsesses, to what end, and they want to benefit from the communion by experiencing changes in their behaviour, awareness and reality. The magician approaches a deity with respectful honesty, not as a servant but as a partner, a lover, a friend and companion. Imagine a self divided by the illusion of separate existence. Consequently, the two poles of human and divine awareness tend to embrace and influence each other. This may seem disrespectful to the religiously minded but the gods seem to appreciate it. In my experience, if you allow me to pronounce my silly and subjective beliefs, many deities enjoy communicating with human minds. They can have sacrifices of candles, dead pigs and sobbing sentimentality at every street corner. They have heard millions of ill-considered demands and have seen more groveling and abasement than anyone can stomach. Most people want and shape deities who are just like caricatures of super-parents, and a god can get sick of this sort of feedback or drown in it.

People who wish to share and increase intelligence are a rare and precious opportunity to the deities. Gods and humans shape each other, and if both parties are intelligent, they will wish to become more intelligent in the process. This implies an entirely different relationship between the human and divine, which are not two distinct phenomena but a flow of awareness.

Coming back to the bards and awenyddion, I would like to propose that if Gerald's account is true, the awenyddion performed as if they were suffering from religious possession, while the bards, who had to remain in a degree of awareness and control (it's dangerous to tell a king everything that comes into your mind. A Welsh proverb relates: *It will never do, to tell all, that is true.*), were more likely in a state of magical obsession. This assumption is confirmed by the fact that the Taliesins frequently referred to events they remembered, be it from this or other lifetimes, and you don't get this effect when you simply blot out your mind and channel anything that comes along. It is also possible that the awenyddion feigned loss of memory. This attitude has the advantage that their clients could not annoy them with further questions after the trance was over. Just for speculations sake, I would like to enquire whether the loss of memory may have been induced by the shaking. Any distraction , when it occurs between distinct states of awareness, can induce a loss of memory. Amnesia, as hypnotherapist Milton Erickson has demonstrated so superbly, is an easy and natural phenomenon.

You see, some items of trance work are not necessarily useful for the conscious mind. If you change some important belief structures, it could be that your deep mind prefers to leave you unaware of the transformation until it has fully happened. The conscious mind can be a nosy and intrusive meddler. Well, some changes simply do not happen when the conscious mind is constantly on the lookout for them. Too much attention, too much desire and too much expectation can ruin any natural development. For this reasons, many magicians employ sigils to communicate suggestions and forget about them directly after the operation. They want to keep the conscious mind ignorant, so that it refrains from well-intended but misguided interference in the process. All magick is half-revealed and half concealed. When I enjoy a hypnotic trance with another person, and when we stimulate the deep mind to perform vital changes of belief and personality, I often provide a lot of distraction when the other person comes out of trance. This is not a tactic to censor memories. It merely gives the deep mind of the other an opportunity to hide some relevant issues from the ego until the willed transformations are fully effected. Sometimes the deep mind of the other uses this opportunity, and parts of the trance are 'forgotten'. Sometimes it allows the memory to remain intact. I think it is a matter of respect for the deep mind of the other to give it the choice how much the ego should be aware of.

In dealing with the prophetic utterances of the bards and awenyddion, it might be considered just how much the prophecy is of a revealing nature (i.e. new data or interpretations are revealed) and how much of it acts as suggestion to stimulate changes. Likewise the prophetic utterances of the bards have the side-effect of confirming belief, thereby shaping and creating reality. The suggestive sort of material does not have to be recalled by the conscious mind of the client, it is enough if the problem is solved. Nor is it of any importance for an awenyddion to recall just which items of sage advice a particular client has received. This gives a measure of privacy to the client, who can be certain that s/he will not be watched by a seer curious to find out if the predictions are coming true. Seen from this point of view, real or pretended forgetfulness may be a useful tactic to make the consultation a functional and mind-changing event.

When it comes to the origin of oracular advice, Gerald was brilliant enough to enquire how the seers actually received their material. First of all, he proposed that the visions are the work of demons, *spirits who are ignorant yet in some way inspired*. This interesting phrase shows how he ran into theological difficulties, attempting to explain a phenomena which impressed him, but which he could not altogether accept or understand. Gerald stated dogmatically that the knowledge of the future is only gods property, but was careful to add that the spirit of the holy ghost could also make prophecies, and that there had been true prophets among the unbelievers as well. This was a daring statement for the time, and reveals that he himself was not quite certain how to judge the nature of the intelligences. To make up for these difficulties, he was quick to supply examples for prophecy in classical history, the Bible and the like.

The Wild Man from the Mountains

In this discussion, several references to Merlin appear. This is an important issue, as Myrddin (Merlin) was acknowledged as one of the greatest of the British prophets.

> He may well have been a true believer, but, you will say, there is no mention of his sanctity or devoutness…We read of the faith of Merlin, and we read of his prophecying; but we do not read that he was saintly or that he performed miracles. You will object that the prophets were not possessed when they prophesied, whereas we read that when Merlin Silvester made his prophecies he was in a frenzy, and in the same way the other soothsayers about whom I have written in this chapter seem to be possessed.

In this instance we are happy to have several long prophecies supposedly made by Myrddin the Mad, who lost his reason in the bloody battle fog of Arderydd, fled in madness from the battlefield and chose to live like a wild man in the isolation of the Caledonian Forest, a shadow among shades. Myrddin, so the legends go, foretold the entire history of the British, his audience was an apple tree, a pig (a wild boar?) and his twin-sister Gwendydd. These poems are preserved in the *Black Book of Carmarthen* and the *Red Book of Hergest*, and it is possible that Gerald had access to this material, or some earlier items. The *Red Book*, poem 2, informs us that Myrddin prophesied out of his grave, and that *the ghosts of the mountain, in Aber Carav* had revealed his knowledge to him. The idea of prophecy coming out of a grave may be interesting here, as the grave signifies the condition when body and personality disintegrate.

Poem 1 of the *Red Book* has Myrddin declare

Since my reason is gone with ghosts of the mountain, and I myself am pensive…

while a later verse has him exclaim
Alas! Fair Gwendydd, great is the

Clouds over Bala.

prognostication of the oracle, and the tales of the Sybil...

The *Black Book*, poem 18, contains the lines

Listen, O little pig! Thou pig of peace! A Sybil has told me a wonderful tale; and I will predict a summer full of fury...Listen, O little pig! Thou blessed little pig! A Sybil has told me a tale which frightens me...

Where could Mad Myrddin have met a Sybil, in his self-chosen isolation in the desolate and wind swept mountain forest? Could this Sybil be a goddess or a spirit? Such questions made Merlin, for all his reputation, an uneasy topic in the eyes of the devout. That his prophecies could not fully satisfy the clergy becomes strikingly obvious when we read that Myrddin, in his grave, refuses to take communion from any monk but from god himself. Nor would the clergy appreciate predictions which proclaimed

Listen, O little pig! It is broad daylight, hark thou to the song of water-birds whose notes are loud! To us there will be years and long days, and iniquitous rulers, and the blasting of fruit, and bishops sheltering thieves, churches desecrated, and monks who will compensate for loads of sins.

The reference to demons, spirits, Sybils and ghosts of the mountain implies the activity of a personified 'outside' agency. This does not necessarily mean that the prophecies were the work of independent beings, it merely implies that the source of the prophecy was represented as existing independently of the seer. The same could be said for all spirits and deities, no matter what religion - we have no way of being certain if we deal with independent intelligence and power which contacts us through our representation, or whether the intelligence and power are our own, represented as being independent. Gerald asked how the utterances were received, and recorded: *They seem to receive this gift of divination through visions which they see in their dreams. Some of them have the impression that honey or sugary milk is being smeared on their mouths; others say that a sheet of paper with words written on it is pressed against their lips.* This, so Gerald says, happens while they are busy in trance prophesying on their clients behalf. What do you make out of it?

Breath of the Awen

The idea of the Awen was central to the vocation of the bards of Britain. The Awen, as the spirit of inspiration, is a common topic in medieval British poetry. Let us look at some references in bardic literature.

The Awen foretells the hastening of the multitude,
Possessed of wealth and peace;
And a bountiful sovereign, and eloquent princes. (BoT 6)

The Awen foretells, the day will come...(BoT6)

The Awen I sing, from the deep I bring it...(BoT7)

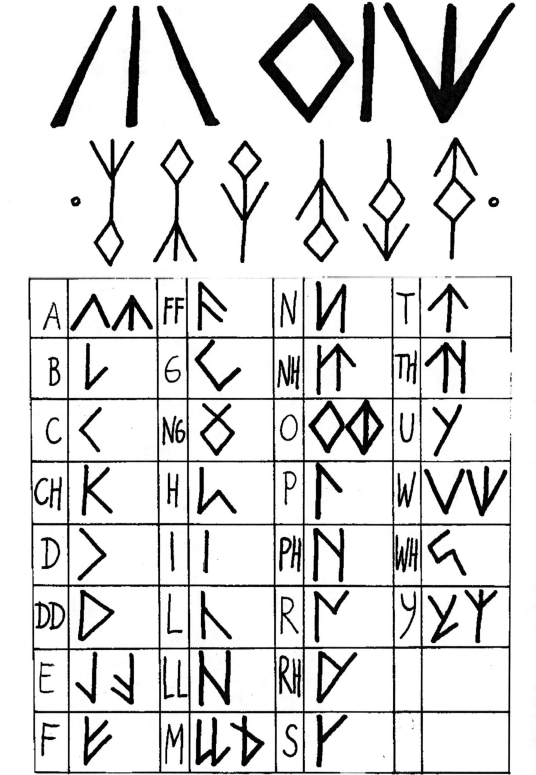

Coelbren of the bards, medieval Wales.

A bard with the breast of an astrologer.
When he recites
The Awen at the setting in of the evening.
(BoT 13)

He (Talhearn) and his virtue gave
Inspiration without mediocrity,
Seven score Ogyrven are in the Awen.
Eight score, of every score it will be one.
(BoT7)

The declaration of a clear song,
Of unbounded Awen (BoT 15)

High is truth when it shines,
Higher when it speaks.
High when came from the cauldron
The three Awens of Gogyrven. (BoT 15)

The extensive booty of the ashen shaft is my
fair Awen. (BoT 37)

Sion Kent (1380 - 1420) composed the
following lines:

Two kinds of Awen truly
There are in the world, and manifest their
course.
The Awen from Christ of joyful discourse
Of a right tendency, a sprightly muse.
There is another Awen not wisely sung,
And they make false and filthy predictions,
This one has been taken by the men of Hu.

Before we explore the Awen further, I
would like to disgress for a moment. Here
is a lovely little path straight into a bramble
thicket. It would be nice to give a simple
explanation of Hu here. This, however, is
next to impossible, as few references to
him survive, and these seem to contradict
each other. The word Hu means *the*, his full
title, *Hu Gadarn*, means The Strong. Hu
Gadarn has been identified as a pagan deity
by several authors. The first reference to
him was made by Iolo Goch, in the 14th C.
who described him as *Constable of golden corn*,
as an emperor of land and sea. A Taliesin
associates Hu with the Isle of Mona
(Anglesey).

Disturbed is the isle of the praise of Hu, the
isle of the severe recompenser
Mona of the good bowls, of active
manliness. The Menei its door...
Disturbed the isle of the praise of Hu, the
isle of the severe ruler. (BoT 21)

I am a bard, I am a harper,
I am a piper, I am a crowder.
Of seven score musicians the very great
Enchanter. There was of the enamelled
honour the privilege,
Hu of the expanded wings. (BoT 48)

Several authors have assumed that Hu
Gadarn is a long forgotten Celtic deity. A
deity named *The Strong* sounds pretty
plausible in a culture which worshipped
gods with names like Sucelos (The Good
Striker) whose emblem was a club.
Nevertheless, the information regarding Hu
is somewhat slim. To make a good case for
him, John Matthews researched an
interesting figure of medieval French
literature, a certain Hugon Le Fort, who
has a contest with Charlemagne. Hugon is
briefly described as seated on a golden
chair and ploughing with a golden plough.
If Hugon were related to Hu Gadarn, we
might be on the track of a surviving pagan
deity. Or could it be a more recent deity,

Detail from the handle of a bronze
jug, Dürrnberg, Austria, 400-380
BCE. Note trefoil at the bottom.

invented by the bards and troubadours? But it gets trickier still. The problem is a song of the British bard Cynddelw, which identifies Hu with Jesus. If you use this identification to make sense of the lines by Sion Kent, it may well be that Kent was not deriding some pagan or heretical poets, but possibly the clergy itself.

But let us return to the breath of the Awen. Two quotations from the Black Book may be worth consideration.
God supreme, be mine the Awen! Amen; fiat!
A successful song of fruitful praise, relating to the bustling course of the host,
According to the sacred ode of Cyridwen, the goddess of various seeds,
The various seeds of poetic harmony, the exalted speech of the graduated minstrel,
Cuhelyn the bard of elegant Cymraec, utterly rejects.
A poem for a favour, the gift of friendship, will not be maintained.
But a composition of thorough praise is being brought to thee...
The most deserving will yield, he will keep his refuge from the insult of the enemy:
He has completely kept the law, completely shown his disposition before the placid Ogyrven.
For a good turn from me, may the gift of Cuhelyn give satisfaction of mind. (BBC 2)

According to the sacred ode of Cyridwen, the Ogyrven of various seeds,-
The various seeds of poetic harmony, the exalted speech of the graduated minstrel,
Cuhelyn the wise, of elegant Cymraec, an exalted possession,
Will skilfully sing; the right of Aedan, the lion, shall be heard. *(BBC 4)*

The Quest for the Muse.

The bards of medieval Britain saw their vocation as a semi-sacred office. While they were more or less Christian in their religious outlook, they also added a number of elements to their lore and ritual practise which go far beyond the regular confines of the faith of their contemporaries. One essential idea is the muse. The Awen as the 'spirit of inspiration' is a rather vague term. As an abstraction, the Awen is too difficult to handle. If you had to rely on your inspiration to be on-its-toes and instantly ready to supply a poem on request, you might be forgiven if you sought for a more reliable idea, if possible one which has a tangible form. Now the term **Awen** can refer to inspiration in its abstract sense, it can also refer to a muse, that is, a spiritual entity which acts as a companion and ally to the bard. To the medieval British bards, one such muse was the eldritch witch Ceridwen. Another may have been the mystrerious (G)ogyrven, whom we shall explore later.

For a start, let us look at the figure of Ceridwen. The word Ceridwen survives in several forms. In medieval British poetry, you can find it as Ceridwen, Keridwen, Kerritwen, Cyridwen, Cariadwen or Caridwen. The meaning of this name is a bit difficult. One possible translation is 'fair and beloved'. Ifor Williams, however, proposed that this name is unsuitable for such an enchantress, and derives it from *cyrrid* and *ben*. The former means *crooked, hooked*, the later means *woman*. If this reconstruction is accurate, the sorceress Ceridwen was actually a 'crooked woman', in short, a hag bent by old age or a person of questionable ethics. Now one could really get into arguing whether Ceridwen was actually fair and beloved or a horrid crooked old crone. May I propose that she was both?

Island Celtic mythology abounds with a certain myth-type which is closely related to the concept of sacred kingship. This is the tale of the ogress, the black giantess, the monstrous lady who challenges the future king to come to bed with her. We shall deal with this myth later on. Suffice it to say that during the night, the bloodthirsty fiend transforms into a lovely young woman who confers the blessing of the kingdom to her spouse. There are quite a few variations to this myth, which we will explore further on, but right here it will do to point out that Ceridwen could appear both in alluring and in terrifying shape, and that both of these masks have a lot to do with inspiration. If we want a good idea about Ceridwen, it might be useful to take a look into the *Hanes Taliesin*, the tale of Taliesin, as it was published in Lady Guest's edition of the *Mabinogi*.

Hanes Taliesin

In times past there lived in Penllyn (Bala Lake) a man of gentle lineage, named Tegid Voel, and his dwelling was in the midst of the Lake Tegid, and his wife was called Caridwen. And there was born to him of his wife a son named Morvran ab Tegid, and also a daughter named Creirwy, the fairest maiden in the world was she; and they had a brother the most ill-favoured man in the world, Avagddu. Now Caridwen his mother thought that he was not likely to be admitted among men of noble birth, by reason of his ugliness, unless he had some exalted merits or knowledge. For it was in the beginning of Arthur's time and of the Round Table.

So she resolved, according to the arts of the books of the Fferyllt, to boil a cauldron of Inspiration and Science for her son, that his reception might be honourable because of his knowledge of the mysteries of the future state of the world. Then she began to boil the cauldron, which from the beginning of its boiling might not cease to boil for a year and a day, until three blessed drops were obtained of the grace of inspiration. And she put Gwion Bach the son of Gwreang of Llanfair in Caereinion, in Powys, to stir the cauldron, and a blind man named Morda to kindle the fire beneath it, and she charged them that they should not suffer it to cease boiling for the space of a year and a day. And she herself, according to the books of the astronomers, and in planetary hours, gathered every day of all charm-bearing herbs. And one day, towards the end of the year, as Caridwen was culling plants and making incantations, it chanced that three drops of the charmed liquor flew out of the cauldron and fell upon the finger of Gwion Bach. And by reason of their great heat he put his finger to his mouth, and the instant he put those marvel-working drops into his mouth, he foresaw everything that was to come, and perceived that his chief care must be to guard against the wiles of Caridwen, for vast was her skill. And in very great fear he fled towards his own land. And the cauldron burst in two, because all the liquor within it except the three charm-bearing drops was poisonous, so that the horses of Gwyddno Garanhir were poisoned by the water of the stream into which the liquor of the cauldron ran, and the confluence of the stream was called the Poison of the Horses of Gwyddno from that time forth. Thereupon came in Caridwen and saw all the toil of a whole year lost. And she seized a billet of wood and struck the blind Morda on the head until one of his eyes fell upon his cheek. And he said, 'Wrongfully hast thou disfigured me, for I am innocent. Thy loss was not because of me.'

'Thou speakest truth,' said Caridwen, 'it was Gwion Bach who robbed me.'

And she went forth after him, running. And he saw her, and changed himself into a hare and fled. But she changed herself into a greyhound and turned him. And he ran towards a river, and became a fish. And she in the form of an otter-bitch chased him under the water, until he was fain to turn himself into a bird of the air. Then she, as a hawk, followed him and gave him no rest in the sky. And just as she was about to stoop on him, and he was in fear of death, he espied a heap of winnowed wheat on the floor of a barn, and he dropped amongst the wheat, and turned himself into one of the grains. Then she transformed herself into a high-crested black hen, and went to the wheat and scratched it with her feet, and found him out and swallowed him. And, as the story says, she bore him nine months, and when she was delivered of him, she could not find it in her heart to kill him, by reason of his beauty. So she wrapped him in a leathern bag , and cast him into the sea to the mercy of God, on the twenty-ninth day of April. And at that time the weir of Gwyddno was on the strand between Dyvi and Aberystwyth, near to his own castle, and the value of an hundred pounds of salmon was taken in that weir every May eve. And in those days Gwyddno had an only son named Elphin, the most hapless of youths, and the most needy. And it grieved his father sore, for he thought that he was born in an evil hour. And by the advice of his council, his father had granted him the drawing of the weir that year, to see if good luck would ever befall him, and to give him something wherewith to begin the world. And the next day, when Elphin went to look, there was nothing in the weir. But as he turned back he perceived the leathern bag upon a pole of the weir. Then said one of the weir-ward unto Elphin, ' Thou wast never unlucky until to-night, and now thou hast destroyed the virtues of the weir, which always yielded the value of an hundred pounds every May-eve, and to-night there is nothing but this leathern skin within it.' 'How now,' said Elphin, 'there may be therein the value of an hundred pounds.'

Well! They took up the leathern bag, and he who opened it saw the forehead of a boy, and said to Elphin, 'Behold a radiant brow!' 'Taliesin be he called,' said Elphin. And he lifted the boy in his arms, and lamenting his mischance, he placed him sorrowfully behind him. And he made his horse amble gently, that before had been trotting, and he carried him as softly as if he had been sitting in the easiest chair in the world. And presently the boy made a Consolation and praise to Elphin, and foretold honour to Elphin; and the Consolation was as you may see...

This is the first part of the story. Let me make some remarks regarding this text. To begin with, the tale of Taliesin is not part of the original *Mabinogi*. Strictly speaking, there are only four tales which may be classed as *The Four Branches of the Mabinogi*. They come from the *Red Book of Hergest*, which includes plenty of other tales, poems and translations of various Latin manuscripts. Lady Guest translated most of these tales and published them all under the name *Mabinogi*, even though many of them are unrelated and come from distinct periods and places. Then she added the Taliesin tale to the lot, as it is such an enchanting and important item of Welsh folk-lore. The Taliesin tale, however, comes from an entirely different source. The manuscript was written in the late 16th C., which makes it rather unreliable if we want to explore the myths associated with Ceridwen some five hundred years earlier. On the other hand, its language is very much in the style of the 9th C., so either we are dealing with old material which has been transcribed, or with a cunning forgery making use of an early and archaic style. I wouldn't dream of voicing an opinion here, as both options are possible. The Taliesin tale, as we have it today, comes from the manuscripts of Llewelyn Sion (born 1540), passed through the collection of Iolo Morgannwg (possibly being edited in the process), from him to Dr. Owen Pughe, and finally to Lady Charlotte Guest and her collaborator, John Jones. The later is another candidate for possible interference, as apparently he added material to the text which did not exist in the original. The poems included in Lady Guest's *Hanes Taliesin* have probably been tampered with, and as most of them do not survive in the original, it is next to impossible to decide which lines are original and which were added by that well meaning Christian scholar. Another version of the tale was recorded by Elis Gruffydd, who lived c. 1490-1552 and included it in his *Chronicle of the World*. Owen John collected another version. Most of these are remarkably congruent, but there are a few significant differences in the texts. The day that Elphin rescued young Taliesin from the weir is not given by Owen John, it's either the 20th or 29th of April in Llewelyn Sion's version while Gruffydd gives the 31rst of October, in which case our Radiant Brow is named at the very beginning of the dark season. Then there is the version that Lewis Morris recorded in 1726. It points at an independent oral tradition. According to Mr. Morris, Taliesin was poet laureate to Maelgwn Gwynedd. Now Prince Elffin happened to be Maelgwn's brother. Elffin found Taliesin in a leather bag in the weir, and Morris proposes that the leather bag may have been a Welsh leather boat, a coracle. Imagine an umbrella floating upside down on the water and yourself standing in it, then you have the idea. Now let us quote from Lewis Morris:

> ...being of a notable genius to poetry and inspired with ye spirit of prophecy he attained to ye greatest perfection in that age. The Cause of Casting him into ye sea was this: He being a poor boy begging his bread: came by chance to Creigiau'r Eryrie where there were two Gwiddans (hags or witches) Boyling a Panfull of Enchanted Liquor: which they could not bring to perfection for want of fuell: Taliesyn asked them if he should

boyl the liquor. And he told them that he had a particular way to make much water boil with little fuell: which they easily granted. Taliesyn gathered up fuell together and bound it in little fagotts and so in a little time (and before they were aware of him) he boyled ye liquor to perfection: and took ye first three drops for himself-the virtue of ye water was such that He that had ye first three drops of it when boyled &c should properly be inspired with ye spirit of divining and this water ye Gwiddan's intended to give to their own sons (and Taliesyn having heard of it) he Endeavoured to make his Escape but was caught by ym and cast into ye sea in a Leather Bagg. &c.

The word Gwiddans may be worth considering. A Gwiddan is a witch or a hag, but not necessarily a human being. Mr. Morris came upon the word Gwidion for 'giants', which suggests a subtle connection between the initiatrixes of Taliesin and the great enchanter and spell crafter Gwydyon. An interesting detail is the fact that the gwiddans appear as a pair. You would expect a single or a triple being in Celtic myth, the occurrence of a pair is not only unusual but also poses the question whether the pair of gwyddans were a couple.

Was Ceridwen a giantess as well? One manuscript, *Aberdar I*, informs us that Gridwen is *a she giant that lived in North Wales*. Now giants are a fascinating topic. Some giants can be seen as nature spirits associated with great destructive forces. Others are spirits of hills and mountains. Much more important for the practising Magickian, however, are the giants of the prehistoric unknown aeons, the primal entities of chaos and creativity who shaped the evolution of human consciousness before the gods of order were invented.

The *Hanes Taliesin* is a story based on a widely known folk-tale pattern. The basic script is called '*The White Snake*' by researchers, and there are dozens of variants to the theme. In *Seidways* I listed a few of them. Think of Finn, who burned his hand while cooking the salmon of wisdom. He tasted the enchanting juice and henceforth, the act of chewing his thumb produced vision and revealed hidden knowledge. Think of Sigurd who slew a dragon and cooked its heart over a fire. His scalded thumb made him understand the language of the birds. Or Erik. This is a story related by Saxo Grammaticus - not a very reliable witness on Pagan mythology, but then, often enough all we have. In his history of *Frodhi III*, we encounter the witch Kraka (Crow). Kraka's son was named Rollir, his half brother was Erik. Let's take a look into the story. Rollir had just been sent home from the forest by his father.

When he saw smoke rising from his mother's house, he approached the door and observed through a tiny gap how his mother was stirring gruel in a misshapen cauldron. Above the cauldron, he observed, were three serpents hanging from a ribbon, their jaws dripping saliva into the vessel. Two were of black colour, the third wore white scales and was hanging above the others. Her tail was coiled while the others were holding the ribbon tied to her belly. The youth instantly recognized that this was sorcery, but was silent about it, lest his mother be accused of witchcraft. He did not know the snakes were harmless nor did he know what virtue the gruel was receiving. Soon enough Ragnar and Erik joined him. Together they went to a chamber and sat around a table. Kraka served the meal, before the youths she placed the cauldron filled with colourful gruel. One part was black, with red and yellow spots, the other pale white, as the gruel had the colours of the serpents. Both tasted the gruel, but Erik, who valued the parts of gruel by their power, not by their colour, swiftly turned the bowl around so that the black gruel came to his side and the white to his brother, speaking 'This is how the stormy sea spins a ship around!'. So each of them ate his part. From eating this gruel Erik attained the height of human wisdom, even the languages of the beasts became known to him. Also he became so eloquent that he could comment on every subject in a speech of knowledge and refinement.

When Kraka came in and found that her stepson had received the black portion, she understood that her sorcery had gone wrong. She humbly asked Erik to swear loyalty to his half-brother Rollir and Erik did so.

In this story, the protagonist, Erik, receives a blessing not meant for him through his superior insight. In the Lewis Morris tale, Taliesyn seeks out the gwiddans on Mount Snowdon and steals the three drops on purpose. Hywel Rheinallt, singing in the 15th C., suggests that Taliesin put his entire hand into the cauldron-again, this does not look like an accident. There is a strangely Promethean element in our story, a glimpse at the myth of the trickster who steals the fire from heaven, or whatever else strikes his fancy. For a full treatment of the topic, let me recommend Juliette Wood's studies of the subject.

Before we continue our journey I would like to point out a few details in the text. Tegid Foel means 'Tegid the Bald', Tegid being the Welsh form of the Roman name Tacitus. Avagddu means 'Overdark', Morvran can be translated as 'Great Raven' or ' Sea-Crow', and Creirwy is 'Dear and beloved'. Gwion Bach means 'Bright and small'. Gwion's blind companion Morda is not that easy to identify. His name appears in a couple of variations - Owen John has Dallmor Dylan, Sion gives Dallmor Dallme, otherwise you find Dallmon Dallmaen. The *Books of the Fferyllt* are not obscure collections of Welsh spells and sorceries but simply the works of Vergil, whom everyone considered a great magician during the medieval period. The tale describes, as you probably noticed, a rite of passage which turned the young beggar Gwion into the enlightened bard Taliesin. It may well be the myth behind the initiation of all the Taliesins. It is certainly no coincidence that Gwion undergoes a change of shape and identity in four elemental realms. We have the hare/greyhound on land, the fish/otter in water, the bird/falcon in the air. The grain of wheat and the red crested black hen may well represent fire. This is not very obvious in the *Hanes Taliesin*. If we look at the earlier songs of the *Book of Taliesin*, especially at *The Hostile Confederacy* (quoted in full further on) that you can find the suggestion that Gwion, as a grain of wheat, was baked in an oven before Ceridwen devoured him. The poem, dating around the 12th C., is a lot earlier than the prose tales and may well reflect a more original type of the legend. More on this ritual, the shape changing and the self-transformation, in the chapter on the ever-hungry-cauldron. While we cannot be certain how much of the tale is a later addition, there are plenty of indications that Ceridwen and some version of the tale of Taliesin was well known to the bards of the Gogynfeirdd period. It was in all likeliness not quite the tale we are acquainted with today. Many references to the matter are so mysterious that they point at an entire body of forgotten mythology. Let me annoy you with further mysteries. Take a look at the following song.

The Chair of Ceridwen
Book of Taliessin 16

Sovereign of the power of the air, thou also
The satisfaction of my transgressions.
At midnight and at matins
There shone my lights.
Courteous the life of Minawg ap Lleu,
Whom I saw here a short while ago.
The end, in the slope of Lleu.
Ardent was his push in combats;
Avagddu my son also.
Happy the Lord made him,
In the competition of songs,
His wisdom was better than mine,
The most skilful man ever heard of.
Gwydyon ap Don, of toiling spirits,
Enchanted a woman from blossoms,
And brought pigs from the south.
Since he had no sheltering cots,

Rapid curves, and plaited chains.
He made the forms of horses
From the springing
Plants, and illustrious saddles.
When are judged the chairs,
Excelling them (will be) mine,
My chair, my cauldron, and my laws,
And my pervading eloquence, meet for the chair.
I am called skilful in the court of Don.
I, and Euronwy, and Euron.
I saw a fierce conflict in Nant Frangcon
On a Sunday, at the time of dawn,
Between the bird of wrath and Gwydyon.
Thursday, certainly, they went to Mona
To obtain whirlings and sorcerers.
Arianrod, of laudable aspect, dawn of serenity,
The greatest disgrace evidently on the side of the Brython,
Hastily sends about his court the stream of a rainbow,
A stream that scares away violence from the earth.
The poison of its former state, about the world, it will leave.
They speak not falsely, the books of Beda.
The chair of the Preserver is here.
And till doom, shall continue in Europa.
May the Trinity grant us
Mercy on the day of judgment.
And fair alms from good men.

Here we are happy to have a piece of poetry directly attributed to Ceridwen, i. e. it is the enchantress herself who is singing. You probably noticed that some elements of the tale are alluded to, such as her son, Avagddu, and her magical cauldron, which is presented as an attribute of the poets vocation. Readers of the *Mabinogi* will also notice that several persons of the fourth branch are mentioned. The poem, however, goes a long way beyond the fourth branch and makes mysterious allusions to events which are completely unknown to us. That Gwydion, as a semi-divine enchanter created a woman out of blossoms, shaped the illusion of horses out of plants and fungi and caused a useless war when he stole the first pigs from south Wales is well known from the fourth branch. The battle of Gwydyon against the bird of wrath in a valley on Mount Snowdon is absent in the surviving manuscripts, and the nature of the rainbow which fair Arianrod binds around the court of the Briton is another tantalizing riddle. Arianrod has been called a moon goddess by a number of fluffy minded researchers, as her name may possibly be translated as 'Silver wheel'.

This was a popular interpretation, as thanks to such romantic idealists as Robert Graves, everybody expected goddesses to be in charge of the moon anyway. Male gods were generally assumed to be solar and active, goddesses were lunar and passive by nature, ah, the simple myths of the nineteenth century. Everybody knew that the people of prehistory were interested in just one thing (you know what), and so they craved fertility cults, mother goddesses, and generally spent the evenings worshipping genitalia. Such ideas can still be found in plenty of popular books on the pagan past. Most modern scholars shy away from these outworn phantasms, as research has clearly shown that we know far less than we ever thought. Though it might be tempting to turn the sorceress Arianrod into a pagan Celtic moon goddess, this is not entirely accurate, as the manuscripts never name her a deity (let alone a lunar deity), and so

far not a single Celtic moon goddess has been found. Arianrod is a semi divine sorceress in the *fourth branch*, living in a secluded castle at the seaside, she is the mother of fair Lleu and one of his worst enemies. Now Lleu is in all likeliness a pale reflection of the great Celtic deity Lug, but this does not automatically turn his mother into a deity. All characters of the fourth branch, while exhibiting more or less divine attributes, are strictly human.

Were they deities in the elder days? Many scholars of the 19th C. were of the opinion that you could see the *Mabinogi* as a medieval rendering of primal Celtic mythology. This hypothesis, still popular among Neo-Celtic Enthusiasts, is not quite the present state of research. The tales of the *Mabinogi* are, first of all, the innovative creation of the gogynfeirdd bards. These were anything but traditionalistic minded custodians of elder lore. In fact, they made use of a lot of older fragments to compose their own brand new mythology. Thus, you can get distorted images of authentic British deities and beliefs floating through a haze of new ideas and fresh inspiration. In several cases, new figures were made up and sometimes an elder figure, whose original mythology had been forgotten, was supplied with a new one. The same problem applies to Ceridwen. Many popular books on Celtic religion parade Ceridwen as a mother goddess, as a fertility goddess, as a goddess of the earth and so on. Some authors go so far to make her a goddess of the Megalith people, a deity to whom the very bluestones were dedicated which were later transported to Salisbury Plain and incorporated in Stonehenge.

All of this is extremely speculative, if not completely nutty. Is Ceridwen a Celtic deity? No, as there is absolutely no evidence for any entity or divinity of such a name in prehistoric Europe. Of the hundreds of Celtic deities whose names and altars are known, none has any similarity to Ceridwen. The name and person first appears rather late in the medieval period, starting possibly in the 9th, but probably in the 12th C. Is Ceridwen a medieval goddess? The answer would be a guarded yes. The bards of the Gogynfeirdd movement definitely saw her as a deity, as she was the muse and initiatrix for the bardic vocation. For those bards, Ceridwen was the personified expression of the Awen, and when they improvised verse or prophecy, it was on Ceridwen that they relied. However, those bards were also Christians, and Christianity is not a religion which tolerates other gods, let alone female ones. As a result, we can be certain that Ceridwen was highly venerated by a number of bards, for whom she functioned as a muse and/or goddess. It is not likely, however, that these bards were keen on discussing their peculiar brand of Christianity with the clergy, or that Ceridwen was known, let alone worshipped by the common people of medieval Britain. In all likeliness, they have never even heard of her. What makes Ceridwen a goddess in the eyes of the Neo-Celtic movement is basically the accumulated errors of several centuries of scholarly plodding.

The historical sciences, like most other branches of learning, undergo regular changes in general dogma. During the last centuries, a number of models were popular which are completely out of date nowadays.

One of them is the fable that any super-human being in folklore was really originally a deity, euhemerized and shrunk into human size and outfit by ill-meaning Christian scribes. To an extent, this theory makes sense. When Snorri explains (*Prose Edda*) that the god Odin was originally a powerful sorcerer who became deified by legend, this rationalization certainly made sense for a Christian audience, which didn't believe in pagan gods anyway. Several churchish writers used this approach, one good example is Saxo Grammaticus, who destroyed a treasure trove of pagan Danish myths by making demons or human heroes out of all pagan gods that got in his way. Given such examples, it was an easy matter to explain all super-human persons as former deities, and quite a few scholars made use of this approach. So, if you encounter a sorceress such as Ceridwen, it's an easy matter to explain her as a goddess in human disguise. And if you know that she collected plants and leaves for her cauldron, why, that obviously makes her an earth or a vegetation deity! Mind you, the dear lady also has a cauldron. Now that's really heavy symbology. We all know what primitive people are always thinking about, so, hooray, let's make her a goddess of fertility and a mother goddess as well! Luckily, this attitude is transforming.

Some historians have actually managed to comprehend that not all super-human entities need to be deities. For one thing, there are plenty of witches and sorcerers in mythology who are possessed of unusual skills but remain human, and for another,

---

Variations of the letters O I V.

plenty of myths make use of the demi-god, or the incarnate deity. Lots of scholars have explained the great Irish hero Cu Chullain as a former deity of the sky, as a god of the sun or of thunder. If you take his myth cycle, however, and retell the tales as if he were a deity, the stories cease to function. The meaning of Cu's super human heroism depends on his humanity, and on his mortality. If you have a half god single handedly fighting the hosts of Ireland, this is extreme heroism. If you have a god doing the same, it's just unfair. So it does not do to turn any unusual mythological creature into a former deity, otherwise you'll end up with a host of deities, none of whom amounts to very much. There are certain attributes which are required by gods. One of them is the ability to do deeds which transcend human ability, another is, that the deity in question is worshipped, receives offerings, has a cult of some sort and can be approached for help. Deities are not just there, what people need is deities who care, who come, and who communicate.

To the Gogynfeirdd bards, Ceridwen, whether she was called a muse or a deity, was certainly a figure of worship and veneration. What makes the situation so difficult is that this attitude is not in tune with the Christian faith, so it may well be that much of the worship of her happened in secret. How did the bards worship her? For one thing, we can be sure they worshipped her with praise and poetry. For another, they sought congress with her in those hours of darkness and silence when they received inspiration from the hidden side of the mind. But look at these lines:

...A battle against the lord of fame, in the dales of the Severn,
Against Brochwel of Powys, that loved my Awen.
A battle in the pleasant course early against Urien,
There falls about our feet blood on destruction.
Shall not my chair be defended from the cauldron of Ceridwen?
May my tongue be free in the sanctuary of the praise of Gogyrwen.
The praise of Gogyrwen is an oblation, which has satisfied
Them, with milk, and dew, and acorns. (BoT 14)

Here we have a reference to what may well be offerings to the deity. Milk and dew and acorns are all sacred substances. Dew in particular was mysterious. Think about this. You go out in the morning and find everything wet. Yet you know for certain that it has not rained during the night! Where did the dew come from? And what about the miracle of milk, or the amazement that a tiny acorn can contain the dream-potential of a mighty tree that lasts for a thousand years?

We could now proceed by saying some clever things about the importance of milk in a pastoral lifestyle, or about the sacred oaks and their use in fattening the flesh of pigs. On the other hand, any person acquainted with the secret language of left-hand-Tantra will be aware that milk, dew and acorns, when they are taken as symbols, are associated with sexual mysteries. These offerings may have plenty of meanings. Dare to guess.

Three Inspirations of Ogyrven

Let us continue with the search for the muse. Look at the lines from the *Black Book* given above. Here you find Ceridwen addressed in one poem as the goddess of many seeds, and in the next poem as *the Ogyrven of many seeds*. In the original manuscript, both expressions read *kyrridven ogyrven amhad*. If you think that things were complicated regarding Ceridwen, you'll soon begin to chortle when we look into Ogyrven. Who or what is this mysterious (G)ogyrven? Some researchers have taken the easy approach, and have solved the problem by claiming that Ogyrven is simply another aspect or form of Ceridwen. This would explain why the two names often turn up in company. The songs by Taliesin often refer to (G)ogyrven, and always associate her with the Awen. Now you might ask (please do it!) how come Ceridwen can be the Ogyrven and the goddess of many seeds.

Does Ogyrven mean goddess? Dr Pugh (*Welsh Dictionary*) explains that *Gogyrven = a spiritual being or form; a personified idea, a prosopopoeia*. If you look up the latter (all right, let me do it for you) you'll find out that a prosopopoeia is a representation in human form, an inanimate or abstract thing given human characteristics, or a person or thing as an embodiment of a quality. Another, and briefer explanation of the word is simply 'personification'. Skene in his kindness pointed out that Ogyrven is associated with a peculiar letter of the Welsh alphabet, and supplied a fitting quotation from a manuscript of the late 15th C. which mentions Gogyrven and links her with the symbol of the three rays. As I could not read it, my editor sought a translator via the Internet. Eventually, he found Sally and her home community, to whom I would like to extend my warmest thanks. Translated, the text reads:

> Three elements of a letter: it is by the combining of one or other of the three that letters are made, namely three shining rays, and of these are made the sixteenth 'gogyrven', that is the sixteenth letter, and by a different art there are twenty-seven (?) 'gogyrven', a sign of the virtue of the one hundred and fourty-seven words at the root of Welsh, from which are derived every other word.

This does not tell us anything about a goddess, but it certainly connects (G)ogyrven with the obscure alphabet of the bards. The letter associated with (G)ogyrven are the three rays of light which descend from above. This sign has been used by Iolo Morgannwg and his associates as a symbol of the Awen. So far we have learned that Ogyrven is a personified idea, a goddess and a letter. Another interpretation I have heard (source unknown) is that (G)ogyrven are little pieces of clay, on which the bards wrote the signs of their alphabet, possibly for use in divination.

Various items from the *Book of Taliesin* raise the possibility that she was one or several muses. Or the muse itself - in this case we could see Ceridwen as the ogyrven (muse) of many seeds. And if Ceridwen was one muse, there must have been more of them. Ah yes, and to screw things up properly I have to mention two little known medieval poems (See R. Gurney 1969). Prince Hywel ab Owain Gwynedd (c.1110-1171), one of the last British poet/ aristocrats, composed two songs which may have to do with our topic. One of them is a love song to a slight young maid who lives in a white fortress next to the church. The poet loudly bemoans the fact that his love is being kept locked in the fortress by her father Ogyrvynn.

The other poem is a love song to Ceridwen. Not the goddess or muse, but a young lady of ten years with whom the poet is desperately in love. It may well be that the two poems are related, and that in Hywel's songs, Ceridwen is the daughter of the rude Ogyrvynn.

Whether the poet is actually speaking of living persons, or whether he uses the names in an allegorical sense is open to discussion. Incidentally, marriages to children were not frowned upon in medieval Wales, and indeed in most of feudal Europe. Be that as it may, here we have an early reference to the two, only that Ogyrven happens to be a male giant in this case. An Ogrvran made it into the Arthurian myths, he is the father of Guinevere, and possibly a giant. Then there is a Seat of Ogrvran in North Wales, local legend considers him a giant as well.

If Ogrvran, Gridwen, the gwiddans and Gwydyon are all giants, it may be useful to understand and approach them as Ancient Ones. As such they come much closer to the nature of true inspiration than if we attempt to label them as deities. Creativity and inspiration are not just poetic moonlight and dewdrops on rose-petals. They are also the dark visions, the nightside fears and the primal urges of the time-before-words. A fully creative mind can think of everything. If you drink from the cauldron you will get the lot.

What I would like to propose in the next pages is extremely speculative. It would be kind if you could listen to my mad fantasies, I would not expect you to take them very seriously. To begin with, the connection between Ogyrven and the letters of the bardic alphabet may seem a bit confusing. The medieval bards made up their own alphabet, the coelbren, and used it like a code for their own communication. The basis for this script are the letters of the Welsh alphabet, but as you can see in the illustration, the runes obviously exerted a certain influence on the shape of these letters. At least the runes come closer to the coelbren than does the Latin alphabet, the North Italian alphabets or the Celtic alphabets you find used on coins or the odd inscription. We have a bizarre text regarding the inner meaning and creation of this bardic alphabet. Sadly, it comes from *Barddas*, that highly questionable compilation of facts and forgeries, based on the manuscripts of Iolo Morgannwg.

Keeping in mind that we are walking on very thin ice here, let us now consider what *Barddas* has to say about the alphabet. The letters, so we are told, were invented by Einiged the Giant, the son of Alser, for the purpose of recording praiseworthy actions and deeds, and inscribed on wooden blocks which are known as coelbren. Bran the Blessed brought the art of preparing vellum for writing from Rome. This looks like an interesting mythological tangle, as Bran the Blessed, as he appears in the second branch of the *Mabinogi*, never went to Rome but to

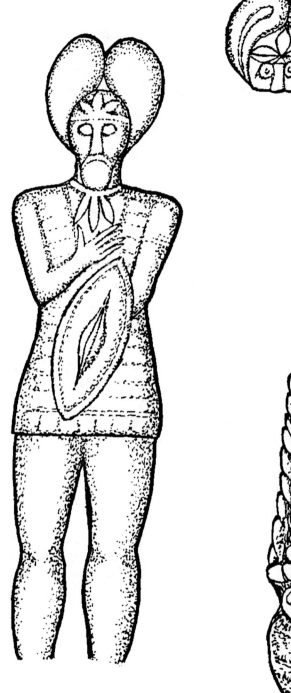

The Glauburg
statue c450BC,
the Pfalzfeld
pillar c400BCE
and the head of
Heidelberg
c450BCE.

Ireland, while the historical Bran (Brennus) who raided and plundered Rome in 387 BCE in all likeliness never traveled to Britain. Be that as it may, the three original letters were obtained by Menw the Aged, who received them directly from the voice of god.

These letters manifested as the triple rays of light, the sign of the Awen. Each of the three rays corresponds to a column and has a sound value. The first column vibrates to the sound of O, the second to the sound of I and the third to the sound of V. The O, by the way, is not written in round shape but with straight lines, it looks like a square standing on a point. As to the V, it is possible to pronounce it not only as 'V' but also as 'U'. These three correspond with the three attributes of god, that is, *love, knowledge and truth*. By the name OIV the universe, the elements and all creatures call god inwardly. From the secret word OIV the 16 letters were formed, the ten primary ones forming the sacred word *Abcedilros*. Later other letters were formed until the alphabet had 24 signs. As *Barddas* points out, only a bard of thorough secrecy can vocalize the name of god out of the three columns, as this feat requires thorough knowledge of their meaning, accent and power. This secret can only be granted by the Awen of god, as only god knows how the sacred name is properly pronounced. The hidden meaning of the 16 letters will then appear in meditation. From the three columns of light, so this tradition claims, comes the custom of revealing wisdom in triads. Thus we learn that the three foundations of the Awen from god are:

to understand the truth, to love the truth and to maintain the truth.

If you allow me to speculate here, I would like to point out that the letters OIV look much as if they were a shortened form of Ogyrven. Was Ogyrven a secret name of god (or a goddess?) for the medieval bards?

The Trefoil Sign

But let us go on further journeys through the thicket. If you look at the sign of the three rays of the Awen, or at the sign of Ogyrven, the first question is where you can find examples. Now there are a number of works of early Celtic art which show a rather similar pattern. Most of these come from the late Hallstatt period with its distinct art and aesthetics. Of course you might argue that it is hardly likely that symbols of the Hallstatt period survived secretly from, say, 500 BCE to the medieval period, when they were resurrected by a group of enterprising and innovative bards. I agree that this is unlikely, and shall continue to voice my speculations asking you to keep an open mind and a critical attitude. Please look at the illustrations. One magnificent sample of a triple-ray item can be found in the Pfalzfeld pillar. This pillar is four sided and made from reddish sandstone. It used to stand before the church in Pfalzfeld, where it suffered from erosion and gradually broke into pieces. The main part is now in the Landesmuseum in Bonn. If you study earlier pictures, you can see that originally the pillar was an obelisk of considerable height. Most of the top broke off and disappeared, and so did parts of the foundation.

The remaining part can be seen in most

books on Celtic art. The design, so you read again and again, of this 'phallic' pillar, shows a male head with a beard on each of the four sides. The head, so the scholars explain, is adorned with a floral crown and placed among a lot of floral growth or fish-bladder symbols, and some of the more dull minded immediately identify the obscure shapes as mistletoe leaves. Underneath the head is a large fleur-de-lis, a trefoil, a plant of three leaves looking much like the Awen sign. Another seems to have graced the upper part of the pillar, though this is not certain, as so much is missing today.

Now there are a number of items on the pillar which are constantly ignored. Maybe those scholars never looked at the design in a suitable trance state or while intoxicated (which the Celts definitely did). For one thing, the head on the pillar is obviously decapitated. This may have a sacred meaning, as the head was the seat of the soul and constituted the cauldron of knowledge. The common Celtic custom of head-hunting and veneration is rather well attested, and the head on the pillar ought to be considered in this light. If the head is chopped off, the trefoil under the neck could represent three streams of blood, or whatever else you get when you cut a head off. The other hidden matter could be called a subliminal. If you have studied Celtic art, you may be aware that many objects can be seen in several ways. There are coins, for example, which show abstract heads. If you look closely into the hair of these figures, you can find deer or dragon heads hidden in the design. This is by no means an exception. Lots of Celtic art is meant to be seen from several points of view to reveal several

layers of meaning. Multiple interpretations are just what makes Celtic art so fertile for the imagination.

While the head on the 'phallic' pillar is male, it rests within a pattern which is definitely not just leaves and bladders. Please look at the design. Can you see the abstract woman hidden in the picture? The head of the man is resting between her thighs. It might be argued that the woman is so abstract, but then, Celtic art can be extremely abstract, just look at some coins. I have showed this hidden design to several people. Most of them couldn't see it at first, but once they had seen it, they found it impossible to ignore.

Then again, the question arises, just what is the meaning of the decapitated head between the thighs of this abstract woman? Personally, I believe that the image shows a death and rebirth scenario, that the head returns to the womb/tomb to find reincarnation on earth. Implied is maybe the idea, that inspiration arises (the Awen type sign) after the head has been cut off and the deceased has returned to the source. A similar idea is expressed by the Indian goddess of wisdom, Chinnamasta, who decapitates herself. Three fountains of blood spring from her neck, feeding the adorants and the goddess with the elixirs of a self freed from ego.

This may sound a bit over the top for most scholars, but it will make sense to any Magicians acquainted with death and resurrection rituals, death-posture trances, chöd self-sacrifice rituals and the like. Many shamans and sorcerers go through a simulated death and rebirth experience, be it through trance, dramatic ritual, hypnosis, drug experience or crisis and disease. Such experiences tend to dissolve the rigid beliefs the ego has fortified itself with, and when ego dies, or is suspended, the self gets a chance to create the world and the personality anew. It is highly likely that Gwion's initiation, as described in the *Hanes Taliesin*, is a distorted account of such an initiation ritual. That death and exhaustion have much to do with the Awen and inspiration is pretty obvious. Many artists need phases of crisis, dissolution or exhaustion before they have a mind empty enough to receive a new impulse. Austin Spare produced some of his finest paintings after simulating his own death in a deep trance state, and used this meditation regularly to stimulate his creativity. Others believe that regular dying improves health and vitality...more on this in the chapter 'The ever-hungry-cauldron'.

The Pfalzfeld pillar is unique, but the image of the head can be traced to other works of art. You have probably heard of the recent excavation at the Glauburg. The Glauburg is a hill rising out of the fertile landscape of the Hessian Wetterau, some 20km from Frankfurt. The hill is long and flat and has been used as a settlement or fortress since the Neolithic. During the Hallstatt period, it was an important power site. As so many people had lived there over the ages, and building activities continued well into the medieval period, few Celtic items could be unearthed, until one jolly day air photographs revealed the vague outline of a burial mound under a nearby field. Generations of farmers had successfully ploughed the mound into the ground, so that its existence was only visible from above. The mound contained several burials and was surrounded by a system of ditches. One of the corpses wore a ceremonial torque (neck-ring) which had three bulbs, looking much like the Awen sign. The item was of gold, but of such fragile strength that it was in all likeliness never worn during life. Golden grave goods of great beauty but little durability can often be found in Hallstatt period mounds, a good example are the golden ornaments on the shoes of the Hochdorf noble which would not have endured walking. Another item the archaeologists unearthed was a life-size sandstone figure of a man (or deity?) who looks a lot like the Pfalzfeld head. The face is very similar and under the throat it has the familiar triple lozenges. On top of the head is a crown or bizarre headdress that looks like the 'thighs' on the Pfalzfeld pillar. While certain scholars knew nothing better than to interpret it as two (gigantic) mistletoe leaves, the press instantly identified it as Mickey Mouse ears. The figure has a floral crown on his brow and ornaments on the back of the head, the bizarre 'ears' of the headdress being large but very thin when seen from the side. Before the body, the figure holds a small stylized shield and has a sword at his side, the latter being short and unobstructive, and being worn on the right side of the body.

This is not a very martial appearance, which would fit what we know of the period, as the Celts of the late Hallstatt time seems to have had peaceful ideas of the otherworld. Most nobles were buried without weapons of war, which points to a belief in an otherlife which has no need for combat.

Top left: Golden torque with three bulbs, Glauburg, Hessen, Germany.

Top right: small figure of man wearing textile armour, top of a bronze jug, Glauburg, Hessen, Germany.

Bottom: two earthenware jugs with trefoil ornament, Dürrnberg, Hallein, Austria.

All items late Hallstatt/ early La Tène time.

You may also wonder about the massive legs. These are not very aesthetic, but they certainly functioned. The Glauberg statue, and its massive thighed counterpart from Hirschlanden, could stand without additional support. Compare this with Roman statues of the same period, which required a background of some sort to prevent them from falling over.

In all likeliness, the statue originally graced the top of the mound. It was not in the open for long, however, as it shows few traces of erosion, so possibly it was hidden in the ditch at the side of the mound where the diggers found it ('Another bloody rock!'). When the Glauburg statue was unearthed, the scholars in charge immediately speculated that the statue may be a representation of the buried noble. That a very similar item used to exist in far away Pfalzfeld, and a similar fragment of a head had been found in Heidelberg, did not stop them. These locations were definitely not ruled by the noble of the Glauburg, so why should the locals bother to put up his image? Nowadays this enthusiastic interpretation is getting a bit shaky, as the Glauburg has by now supplied fragments of several other statues of the same appearance. Not to mention that the headdress can also be seen on a couple of items found in the mound of Waldalgesheim, near Mainz. This points at a common religious tradition, and not at a personality cult of a specific individual.

Apparently a figure with three rays or leaves under its throat, a floral brow and a bizarre headdress was a common motif in the late Hallstatt time. On the Pfalzfeld pillar you see the person/entity/deity in its decapitated state, on the Glauburg statues the bearer still holds on to his head, though the signs of times-to-come are obvious already.

Of course I would not dream of advancing an opinion whether the figure is really a noble, a deity or some exalted figure, such as a priest or poet. I have my suspicions - strange things happen when you use the symbols as gateways for astral projection or assume the god-form of the statue - but it wouldn't be fair to annoy you with them. It's much better if you do your own research and dreaming. Mind you, the flowers around the brow may well remind you of Taliesin, the bright, radiant or precious brow, bringing to mind the floral wreaths worn by poets in the classical world.

And while we are busy dreaming and speculating, let me introduce another question. The trefoil coming out of the throat of the figures looks a bit like the symbol of the lily. You may be acquainted with this sign, it is known as the Lily of France, for instance, and used by all sorts of folk including boy-scouts. What did this sign mean during the Hallstatt period? We have no means of being certain. It may be of interest, that it can be connected with intoxication. Tombs from the famous Dürrnberg near Hallein contained earthenware jugs filled with what was probably mead. If you visualize these jugs as figures, you can find three large Awen-type lozenges coming out of the collar/torque. Here we have a link between the seat of speech (the throat) which allows the Awen to manifest in free-flowing poetry, and the draught of intoxication.

Further support for this idea can be found

in one of the wine flagons from the Glauburg mound. You wouldn't see this in a photograph, but when you cautiously examine the end of the spout, you could discern a fine trefoil design over which the cherished mead poured on its way into a drinking vessel.

What do you make of this theory? And while we are at it, let me add something really bizarre. Here is some synchronicity, supplied by kind spirits who know the sort of nutty stuff I'm interested in. Recently, while I was researching legends from Frankfurt, I came upon a tale of Doctor Faust. Faust, as you may know, was not an invention of Goethe but a historical person who spent most of his life touring middle Europe selling sorceries, telling tall tales and exploiting the naive. Well, the legend goes that one day, Doctor Faust came to Frankfurt. As he was walking through the trader halls, he heard some folk gossiping. There were three mighty magicians in town, the traders said, who had taken up their quarters in a guest-house close to the Jewish alley. Every day they would permit the public to participate in a strange ritual. This was enough to excite Doctor Faust, who was never a happy man when other sorcerers were mentioned.

So, early the next morn, found Faust hurrying to the performance. The three sorcerers had taken their quarters in a large and lavish room, and were about to have a shave when Faust arrived. For this purpose, they had engaged a barber, and all doors and windows were widely open, so that the public could come in and watch. To begin with, one of the three took a seat. Another reached for a large sword, and wielding it

with passion, cut off his colleague's head. While the corpse collapsed, the barber reached for the head, placed it on a table, and began to shave the beard. Then he cut the hair and kneaded the cheeks to make them look red and cheerful. Finally, he returned the head to the sword wielder, who replaced it on the neck, and, lo and behold, the dead man came to life again, looking happy and well groomed.

Faust observed this piece of magic with ill-concealed envy. Then he happened to notice something even more unusual. As soon as one of the mages lost his head, a lily appeared in a bowl of water which was standing on the table. When the head was replaced, and the mage came to life, the lily disappeared. This naturally aroused Faust's curiosity. When the next mage had been decapitated and was being shaved, Faust cautiously approached the table and cut through the stalk of the lily in its bowl. Nobody happened to notice this transaction, so when the sorcerers tried to put the head back on, the damn thing kept falling off again. This made them realize that one in the audience had seen through their game, and humbly apologized for having failed to realize that another sorcerer was present.

Faust, feeling very proud of himself, slipped away unseen. What makes this tale so interesting is the way it combines the symbol of the lily with decapitation. The lily, so the text said, was a symbol of life, and especially of eternal life, so when Faust severed the stalk, the head could not come to life again.

Deity of the Poets

After we have looked into the muses venerated by the British bards, it may be useful to take a look across the Irish channel and wonder whether the filid may have adored a poet's deity as well. The answer is much easier than in Britain and Wales. To begin with, it may be useful to take a look at the Tuatha De Danann. In pre-Christian Ireland, a wide range of deities received offerings and worship. Then St. Patrick put a stop to suchlike fun festivities and taught the people to kneel and grovel before their god. The filid accepted this conversion, but as custodians of history they did not forget that before the coming of bright Christ, things had been a lot different. In their legends, they commemorated the pagan deities. These are basically a group of figures, or a family, known as the people of the goddess Danann. Here we have a first connection to the faith of the British Celts: in the *Mabinogi*, a number of semi-divine persons (Gwydyon, Govannon, Arianrod) come from the family of Don.

There were several fascinating deities in ancient Ireland. It would easily exceed the scope of this book to explore the lot of them, so I'll leave you to do some reading and thinking on your own. Suffice it to say that the scholars of the 19th century were rather over-enthusiastic in their treatment of the Tuatha De. It was the easiest thing in the world to generalize that all members of the divine family are automatically ancient Celtic deities. Modern research points out that things are more complicated. Yes, there are some candidates among the Tuatha De who are closely related to the gods of the British or even earlier, the gods of ancient

Gaul. The Irish smith of the gods Goibhniu has a British parallel in the master-smith Govannon son of Don (in whose fortress Taliesin received some of his initiations), in the Gaulish world the name *Goban-, latinized as the popular god Volcanus, is a close relation. Goban (literally: smith) was a popular name in ancient Gaul. When archaeologists excavated the early medieval shrine of St. Gobnet in Ballyvourney, Country Cork, they found a complex pre-Christian industrial site underneath, containing at least 137 forges (Hutton).

Radiant Lugh of the Irish, a god of cunning, skill and shining excellence in many crafts, has a pale reflection in the British Lleu, fosterson of Gwydyon. In a similar fashion, the Irish god of the sea, Manannan, has a counterpart in the British half-god Manawyddan son of Llyr. The later two, however, can not only serve as examples for deities surviving in human form. On close examination you can also observe that the Irish and the British versions have very little in common. The Irish Manannan is a god of the great oceans which he travels in his enchanted chariot. The British Manawyddan is a super human sorcerer, not a deity, and has next to nothing to do with the sea. Lugh of the Irish is a leader of the gods, a half giant and trickster. Lugus was also an important deity among the Celts of Noricum and received veneration in several places on the continent. Maybe he was a similar god there, and maybe he wasn't, as, so sorry, none of his myths or rituals have survived. A strange folk-myth from the Vogelsberg mountain range in Hessen claims that the locals venerated a deity called Heillug who was adored as an idol

Two items from the burial of the 'Lady of
Reinheim', Saarland, Germany, 370-320 BCE.
Top: bronze mirror with head, diameter 18,9 cm.
Bottom: bronze jug topped by a horse with
human head, height 51.5 cm.

with a copper bull's head. At nighttime, fires were lit within the head so that its eyes shone. Neither the Irish Lugh nor the Welsh Lleu have any relation to bulls, but as their names mean something like light, shining, the glowing idol may well come from the same root.

Lleu in Wales is a gifted human being with some supernatural characteristics and a few interesting problems with women. His one contribution to divine behaviour is that, on being wounded by a poisoned spear, he transforms into an eagle and flies away to the otherworld. There he sits on an oak and rots till his uncle Gwydyon, being guided by a hungry sow, comes to rescue him. If you look for deities closer to the Irish Lugh you can find them more easily in the Scandinavian trickster gods Loki and Odin. Not to mention that the closest parallel to the British half-god Gwydyon son of Don is the common Germanic Wodan/Odin, god of enchantment, rage, ecstasy, trickery and illusion. The Langobardian writers Paulus Diaconus recorded that the Germans (in this case probably the Alemanni and Bavarians) venerate Wodan, who is called Mercurius by the Romans, under the name Gwodan. It is not far from Gwodan to Gwydyon, especially if you consider that both are associated with sorcery, spell-craft, enchantment, eloquence, shape-shifting and so on. Thus you can see that there was a connection, or a common origin, or perhaps some cultural exchange, but that by the time the myths were recorded, most of the essentials had long been forgotten.

Then there is the fact that a good many members of the Tuatha De have very few,

if any, divine qualities. Worse yet, the stories collected by the filid have a slightly contrived element to them. They do not seem like precise records of an elder faith but like a talented historian's efforts to reconstruct a pagan mythology out of a lot of odds and ends. You have a similar case in the *Prose Edda* which learned Snorri compiled in medieval Iceland to give a record of the faith of his pre-Christian ancestors.

The question marks raised by the lore of the Tuatha De have increased so much that a number of scholars speculated that the Tuatha De Danann may have been no gods at all. To trace a religion you need gods, but you also need evidence that these gods were adored, that they received offerings, that there were rituals of sorts or that people approached them for help. With most of the Tuatha De, this evidence is lacking, and it wouldn't surprise me if they were simply made up for the sake of a good story. On the other hand, a number of Tuatha De exhibit good evidence that there was a religion associated with them. To begin with, we can look at Cormac's records. The good bishop recorded that Danu, or Anu, is the *Mater Deorum Hibernensium*, i.e. the Mother of the Gods of Ireland. The *Coir Anmann* (14th C) calls her a goddess of fertility, to whom the province of Munster owes its wealth. Here we may be on the track of an Indo European deity. The Indian *Rig Veda* has a goddess Danu, whose name may be translated as 'stream' or 'waters from heaven'. Related may be the Danube river, the river Don in Russia, the Dnieper river, the Dniester river and the British river Don. Then there is the Celtic goddess

Arduinna, who was the patroness of the Ardennes mountains, and whom the Romans identified with the virgin huntress Diana. The mother Danu (or later Danann) may well be a former deity. Her people were accounted for in several ways. Tuan the shape changer recorded that the Tuatha De Danann came from the skies: *on account of their intelligence and the excellence of their knowledge.* This makes them extraterrestrials. Other authors were more cautious and claimed that the people of Danu came from Spain, from the south, from Skythia, from Denmark and elsewhere. Most of the filid do not refer to the Tuatha De as deities, but give semi divine roles to them. A writer of the 15th century mentions that the Tuatha De were worshipped (see Rees) and a poet writing around AD1000 states that though he enumerates them, he does not worship them, thereby giving evidence that obviously some people did.

It may be interesting to take a look at a little known manuscript here. There is *A Tuath De Miscellany*, based on versions from the *Lebar Gabala*, translated by John Carey and dating around AD1100. The short text lists members of the Tuatha De Danann and tells us in line 11. *Those were the Tuatha De, the professionals were gods, while the farmers were non-gods.* While this was not very kind on the farmers, it does show that as early as 1100, some people were aware that the traditional lists of the Tuatha De contain deities and non-deities.

Let us now take a look at the best known pagan deity of Ireland. This is the blessed Brigid, Brighit, Brighid, Bride. The name derives from an elder form, * Briganti, which may mean high, exalted or bright. The title was possibly used for several Celtic goddesses. The *Miscellany* introduces her in line

1. Brigit the Poetess, Daughter of the Dagda. 2. With her were Fe and Men, the Kings of Oxen, from whom is named Femen. 3. With her was Triath, the King of Boars, from whom is named Treithirne. 4. With her were heard the three voices of the devil after transgression in Ireland: whistling and wailing and outcry.

It certainly says a lot that the poet who composed the *Miscellany* named Brigit first of all gods. She was a special deity to him, and this goes for many of the filid. Here we have the words of Cormac again, who wrote in his *Glossary:*

Brigit: A goddess whom the filid used to worship…therefore they used to call her Dea Poetarum, her two sisters, also named Brigit, excelled in medicine and smithcraft.

Cormac is an excellent witness, as he was a fili, a historian, a devout Christian bishop and aristocrat. As such, he had access to plenty of old lore. If he is ready to name Brigit a deity, and admit that she used to be worshipped, this surely counts for something. His lines have served to identify Brigit as a triple goddess. Robert Graves made use of them, and a mistranslated line purporting that she was goddess to all of the Irish, to establish his own personal vision of a triple moon-goddess.

In Graves' *White Goddess* you can find lots of stuff on a Brigit who would have come as a real surprise to the filid. I mention this matter, as Graves had such an immense influence on early Wicca, and his *White Goddess* is full of the most mind blowing errors. In Graves version, Brigit is a triple goddess. Unlike Cormac's account, Graves portrays her not as a poetess, a smith and a healer (all three adult craftswomen) but gets her mixed up with the matronae, the triple mother goddesses favoured by the Rhineland Celts, and his own delirious visions of near eastern moon deities. As a result, his triple Brigit appears in the roles of virgin, mother and crone (to quote Astrid: The three times in the life of a woman when she has least fun). This is common gospel in Wicca and similar neo pagan cults but there is not a shred of evidence in favour of it. In fact we can't even be sure that Brigit was a triple goddess. Ronald Hutton cites a medieval inventory of saints which lists ten different Brighits, twelve Brigs and three known as both. Other documents supply a Brig Ambue, goddess of justice, and Brig Briugu, the provider. Related to them may or may not be a British deity called Brigantia, worshipped by the Brigantes tribe and possibly associated with the rivers Brent and Braint. The Briganti were a north British people whose history was partly recorded in Tacitus' *Annals*. After the Roman invasion in AD43 their queen Cartimandua collaborated with the invaders. This friendly attitude seems to have lasted only for a few years, as between 48-69AD, we find the Briganti in open warfare against the Romans. There are just seven inscriptions to her, two of them identifying her as a goddess of victory. As such she was shown in the shape of Minerva/Athena (see illustration). Can a war-goddess function as a deity of poets? Geoffrey of Monmouth evidently thought so when he recorded that Taliesin was taught and inspired by Minerva. When Christianity was introduced to the Irish, the former pagan deity Brigit, of whom we know so little, was turned into several female saints. The most famous of them is said to have lived in the 5th century she must have been a contemporary of St. Patrick. As her hagiography goes, the dear lady was the daughter of a slave woman toiling at the fortress of a chieftain called Dubhthach. The latter fathered Brigit, and when the child was born, had her raised by a Druid. In spite of her foster father's occupation, young Brigit wanted to be baptized, and apparently the Druid allowed it. As she grew up, she became famous for giving things away to the poor and needy. Her father Dubhthach grew so annoyed about this habit that he tried to sell her to the king of Leinster. The Leabhar Breac gives the scene:

> Said Dubhthach to Brigit, 'Not for honour or reference to thee art thou carried in a chariot, but to take thee, to sell thee to grind the quern for Dunlang mac Enda, King of Leinster' When they came to the king's fortress Dubhthach went in to the king, and Brigit remained in her chariot at the fortress door. Dubhthach had left his sword in the chariot near Brigit. A leper came to Brigit to ask an alms. She gave him Dubhthach's sword.

On coming out to fetch her, Dubhthach saw the sword missing and had a fit of rage.

Statue of Brigantia, 3 century CE, Birrens, Dumfriesshire, Britain. The image is a close copy of the goddess Minerva / Athena, complete with cloak, helmet, spear and fear inspiring Medusa head. If it were not for the inscription, we would not even know it shows a Celtic goddess.

King Dunlag, however, was more sensible. First he refused to buy her, fearing that she might squander his wealth even faster than that of her father. On examination of the girl he declared that she had *a merit higher before god than before men.* So Brigit was liberated from slavery and granted royal permission to set up a convent. She chose the plains of Kildare, where there was a famous race track, the buildings being erected close to an ancient oak. Local legends associate her with the race course, and describe her as riding her chariot across the plains. This fits neatly a local tradition that in times of war, Brigit would appear like a raging war goddess to lead the locals to triumph. The chronology of St. Brigit has her become a nun c. 467. Her hagiography informs us that she met St. Patrick once, when he gave a non-stop sermon that lasted for three days and nights. During the event, she fell asleep, and while the holy men preached, she had a number of prophetic dreams. These involved white, dark and black oxen in corn fields, savage animals like dogs and wolves fighting each other, and in another version, a complicated assemblage of sowers and ploughmen doing their highly symbolic job. After she woke, she apologized for having fallen asleep. St. Patrick, however, asked to be told the dreams and declared that she had foreseen the future fate and doom of the Irish church.

This story, though full of Christian elements, includes one pagan motif. It's the belief in oracles obtained by dreams. If we can trust the manuscripts, a ritual of dream incubation may have been used to chose the kings of Ireland (see the chapter on divination), and here we have St. Brigit,

patroness and deity of the poets, who has a deep trance vision after being hypnotized by a monotonous long sermon.

In her monastery in Kildare, the saintly lady had establishments for Christians of both sexes. Soon enough, the religious community became such a center of influence that around it grew a large settlement. It even had a school of metal-making under the patronage of the good saint, maybe a memory of the association of the deity with smiths.

When St. Brigit died around 525, her reputation was well established all over Ireland and to this day she is as important to Irish Christianity as the Virgin Mary, if not more so. Before we look at the folk lore, I would like to mention that there is an episode that tells us that a pillar of flame rose from St. Brigit's head. This is not far from the fire of inspiration that flamed in the head of many a poet. Fire is often associated with her. We find fire in smithcraft, and there is the legend told by Gerald of Wales that she had a perpetual ashless fire, blown by fans and bellows, which was guarded by twenty nuns, of whom she was one. And fire is in the poet's art. Nede chanted that he sings straight from the heart of the fire.

If we consult Carmichael's *Carmina Gadelica*, we can find references to the blessed Bride in dozens of spells, blessings and folk customs of Scotland. She often appears in company of the Virgin Mary, and legend has it that she acted as her midwife. Bride was famous for plenty of enchanted objects, such as a bright staff. This was usually a peeled wand of birch, broom, bramble, white willow, very similar to the white wands handed to the Irish kings on their inauguration, to symbolize that their reign should be straight and peaceful. Folk-spells also mention her mantle, lorica, corslet and bed. In folk belief, Bride presided over all crafts, over art, over all beauty, and her reign extended from beneath the sky to beneath the sea. Upon birth, the Highlanders would anoint the brow of a babe with the three drops of Bride, an interesting parallel to the three drops of Ogyrven's Awen bursting out of the cauldron.

Then there are the feasts of Bride at Imbolc (lit. in milk, i.e. the season when the ewes produce milk, this being a sign that soon young sheep would be born and spring begin). Imbolc, at the first (or 13th) of February, was the symbolic end of the Gaelic winter and the beginning of spring. It's Catholic name, candlemass, associates it with her fiery nature. Mind you, it takes a lot of fire to tame the Gaelic winter, *the dead quarter of the year*. This is not the gentle spring of the Mediterranean calendars but the fiercely struggling spring of a people who can expect heavy snowfall till the end of April.

Ritual: Bride's Bed

During the night before Imbolc, the Highlanders used to prepare a bed for Bride. This is a charming ritual and perhaps you'll like to join in. There are plenty of variations in Scotland and Ireland, here is a workable synopsis. In general, the night before Bride's day (nowadays the night before Feb. 1st), the old women made a figure of Bride. This could be formed out of an artfully plaited sheaf of corn, dressed up with pieces of cloth, or formed out of oats. You can make a Bride out of porridge or use flour and water, which will produce smoother surfaces for really smoth results try marzipan. The Bride is placed on an elaborate bed. The old ladies of the isles used a basket shaped like a cradle. The bed was made with much loving care. It contained ribbons of cloth, the first early flowers, crystals from the mountains and shells from the sea. Straw ornaments are another popular element, or any beautiful object. On Bride's breast is a small crystal, if available, or a bright shell from the sea, called *the guiding star of Bride*. When the *dealbh Bride* (the icon of Bride) is ready, one of the crones went to the door and called softly into the night 'Bride's bed is ready'. Another one, standing behind her, replied: 'Let Bride come in, Bride is welcome.' Then the woman at the door called out: 'Bride! Bride, come thou in, thy bed is made. Preserve the house for the Trinity.' Then they place the white (peeled) wand in Bride's hand. On the hearth, they leveled the ashes. The next day they carefully searched them for signs left by the goddess. Wand marks ensure good luck but even better is a footprint. When no signs can be found, so Carmichael tells us, the family had to regain Bride's favour by offering incense on the hearth at night and sacrificing a cockerel by burying it alive near the junction of three rivers.

Of course the rite of Bride exists in countless variations. In some districts girls and young women made a figure of Bride out of straw and ribbons and took her for a walk round the village. Each house was expected to offer a gift to Bride, be it foodstuff, drink or any beautiful object, be it a pin, a pebble or a flower. After going round the women retired to a house where they prepared the feast of Bride. Later on the lads came round and asked for Bride's permission to join in, then it was drinking and dancing and singing songs till morning. In the dawn they formed a circle and sang a hymn to greet the day of the foster mother of Christ, later the leftover foodstuff was distributed to the poor. Some left ribbons hanging out of their windows. When Bride passed the window in the night, she touched the ribbons. If you tie one around your head and offer a bit of prayer, headache disappears.

The Personal Muse

A Welsh proverb tells us that the three qualities that make up the Awen are *knowledge, thought and inspiration*. This simple piece of data contains some amazing insights into the nature of the mind. What people loosely describe as thinking is generally a number of more or less complicated activities making use of several sensory systems. A thought cannot be thought unless it is represented in some way. For this purpose, people employ inner vision, inner speech and inner feelings and/or emotions. These sensory systems create a representation in the mind. The thought is not the representation, but without a representation you couldn't think it anyway. Most people do this sort of thing, but the way they do it, how they do it, in what order and to what effect differs enormously. Some are aware of several sensory channels. Some are only aware of their inner voices, or of their inner pictures or feelings, and the resulting chain of thoughts may well be somewhat one-sided or restricted. Each sensory system has its strengths and shortcomings.

Think of the question of quality. Some represent their thoughts with great vividness, others are more restrained. The former are easily excited, the latter may seem withdrawn and distant. The better sort of magician is aware of these individual differences. In thinking, remembering and receiving inspiration, s/h makes use of as many sensory systems as possible. This gives a very convincing representation, or one that seems 'real', whatever that may be. We tend to do two sorts of thinking. One is based on stored memory, the other on constructive, creative thought. If you have an opinion, know about a topic or recall an incident you are making use of memory. Everything you know about the world is memory, and so is everything you know about yourself. Unlike what most people think, however, memory is not simply a device for storing information. Yes, the information is stored in some cryptic way, but it is not stored in a form you could actually think consciously. Your deep mind creates the memory you recall out of stored data. The data, so we hope, is more or less reliable, but the shape the deep mind makes up for it usually involves items that were not stored that specifically.

In re-constructing a scene or event or piece of information, some of the representation is always creative. On the other hand, when you use thought in a constructive way, you make use of items that come from your memory. If you dream about the future you are evidently constructing images, but the way you do so depends very much on your assessment of what the future may be like. This process involves estimations of past memory and future possibility. The result is a myth, and definitely unlike anything you are going to experience, but to lots of people such a myth is as convincing as if it actually happened . So what we perceive as the two basic forces of thinking are construction and recall.

These are fine for a start, but if you wish to taste and share the Awen, what you need is the element of inspiration. Inspiration is anything you personally couldn't think of, i.e. information coming from 'outside' of your ego. Inspiration means literally that you are inspired by a spirit, i.e. an unembodied entity. This is anything but a metaphor: we are in the realm of the Shamans here. But what, I hope you are asking, is a spirit? As I had to repeat in most of my books, there are many explanations possible. Most of them boil down to the insight that spirits (and gods, giants, demons etc.) may be

1. Independent entities dwelling on another plane but able to influence ours,

2. Imaginary figures invented to represent abilities, instincts and forces of the deep mind (subconscious self) to our rather limited conscious minds or

3. Both, as the deep mind is not just yours or mine but in constant interaction with the deep minds of all life-forms. As all selfs come from one consciousness, a spirit or god may be independent of you and still be bound by bonds of mutual selfhood. You may seem apart, but the parts that communicate are shared. This goes for the spirits, but it also applies to other people, beings, entities and so on.

And it especially applies to muses. Gogyrven, as you may recall from Dr Pughe's dictionary, is a spiritual being, but also a personified idea. This description is not a contradiction, if you think it is, you ought to get more knots into your brain so that the Celtic can flow more easily. For a start, a muse is much like a spirit helper for the bard or poet. Here we are again close to shamanism. The bard, like the Shaman, needs at least one associate in the otherworld to whom s/he can turn for help, healing and inspiration. In Crowleyan lore, such a being may be called the Holy Guardian Angel. If you know Crowley, you will be aware that his idea of an angel is a long way from the bloodless creatures envisioned by New Age goody-goody thought. The word angel means 'messenger', and as we all know, message and messenger tend to influence each other. Crowley's angel is a messenger of the True Will, the original self-nature. Its not good or bad, it's not nice or nasty. It can be any of these, or none, but it is specifically that what you need to learn and develop. The mask assumed by your Holy Guardian Angel depends on the mask you are wearing, and on the will you share with your deep mind and the universe in general.

With the muse, similar difficulties arise. Please pause now to think of a muse. How would you imagine your muse? Do this before you go on. Ready?

Whatever shape you imagined, it will be a shape that seems attractive to you. A muse is, after all, a being that inspires poetry, tales and myths, and nobody, least of all you, would bother to make poems for a being whom you don't like. A good muse is a creature that makes you want to be creative. By the same mouth, a muse embodies whatever you need to get going. Think of human muses. Plenty of poets saw their beloved ones as muses, if only because they wanted to do something to impress. Your partner can be your muse, or your lover, or any good friend, provided s/he inspires you to act, create, shape, form or whatever.

Sometimes opponents and rivals can be muses, if only to make you learn how to do it better. Humans can fulfill the function of muses. Examples of this abound in life, they can also be found in the poems attributed to mad Myrddin. One old song has Myrddin's sister approach the aged seer, who has just reclined in his newly dug grave. Hearing his sister plead for true prophecy, the lunatic sage looks out of his earth hole and recites the history of Britain till doomsday. In this song Gwendydd functions as the muse for Myrddin, and when she asks the source of his inspiration, he cites his muses: the ghosts of the mountain and a sybil who sang a song to him. Another song has Myrddin and Taliesin chanting prophecy in alternation. The two inspire each other into a frenzy of violent prophecy, here we have two bards acting as muses for each other.

While a living person can act as a muse for you, this is also possible with an imaginary one. One thing I do before I write a complicated text is to tell the tale to a couple of imaginary persons. Watching their response tells me a lot. Or I go for a walk imagining being in the compnay of a person from another culture and age, or maybe an alien. I watch what makes them respond and react. Usually it's something fascinating which I overlooked before. We all overlook so much, and take so many miracles for granted. The poets knew how many miracles fade into uncaring routine mindedness. We can remind each other to wake up.

Return to the madman of the Caledonian forest. Not only Taliesin or his sister inspired mad Myrddin. Then there were the crazy times when Myrddin dwelled all alone in the mountains of Scotland, living like a beast among the deer and wolves of the wilderness. Here our inspired prophet sang his visions to the unusual audience of a pig, an apple tree and, if we can trust Geoffrey, an aged wolf. This is a case of animals acting as a muse. As most real animals and trees have little interest in the future fate of kingdoms, it may be assumed that they were spirit animals, or totem spirits.

A similar tradition has survived in North Germanic mythology, where you find the hero's fylgia (spirit helper) appear as a wild beast, usually a wolf, lynx, bear, swan, eagle or dragon. Plenty of elite warriors used to trance-form their consciousness into fylgia obsession when a fit of berserk rage was needed. Others went into a trance and assumed the fylgia's shape in the astral world (the realm of dreams and imagination) to work fighting magic against their enemies.

Island Celtic mythology contains many hints that make the existence of similar concepts (and spirits) likely. A good example is the Irish poem of the *Hawk of Achill*. The tale, extensively quoted by John Matthews, relates how the hawk, who happens to be one of the oldest creatures in the world, pecks out the eye of an aged seer. Then the two have a memory contest, starting out by telling the oldest stories in the world and proceeding to the painful present. Finally they come to conclude their ecstatic frenzy by sharing a lengthy and complicated prophecy of doom and destruction. For some mysterious reason they both drop dead, which goes to show that their lives are closely entwined. Similarly, to a North German hero, the disappearance of the fylgia meant death would soon approach.

While muses may have appeared as animal spirits in some cases, most of them tend to be more or less humanoid. Their appearance has much to do with desirability and attractiveness. What seems attractive to you is the ideal shape for their incarnation, as it invites attention and belief. Spirits and gods feed on attention, but attention only works when it is energized by passionate emotion. Strong or refined feelings are the currency of exchange with the otherworldly ones. The flow goes both ways, you have to care about whoever you seek to invoke. As a result, quite a few imagine their muses like perfect lovers. This brings them close to the function enjoyed by succubi and incubi. Perhaps this sounds over the top to you, but a muse and a demon lover can have a lot in common. Let me quote WB Yeats on the subject:

The Leanhaun Shee (Ir. Leanhaun sidhe, i.e. fairy mistress)This spirit seeks the love of men. If they refuse she is their slave, if they consent, they are hers, and can only escape by finding one to take their place. Her lovers waste away, for she lives on their life. Most of the Gaelic poets, down to quite recent times, have had a Leanhaun Shee, for she gives inspiration to her slaves and is indeed the Gaelic muse - this malignant fairy. Her lovers, the Gaelic poets, died young. She grew restless, and carried them away to other worlds, for death does not destroy her powers.

Now Yeats, as a member of the Golden Dawn, was not just speaking as a romantic poet when he wrote these lines. As a well informed, but somewhat hesitant sorcerer, he was aware that these matters were not just metaphors. Inspiration from the Leanhaun Shee works. Not quite as Mr. Yeats had it, as the relationship is definitely not based on slavery but on true will. How this works is something you will explore together with your muse. Suffice it to say that the poets die young, even if they make it to old age, and that they die young repeatedly, as with each rebirth they come closer to the essence of the mystery. Keep in mind that death does not destroy her powers. Like the Holy Guardian Angel, the muse can accompany a soul from life to life, stimulating intuition, evolution and intelligence. While not every muse makes its poet wither like a leaf in autumn, most of them can and should be drastic in their behaviour. The Gogynfeirdd poets saw Ceridwen as their muse, and as the muse of their vocation, but they were aware that she has a darksome nature when it comes to initiation.

In the *Hanes Taliesin*, Ceridwen tries to kill Gwion, and succeeds. It is through dying and being reborn in the nourishing darkness of her womb that Gwion attains to the degree of spiritual ripeness that enables him to survive his ordeal in the leather bag. You could consider that Ceridwen is doing Gwion a kindness, but in the process she certainly gave him hell. The muse of the bards is no sweat and translucent ideal. She can appear as a sorceress, as a giantess or as a deity. She can be kind and gentle, but she can also appear in terrifying guise and scare you till all pretense falls away. In this sense she is not unlike the terrible deities of death and destruction who liberate the soul from the confines of self-made illusions. Kali has a black colour, Helja is both black and white and Ceridwen appears as a screeching black hag in a poem from the *Hanes Taliesin.*

The goddess or giantess with her two moods is a common element in Island Celtic mythology. Think of the shape-changing giantess in the tale of Njall (who became high king of Ireland after just one night in her embrace), the Lady Ragnell who was married to Sir Gawain, the ogress bedded by King Henry in a folk song or the dark, bald lady who accompanies the holy grail (and a collection of blood dripping weapons and/or chariots full of bleeding heads) in the tales of the continental troubadours. Her winter side is dark and terrifying. She has eyes as big as soup-plates, a mouth full of sharp teeth that splits the head in a ear-to-ear grin, her skin is black, her breasts worn and drained, her ribs stand out and her belly is flat with hunger. Like sticks her legs, the knees all bloated and swollen, the spine crooked and the hands reaching out like twisted claws. Would you care for a kiss?

The summer side appears gentle and loving. Here she is the fairest maiden in the world, her eyes aflame with sparkling joy. Her clothes are the rich greens of the summertime, the ornaments a shower of blossoms and fruit cascading over her mantle. Usually she embodies the sanctity of the land. In several myths there are kings or nobles who have to wed her (in her terrifying shape) before she can transform and show the benevolent side of her nature (see Loomis).

Maybe the bards enjoyed similar beliefs about their muses. I suspect that they imagined muses suiting their sexual orientation. In this sense it becomes obvious why most bards, as they were men, envisioned her in feminine form. There were some female bards and visionaries around in the medieval period, not many, but enough to show that the profession was not totally sexistic. Whether there were female bards in the pre-historic period is anybody's guess, but the evidence for mad prophetic priestesses is pretty good. In all likeliness, their muse may have appeared male. This may be a key to the question why the sex of Ogyrven is such a riddle: people find what they are looking for. And it explains why Ogyrven is both a spirit and a personified idea. For you, Ogyrven will appear in shapes crafted out of your own hopes, desires and fears. It is your shape, it is a shape for self to project itself in the guise of all-otherness, and of course this shape is artificial and totally subjective.

On the other hand the same applies to all poets, each of them irresistibly attracted to a lucid vision of utter subjectivity. As the muse is of our nature, it is at once always present and yet elusive. And again, just because you made up a shape for the muse to manifest in, it does not mean that what manifests is also of your own making. Your projected dreams do not create the deity but give flesh to it. You shape the form, but the form is moved by the spirit. When the flesh supplies a mode of interaction, the prosopopoeia comes to life and speaks the wisdom of the deep. Often enough, the muse will need more than one face to do her work. S/he can be a fleeting range of subtle faces and figures.

Muses are not only authors of inspiration, however, they are also stimulate evolution. Ceridwen may supply the material that goes into the cauldron, and likewise she supplies a hut for the boiling and food for Gwion. It is Gwion who has to feed the fire, who supplies the fuel and who stirs the broth for an entire year. His yoga is constant attention, never ceasing watchfulness and care. The muse may offer inspiration, the mind has to prepare the elixir. This process is not necessarily nice. A good muse is capable of teaching by means of joy, rapture, confusion, problems, exhaustion, ordeal and trickery. Think of yourself. How often have your spirits provided the very crisis you didn't like but needed nevertheless? The Celtic muses are not fluffy minded romantic girlies. They work their spell with passion and determination. Real poetry, real art and real magick come from the source of life and death. So take another look. Go inward and consider. Which deities do you like to have a chat with? Who of them surprises you frequently? Who asks the impossible questions? Who makes you think, doubt, and think again? The muse need not be anybody new. You know her/him already. Have known it for ever. Just find out who answers to your call, who gives you fresh insights, and there you have it, this is your muse, and it is you beyond yourself. Of course this sounds dangerously like having

to do some practise, doesn't it? Before you know you'll be busy having your very own subjective experiences.

To begin with, there may be two basic forms of inspiration, the face and hands of the muse. Direct inspiration is what happens when you channel some consciousness, when you trance and meet your deities, when you are obsessed by them. In all of these cases there is a specific source of your inspiration, and you are in direct contact with it. Indirect inspiration uses another medium. You find it when a sight reminds you of something, when the universe is telling you something. Some gods or muses send gifts, some send events and some send whatever comes in handy. Let's assume that we start out with the indirect approach. If you want the world to inspire some interesting insights in your mind, the first thing to do is to tell the deep mind what you expect of it. What sort of inspiration do you want (or need)? If you can specify what you want, and how you intend to use it, your deep mind will have some idea of your desire. Likewise, your conscious mind begins to expect something, and starts to watch out for the very stuff it needs. You can do this with yourself, you can speak with your deep mind like you speak with a close friend.

And watch out for the response. Or you can go one step further and speak with your muse. An example. As you set out to go for a walk, tell the muse what in particular interests you, what sort of inspiration you are hunting. Ask her/him to provide the sort of experience you need, be it to inspire, teach or transform you. Then dedicate the walk to the muse and go out adventuring till you find whatever you set out for.

Last, give your thanks and share the joy. The process can be used to find inspiration for all sorts of art forms. It can also be used to ask for the sort of inspiring insights that transform the seeker. You can make it easy to recall the influence of the muse if you wear an article of clothing or talisman to remind you of her presence. Much of the magick depends on keeping the cauldron stirred. If you wish to work on a great art project or if you simply wish to obsess yourself for fun and entertainment, it is useful to think of your object frequently. If you keep giving the brain a good stir from time to time, the broth stays in motion and the elixir ripens. When, in daily life, your attention goes round and round the cauldron, new things rise from the deep while others are swallowed up and sucked into the pulsing center of infinity.

The muse is not just a source of inspiration but also a force that initiates and refines the bard so that the inspiration can flow easily into a clear and open mind. The first work of art of every artist is always the conscious mind, the personality. Identity is the first illusion, and the muse is very helpful in getting over it. You'll find out.

If you want direct inspiration, and even better direct contact with the inspiring agencies, it can be helpful to consider a few points. Many bards sought inspiration in darkness, silence and solitude. These terms refer to conditions, but they are even more important for the consciousness states they represent. How can you embody darkness, silence and solitude? How can you go beyond whatever you are to open up to the next step?

What else can you do? How about an offer of milk, dew and acorns? How about composing a poem? How about making music, dancing and singing? One way or another you can begin to pray and invoke. If you don't know how to do this, you can read it up in *Visual Magick*. Here it should suffice to say that the thing to aim for is not necessarily grandiose language. Simply speak from the heart. Your words don't have to be perfectly worked out, the important thing is that you speak passionately, with energy, and love, and desire. A good invocation produces emotion. It doesn't matter just how you produce emotion, do anything that works. If your approach is classical, you can make use of a dramatic voice, of gestures, offerings, candles, magickal weapons and the like. If its more shamanistic, you might enjoy a bit of dancing and chanting, followed by a shaking trance and a number of amazing astral visions. Or you could do the natural thing, and make up for lack of technique by being utterly honest and direct.

Many ways are possible. The main thing is that you call your muse and that imbue the call with lust and joy and love. Or any other emotion that suits your idea of your muse. Then you could close your eyes and direct your awareness into the deep. Using the eyes of the imagination, you can observe how your muse begins to develop. It's not fully there in the beginning, as its astral (imaginary) form has not stabilized, but if you meet her/him a couple of times, you'll find that the vision becomes surprisingly stable. Let me repeat that the vision is very much of your own making. At first. And that what inhabits the vision is definitely not your ego. Not the you who has a name, a form a shape, a history. Maybe it is part of the deep mind, maybe it is an independent entity, maybe both or neither. Do you need to know? Would you believe it? When you want an answer, ask your muse.

Now there are mages who tend towards shyness. They are like so many beginners in art schools, who take a great big piece of paper and draw a tiny figure into a corner. If you want to enjoy your magick, and this is what we are here for, we may as well make it impressive. Ogyrven is a god/dess, giant/ess (or primal chaos alien if you like), and as such she deserves a strong and dramatic appearance. This is not the time for half hearted pictures. Make the vision large and colourful, bring it up close and wrap it around you. It's the very moment you turn on the volume and feel this aura and see this face and go for it.

Anything can happen. If you are an experienced Magician, you will be wise to the fact that some enchantments are easy and some may take a bit of practise. It takes time to come to terms with a new spirit, friend or deity. In this place it can happen that your muse takes longer to assume a more or less constant form than a deity would. Deities are usually well-established figures while the muse, like the Holy Guardian Angel, is a very intimate experience. Maybe your muse likes to change face and appearance from time to time. And just how constant is her voice?

Now the skeptically-minded may enquire how to be sure whether one has really made contact with the muse. Well, in a thoroughly subjective world full of original realities, it is next to impossible to be sure of anything.

What you can do to test your contact, however, is to ask lots of questions. Listen carefully. Are you learning anything new? If you do, then you stand a good chance of being inspired, or challenged, or confused. Anything that stimulates creativity is a boon. We can't be sure whether the bards were really inspired by their muse, and neither were they. The important thing is not whether the muse is real (or whether you are...no, I don't take any bets), but what influence s/he exerts on your mind and your reality.

Then there is poetry. My muse is pretty good at extended bouts of free-style chaos ranting. Often enough it sounds like Joyce, Thomas and Wilson going on a roller-coster ride. Much of it is meaningless, or riddling, or simply confusing for me, but in between the odd stuff I come upon imags that are fascinatingly alive and lucid. The flow of creativity may be just like that. There was a time when I spent half an hour each day lying on my back in a gentle trance state simply observing my thoughts without interfering (this is the hard part). The thoughts that went through my mind were often extremely chaotic and seemingly disconnected, like garbled dream images reflected on the half-sleeping mind. Yet there are patterns wherever one seeks for them. Creativity is often so chaotic that it appears random. It has its good and bad bits, but mostly the bits are so many and they come rushing along all at once. If lots of ideas are combined with each other, the odd inspiration is bound to happen. And here we come to the songs of Taliesin again. Many of them seem garbled, confused or badly censored. We could explain a lot by pointing at faulty recall, confused scribes, tattered manuscripts and eager churchmen. There is another approach. What if the poems constitute genuine outbursts of poetic frenzy in a dark and mysterious speech? What if they never were entirely meaningful? Like the cauldron of the mind, these songs sparkle and foam as bubbles are swept to the surface and alluring fumes dance on the seething fluids.

Here is another Taliesin song that can do with being read several times. You'll find a lot of references to the Awen in it, to Ogyrven, to shape-changes, the proto-*Hanes Taliesin* and to the great and wonderful riddle of the world. For some mysterious reason it has become known as *The Hostile Confederacy*, as some commentators believed that it constitutes one of the items the mythical Taliesin sang to challenge the uninspired bards at Maelgwn's court. Are you up to some riddles? Enjoy!

The Hostile Confederacy

Book of Taliessin 7
A bard there is here, who has not sung, what he shall have to sing;
Let him sing; when he shall have finished,
An astrologer then he may be.
The generous ones refuse me.
There will not be one that will give.
Through the language of Taliessin,
It was a bright day
When Kian did
Praise the multitude.
There will be slaughter, let there be the speech of Avagddu.
But if he ingeniously brings
The requisites forward,
Gwiawn will declare,
O the deep that will come!

He would make the dead alive,
And destitute of wealth he is.
They will not make their cauldrons,
That will boil without fire.
They will make their metals
In age of ages.
Thy pace that bears thee
From the deep of panegyric,
Is it not the hostile confederacy?
What its custom?
So much of national song
Your tongue has given.
Why will ye not recite an oration
Of blessing over the liquor of brightness?
The theme of every one's rhapsody.
I shall be there according to custom,
He was a profound judge.
He came after his periodical custom,
The third of the equal judges.
Three score years
I have supported an earthly scene,
In the water of law and the multitude.
In the element of lands.
A hundred servants surrounded,
A hundred kings made vows.
A hundred they are that went,
A hundred they are that came.
A hundred minstrels sang,
And he foretold of them.
Lladdon, the daughter of the stream,
Little was her desire
For gold and silver,
Who is the living one that left her?
Blood on the breast;
He will probably be spoken of,
He will be greatly praised.
I am Taliessin,
I will delineate the true lineage
Continuing until the end,
In the pattern of Elphin.
Is not the tribute
Of counted gold a debt?
When is hated and not loved,
Perjury and treason,

I desire not advantage,
Through the fluctuation of our song.
The brother that freely greets,
From me no one shall know.
The wise man of the primary science,
The astrologer reasoned,
About wrath, about the resolvent,
About the man describing windings.
About men well versed in praise.
Let us proceed, God it is,
Through the language of Talhaearn,
Baptism was the day of judgment,
That judged the characteristics
Of the force of poetry.
He and his virtue gave
Inspiration without mediocrity,
Seven score Ogyrven
Are in the Awen.
Eight score, of every score it will be one.
In the deep it will cease from ire;
In the deep it will be excessively angry;
In the deep, below the earth;
In the sky, above the earth.
There is one that knows
What sadness is,
Better than joy.
I know the law of the graces of the Awen,
when it flows,
Concerning skilful payments,
Concerning happy days,
Concerning a tranquil life,
Concerning the protection of ages.
Concerning what beseems kings; how long
their consolation.
Concerning similar things, that are on the
face of the earth.
Magnificent astronomy, when communicated,
Sees all that is high.
When the mind is active,
When the sea is pleasant,
When the race is valiant,
When the high one is supplicated,
Or the sun when it is given,
When it covers the land.

Covering land of what extent?
When was drawn the bird of wrath,
The bird of wrath when it was drawn.
When the earth is green.
Who chaunted songs?
Songs who chaunted?
If true, who has considered them?
It has been considered in books,
How many winds, how many streams,
How many streams, how many winds.
How many rivers in their courses,
How many rivers there are.
The earth, what its breadth;
Or what its thickness.
I know the noise of the blades,
Crimson on all sides, about the floor.
I know the regulator,
Between heaven and earth;
When an opposite hill is echoing,
When devastation urges onward,
When the silvery (vault) is shining,
When the dell shall be gloomy.
The breath when it is black,
When is best that has been.
A cow, when it is horned,
A wife, when she is lovely,
Milk, when it is white,
When the holly is green,
When is bearded the kid
In the multitude of fields,
When it is bearded,
When the cow-parsnip is created,
When is revolving the wheel,
When the mallet is flat,
When is spotted the little roebuck,
When the salt is brine,
Ale, when it is of an active quality.
When is of purplish hue the alder.
When is green the linnet,
When are red the hips,
Or a woman when restless,
When the night comes on.
What reserve there is in the hour of flowing,
No one knows whence the bosom of the sun

is made ruddy.
A stain on a new garment,
It is difficult to remove it.
The string of a harp, why it complains,
The cuckoo, why it complains, why it sings.
Why keepeth the agreeable,
Why have left the camp
Geraint and Arman.
What brings out the sparkle
From hard working of the stones.
When is sweet smelling the goat's-beard
plant;
When the crows are of a waxen hue.
Talhayarn is
The greatest astronomer.
What is the imagination of trees.
From the muse the agreement of the day.
I know good and evil.

. . . .
. . . .

The bowl of whom has flowed,
What dawn has finished,
Who preached,
Eli and Eneas:
I know the cuckoos of summer,
(Where) they will be in the winter.
The Awen I sing,
From the deep I bring it,
A river while it flows,
I know its extent;
I know when it disappears;
I know when it fills;
I know when it overflows;
I know when it shrinks;
I know what base
There is beneath the sea.
I know their equivalent,
Every one in its retinue;
How many were heard in a day,
How many days in a year.
How many shafts in a battle,
How many drops in a shower.
Mildly he divided them.
A great mockery, the partial stirring up of a

disgrace,
The vicious muse of Gwydyon.
I know the one,
That filled the river,
On the people of Pharaoh.
Who brought the windings
Of present reasons.
What was the active patience,
When heaven was upreared.
What was a sail-staff
From earth to sky.
How many fingers about the cauldron,
About one, about the hand,
What name the two words
Will not deliver in one cauldron.
When the sea is turning round,
When black are the fish.
Marine food shall be their flesh,
Until it is transformed,
When fish shall contain it.
When the foot of the white swan is black,
Four-sided the sharp spear.
The tribe of heaven will not put down.
Which are the four elements.
Their end is not known.
What pigs, or what wandering of stags.
I salute thee, Bard of the border.
May he increase thee, (whose) bones (are of)
mist.
(Where) two cataracts of wind fall.
My mind has been expressed
In Hebrew, in Hebraic.
In Hebraic, in Hebrew,
Laudatu, Laudate Jesu.
A second time was I formed.
I have been a blue salmon.
I have been a dog; I have been a stag;
I have been a roebuck on a mountain.
I have been a stock, I have been a spade;
I have been an axe in the hand;
I have been a pin in a forceps,
A year and a half;
I have been a speckled white cock
Upon hens in Eiddyn.

I have been a stallion over a stud.
I have been a violent bull,
I have been a buck of yellow hue,
As it is feeding.
I have been a grain discovered,
Which grew on a hill.
He that reaped me placed me,
Into a smoke-hole driving me.
Exerting of the hand,
In afflicting me,
A hen received me,
With ruddy claws, (and) parting comb.
I rested nine nights.
In her womb a child,
I have been matured,
I have been an offering before the Guledig,
I have been dead, I have been alive.
A branch there was to me of ivy,
I have been a convoy,
Before God I have been poor.
Again advised me the cherisher
With ruddy claws; of what she gave me
Scarcely can be recounted;
Greatly will it be praised.
I am Taliessin.
I will delineate the true lineage,
That will continue to the end,
In the pattern of Elphin.

Coins 8, boars
top r: Britain, boar head
center l: Armorici, gold, 15 mm, note serpents and
unknown object between boar legs
center r: , bronze, 20 mm, another object between legs
bottom l: Britain? Silver, 15 mm, usually identified as
boar, my guess is hedgehog

8. Taliesin Penbeirdd

Much of British poetry revolves around a bard called Taliesin. The name also appears as Taliessin, Talyessin, Taliesson, Theliessin, Talyes, Taliess, Telesinus and Talgesinus. You read some of his obscure poetry earlier on, it's not that easy to understand, but certainly stimulating. To simplify things, this bard was at one time a brilliant poet, a wizard, but also an immortal sentience, a semi-divine entity, and a reincarnate shape shifter. This may seem a bit confusing to you, yes, I agree, and so we shall delve into the mystery step by step. Things are easier to digest when they come in bite size portions. Let's start leisurely. What has come to us under the name of Taliesin is a blend of several persons, histories and traditions. You could think of one as the mythical Taliesin. This is the Taliesin whom we know from the *Hanes Taliesin*. First Gwion Bach, a beggar on the road, a servant stirring the cauldron of Ceridwen. Chance initiated by three drops of sorcerous elixir. Shape-changed, hunted, devoured, reborn, cast into the sea, saved, named and reared by Elphin. In contest with the bards of Maelgwn. Immortal sentience, all-knowing, divine. The 16th century *Hanes Taliesin* reveals this persona in a number of mysterious but enchanting poems. Earlier material, and certainly more reliable stuff, appears scattered through the *Book of Taliesin* itself. This item, however, puts us on the track of one or more persons who chanted and wrote under the name Taliesin over the centuries.

Who is the Historical Taliesin?

This question has inspired (and deluded) a lot of researchers. Let's take a look at the *Book of Taliesin*. The manuscript *Llyfr Taliessin* is a collection of songs and poems dating from the late 13th century. The original supposedly contained 77 items, but as the manuscript is damaged, not all of these survive. Only one copy of the manuscript exists, so we have no idea whether the scribe was any good. The material falls into several categories. One is the mythical material alluded to earlier. It contains some historic references, but not enough to make it reliable. More typical is the appearance of legendary or mythical figures, such as Arthur, Gwydyon, Lleu, Govannon, Dylan, Arianrod, Beli, Pwyll, Pryderi and other heroes of the *Mabinogi*. Then there are several religious poems, historical songs praising warlords, lists of tombs, horses, regents, riddles and some odd things like a poem praising a Roman friend, or heroic myths based on a highly imaginary Alexander. The poems are anything but organized and come from various periods between the 6th and the 13th century.

The first enthusiasts who explored the material were quick to realize this. If the *Book of Taliesin* was a collection, who could be considered the first of its authors? One group of songs stood out as particularly archaic. These were historical battle poems addressed to a number of British lords living around the end of the 6th century. You may recall that 'Nennius', writing around the 9th century, informs us that in the time of Ida, the British bards Talhaiarn Cataguen, Neirin, Bluchbard and Taliesin were famed for their poetry. Ida's 12 year reign was in the mid 6th century, he died around 560. So here we have our first record of a famed bard called Taliesin. When we look into the praise songs associated with the nobles of the period, we learn more about Taliesin as a human being. It's a bit of a disappointment, but the earliest Taliesin is simply a brilliant poet with nothing but warfare, politics and generous wages in his all too simple head. He rarely sings about himself, still, there are a few insights that appear here and there in the blood splattered verses. Most of the poems associated with the 6th century bard are addressed to the regents Cynan Garwyn, King of Powys, and Urien of Rheged. Taliesin tells us that he is a stranger in Rheged, it is likely that he came to the north of Britain after dwelling in Powys. Where Rheged exactly was is an open question, most scholars propose somewhere between Wales and Scotland. Cynan was a powerful ruler in his time, he made generous gifts to Taliesin, and was celebrated as one who carried war against the men of Gwent, the dwellers of the Wye valley, the lands of Brycheiniawg and the folk of Cornwall. He also may have had a bit of warfare against the Anglo-Saxons, when he wasn't busy fighting his relations. Take a look at the time. Earlier on, Arthur (real or imaginary) had scored a number of victories against the Anglo-Saxons and succeeded to drive them from the heartland of Britain. After his death, an uneasy peace prevailed. The Saxons of the Thames valley had given signs of subservience and been allowed to exist in a much reduced and humbled status. Then a plague swept across the country and did much to reduce the population and its martial enthusiasm. This state did not last for long. Soon enough, the Saxon lords clamoured for war and once again the British began to feel the pressure from the east. It was not felt like much of a threat. If we can trust the songs, the British were optimistic and expected to conquer the foreigners once and for all. It was generally prophesied that a strong leader would unite the British and lead them to triumph over the invaders.

When we examine the songs addressed to Urien of Rheged, a clearer picture emerges. When Taliesin came to Rheged,

Urien the strong, Bull-Protector of the Island, was already an old man with an amazing reputation. Poem after poem Taliesin exclaims his amazement that Urien in his old age could fight his numerous enemies so devastatingly. It is not certain if Taliesin accompanied Urien during the battles. He occasionally uses the form 'I have seen…' but this could be a metaphor for poetic vision. In one touching poem the bard remains in Urien's stronghold and waits for news from the front. How will Urien return to his castle? Will he come riding in glory and triumph, or will he be carried on a stretcher, his white hair clotted with blood, his radiant face forever pale, leaving the poet and the country in hopeless misery? Finally a great outcry is heard. The bard sends a servant to find out what had happened and is relieved that Urien has once again come home victorious.

Urien must have been an impressive ruler. Taliesin praises him, much as the custom of the time demanded, as a violent and cruel fighter, but also as a generous and friendly provider. These were the two main functions of royalty in the time. No doubt old Urien was a skilled politician as well, but this quality was nothing the bards bothered to chant about. Urien granted lands to Taliesin around Llywyfenydd. Taliesin accepted them, but sang that their rightful owner remains Urien. It seems that Urien had quarrels with his sons Owain and Elffin, who lived north of his country, and to whom he had to grant much of his kingdom over the years. Taliesin sang that he had no sympathy for them, nor that he would travel to their realm in the north, but when Urien was finally slain, (possibly) he continued to sing for Urien's heir, Owain. There is a death song by a Taliesin praising Owain. It is no way certain whether Owain survived Urien or fell in the same battle, not that it matters much. Maybe the association of the mythical Taliesin with a prince called Elffin comes from a vague memory or Urien's son. In spite of all his family problems, Urien joined forces with a couple of British kings and died in a battle against Deoderic, the son of Ida, in Lindisfarne. It seems that his death happened at the hands of a British king called Morgan, who was jealous that Urien had been granted the title gwledig, i.e. supreme leader.

Two songs that seem to belong to the same period have Taliesin praising the fierce king Gwallawg of Elfed (Leeds?), mind you, Urien didn't like Gwallawg much, so when Taliesin came home to Rheged he had to make a song to apologize. It may well be that he returned to Gwallawg's patronship after the death of Urien and Owain (see Pennar 1988).

A similar historical tradition (if trustworthy), coming from the pen of Llewelyn Sion (late 16th C.) has it that Talhaiarn held the bardic chair at Urien's court at Caer Gwyroswydd before Taliesin. After Talahiarn's death, Taliesin presided in three bardic chairs: Caerleon-upon-Usk, Chair of Rheged at Bangor Teivy, and finally he was invited to Arvon, where he was granted land. According to this account, Maelgwn Gwynedd desired this property, which caused virulent animosity between king and bard. Maelgwn in his characteristic megalomania took the property by force, and Taliesin in return cursed him so that vad velen, the yellow plague, came to Rhos.

Whoever saw it was doomed to certain death. Maelwn sought to escape his fate by hiding in the church of Rhos, but in his curiosity he could not resist the temptation to look through the keyhole, well, as he looked out the plague looked in, and this finished him. Finally Taliesin, so Sion had it, retired to Caer Gwyroswydd.

Lastly, there is a brief reference in the *Dream of Rhonabwy*, telling us that Taliesin had a son called Avaon. The text also refers to Prince Elphin as a *perverse and overanxious lad*, without explanation. Taliesin is especially associated with the countryside near Geirionwyd. This is one of the most beautiful districts in northern Wales. From his home, Taliesin could have walked to the Fairy Glen, or to a strange pool where in elder days a monstrous serpent, the addanc of the deep, used to dwell. The locals, so the folk tales say, used to placate the raging reptile with the odd virgin, well, one day they decided to change their policy. The last virgin for miles and miles had to sit at the lakeside. As soon as the monstrous serpent began to drag itself out of the lake, armed men came running and tied it up in nets and chains. Thus it was bound to a huge cart, and two famed oxen were set to pull it out of the lake and to a better habitation. The two oxen, by the way, happened to be the kings Nynaw and Peibiaw, who had quarreled and boasted so much regarding their wonderful treasures that god in his wisdom transformed them into oxen. Now the oxens pulled with all their might, and so did the locals, and soon enough the toxic addanc was on its way. The big problem was where to get rid of it. The snake catchers dragged their prey across Wales, but found no place to dispose of it. Ultimately they dragged the poor beasty all the way up mount Snowdon, where they released the chains and fetters, and the snake slid into the blue-green waters of Snowdon's highest lake, where it is resting peacefully to this very day. Apart from being a colourful story, you might be excused for finding evidence for serpent worship in this tale. And isn't it convenient that our dear Taliesin, who called himself a serpent (at least three times) happened to live at such a fitting site?

So much for the historical bits and pieces. It was a great temptation to the early scholars to class all songs of the *Book of Taliesin* as original 6th century poetry. With such a formidable age, the mystical songs could be expected to contain a lot of long forgotten pagan lore. It is hardly surprising that many excitable historians saw the long desired gnosis of British Druidry before their eyes. Since then, linguistic and historical analysis has shattered a good many hopeful dreams. The earliest stuff, as we have seen, belongs to the group of poems relating to Urien of Rheged, while the enchanting 'pagan' material comes from the Gogynfeirdd period between the 11th and 13th century. For linguistic reasons Sir Ifor Williams proposed that only a dozen songs can be attributed to the 6th C. bard. Modern researchers like Toby Griffen are even more cautious. Even among the bulk of Urien, Owein, Cynan and Gwallawg poems, only a very few songs have the linguistic structure of the late 6th C. Others were written in the 7th C. and later. In each case, the author wrote as Taliesin, and all of these poems are united in the singular *Book of Taliesin*. This

Rowan knot.

has led to a certain scholarly trend to identify the later poems as forgeries. Taliesin, so it may be reasoned, had such a fame during his lifetime that later bards passed their own efforts as original songs coming from the 6th C. master-bard. Another explanation was sought in the political history of the British. In 1792, Edward Jones noted that after the disintegration of princely government in Wales (i. e. with the death of Llywelyn ap Gruffyd, 1282):

Such was the tyranny exercised by the English over the conquered nation that the bards who were born 'since Cambria's fatal day' might be said to raise under the influence of a baleful and malignant star. They were reduced to possess their sacred art in obscurity and sorrow, and constrained to suppress the indignation that would burst forth in the most animated strains against their ungenerous and cruel oppressors. Yet they were neither silent nor inactive. That their poetry might breathe with impunity the spirit of their patriotism, they became dark, prophetic and oracular. As the monks of the Welsh church, in their controversy with Rome, had written to countenance their doctrines several religious poems which they feigned to be the work of Taliesin, the bards now ascribed many of their political writings to the same venerable author.

What a touching story. It seemed eminently convincing in the days of romantical scholarship, and to an extend there may be truth to this simplification, but then, as you doubtlessly noticed, a political motif does not explain everything. Of course there were bards who produced prophecies under the name of Taliesin. So were some monks, possibly Master John of St. Davies is an author of a religious Taliesin poem which I won't bother you with. On the other hand we can't agree that every obscure item in the Taliesin's poems is a political reference in an occult and forbidden code. Too many songs involve elements that are typical for shamanic prayer and invocation, I'll treat you to some examples further on. Nor is the material ascribed to the mythical Taliesin in any way typical for the faith of so called Celtic Christianity. Not one word in Taliesin poems reflects the great conflict of the churches regarding the correct date of Easter. Indeed several Taliesin songs contain severe criticism of the church and of the monks. Yes, things are never quite as simple as they seem. Be that as it may, there were dozens of authors who wrote under the name of Taliesin over the centuries. You could call them forgers. But is this really such a good idea?

The Mythical Taliesin

Pause a moment and think of the mythical Taliesin. We know enough of the historical bards to be sure that the myth of Taliesin, or some form of it, was well known to them. The mythical Taliesin, as they were probably aware of, was much more than a single human being. Not a single person but a consciousness that had been around from the dawn of time, reborn and reshaped time and time again. In the *Hanes Taliesin*, the bard introduces himself to the unfriendly king Maelgwn and his arrogant court bards

by chanting:
Primary chief bard am I to Elphin,
And my original country is the region of the
summer stars;
Idno and Heinin called me Merddin,
At length every king will call me Taliesin.
I was with my Lord in the highest sphere,
On the fall of Lucifer into the depth of hell;
I have borne a banner before Alexander;
I know the names of the stars from north to
south;
I have been on the galaxy at the throne of
the Distributor;
I was in Canaan when Absalom was slain;
I conveyed the divine spirit to the level of
the vale of Hebron;
I was in the court of Don before the birth of
Gwydion.
I was instructor to Eli and Enoc;
I have been winged by the genius of the
splendid crosier;
I have been loquacious prior to being gifted
with speech;
I was at the place of the crucification of the
merciful Son of God;
I have been three periods in the prison of
Arianrod;
I have been the chief director of the work of
the tower of Nimrod;
I am a wonder whose origin is not known.
I have been in Asia with Noah in the ark,
I have seen the destruction of Sodom and
Gomorra;
I have been in India when Roma was built,
I am now come here to the remnant of
Troia.
I have been with my Lord in the manger of
the ass;
I have strengthened Moses through the
waters of Jordan;
I have been in the firmament with Mary
Magdalene;
I have obtained the muse from the cauldron
of Ceridwen;

I have been bard of the harp to Lleon of
Lochlin.
I have been on the White Hill, in the court
of Cynvelyn,
For a day and a year in stocks and fetters,
I have suffered hunger for the son of the
Virgin.
I have been fostered in the land of the deity,
I have been teacher to all intelligences,
I am able to instruct the whole universe.
I shall be until the day of doom on the face
of the earth;
And it is not known whether my body is
flesh or fish.
Then I was for nine months
In the womb of the hag Ceridwen;
I was originally little Gwion,
And at length I am Taliesin.

Taliesin certainly got around. As this poem makes abundantly clear, you could expect to meet Taliesin present and poetic at every important event in history, no matter the time or place. Before we move on, let me add a few notes to this poem. It comes from the Lady Guest translation of the *Hanes Taliesin* and is much younger than the poems of the *Book of Taliesin*.

The poem starts by identifying the origin of the bard: the original country is the realm of the summer stars. This makes Taliesin an extraterrestrial sentience. At a guess I would propose that the summer stars are the ones you can see when you go out of the smoky hall in the middle of the night and look straight up. The pole star, the wain and draco are glittering in frosty brilliance in the sky, while Caer Gwydyon, splendid court wrought by the great enchanter (the milky way) stretches across the jeweled firmament. Much as I like the interpretation reading *the summer stars*, I have to point out that the lines can also be read *My accustomed country is the land of the Cherubim*, as Nash did. In this case, the aliens appear as angels. Whatever interpretation you favour, the fact remains that Taliesin's source, or dwelling space, is of extraterrestrial nature. This may remind you of the Irish filid who believed that poets are born and raised in the otherworld.

The next lines refer possibly to *Iddno and Heinin*. Another reading of the manuscript provides *Johannes the Diviner* (Nash), not the Biblical character but Master John of St. Davids, a churchman and famous poet of the 12th century. Somehow Taliesin is identified with the mountain sage, mad Myrddin in these lines, or vice versa. Further evidence for the connection between the two can be found in their dialogue (*Black Book*), which ends by hinting that some sort of authority would go to Myrddin from Taliesin, and in the *Vita Merlini*, where the two meet and have a long discourse regarding natural history, ornithology and all sorts of sacred springs.

Then we find reference to Alexander the Great, a person of great importance in medieval myth. Alexander employed a lot of Celtic mercenaries in his world-conquering armies, which may or may not have been known to the bards. Nash reads that Taliesin was *on a horse's crupper of Eli and Enoch*, and notes that both were taken to heaven in a chariot. Caer Arianrod may be the seaside castle of the *Mabinogi*, but it could also be the constellation of the Northern Crown, if we can trust Dr. Owen's research. Likewise, Llys Don, the Palace of Don, is probably Cassiopeia.

The remnant of Troia is Britain, medieval belief had it that the survivors of the Troyan war finally settled on this island. Then there are the Biblical references. Some of them seem rather unusual. Moses, for example, did not make it through the waters of the Jordan. If Taliesin helped him across, does this mean that he killed him? And what do you make out of being in heaven with Mary Magdalene? Wasn't she possessed by seven demons (gods?) before she got religion? Nash proposed it should read *at the cross*, but noted that the words do mean *in heaven*. The overseer of Nimrod's tower, as you may recall from the lore of the filid, was also the master poet who began the craft of poetry and created Gaelic. Is this a parallel belief from Wales? Finally, the translation given by Nash ends in some lines that are unlike the Lady Guest version, and well worth considering for their stellar significance. The reference is to Caer Sidin, in all likeliness a term for the galaxy itself.

I have been instructed
In the whole system of the universe;
I shall be till the day of judgement
On the face of the earth.
I have been in an uneasy chair
Above Caer Sidin,
And the whirling round without motion
Between three elements.
It is not the wonder of the world
That cannot be discovered.

Why these lines look so different in Lady Guest's version is beyond my comprehension. Perhaps it helps when we recall that the poetic material she published is in all likeliness a bit damaged by the overeager editing of her collaborator. The *Hanes Taliesin* also has the bard state: *Three times I have been born, I know by meditation*; well, three times is not exactly much, considering all the claims you read earlier. But maybe he was alluding to birth one as Gwion, birth two as Ceridwen's nameless child and birth three as Taliesin out of the waters of the great sea. Earlier bardic sources add to the list of incarnations. Triad 87 has:

Three Skilful Bards were at Arthur's Court:
Myrddin son of Morfryn,
Myrddin Emrys,
and Taliesin.

In a mythical sense this is true enough, as Taliesin was everywhere anyway. For the late 6th century bard this would have been a little early, Arthur was long dead when Urien reigned. But the triad is not that reliable in other respects either: Myrddin son of Morfryn lived in the late 6th century, while Myrddin Emrys, Merlin Ambrosius, is the wonderful child who prophecied to King Vortigern before the days of Uther Pendragon and his son Arthur. A Taliesin composed a death song for Uther Pendragon. Another Taliesin accompanied Arthur on a journey to one or several otherworlds. There they evidently got into trouble, as only seven survivors made it back to Britain. This is one of the earliest Arthurian myths, you can find it in song 30 of the *Book of Taliesin*, dating around the 9th century.

Sadly, the full story is nowhere recorded. Taliesin was also one of the seven survivors of that futile war between the Welsh and the Irish told in the Second Branch of the *Mabinogi*. There are some intriguing parallels between the two traditions. Let me continue with a few lines from song 14 from the *Book of Taliesin*. The song begins by reciting how the seer has witnessed the battle against the sons of Llyr in Ebyr Henvelen. Then he announces that Brochwel of Powys loved his Awen, and invokes the muse:

Shall not my chair be defended from the cauldron of Ceridwen?
May my tongue be free in the sanctuary of the praise of Gogyrwen.
The praise of Gogyrwen is an oblation, which has satisfied
Them, with milk, and dew, and acorns.

A few optimistic lines on war against the Saxons follow, then Taliesin launches on a journey through time:

I came to Deganwy to contend
With Maelgwn, the greatest in delinquencies,
I liberated my lord in the presence of the distributor,
Elphin, the sovereign of greatly aspiring ones.
There are to me three chairs, regular, accordant,
And until doom they will continue with the singers.
I have been in the battle of Godeu, with Lleu and Gwydion,
They changed the form of the elementary trees and sedges.
I have been with Bran in Iwerdon.
I saw when was killed Morddwydtyllon...

The battle of Godeu, as you will read later, is not a historical event but a mythical one. Bran's journey to Iwerdon (Ireland) is the subject of the second branch of the *Mabinogi*. Morddwydtyllon is a name of Bran, it possibly means pierced thigh, and refers to Bran's death by a poisoned dart. A wounded thigh or leg is one of the major attributes of the kings who guard the grail, and indeed several of them are called by names that sound much like Bran. In these verses we are at the root of what later became the flourishing tree of grail romances.

Now follow a few lines on Welsh nationalism and finally the poem ends in a description of the stellar otherworld not unlike the lines translated by Nash:

And about the boundary of Prydain,
beautiful its towns,
There is a battle against chiefs above the
mead-vessels,
In the festivals of the Distributor, who
bestowed gifts upon me.
The chief astrologers received wonderful
gifts.
Complete is my chair in Caer Sidi,
No one will be afflicted with disease or old
age that may be in it.
It is known to Manawyd and Pryderi.
Three utterances, around the fire, will he
sing before it,
And around its borders are the streams of
the ocean.
And the fruitful fountain is above it,
Is sweeter than white wine the liquor therein.

If anything, the evidence shows that the bards did not necessarily think of Taliesin as a single person. If the mythical bard appeared and participated all through history, it may be understandable that more than one person produced poetic material under the name. Not as a forgery. Forgery implies that an original exists. In our model, every single Taliesin is the original. When

we speak of Taliesin, are we using a name or a title? Usually, Taliesin is translated as *bright, radiant, beautiful brow*. Williams remarked that the name can have a double meaning. Tal (brow) can also mean worth, value. Thus, when Gwyddno asks his son Elphin what he got from the weir, the latter replies: *'A poet.' 'Alas'*, said the father, *'what is a thing like that worth?'* Taliesin's reply: *'He is worth more than you ever got out of the weir'*. The *worth* (value) is a pun on the word tal. Thus, Taliesin could also mean *fine value*. The radiant brow could also be a radiant worth or value. This makes Professor Griffen speculate that the supposed name may refer to a poet wearing some ornamental crown, laurel or coronet. He hypothesizes that Taliesin may have been the crowned bard of the age and asks:

Who was the sixth century bard whom Aneirin knew as (the) Taliesin? Since nothing survives from the period except Canu Aneirin, we have no way of knowing. In fact, we do not even know how many Taliesins may have been crowned by how many different rulers (?) at the time of Aneirin. Nor do we know if the title had become so metaphorical by this time that Aneirin's Taliesin may have simply assumed it himself.

Though there is no hard evidence that the penbeirdd, the Head of the Bards, wore a ceremonial headdress, the notion of a lineage of Taliesins makes a lot more sense than the popular vision of a single bard and

Faces in the rocks. Llyn Peninsula, Wales.

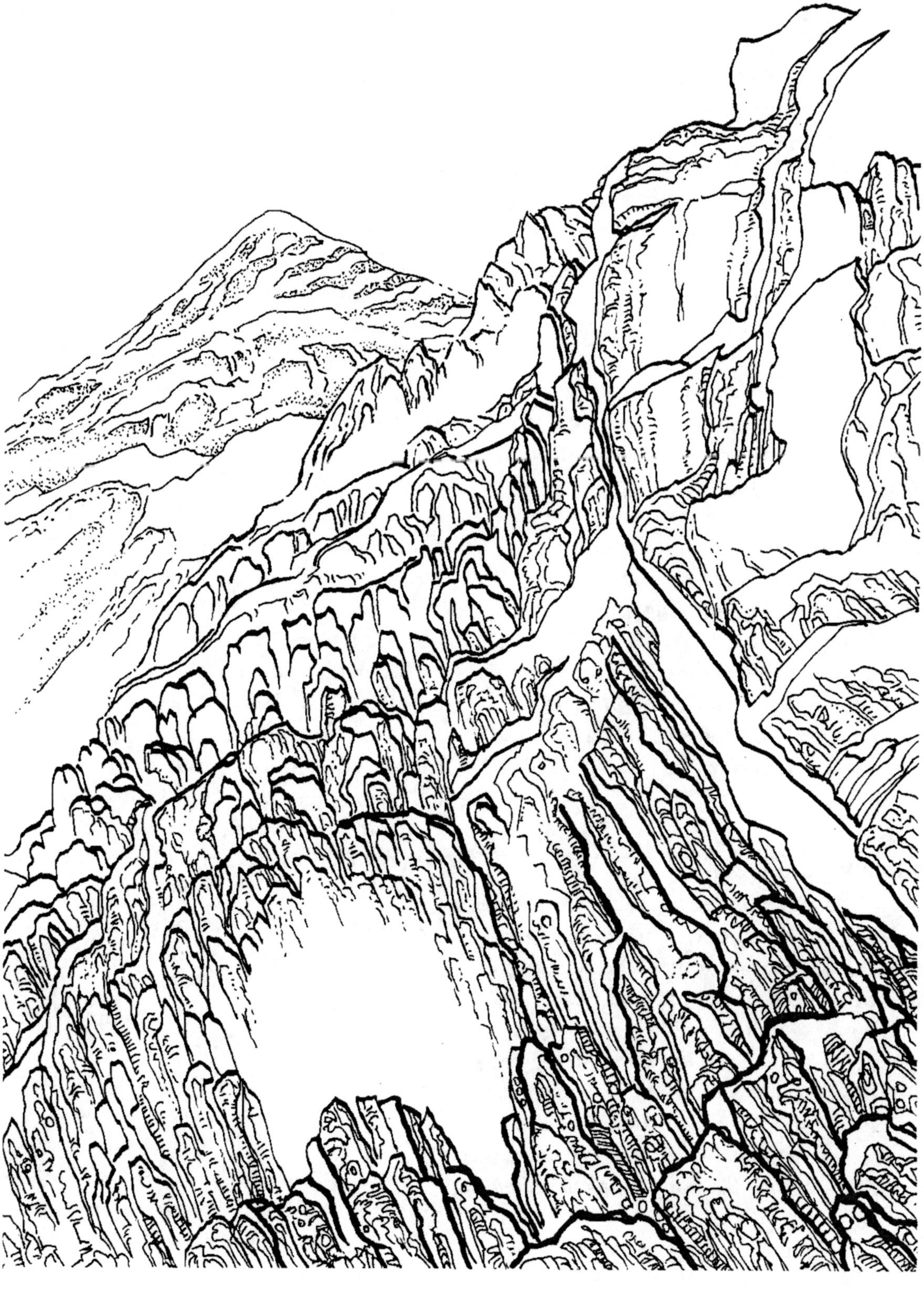

his copyists. The idea of a lineage is itself a link across time. What if the Taliesins shared a consciousness? All Taliesins had their title from the myth of the elixir and the cauldron, though in each case the particular vision differed. Maybe they all dreamed the vision in their initiation, maybe they experienced the transformation in a ritual, in dramatic acting, in an astral journey, a hypnotic trance or a drug journey. They shared a common origin myth, from which they derived their inspired status. What if their common origin was a special awareness, a illuminating experience setting their minds on fire with poetic inspiration? If there were enough of them, over the ages, we can be sure that one or another was around at many important times in history. Each time a different person. Each time the same instant of inspiration, the same nameless, wordless self waking to soar on wings of darkness through the labyrinths of form and meaning. If you want a reincarnation concept in Island Celtic myth, why has this one been overlooked so often?

Trouble with Maelgwn

By now, you may wonder what all the trouble with Maelgwn was about. You met Maelgwn earlier on. Remember how he became high king after floating on his chair with its waxen wings, and how Gildas raved against his vanity and his ungodly ways. Maelgwn, so Gildas recorded, prefered to listen to his own praise songs (rather than to those praising Christ) performed by *the rascally crew yelling forth, like Bacchanalian revellers, full of lies and foaming phlegm, as to besmear everyone near them.* So much for the court bards.

Then there was the peccadillo of murdering a nephew to marry his wife, and polygamy in general. What annoyed Gildas most was that Maelgwn, in his youth, had taken Christian oaths and had retired to cloisters, from where he emerged to begin a violent but extremely successful career. Other writers weren't kind with him either. Geoffrey, for what it's worth, calls him Malgo and states that he had two sons, Ennianus and Run. He was the most handsome leader among the British. He fought with great courage and was generous, as befits a great king. In Geoffrey's opinion, Maelgwn made himself hateful to god by homosexuality. He becomes totally untrustworthy when he has Maelgwn conquer all of Britain, as well as Ireland, the Orkneys, Iceland, Gotland, Denmark and Norway.

Arthurian enthusiasts will be delighted to learn that several genealogies mention Maelgwn. In *Mostyn ms. 117* we read Maelgwn Son of Cadwallon Long Hand, the fourth king in Britain after Arthur. *Jesus College ms. 20* has: Constantinus father of Constans the Monk, father of Gwrtheyrn, father of Gwrthefyr the Blessed, father of Emrys the Sovereign, father of Uthr Pendragon (Uthur Pendreic), father of Arthur, father of Constantinus, father of Aurelius, father of Ivor, father of Maelgwn of Gwynedd. Not very trustworthy either. Gwrtheirn is Vortigern in Geoffrey's tale, where he comes to kingship by cunningly murdering the rightful ruler Constans. He is famous for making the fatal error of allowing Saxon warriors to settle in Britain, on the condition that they would repel all other invaders. Most medieval histories blame him for this policy. They rarely take into account that in Gwrtheyrn's time, few able warriors were available in Britain. When the Roman empire was in its final death throes, any amount of young men were drafted from the outer provinces to serve in the last power struggles on the continent. As soon as the last legions had left, all sorts of marauders came over the seaways, and Gwrtheyrn could not have handled them with the forces he could muster.*

Anyway, Maelgwn was an impressive historic person who held court, so it is said, at Deganwy in North Wales. If he really died from the yellow plague, this happened in the year 586, according to the chronology in the *Red Book of Hergest*.

As Sion told us, Maelgwn and Taliesin had a row as Maelgwn had occupied lands granted to Taliesin, and Taliesin retaliated by cursing him to suffer from the yellow plague. The *Hanes Taliesin* offers an entirely different story. Let's find out how the story progressed. As you remember, Prince Elphin, son of Gwyddno Garanhir, had picked up the leather bag in the weir and found a babe with a radiant brow in it. He named it Taliesin, and the child replied

---

* *Gwerthefyr is Vortimer in Geoffrey's account. He fiercely fought Saxons, maybe to make up for his father's policy. Before his death he decreed that his bones should be buried in every seaport around the British Isles, as a spell against the foreign invaders. Some legends have it that the bone spell was never completed, others that the bones were mishandled, leading to a swift return of the oppressing Anglo-Saxons. Then Gwrtheyrn returned to the throne, and was a major nuisance to people like young Merlin, till finally Ambrosius Aurelianus (Emrys Wledig) burned him to death in his impregnable tower.*

'Taliesin it is' and launched into his first song, to console Elphin for the loss of salmons he had suffered. Elphin took the infant home and gave it to his wife, who lovingly reared it. When Taliesin was thirteen years old, it happened that Elphin was invited to the court of his uncle, Maelgwn, for the Christmastide celebration. Elphin went, and found the party loud and furious. As the *Hanes* tells us:

> Now at the time the bards were in great favour with the exalted of the kingdom; and then none performed the office of those who are now called heralds, unless they were learned men, not only expert in the service of kings and princes, but studious and well versed in the lineage, and the arms, and exploits of princes and kings, and in discussions concerning foreign kingdoms, and the ancient things of this kingdom, and chiefly in the annals of the first nobles; and also were prepared always with their answers in various languages, Latin, French, Welsh and English. And together with this they were great chroniclers, and recorders, and skilful in framing verses, and ready in making englyns in every one of these languages. Now of these there were at the feast within the palace of Maelgwn as many as four and twenty, and chief of them all, was one named Heinin Vardd.

This is an excellent description of the bardic craft at the time. The bards and nobles were all abuzz discussing such exciting topics as:

Is there in the whole world a king so

great as Maelgn, or one on whom Heaven has bestowed so many spiritual gifts as upon him? First, form, and beauty, and meekness, and strength, beside all the powers of the soul?' And together with this they said that Heaven had given one gift that exceeded all the others, which was the beauty, and comeliness, and grace, and wisdom, and modesty of the queen; whose virtues surpassed those of all the ladies and noble maidens throughout the whole kingdom. And with this they put questions one to another amongst themselves, Who had braver men? Who had fairer or swifter horses or greyhounds? Who had more skilful or wiser bards-than Maelgwn?

It must have been a rip-roaring success of a party. Elphin, by then rather drunk, thought similarly. Sadly, he also said what he thought:

Of a truth none but a king may vie with a king; but were he not a king, I would say that my wife is as virtuous as any lady in the kingdom, and also that I have a bard who is more skilful than all the kings bards.

Very polite but nevertheless a fatal mistake. Soon enough word had reached Maelgwn himself, who threw an impressive fit of rage and locked Elphin in the deepest dungeon of the fortress tower. It is said that Elphin was chained with silver fetters, on account of his nobility.

Maelgwn in the meantime send word to his son Rhun, *the most graceless man in the world*, with a well deserved reputation for coercion and rape, to *enquire into the demeanour of Elphin's wife*. But while Rhun was speedily riding towards Caer Garanhir, our boy Taliesin had already foreseen the impeding danger and warned the princess. Together they made up a young maid to look like the princess, while the lady herself assumed the shape of the maid. Some of this was a matter of dress and make-up, but most of it came from Taliesin's sorcery. When Rhun came rushing in, all had been prepared in advance. The lout sat down at the table and began to jest with the would-be-princess, while the real princess was serving food and wine for them. Finally Rhun slipped a sleeping powder into the drink, and when his victim slid to the ground, cut off her little finger, with Elphin's signet ring, to prove that she had been in his power.

Gleefully he rode home to Deganwy, where Maelgwn had Elphin released to show him the cruel trophy. Elphin, however, refused to give in. Looking briefly at the finger, he admitted that the ring was his, but that the finger could never be his wife's. First, his wife had such dainty hands that the ring would not even hold on her thumb, second, the nail had not been pared for a month, whereas the Princess was known to cut her nails every Saturday. (Care of finger nails, by the way, was an important matter for most Island Celts. Irish law made it a criminal offence to damage someone's finger nail and calling a person 'ragged nails' was an insult.) Last, there were bits of rye dough under the nail, and the Princess was not given to baking her own bread. This bold statement made Maelgwn mightily wrath, and he had Elphin locked up again until the skill of his bard were proven. At home in Caer Garanhir, Taliesin knew everything that was happening in far away

Deganwy. He knew that he had to go to best Maelgwn's bards, and sang a song declaring his intentions:

A journey will I perform,
And to the gate I will come;
The hall I will enter,
And my song I will sing;
My speech I will pronounce
To silence royal bards.
In the presence of their chief,
I will greet to deride,
Upon them I will break
And Elphin I will free.
Should contention arise,
In presence of the prince,
With summons to the bards
For the sweet flowing song,
And wizards posing lore
And wisdom of Druids.
In the court of the sons of the distributor
Some are who did appear
Intent on wily schemes,
By craft and tricking means,
In pangs of affliction
To wrong the innocent,
Let the fools be silent,
As erst in Badon's fight,
With Arthur of liberal ones
The head, with long red blades;
Through feats of testy men,
And a chief with his foes.
Woe be to them, the fools,
When revenge comes on them.
I Taliesin, chief of bards,
With a sapient druid's words,
Will set kind Elphin free
From haughty tyrant's bonds.
To their fell and chilling cry,
By the act of a surprising steed,
From the far distant North,
There soon shall be an end.
Let neither grace nor health
Be to Maelgwn Gwynedd,

For this force and this wrong;
And be extremes of ills
And an avenged end
To Rhun and all his race:
Short be his course of life,
Be all his lands laid waste;
And long exile be assigned
To Maelgwn Gwynedd!

The song, as you noticed, is a spell, a prophecy and ends in a passionate curse. The Druidic references are especially interesting. It's regrettable that the manuscript is so late and has possibly been tampered with. But let us continue with the story.

As soon as Taliesin entered the hall, he placed himself in a quiet corner, near the place where the bards and the minstrels where wont to come to in doing their service and duty to the king, as is the custom at high festivals when the bounty is proclaimed. And so, when the bards and the heralds came to cry largesse and to proclaim the power of the king and his strength, at the moment that they passed by the corner wherein he was crouching, Taliesin pouted out his lipsd after them, and played 'Blerwm,'blerwm,' with his finger upon his lips. Neither took they much notice of him as they went by, but proceeded forward till they came before the king, unto whom they made their obeisance with their bodies, as they were wont, without speaking a single word, but pouting out their lips, and making mouths at the king, playing 'Blerwm,'blerwm,' upon their lips with their fingers, as they had seen the boy do elsewhere. This sight caused the king to wonder and to deem within himself that they were drunk with many liquors. Wherefore he commanded one of his lords, who served at the board, to go to them and to desire them to collect their wits, and to consider where they stood, and what it was fitting for them to do. And this lord did so gladly. But they ceased not from their folly any more than before. Whereupon he sent to them a second time, and a third, desiring them to go forth from the hall. At the last the king ordered one of his squires to give a blow to the chief of them named Heinin Vardd; and the squire took a broom, and struck him on the head, so that he fell back in his seat. Then he arose and went on his knees, and besought leave of the king's grace to show that this their fault was not through want of knowledge, neither through drunkenness, but by the influence of some spirit that was in the hall. And after this Heinin spoke on this wise. 'Oh honourable king, be it known to your grace, that not from the strength of drink, or of too much liquor, are we dumb, without power of speech like drunken men, but through the influence of a spirit that sits in the corner yonder in the form of a child.'

Forthwith the king commanded the squire to fetch him; and he went to the nook where Taliesin sat, and brought him before the king, who asked him what he was, and whence he came. And he answered the king in verse... Primary bard am I to Elphin...And when the king and his nobles had heard this song, they wondered much, for they had never heard the like from a boy as young as he. And when the king knew that he was the bard

of Elphin, he bade Heinin, his first and wisest bard, to answer Taliesin, and to strive with him. But when he came he could do no other, but play 'Blerwm' on his lips; and when he sent for the others of the four and twenty bards, they all did likewise, and could do no other. And Maelgwn asked the boy what was his errand, and he answered him in song...

What you have just read is more than folklore. Some elements of the tale are worth considering. When Taliesin appears, he hides in a dark corner. It is no coincidence that before the spell contest, the bard finds inspiration and insight in a dark and shady place. From this state of darkness, dark and overdark (Avagddu), the wonderous child makes mind numbing spells. The gesture is not coincidental either. Gwion became enlightened after his scalded finger came to his lips. Here a finger is playing on the lips, making a buzzing drone, and the gesture of true initiation is precisely what turns the court bards speechless. (Note: playing with a finger on the lips, especially when holding it parallel to the mouth and singing or chanting is a valuable technique of trance music. Try it!) When Heinin, chief of bards comes to his senses, he immediately recognizes that the source of his trouble is a spirit in the form of a child. Challenged by this accusation, Taliesin retorts with a song that reveals him as an entirely otherworldly, immortal sentience. The Hanes Taliesin supplies several songs which Taliesin is said to have sung to spite arrogant Maelgwn and his overbearing bards. The songs from the earlier Book of Taliesin likewise contain references to Taliesin's contest. It was a popular motif to invent poetry for. One

Swamp guardians.

characteristic of the contest songs is that they frequently insult the royal bards. Here are some passages from the Hanes Taliesin:

If thou art a bard completely imbued
With genius not to be controlled,
Be thou not untractable
Within the court of thy king...

It is certain you know not
How to understand the song I utter,
Nor clearly how to discriminate
Between the truth and what is false;
Puny bards, crows of the district,
Why do you not take to flight?
A bard that will not silence me,
Silence may he not obtain,
Till he goes to be covered
Under gravel and pebbles...

Minstrels persevere in their false custom,
Immoral ditties are their delight;
Vain and tasteless praise they recite;
Falsehood at all times they utter;
The innocent persons they ridicule;
Married women they destroy,
Innocent virgins of Mary they corrupt;
As they pass their lives away in vanity...

These samples should suffice for the moment. What we have in these lines are in reality two topics. One of them is the bardic contest, an ancient ritual to determine the proper head of the bards. The other is a spate of all-purpose criticism uttered by Taliesin to make absolutely clear just what he dislikes about his colleagues. The poetry of the *Book of Taliesin* supplies plenty of evidence that our poet was anything but a silent bystander. Like the rebel of all ages, he takes a stand and refuses to soften his words. Taliesin is not a meek singer, and this is an important element of his office.

The Penbeirdd (penceirdd), the head of the bards, has to be ready to criticize, to spell-cast and to correct those around him, be it the war loving princes, blundering kings or overbearing fellow bards. When a king goes erring, the bard had to talk sense into him. It may be for this reason that the head of the bards had an authority equal to royalty. Consider this carefully. Certainly the bards were being paid for praise songs, but then their employers could not automatically rest assured that they would always be praised. There had to be a grain of truth in the praise, otherwise the king could expect a shattering satire instead.

Chair of the Bards

Rowlands (1985) notes that in the 13th Century when the manuscript of the *Book of Taliesin* was compiled, the bardic order in each county was lead by a Penceirdd. This august personage also trained the apprentice bards, and received 24 pence after they had completed their education. The number 24 does not appear like a coincidence, remember that Maelgwn also had 24 bards. In this late period, a pencerdd was basically a bard who had won a chair. The bardic chair was a function, but it also served as a symbol for the seat of inspiration. The gogynfeirdd bards in particular made use of the chair as a metaphor. Let me disgress a little to name some of the chairs that appear in Celtic mythology. Bards had chairs, so did kings and selected heroes.

A song entitled *The Chair of the Sovereign* (BoT 15) tells us about the seat of the Guledig, the great king. As could have been expected, the honour of reigning depends pretty much on the opinion of the bards in charge. A royal seat, after all, is not simply a gilded chair but a stance in life, a task and a responsibility. Taliesin sang:

He deserves not the chair
That keeps not my word.
With me is the splendid chair,
The inspiration of fluent (and) urgent song.

The poem mentions several rulers and Arthur, the Guledig, and hints at the nature of the royal chair:

Let the billow cover over the shingle,
That the land becomes ocean,
So that it leaves not the cliffs,
Nor hill nor dale,
Nor the least of shelter,
Against the wind when it shall rage.
The chair of the sovereign
He that keeps it is skilful.

These lines remind me of walking in the howling gale and drenching downpour on Mount Snowdon, the highest peak in Wales. According to a local tradition, Arthur had his last battle against the treacherous Mordred high up on the mountainside one gloomy day in late autumn. One of Snowdon's lakes, so it is said, is the very place where the dying Arthur was taken aboard the boat that took him to enchanted Avalon, and several legends claim that Arthur and his finest warriors are sleeping in a cave high up the mountain where they wait for the very day when they will awake to drive the Saxons out of Britain. Considering traffic in and around London they may as well stay in bed. This makes Snowdon a likely candidate for the seat of the sovereign, the chair of the Guledig. It is a dangerous seat, but so are most chairs in

Celtic myth.

In the *Mabinogi*, first branch, you may encounter the dangerous seat on the hill above Arberth. Any noble who spends a night seated in it may expect to see a miracle or to receive a lethal blow. Pryderi and Kigva, Manawyddan and Rhiannon tried for entertainment's sake. They found a heavy mist descending, and when the next morning the fog disappeared, their country had become a desolate wasteland devoid of all inhabitants. Arthur's table had a dangerous seat which did horrible things to any knight who wrongly sat down in it. The grail castle has a dangerous seat where chosen knights were allowed to spend a night in vigil and prayer. In some versions this happened to be a dangerous bed which promised wild visions but also fatal injuries if the sleeper was not pure enough. The *Prose Lancelot* has Sir Gawain lie down on one such item of lethal furniture, the Couch Adventurous. As soon as Sir Gawain reclined, he was mortally wounded by a burning lance that went straight through his shield and armour. Next appeared a terrifying dragon which spat out 500 young dragons. The dragon fought a leopard and then proceeded to devour its own young. Twelve lamenting maidens marched through the chamber. Then a huge knight appeared, and Sir Gawain fought him successfully, in spite of losing blood all the while, and finally a processions of damsels, carrying the grail itself, cured the poor hero so that he felt no more of his injuries and sank into comatose sleep. The next morning he awoke, in one piece but not in the castle where he had spent the night before. He found himself in the vilest cart in the world, pulled by a half starved horse, and as he was dragged through the streets, the villagers pelted him with all the muck they could find.

In Irish myth, Cuchulain has to keep watch in a dangerous seat at Cu Roi's castle, and spends the night battling apparitions and phantoms.

A middle European tradition has it that some Celtic hill fortresses had special royal seats (usually impressive rocks) from where the regents could gaze over their realm. It is said that these kings ruled as far as their gaze reached. This seems like a ritual and reminds us of Irish kings who had to be up on the ramparts of their forts each sunrise. This was to make sure that the monstrous Fomors had not invaded the land overnight.

The highest mountain in the Taunus (Hessen, Germany) is topped by a large rock which is called the seat or bed of Brunhild. This is not the Brunhild of the *Edda* or the *Nibelungenlied*, but the wife of Siegbert, King of Austrasia. Legend has it that the Frankish queen used to travel to the mountaintop when the weather was kind. Then she had her bed prepared on top of the rock. What purpose may she have had? Spending a night on a mountaintop is not just a harmless habit, it's a pagan ritual closely connected with the rite of utiseta (to sit outside) attested in Nordic sagas. Who spends the night out of doors, in darkness and solitude, is said to perceive strange visions and to get a glimpse of the future. While we have no idea what Brunhild did on her mountaintop seat under the sparkle of the summer stars, we do know that in the year 613, when she was 80 years old, the noble lady was accused of murdering ten members of the royal family by poison. She was tortured for three days, quartered

by horses and finally her mortal remains were burned to ashes and thrown into the wind. This is not exactly a punishment for murder, witchcraft seems more likely.

Then there is the seat of the giant Idris, Cader Idris, a magnificent mountain in Wales. In olden times, so the story goes, Idris used to climb this mountain to study the stars.

Avebury offers a megalith called the Devil's Seat. It's a dangerous place indeed, as women who sit there are in danger of becoming pregnant. On the other hand it's just the place to be initiated into neo-chaotic Druidry, so I've been told.

Finally, there is the Chair of Ceridwen, which is not a chair but the bardic vocation itself. The bardic chair, or the chair of the penceirdd, is likewise not only a seat of status and an office, but also an obligation. It has to be won, but once won, it has to be kept.

Ritual: Chick of the Chair

According to Nash, there was a bardic ritual. The higher and lower bardic order chose a cyff cler (a butt), who was to be ridiculed. A year and a day before the great event, a pencerdd was informed that the role would be his, and that he ought to prepare himself. When the important day came, the cyff cler took a seat in the middle of the hall. The bards assembled around him and attacked him with ridicule and satire. He had to remain silent during the onslaught, which, so we learn, earned him a considerable fee. The next day he answered his revilers and returned the scorn and insults. Taliesin in *The Fold of the Bards* (Nash) sings:

I am the bard of the hall,
I am the cyff of the chair,
I am able to stop the tongues of the bards.

To answer back in style, a bard had to be acquainted with an immense number of verses, from which s/he could improvise replies, the spontaneous poems, the pennillion. Then there is the fact that the cyff of the ritual was informed about what was to happen one year in advance. If you were to be the target of this rite, how would you prepare for it? The easiest way is to consider just what the satirists might ridicule. The cyff had one year to recognize personality flaws and to accept or change them. A year is a long time, and you can change a lot of your personality over such a span. In this sense, the year was a period of refinement. Of course it was also a year to learn about the flaws and shortcomings of those who were to ridicule you, which came in handy on the second day.

Please consider the effect of this ritual. Pause now and imagine that it is you who are sitting in the chair, assaulted by a bunch of sharp tongued satirists with wide experience and no scruples. Imagine what they would sing about you, about your life, your work, your principles, your personal problems. How can your ego be insulted? What would really make you angry? How could they force you out of your composed silence?

Think carefully, look at yourself out of the eyes of someone else. If you like to experience this fully, dissociate from your own point of view. Imagine you are a bard and compose insults and ridicule that hurt your ego. Can you see yourself through the eyes of a satirist? How many unjust accusations can you swallow? The bards who made up this ritual knew quite a lot about ego. They knew how tempting it can be to let the ego bloat itself with pride and self-importance. What a master-bard needs, first of all, is a sense of humility, i.e. a certain understanding of his/her place in the larger scale of things. Humans, for example, are valuable to feed bacteria and worms. If you suffer grandiose visions, if you see beyond humanities narrow horizons, if you transcend personality and spurt forth wisdom and poesy, it can be one hell of a temptation to be proud of it. This pride is a trap and effectively aborts all future evolution. On the other hand, too little ego and you may find that nobody listens to your vision, as they are too busy walking all over you. Humility is not making yourself too small. It's finding a workable balance between a bloated and a shriveled ego, it's knowing ones faults, listening to criticism and doing something to improve the situation.

Can you actually enjoy hearing someone criticize you? Can you learn something new? Can you calm your temper and understand what your audience is telling you, no matter how distorted it may seem? It's a skill well worth developing. When I am criticized, I generally tend to dissociate, i.e. I step beside myself so that I can watch myself and the other party while the criticism goes on. This is a useful tactic in that it reduces the emotional impact and permits me to keep a clear and open mind. Not to find excuses or devastating retorts but simply to listen and learn. Criticism is often useful feedback, no matter if it seems unjust or mistaken. Even if it is based on sheer misunderstanding and gross exaggeration, it can be useful to teach you what somebody else is thinking. If you get emotional, you are not likely to learn anything. If you manage to keep calm, you may learn what is behind all the upset.

The rite of the cyff in the chair is an excellent remedy to overbearing pride. Anyone who seeks the rank of the chief bard is well advised to undergo some such situation. If you can't find people who are willing to criticize you roughly enough, ask your gods and spirits. They know much dodgier things about you than your friends and colleagues. Above all, remain silent, and listen to what they say. The perfect balance is between opinions, in the perfect realm of suspended belief. This is not just an attitude, it is a state of mind.

The word Cyff, however, means not just a butt, or a target for satire. An alternate meaning is a chick. In Skene's version of the text, the lines refer to the *chick of the chair*. Remember how Ceridwen transformed into a black hen with a fiery comb to devour young Gwion. When she gave birth to him nine months later, he had indeed become her chick. The butt of the satirists is the child of the poetic goddess herself. As you like riddles so much (why else did you persist in reading up to here?) I'll quote the whole song.

The Fold of the Bards

Book of Taliessin 3

Meditating were my thoughts
On the vain poetry of the bards of Brython.
Making the best of themselves in the chief convention.
Enough, the care of the smith's sledge-hammer.

I am in want of a stick, straitened in song,
The fold of the bards, who knows it not?
Fifteen thousand over it
Adjusting it.
I am a harmonious one; I am a clear singer.
I am steel; I am a druid.
I am an artificer; I am a scientific one.
I am a serpent; I am love; I will indulge in feasting.
I am not a confused bard drivelling,
When songsters sing a song by memory,
They will not make wonderful cries;
May I be receiving them.
Like receiving clothes without a hand,
Like sinking in a lake without swimming,
The stream boldly rises tumultuously in degree.
High in the blood of sea-board towns.
The rock wave-surrounded, by great arrangement,
Will convey for us a defence, a protection from the enemy.
The rock of the chief proprietor, the head of tranquillity.
The intoxication of meads will cause us to speak.
I am a cell, I am a cleft, I am a restoration,
I am the depository of song; I am a literary man;
I love the high trees, that afford a protection above,
And a bard that composes, without earning anger;
I love not him that causes contention;
He that speaks ill of the skilful shall not possess mead.
It is a fit time to go to the drinking,
With the skilful men, about art,
And a hundred knots, the custom of the country,
The shepherd of the districts, support of gates,
Like going without a foot to battle.
He would not journey without a foot.

Coins 9 top l & r (front & reverse) Helvetii. Capricorn? center l & r (front & reverse): Helvetii, compare feathered bull with Mogh Ruith legend bottom l: Leuci, boar bottom r: Leuci boar

He would not breed nuts without trees,
Like seeking for ants in the heath.
Like an instrument of foolish spoil,
Like the retinue of an army without a head,
Like feeding the unsheltered on lichen.
Like ridging furrows from the country
Like reaching the sky with a hook,
Like deprecating with the blood of thistles,
Like making light for the blind,
Like sharing clothes to the naked,
Like spreading buttermilk on the sands,
Like feeding fish upon milk,
Like roofing a hall with leaves,
Like killing a tortoise with rods.
Like dissolving riches before a word.
I am a bard of the hall, I am a chick of the chair.
I will cause to loquacious bards a hindrance.
Before I am dragged to my harsh reward,
May we buy thee, that wilt protect us, thou son of Mary.

Again, the basic topic of this song is the contest between young Taliesin and Maelgwn's bards. In another sense, the poem could refer to any of the rituals of satire that authorized the penceirdd to keep the bardic chair. As you can see, the lines are not only full of criticism for the bardic vocation. They are also full of riddles. John Matthews (1991) suggests that doing the things mentioned in the lines beginning with *Like*... would be an utter waste of time. I can't quite agree with this interpretation. In many cases it may be useless to do so, but then, plenty of unsheltered did feed on lichen in early medieval Britain. Leaves can be made into a roof (for a night or two), or would you prefer to consider that the mighty beeches in the forest form a natural roof above wide halls? Riches are dissolved before a word,

when the king pays the bard. Even the lines referring to going to battle without a foot are not as simple as they seem. One who goes to battle without a foot is the serpent, another is the ruler of the monstrous Fomors in ancient Ireland, Cichol the Footless, maybe also a serpent. Or are we dealing with a reference to the function of the footholder? This person had the office of holding the feet of the high king in her or his lap from the time of the evening meal till bed. You can find reference to it in the fourth branch of the *Mabinogi* and in the venerable laws of Hywel Dda. Maybe the king with his feet off the ground was off duty. At this time, people with important needs could appeal to the foot holder, who was not as dangerous to approach as the king himself. In wartime, the footholder stayed at home. What is your explanation? Do yourself a favour and think about it. So much is lost in Taliesin poetry when you simply skip over the pages. The riddles in Taliesin's songs have more than one purpose. When you have considered for a while, we'll continue to the art of riddlemagick itself.

A Torrent of Questions

We have come to that point in the *Hanes Taliesin* where the young and ageless bard ridiculed the bards of Maelgwn's court for their ignorance, their arrogance and sins. Yet how could he bring the game to an end and free Elphin from his silver shackles? Riddle after riddle came flowing from the lips of the all-knowing youth, but the bards remained speechless, incapable to utter a word. Then he finally chanted a lengthy song (no doubt frothing mightily) that can be understood as a riddle, an invocation, a spell and a curse. Here are the first lines:

Discover thou what is
The strong creature from before the flood,
Without flesh, without bone,
Without vein, without blood,
Without head, without feet;
It will neither be older nor younger
Than at the beginning;
For fear of a denial,
There are no rude wants
With creatures.
Great God! How the sea whitens
When first it come!
Great are its gusts
When it comes from the south;
Great are its evaporations
When it strikes on coasts.
It is in the field, it is in the wood,
Without hand and without foot,
Without signs of old age,
Though it be coeval
With the five ages or periods;
And older still,
Though they be numberless years.
It is also as wide
As the surface of the earth;
And it was not born,
Nor was it seen.
It will cause consternation
Wherever God willeth.
On sea, and on land,
It neither sees, nor is it seen...
One being has prepared it,
Out of all-creatures,
By a tremenduous blast,
To wreck vengeance
On Maelgwn Gwynedd.

And while he was thus singing his verse near the door there arose a mighty storm of wind, so that the king and all his nobles thought that the castle would fall upon their heads. And the king caused them to fetch Elphin in haste from his dungeon, and placed him before Taliesin. And it is said that immediately he sang a verse, so that the chains opened from about his feet. And afterwards he sang the ode which is called 'The Excellence of the Bards'. And after that he sang the address which is called 'The Reproof of the Bards'. Then he sang the piece called 'The Spite of the Bards'. Taliesin having set his master free from prison, and having protected the innocence of his wife, and silenced the Bards so that not one of them dared to say a word, now brought Elphin's wife before them, and shewed that she had not one finger wanting. Right glad was Elphin, right glad was Taliesin.

The answer to the riddle is, of course, the wind. The *Chant to the Wind (Can y Gwynt)* appears in fairly similar form both in the *Hanes Taliesin* and in the *Book of Taliesin*, it is the only poetic piece which appears in both manuscripts. What makes the riddle such an impressive piece of magick is that its answer appears ready for direct experience. Right at the beginning the listeners are told that they are to discover the answer. As they cannot guess, they cannot bind the spell, and before long the roof starts to fall in. Mind you, the wind conjured by our bard is by no means the gentle breeze that sweeps across shady dales and fertile meadowland. It is the primal, pre-create storm of the beginning, oldest of all forces, total, uncontrollable and overwhelming. Here we find a Taliesin who does not care to prove his superiority by singing tunes, this sorcerer is ready to bury the court of the high king in a heap of falling rocks.

The myths of ancient Europe contain a number of riddle games which come close to rituals. The Icelandic *Eddas*, for instance, have several allusions to this topic. The *Gylfaginning*, compiled and edited by Snorri Sturlason (1178-1241), has a riddle contest as its very frame. It begins with the tale of King Gylfi, who changed his shape and travelled to Asgard, the home of the gods, to find out about the power and nature of the pagan deities. As the Nordic gods were rather well informed, they met Gylfi's deception by a glamour of their own.

Gylfi walked into the royal halls of Asgard disguised as a humble traveler. He approaches the high chair of the king of the gods, only to find that there are three regents seated on the throne: Har (High), Iafnhar (Equally High) and Thridi (The Third). All of these, so the story hints later on, are aspects of Odin. Har offers refreshment to Gylfi, but Gylfi refuses on the grounds that he has come for knowledge. So he is allowed to ask questions, and the three faces of the deity reply with answers. As Odin appears in three personalities, it is often from several points of view that the answer is given.

Similar patterns appear in several songs of the earlier *Poetic Edda*. The *Vafthrudnismal* has Odin (also in disguise) travel to the court of the giant Vafthrudnir, who is wise in ancient knowledge. The song takes the shape of a contest: he who cannot answer a question is to lose his head. In the end, the giant fails to answer a question which cannot be answered. Instead he guesses the identity of his guest. It is not recorded whether the dangerous game ends in a slaying. Or think of the *Alwismal*, where you have the thunder god Thor riddling an all-knowing dwarf on the lore of the many life forms in the nine worlds. This song is one of the most important ones in the entire *Edda*, as it records how the various creatures of the Nordic cosmology perceive reality. It says so much about the differences in consciousness between gods, humans, giants, elves, dwarves etc. that I find it next to miraculous that most writers on Nordic Mythology tend to ignore it. This riddle contest ends in defeat for the dwarf. Though he answers all questions correctly, he fails to observe that the night ends and the sun shines into the hall, thus, the poor fool is overpowered by daylight and petrifies.

In the *Fiölsvinsmal*, a riddle contest reveals the hidden identity of a hero and breaks a malignant spell. An evil spell uttered by a sorcerous lady called Busla (*Bosasaga*) ends in a riddle, too. If the king whom she cursed is able to understand the hidden meaning of several runes, he may break the spell. As he cannot, he is doomed to do her will. The existence of so many examples of ritual riddle games shows that we are dealing with a common and popular tradition. The next question is obviously whether a similar custom can be traced in the myths of the Island Celts. Taliesin's riddles come readily to mind. In Maelgwn's castle, the bard, looking to all observers like an innocent youth, taunts the prestigious court bards for their ignorance. You stumbled over a lot of these questions earlier on. Well, there are plenty more of them, the entire stock of late Taliesin poetry is brimming full of them, so let's have another batch. Here is the beginning of song 1 of the *Book of Taliesin*. What do you make out of it?

A primitive and ingenious address, when thoroughly elucidated.
Which was first, is it darkness, is it light?
Or Adam, when he existed, on what day was he created?
Or under the earth's surface, what the foundation?
He who is a legionary will receive no instruction.
Est qui peccator in many things,
Will lose the heavenly country, the community of priests.
In the morning no one comes
If they sing of three spheres.
Angles and Gallwydel,
Let them make their war.
Whence come night and day?
Whence will the eagle become gray?
Whence is it the night is dark?
Whence is it that the linnet is green?
The ebullition of the sea,
How is it not seen?
There are three fountains
In the mountain of roses,
There is a Caer of defence
Under the ocean's wave.
Illusive greeter,
What is the porter's name?
Who was confessor
To the gracious Son of Mary?
What was the most beneficial measure
Which Adam accomplished?
Who will measure Uffern?
How thick its veil?
How wide its mouth?
What the size of its stones?
Or the tops of its whirling trees?
Who bends them so crooked?
Or what fumes may be?
About their stems?
Is it Lleu and Gwydyon

That perform their arts?
Or do they know books
When they do?
Whence come night and flood?
How they disappear?
Whither flies night from day;
And how is it not seen?

As you can see, there are plenty of mysteries hidden in these altogether too brief lines. If you are new to bardic poetry, you will feel confused, if you have years of experience, it'll be pretty much the same, only that your confusion will be more sophisticated. What emerges with some clarity are a number of references to several otherworldly places. One of them is an underworld deep beneath the waves. Another is the mountain of roses with its three springs, a topic that also appears in a song from the *Hanes Taliesin*. Last, there is Uffern itself. Uffern was a dark and cold otherworld in bardic myth, a cold hell of which we only know that a Taliesin sang (BoT10):
May I not fall into the embrace of the swamp,
Into the mob that peoples the depths of Uffern.

One of the earliest mythical Taliesin songs adds (BoT30):

And before the gate of Uffern the lamp was burning
and adds that of all who went there in Arthur's ill-fated expedition, only seven returned.

This is not exactly much, but at least it says more than the later interpretations. When the British were forced to accept

Christianity, Uffern became synonymous with the Christian concept of hell. Thus the British were taught, that one jolly day, Christ and his victorious war band rode to conquer Uffern, from where they released the souls of all poor sinners (i.e. those who had not been baptized). But let us look at the other enigmas in the text. Right at the beginning, our poet asks several questions which are simple and cosmic. From where do night and day come? What colours an eagle grey and a linnet green? Take a book on ornithology and look at the linnet. Then think about that question again. While we are lucky to know that Gwydyon and Lleu were two of the most important characters of British myth, and that their books were in all likeliness volumes on sorcery, we have no such myths for the simple cosmic questions. It is possible that there were originally myths for all of these questions. I find it more likely that they were made up as the poet went along. This takes us out of the usual interpretation of the material.

Many authors have assumed that Taliesin knew all the answers. As an ever lasting presence I should hope s/he did, but as a human being, this does not seem too likely. What is the purpose of so many riddles? Is our bard simply showing off with his superior knowledge? Or are we on the trace of an entirely different phenomena? Look at the Christian lines in our poem. Who was the confessor of Jesus while he died on the cross? The answer could be no-one, or it could be god, or maybe the cross-tree itself, if you prefer a shamanic way of thinking. Whatever you reply, the fact remains that Jesus did not confess properly. Now the rules of the Catholic game have it that anyone who wants to go to heaven has to confess first. If Jesus, who started the religion, did not, what happened to him? If you persist in thinking along these lines, you may well encounter thoughts which are anything but acceptable to the clergy. The same goes for the lines on Adam. The deed of Adam that comes to mind is generally his sin, the forbidden bite from the apple that taught the knowledge of good and evil. Another paradox: how can a sin be the best accomplishment? Did Adam obey god's will when he acted against divine regulations? If you think about it for a while, you may get the idea that blind obedience to god's commandments is not necessarily what god wants. If you continue on this road, you may learn a lot about god, sin and disobedience and free will, but you will certainly collide with the regular teachings of the church. Plenty of Taliesins ranted against the church, not necessarily because they considered themselves pagans, but as they thought their own idea of Christianity a lot superior to that demanded by the clergy. However you think about it, such questions do not make for blind faith and sheep-like docility. They show where religious logic is in knots and, instead of offering answers, make the audience think.

We find similar methods in a number of eastern religions. Some shamans of ancient China chanted songs full of questions and riddles that sound like direct quotes from Taliesin. In the *Chu Ci*, the *Songs of the South*, attributed to Qu Yuan, you can find the song *Tian Wen* (*Heavenly Questions*). Here a few lines in the translation of David Hawkes (1985):

Who passed down the story of the far-off, ancient beginning of things? How can we be sure what it was like before the sky above and the earth below had taken shape?…What manner of things are the darkness and the light? How did Yin and Yang come together, and how could they originate and transform all things that are by their commingling? Whose compass measured out the ninefold heavens? Whose work was this, and how did he accomplish it? Where were the circling cords fastened, and where was the sky's pole fixed?

The whole song consists of 172 questions, surely enough to blow anybody's mind. Many of them are just as simple and perplexing as the ones asked by Taliesin, or like the riddles of the origin that appear so prominently in the *Eddas*. It could be argued that each question has an answer, if we accept a superficial mythological interpretation. For example we could answer that it was Fu Hsi's compass that measured the primal heaven. To accept this interpretation at its face value, however, is to accept Fu Hsi, a totally mythical shape-shifting chaos creature with the body of a dragon-serpent, as if s/he were a normal person living next door.

When the Norse myths propose that sun and moon rush over the windswept width of the sky in horse-drawn chariots as they are pursued by a pair of wolves, we come to a similar impasse. Anybody who accepts invisible horses, chariots and wolves as the real thing is a candidate for religious faith, but certainly not suitable for the job of a shaman or sorcerer. Good Magicians or bards need a precise way of distinguishing between levels of relative truth, if they start

to mix the planes by confusing the truth of one reality with that of another, they soon come to a messy end. It is precisely as magick makes use of so much fantastic imagery that a good mage has to know more about consensual reality than the simple people who think it is the only reality there is. The bards and Druids doubtlessly had a lot of fantastic answers to the impossible questions, but if they knew their business, they also knew the limits of each explanation. However you answer a cosmic question, you will find that behind each answer, no matter how convenient, at least three new questions are lurking.

As more recent examples, the koan (barrier) questions of the Chinese and Japanese Buddhists come to mind. For hundreds of years, starting around the Sung dynasty, students of Chan and Zen have been given crazy little anecdotes and bizarre questions to unhinge their minds and to upset their ordinary, routine way of thinking.

What is the meaning of life? What was your face before you were conceived? How can you pass through the gate-less gate? What is your true nature? Why has the red-bearded foreigner a red beard? What is the Buddha? Has a dog Buddha nature? What is the way? Answer any of these once and for all, and you are lost. The glib answer, the clever answer, the easy answer, they all spring from the wrong mind. When you seek for enlightenment, you are likely to find it (and yourself) the very moment you cease to think as you always do. The instant of enlightenment is not as anyone would have it. It is not a goal, it has no purpose, and there is nobody around to achieve it. Persistence in dualistic thought blinds the mind to direct experience. If I talk sense, I delude you. The ultimate question is no question, the end of the journey is exactly here, but you are gone before you ever came. If you understand this, you will disagree, and so do I.

All initiatory systems which aim at direct insight (unlike the common religious goal of faith and obedience) make use of paradox, meta-paradox and multiples thereof. Religion often claims to supply the answers to the great questions. Exposed to a doubting mind, such answers soon turn into rags and tatters. By contrast, systems of enlightenment tend to favour continuous doubting. This is not the simple doubt of the materialist or the atheist, but the superior doubt that comes when you doubt all, including your own doubt, and that also, and go beyond that. One way to hop into the abyss is to ask 'why?' until your mind comes apart. Most thinkers stop before they reach this point. They limit themselves to a handful of harmless 'whys' and ignore the others that threaten their own world view. If you ask why with persistence, you may catapult your mind into a crisis of such intensity that it destroys your world and yourself. If this happens on the physical plane (madness and death), the whole effort was a failure. If you find your beliefs about yourself and everything disintegrate, and yet something nameless, unborn and wonderful continues, it may well be that you are on the right way.

Forget the 'you' and the 'way', and there appears what Kenneth Grant calls a *Solution of Continuity*. This is the main reason why students of Chan and Zen are pestered with impossible questions. These systems of enlightenment make use of doubt, crisis and confusion to free the self from the shackles of thought, belief and personality. Seen in this light, Taliesin's questions are just as useful as the ones asked by the great Buddhist teachers. If you find a sensible or rational answer, you simply haven't grasped what the question was good for.

Exercise: Riddle Magick

So we come to three simple little exercises. First of all, pick any of the typical Taliesin questions and ponder it really deeply. Reject all superficial answers. Go deeper. Persist. Think about it day and night. This is not a party game. Some adherents of the Eastern systems struggle with their koans as if more than their life depends on it. It does. Like the Nordic riddle contests, a true answer can be a matter of life and death. If you want to get out of your mind, an impossible question is just the thing to set you free.

Second, such questions have enormous surprise value. A well timed question can come like a bucket of cold water. Treat your friends to cosmic questions when they least expect it, when they think they know what they are doing, when they are overly settled in their ways, or when they are sensitive and really close to understanding. Ask them to do the same for you. This is something that is a blessing to anyone, no matter how advanced along the path. I love it when I am surprised by really simple and overwhelming questions. Not so much to answer them, but for the fact that they awaken me from whatever routine my mind is in. Anad once completely upset me by asking 'Who are you?' while we were riding a train and I was thinking I knew what I was thinking. I returned the kindness when I

Coins 10: top l & r (front & reverse): Bellovaci; center l & r (front & reverse): Senones; bottom l & r (front & reverse): Caletes, bronze;

asked her, in a sensitive moment, just where her Holy Guardian Angel is, who it is, and what it is doing NOW? Such questions seem simple. They work wonders when the mind is not expecting them.

A third use of this method can be made in meditation. Let me suggest that you go for a walk. Go slowly. Look around, see, hear, feel and sense the world. How many questions can you find? Why is the sky blue? How do seeds know which way is up? What tells the plant how and where to grow a thorn? What heals a wound? What intelligence causes growth, and what makes growth stop again? Who teaches songs to birds, and when did it start? When does random behaviour become meaningful? Is the light we see in our minds? What makes the nettle sting? How do toads hibernate? How fast is time to the mayfly, the mole or the mighty oak? What makes fluids spiral in regular turbulence? How do things fall to the ground? When is the beginning of feed-back loops? Where do your thoughts come from, and where do they go? Who is the thinker, and who is the thought? Is a thought real? Is the thought of a toad as real as the thought of a human? Where is the mind of a stone? What is it that you always overlook? These questions are not necessarily there to be answered. Instead, they reveal how many miracles exist. As you continue to ask such questions, you may induce a trance of wonder. The riddle trance is a state of consciousness, ever old, ever young, and always on the pivot between worlds. Impossible questions, shunned by most people, can be like friends who accompany you through life. They are reliable, they can be trusted and they always work. This, if anything, is useful to keep the mind young and the world fascinating.

A Question of Identity.

So far, we have encountered Taliesin as several persons. To begin with, in the mythical account we have the thief and beggar Gwion who endures the ordeal of keeping the cauldron hot and stirred for a year and a day. Gwion, as a normal human being, disintegrates as soon as he partakes of the three blessed drops of secret elixir. The initiation is not completed by the drink, however. A single initiation is never enough. Having become all-knowing, the lad is forced to put his newly gained vision to test when Ceridwen attempts to kill him. In the *Hanes*, he is chased through the realm of solid matter, fluid water and gaseous air. Finally he transforms into life-in-potential, and becomes a grain of wheat. This indicates a massive shift of consciousness from active to passive. No doubt you can imagine being an animal, such as a hare, a trout, a bird in the air. As a grain, our nameless initiate is not even a plant, but simply a plant in potential. In this shape, simple and nameless, he is devoured by Ceridwen, who bears him in her womb till he is ripe for reincarnation.

If I may indulge in happy subjectivity at this point, I could tell you that I recall something very similar from the time before I was conceived. Prior to incarnation, between lifetimes, I was the total of all personalities I had ever been. Then, as I was sucked down the spiraling vortex and into my mother's womb I became simple and ever simpler until I forgot the lot. Arriving in the womb I was but a few cells, without a name, a concept of identity or a single meaningful thought. A grain of wheat is an excellent metaphor for this awareness. The womb consciousness seems to be so simple and silent as the babe, when it is born, has to have a really open mind to learn the world anew. If you brought along all the knowledge, the experience and the rubbish of your past lives, you wouldn't get a proper chance to learn.

It would be a simple matter to think that Gwion's initiation ends in the forbidden drink, and that everything afterwards is due to Ceridwen's anger and lust for revenge. If you have gone through initiatory experiences, you will be aware that a single rite, a single vision or a single deed of power is never all there is to it. A good initiation is continuous, it goes on and on, leading the initiate from one mind transforming experience to the next. In this perspective, the three drops are just the beginning of the game. Now there is another sort of initiation implied in the *Hanes Taliesin*. It is not often commented upon, but should be considered nevertheless. By our account, young Gwion is a good looking lad, and the name Gwion Bach (Bright and Small) can be interpreted in several ways. Likewise Ceridwen can be a horrible crooked crone, but her name might also be translated 'fair and beloved'.

Have you ever wondered about the sexual metaphor of stirring a cauldron for a year and a day? Knowing my readers, yes, you probably did, especially as Ceridwen's husband Tegid the Bald is so conspicuously absent in the myth. You can find a similar symbolism if you contemplate the three sacred letters OIV. At this point we have to leave Lady Guest's popular translation of

the *Hanes* and take a look at Nash's version. Lady Guest cleaned up a lot of minor matters in her rendering of the *Mabinogi* to suit the taste of the time while Nash was more concerned to provide a scholarly treatment.

Here is the poetic History of Taliesin:

Before I was formed into the form of a handsome man,
I did penance in the hall of Caridwen.
Though small in appearance, a festival was my reception.
I was (placed) high above the floor of the hall of my chief;
My ransom was set apart by reason of my sweet song;
And by law without speech I was set at liberty.
The old hag, black her appearance when irritated;
Dreadful were her screams when pursuing me.
I fled with vigour, I fled as a frog;
I fled in the semblance of a raven, scarcely finding rest;
I fled vehemently; I fled as a chain;
I fled as a roe into an entangled thicket;
I fled as a wolf cub, I fled as a wolf in a wilderness;
I fled as a thrush, the interpreter of omens;
I fled as a fox, leaping and turning;
I fled as a marten, which did not avail;
I fled as a squirrel, that vainly hides;
I fled as an antlered stag of free course;
I fled as iron in a glowing fire;
I fled as a spear head, woe to him who desires it;
I fled as a bull fierce in fighting;
I fled as a bristly boar seen in a ravine;
I fled as a white grain of pure wheat,
on the skirt of a hempen sheet entangled,
That seemed of the size of a mare's foal,
That was flowing in like a ship on the waters.
Into a dark leather bag was I thrown,

And on a boundless sea was I set adrift.
It was good tidings when I was entangled in
the branch.
And God the Lord set me at liberty.

Again, several elements in the poem
shout for attention. The first lines imply
that Gwion was a prisoner in Ceridwen's
hall, but that he was also received with
festivity, ransomed by song and released by
wordless mind shattering insight. His role
is more and less than a servant, in fact, he is
treated more like an initiate, or a sacrifice,
than as a simple hired hand. After receiving
his mind-opening taste of the enchanted
fluids, he is chased in the shape of numerous
beasts and several objects (watch out for
symbolism). Not just three or four animals:
our hero has to pass through much of the
fauna of the Welsh countryside. His
initiation continues as each animal supplies
its own perception of reality. Very similar
practices appear prominently in the
initiations of countless shamanic cultures. I
wouldn't claim that Taliesin is simply a
shaman, as the bard is definitely not a tribal
healer, but that he underwent a number of
shamanic experiences in his initiations.
Countless shamans all over the world have
chanted of their activities in various animal
forms, or have assumed the form of their
animal spirits as they chanted and
hypnotized themselves. You find references
to Taliesin's other lives scattered through
several songs (so you'll forgive me for not
quoting the lot in this place). Let me quote
lines by the famous Mazatec healer Maria
Sabina instead, who regularly ate
hallucinogenic mushrooms containing
psilocybin to attain states of enlightenment:

…Eagle woman am I,
Opossum woman am I,
Woman who examines am I,
Hunting dog woman am I…
Woman who thunders am I, woman who
sounds am I,
Spider woman am I, hummingbird woman
am I,
Eagle woman am I, important eagle woman
am I,
Whirling woman of the whirlwind am I,
Woman of a sacred enchanted place am I,
Woman of the shooting stars am I…

The repetitive nature of the verses, the
hypnotic simplicity, the use of set formula
to induce trance states all appear very similar
to the lines composed by some Taliesins.
Magic mushrooms with similar chemistry
as those used by Mesoamerican healers are
available in Britain and middle Europe, but
if we simply blame such insights on
psychoactives, we are forgetting that very
similar states can be produced by the brain
without ingesting toxic substances. Plenty
of shamans have attained very similar
experiences of multiple identity, and
survived the flood of new experiences by
blending and harmonizing them in the
cauldron of the mind. The idea that the soul
can assume the shape of an animal is
international and widely popular. In ancient
Europe you find it in the fylgia, the guardian
spirit of the Nordic warriors, it was usually
a bear, wolf, lynx, dragon, eagle or some
other fierce animal. Disappearance of the
fylgia implied that death would occur soon.
Likewise, the Germanic deities frequently
transform into animal shape, and the more
sorcerous a god is, the more animals appear
in the list. Odin/Wodan, archetype of the
shamanic shapeshifter, sorcerer, spellbinder

and astral traveler appears not only as wolf and raven but also as worm, fish, beast and bird when he travels through the otherworlds. Loki as a classical trickster deity appears as horse, seal, bird, salmon and mosquito. Freya, goddess of love, is accompanied by cats and boars, and keeps a falcon costume for long journeys in her wardrobe.

The *Mabinogi* also lists several human/ animal transformations, such as the case when Gwydyon and Gilvaethwy are perforce transformed into deer, wild boar and wolves by the ancient enchanter Math. He punished them with these transformations for the rape of his foot-holder, Lady Goewin. Again, the punishment is also an initiation, and when the two louts are allowed to become human after three years in the wild forest, they appear humble indeed. Similar tales abound in Island Celtic literature, be it in the animal lives of Tuan Mac Cairel, the shape shifting swine-herds of Ireland, Etain's life as a melodious fly, Llew's after-death existence as an eagle or in mad Myrddin running with the deer in the Caledonian forest.

Witches were renowned for animal forms, cats and hares being especially popular when it came to travel overland or to steal a neighbour's cream. Likewise, common folk-myths have the soul appear in the shape of a mouse, a serpent or a butterfly. Similar shapes are assumed by tribal sorcerers in Africa and elsewhere when the journey leads them to realms that are forbidden to humans. One healer of the *Kung pointed out that in the realm of the dead, a human form means that you have to die. By going there in the form of a toxic mamba serpent, he is able to survive the transition and to return to the world of the living alive (see Halifax 1979).

Thus, to the shamanic healer, a repertoire of animal helpers and animal forms is essential for survival. Taliesin has been around everywhere and has been just about anything. Ceridwen did the dear lad a great favour when she pursued him so vigorously through a pageant of alternate existences. Finally, she devoured him-again, this is a typical element of shamanism, would-be-shamans are often devoured by a number of not-too-friendly spirits-and brought him to life as her own child. As a babe, very young, very old, nameless and thoroughly open-minded, she wraps him up and sends him to float across the bottomless world ocean. This completes his initiation: In a small and dark cell the bard ripens for reality. As I proposed in *Seidways*, we can view Avagddu, Gwion and Taliesin as three faces of the bard. Gwion as the human being, the beggar on the dusty road between sunrise and sunset, Avagddu (Over-dark) as the crazy one, the ugly brute, the nightside dweller between worlds, and finally Taliesin (Bright Brow) as the enlightened visionary seer and singer. In the process of his initiation, Gwion undergoes several phases of being Over-dark, be it while he stirs the cauldron in the smoky gloom, be it in the womb of the dark hag, in the leather bag drifting through the ocean and when he spell-binds Maelgwn's bards before the contest. That extended periods in total darkness were used in the training of some Irish poets in the early 18th century appears from the *Memories of the Marquis of Clanricarde* (1722). You can find the full text on the subject in John Matthews (1991), it is well worth

A knot of
bones and
berries.

reading. Rowlands (1985) also refers to this subject and proposes that similar methods may well have been used in the training of the British bards. He cites Iolo Goch (c. 1320-1398): *Elegy to the Sons of Tudor Ap Goronwy* where you can find the innocent line:

Anglesey with the green nape used to be called the dark island, cell of song.

Mona, or Anglesey may remind you of the last Druidic stronghold in Britain, raided by the Roman legions to crush the cult once and for all in the year 60. That bards were trained in this place is not unlikely, as the island was more fertile and wealthy than all the rest of Wales.

Retiring to dark places in order to invoke inspiration seems to have been a popular activity for bards and poets. It is precisely from total darkness that bright and fluent song and vision can arise. In this sense, the bards did not only undergo darkness once but sought it repeatedly when they composed their enchantments. Likewise, after a period of brilliance, it can be only too natural to retire into darkness and emptiness to restore the inner balance. Taliesin (dayside) and Avagddu (nightside) may refer to the two faces of the ecstatic vision, while Gwion, as the human persona, goes to work and keeps the fire burning and the broth stirred. This leads us to the question of the nature of a soul that knows so many permutations. Who is the real self behind the dance of all the masks? What is your answer to the question? If you can name it, you are bound to be wrong. Nash came very close to the answer when he translated a Taliesin line as *There is nothing in which I have not been.*

While having been everything, the bard is essentially not. This is the truth that most shape shifters and astral travelers encounter if they persist in their trance journeys for long enough. What happens if you dance your way from form to form? Who moves from bird to beast, from human to object, from tree to stone to stellar fire? Who is it that lives in hundreds of lifetimes, each of them in a different ego? Who is it that returns from the journey? Who sings the song of these experiences and who listens and understands?

Knowest thou what thou art
When thou art sleeping?
Whether a body or a soul,
Or a secresy of perception? (BoT 9)

The ability to assume any form and to sense in every consciousness, to experience every period in time, to die and to be reborn again and again comes precisely from being no-body, no-name, no-shape, no-personality. Nothing is a key to this state, only that nothing is too positive a concept, as the true nature we are talking about is beyond the limitations of conceptual thought. The nothing you can think is not nothing enough. Essentially, the self is consciousness without shape, all present, unformed, unknown, unborn and undying. All shapes that you perceive, all forms you encounter, all beings you meet, all personalities you identify with are glamours cast off like phantoms from the primal well of sheer awareness. This is what constitutes the essence of Taliesin, and the same goes for you and me and every other dancer in this weaving of realities.

Hoard of
Großbissendorf
Top l. unknown
tribe,
Großbissendorf,
Neumarkt,
Bavaria, gold, 18
mm, trefoil
symbol.
Top r. unknown
tribe,
Großbissendorf,
Neumarkt,
Bavaria, gold, 16
mm, swastika.
Center l.
unknown tribe,
Großbissendorf,
Neumarkt,
Bavaria, gold, 16
mm.
Center r.
unknown tribe,
Großbissendorf,
Neumarkt,
Bavaria, gold,
stylized bird
head in profile?
Bottom l.
unknown tribe,
Großbissendorf,
Neumarkt,
Bavaria, gold,
stylized trefoil
transformed into
an
anthropomorphic
figure, goddess?
Bottom r.
unknown tribe,
Großbissendorf,
Neumarkt,
Bavaria, gold, 16
mm.

9. Enchantment

The Fire of Motivation

I am not a mute artist,
Conspicuous among the bards of the people.
I animate the bold,
I influence the heedless;
I wake up the looker on,
The enlightener of bold kings. (BoT 13)

The bards of Britain and the Filid of Ireland were adepts at motivating people. You read earlier on how the praise songs worked their spell to motivate nobles to deeds of reckless heroism. You could call this the bright side of the Awen, the enchantment wrought by lucid vision and glamorous fascination. Praise-songs motivate the hearer to hurry towards a goal. If the goal is defined in attractive form, and if the vision is brilliant enough, many fall to its alluring fascination and struggle to attain it, no matter the cost. On the other hand, the spells wrought by the Awen could also promise doom and destruction. Hidden in the twilight, in the twisted growth, in misty glades and forsaken solitude, you can encounter the other face of the muse. Bards and poets used satire, curses and darksome spellwork to threaten, hurt and destroy. In this way they could move minds by means of promise and of punishment.

Before we go into the historic evidence for such activities, I would like to ask you to pause a moment and to consider. How do these two forces influence your life? As you probably guessed by now, we are all bards and poets in that we weave the spells, songs and stories that make up our life's texture. What the bards did for the 'heroic society' is not that different from what everybody does right up there in the mind. We are myth makers and myth livers. The main difference is that the bards did this sort of thing for other people, while you will be focused on your own dream of life. Apart from that, the mechanisms are pretty much the same.

In their praise songs, the bards and filid made use of several tactics to motivate the audience. Let's take a look at them. One way to motivate was to recall the heroic deeds of the *ancestors*. Here are some lines a Taliesin composed as a death song for Uther Pendragon:

Is it not I that have destroyed a hundred Caers?
Is it not I that slew a hundred governors?
Is it not I that have given a hundred veils?
Is it not I that cut off a hundred heads?
(BoT 48)

Clearly, old Uther, father of Arthur, the Bear of Britain, had a fantastic reputation. Most heroes had, provided they were dead for long enough. When bards sang of the ancestors, they took care to make them really impressive.

These shining examples of heroic virtue and generosity were a lot larger than life, so large in its literal sense that we find several Irish and Welsh myths relating that the heroes of the elder days were of a much superior size and walked the earth like giants. What happens in your mind when you make a vision or inner picture larger? Imagine a person. How large is your image? Now increase the size. Make it bigger. Does this alter your experience? Think of a deity. How tall is it? Increase the size. How is your emotional response changing? Most people respond much stronger to bigger images. You can increase this effect by making the image brighter, and bringing it closer to you. From where do you see it? From above, eye-level, the sides or below? Try out different perspectives. How can you make it really impressive? And what happens when you make it too big? We do plenty of amazing things in our minds. The bards and filid knew how to do them for

their audience as well.

Another motivation was to invoke the *race* and *nationality*. This particular figment of imagination reflects a belief in a group self (and depends a lot on how the group defines itself). If a race was called valiant or invincible, its members had better live up to it. You can call this patriotism or mass hallucination, depending whether you view it from inside or outside the group.

Then there was *religion*. As long as the British were Christians, and the Anglo-Saxons were pagans, it was a useful stratagem to call on god for a bit of righteous warfare.

From the agitation of fire, smoke will be raised,
And God our creator will defend us.
(BoT 10)

Then as now it's an easy matter to motivate the faithful to war when the deity concerned approves of it. Most deities don't, but people just don't listen.

Mind you, I can't quite believe that the monarchs or their bards always took nationality or faith so seriously. Modern pagans often assume that the British and the Anglo-Saxons were traditional enemies, or generalize from this hypothesis that the so called 'Germans' and the so called 'Celts' of earlier times were always hostile to each other. This was certainly not the case in prehistory, and it was not always the case in Britain either. Read the venerable Bede, and you can find the old saint ranting against a British lord (Christian) who allied with a Saxon lord (pagan) to attack another British lord (and fellow Christian). He also goes on about various alliances between Saxons, Angles and Picts, the latter being, according to recent studies, another Celtic tribe. Alliances in medieval Britain were always shaky, and nationality or faith tended to mean very little when rulers went about having at least one profitable war each year.

Prophecy is another interesting motivation. Faith in prophecy implies that the future can be known or made. As we all know, the oracle is always right, one way or another. Prophecy makes use of future imagination uttered in a form of absolute certainty. A bard in oracular frenzy must have been an impressive sight to behold. Ecstatic madness, spittle flying, rolling eyes and wild trembling…anything to get the good old imagination going. 'Crazy' behaviour can be just the thing to kick the mind out of its narrow confinement of rules and regulations into a world where perception is direct, spontaneous and completely uninhibited. Shaking in particular is a useful technique to change consciousness drastically and to amplify vision and imagination. I won't detail how to learn shaking trance, as this topic has been treated in depth in *Seidways*. While ecstatic madness can be useful to create an interesting state of mind in the shaman, prophet or bard, it is also useful to impress the audience. Dramatic behaviour is expected from spirit mediums in many Asian or African countries. What constitutes trance and prophecy differs enormously from culture to culture. In some lands a holy person is expected to remain utterly serene and composed in ritual, in others you have wild folk who shake and tremble as the spirit moves them. What would impress you more?

Whatever your reaction, it doesn't say one bit about the validity of the oracular message. It says a lot about your expectations. Think about it. Are you aware how you live up to whatever you expect or believe? How about expecting something entirely different, and treating yourself to a surprise?

This brings us to *spell-craft*. As everybody knew, the sacred song of the inspired poet can make things happen. Here we have a present activity that results in a magically transformed future. Finally, think of the most direct form of motivation: the *inflated ego*. Make a pause now and imagine what you look like. Walk around yourself, take a good look from all directions. Do you like what you see? Could you do with some improvements? Now change the image. Make yourself look the way you would like to look. How would you look if you had excellent posture, if you exercised more often, if you had a healthier outlook on life? What else do you want? Happiness, curiosity, excitement, insight, humour? Play around with the image. Now bring it closer. Make it brighter, a bit bigger…would you enjoy more colour? More energy? Are you laughing? Give this self image of yours something good to feel. Is it smiling? Come on, is it only smiling? How about something stronger? How would you like intense rapturous joy? Did you know that the natural condition of humanity is sheer ecstatic joy and intense curiosity and wonder? Build that into the image…make it really attractive…is this what you would like to become? Is this a good direction for your journey? If its what you will, put the image into your close future and go for it.

The bards made use of very similar methods to create glamorous personalities for their clients. *A coffin to everyone his ambition.* (BoT 11).

If a noble was praised for certain qualities, such as cruelty and battle-cunning, living up to them was the only option. One of the first Taliesins chanted for his patron Urien of Rheged:

He slays, he plagues,
He cherishes, he honours,
He honours, he cherishes,
He slays before him…
I also will praise
Thy deeds.
And until I fail in old age,
In the sore necessity of death,
May I not be smiling,
If I praise not Urien. (BoT 33)

Being forced to live in a mask dictated by public relations is never very easy. It must have been especially unpleasant when the bard sang of the king's generosity. Such songs could be costly. One of the earlier Taliesins boasted of having received 100 steeds with silver trappings, 100 purple robes, 100 armbands, 50 brooches and an incomparable sword from Cynan Garwyn. I wonder if it ruined his host.

In dealing with an inflated ego, we are obviously on dangerous ground. The vision can be so tempting, so convincing, and this is where people cease to consider alternatives. If you create wonderful visions of yourself, better be sure that you choose wisely. Plenty of people use suggestion, positive thinking and amplified imagination to make total idiots out of themselves. Few bother to consider if their new personality is such a wise choice.

Make yourself someone who likes to learn and laugh. This is not what the bards were motivating their mead besotted nobles to, but then I am sure that you can think of lots of better activities than battle frenzy and mindless pillaging.

What do you aim for in life? What do you want to achieve? Write down some of your goals, the small and the big ones, the vague and the specific. If you like to, you can underline what seems especially important for the fulfillment of your will. What is essential for you? What is open to debate? And just what is extra?

How did you frame your will? Are your goals images that motivate you to go towards them? Or are they expressed as images you would rather avoid? The difference says a lot about the way you motivate yourself.

It's a sad fact that most people in our society use too much negative motivation. Think of your loved ones. What motivates you to be with them? Do you enjoy to share good times together (positive motivation: an attractive goal) or is it better than loneliness (negative motivation: an unattractive option that you'd rather avoid)? Do you work to achieve something worthwhile (positive motivation) or to avoid something horrible such as poverty? Do you read this book to gain something new and valuable or do you fear to be uninformed or bored? If I ask you to try this exercise, do you think you can profit from it or do you fear you'd miss something you paid for? This sort of thing goes on all of the time. When you get up out of bed, is it because you look forward to doing something valuable or pleasant, or is it that you fear to miss something, or to be mauled by your employer? Would you exercise as your body enjoys the experience or do you force yourself to move as you fear overweight, ill-health and low energy? In terms of bardic enchantment, do you strive for a good reputation, fame, glory and pleasure? Or do you fear ridicule, scorn, shame and pain?

How do you motivate yourself for the essential things in life? Usually, people use both tactics for different outcomes. Most folk have a handful of activities they move towards, and a lot of other issues they struggle to avoid. Now I wont counsel that you brainwash yourself to desire something that is obnoxious to you. If you have a horrid job, it's hardly any use to hypnotize yourself that this is what you crave to do. It might be worth considering how to improve the job so it is more fun, however, or to look out for a better one.

Then there are activities which are unpleasant but can't be avoided. This sort of thing looks like negative motivation, but then again, you can turn it into positive motivation by making it attractive. An unpleasant task may be no fun while you are at it, but it can be a pleasure if it yields something valuable, if it becomes a good story, or if you reward yourself with something joyous afterwards. The last strategy is used by lots of people, it's called 'getting it over with'. How well it works depends on how efficiently you reward yourself. Many do this half heartedly. They imagine something attractive after the chore. If the ordeal is too strong, or lasts too long, the reward may not be sufficient to pull them through. Why reward yourself afterwards? How about enjoying the reward

while you are at it? It can be useful to break down the unhappy job into smaller units. If you congratulate yourself to every step you have completed, and imagine the good stuff to come closer with each obstacle you have mastered, you may find that the unpleasant job is done pretty soon. You can do this in your mind. Make a compelling vision and get access to all the good feelings that are ready for you. You can enjoy having completed a step, or a unit, but you can also enjoy completing it, in the certain knowledge that better things are waiting for you. How can you reward yourself more wisely?

On the other hand, some folk prefer to plod through an unhappy task resenting it all the time. They make up representations of things they might be enjoying if they didn't do this horrible stuff, and of course the better they hallucinate what they are missing, the worse does the task become. Or think of the Castaneda tactic of redefining every difficulty as a 'challenge'. This frame implies that you are challenged (by whom? About what?), and that if you solve the problem, you may win in your own self esteem, or whatever else you use to keep your ego bright and shiny. Some find this useful. I agree it can be, on occasion, but on the whole it is not that elegant. The whole frame implies so much strain and tension, and turns everyday matters into a life and death struggle. Too much 'challenge' and you may find yourself getting very tense and edgy. If you like drama to motivate you, you can have that, and plenty of it. I prefer to enjoy what I'm doing, and to take matters less seriously.

So, in motivating yourself, you can use

Couldron of the Gods

pleasure (rewards) and pain (punishment). You could also use this chance to consider the outcome. If you motivate yourself to achieve something by moving towards it, chances are that you'll get it sooner or later. If you motivate yourself by avoiding something unpleasant, you will probably avoid that, but this does not mean that you'll get what you really want. Avoiding errors does not mean that you do something good, let alone excellently. It's like walking backwards. If you walk backwards you can avoid being caught by nasty things coming after you, but you won't necessarily get anywhere you want to go. So how about looking at your list again? How can you frame the negative goals (avoiding xyz) so they become positive goals that attract you? And while we're at it, how can you frame the positive goals so you can be certain that they are worth getting?

And what can attract you once you are there? Remember that evolution is not just a matter of reaching a goal and then you have it and its over. It can be very unpleasant to reach all of your goals. Some goals last a lifetime. Some are like stepping stones across a sparkling brook. Some lose most of their attraction when you examine closely. Much better is a direction in which you can develop, a path that continues, and a future that holds new sensations and new surprises unfolding as you go along. A system has to be open to avoid stagnation and entropy.

The Gift of the Nettle

The bards and poets used both forms of motivation to move their audience. On one hand they gratified and caused pleasure when they praised a given noble. On the other hand they punished by using satire and ridicule. If you read this book as a magicians, you will be aware that each of these two tactics relies on the ego. Either ego is praised, so it can bloat itself with pride, or ego is punished until it becomes small and shameful. This sort of thing works wonders on ordinary people and ordinary warriors, it is not especially valuable for a magician seeking to go beyond ego altogether. It would be interesting to know if the more refined bards themselves could be caught in such a simple snare. For the fun of it you could take another look at the catalogue of bardic motivation methods. Which of these approaches could motivate you? What snare can catch and hold your ego?

So far, we had some examples for the way the bardic audience was moved by praise. When we examine the way ridicule and curses were used, we get into deeper waters.

An Irish manuscript dating around 1100 contains a curious tale. One Samhain, when the sky had turned bleak and the cold winds began to howl, the master poet Dallan Forgail came to the court of Mongan, king of Ulster. As was the custom of the master poets, Dallan sought to spend the dark season between November and May in the comfort of a royal hall. Great was the hospitality in the brightly lit chambers of Mongan's castle. The ale was strong, the company cheerful, and Dallan was received as a guest of honour. As payment for the royal generosity, Mongan told tales. He told a tale each night, and would have continued in this fashion till summer began

Coins 12, birds
top: Bellovaci, gold, 18 mm, head with hand-
bird and three drops. Compare with Taliesin
tale.
center L: Vindelici, gold, 17 mm, very
common image of bird head and moons
center r: Carnuti, bronze, 16 mm, bird of prey
with lizard
bottom: Carnuti, bronze, 15 mm, bird of prey
with small bird. Another type shows snake.

and the Beltain fires were lit. Sadly, before the warm season returned, the king and the poet came to have a quarrel about the final resting place of a certain hero. Dallan knew the place, but the king knew better, and before long, harsh words were said. As both parties could offer no proof of their allegations, it did not take long before the king was hollering wrathfully. Himself a man of overbearing pride, Dallan threatened to satirize king Mongan, as well as the kings ancestors, and to curse the rivers to be fishless, the woods fruitless and the plains barren for ever.

King Mongan, shocked by this proposal, came out of his rage and attempted to soothe the poet. In vain he offered to pay a price of 7, then 14, then 21 bondmaids to the angry poet. Dallan would not accept it. His pride had suffered and the king was to pay for it. A couple of slave girls could hardly make up for the damage. Mongan, seeing that the poet remained unmoved, offered a third of the kingdom, then half of it, and finally broke down to pledge all. 'Take my land!' shouted the king in his rage 'but leave me my liberty and my wife!' The master poet, however, remained as revengeful as ever. He had long fancied the queen's beauty and now saw a chance to win her and to break the king's pride for ever.

While the former King left the realm in shame, Dallan took the royal seat and the queen, who was sorrowful and wept every day. Eventually, it turned out that Dallan had been wrong in the first place. He became famous for unjust insolence and overbearing pride. His tale was passed from poet to poet, and eventually his real name was forgotten. His legendary name, Dallan, means 'blind'. His pupil, Senchan Torpeist succeeded him to the office of the head ollamh of Ireland. Being just as arrogant as his master he was later satirized himself.

Here we have an interesting example of the power enjoyed by the Irish poets. As you may notice, part of the threat was to satirize the king and the royal family. What was the power of satire? In our days, people are used to being joked about. Politicians and celebrities have to expect and live with ridicule, and possibly this state of affairs is useful to keep them from becoming too proud and self-important. In Celtic society, as far as we know, an entirely different outlook prevailed. If you have lots of nobles who live for their own grand reputation, the very idea of someone being satirized can be enough to constitute a very real threat. To the victim, a satire was anything but a laughing matter. To be ridiculed was to suffer, not only in pride and reputation but also physically. It follows that anything which hurts a king is also likely to hurt the kingdom. In this sense, it is only too understandable when Dallan threatens to curse the land with barrenness. The people of the time took such threats very seriously. Take a look at the final battle fought by the semi-divine hero Cu Chullain. During the fight, Cu is taunted by satirists to give up his enchanted spear or to suffer insult and ridicule. In a fit of rage he kills two of the satirists, but finally gives in to the third, who threatens to revile Cu's race itself. This deed turns out fatal. Once Cu releases the spear, it is taken up by the warrior Lugaid and used to disembowel its former owner. Cu gives a mighty scream and angrily walks off to a nearby lake, where he has a wash and a lie down.

In the *Tain*, Queen Medb sends Druids, enchanters and magicians to Ferdiad, whom she wishes to fight against the invincible Cu. Against his will he goes to the encounter (Cu was a close friend and foster-brother) as otherwise the *Glam Dicenn* (satire) would make three terrible blisters break out on his face. These would have killed him within nine days. Rather than die with three blisters, Ferdiad prefers to die as mincemeat.

In the mythical prehistory of Ireland, the People of the goddess Danann fought a long lasting war against a race of elder creatures who seem to have come from under the sea. Chief of these beings, the Fomors, was one called Bres who was the very epitome of good looks. In this matter he was very unlike most of his relations, some of whom had bull heads or crept around like footless serpents. Now Bres was good-looking but also very unjust, in that he demanded exceptional taxes and offerings and sacrifices. The Tuatha De Danann, seeking to righten the situation, sent their poet, Cairbre son of Etain, to negotiate. Instead of getting the respect due to a poet, Cairbre was received shamefully.

He entered a cabin narrow, black, dark, wherein there was neither fire nor furniture nor bed. Three small cakes, and they dry, were brought to him on a little dish. On the morrow he arose and he was not thankful. As he went across the enclosure, he said:
Without food quickly on a dish:
Without a cow's milk whereon a calf grows:
Without a man's abode in the gloom of night:
Without paying company of story-tellers, let that be Bres's condition.
Let there be no increase in Bres.
Now that was true. Naught save decay was on Bres from that hour. That is the first satire that was ever made in Ireland. (The Second Battle of Mag Tured, transl. Cross and Slover)

The poets called this sort of thing satire, but evidently it was not meant to make anyone laugh. Closer to the mark would be the term curse. Now perhaps you would like to know how a proper cursing was done. Cairbre did it simply by voicing his ill wishes, and this seems to have sufficed, maybe as he came from the tribe of the people of Danann and was consequently a deity, or at least a semi-divine figure. What about the more humble satires uttered by human poets?

The Irish Filid had complex ritual called *Glaim Dichin* or *Glam Dicenn* (see D. Hyde 1899). Like the *Aer*, the satire, it was a legal means by which a poet could force nobles to make up for misdeeds or lacking payment, provided his cause was a just one. This practise was discontinued in historical times, as the poets often made unreasonable demands, so that laws had to be passed which fixed specific prices for poetic ranks. Much of this was against the will of the poets, but then, they couldn't help it, public opinion being very much against them. A 12th century song attributed to St. Columban contains some valuable references to *Glam Dicenn* . The Irish, so the man of god said, would die if they were satirized, or they would suffer from three blisters in their faces, called disgrace, blemish and ugliness. If the poet unjustly satirized a person, however, he would receive the blisters himself. This sort of thing is frequently alluded to. When Sencha, son of Ailills spoke a false verdict, three blisters appeared in his face. Sen MacAige made a false verdict and a blister grew in his face. When he reconsidered, the blister disappeared. So much for psycho-somatic reactions.

Another painful episode. When a woman promised to King Conchobar refused to sleep with the poet Aithirne Ailgesach and his two sons (who were all in love with her), the latter sang three satires that caused the three blisters disgrace, blemish and ugliness (in black, red and white) to ruin her face. She died of shame. Cathbad, Druid of Ulster, said that Aithirne would send wild beasts:

> satire, shame and misery, curse, fire and bitter words. His six children of dishonesty are called stinginess, contradiction, refusal, hardness, stubbornness and greed and they are so good at it that they will wage war against you.

Aithirne made a nuisance out of himself by touring various provinces of Ireland. He threatened people with his malignant satire and coerced them to offer gifts, even if it ruined whole districts. In Leinster he asked the men to give up their wives or an eye, and when he came to a district that had nothing whatsoever to offer, he demanded that the most precious jewel of the hill should be given to him, or else. Laughing gleefully he declared that nobody knows the nature of this hill and its location. Was he talking about a hill, a mound or the head-hill rising above the shoulders? Finally the Ulstermen did everyone a favour by slaying Aithirne and his spawn.

Here is another tale of a poet who abused his power. Let's take a look into *Cormac's Glossary*. Nede was one of the greatest filid of Ireland. Several of the most magical songs of the Green Island are attributed to him, and these manifest a degree of wisdom that far exceeds the horizon of most poets. Maybe he actually wrote some of them. Maybe he was simply the model for the perfect poet. Nevertheless, in later life he committed a very stupid blunder. King Caier had adopted Nede as he had no son of his own. One day, so it is said, the Queen herself approached the poet and offered him a silver apple if he would lie with her. Nede refused her. Then she offered that he would be king after Caier. 'How can this be?' said Nede. 'Satirize him,' said the queen, 'and he will suffer a blemish. A blemished man cannot remain king.' 'I cannot satirize him,' pondered Nede, 'as whatever I may wish for, he is certain to give it to me.' 'Ask for his dagger,' said the queen,' he is bound by geas (taboo), he cannot give his dagger away.' Nede considered this. How could he lose? A king who broke a geas was as good as dead anyway. So Nede went to the king to ask for the dagger. The king, bewailing fate, refused him. So Nede made a *Glam Dicenn* against the king.

Singing angrily, he fated the king to suffer evil, shortness of life and death, to be hewn down by the blades of battle, to be rejected by country and earth and to rest finally under soil and rock and ruins. The next day Caier went to a spring. He saw his face in the water, and there were three blisters on it, red, green and white, called shame, stain and ugliness. He had received a blemish and was not fit to govern any longer. So King Caier secretly left the land and traveled to Dun Cermnai where he hid himself in sorrow. He felt so ashamed of his blisters that he assumed another name and henceforth shunned company. Nede, having unjustly cursed a king, proceeded to marry the queen and assumed the kingship.

After a year, Nede made a journey to Dun Cermnai. The former poet had begun to feel a bit uneasy about the way he had mistreated his adopted father. He had heard rumours about a strange refugee living at the court and decided to go there. Seeing the royal chariot approach, the former King Caier muttered 'We used to travel in this chariot' but a warrior overheard him and spoke 'These are the words of a former king!' Caier howled mightily in his shame, ran off and hid in a hole in cleft rock. Nede entered the stronghold and used one of Caier's dogs to find its owner's hiding place. The former poet rushed to embrace the old man, but Caier simply dropped dead. The rock around him grew so hot that it burned, boiled, and burst apart. A splinter struck Nede right through an eye. He said 'Ouch', composed a final poem and died.

The Rite of Cursing

To begin with, the poet had to fast on the land of the king who had offended him. Fasting in itself was a magickal act. You can find it regularily in Irish mythology,

especially when visionaries seek to change shape, trance or prophecy.

A good example for fasting occurs in the tale of Tuan mac Cairill. First, the tired and exhausted Tuan retired to a cave where he fasted for three days and slept. When he woke, he had recovered his former health, but he had also transformed into a stag. After a lifetime among the deer of Ireland, he returned to the cave where fasting and sleep changed him into a boar. Later, Tuan in boar shape fasted and transformed into a hawk, and finally into a salmon (see *Seidways*).

Fasting, seclusion, darkness, exhaustion and a sleep-like trance state play important parts in the initiations of many shamans, be it in Siberia and elsewhere. Under the proper conditions, and given a suitable frame of belief and expectations, such initiation/ ordeals can suspend the everyday personality of the initiate and open her/his mind to inspiration and recognition of the original self. As some recent studies indicate, prolonged fasting can alter the serotonine balance in the brain, which may lead to similar experiences as LSD. In this case, we may propose that our poet or vision-seeker is tripping, even though no drugs as such were ingested. Mind you, fasting by itself is no guarantee for earth shaking visions and fancy illuminations. The same goes for isolation, exhaustion and the like. It takes a skilled mind to make use of fasting and exhaustion. Initiation is never an automatic process. Some of it has to be worked consciously, some of it needs the blessing of the deep. The use of such methods necessitates experience, otherwise one ends up sick and miserable and as stupid as on every other day. To make use of fasting for purification or changes of consciousness is an old method. It is not necessarily a Christian custom, though the Christians were certainly aware of it. You can find it mentioned in old Pliny's account of Druidic ritual. It would be interesting to learn just what constituted fasting to the Celtic seers and visionaries. Some medieval authors use the word for a complete abstention from any food, others mean minimal meals, or forbid certain foodstuffs, such as meat and strong liquor.

Fasting was not just a means of altering consciousness, however. It also constituted a symbolic act of protest and carried a message of accusation. The modern practise of hunger-strikes, well known from political prisoners in Ireland and elsewhere, may have its roots in the medieval gnosis of the filid.

To proceed with the cursing, the poet had to make sure his cause was a just one. In this dire case, he needed the consent of 30 laymen, 30 bishops and 30 poets. This may sound like a difficult task, but in the days when the poets made the laws, the consent could not be withheld when a poet had been cheated of his wages. The injured poet had to ascend a hill on the boundary of seven lands on sunrise. He had to be in the company of six poets of different rank, so that all the seven ranks of the poetic art were represented. Each poet turned to face one land, the ollamh facing the seat of the king against whom the curse was aimed. In their middle, so that their backs were turned to it, had to be a hawthorn. This tree has quite a reputation in Irish poetry. The ogham alphabet associates it with the letter H and

calls it a *pack of wolves, a terror to any one,* and comments *blanched is a man's face when he is encompassed with fear and terror.* As the *Auraicept* points out repeatedly, the letter H is not pronounced. Instead, it is often used to delete the sound which comes prior to it.

Next, the ritual requires a wind blowing from the north. This is not only a cold wind, it also comes from the black direction of the compass. Some Irish texts call satire a black art. Each poet holds a stone with a hole (such stones appear prominently in plenty of European cultures as charm givers and breakers of ill influences) and a thorn, presumably from the bush. The genital symbolism of this combination is obvious. The poets each sang a verse of the curse, the ollamh starting. According to the poetic hierarchy, the lowest rank, the focloc, injured the king's robes. The macfuirmedh injured the king's hound, the doss the king's arms, the cana the king's wife, the cli the king's son, the anrath the king's steed while the top rank, the ollamh, cursed the king himself. Finally they earthed the rite by placing the stones and the thorns under the stem of the hawthorn. This rite was known to be utterly lethal provided the poet had been treated unjustly in the first place. If the poets were wrong, however, they could expect the ground to open up and to swallow them. Evidently, a rite of such magnitude was not an everyday matter but a practise reserved for those who really deserved it. You may estimate how much the effect of this rite was dreaded when you consider how difficult it was to carry it out. Complication can raise expectation, it can also give enraged sorcerers a time to calm down and consider.

Coins 13, horses
top: unknown, Gaul, silver
center l: Boii, siver, 15 mm, note double tail
center r: Turoni, gold, 23 mm, note horse goddess,
thumb gesture and abstract eye-images
bottom: unknown, Gaul, silver, 15 mm, note large fish

A hole stone in malignant use appears in the medieval Irish tale *The Pursuit of Dermat and Grania* (*Book of Leinster*, c.1130). In one curious episode, the hero Finn sets out to crush his rival Dermat by means of sorcery. First, he travels to the otherworld, to the Land of Promise, where his old nurse lives. Hearing how Finn had been insulted, the old lady immediately agrees to come to Ireland with him. Let me quote P. W. Joyce's translation:

> Next day, they set out, Finn and his people and his nurse; and it is not told how they fared till they reached Brugh of the Boyne. And the men of Erin knew not that they had come thither, for the witch-hag threw a druidical mist round them, so that no man might see them. It chanced that Dermat hunted that day in the forest, alone; for Oscar had gone from Brugh the day before. When this was known to the witch-hag, she caused herself to fly into the air by magic, on a water-lily, having by her spells turned the pale leaf into a broad millstone with a hole in the middle. And, rising over the tops of the trees, she floated on the clear, cold wind, till she came straight over the hero. Then, standing on the flat millstone, she began to aim deadly poisoned darts at him through the hole. And no distress Dermat ever suffered could compare with this; for the darts stung him even through his shield and armour, the witch having breathed venomous spells on them. Seeing at last that there was no escape from death unless he could slay the witch-hag, he seized the Ga-Derg, and, leaning backwards, flung it with sure aim at the millstone, so that it went right through the hole, and pierced the hag; and she fell dead at Dermat's feet. Then he beheaded her and brought the head to Angus of the Brugh...

In both cases we had a hole stone being used to aim darts or pointy thorns at an enemy. The filid's chanting has its parallel in the noxious spells the witch breathed on her arrows. It's the blend of breath (vitality, life energy), words (symbols in a special form) and intent (strong emotions) that gives potency to the curse. Against this enchantment the king in his mighty fortress with its towers and walls is as unprotected as Dermait in his warrior's armour. What wins his battle is the fact that he can interact with the witch on a mutual plane, and that she comes close enough to be struck. Most satirized kings were not that lucky. As a side remark I would like to add that Finn, who had ordered the assassination, was not just a leader of warriors but also an inspired seer and poet, hence he has a nurse in the otherworld where the true poets and visionaries are born. Also, what shall we make of the water lily? Perhaps the plant was used as its broad, rounded leaves resemble the millstone it was turned into. Just as possibly it may be a reference to the witch's trance practise. Was the hag tripping while she laid her curse? Several species of the nymphaecea family (water-lilies) contain apomorphine, nuciferine and nornuciferine in their roots. This made them popular hallucinogenics in the old and new world, you can find evidence for their use in ancient Egypt, Greece, India, China and Mexico.

It might be worth noting that, while

every poet could make use of satire, it was considered pretty bad manners to do so too frequently. There were professional satirists in medieval Ireland, but these enjoyed a very low social status. These unfree musicians travelled the country in bands to provide crude entertainment. Irish laws, written by the filid, class them with *the sons of death and bad men*. Sons of death, by the way, are bands of outcast criminals living on the borders of kingdoms or hiding in deep forests. Regarding the satirists, it seems that they were occasionally employed in ritual. A. and B. Rees (1961) mention such an event:

> There is an account of a band of nine of them, jet-black and hairy, chanting from nightfall till dawn upon the grave of a king after his burial. They are likened to demons of hell, and when they are dispersed by Mass and holy water they appear in the air above in the form of jet-black birds.

Here we have a ritual of exorcism. I would guess that the dark buffoons represented evil spirits, possibly demons hungry for the soul of the dead king. In the medieval ages, a prevalent belief had it that the night after burial, the devil or his minions would come for the soul of the deceased. For such reasons, and knowing fully well how many misdeeds he had committed during his reign, King John 'Lackland' had his own body buried right next to Saint Wulfstan. He hoped that the presence of the famous saint would keep the devil at bay. In a similar fashion, I could imagine that the jesters were employed to symbolize demons, only to drive them out ceremonially thanks to the powers of the church.

When we come to the British bards, the evidence for ritual cursing is harder to detect. Satire, in all its forms, was a well known element of the bardic craft, and many a noble warrior feared to become the victim of biting words and bitter jokes. Taliesin himself claimed that one of the faculties that made up his nature was the flowering nettle. Could the stinging nettle represent the power to satirize others? We often find the Taliesins criticizing the misdeeds of their society. There are plenty of topics that aroused their wrath. Typical targets are wealthy and corrupt monks, the learned (but uninspired) priests, false bards lacking in art, subtlety and humility, faithless warriors, cheap entertainers, oath breaking kings and so on. In BoT 13, a Taliesin calls himself *the agitator of the praise of god the Ruler*. In BoT 33, a Taliesin thanks King Urien for having listened to his *vehement animosities*. Plenty of Taliesin songs ridicule the bardic vocation itself. Whatever you may say about the bards, they could be loud and bitter when angered.

Now what about cursing? Sadly, we have no such bardic ritual as the Irish poets kindly preserved. However, there is a part of the *Book of Anerin* (71) that comes pretty close. As you may recall, Anerin was a singer, possibly a cleric, who survived the great (i.e. futile) battle of Gododdin and composed an elegy for his slain friends and relations. When commemorating the bard Owain, Aneirin sang:

He fell headlong down the precipice;
Song did not support his noble head:

It was a violation of privilege to kill him
when bearing the branch,
It was the usage that Owain should ascend
upon the course,
And extend, before the onset, the best
branch,
And that he should pursue the study of meet
and learned strains,
An excellent man was he, the assuager of
tumult and battle,
His grasp dreaded a sword;
In his hand he bore an empty corselet.

In Steve Short's translation, the meaning
is rendered somewhat more sorcerous:

...It was his custom to climb
the hill above a battle
where, bending branches,
he'd make a shelter from which
with his songs of death
he would press destruction on
all our enemies...

While it might be debated whether the
branches were bent to form a rude hut (a
sacred space), extended like a magic wand
to direct a curse, or whether the bard himself
was under the branch, much like the Irish
poets traveled under branches of gold, silver
or copper, it still remains that the warriors
of Gododdin expected one of their number
to leave the actual battlefield to do a bit of
cursing on their behalf. It might remind
you of the middle American soccer teams
who have their own Voodoo, Macumba or
Santeiria priests plus drummers in the
stadium. Sadly, we do not know how Owain
directed curses against his enemies. Nor is
it certain if all bards were expected to spend
the battle cursing from the bushes. Meirion
Pennar in his translations of early Taliesin
poems points out that the lines *I know that
a war is being mooted, and the amount I say will
be annihilated* ought to read *the amount I
destroy will be annihilated*. In his opinion this
amounts to sympathetic magic. This
comparison is just, as the words of the
inspired poet proclaim a prophecy, and as
the prophecy, born out of the secret well of
the Awen, is true, so is its effect on the
enemy hosts. That Taliesin, or at least some
of them, were adept in magical fighting is
more than likely. Nevertheless some of them
also joined the carnage. There is evidence
for bards wielding swords and spears, so we
might assume that the spell-working was
not their only contribution to the slaughter.
We have some lines in which a Taliesin
curses the Anglo-Saxons:

Saxons on all sides into disgrace will come;
Their age has passed away; there is not a
country...
Let a bush be their shelter in reward of their
bad faith.
Let the sea be, let an anchor be, their
counsellors.
Let gore be, let death be, their auxiliary.
(BoT 6)

They come from a lengthy item called
The Omen of Prydein the Great. A Taliesin
composed it, as a prophecy, to show how in
future the Celtic races of the British Isles
would unite to deliver a crushing defeat to
the invading Anglo-Saxons. As it turned
out, the prophecy was almost successful. A
lot of warriors believed it faithfully, and
duly gathered for that final battle. Sadly,
the troops were not that well organized.
Some fought, others came too late and a
number of participants decided to stay home
in the last moment. Those who actually

made it to the battlefield in time were slaughtered. The prophecy resulted in a bloody defeat, and before the British got another chance to regain their freedom, the Normans came over and put a stop to Anglo-Saxon rule.

Speaking of the Taliesins, it may be useful to consider a neat little curse uttered by their mythical ancestor, the Taliesin of the *Hanes Taliesin*. In the second part of the tale, we find Taliesin at the court of Maelgwn Gwynedd, where he has a magical and poetical contest with the bards of the court to free his patron Elphin from Maelgwn's dungeon. During the contest, the courtly bards are struck speechless, while Taliesin recites his bright poetry with the eloquence of the white waves as they rush towards the shore in sparkle and splendour. Facing high king Maelgwn, Taliesin exclaims:

Be silent, then, ye unlucky rhyming bards,
For ye cannot judge between truth and
falsehood.
If you be primary bards formed by Heaven,
Tell your king what his fate will be.
It is I who am a diviner and a leading bard,
And know every passage in the country of
your king;
I shall liberate Elphin from the belly of the
stone tower;
And will tell your king what will befall him.
A most strange creature will come from the
sea marsh of Rhiannedd
As a punishment of iniquity on Maelgwn
Gwynedd;
His hair, his teeth, and his eyes being as
gold,
And this will bring destruction upon
Maelgwn Gwynedd.

These words, be they a prophecy or a curse, turned out remarkably accurate. A few years later a plague came to Britain. It is hard to estimate in our day what specific plague it was, but the result was a massive loss of lives among British and Anglo-Saxons. So many died that for years, the hostilities between the warring cultures ceased. Maelgwn in his desperation sought the refuge of the church of Rhos. Guarded by his fiercest fighters, he locked himself in the chapel and sought safety in prayer. His subjects found him so, lying next to the altar, in a deep trance or swoon. They sought to wake their lord, but failed in the attempt. In the church of Rhos, Maelgwn slept his long sleep, and he never woke up again.

Before we leave the subject of cursing, I would like to point out that such rites are by no means an invention of the medieval Celts. We have some evidence that cursing was already popular during the Roman occupation. Ronald Hutton's invaluable *Pagan Religions* mentions two leaden tablets. One was found at Uley (Gloucestershire). It has an inscription declaring that the writer, a lady called Saturnia, had lost a valuable linen cloth by theft. She requests the god of Uley temple to punish the evildoer. The inscription contains some confusion, as the deity concerned is first addressed as Mars, then as Silvanus and finally as Mercury (whose shrine it actually was).

A tablet of a lead and tin alloy was found in the sacred spring at Bath. The inscription reads:

Basilia gives to the temple of Mars her silver ring, so long as anybody, slave or free, who knows where it is and says nothing, may be cursed in blood and eyes and have their guts eaten away...

Finally let's look at a Celtic lead tablet uncovered in a grave from Praunheim, Frankfurt, c. 100, with a somewhat eroded inscription:

I ask you, gods of death,...you gods of the underworld,...Fronto, the enemy (in court) of Sextus shall be powerless, shall not speak against Sextus, shall become mute when he steps up.

The reverse side, almost illegible, contains the lines *he shall be dumb and unable to speak or do anything...* Think about it. For one thing, lead is a heavy and highly endurable material. Whatever you record in this medium, it is bound to last a while. For another, it is given to the deep. In the second sample, the message was cast into the sacred spring, probably as springs and wells are gateways to the otherworld. The last example is a lot more doomful. It may be speculated whether our charming Mr. Sextus buried it in some suitable grave to make sure that the gods of deathland get the message. I wonder what he bribed them with, and what price he finally paid for his request.

Bright Blessings.

Just as the forces of evil, doom and destruction could be harnessed by such arts as satire and cursing, the forces of joy, love and divine sanction could be invoked by the art of blessing. A blessing is pretty much the same thing as a curse, only that it uses different energies and divine personages to achieve an altogether happier result. Think of it as a well expressed wish that tends to come true. To begin with, a proper blessing ought to come from some holy person or priest. This gives the church a monopoly on blessings. It probably won't surprise you that the British bards felt quite holy enough to join this game, and to promise all sorts of benefits to the hearer of their poetry. A Taliesin actually declared that those who hear his bardic books would obtain the region of heaven, the best of all abodes. This is a strong medicine, considering that he was not even a minister of the church, and no doubt the clergy resented it. You can find some blessings in the religious songs of the *Black Book*, but many of these seem to come from the pens of monks and priests, i.e. people who are more or less expected to bless and work miracles. Something that comes close to blessings, without actually naming the word, is a long poem by one of the Taliesins (BoT 4). Let me quote some of the lines:

A pleasant virtue, extreme penance to an extreme course;
Also pleasant, when God is delivering me.
Pleasant, the carousal that hinders not mental exertion;
Also pleasant, to drink together about horns.
Pleasant is Nud, the superior wolf-lord;
Also pleasant, a generous one at Candlemas tide.
Pleasant, berries in the time of harvest;
Also pleasant, wheat upon the stalk.
Pleasant, the sun moving in the firmament;
Also pleasant, the retaliators of outcries.
Pleasant, a steed with a thick mane in a tangle;
Also pleasant, crackling fuel.

Pleasant, desire, and silver fringes;
Also pleasant, the conjugal ring.
Pleasant, the eagle on the shore of the sea when it flows;
Also pleasant, sea-gulls playing.
Pleasant, a horse with gold-enamelled trappings;
Also pleasant, to be honest in a breach.
Pleasant, liquors of the mead-brewer to the multitude;
Also pleasant, a songster generous, amiable.
Pleasant the open field to cuckoos and the nightingale;
Also pleasant when the weather is serene...

So much for the pleasant things. The full poem is about three times as long, and no doubt it could be extended. Would you call it a blessing? Whatever it may be, it certainly has its uses as a trance induction. How about an experiment? Take a look at the place where you are. What seems pleasant for you? What is enjoyable? What do you appreciate? Use the simple formula that Taliesin made use of and speak poetically. Think of it as an invocation if you want a magical frame, or as a form of self-hypnosis, if you prefer a therapeutic approach. It takes a bit of practise, but before long you'll find yourself improvising and speaking free and fast. Now try this as you go for a walk. What is pleasant to you? Name what you enjoy, what you like, what you desire. Find plenty of pleasant things, name them and find more. People generally tend to find what they are looking for. If you search pleasant things, you are bound to discover a lot. Big and small, important and optional, the world is full of the most amazing possibilities. The senses, avenues of perception and thought, can be fine

tuned. Wherever you may be, there is an immense wealth of fascinating sensory experiences waiting to be discovered. You can do so anytime. Just go for a walk with Taliesin and find out how much there is to enjoy.

Lorica

When blessings are applied to one's own person, they come close to a sort of protective magick technically called *lorica* (Latin: a breastplate). Several examples can be found in earliest Irish literature. Here is an example that abounds with enchanting pagan elements, translated after the German version of J. Pokorny (1944).

I invoke the seven daughters of the sea,
Who weave the strings of fate for men.
Three deaths shall be taken from me,
Three lives shall I receive,
And seven waves of fullness shall be given to me.
Ghosts may not harm me,
When I go my way in shimmering, stainless armour.
My honour shall not be slighted.
Life shall be granted to me, death shall not come to me,
Until I am old.
I invoke the silver warrior,
Who does not die, nor will ever die.
A time be granted to me,
Of the goodness of white bronze.
May my shape be exalted,
May my rights remain granted,
May my strength increase,
May my grave remain unprepared.
Death shall not reach me on the journey,
My return be secure.
The double-headed snake shall not grasp me,
Nor the grim black worm,

Nor the headless black beetle.
No thief shall harm me,
Nor groups of women,
Nor hosts under arms.
The king of all beings shall increase my time.
I invoke Senach, who survived seven ages,
Who was nourished by fairies on breasts of
fullness,
May my seven candles not be extinguished!
I am an impregnable fortress,
I am an immovable rock,
I am a precious stone,
I am the embodiment of seven treasures.
May I be a hundred in riches, in years,
One hundred after another!

Such spells of protection remained
fashionable when Christianity came to
dominate the green island. Several examples
of old Irish lorica invoked the blessing of
god, angels and saints. Occasionally, they
constitute a weird mixture of Christian and
pagan elements. Here is a useful passage
from a lorica attributed to Saint Patrick. As
the story goes, the saintly man was
journeying in the company of freshly
converted believers when they stumbled
into an ambush set by King Logaire. Saint
Patrick instantly improvised a spell of
protection which turned his group into deer,
allowing them to escape unharmed. Most
of this poem is based on strictly Christian
ideology, apart from the following lines
which give a neat summary of nine pagan
elements (after Pokorny):

I arm myself today,
With the strength of the heavens,
The light of the sun,
The gleam of the moon,
The brightness of fire,
The swiftness of lightning,
The rush of the wind,
The depth of the sea,
The firmness of earth,
The hardness of rock.

Blessings of such nature continued for a
long time in the songs and prayers of the
simple folk in the Scottish Highlands. When
Alexander Carmichael (1832-1912) set out
to collect the folklore of the Highland Gaels,
he discovered an immense wealth of curious
prayers, rituals and all-purpose spells. He
smoothed them down to an extent, as was
expected of a scholar of his time, and
published the lot under the title *Carmina
Gaedelica*. If you care to read about ancient
Gaelic traditions and curious semi-pagan
rites and superstitions, the *Carmina* is just
the work for you. It contains such a wealth
of useful items that I suggest you get yourself
a copy of the work and enjoy it at leisure.
Of the numerous spells and songs I have
selected a few samples that show some of
the essentials of spell-craft. Take a look at
this blessing:

I bathe my palms
In showers of wine,
In the lustral fire, In the seven elements,
In the juice of the rasps,
In the milk of honey,
And I place the nine pure choice graces
In thy fair fond face,
The grace of form,
The grace of voice,
The grace of fortune,
The grace of goodness,
The grace of wisdom,
The grace of charity,
The grace of choice maidenliness,
The grace of whole-souled loveliness,
The grace of godly speech.

Winter boar.

Dark is yonder town,
Dark are those therein,
Thou art the brown swan,
Going in among them.
Their hearts are under thy control,
Their tongues are beneath thy sole,
Nor will they ever utter a word
To give thee offence...
Thine is the skill of the Fairy woman,
Thine is the virtue of Bride the calm,
Thine is the faith of Mary the mild,
Thine is the tact of the woman of Greece,
Thine is the beauty of Emir the lovely,
Thine is the tenderness of Darthula
delightful,
Thine is the courage of Medbh the strong,
Thine is the charm of Binne-Bheul.
Thou art the joy of all joyous things,
Thou art the light of the beam of the sun,
Thou art the door of the chief of hospitality,
Thou art the surpassing star of guidance,
Thou art the step of the deer of the hill,
Thou art the step of the steed on the plain,
Thou art of the grace of the swan of
swimming,
Thou art the loveliness of all lovely desires...

There were several versions of this blessing in vogue in the Highlands. In Tiree boys and girls were blessed with this poem, in Uist young men and maidens. This version dates from the early 19th C. It came from a crofter who had learned it from the widely known Catherine Macaulay, who spent much of the year visiting homesteads where she told tales and sang songs. In this, she evidently followed the traditions earlier perpetuated by bards and filid. I have no idea how the good lady was trained, but the blessing she used show her as a poet of considerable learning. There are several methods involved in this poem. To begin

with, the singer symbolically purifies herself. Then she invokes a number of forces and qualities, and bestows them. In the process she makes use of analogy ('Thine is...', 'Thou art...'), be it with forces, events or entities. The evil forces of opposition are named and identified, then the singer announces that they will be controlled. A number of semi divine persons are called upon who supply encouragement, shining examples and give their sanction to the event. Some of them are half-gods of pagan mythology, such as the tempestuous Queen Medbh, others are spiritual beings from Christian religion, like Mary, or enjoy a curious in-between status, such as St. Bride, who began her career as a pagan Celtic deity. What other forms of encouragement can you observe? Before you buzz off to the next passage, I would like to ask you to treat yourself to more experience. You have seen how the blessing is composed, and how it uses various stylistic elements. How about composing a blessing that suits you better? Do I hear you squeaking? Come on! Simply make up a good blessing, learn it by heart and use it to bless yourself twice a day for two weeks. You'll understand blessing-magick much better by then. Once it works you can use it to bless others as well.

Greetings for Sun and Moon

The highland folk did not only use blessings on various occasions, they also had plenty of songs and prayers to mark important events. As their culture was so closely connected with the seasons and the tides, the calendar, and its natural expression, the lunar cycle, was really important. To begin with, there are so many rhymes addressed to the moon that Carmichael suspected a case of half-forgotten moon worship. The moon influenced most of the rural activities. In the highlands, no wood was cut nor plants were collected when the moon was waning. Likewise, animals were not slaughtered, as the waning moon was certain to ruin the flesh. The idea behind this is basically, that when the moon dwindles, so do other things in nature. Trees cut during the waning moon supply brittle wood, plants tend to rot. The Highlanders believed that the waning moon dries the plants and makes the sap go into the roots. This was useful if peat had to be cut, in some districts the waning moon was also a good time for ploughing. It's no use planting when the moon wanes, as the energy of the time favours reduction, not increase. On the other hand, once the moon has reached its minimum, increase is bound to follow. Things begun during the waxing moon were generally under a good sign. Planting and sowing were done when the moon increased, with the exception of some plants such as onion and cabbage (McNeill, 1957, remarks that these tend to run to seed if sown in the increase). Marriages were fastened and journeys began. The new moon itself was greeted like a friend or guide. The first sight of the new moon usually demanded a verse. Some turned a coin in their pocket thrice, to make their finances increase. New moon was also a good season to cut hair, corn, wheat, peat, sheep wool and the like. Here is part of a popular moon-rhyme.

Hail to thee, thou new moon,
Guiding jewel of gentleness!
I am bending to thee my knee,

I am offering thee my love…
Hail to thee, thou new moon,
Joyful maiden of my love!
Hail to thee, thou new moon,
Joyful maiden of the graces!
…Thou queen-maiden of guidance,
Thou queen-maiden of good fortune,
Thou queen-maiden my beloved,
Thou new moon of the seasons!

Similar traditions of moon-enchantment can be found in many European countries. In spell-making, some country witches took an item that represented the victim (such as hair, finger nail parings, a piece of cloth, a sample of handwriting, etc.) and placed it in the light of the waning moon with a bit of ritual. As a result, the victim could be expected to suffer from weakness and general decay. Using the increasing moon's light, the opposite effect could be achieved, this can be useful to strengthen a person recovering from an illness. Likewise, a common belief has it that you can get rid of things when the moon helps. Spells to banish a bad husband or a cluster of warts work more easily when the moon happens to be waning. The sun was of similar importance. Seeing the sun rise, the old men of the isles used to uncover their heads and to hum a private little hymn. Carmichael gives two examples, here is one:

Hail to thee, thou sun of the seasons,
As thou traversest the skies aloft;
Thy steps are strong on the wing of the heavens,
Thou art the glorious mother of the stars.
Thou liest down in the destructive ocean
Without impairment and without fear;
Thou risest up on the peaceful wave-crest

Like a queenly maiden in bloom.

Such poetry is not only a fitting expression for a deep felt love for nature. If you want to find out how it works magically, there is no better way than to do it yourself. If you greet the sun and the moon every day, you may find that this simple gesture can produce a spell of enchantment that makes life happier. There are several other uses to this, but I won't spoil your fun by telling. Suffice it to say that many religions make use of a regular ritual timetable in order to put more blessing into the day. Make up your own blessings and use them!

Spells of Healing

That suggestion can be a powerful device to effect changes was well known in Celtic cultures. Just like the cursing, and the use of magical plant talismans, its use can be traced to the earliest period of written history. We don't have much material for this, but at least enough to show that some folk in the Roman period were happily using spells to influence diseases. The Gaulish healer Marcellus Empiricus, otherwise named Burdigalensis (after his home town Bordeaux) published a compilation of such spells in the 4th Century, during the reign of Theodosius. A good example for his recipes is his cure of agnail. The patient is to touch a wall with the afflicted finger. On withdrawing, he is to repeat thrice: ' *Pu, pu, pu, nevermore I wish to see you, creep through the wall!*'. To cure podagra, the patient has to say '*Flee, flee podagra, and all nerve pains from my feet and out of all my members!*' A couple of repetitions for good measure may well accelerate the cure. With swollen tonsils, the spell makes use of counting. The cunning Marcellus has the patient count backwards nine sore tonsils, eight sore tonsils, seven sore tonsils until finally zero sore tonsils remain and health is recovered. Very similar spells were widely used by other cultures of antiquity, such as the Greeks and Romans. Here is an example with a strong pagan flavour. In the 10th century an anonymous author copied two spells on a Christian manuscript kept at Merseburg in Germany. This is the second of the two:

Phol and Uodan (Wodan) drove to the forest
Then (it happened that) Balder's foal sprained its foot.
Sinthgunt chanted over it, and her sister Sunna (sun),
Friia chanted over it, and her sister Uolla (Holle, Helja);
Uodan chanted over it, as he could do so well,:
Be there healing of the leg, be there healing of the blood,
Be there healing of the limb,
Leg to leg, blood to blood,
Limb to limbs, as if they were glued together.

It would be tempting to analyze this spell in full detail here, especially as it contains several elements of pagan Germanic belief you can't find in Scandinavian lore. Several of the deities are unknown nowadays, but then, a good spell does not necessarily rely on conscious knowledge. The 10th century scribe needs not have known all details, but he was certainly of the opinion that the spell was valuable. Just look at the pattern. To begin with, you have an example: a story is told. The story is that of an accident which presumably parallels the accident suffered by the patient. Next, the story is made important by introducing a number of important deities into it. This tells the patient not to worry overmuch, as the same thing has happened to the gods. There is a divine precedent. The introduction of deities ensures that the spell is powerful in a religious sense. If you have faith in Wodan you can rest assured the spell will work. Difficulties are mentioned: several deities work on the job before Wodan finally gets it done. This strategy is a highly elegant approach. Most people who suffer from a disease or malady tend to believe that their affliction is a lot worse than anything which happened to other people. Consequently, the spell numbers several attempts at healing before the desired result is effected.

In a similar fashion, hypnotherapist Milton Erickson occasionally suggested that his patients would improve, then have a bit of trouble, and come to a healing finally. When he treated persons who wanted to lose weight, he did not suggest that the desired weight would be reached in one go but that the patient would have a couple of setbacks on the way. This can be very useful when you deal with someone who is skeptical and uneasy. A person suffering from an injured leg or an open wound may well be a bit skeptical about any healing spell, so if you allow for some minor difficulties before all ends well, you are pacing what the patient expects anyway.

Finally, the end of the spell is a direct quotation of what Wodan said and what the healer or enchanter is saying in the god's name (and with the god's authority). Here the words become a simple and direct suggestion that tells the deep mind what it should do. This is in marked contrast to the complicated names you find in the first part. All in all, the spell shows a lot of refinement and seems much more convincing than the blunt lines we have from Marcellus.

Now the Merseburg healing is by no means unique. A very similar pattern can be observed in many European spells between the medieval period and the last century, and probably some such spells are still in use in out-of-the-way places. Alexander Carmichael collected several very similar items in the Scottish highlands. Most of them are perfect counterparts of the Merseburg spell, only that it is Christ who finds the legs of his horses injured, so

He put marrow to marrow,
He put pith to pith,
He put bone to bone,
He put tallow to tallow,
He put flesh to flesh,
He put fat to fat,
He put skin to skin,
He put hair to hair,
He put warm to warm,
He put cool to cool...

You may notice that in this case, the approach is more single-minded, and that the healing can be visualized in more detail. Again, the language is simple and the words have a certain repetitive quality. How many repetitions a given patient (or horse) needs may be open to individual requirements. Other versions had it that the barely Christianized Gaelic goddess Bride worked the job.

Bride went out
In the morning early,
With a pair of horses;
One broke his leg,
With much ado,
That was apart,
She put bone to bone,
She put flesh to flesh,
She put sinew to sinew,
She put vein to vein;
As she healed that
May I heal this.

While Christ as the most powerful deity could be trusted to work the spell, Bride, who appears as patroness of healers, smiths and poets could be relied upon even more.

The rune made by the holy maiden Bride
To the lame mariner,
For knee, for crookedness, for crippledness,
For the nine painful diseases, for the three venomous diseases,
Refuse it not to beast, deny it not to dame...

In some cases the efficiency of the operation was enhanced by deeds of holiness, such as saying a number of rosaries. This is not required when you enchant a horse, but may well work with humans, most of whom have a firm belief that simple things don't work unless they are accompanied by a measure of mystery and complication. Lists of step-by-step improvements, such as the text above, exist in countless versions. A 9th century spell from Vienna uses the process against sciatica:

Go out, worm, with nine wormlings, from marrow into bone, from bone to flesh, from flesh to skin, out of the skin into this arrow. Lord, make it thus.

When the disease in the shape of the worms has moved into the arrow it is ritually shot away as far as possible. Similar disease extraction rites are common shamanic practise in central Asia. The credibility of the healer is of vital importance. One family of Welsh healers acquired its skill after eating eagle flesh. Nine generations of healers were enabled to cure shingles. In the process, the healer breathed on the inflamed part and invoked a pair of eagles to carry the disease over nine seas, nine mountains and nine acres of unprofitable land (see Owen). The physicians acquired their healing skills from having a fairy lady in their ancestry. Being somewhat more than human is a quality that has given many a healer an aura of authority.

Gesture

Another useful element of spellwork is a gesture. If you fix a suggestion in words this may be nice for a start, but if your body congruently adds its own contribution, or if the spell involves a visual element (such as written words) you are allowing more senses to participate. One popular approach among the Gaelic Celts is circumambulations. Plenty of religious and sorcerous rituals began with walking deosil (in the sun's direction) three times around the focus of the rite. This could be an altar, a fire, a holy well, a stone, a tree, a building or a church. Deosil circles have a long tradition, especially in Ireland, where from elder times the custom prevailed that an approaching war-chariot would signal benign intentions by showing its right side. Challenges, insults and curses were delivered by approaching with the left side showing. The same custom appears in folk sorceries. Spells for healing and blessing needed deosil circles, spells of death and destruction widdershins circumambulations. To ensure a good birth, expectant mothers used to walk thrice deosil around the church. Marriage parties danced three times deosil around the house before going in, infants were protected from the grasp of the fairies by waving a flaming torch around them thrice deosil directly after birth. Three repetitions fix many a spell, and if you accompany this by walking in a circle or spinning on a spot, your rite may well gain in the process.

A Welsh tradition has it that sorcerers utter their spells in one such posture. You have to stand on one leg and keep one hand behind your back, and one eye shut. Then, as you chant or mutter your spell, you hop around in a circle three times. This, if anything, is a strong signal to the deep mind to treat the spell's words as a message of some importance. On the other hand it can do interesting things to hemispheric brain/body coordination, depending on the choice of leg, hand, eye and direction. Finally, spinning or walking in a circle is such a lovely way to dissociate everyday awareness. Many Magicians draw circles around their ritual space. Well, it can be fun to walk around a circle once, but it's a lot better if you go around for a while, ringing a bell and praying or chanting. If you persist you'll get giddy, a word originally meaning obsessed by god. This confuses the ego and opens the mind for new sensations. Going round in circles is also good policy during extended rituals as a bit of confusion and dizziness can work wonders to keep up the excitement.

If you fix a spell, going round faster and faster can produce a climax. Or you could link the rite of circling with a specific object. A look into folk tales. In southern Hessen, one of the most famous conjurers was a man called Struwel. One night three drunken lads coerced him to raise the three ancient knights from the crypt of Auerbach castle. Struwel agreed with some hesitation, drew a circle on the ground with a coal, bent a willow rod and began to draw signs into the air while walking ever faster deosil. This went on for a while until the door broke open and three skeletons in rusty armour marched in. The lads fainted but Struwel turned on his heel and ran widdershins as fast as he could. The apparitions likewise turned around and marched silently back to their tombs. Finally Struwel exclaimed 'Now they are reclining again' and collapsed like a corpse. Ah yes, and going or dancing in a circle is also useful to end a ritual or meditation.

Let's have a look at another little healing rite, the spell of the red water. In Scotland the wise women made a basin out of their hands to collect the urine of a sick cow. Then they hurled the urine into water, as water was certain to carry the disease demon away. They washed their hands and formed them into a trumpet. Turning to face the sun, they held their hands before the mouth and yelled the spell as loud as they could. The rune includes the lines:

Great wave, red wave,
Strength of sea, strength of ocean,
The nine wells of Mac Lir,
Help on thee to pour,
Put stop to thy blood,

Put flood to thy urine.

Perhaps this ritual is of some antiquity, as it invokes a Gaelic deity, the god of the great oceans, Manannan Mac Lir. Maybe he is involved as urine and sea water have an affinity, they both contain salt.

Nightfears, Evil Eye and Spells of Destruction

The country people of the Celto/Germanic cultures were generally not very happy about the dark and all the dangers lurking in it. Many a bold Highlander dreaded to go out in the night before the cock had called. The night was bound to be full of dangerous apparitions, of ghosts, phantasms or beings belonging to other worlds. The fairies, respectfully called 'the Good Neighbours', were primarily a source of terror. Changing children, shooting arrows of poison and disease or simply bringing bad luck were parts of their trivial pursuit. It says a lot that so many placating titles were made up for them. The shining ones, the beautiful folk, the fair ones…make up a fancy title and use it respectfully, leave out a saucer of milk, protect your front door with a piece of cold iron…there is real fear behind such customs. Whenever a malady could not be accounted for, you could be sure the good neighbours were blamed for it.

The charm made by Fionn son of Curnhall
For his own sister dear,
Against rose, against pang, against reddening,
Against surly creatures of the mountain;
Against the fairy elfin arrows,
Against elfin arrows charmed,
Against piercing arrows of a fairy host,

Against harassing arrows on the journey…
(spell against rose recorded by Carmichael).

Even Ireland's greatest hero, the invincible Cuchullain was spell struck by a pair of elfish ladies who came from the otherworld, beat him with enchanted whips and took his spirit away.

Then there were the shades of distant ancestors, the souls of suicides, malignant nature spirits and of course the witches and sorcerers in league with the dark. Wherever you encounter the unknown, you also encounter your own fears magnified. No doubt the ancient Celts did much as most other cultures, and attributed maladies, plagues, strange accidents and strokes of ill luck to the working of malignant entities. Well, if you invent (or discover) a bunch of nightside monstrosities, it may be sound practise to invent a bit of magick to keep them at bay. One method of doing this is to forbid the evil deed using a spell.

Mother of Pain, Mother of Berries,
you wish to lick blood,
to kill the heart,
to tear the limbs,
to stretch the skin!
You may not do it,
you shall rest,
in the name of God.

This cheerful item comes from Siebenbürgen. Another method was to delay the approach of the fiend. Here is an example from the Rhineland:

Beyond the horizon. Center design based on a silver coin of the Tectosagi

Nightmare, you evil beast,
don't come here in the night,
All waters shall you wade through,
All trees shall you strip,
All flowers shall you pluck,
All hollows shall you lick,
All shrubs shall you creep through,
All puddles you shall drink,
All stalks you shall count,
Don't come to torture me at night.

We may assume that the nightmare had a busy time completing these tasks and that morning broke before she could come round for a visit and a squeeze. The evil spirit, demons and devils could also be forced to go to specific places. Sending demons into swine was a popular practise in the ancient Greek and Roman world. Running water also did the job, especially for those who knew the sanctity of water. Diseases were bound into suitable trees. Many a devil was told to *go across stick and stone into the wild forest.* Or into the desert, the wasteland or the swamp, it depends on what the locals have handy and rather do without. For a long list of suitable locations see the Vipunen passages in the *Kalevala.*

If you expect danger, another thing you could do is to ask spirits or deities to protect you while you sleep. To invoke divine protection is a common practise. A rhyme from the Rhineland calls for a protective flock of 14 angels. A shorter spell from Austria invokes seven of them. Carmichael recorded very similar material in Scotland and the Isles. In all examples, the sleeper surrounds the bed with a number of powerful spiritual entities, be it angels, saints, figures from holy writ or whatever. This could well be a custom predating Christianity. The other thing to do was to return the evil influence. This was especially favoured when some human being was believed to be the cause of trouble.

Curses were and still are a popular idea in Celtic countries. Here is a Welsh curse used by the witches and warlocks of Llanddona in Anglesey:

May he wander for ages many,
And at every step a style,
At every stile a fall,
At every fall a broken bone,
Not the largest nor the least bone,
But the chief neck bone every time.

The only safeguard against abusing such curses is the sure knowledge that, should the cursing fail, the evil would inevitably recoil on the spell-caster. Those who are tempted to use such a curse on their real or imaginary foes should consider something simple. Usually the very people who seem to deserve a cursing are already so self-cursed that your effort will only make things worse. How about trying a healing instead?

Casting the evil eye is another ancient practise. The influence of the eye shows when a person or beast is often sick, yawns, vomits, feels weak and finds life a pointless chore. Well, this probably goes for most of the population, and for good reason. The trouble is that the evil eye is so contagious. Most folk who suffer from it tend to do their best to make their company suffer likewise. Returning the spell to its sender one of the most common bits of spellcraft anywhere in Europe. I wouldn't like to go into this topic in detail, as it is rather extensive but also very repetitive and dull.

Most spells against the eye are anything but original. They do work, otherwise they would have long been replaced by more efficient items, but there is a lot to them which could be improved by any creative mage. Instead of the boring items, let me quote from Carmichael one of the finest and most poetic examples of evil eye removal. You can read it as an example for a powerful and dramatic spell. You might also do yourself a favour and wonder whether it contains one of those lists of Celtic 'elements'. Study it patiently. What can you discover that other researchers overlooked?

I trample upon the eye,
As tramples the duck upon the lake,
As tramples the swan upon the water,
As tramples the horse upon the plain,
As tramples the cow upon the iuc,
As tramples the host of the elements,
As tramples the host of the elements.
Power of wind I have over it,
Power of wrath I have over it,
Power of fire I have over it,
Power of thunder I have over it,
Power of lightning I have over it,
Power of storms I have over it,
Power of moon I have over it,
Power of sun I have over it,
Power of stars I have over it,
Power of firmament I have over it,
Power of the heavens
And of the worlds I have over it.
A portion of it upon the grey stones,
A portion of it upon the steep hills,
A portion of it upon the fast falls,
A portion of it upon the fair meads,
A portion of it upon the great salt sea,
She herself is the best instrument to carry it,
The great salt sea,
The best instrument to carry it.

The verses were repeated during a complicated ritual. To begin with, the enchanter collects water in a pure stream with a wooden ladle, all the while invoking the trinity. The ladle has to be made of wood, and the stream should be one over which the living and dead cross. Taking the water indoors, a wife's gold ring, a piece of gold, silver and copper are put into the ladle. The water is crossed and the rhyme intoned slowly. This is an unusual element, as spells that break an evil influence are often uttered fast and dramatically. Then the water is given to the patient to drink. The rest of it is poured over some large stone indoors or outdoors, it is said to crack the rock if the cursing had been severe.

In some versions of the rite, the character or sex of the caster of the eye was divined by examining the ladle, cautiously observing which bit of metal (if any) stuck to it. Not that this is needed, I bet that most patients had their own suspicions when it came to laying the blame on some convenient evildoer.

Magical Battles

The deflection of the evil eye is a bit of folksy spellcraft echoing a much more potent sorcery woven by adepts in the magical arts to assault each other. There are plenty of legends telling how god's own saints battled with herectics, pagan enchanters and assorted unbelievers. These echo earlier traditions of fighting between wonder workers. Caesar tells us that the Gaulish Druids used to fight it out when they couldn't make up their minds regarding superior rank. In Irish myth, we encounter Druids from various provinces who have nothing better to do than to assault the folks across the border for the sake of political profit. While this is certainly a deplorable waste of good talent for shabby ends, it does supply us with some examples of what the filid thought Druidic spellcraft is all about. I emphasize the filid in this case, as it is they, the medieval poets, who wrote down the accounts of these sorcerous battles. Some interpreters chose to see them as examples for Druidic traditions. While this may or may not be the case, we cannot be certain, as we only have the poet's words on the subject, the Druids having died out centuries earlier. One particularly lucid example can be found in *Forbhais Droma Damhghaire*, the account of the siege of Knocklong. Here we find high king Cormac MacAirt setting out with his troops and Druids to invade the province of Munster to force king Fiacha to pay more taxes than could justly be demanded. The Druids take a very active part in this enterprise, as their enchantment almost destroys the fertile land of Munster. To counter the superior might of Cormac's Druids, the Munstermen seek out the old, blind Druid Mogh Ruith whom they coerce to come out of his retirement for the sake of a good wage.

In one episode of the epic, Mogh goes to confront his foes at a ford. Though the old Druid is not in a state to fight, he wears all equipment a warrior would carry, such as a shield, a sword and a couple of poisoned spears. With him is his disciple Ceann Mor. The latter is a bit shy, as he has never fought in single combat before, and dreads to face the mighty champion Colpa, well known as a man-slayer and sorcerer. As they reach the ford, Mogh Ruith speaks to his disciple:

'Bring me my poison-stone, my hand-stone, my hundred-fighter, my destruction of my enemies.'

Ceann does so, and Mogh puts a venomous spell on it:

I beseech my Hand-Stone -
That it be not a flying shadow;
Be it as a brand to rout the foes
In brave battle.
My fiery hard stone -
Be it a red water-snake -
Woe to him around whom it coils,
Betwixt the swelling waves.
Be it a sea-eel -
Be it a vulture among vultures,
Which shall separate body from soul.
Be it an adder of nine coils,
Around the body of gigantic Colpa,
from the ground to his head,
The smooth spear-headed reptile.
The spear-armed, royal, stout wheel
Shall be as a galling, strong, thorny briar;
Woe is he around whom it shall come,
My fiery, stout, powerful dragon.
Nobles and warriors shall relate
The woe of those whom it shall reach;
The high valour of Colpa and Lorga;
It shall dash against the rock.
The bonds which it binds on,
Are like the honey-suckle round the tree.
Their ravages shall be checked;
Their deeds shall be made to fail;
Their bodies shall be food for wolves;
At a great ford of slaughter.
So that children might bear away,
Their trophies and their heads.
(quoted after O'Duinn's excellent translation).

Coins 14

top l & top r (front & reverse): Boii, Bohemia, gold, 16 mm. The female head is loosely based on a Greek Athena coin, the raven is a Celtic original. A prototype of the Morrigu?

center l: unknown, Danube, silver, 23 mm. Horse goddess, Equona?

center r: unknown, Rhineland, gold, 15 mm

bottom l: Aulerci Eburovices, gold, note tattoos or scarification, very common for this tribe

bottom r: Belgae, coastal region, gold, 18 mm, wild rider. Note Lyre symbol.

As Colpa approaches them, he finds his way full of obstacles. Mogh Ruith is breathing a magical breath northwards against him, which turns stones and sand into scorching fireballs and the very sedges become raging dogs. When he reaches the ford he sees that Mogh Ruith has turned his appearance into that of a giant. This amazes Colpa, as he had expected a blind elder, not a towering warrior. Ceann Mor, after throwing the enchanted hand-stone into the ford, swiftly changes a rock into his own shape, while he himself hides in the shape of a rock. Colpa, fooled by the shape change, delivers three devastating blows against what he believes to be Ceann, only to find the waters of the ford rising in a howling storm-tide of dreadful destruction and maddening rage. Out of the churning currents arises a mighty eel, winds itself around Colpa and smashes his weapons and armour. It coils itself around the struggling warrior in nine suffocating knots and bears him down under the water's surface. When Colpa's head emerges, grasping for breath, Ceann Mor takes the weapons of his mentor, pierces his opponent with a poisoned spear and chops off his head with a mighty sword-blow.

10. Tales of Transformation

A Net of Romance

Once upon a time there were two brothers who collected tales. We could begin a tale of enchantment in this way, and indeed a tale it became. The two brothers I am speaking of are two of the Grimm brothers, Jacob and Wilhelm, whose name has become such a byword for folk tales. Jacob (1785-1863) and Wilhelm (1786-1859) came from the small town of Hanau close to Frankfurt, where they spent their first years in respectable poverty. This turned out to be sound practise, as later life wasn't much better. Their family moved to Steinau and later to Kassel in northern Hessen where our protagonists attended school and received a good classical education. As good as they could afford, that is, their father having died earlier. In Marburg they attended university, which turned out to be a hopeless struggle. The Grimms tried to learn law, but their inquisitive and romantic minds simply could not cope with such a dry subject. What fascinated them was classical culture, old history and folklore. So it was Professor von Savigny who taught them 'proper historical thinking' while his brother in law, Clemens Brentano, introduced them to old German literature. It turned out to be a fatal deed. Brentano had been busy studying folklore, and under his direction, Jacob and Wilhelm began to collect songs, ballads, place tales and legends, which were to be published by Brentano at a later date. In our days, folk lore has long been accepted as a serious topic for ethnographic studies. When the Grimm brothers were young, this was definitely not the case. Around 1807, when they began to collect, very few educated people gave a damn for childish stories. Folk tales were regarded as primitive entertainment for illiterate crusties and their kids. Such matters did not concern scholars who cared for their academic reputation. Before sending the Grimm brothers out among the natives, Brentano kindly showed them two folk tales which were the sort of material he was interested in. These were 'The Fisher and his Wife' and that macabre tale of death and resurrection, 'The Juniper Tree'. As both tales were in dialect they seemed impressively crude. The Grimm brothers assumed that this stuff was the real thing, recorded directly from the mouth of common people, and set out to find similar items.

They did not know that both tales had earlier been edited and streamlined by a Mr. Runge, who was a poet of sorts. As a result, the Grimms thought that real folk-tales are well organized, clean, with a proper plot and well defined beginnings and ends. Such items were hard to find. To begin with, their research produced little but frustration. The common folk of their time were shy about telling children's stories to studied gentlemen from the university who wore their hair like hippies and didn't even have a solid accent (the sort you can use to bend a horseshoe around and to clobber others over the head). When the Grimms advertised in the local newspapers, they only reached that part of the population which read, and this was the very sort which did not recall folk tales. Even visits to homes for the elderly proved to be disappointments.

Then, gradually, the first handful of tales emerged. Several of these came from the Huguenots who had been violently expelled from France and found a new home in Hessen. The Grimms felt very happy about this material, and were all set to sift it for ancient Germanic elements, when they discovered that the Huguenots were well acquainted with the folk tales of Charles Perrault. The precious items of oral history were retold stories from a French book. By

1810, the Grimms had painstakingly collected some 50 tales, many of them very crude and short. They sent the fruit of their efforts to Brentano, who chose to forget his earlier intentions to publish them. These early tales are a far cry from the folk tales you find in the collections nowadays. They were simple, sometimes confused, very brief, rough and a long way from the refined 'simple' prose which defines the later versions.

In 1812, a wealthy friend found a publisher for the collection. This must have been a difficult task, as the subject of the book seemed anything but auspicious. The collection had by then grown to include c.100 tales. The Grimm brothers saw their book as a scientific study and imagined their future readers to come from the academic world. The Grimms did not see themselves as storytellers but as scholars. They wrote on German mythology (three massive volumes which make for easy bedtime reading, provided you are fluent in Latin and old Greek), a German grammar, studies on Irish and Scotch fairies, on the *Edda*, the *Kalevala*, the old English rune poem, Danish heroic sagas and, as their masterpiece, they began the first dictionary of the German language. This project turned out to be totally overwhelming. For all their obsessive effort, the two only managed to get to the letter D. This was pretty good going and started a fashion, as other countries soon decided that they needed similar dictionaries for their own tongues. The Grimms had little hope that more than a handful of scholars would care for their *Children's and House tales*. For one thing, such tales were of little interest to adults.

For another, the stories were not smooth enough. Some even involved subjects which are not mentioned in polite society.

As soon as the book appeared, the Grimms had to listen to critics who derided them for the crudeness of their material. So they worked on the tales and issued another edition in 1825. This version did not include the voluminous notes. The tales had been edited and the price was much reduced. It was criticized for containing offensive material, for being ethically suspect and vulgar. Nevertheless it began to sell, if slowly. Then followed the edition of 1837, which became a great success. At long last, the public was beginning to wake up. The times were ripe.

After all the trouble with Napoleon, a somewhat war-worn Europe was redefining its borders, both on the map and in the mind. Humanistic philosophy (a sticky subject) introduced the idea that children ought to have some education. This turned out to be a problem for the middle classes. The upper classes could afford private tutors, the lower classes sent the kids to work as early as possible. The middle classes had to do the educating pretty much on their own and were completely out of their depth. There were no children's books around, and many a mother despaired at the question what to tell the kids before bed. The Grimm tales filled a gap and provided literature for the young. The work, by now much extended, became a best-seller.

To make the book more palatable for the ordinary reader, all scholarly items were taken out. Likewise, the Grimms decided to edit the tales to a much greater extent. If you publish for an academic audience you can get away with material which simply wouldn't have done in a bonny bourgeois household. Wilhelm Grimm edited the tales, and introduced plenty of minor changes. A number of undesirable pregnancies and rude deeds had to be eliminated, and a host of cruel mothers were transformed into cruel step-mothers: sound policy, when it is basically the mothers who read the tales to their kids. The familiar 'Once upon a time' formula was applied to every tale, diminutives were liberally scattered around and finally the collection became a perfect reflection of 19th century taste.

So much interference may seem offensive to a scholar of our age, but at the time of publication, the Grimms were accused of being reluctant to eliminate undesirable elements. So much for the *Children and House tales*. The Grimm brothers did their job and then continued with more sober-minded topics. They had not expected to publish a bestseller and neither could they expect the myth-making that follows.

Stories are strange things. They develop, they assume form, they evolve and then they sink into some suitable brain and begin to transform the myth that people term reality. With growing interest in the folk tales, the Grimm brothers themselves were caught in a web not of their own making. Popular belief began to envision them as traveling through tiny villages and settlements, where they could be seen sitting in peasant huts, carefully recording the secret lore of simple people. What a feast for the romantic! Imagine Jacob and Wilhelm, sitting in some wattled cottage or pig sty in their poor but clean coats, notebooks on their laps, listening with a faraway expression on their faces. Imagine the drooling old crone, the horde of awed children, the parents, hard working but honest, the rapt smile on the face of the cow next door. This is what it should have been like, and of course such a tale survives much easier than prosaic reality.

Where did the Grimms find their tales? Some were received orally, others came from books, and still others were supplied by interested scholars who corresponded with the Grimms. This was not romantic enough by half. Popular opinion demanded archetypal story tellers, and where these were lacking, simply made them up. One of their informers, Dorothea Viehmann, was turned into a crone who lived at the edge of the forest and to whose house the Grimms came like pilgrims to find lost treasures of oral literature. In sober minded reality, Ms. Viehmann used to sell vegetables in the market. She used to visit the Grimms afterwards, to have a good chat and to sell them the shoddy stuff which hadn't sold as horses had sat on it. This tells us something about the income the Grimms enjoyed most of the time, it also shows that she was not as remote from the world as is often assumed. Also, she was from Huguenot origin and of the half dozen tales she actually passed to the Grimms, several turned out to come straight from Perrault's book. Other informers of some reputation - old wives, retired soldiers and the like - were completely fictional. Their myths are alive and well today.

Then there was the question of authenticity. 1815, Wilhelm Grimm in all honesty pointed out that only some material was left in the prose it in the original condition. Later generations ignored this announcement, and declared that the Grimm tales were all in the truest oral tradition. The glamour of the tales was simply too strong. Myths are contagious, they tend to alter the reality flow and attract suitable archetypes. While I am sure that most of you have encountered Grimm's fairy tales (after the *Bible*, they are the second best selling book in the world), few of you have presumably seen the tales in their early form. Let me use this opportunity to quote one.

The Stupid One.

Once upon a time there was a Hans who was so incredibly stupid that his father sent him into the wide world. He runs along until he comes to the shore of the ocean where he sits down and hungers. Then an ugly toad appears and croaks: embrace me and come down! So she comes twice, but when she comes the third time he follows her. He sinks down and comes to a beautiful palace under the sea. Here he serves the toad. Finally she asks him to wrestle, and he wrestles, and the toad becomes a beautiful girl and the palace with all its gardens is on earth. Hans becomes clever, goes to his father and inherits the kingdom.

Nice, isn't it? This tale is full of interesting shamanic elements but a far cry from what a well told tale should be like. Notice the shamanic elements - the 'stupidity' of the protagonist, the journey, exhaustion, crisis, fasting, appearance of a spirit, serving the spirit, then fighting it and finally the transformation and the way the underwater

Coins 15
top l: Unelli, gold, 15 mm,
masked rider with animal head and drum (!)
top r: Viromandui, bronze, 18 mm, vegetation deity!
center l: Veliocassi, gold, 18 mm
center r: unknown, Britain, gold, solar deity!
bottom l: Taurisci (!), Austria, silver, 24 mm. Left side of coin badly worn. Note 29 circles in central bar: lunar symbolism!
Bottom r: unknown, Czech, silver, 29 mm, monster devouring legs, MACCIUS

palace tranforms to become dry land and part of everyday reality. That's quite a bit of hidden lore in a short story told to children to shut them up. It appears in an early edition of Grimm's tales but was soon taken out again as it was simply too crude. From what I know, it seems that the Grimms received it from the countryside near Kassel, in northern Hessen, where the locals had dark rain drenched forests and no idea that toads do not live in the ocean.

Oral Tradition

This leads us to the next issue. How genuine are old tales? How reliable is the oral tradition? Let's stroll down memory lane and take a look at the medieval bards. As you may recall, the Island Celtic bards and poets were required to memorize an immense amount of data. These tales, so some researchers propose, were passed from teacher to student with amazing clarity and stickling for detail. You may be excused if you wonder how modern experts can know this. Let's look at some sources. For a start we have Caesar commenting on the Druids of Gaul:

> Report says that in the schools of the Druids they learn by heart a great number of verses, and therefore some persons remain twenty years under training. And they do not think it proper to commit these utterances to writing, although in almost all other matters, and in their public and private accounts, they make use of Greek letters. I believe that they have adopted the practise for two reasons-that they do not wish the rule to

become common property, nor those who learn the rule to rely on writing and so neglect the cultivation of the memory... (De Bello Gallico, 6, 14, transl. H. Edwards, in Kendrick 1927).

Sadly, Caesar does not tell us what the verses of the Druids were all about. Did they simply contain teachings on the nature of the soul, on reincarnation and the ways of the gods? Given a training of twenty years, a lot of topics may be likely. With the British bards and the Irish poets, who underwent training periods of similar length, some of the topics are known. The bards and poets were taught history, heroic poetry, mythology and the like. They also learned the lore of places, proverbs, law texts and a lot of crooked etymology.

Some have claimed that the teachings of the bards were basically Druidic, as both professions needed a similar amount of verse memorization to reach the top rank. This argument is a bit shaky, as the Druids functioned in offices which were never held by bards or poets. One Druidic function was healing, for instance, and the bards knew little about medicine, nor were they expected to. On the other hand, a well trained poet was expected to have a certain fluency in Latin, Greek and Hebrew. If this was required of Druids, nobody has bothered to record it. Versification simply shows that some people find verses easier to memorize than prose. Old Irish literature contains a surprising amount of verse between sections of driest prose. Some took the verse as a means of making the prose seem more attractive. More recent studies speculate that in the original, possibly the entire tale was in verse, and that the bits of prose were inserted where the original poetry had been forgotten. This style is characteristic for the elder manuscripts, and was copied by more recent authors, up to the 18th century, who sought to make their work more archaic.

Old British and Irish literature was often recorded after having been on the lips of storytellers for decades, if not centuries. Precision in story telling was an important topic and no laughing matter. A tale from the *Yellow Book of Lecan* (c. late 14th century) describes a feast at Tara. As the story goes, the Irish nobility assembled to divide the island into districts. This was a problematic affair, and had a lot of religious implications, as the just division of the land was needed to maintain the divine balance. It also tied in with such topics as war and taxes, so no doubt there were plenty of serious minded folk assembled who drank little and scowled much.

To find out about the proper division, the Irish relied on their knowledge of the past. This proved to be a problem, as knowledge about proto-history was lacking and even the eldest could not remember what the original order of the island districts had been. The poets, well aware of the shortcomings of their precious lore, suggested that the oldest man on the island ought to be found. This character retold a tale of greatest ancestry. In his days, so he said, the Irish had been visited by an otherworldly giant named Trefuilngid Tre-Eochair who was of great size and held an enchanted branch in his hand. The branch had the virtue that it carried magical nuts, apples and acorns, which were all the food

that Trefuilngid ever needed. Holding his twig of office, the branch bearer declared the entire history of Ireland to the assembled poets, judges and nobles, who had to admit that, to their shame, their precious oral tradition contained very little of it.

This may be the first appearance of the branch bearer in written history, and maybe the source of the legend which claims that the Irish poets travelled under artfully crafted branches of gold, silver and copper. It also shows that the Irish poets, who kept such tales alive, did not have much trust in the exactness of their own oral history. Likewise, when the Irish poets assembled to recollect the tale of the cattle raid of Cuailnge, they found that their stories contained many gaps and holes. To fill these, they made use of necromancy. A poet named Muirgen approached the grave stone of Fergus mac Roich, who had been a major protagonist of the tale.

Muirgen chanted a poem to the gravestone as though it were Fergus himself. He said to it:

If this your royal rock
were your own self mac Roich
halted here with sages
searching for a roof
Cuailnge we'd recover
plain and perfect Fergus.

A great mist suddenly formed around him-for the space of three days and nights he could not be found. And the figure of Fergus approached him in fierce majesty, with a head of brown hair, in a green cloak and a red-embroidered hooded tunic, with gold-hilted sword and bronze blunt sandals. Fergus recited him the whole Tain, how everything had happened, from start to finish.

(The Tain, transl. T. Kinsella, 1969).

The Irish poets were willing to admit that their cherished lore could be faulty and misleading, but they were just as ready to declare that the newly regained version was flawless and perfect. How precise is story telling from memory? The training schedule for Irish poets burdened the budding File with twenty stories plus six metres and a lot of convoluted grammar in the first year. By contrast, a fully trained Ollamh was expected to be ready with 250 prime stories, 100 secondary stories, not to mention 350 types of versification. Such a feat of learning can be interpreted in several ways. Maybe the Ollamh knew all those stories by heart, word for word and line after line, as is proposed by those who believe that oral history is passed on in complete precision.

Maybe he was only familiar with the frame of the story and the plot, and filled in the details spontaneously by making use of a large stock of useful metaphors. Both forms of oral tradition can be found on this planet. Homer, for instance, had a huge repertoire of lines which he used freely to describe the sort of events which happen frequently. His verses on feasting, ship journeys and the rosy fingers of dawn are woefully repetitive. The same method was used by the singers around the Baltic (see the *Kalevala*), who had a large hoard of useful lines which they assembled as it suited the story.

It is a tough question whether the Island Celtic storytellers and singers memorized their lore perfectly or whether they built it up using prefabricated material. There is a fierce academic debate regarding this question. The clash of faiths goes as follows. One camp proposes that the tales and songs of medieval literature are all perfectly preserved goodies from Celtic prehistory which were faithfully passed along over the centuries until finally put down on vellum by scribes. This attitude was quite popular in the last century, as the scholars of the time *wanted* original material, no matter the price. More recent (and less romantic) studies take a different perspective. The medieval texts do contain modern elements.

Some elements, such as the Christian references, can easily be blamed on the scholarly scribes who wrote down the old material, doubtlessly editing and deleting as they went along. Using this theory, it was easy to blame all confusion on monkish errors and censorship. On the other hand it turned out that it is remarkably hard to prove that such editing actually happened. You have to have an original to see where the later copies were tampered with, and such originals are still lacking. To explain difficult lines by inventing an unproved censorship is not very scientific, though it does have its attractions.

Evolution of Song

Take the Taliesin songs. How old may they be? The early Celtic scholars pounced on the fact that a Taliesin lived in the 6th century and declared that everything in the *Book of Taliesin* comes from this period. Sadly, the text contains plenty of remarks on matters and persons which did not exist in the 6th century, such as Cadwallawn,

Cadwalladyr, Bede, Henry I or II and others. This led to the assumption that, while the songs are mainly 6th century, a number of later hands have added to them. As some of the most enchanting Taliesin songs look completely garbled and confused, this interpretation had its own charm.

Linguistic analysis soon brought down that theory, as it is far too simple. Over the centuries, the Welsh language underwent a number of changes, some of them radically altering accent and pronunciation. Lines that rhymed in the 6th century did not fit the pronunciation en vogue a few centuries later, that is, the poets could not sing them properly any more, and their audience didn't understand many of the words. Sooner or later not even the bards understood the words of their ancestors, which led to a number of interesting errors. This indicates that bardic lore was probably innovated regularly, much to the disgust of modern Neo-Celtic traditionalists. Even if the ideas of a Taliesin poem may be of antiquity, they are certainly not in that ancient form any more. If we study the old elements of the *Battle of the Trees* or the *Hostile Conspiracy*, we have to keep in mind that they are in the language of the high medieval period. Maybe there were bards who re-rhymed such songs to keep them up to date, but necessarily, each time a re-rhyming took place, some of the original information was distorted or lost. That the Taliesin songs are often so thoroughly confused may point at regular transformation of the original material. On the other hand it may be modern thinking which postulates that a song starts out meaningful and then becomes tangled up.

Who did the Taliesins sing for? For the proud warriors who got blind drunk in the great smoke filled halls, for the kings and chieftains who paid for the performance? Sometimes I wonder whether the Taliesins chanted for the semi-educated nobles or whether their real audience was a handful of highly trained bards who could be expected to understand subtle allusions and obscure references. We are not dealing with pop songs but with inspired utterances made by the penbeirdd, the Head of the Bards. If you recall the chapter on prophecy you may remember that the Welsh poets, the Awenyddion, gave their oracles in meaningless ranting and crazed allusions. Maybe the Taliesin songs have never had a meaningful arrangement to begin with.

But let us take a closer look at the way in which oral history transformed. There are old Irish tales which seem to have influenced and shaped later Welsh tales. These were retold at the courts of Brittany, passed to the troubadours who toured France and Germany, and underwent plenty of changes on the way.

The Once and Future King

The myth of good old King Arthur is the best example for this process. In the early 6th century, when Arthur fought the Saxons (provided he existed at all), few people outside of Britain had ever heard of him. By the 13th century, the continuous retelling of Arthurian sagas had made the topic popular at every European court. These tales did not only move from Britain to mainland Europe, they also returned to Britain. Many of the noble knights of Arthurs court began as heroes of Irish myth, had their name and nature turned into some Welsh form, were renamed by continental storytellers and returned to Britain in such a grotesque form that nobody recognized them. This topic can be studied at great length in the works of Loomis. Such transformations point at a living and adaptable form of tale-transmission. Likewise, many of the troubardours had their own favourite knights in the Arthurian court. Sir Kai, who appears as a model for the ruthless, efficient warrior in Welsh bardic poetry was turned into a fumbling dolt by later authors. Sir Gawain, appearing in the early myths as a semi-divine hero, became a bad loser once the troubardours had invented the figure of Sir Launcelot and attributed all heroic glory to their new brain-child. And fierce Medrawd, who may well have fought at Arthur's side at Camlan (according to the early bards) was turned into the evil and degenerate Sir Mordred who caused Arthur's downfall.

Stories keep transforming, so that the deeds attributed to one hero may be associated with another only a century later. If a given hero reaches a certain weight, other tales tend to fall into his myth cycle, thereby increasing density, mass and gravitational pull. And when it came to stories of the graal the different interpretations of the enchanted vessel clearly show that some folk made up their stories as they went along. Or take a look at the so called *Welsh Triads*, a collection of brief lists recorded between the 13th and 17th century Remember how fond the Celto/ Germanic people are of trinities? Each triad gives a list of usually three persons. You get triads with titles like:

The three red reapers of the island Prydain, the three golden shoemakers, three battle-horsemen, three arrogant men, three powerful swineherds, three men who performed the three fortunate assassinations, three unfortunate hatchet-blows, three oppressions that came to the isle, three concealments and three disclosures, three prominent oxen, three bestowed horses, three women who received the beauty of Eve, three exalted prisoners, three prostrate kings, three harmful blows, three great queens of Arthur's court, three amazons, three golden corpses, three wild spectres, three unrestrained guests of Arthur's court, three defilements of the (river) Severn, three men of the isle of Britain who were most courteous to guests and strangers, three futile battles, three knights who won the graal, three skilful bards, three perpetual harmonies, three people who broke their hearts from bewilderment, three frivolous bards, three great feasts and so on.

In most cases, the text amounts to very little, just a few names and maybe a short note. The three golden shoemakers of the island of Britain, for example are:

Caswallan son of Beli, when he went to Rome to seek Fflur; and Manawydan son of Llyr, when the enchantment was on Dyfed; and Lleu Skilful-Hand, when he and Gwydion were seeking a name and arms from his mother Ar(i)anrhod.
The Three Fair Maidens of the Isle of Britain: Creirwy, daughter of Ceridwen; and Ar(i)anrhod daughter of Don, and

Coins 16
top l: Ile de Bretagne, bronze, stylized head
top r: Ile de Bretagne, bronze, a bard? Note sign coming out of mouth, breath, speech!
center l: Ile de Bretagne, silver, bull
center r: Ile de Bretagne, bronze, wheel and flames!
bottom l: Ile de Bretagne, gold, stylized leaf. Probably related to the sharp-edged wine leaf coin of Verica, Britain, VIRI; bottom r: Ile de Bretagne, silver, compare with image on Gundestrup cauldron

Gwen daughter of Cywryd son of Crydon.

Only in a very few cases are the commentaries extensive enough to supply some sense for the uninitiated. The result is a bardic book which was definitely not meant as easy reading. The purpose of the *Welsh Triads*, as far as we know, was to provide the bards with an organizing structure for their tales and songs. The readers were expected to know all the details of the legends, so that they only required a bit of help in memorization. Even if they didn't know all of the tales, they found that the triads tend to stimulate imagination.

Our next question concerns the validity of historical data in the bardic tradition. This is a troublesome subject which has upset a good many scholars and Celtic enthusiasts. Professor Jackson proposed that Irish myth is a *'window to the iron age'*, an opinion which was shared by plenty of romantics. The assumption that you can find ancient Celtic traditions in old Irish lore is so tempting, especially as those violent tales seem so rough, unpolished and their protagonists behave like vain-glorious savages. The heroes of Irish tales seem so much like what the classical authors wrote about the Celts of the pre-Roman period. But how accurate was the knowledge of the medieval Irish poets regarding their own pre-history?

To begin with, the poets pretended to know everything. A fully trained poet was expected to know the etymology of all words in his language, and when this was not the case, went to great lengths to make it up. Most of early Irish etymology is a horrid mess, showing that the poets knew less than they were ready to admit. Or think of origin. Many poets claimed that the Skythians were the ancestors of the Scots. This seemed so simple and obvious. The poets were acquainted with Herodotus' account of the fierce horse-riding Skythians living on the Black Sea, and as the name seemed so similar, it was easy to make up a connection which is completely spurious. The swords in Irish sagas are generally long, archaeological excavations tend to unearth short ones. The forked multi-pointed spears of Irish myth have not so far been found, maybe they never existed, save as symbols for divine lightning bolts. Ronald Hutton points out that the medieval Irish scribes correctly identified a number of important ancient sites in Ireland. However they turned them into great royal halls. Excavations show that most of them were dedicated to complex ceremonies, but had no such buildings. Then there are the parallels you can find between classical accounts and the Irish tales. Diodorus, writing in the 1rst century BCE, tells us about Celtic warriors:

When the armies are drawn up in battle array they are wont to advance before the battleline and to challenge the bravest of their opponents to single combat, at the same time brandishing before them their arms so as to terrify their foes. And when someone accepts their challenge to battle, they loudly proclaim their own valorous qualities, at the same time abusing and making little of their opponent and generally attempting to rob him beforehand of his fighting spirit.

This colourful ritual is a common element in Irish heroic tales. Or consider these lines by Athanaeus, who quoted from the lost works of Poseidonios in the 2nd century BCE:

> When the hindquarters were served, the bravest hero took the thigh piece, and if another man claimed it, they stood up and fought in single combat to the death.

The quarrel about the 'hero's portion' comes up in Irish myth, where the boldest of heroes are ready to kill each other for the honour of cutting a choice bit of pork. Such parallels have often be used to show that medieval Irish lore contained plenty of ancient pagan elements. Some scholars went completely over the top and proposed that such behaviour, if it can be attested for ancient Gaul and medieval Ireland, was probably typical for the entire 'Celtic World', whatever that may be. The problem is that we cannot be sure from where the medieval poets derived their information. It is possible that they made use of ancient oral traditions. It is just as possible that they read the classical authors and reconstructed their past history accordingly. This may seem bizarre to modern Celtic enthusiasts, but many medieval poets were familiar with the classical authors, in fact, they often knew more about classical history than they knew about the original traditions of their homeland.

When we examine medieval Welsh literature, the situation is even more difficult. The refined knights you encounter in such romances as *Peredur*, *Geraint* and *Owein* owe more to the tales of the continental troubardours and to the medieval tradition of chivalry than to the Celtic past of pagan Britain. While Celtic nationalism in the last century insisted on a pure transmission of pagan Celtic lore, in this century the scholarly trend goes in the other direction and points at the modern and European elements in island Celtic lore. This is hardly surprising. People tend to find what they are looking for.

May I propose that we leave the question to some future generation and focus on more profitable issues, such as the question 'What can we learn and use practically?' Personally I don't care much whether such splendid inventions as tree-oghams or Imbas Forosnai-divination were developed by pre-Roman Celts or by the christianized people of later ages: they are elegant, and they happen to work. What is your attitude in these matters? Do you think that an ancient piece of Celtic magick is more attractive than a bit of medieval enchantment? Is great age a guarantee for efficiency?

Exercise: The Time Frame

After so much theory you are no doubt eager to play around with your mind. Let's use this opportunity and find out how you organize your preferences. Select some simple magickal practise or ritual. It could be something simple, like making a talisman out of flowers and suchlike, or a more complicated rite, such as the mistletoe cutting as described by Pliny. It could be a simple technique of meditation or a complicated astral ceremony. Have you found a bit of magick to play around with? First of all imagine that the practise is 10,000 years old and was developed at the end of the last ice age. Make up a vision of our Paleolithic ancestors doing their thing and include your practise in their program. Next, shift the practise into a younger period, say, 5,700 BCE when the first Neolithic communities developed in Central Europe. Does it make a difference to your estimation of the practise? Now let us shift the practise into the Hallstatt time. Imagine a bunch of jolly Celts inventing it. What happens when you imagine the practise was invented in a medieval setting? Or when you imagine that it was invented by a mage of the last century? Now for the present. Imagine that you go to some occult bookshop, or better a semi-occult bookshop (the really occult bookshops are the ones you never find). Lying on the counter you can see this book. It's a new publication, telling you about this new technique, which has just been invented. Does it seem inviting? Go further. Imagine the technique will be invented in a decade. Thanks to your great good luck and time-traveling skills you may learn it today! Last, imagine that the technique comes from the future in a thousand years when people are really advanced. In each time-frame, the technique remains the same, but its setting and its aesthetic form vary.

So do the people you imagine. Let me suggest that you make notes about your visions and that you go through the process with several magickal techniques. Before long you will find out what setting seems most impressive to you. The same goes for the folk who do it. Is a given rite more attractive if invented by an ice-age hunter, by a farmer of the megalith period or by a medieval songster? Would you prefer it to come from 'primitive' people of the 'noble savage' category? Or from futuristic folk who travel around the universe in fantastic spaceships? Which origin makes it most impressive? The answer to this questrion tells us nothing about the actual age of the rite. However it says a lot about your unconscious prejudices. Something magickal happens in the minds of people when they project the origin of a given rite into a specific setting. They tend to forget the validity of the rite itself and respond to their estimation of the setting. If you sell the *Mabinogi* as ancient Celtic mythology you will find more customers than if you point out that the book comes from chivalrous Wales and was assembled and edited by well educated medieval Christian poets. People show a lot of prejudice when they evaluate. Some admire a mystical past, others feel attracted to the glamours of the far future.

Exercise: The Cultural Frame

Then there are the problems of cultural prejudice. A good many modern enthusiasts tend to glorify the so called Celtic and Germanic people while deriding the so called Romans. This leads to very simple visions of the past. On one side you get mystical Celts standing hip-deep in the accumulated wisdom of the Druids, on the other the Roman culture, callous, arrogant and thoroughly decadent. If you subscribe to this view, please close your eyes now and imagine some Roman and Celtic people. How did the Romans look like in your representation? Were they all small dark haired Italians? Did any of them have kind faces? Do they look as if they had families at home whom they cared for? Just who are those 'Romans'?

The Roman empire was not won by a lot of central Italians. Caesar, for example, had only a single Legion when he set out to conquer Gaul. Being a cunning sod, he did not set out to conquer all of Gaul in one go. Instead he divided his unlimited ambitions into smaller chunks, and proceeded with the conquest step by step. This was sound policy, as it is much easier to enjoy a meal if you eat it bite after bite. Whenever Caesar crushed a province, he immediately recruited new soldiers from the conquered. The locals, mainly young men with few hopes of inheritance, joined the legion en masse and did their best to push the frontiers further. It did not bother them that they were actually fighting other 'Celtic' people, just as it didn't upset the Welsh archers when they conquered the Scots for the English crown. It was mainly Gaulish warriors, fighting under Roman command, who conquered Gaul.

After the occupation, the nobles of Britain did not have to be forced to learn Latin and to decorate their homes in Roman style. People were in favour of imported wine and Mediterranean luxuries, they also appreciated innovations such as chimneys, glass windows and roads that lasted for more than one rainy season.

Finally, when the empire disintegrated, its former members saw themselves as 'Roman citizens', no matter whether they lived in Cumbria, Mauretania or Mesopotamia. This is historical reality, but a far cry from the reality of the neo-Celticist fringe. In the eyes of many pagans, the issue is still framed as 'us against them'.

If you believe that the Romans did something horrible to us, it may be fun to find out how you do this. Go inward and take a good look at your visions of the Roman conquest. What do you see? A lot of cruel dark-haired soldiers in heavy armour cutting down badly armed civilians? Do the victims look like people whom you like? Do you identify with those who were slain, tortured or sold into slavery? Now try the other extreme. What do you think was it like when Celtic warriors plundered Rome in 387 BCE and Macedonia in 279 BCE? Do yourself a favour and examine your visions in detail. What is the difference between Roman and Celtic war crimes? I've heard neo pagans getting quite angry when they talked about the way the Roman armies slaughtered the Druids of Mona, and expressing gleeful pride when discussing the way Celtic armies went pillaging in the sunny south. Does it make much of a difference if one is slain, enslaved or raped by a Roman or a Celtic warrior? Do you identify with one group because they are from a certain culture? What about winners and losers? Do you have a preference for the underdogs? Or is it the successful who come out best in your imagination? Were the Romans better or worse than their opponents? Whatever your answer may be, it says a lot about the way you organize your beliefs. If you really want to find out what things were like, you have to see them from as many points of view as possible. This is a key to understanding, and as every master of the temple knows, multiple points of view are only possible if *you* with all your prejudices and personal opinions are absent.

Multiple points of view produce more

Coins 17, Variations of a theme. All coins Boii, Bohemia. The classic "Rainbow Cups". Rainbows, torques or cauldrons! Note bottom r with stylized lyre shape and moons.

data than any single evaluation. This is understanding itself, what comes next is wisdom, i. e. the choice which point of view (or opinion) you need to do your true will. No point of view is truer than another, but some of them function more easily under specific circumstances. So, if you find yourself sneering at some magickal practise because it comes from the wrong culture, or happens to be only a week old, how about taking your representation and putting it into a new form?

Shaping Reality

Stories transform people's representation of events, and thereby shape the reality in which they believe. Sometimes an impressive story can do this so convincingly that it blinds us to further research. Consider the mistletoe ritual which dear old Pliny recorded so carefully. This picturesque account has coloured scholar's opinion to such an extent, that for two centuries experts have interpreted every bit of floral ornament in Celtic art (no matter from when and where) as mistletoe. Who knows how many plants and trees were sacred to the various Celtic people? Who knows how many healing plants were used? No matter what the archaeologists uncover, you can be sure that some learned fool calls it mistletoe. A story is not just a certain amount of information. Stories come to life and colour memory and imagination. A well told tale can reach levels of the deep mind which are inaccessible to commonplace information. Likewise, a couple of dry facts are much harder to recall than any colourful story. Memory works like that. If you want to

recall dry facts, tie them up in an interesting tale. To many early cultures, stories were not just information and entertainment. There was a special magick to stories. Think of the way the British warriors, many of them of noble birth, valued their reputation. A reputation, however, depends on story telling. The nobles needed the bards to perpetuate the songs and tales of their heroic deeds. Now you can invent a glorious story to bolster up your image. If you tell it often enough, however, it can happen that you begin to believe it yourself. From that point, the story becomes a hypnotic suggestion. If a bard praised a given warrior for a number of violent deeds, or if a noble boasted loud enough, he was expected to live up to his reputation. The result is a feedback system. The great heroes produced a radiant image of their own valour, and identified with it. They went into a 'larger than life' representation and lived up to it. You might compare this to positive thinking, only that it was not done in one head but confirmed by a lot of like-minded battle hungry dolts. When spring came, and the treasure chests of the royalty were empty, the season of warfare began and the wild boasts of the mead-besodden winter-evenings were put to test. The warriors fought, and often recklessly, with total disregards for their own safety. In the process, a lot of them lost important parts of their anatomy. Quite a few lost their heads, but then, what matters a swift death, which is as inevitable as rain, when death was followed by everlasting praise in the songs of the bards? Many of those brave fighters were thoroughly scared of growing old and infirm. A short and vivid life full of spectacular deeds seemed much more tempting. They wanted to live a good story.

Exercise: Your Story

Please pause now and think about it. What sort of story will your life make? How many good tales do your memories yield? Stories of excitement, of transformation, of sudden surprises and funny events? Stories of love and feasting, of enchantment, ordeal and inspiration? Which stories of your life do you value most? If you were quite thorough with this, you could use this opportunity to recall a number of your personal stories. You could even list them briefly, and find out whether the exciting, the tragic or the funny tales are in the majority. You could also decide what sort of stories you would like to live and set out to do so. So, if you find yourself stuck in some boring or dull period, you could do yourself a favour and go out to live a story that may be worth telling one day. You could also take a closer look at daily events-which of them make good stories? Take something that happened to you the other day. Can you retell it as a tragedy, a drama, a fairy tale or a satire? There ought to be more funny stories around. Too many people tell themselves tales that bring them down. Too many people cultivate an inner voice which recalls all sorts of miserable and negative events. Some list their failures, others list their fears. How about turning the horrid stuff into bizarre and funny stories? Can you laugh about yourself? Can you take a look at yourself when you are feeling really miserable or frustrated, and see the absurdity of it all? Can you turn a horrible event into a funny one while it happens by thinking of

how the tale of it might be told? Which moments have entertainment value? You don't have to wait for them to turn up. If you are cunning, you can make them happen. You can also improve on them. If you notice what tale you are in at a given moment you can decide if you like it, and turn it into a story that suits you better. This is your choice, your freedom and your responsibility. You are the bard, you are the storyteller. You are in charge of your life and the tales you participate in.

Ritual Story-telling

Let's take a look at the role of the story-teller in ancient Europe. The Irish Ollamh had to have a repertoire of 250 prime stories and 100 secondary ones. We know about the prime stories that they were organized in specific groups. The *Book of Leinster* (*Lebor Laignech*, c.1160) gives twelve headings for prime stories:

> destructions, cattle-raids, courtships, battles, caves, voyages, violent deaths, feasts, sieges, adventures, elopements and slaughters.

Another section of the same manuscript gives five additional categories:

> irruptions, visions, loves, expeditions and invasions.

As you can see, most of the topics come under the general heading 'sport news'. These categories tell us that the stories were organized by function. It is not unlikely that the storyteller selected a tale to suit the general mood of the audience. The grouping of the prime tales under the various headings allowed the poets easy access to stories to suit any occasion. That the groups of tales are organized by function may well be worth thinking about. In our time, stories are often organized around persons or places. Take a look at the 17 categories cited by the *Book of Leinster*. What are your own cattle-raids, elopements and adventures? What anecdotes of your life would fit into the poetic categories?

While the prime stories pose some questions, as many of them have not survived to our age, the secondary ones are even more mysterious. As the secondary tales are not listed anywhere, we have no idea what was in them. Whether they contained important or unimportant material is anyone's guess. Secondary tales sounds a bit disappointing, but then you should recall that only the four top ranks of poetry where entitled to tell them. How would you organize your life history into prime and secondary tales?

Story telling itself was a ritual. Today a lot of people don't feel at home unless they have the TV blabbering away in the other room. The media are drowning us in a flood of easily digestible story material so that people tend to suffer from overload. In the olden days, a story was an event and good storytellers were welcome. Information was a highly valued commodity. To begin with, the audience was expected to listen in silence. This rule applied to the nobles who listened to the top-poets in the torch-lit halls of the kings, it also went for simple folk squatting around peat fires. While new stories had their attraction, the old ones certainly remained popular. This may be due to the way the mind makes the story come to life.

The Enchantment

In itself, the act of storytelling is a fairly simple matter. You have one person, who has a number of inner experiences (memory and imagination) and who communicates these using an abstract and highly arbitrary system involving semantic symbols (words) as well as inflection, tonality, accent, pronunciation, tempo, emphasis, body-posture, gesture and so on. These means of transition are not the story. The story is what the story teller has in the mind. The story is what happens in the minds of the audience. The story is the enchantment that flows between teller and listener, passing from mind to mind and shaping itself anew for each new brain. Each story is unique for each person who experiences it. The mind that makes sense out of the words and gestures is your mind, so what you experience is largely of your own making. You make sense of the tale by perceiving it with your inner senses. Within your very own brain you see pictures, you listen to sound, you feel and participate in emotions. Sometimes you even smell or taste. All of this is subjective.

You could call it imagination or daydreaming if you like. You could also call it hypnosis or trance magick. This happens all the time. You can't read or hear a single sentence without representing its meaning in your inner senses. The representation is yours, is your own work of art. If you listen to a story once, it may be a more or less vivid event, depending on how well it was told, how much it interested you, and how intensely you represented the contents in your inner senses. If you recall the story to yourself the next day, this may stabilize your memory. If you hear it retold a number of times, the inner senses will amplify it even more. Thus, hearing an old tale retold needs not be boring. It could just as well be that some tales ripen if they are imagined often enough. This happens to the audience, but it happens even more intensely to the poet who tells the tale so often that s/he can practically move in and live there.

In Scotland, guests who came to a house could expect to be entertained with a story, but were expected to return the kindness. A Scot's proverb warns us: *First story from the host, story till day from the guest.* Storytellers could expect a warm welcome, in some cases they could expect a sore throat as well. The traditional welcome for bards and storytellers appears briefly in the 4th branch of the *Mabinogi*. Here we encounter the cunning enchanter Gwydyon and his like minded friends, who set out to steal the wonderful pigs which Pwyll and Pryderi of the southern Welsh dynasty had received from the otherworld. The pigs were something really new. Pwyll had received them from Arawn (Silver-Tongue?) the ruler of Annwvn, as a gift. To make sure that they would be received in friendship, Gwydyon's band of troublemakers disguised themselves as bards. In this guise, they easily secured a friendly welcome.

Gwydyon was soon asked to tell a tale, which he did with all the charm and passion of a professional. Like a professional bard he also asked for an immensely high wage afterwards, namely those precious pigs which he desired and which Pryderi had sworn not to give away. As denying a bard's request was next to impossible, this put Pryderi into a very difficult spot. He could not give the pigs without breaking his word, but neither could he deny that golden tongued enchanter. To make things easy, Gwydyon proposed to pay for the pigs. His offer consisted of noble horses with luxurious saddles and trappings, all of them so valuable that Pryderi and his nobles could hardly believe their eyes. Blinded by shining gold and glimmering jewels they gave in. Little did they know that the horses and their equipment had been spell-crafted out of plants and fungi. Now spells of illusion rarely last for very long. They found out about that the morning after, when Gwydyon, his cronies and the cherished pigs were well on the way to the north.

In Wales, a story or tale is called Cyfarwyddyd, meaning *guidance, direction, instruction, knowledge* and *skill.* The storyteller was called a Cyfarwydd, this is a bardic rank. At the root of both words is arwydd: *a sign, symbol, manifestation, omen, miracle.* Go over these words slowly and consider them. How can a tale be a sign, a miracle, what may it manifest or symbolize? Think of some tales you know and evaluate them accordingly. What is the magick hidden in them? What manifestation could they effect?

Storytelling is often limited to certain occasions. Many cultures have stories which may only be told at night, or in winter, or during specific ceremonies. Sometimes the telling of a story is limited to certain persons, professions, sexes, age-groups, social classes and so on. All of this shows the special status attached to the act of storytelling. In ancient India, certain stories were known to confer blessings. The Hindus believed (and some of them still do) that listening to the ancient epics *Mahabharata* and the

Coins 18: top l: Boii, star; top r: Boii, star; center l: Boii, trefoil; center r: Boii, torque and lyre; bottom l: Boii, abstract design suggests owl face; bottom r: Vindelici, gold, 16 mm, trefoil, reverse of deer on coins 5 bottom left.

Ramayana confers blessings and divine protection. Both of these tales are rather voluminous (the *Mahabharata* contains 100,000 verses). They contain story elements, history, law, folk customs, religious precedents but also countless bits of good advice. As my editor, Mr. Morgan once told me, a king could expect success in war after listening to the *Mahabharata*. This was due to the fact that the gods smile on kings who know when to listen to traditional lore, but also due to a lot of practical military and strategic advice hidden in the tale.

The brilliant early Indian collection *Tales of the Corpse* (*Vetalapancavinsati*, available in several versions and translations) is known to scare demons and evil spirits away, it frees from sins and suffering. The medieval compilation *Srimad Devi Bhagawatam* is known to release the listener from illusions and liberates the soul instantly from karmic bonds and fetters. The massive work is also a treasure trove for all who seek the little bits of practical ritual required for the worship of the great Indian goddess Devi, and all the goddesses the Devi was created out of. In all of these cases some blessing can be expected by casual listeners, but those who bother to listen to the entire work with focused attention partake of the story as if they would participate in an extended ceremony.

The storytelling can be a ceremony, it can be an act of worship and a work of magick which transforms the world. A similar tradition of sacral storytelling can be found in medieval Ireland. The best known epic of Irish literature is that violent saga of heroism and wholesale slaughter, the *Tain Bo Cuailnge* (*The Cattle Raid of Cuailnge*). The manuscript version of the epic which can be found in the *Book of Leinster* contains a final note, a finit, in Irish:

A blessing on everyone who will memorize the Tain faithfully in this form, and not put any other form on it.

Here we have good evidence that the form of the tale itself was considered sacred. It is also possible that the Irish scribe who wrote the note believed the *Tain* to be true. To the Irish finit, a later hand added a finit in Latin. It shows a more sober minded attitude:

I who have copied down this story, or more accurately fantasy, do not credit the details of the story, or fantasy. Some things in it are devilish lies, and some poetical figments; some seem possible and others not; some are for the enjoyment of idiots. (transl. Kinsella).

However much the scribe disagreed with some elements of the tale, he still felt obliged to keep his material as it was. This says something for his open-mindedness, it would have been much easier to cut out the offensive passages than to copy them in detail. You can take it as evidence that not all monkish scribes censored pagan ideology. There is an Irish tradition which states that whoever listens to the whole *Tain* is protected from all evil for the span of one year. This seems quite an achievement for a story.

A similar effect was ascribed to a number of old Irish works. A poem ascribed to St. Patrick informs us that anyone who listens to *The Fosterage of the House of the Two Methers* shall have good luck on dangerous journeys, during hunts and while visiting banquetting houses. It blesses those who marry, it blesses the king who listens (without interruption) and it frees captives from bondage. A similar tradition of sacral storytelling can be found in the poetic *Edda*. Read the *Grimnismal* and find out how the disguised god Odin confers kingship to a youth of his choice through an act of storytelling in verse. In the process, the future king is initiated into the gnosis of the divine otherworlds while the old king falls into his own sword and dies. Is storytelling part of the inauguration ceremony? Another blessing appears at the end of the *Havamal* (*The Song of the High One*, ie. Odin). It assures the listener of a long life. In Britain, Taliesin tops it all by chanting

Book learning scarcely tells me
Of severe afflictions after death-bed;
And such as have heard my bardic books
They shall obtain the region of heaven, the best of all abodes. (BoT 1)

Think about it. Taliesin was neither a saint nor a churchman. If he promises salvation for those who listen to his works, he implies that his works are on one level, if not superior, to the *Bible* itself. It seems likely that the medieval bards had a full repertoire of wonder-working tales. Specific Irish tales were known to make kings victorious, marriages fruitful, blessed new houses (if told during the first night there) and hallowed fresh ale. Considering the sacredness of storytelling in a number of ancient Indo-European cultures, it may be likely that the pre-literate Celto/Germanic

people of central Europe had similar traditions.

Therapeutic Storytelling

We have taken a look at the way stories were used to shape belief and reality. Some of you may think that the magick of tales is only a minor matter rating on a level with spell-crafting and dowsing. On the contrary I would propose that stories are so magickal that they shape group reality. No matter what 'objective' scientists believe, most of reality is not measurable but a matter of consensus. The mass media of our days, while scoring very low on a factual level, are popular enough to shape the opinions and beliefs of millions. It is these people, the shallow minded majority, who form and confirm the myth called reality. This is a feedback process. The people believe in the media and the media supply what the people want to believe in. Luckily, not all newspapers and TV programs agree with each other, and thank gods there are more reliable sources of information in our days.

In the days of bardic storytelling, data was a lot harder to find, and the word of the intellectual (bard or poet) carried a lot of weight. Bardic poetry confirmed the purpose of the so-called heroic society, it inspired the audience to certain forms of conduct while tabooing other deeds. In this sense bardic magick created an entire worldview for a whole society. This is certainly high magick. It is not the sort of magick you can use to achieve odds and ends. It is the kind of magick that ought to set you thinking how the bards of today, mass media, are shaping your reality. Where does consensual reality offer freedom of choice to you and where is it limiting your development? Take a good look at the simple, ordinary ideas which you always take for granted. Probably some storytellers are responsible for them. Mind you, there is one important difference between the bards of old and the media of today. The bards went through a process of spiritual initiation and refinement in their training, and produced plenty of inspired art. Modern journalists basically learn to recognize the fundamental kicks their audience hungers for, meet at the lowest possible level and turn dross into gold. So much for magick on a huge scale. Let us now look at the way stories work on the small scale, and how they can be introduced into your personal magickal practise.

Story telling is invaluable for refined hypnotherapy. Most of you will have some idea about hypnosis and the way suggestions can be used to stimulate change and healing. In the early days of hypnosis, the pioneers had very few techniques to induce trance states and healing processes. They had a simple method, called direct suggestion, and applied it like a sledge hammer. The very first hypnotists simply repeated orders. 'Go into trance. Go deeper. Calm down. Feel relaxed. Your eyes close. Hear my voice. Breathe deeply. Go deeper into trance. Obey my commands.' Such simple suggestions were repeated continuously, if need be for hours or days, until the patient either trances or walks out. Consequently, the experts of the time decided that some people can be hypnotized while others cannot. They thought that the ability to be hypnotized depends on the patient, and

that their own moronic inflexibility had nothing to do with it.

When the patient had achieved some sort of trance, the therapists tested whether it was deep enough. In those days, it was common superstition that deep trances equal deep transformations while shallow trances are ineffectual. To test trance depth, the therapists invented a lot of absurd practises, such as arm levitation, anesthesia, paralysis and the like. If the patient was obedient, this was considered as a good trance, if not, there was 'resistance', which, as we all know, is a three headed slimy monster with wings, claws and a terrible sense of humour.

People showing resistance were classed as bad subjects, screamed at and thrown out. Those who did well in trance depth received instructions regarding the changes they sought. You could expect stuff like 'the desk is tidy.' 'smoking is bad.' 'I get better every day', 'Duty is pleasure' and so on. Such commands were thought to build character. Following the rule 'more is better', they were repeated hundreds of times, week after week, until the desired change set in or the patient sought another therapist.

I once read a book on hypnosis in Russia which included the hint that real hypnosis requires the hypnotist to appear authoritative, totally certain with a sinister look in his eyes. To achieve this, the reader was asked to cultivate dark, bushy eyebrows, and to grow a proper hypnotist's beard. In Russia under the tutelage of the good Dr. Pavlov, patients could expect such suggestions as 'Comrade Olga, you are ordered into trance now!' Coue, from the

French school of early mind benders, proposed that people should repeat suggestions to themselves (this began the history of self-hypnosis), and that mothers should sneak into their kid's bedrooms to whisper suggestions whilst they slept.

Nowadays hypnotherapy is quite a different matter. The authoritative approach, which worked so wonderfully in dictatorships and feudal systems, is rather inefficient in the modern world. When all the media clamour that you should be an individual, go your own way and consume the following products, ordering people into trance is not very fitting. Likewise, doctors have lost a lot of their semi-divine status, so a suggestion is not taken as gospel any more. Modern hypnotherapy owes a lot to such researchers as Milton H. Erickson and the brilliant pioneers of Neuro Linguistic Programming (NLP), John Grinder and Richard Bandler.

In the modern approach, patients are not treated using standard strategies. People are unique, every individual having original experiences, memories and personality traits. It follows that a standard cure is impossible, and that each patient has to have custom-tailored therapy, and the sort of suggestions s/he wants to respond to. Some people like to be told what they should do, and are happy when they get direct suggestions sounding like commands. Other folk (by now in the majority) do not want to be ordered around. In the old days they

were thought unhypnotizable, today we only have to code the suggestions in a more appropriate form and off they go into trance. If a person shows resistance, this is generally evidence that the therapist is not flexible enough or tries to force the patient to do something offensive.

Hypnosis is not a form of mind control nor a contest of will-power. It is a graceful method of communication involving plenty of feedback. Where the old hypnotists believed that they had to control and imprint the mind of the patient, modern therapists take the attitude that healer and patient want to cooperate. Erickson himself proposed that the therapist is unimportant and merely provides a setting in which the patient can induce whatever changes s/he wills.

One of the ways in which the therapist can offer freedom of choice to the patient is by the use of indirect or undefined suggestions. Keep in mind that the therapist is not all-knowing. If you try to make a person change in the way you will, it is more than likely that it won't work. Even with the best of intentions you cannot know exactly what the patient needs. This is pretty much the same thing that lies behind sigil magick. If you form a sigil you are asking your deep mind (or the gods, spirits etc) to do something for you. You ask the deep mind as the conscious mind didn't get anywhere. Usually, the deep mind is much better informed than the conscious mind

What is the chief problem in magickal evolution? Not demons or angels, not wrathful deities or wriggly things from in-between. It is simply the ordinary human personality, the mask of identity held together by habitual thinking and rigid belief. This creature can do with a bit of confusion from time to time. How about confusing yourself on purpose?

(the personality or ego). It has the resources, the understanding and wisdom and it knows much better what is good for you than you do. A well shaped sigil can stimulate the deep mind to produce changes which seem magickal to the uninitiated. Part of its efficiency comes from the fact that the sigil is forgotten after transmission, so that the deep can go to work without interference from the ego.

In a similar fashion, a good hypnotherapist does not insist on knowing better. It is much more efficient to ask the deep mind of the patient to find its own solutions and to effect the transformations it really needs. One method to effect this is to use open suggestions. Let me improvise an example:

'and as you are feeling that you are going deeper and your body breathes gently and your muscles relax you may find that your deep mind is beginning to explore the changes which are really important for you now and that it finds access to the very resources that work for you and you can expect that they will work even better for you in future as you go about your business and suddenly you realize that the things which had been difficult before are so different now as you notice what has happened and begin to enjoy it. Your deep mind knows what changes you need and right now it can decide on three character traits it would like to transform and as you are listening to my voice you are beginning to sense that this is happening now and that you can expect a pleasant surprise soon so you may as well enjoy this good feeling now and perhaps you want to dream something pleasant now or recall a memory while your

deep mind is busy healing you and doing all those things that do you good. You can take the time now to allow this process to work so well and when your deep mind has done its job you may find that you wake from your dreams and come out of trance feeling refreshed and renewed when you are ready and look forward to the blessings of the deep transform your life now...'

In these lines you can find several elements of hypnotic speech patterns. Some of them make use of odd grammar, of hidden implications, of experiences which can be verified and others which cannot. If you look closely at this text you will notice that, while it sounds specific and meaningful, most of it is just a lot of glittery soap bubbles. Good hypnotic language is often artfully undefined. The lines make no sense to patient or therapist apart from the fact that they stimulate certain internal processes. They make the deep mind (whatever that may really be) begin to search for aspects of the personality that need an update, and to change them, while the patient experiences unspecified dreams or memories or simply enjoys that relaxed feeling that comes with such a trance. I did not specify what should change, how it should change or why it should change. I implied, however, that change will occur now, and that it is to be a pleasant change for the better (whatever that may constitute of).

By being artfully undefined, the therapist avoids the pitfall of 'knowing better' and undue meddling. Thanks to vague suggestions, the patient can get exactly the therapeutic changes s/he needs. The therapist needs not know what is being

Coins 19
top l: Tectosagi?
top r: unknown, north of the Danube
center l: unknown, Taunus, very common in
central Germany, related to Boii coins?
center R: Eburones, triscel
bottom l: Iceni, Britain
bottom r. Iceni, Britain

done and neither has the patient to be aware what transformations occur. The vital thing is that the proper changes happen, and this is what the magick is all about.

Hypnosis as such is just one method of inducing useful and entertaining trance states. If you wish to help some person to transform, you can do this in a normal hypnotic trance setting. You could also do it more elegantly. In some cases it may be useful to do the whole routine, and to induce a trance after allowing the patient to relax, calm down, become slower and so on. At other times, this approach is simply too rigidly ritualistic. This can especially be the case when the person hypnotized has a deep dislike for hypnosis or feels terrified. Thanks to the way the media have presented hypnosis, most people in our society view it in a negative way. They think that hypnosis is forcing other people to do things they don't want to do. They believe that people can be hypnotized to commit crimes, and that, in trance, they would be somehow vulnerable to any malign influence.

This sort of myth is popular and totally wrong. If you want to make people do things that go against their principles, coerce them in the waking state. This is what bosses, governments and authority figures do, and it works pretty well. In trance, most people are a lot more intelligent than in daily life, they are in touch with their essential nature and recognize manipulation more easily than when they go to work or watch TV.

Should a person fear hypnosis or resent interference, it can be useful to code suggestions in such a way that they are not recognized as such. There are some therapists who use story telling for this purpose. To begin with, a story is something harmless. If you listen you don't have to go through trance inductions and you can think of yourself as a listener, not as a patient, which is a great relief. Likewise, the therapist appears like an entertainer. While entertaining, a well told story induces a trance state. Think about it. Erickson defined trance as a state of focused attention. In trance, your general awareness is reduced while some specific item of awareness is perceived more intently. People in trance often have some very intense experiences while others go by unnoticed. This explains why pain control by hypnosis is possible. The pain is not really controlled. It is simply reduced and forgotten as other sensations appear more fascinating. Attention shifts elsewhere, or, as a Chinese martial arts saying goes: *If you think of the pain it hurts twice as much.*

In the same way I could say that the writing trance I experience while typing these lines involves a degree of physical anesthesia. While my mind is busy with its narrow focus (the words, inner language, the fingers on the keyboard) I tend to forget my body and generally don't notice whether I'm hungry or tired or need a bit of motion. Can you recall reading an exciting book, a book that was so fascinating that you just couldn't stop reading? What a wonderful example for a deep hypnotic trance! While enjoying a story, you receive words, gestures and a number of subtle informations communicated by means of pronunciation, tonality, speed, emphasis and so on. When you read, you get even less to work with: just the words, and you can make up any voice that sounds fitting. Whatever you receive, it is not the story. The story is what your brain produces out of the various information outlets. You bring the words to life, you represent events in your inner senses (this is called making sense) and you experience genuine emotions as a result of your inventiveness.

Most literate folk take this for granted, few of them consider that reading or listening to a story is an exercise in applied hallucination. Think of some exciting novel, one that really touched your emotions. Isn't it amazing how strongly you can feel about persons whom you make up right in your mind? Isn't it strange that a story can brighten up your day, or bring you completely down? Some stories make people laugh or weep. Pretty strong hallucinations, eh?

Some therapists have perfected the art of story telling to such a degree that their patients do not notice that they are being hypnotized. This approach was developed into a high art by Milton H. Erickson, who told tale after tale during therapy. Erickson, sitting in his wheelchair, staring at the ground and mumbling vaguely, had found that he could bore patients into trance. Listening to one story after another, the patients soon began to doze and dream, they tranced out without ever needing to be told to. After the session, they usually found that they could recall very few of Erickson's stories, and many of them left the practice with a distinct feeling of disappointment. In the opinion of their conscious minds, the doctor had not done anything. Days or months later they suddenly realized that their lives had undergone a change for the better, or they began to recall tales which suddenly made lots of sense for their well being.

Erickson used this method on patients who were difficult or none too intelligent. He also used it to train other therapists. In his teaching workshops, he very rarely bothered to give explicit instructions. When a therapist asked how to do something, the usual response was yet another story. You can treat yourself to such a learning experience by reading *A Six Day Seminary with Milton H. Erickson* if you want to enjoy something immensely valuable. When Erickson told his tales, the audience dozed or daydreamed. They hardly had a choice about it. At the same time, their deep minds were really busy filtering important information and acquiring new sets of behaviour. In this sense, Erickson's tales worked a lot like sigils. They bypassed the censors of the conscious personality and sank into the deep to effect changes and healing. And just why do you think my books are so full of odd stories?

Therapeutic Functions

In therapy, storytelling can be used to produce several effects.

Diagnosis. A story can elicit responses from the audience. By observing the client's reactions you can gather information which is difficult to access otherwise. You can watch what the listener responds to consciously, and find out at which points of your tale the listener's deep mind gives subliminal clues. Watch out for body symmetry, posture, attentiveness, gestures and so on.

Confusion. When people have problems, part of their trouble tends to come from the way in which they think about their problems. Thoughts are not entities as such, they come in a certain form. In order to think thoughts, you have to make sense out of them, i.e. you have to shape them using the sensual channels of your imagination. The way in which you represent a given thought influences your thinking. When a certain thought has been thought repeatedly, it can become so rigid that it is hard to think otherwise.

> Many people, when they try to solve a problem, stay within the confines of the situation. If you can get them to step outside, you are showing them, 'you can step beyond the immediate confines of that emotional problem.' All of a sudden they realize there are other views, other possibilities, other understandings. You're merely telling them, or forcing them, to step beyond the immediate confines of that emotional configuration. (Erickson in Haley 1985)

Stories can induce confusion, and confusion can throw the listener right out of the usual routine thinking and open the mind for new insights and possibilities. You can use a story that confuses the conscious mind of your listener, and communicate a number of useful suggestions to the deep mind in the process. You could also invent long and complicated sagas, wrapping tales within tales within tales until the listener is thoroughly perplexed. Both the conscious mind and the deep mind will be searching for a meaning. Its not that important to

supply the conscious mind with meaning, but it can be handy to give meaningful messages to the deep mind in the process. As all stories have several levels of meaning, the meaning for the surface needs not be identical with the meaning for the deep. Confusion is not only valuable in therapy. It is also invaluable in magick and mysticism. What is te chief problem in magickal evolution? Not demons or angels, not wrathful deities or wriggly things from in-between. It is simply the ordinary human personality, the mask of identity held together by habitual thinking and rigid belief. This creature can do with a bit of confusion from time to time. How about confusing yourself on purpose?

Problem solving. Stories can carry advice and solutions. In the worst case, you can observe this formula in simple moral tales. This sort of thing is hardly efficient. If you can't ask the listener 'How about doing so and so?' directly, and wrap the matter up in a sticky little story instead, the analogy will be glaringly obvious and the client may easily detest this. Likewise, any bit of advice which *you* offer may be totally beside the point. You are only guessing. Instead of offering a solution you could tell a story that stimulates the listener to fresh thinking. Multiple choices, for example, are a much safer bet than any single solution. Stimulation is more graceful than coercion.

> In trance induction, the inexperienced hypnotist often tries to direct or bend the subject's behaviour to fit his conception of how a subject 'should' behave. There should be a constant

minimalization of the role of the hypnotist and a constant enlargement in the subject's role. (Erickson in Bandler & Grinder, 1975).

Artful Vagueness.

In many forms of art you can observe a dynamic interplay between suggestion and definition. Think of a Chinese landscape painting. Much of its charm comes from the fact that the scenery cannot be fully seen. Clouds veil parts of towering mountains, a tangle of vegetation hides the path, inaccessible sites allure with their mystery. Such elements are not coincidental. The traditional rules for Chinese landscape painting demand that a good picture should include such items, just as it should show some human beings, a building and a dynamic energy flow in the scenery.

Or think of landscapes done in watercolour. Compare them to landscapes done with a pen. What is the difference? In one case you have a vague image that invites suggestion, in the other the image is sharply defined. Pictures can define what happens and they can suggest it.

The same forces are at play in storytelling. If the persons in a tale are well defined, this may make the audience respond to their personality traits. If you want a hero whom people identify with, you have to be very precisely balanced between definition and suggestion. Too much detail and you may offend some of the listeners, too little detail and your hero becomes a cardboard character. A hero with too much personality may be original and convincing, but hardly popular.

Let me tell you about dear old king Arthur now. Ever heard of him? Nennius, writing around 830 mentions him briefly as a *dux bellorum*, a war-leader. He fought 12 battles against various Anglo-Saxons, and hunted a pig called Troynt. When fighting he sometimes carried an image of the virgin, and once he journeyed to Jerusalem to obtain a cross. Not much information, but enough to start a legend in a time that was hungry for legends.

The original Arthur was a humble character. His contemporary Gildas, writing wrathfully about the monarchy of Britain, does not even bother to mention him (good evidence that Arthur, if he existed at all, was no king). Lambert of St. Omer dismissed him as 'a soldier.' This wasn't much material to build a myth. Did Arthur exist at all? In the period associated with him, the early sixth century, there is no record of him whatsoever. This may mean a lot or very little, as so precariously few documents have come to us from that period. Historians are not very happy abot the post-Roman years in Britain, when history writing went rapidly downhill and illiteracy became the rule. There is indirect evidence, however. The name Arthur became very popular in the generation that lived after him. The written records of the next centuries hardly ever mention him. Then came the transformation.

Whoever Arthur may have been originally, his legend, recorded by Nennius, shows him as a highly successful fighter against the dreaded Anglo-Saxon invaders. This made him popular with the Welsh and the British. As time went by, more and more legends were added to his myth.

Geoffrey of Monmouth (c.1100-1155) published a bizarre pseudo history called *The History of the Kings of Britain* which became a bestseller. It contained a large section on King Arthur who had become a national hero. Others copied from Geoffrey and the continental troubadours with their grail stories did the rest.

Arthur was not only a king of early history, in reality he was an emperor. Had he not personally conquered Britain and Ireland, Scandinavia, Germany, France and indeed the mighty Roman empire itself? Had he not single-handedly destroyed giants, humbled tyrants and freed the downtrodden from ill-mannered dragons? Arthur was real to these people. Arthur the noble, the just ruler, head of the most glamorous court of chivalrous Europe, founder of the round table.

Before long, Arthur and his gallant knights were celebrated in every European court. The troubadours, traveling from castle to castle, made the story popular. They brought a myth to life which inspired plenty of aristocrats to imitate Arthur and his brave company. A host of stories grew around Arthur the perfect regent which would have come as a surprise to the original 6th century war leader. One of the reasons the Arthur story was so successful was that its focus had so little personality. Many people could identify with Arthur, as they could make up their own Arthur in their own minds. Imagine a bard telling you:

'Once upon a time there was a great and noble king whose name was Arthur. He was a strong fighter and a wise ruler whose justice was admired by everyone. His fame reached so far that knights came traveling from all quarters of the world. They wanted to join Arthur's company and sit at the round table where all men are equals. Arthur held court at Camelot and it was the greatest honour to join his company. Arthur loved his subjects and did everything to improve their condition. Whenever he heard of some evil being done, he sent out a knight to punish the evildoer.'

This tells us very little about Arthur's personality. It invites you to hallucinate a perfect monarch who miraculously happens to have your very own idea of justice. The Arthur you made up is your Arthur. If you play the game, you have to instil him with your own virtues and prejudices. Given such a nondescript Arthur, lots of people will happily hallucinate whaever they want. Let me go into the other extreme. What about an Arthur who has personal traits? Luckily, there are plenty of odd details in medieval literature. Some of them sound pretty crazy. Now imagine you hear your bard saying:

'Arthur? He wasn't a bad guy, you know. Sort of big. Longest legs you've ever seen. Kept knocking his head against doorframes-lots of dents in it. And a bit shy. His father was a menace. They called him the Terrible, but only behind his back. Horrible temper. Always fell from horses and got mad if anyone laughed. So Arthur was raised by other folk. Never got over it, but there you have it, he couldn't help it. He had a good court, though. Big castle. 15 rooms altogether, and three of them had heating. Rushes on the floor, lots of fancy food and no sanitary arrangements. Next river was a bit downhill, not that much, I say, but who got around to washing those days? Old Art was always out and about fighting. They said that for seven years nothing grew wherever he walked. Didn't dare to, really. Here a giant, there a dragon, then the Saxons-they kept coming over, but Art beat them soundly. Twelve big battles isn't bad for a lifetime. Of course sometimes we went over for a bit of war on their side of the Channel. Good times they were. I remember when he became devout. He had this terrible quarrel with a saint…Padarn the bugger was called. Came from Rome in the fanciest tunic you have ever seen-tassels and buttons and stuff. Arthur wanted it, but Padarn wouldn't hand it over. They had an awful row, and Padarn won. Cursed Arthur right into the ground. Well, old Art wasn't that stupid for a king. He decided to outfaith him. Went to Jerusalem and brought back this big cross. At Mount Badon he cracked a lot of Saxon heads with it. And his shield! Had the Virgin Mary on it, with golden hair and big boobs. Of course he was right jealous about it. Anyone daring to scratch that picture, off goes the head. But he wasn't always fighting. We had parties, you see, and old Art wasn't such a bad guy when it came to drinking. He liked his big graal of mead as well as the next fellow. That, and soccer. They used heads in those days, you know, plenty of heads around. Lots of good knights too. Sir Kei was so hot that he could melt his way through a snow-heap. And old Lancelot…always after the queen. Good fighter though. Sad that he had this identity problem. Sometimes it made him right mad. You see, he hadn't been invented at the time, that was several centuries later, and he never got over it. The ladies weren't bad either. Arthur had three queens, each of them called Gwenhwyfar and three mistresses, I forgot who. He used to walk into ladies boudoirs in his cloak of invisibility. And he always fancied himself something of a bard. Made godawful poems when he was drunk, it happened almost every night. Much better at fighting really…we bards had to drink a lot to tolerate his metre. Then he screwed up this expedition to the otherworld, well, lets pretend it never happened. Conquered most of Europe, though. Gaul and Germany, Italy and Greece, even Norway and Iceland. His big trouble was pigs. Pigs and women. He kept going out to hunt pigs. Total failure. Didn't even manage to steal the swine of king March. Well, we all have our little problems. In the end they killed him stone dead. That was at Camlan. Awful show. Most futile battle I've ever been in. But there you are, he wasn't bad for a king. They dumped him into a hole at Glastonbury. Old Bedwyr pinched the sword and sold it; we drank for three weeks on the money.'

This sort of tale has more life in it, but it wouldn't make anyone hallucinate a perfect monarch, let alone identify with him. Everybody likes the idea of a just and generous ruler, but your ideas on justice will differ from mine and both of us will be a long way from the legal philosophy of the 6th Century.

Tools for Hallucination

Thus we arrive at the first essential in magickal or therapeutic storytelling. Allow the audience to hallucinate. Don't be too

Coins 20, all coins
Ile de Bretagne,
gold. Note that the
symbolism revolves
on a pair of "moon-
sickles" (?). The
rectangles in the
bottom coins are not
symmetrical.

specific or you will lose them. Give them the freedom to invent their own characters, setting and atmosphere. If you tell a story to yourself you can be as specific as you like. If you have specific visions, it's sound practise to use specific language. If you tell a tale for others you have to be more vague. This way they can make up the specific visions they like and everybody is happy.

If you describe scenery, for instance, it is useful to stick to essentials. If you talk of the seaside, you can mention the waves that come rolling in, the sound of the surf, the hissing of the foam, the fresh damp air, the calls of water-birds, the smell of salt and iodine, the wide horizon. Such sensations are pretty natural for the seaside. You may have noticed that I did not specify the sort of shore, the time of day, the climate, animal life, tourist activity and similar details. I mentioned 'the sound of the surf'. I did not specify what sound, nor did I state what sort of waves make it. All I know is that you get some waves at the seaside, and that they make some sound.

When you imagine a wide empty shore and a grey rainsoaked pebbly beach and I suddenly talk about towering brownish cliffs in the sunshine, this will interrupt your imagination and necessitate a bit of constructive re-thinking. In short, it disrupts your trance. It can be a lot more elegant to be so unspecific that each listener makes up the very seaside that s/he likes best. The trick lies in knowing when you have to give detail and when you can leave it to the audience. Should your story involve someone falling from a cliff, you have to introduce that feature of the scenery so early that the audience has time to integrate

it in the dreaming. You can tell them that its a terribly high cliff, and everyone will imagine what s/he believes to be terribly high. You don't have to specify what seems high to you. In the same way a horrible monster is more horrible when everyone gives shape to her/his own nightmares. If you try to describe what seems horrible for you, most of the audience will be disappointed.

Similarly, activities need not be specified very much. **Unspecified verbs** are useful for this. If you hear that Arthur fought the Saxons, 'fighting' is unspecified. You get no data on how he fought, and when, whether he did it all alone, how often, and what it was like. The listener, naively assuming to know what 'fighting' is like, hallucinates whatever s/he likes.

Then there are **nominalizations**. This is even more fun. The term comes from modern linguistics and is frequently used in NLP literature (Read *The Structure of Magic* by Bandler and Grinder for an enlightening experience). You get a nominalization when you take an activity (a verb) and turn it into a noun. In the process, it seems to become more real. 'To love' (an activity) is transformed into 'love'. May I ask you what love is? You know what the word means to you, I know what it means to me, and if we use the word in conversation, we are both likely to hallucinate that we know what the other is talking about.

Nominalizations are essential in magick. Ever heard such words as self, consciousness, will, love, understanding, doubt, wisdom, knowledge, strength, compassion, desire, pleasure, trance, ecstasy, rapture, delight, lust, healing…?

Every simple invocation contains such stuff. It means very little (and a real lot) and it certainly produces effects.

Nominalizations are also vital for political speeches. Freedom. Control. Pride. Duty. Hope. System. Commitment. Obligation. Choice. Stability. Responsibility. Progress. Security. Tolerance. Lovely, isn't it? It sounds so real. You can get people to kill each other for a 'freedom' which has never been defined. What is freedom? Look at the original verb. I am free to do xyz. Everybody wants to be free to do xyz. Thus, the politician who promises 'freedom' expects that every voter will fill the word with tantalizing delusions.

If your story involves a person feeling love, fear, hunger, sorrow or whatever, the audience is bound to insert their own ideas into these terms. You can use this moment to learn something useful. Please take a pen and paper and make a list of at least 300 nominalizations, plus the verbs they were formed out of. You'll find that it's a lot of fun. It's completely amazing how many hallucinations are required to make sense of simple phrases.

If you are not sure if you are dealing with a noun or an nominalization, there is a simple NLP trick to find out. Ask yourself if you can put it in a wheelbarrow. You can put an elephant in a wheelbarrow, but you can't fill a wheelbarrow with optimism, truth, identity, excitement or depression. Take some newspaper texts and underline all nominalizations. Listen to advertisers, politicians, philosophers and therapists. And let me end this by telling you of a friend called Astrid. As I was hypnotizing her, I had this crazy idea and told her to go to the House of the Spirits. I had no idea where this would take her. For me, the House of the Spirits is a useful place in the imagination where I go to have a chat or a drink with the spirits. Usually it appears as a small reed-thatched hut standing on poles in twilighty swampland. For her, the house of spirits was a mega-sized transparent dome. Hundreds of spirits were walking in and out. I asked her 'What spirits are they?' and she answered 'They are all nominalizations'.

Stories and Self-Hypnosis

You can use this opportunity to experiment. Take a simple story. A useful example would be the story of the stupid Hans which you read earlier. How can you turn this dry summary into an enchanting experience? Read it a few times until you know the order of events. Then tell the story to yourself. Repeat it. Close your eyes if you like and describe what you sense.

What visions come with the story? If you tell it to yourself a couple of times you will find that more and more lucid visions develop in your imagination. At the same time the story line develops and the gaps are filled with suitable details. You can amplify them. Every inner vision can be made more impressive if you find out what turns you on. Do you find big pictures more impressive than small ones, do you prefer strong colour to dullness, how about making the scene come closer? Would you prefer more lucidity, more contrast, more detail? Is the episode flashing by or can you watch events leisurely? How fast is your story? How about adding shine and sparkle? What else can you do to make the imagination more impressive? How about perspective? Does it get stronger when you see the story from above, sideways, eye-level or from below?

This may be one of the most important techniques for your magick. You can make your inner visions more exciting, this is sound policy with entertaining memories and pleasant thoughts. With unpleasant memories it can be a relief to do the opposite, that is, to make the images less exciting. What makes an image exciting for you and what reduces its effect? I cannot tell you what you like, but luckily, you can. Use the images of the tale to explore the way your mind codes data using representation. What turns you on? And what turns you off? Be so kind to list what you do and what seems most impressive. You can use it for other stories, and for the tales you make up while you go through life.

You can also play around with the other inner senses. Every inner sense has these fine distinctions. In technical NLP language the sensory channels are referred to as the modalities while the little differences within each sensory modality are called the submodalities. How about making the sound louder, and bringing it closer? From where does it come? Within your body? Outside of your body? From what direction? Is it clear or muffled, constant or changeable? And what about the kinesthetic sensations? From where does a feeling come, how well is it defined, does it pulse, is there a rhythm, how much pressure and solidity and texture do you sense? When you speak of burning sunshine, pouring rain, the weary long road and the hungry belly of Hans, can you do it so that you feel what you are talking about?

Most people think that their thoughts are just there. Maybe they like some, maybe they loathe others. Very few bother to find out that thoughts can be changed when you change the way you are thinking. If you don't like the quality of your inner visions, or if a story only produces unconvincing, half-hearted imagery, what about saying Yes! Now is the time to turn on my imagination! Now is the moment to make my inner visions really good! And this is true. You can do it. You have been doing it all your life, only that you rarely noticed what you were doing. Lots of people make huge, colourful bright pictures of events they don't like and bring them really close. Then they practically go nuts with worry. Others hardly dare to imagine what something good may be like. They produce a flimsy, pale picture somewhere in the far distance and then complain that it doesn't seem attractive. In the real world, nothing is attractive or unattractive. It's happening up there, all in your mind. You are doing it, and if you don't like what you are doing, do it differently and better.

In magick, it is important that you can make your imagination so impressive that it carries you away. This is what enthusiasm is all about. If you practise with a story, make it as impressive as you can. Use all the tricks that work for you. Use all the senses. When Hans comes to the seaside, you can see the sea, you can hear it and you can feel it. Maybe you even can smell and taste the salty freshness of the air. If you experience a given thought in several senses at once, it appears more 'real' to you than a representation in a single sensory system.

Aim for emotion.

A good story should be touching. It should elicit a genuine emotional response from you. Some stories do this naturally. You can make it stronger by amplifying the representation. Other stories are shy at first. You have to warm them up and improve them a bit to produce lively visions and strong emotions. Incidentally, if you imagine the story well, you may find yourself in a trance state. It could be a light or a deep trance, depending on how closely you associate with the story and how much of the world around you is dissociated (or ignored). The more attractive you make your story, the deeper will it put you in trance. For a practical introduction to submodalities read Richard Bandler's *Using Your Brain For A Change*.

Sometimes you start to tell yourself a story. By the time you have warmed up you become more caught up with it, and when the outside world calls for your attention, you may find it hard to stop the tale. Once started, a story can achieve a lot of momentum. Somehow the deep mind likes to complete stories. If you break off at some point, the deep mind of the listener will be obliged to make sense of the tale by inventing its outcome. Please tell yourself the story until it is as real as a dream. By then you will have given it a lot of your life. Reciprocally, the story will show you some of its hidden enchantment. It is at this point that we leave therapy and similar fun activities.

Stories as Spirits

Magickally speaking, a story is a spirit. Stories are born, they develop, the mix, breed, throw out countless mutations and infest as many minds as they can. Some stories can be completely obsessive. Think of them as living entities. To practise storytelling is a form of invocation, the act of telling itself is a communion which feeds the teller, the story spirit and the audience. In the guise of stories, information survives and continues. May I call it an unembodied life-form adapted to communicate ideas across the centuries? We can use storytelling to improve ritual. How about using stories as invocations? Many ancient tales deal with deities. You can use them as sources of information to get some idea about the nature of your gods. You can also tell the story to make contact easier. It works pretty well when combined with a bit of prayer. Anything that focuses attention and produces emotion can be used as an offering to the gods. If you wish to contact a new deity, how about telling its stories until communication occurs naturally?

Let us go a little further. Think of your childhood. Can you recall the tales and stories that inspired you ? What obsessions and secret meanings were hidden in the tales? And which of your later-life obsessions appeared in your choice of childhood literature? Can you recall the books, movies and stories that shaped your life?

And what of the tales you made up as a motivation strategy? Lots of people daydream. Some have specific daydreams, others just hazy bits of mental flotsam. Some dream when they are young but give it up as they grow older. Some become scared of dreaming as they dread disappointment. Some go for big, colourful daydreams while others feel safer with small and easily controllable bits of wishful thinking. Whatever your choice may be, it produces the life you are living. Are you happy with it? Or could you dream of something better? Think of being very much in love. What stories did you make up for yourself? Or think of the other extreme. How about worrying? What stories do you invent to get a good worry going? And what tales can you tell yourself to achieve your ambitions?

Enchanting Others.

Once you have experienced your story a number of times on your own you may enjoy sharing it with others. Several tactics can be used to make storytelling an act of magick. One useful item is a **ritual setting**. If you begin your tale with a set formula, such as 'Once upon a time' your audience gets a clear signal to listen attentively. The same goes for a set formula at the end of the tale.

Pauses are another interesting matter. Sometimes a pause is unavoidable. Maybe you are busy telling a six hour saga and find that you need a break. Maybe the phone rings or you have to answer the door. If you simply stop, some of your audience may dislike this. If you interrupt a ritual (be it a ceremony, storytelling or hypnotic trance) without giving the other persons a script for future behaviour, anything can happen. Some may lose interest and walk away, others may call for you to continue. If you announce the pause as something that goes on for a certain time span and that the story, ritual or trance will continue then, the pause is not an interruption any more

but a part of the program.

This is also useful for self hypnosis and certain obsessive trances. Imagine you have been out in the forest in a wild Shamanic trance. After a few hours, you decide that you will have to go home, maybe as you're cold or hungry. On the other hand it would be a shame to stop trancing altogether. How can you do it? One way is to stop the trance, to go home, and to resume it at your destination. This implies effort. First you have to dissociate your trance and associate with whatever you need to ride a train or drive a car. Then at home you have to dissociate the transit-reality and associate with your original trance again. Such changes can cost a lot of energy. They can also be frustrating, as you can't be sure that you'll get into the desired trance again when you are home.

Now try this. Instead of getting out of trance you could suspend it. If you ask your deep mind to suspend the Shamanic trance for long enough to drive home, and to resume it in full power as soon as you are there, you may find the transition a lot easier. There will be less conflict. You won't have to stop and start again, you can simply continue where you left off.

Adaptation. Next, consider the audience. If you want a full effect you will have to adapt the story to the folk who listen. To a sense you adapt it when you talk vague and unspecified. To another you can use the language structures your listeners respond to. You can make a given person of your tale attractive or loathsome if you associate it with behaviour the audience reacts to. This is especially efficient when it happens unconsciously. If you give your character a way of thinking your listeners feel comfortable with, that character stands a good chance of getting affection. If the hearer prefers to think in visual form, a fictional person who also thinks visually will seem sympathetic. You could use expressions such as 'he saw', 'it was obvious', 'insight', 'clarity', 'contrast', 'take a look', 'it appeared' and other visual terms to make this convincing. By contrast, a highly kinesthetic thinker will prefer to identify with someone who 'has a grip on reality', 'feels strongly', 'weighs matters', 'holds on', has 'firm convictions', is 'in touch', 'takes a stand' etc.

Acoustic thinkers also come up once in a while, but you rarely meet them, unless you know plenty of musicians. In other cultures this may be different. To make such folk happy, use expressions such as 'harmony', 'sounds good', 'discord', 'in tune', 'resonance', 'pitch' etc. If the hearer is unaware of this trait, the identification will work twice as well. Think of cheap fantasy literature. There are plenty of tales of swashbuckling derring-do being devoured by shy young intellectuals. How can they identify with heroes whose lifestyle is the exact opposite of their own? The trick lies in the process. Fantasy literature is not written by action men but by intellectuals. Many heroes of fantasy literature act like barbarians but think like intellectuals. The same can be observed in popular historical novels. Their characters act as if they came from another time, but their way of thinking is usually pretty modern. If you wish to custom tailor a story for a specific person, make use of that persons subconscious habits.

For therapy, this sort of secret marking is essential. If you want to communicate suggestions, the thing is to do it gently and subtly. A direct analogy is almost always resented and may result in the very form of behaviour which is of no use anyway. A **hidden analogy** can be a lot more useful. Thus, if you are stuck in love-sickness and I want to stimulate your fresh thinking, I wouldn't be so daft to tell you a tale of lovesick people. It would be much more efficient to tell a tale that seems to have nothing in common with the problem. I could tell you the adventures of the small blue stone and how it traveled through the wide world. Your deep mind will realize that on the whole, small blue stones won't go traveling nor do they have adventures. As a result, the deep mind will look for a hidden meaning in the tale. If it can't find any it will make it up. Give it something useful to make up from!

Neither is it necessary to mention love-sickness at all. Instead, the small blue stone may go through a lot of experiences that seem unhappy at first, but lead to important changes. Here **quotations** come in. You can say what you like if you disguise it as a quote. 'You idiot!', said the stone to itself, 'Go out and have fun! If you wait any longer you'll petrify!' In this fashion you can insert direct suggestion into your tale without ever appearing to do so.

Another way to offer suggestions was developed by Milton Erickson. Bandler and Grinder call this approach analogical marking or imbedded commands. When telling a tale, Erickson used to emphasize useful suggestive elements by marking them with a hidden signal. There are lots of ways you can do this. Erickson, who spent much of his life in a semi-paralyzed condition, used very subtle signals. Sometimes he emphasized a few words by moving his head to another angle, which made his voice sound slightly different. Sometimes he used tiny gestures, pauses or gentle changes in tonality. The main thing is that you mark the decisive passages so subtly that the conscious mind does not notice. The deep mind, however, will soon become aware that some words come with this special signal, and will put their meaning together. Let me annoy you with another example.

A Forest Walk

Would you like to *come with me* to the forest? Not far from my home are mountains. They are *comfortable* and pleasing mountains that *feel good* and have just the right size to wander through the green and *enjoy a real change of consciousness*. I wonder if you have ever been to a large forest. The trees *stretch out* for miles and miles and as you can walk you can *rest and relax* and you can *discover new things* as you *find your own way* through the wild wood. Perhaps you can guess how good it feels when you *go exploring* and you know that *you have lots of time* and that *you are comfortable* in the wide world of nature.

There are so many different sorts of trees in the forest. Some of them tower high above you and they *sway gently* and there are smaller trees around that grow *further down* and there is so much more as you *go deeper and deeper* into the heart of the forest. You might enjoy to *sense this deeply peaceful mood* as you look through the trees and feel your feet *go quietly* and gently as you *find your own path*. If you *listen closely* you can hear a blackbird singing far away, and finches fly between the branches, but much closer to you is this great refreshing silence that makes *you relax* and *calm down* and *enjoy the good feelings*.

In the twilight *deeper now* under the trees you can see big rocks, and these rocks are very peaceful and patient as they *rest and listen* to the song of the birds. Now a rock is not a human, but a rock has its own good feelings and enjoys to *listen and dream* as it is *at rest and very comfortable*. Sometimes a rock moves a little bit but then it becomes *calm and quiet again* and perhaps you may wonder what rocks feel as they *sleep and dream*. Perhaps they make you think that you would like to *slow down and dream* and you know that *time passes differently* when you *rest and relax* in the forest. A rock can *enjoy being slow*, as it has lots of time while the wind makes the trees *sway gently* and *time slows down* and *you can enjoy this*. *Deep down* in the shady heart of the forest there are many paths you can *choose and explore* and many wonderful places you can *discover*. Few know that you can *find what you need* when you *leave the main road* and follow the straying little paths, and perhaps you would like to *learn the secrets* the forest holds for you. At first you *feel confused*, then it begins to *make sense* and all of a sudden you discover that you have come to *find a nice surprise* waiting for you. Everyone likes a nice surprise. I have no idea if you will *find a great surprise* or whether you prefer another surprise, but *deep down* you will *find what you are looking for and enjoy it*.

What was this reading experience like for you? No doubt you hallucinate lots of forest which you made up all in your own mind. You can see that the suggestions and imbedded commands in italics can be used for a number of purposes. Some of them (going down, becoming silent, resting, relaxation, time distortion etc.) are useful to make the trance deeper. Others stimulate fresh thinking, hint at new directions and finally the deep mind is asked to come up with a nice surprise. If you want to learn this method, I suggest you begin by reading the text aloud. Whenever you wish to emphasize a given suggestion, mark it with a tiny gesture, or with a slight change in tonality or volume. Use the same signal every time, so the deep mind of the listener notices that something is happening regularly. Then write some texts of your own and fill them with hidden suggestions. Practise with them until the marking happens really fluently.

A variety of literary styles are useful. You could hide anything in a chapter of James Joyce or a song by Taliesin. Erickson invented the technique when he studied the word salad that some clinical patients produce. Then in turn he sat down and composed his own word salad, taking care to fill it with therapeutic suggestions to the brim. The patients reacted favourably. It is doubtful that they made sense out of the surface meaning of the text, but subconsciously they picked up the bits that were useful and responded to them.

One person whom Erickson experi-mented with was his secretary. The dear lady frequently suffered from headaches. So Erickson composed a text which was finest quality surrealistic word salad, and read it aloud so she could type it. At the same time, the headache disappeared. Typing similar texts, without hidden suggestions, made no difference on her headache.

Finally, I wish to remind you of a vital element of story telling. No matter whether you do a ritual invocation, talk a person into trance or tell a story, do it **congruently**. If you want to calm and slow another, use a calm and slow way of speaking. If you want to surprise and excite, allow your whole being to express this excitement. If you want to invoke a deity or spirit, get into its mood. It's no use to address a trickster god in a reasonable way, nor does it work to pray to a war god if your voice sounds timid and squeaky. You get much further when you live the mood. As a story usually goes through several emotions, you would do well to experience them fully. Slow down in the gentle passages and speed up when things become exciting. Give different voices to your characters and assume their movements. A storyteller is always something of an actor. S/he is also something of a Magickian, in that the story (a spirit) can be an initiation and transform the world.

11. The Secret Arts

Part of the education of a good poet or bard were a number of activities which may be loosely classed as divination. Pause a moment and consider just what divination means to you. Is it fortune telling? Prediction? Prophecy? Or does it include other skills - inspiration, creative vision, reinterpretation of the world? What did it mean to the people of Britain and Ireland? And what did it mean in the centuries before the Roman occupation? We are lucky that the classical histographers have mentioned divination so frequently. We can be moderately certain that the Druids of Gaul divined by seeking omina, be it from the flight and behaviour of birds, be it from the death throes of dying prisoners. No details regarding such techniques survive. Regarding the birds, a number of birds and animals were deemed auspicious and unlucky, and are still regarded so, in rural parts of Scotland, Ireland and Wales. Especially the behaviour of crows, ravens and magpies (all of them 'devil's birds') was regarded with interest, and the existence of so many different magpie rhymes is a good indication that this may be an older tradition having undergone diversification in a number of districts. My favourite verse comes from Scotland and goes as follows:

One for sorrow, two for mirth,
three for a wedding, four for as birth,
five for silver, six for gold,
seven for a secret not to be told,
eight for heaven, nine for hell,
and ten for the devil himsel'

It works wonders in making long car or train rides more exciting. Once you make it a habit to count magpies you'll be amazed how many live in your neighbourhood. You may also finds that magpie spotting can be a compulsive habit. Would you care for a bit of obsession to make your life more exciting? Magpie's are just the thing to brighten up a dull life. Wolfram von Eschenbach, always a bit peculiar in his imagery, makes the magpie a symbol of the perfect human being - partly white, of heavenly nature, partly black, of hellish nature, and able to fly.

The members of the crow family feature popularly in the divination of a good many people, including the rama (shamans) of Nepal, who listen to the raven's croaks and calls, move their hands in a complicated sign language and receive such news as:

It's sending; the message is not here yet. The raven says, in the west someone has died. A good person comes from the south. In the west, rain will fall today...from the west come bad news about the death of a person and a cow. *(after Oppitz, 1981).*

It is not unlikely that Druidic augury had a similar style. Count Tolstoy even offers an auguration from the complex call of the capercaille. In his novel of Myrddin, the Druids are busy listening to the length of the pauses between the clicking, plop, and the scraping to divine the outcome of the next war. Or think of the common tradition that the melancholy call of the small owls portends death. Or those simple folk who count the calls of the first cuckoo and believe that they equal the number of years still due to them.

Most people in ancient Europe were concerned about lucky and unlucky signs. Where we find evidence for divination from omina, however, the usual approach is to watch out for signs, but not to believe in them unless they are supported by other signs. This approach is useful for many forms of divination. As you are undoubtedly eager to enjoy yourself and to experiment, let's take a look at a form of divination that has survived in the Gaelic countries well into the last century and put it into practise.

The Frith

Here is a ritual that was used especially around the quarter days to obtain a sign for the next season. It was commonly done on the first Monday of the quarter, but it may as well be used as an oracle for a month, a week or a day. The frithir (augurer) prepared by fasting. S/he got up early in the morning, before sunrise, and walked to the house door with bare head and feet and closed eyes. S/he opened the door, keeping the eyes shut, and stepped into the middle of the door-frame, extending a hand to each jamb. This placed the diviner between worlds. In-between-ness is essential for many forms of magic and divination, it signifies a state when the flow of reality is undefined and anything can happen. Holding on to the sides of the door, the frithir recited a prayer *to the god of the unseen to show him his quest and to grant him his augury* (MacNeill).

This duly spoken, the frithir opened her/his eyes and stared straight ahead. It may be useful to stare in absolute silence. If you shut up your inner voices for a minute, you will be able to see more intently. Whatever came into sight was taken as a sign. Sometimes this was an event of symbolic nature. More commonly it was simply a person or beast. Whatever it was, it had a meaning. A good frithir knew a wide range of sights and what they portended. Birds

Voices of the waterfall. Cader Idris, Wales.

were generally good, but crows were difficult. A crow was often a sign for danger, possibly disaster, while the hooded crow could be a representative of the hungry hag, the Cailleagh or the Morrigan. The raven could be very unlucky, but some crafty Highlanders disagree, as they believe it to house the soul of King Arthur. An untimely owl, seen or heard in daytime was always risky. Luckily, the danger could be thwarted by making a knot in a handkerchief or by throwing salt into the fire. Swifts were the souls of the damned, speckled birds create confusion. Seagulls occasionally housed the souls of drowned fishermen and could count as a warning. Any bird flying widdershins was a certain sign of trouble, and in danger of being pelted with stones. Hares and cats were often unlucky, maybe as they were closely associated with witches. A bee coming into a house was excellent luck. Cockerels were lucky provided they behaved normally. If they crowed between nightfall and midnight this was a danger sign, if they crowed near the door, a visitor was approaching.

People were judged according to activity, so that a person standing implied good health, a person lying symbolized disease. Hair colour was an important element, and direction. It would be rather useless to go into details here. If you explore this technique, as I hope you will, a number of typical sights and omina will appear before your eyes. You will learn what is likely to happen in front of your door, and what meaning you can attribute to it. It will be your very own creative language of signs, and a special way in which the universe can communicate to you. Is the vision coincidental or do you subconsciously chose the right moment to look out? To what extent will your prayer make things happen? Whatever it may be, it certainly makes sense if you are willing to make it so. Divination tends to shape the way in which we interprete reality.

Of course the frith was done differently in various parts of the countryside. A variation from South Uist requires the frithir to walk round the house sunwise with closed eyes, reciting Hail Mary until s/he safely arrives at the door sill. Then the seer looks through a circle made of finger and thumb, and receives an answer from the very first object on which the eye rests. Looking through such a circle is a practise that appears in several Central European forms of divination. In each case a frame is used to define a vision - be it that the seer looks through a tube formed by the hands, through the bent elbow of another or bends down to look through between the legs. This frame defines the range of the vision, it can also be of use when it comes to creative hallucination.

When you find this divination in legend, it is usually fighting armies that appear before the eyes of the seer. Sometimes it is real armies, at others, the diviner sees the wild hunt roaring past in all its crazed splendour and terrifying exhileration. You even find such methods in spells to make the elves visible. This means that the circle is not just an element to confine the eye, it is also a space in which the mind can project its dreams and premonitions. This is not far from looking into a crystal ball, a pool of ink or a mirror. The frithir, if we can trust the record, generally saw something material and symbolic. The person gazing through the ring may well neglect the physical objects in sight and focus with the eyes of imagination. Imagination produces vision, and it is a wise seer who knows when to observe the external world, when to ignore it, and when to blend its images with the bright vision of magical imagination. The ring also has the advantage that it keeps your attention on what you are doing. When seeking vision by empty-mindedness and self-hypnosis, it can be so easy to lose oneself in a stream of images and thoughts. If you open your mind to receive data, chances are that you will get all sorts of stuff, and not just the material you are looking for. This can easily result in drifting, daydreaming and forgetting what you initially sought to learn. If you have such a frame as a ring of thumb and fingers before your eyes, it will help to keep the object of your divination in mind.

In the frith prayers recorded by Carmichael, a divine precedent is alluded to. One day young Jesus was missing, so Mary made an augury and gazed downward through her palm. She saw Jesus in the temple, disputing with frowning doctors, and went to fetch her child home. Or you have Bride who forms a pipe with her palms, gazes through, and sees her foster son Jesus at the side of a well, teaching and lecturing. Yet another version has the diviner form a tube with the left hand and blow through it in the name of the trinity three times to start the visions. Each of these cases does without objects seen in the external world. The vision, though observed between the fingers of the hand, comes from the imagination.

Imagination is the key to the more refined forms of divination. Like all subtle skills, it requires training and experience to function properly. It also requires a measure of detachment, as a diviner who is caught up in a problem hasn't got the open mind needed to perceive an answer. Visionary divination often involves activities or conditions that make dreaming easier. Water has such qualities, and consequently the bards and poets often sought their inspiration in the narrow range between water and land, between the fluid and the solid. Here we have Taliesin's cream coloured steed racing, swifter than a screeching gull between the sand and the foaming sea. Here we have the Irish poet Nede walking. As he heard the waves sighing and mourning, he cast a spell on the sea, and the waves revealed to him that his father had died.

And here we have the wise women of the Suebi seeking hidden knowledge. As Plutarch tells us, the Suebian king Ariovist was getting ready for a decisive battle against Julius Caesar when the seeresses of his tribe decreed it dangerous to do battle before the new moon. They had obtained this knowledge from the eddies, turbulences and the roaring voice of water. How can water reveal so much? We could propose something crude and ominous, such as a system of meanings going 'strong ripples from north east mean so and so'. I find it much more likely that they used the monotonous motions of the water as a trance inducing mind-machine. If you have an eddying stream available, go there, sit down on the banks, ask your question, gaze into the swirling spirals and empty your mind. If the sun is glittering on the water, you may well find that the sparkle and foam induce a pleasant and half-sleeping state of mind. Your eyes may gradually want to close, and when they do, the imagination takes over. Flickering lights in a regular and rhythmic motion may be the very thing to induce trances naturally. Or listen to a waterfall. The 'pink noise' coming from the cascading fluids is the very substance to produce convincing auditory hallucinations. You can hear voices singing and speaking - the very thing for those who want an acoustic answer to their questions. Caesar's account of the incident differs from Plutarch's. In his book, it was the Suebian mothers who divined the will of the gods using lots (runes?) and divination. They also cast lots to determine auspicious days for human sacrifices. This account was often taken as evidence for early rune divination among the Germans. The Suebi, as Caesar shows them, were a fierce and primitive German tribe, a branch of which had invaded Gaul and interfered with his own interests. He attributes a grotesque savagery to them, in strong contrast with the more cultivated barbarians of Gaul. Recent studies show that the Suebi were an agglomeration of tribes living in south west Germany, many of them, like the Nemeti and Triboci, of Celtic origin. The 'name' of the Suebian 'king' turns out to be a Celtic title: Ar (war) iubaist (leader). The name of their goddess, Nerthus (see Tacitus for an account of the cult) is relate to the Celtic *nerto-, power, strength, and *narito- magically stengthened, from IE *ner- creative force, magical power (Meid 1992). So we have the Celto-Germanic Suebi

casting lots. How these lots were related to the Germanic runes is an enigmatic question. Several rune names show the influence of the Celtic language. This means that amongt some Celts, a runic system of symbols and names was used. It influenced what later became the futharc alphabet. Possibly divination by casting staffs or lots were a lot more common among the Celts of central Europe than we may ever know. How did the lots look? What signs were carved on them? What signs would you carve?

According to the *Auraicept*, the filid had several divinatory methods in their program. They were mastered by the top ranks, the ollam, after a minimum of eight years of poetic study. Here the methods are named tenmlaida, immas forosnai and dichetal do chennaib. Several variant forms are on record. Lets look at them more closely.

Imbas Forosna

This is described in some detail by Cormac. He claims that St. Patrick outlawed it, which makes Maier wonder to what extent Cormac was informed about a practise that, according to him, had been abolished for more than four centuries. There are some slight differences between the manuscripts, but basically the rite happened as follows.

This is the way it is to be done. The poet chews a piece of the flesh of a red pig, or of a dog or a cat, and brings it afterwards on a flag (stone) behind the door, and chants an incantation upon it, and offers it to idol gods; and his idol gods are brought to him, but he finds them not on the morrow (?). And he pronounces incantations on his two palms; and his idol gods are also brought to him, in order that his sleep may not be interrupted. And he lays his two palms on his two cheeks, and thus falls asleep. And he is watched in order that no one may disturb or interrupt him, until everything about which he is engaged is revealed to him, which may be a minute, or two, or three, or as long as the ceremony requires - one palm over the other across the cheeks. (quoted after Bonwick)

In Whitley Stokes translation the diviner calls the idol gods to him and leaves them not on the morrow. The divination, lasting only minutes (the term nomad may possibly mean 'a moment') in the version given above, takes three days and nights in other versions. The red flesh may well be raw. Then there is O'Curry's translation, which holds that the diviner retires into a bed behind the door, and postulates that he takes the idol gods to bed with him. Given these details, and a bit of healthy doubt regarding Bishop Cormac's knowledge, we can easily create a trance divination based on Imbas Forosna. I have detailed this in *Seidways*, forgive me for repeating myself. To begin with, take a look at the term. Imbas forosna has been identified as *the light of foresight* (Kinsella), the word imbas being a probable relation of the British term awen. Imbas forosna is a rite of divination, but also of inspiration. You can use it to find out about the hidden side of things. You can also make it a meditation to stimulate any sort of creative thinking.

To begin with, retire to a place where you enjoy a measure of peace. Close the door and place an offering behind the jamb on a flat stone and invoke your gods, if you feel traditional. If you don't, use a trick from M. Bertiaux's voodoo: rub your palms together until they tingle and glow. Invoke the gods of your circle, speaking freely and passionately. Hold out the palms so they may partake of the energy that comes streaming. Or combine both methods. Make it an offering of love, attention and energy. This is what the gods want, and what they respond to. If you want to do it in Cormac's style, chewing and offering fresh raw meat is the task of the day. Considering the quality of meat you get in the shops, and what pigs, cats and dogs are fed with, I wouldn't recommend it. Nevertheless, it may be worth thinking about the nature of the animals. Pig, cat and dog all have a somewhat otherworldly character, and fresh meat is certainly stronger in vitality than the cooked variety. As bio-energy (Ch'i, vitality) is one of the essentials for a good contact with deities, the palm rubbing technique is a useful alternative.

Next, make contact with the gods. The text implies that the gods appear, be it materially as idols or as images in the mind. If you have some experience in practical magick, a number of your deities will come to mind and body. Tell them what you want to know. Keep this question short, simple and precise. Sit or recline in some posture that allows you to hold your hands to your face. This is not altogether comfortable, so we can dismiss Cormac's idea of the poet going to sleep in this posture. I prefer to sit on the ground, leaning against a wall, so I can rest my arms on my elbows. This is as I like long visions, if you prefer three minute insights, you can do it in any other posture. Hold your palms in front of your face and breathe on them. Look into the palms and ask your question. You can say it, imagine it, or even imagine that you write it on your hands. Repeat this for a while. Then bring your hands closer and rest them on your face. I like to press the bases of my hands against the cheeks, so that the fingers loosely shadow the eyes. I keep them relaxed and apart, so that a measure of air and light come in. Now close your eyes slowly. Twilight falls and the darkened fingers loom like towering trees in a nemeton of shadows. As you gaze into the *cauldrons of five trees*, between light and dark, between tension and relaxation, the answer comes flowing from the palms. It is an answer that suits your imagination. You will notice that the strange posture has the advantage of keeping the question in the forefront of your attention. It also produces a circuit: you ask yourself (the gods, deep mind, muse etc.) by asking into your hands, and from the palms of your hands the answer comes to your imagination.

End the rite when you have learned enough. Rub your hands, give your thanks and get up slowly. The importance of this rite is that it produces wonderfully stimulating visions. What can you use it for? Queen Medb coerced young Lady Fedelm (who had been to Scotland to learn verse and vision) to use Imbas Forosnai to foretell the fate of her army. Fedelm gazed and muttered 'I see crimson, I see blood!' Medb, undaunted by this prospect, ordered Fedelm to continue. Again and again the seeress gazed into crimson blood, until finally a vision appeared and she beheld Cu Chullain in full fighting rage, shaking and screaming, as he single-handedly opposed Medb's troops. Not every vision appears fully developed. It can happen that you gaze, but fail to see anything. Maybe you are overlooking a feeling, or missing something worth listening to. Whatever you perceive, you can explore it. Your sense interact with each other. Sound, feeling, vision, smell and taste can evoke each other. If you receive one of them, go into it until it leads to the others and the vision involves all senses.. If you see a colour, stay with it, keep asking, keep your mind open, and before long, images appear. If you feel something, this feeling may be the key leading to your answer. Give yourself time. It takes practise to develop any divinatory system. You will find that the imagination tends to work more easily the more you employ it. If you use Imbas Forosna to foretell the future, you are abusing it. Much more important for the mage, poet and bard is the use of vision to illuminate the present. What do you want to know? What do you wish to remember? The nature of a place, a comment on a pressing personal problem, a better way to work a rite, a new method of trance induction, learning something you never knew about yourself, creating a new piece of art, a tune, a song, a poem or a painting…what else can you learn now you can do it? Give your creativity a chance, taker a piece of paper and list at least 30 things you would like to learn about. When you have done that, burn the paper and invent another hundred. The only limit of your creativity is the limit that

Coins 21
top l: Salassi, draw
this image properly as
an equilateral triangle
and you'll discover a
lot of interesting
geometry. Obviously
a Celtic version of the
Chinese Tangram
puzzle.
top r: Salassi. Several
versions of this were
popular.
center l: Ile de
Bretagne, tree and
moon
center r: unknown,
very stylized tree and
circles (fruit?)
bottom l: unknown,
possibly Tectosagi,
found in sacrifical
deposit at enclosure of
Saint-Louis
bottom r: Ile de
Bretagne

you impose. It's your choice. You'll be amazed how much you find once you start looking.

Leaving the subject, I would draw your attention to the Irish hero Finn. Much like Gwion in Britain, Finn received his Imbas when he cooked an enchanted salmon of knowledge, burned his thumb and put it into his mouth to cool it. In later life, Finn could see visions whenever he put his thumb in his mouth. Some versions have it that he also chewed it. This turned out eminently practical when it came to identifying headless corpses and looking into the fairy world. Bonwick mentions an episode when Finn, invited to take a seat beside an exceptionally fair lady, suspiciously chews his thumb. Instantly the lady transforms into a malignant crone. When Dermad and Greine fled from Finn, they knew that he would use his visionary thumb-chewing to detect their hiding places. That night she slept on rushes and he slept on a bag of sand. Finn, finding out that one was on rushes, the other on sand, promptly assumed that they had split and sent his troops in the wrong direction.   Is it possible that the Taliesins used a similar gesture when they became oracular?

Dichetal Di Chennaib

This was the only form of divination permitted to the filid by St. Patrick, as it makes do without sacrifice to idols. Cormac informs us that it was a divination from the ends of the fingers. One possible answer to how this might work is given in the chapter on trees. The fingertips lead us to the next type of divination, indicating that there

may have been some confusion of terms.

Teinm Laeda

This is a method that was outlawed by St. Patrick, if we can trust *Cormac's Glossary*, as it involved sacrifice to pagan deities. It is mentioned in the *Senchas Mar*, the famed early eight century compilation of Irish law texts. Teinm Laeda was used by the learned poet to compose a poem without thinking. Before St. Patrick, the poet used to take a wand and place it on the head or body of the person he wanted to know about. In a minute or two the name of the person was revealed, as well as the ancestry and every unknown thing. After the introduction of Christianity, the staffs went out of use. Instead, the poets made verses at once with the ends of their fingers (or bones) without studying, and they composed and spoke at the same time.

The *Senchas Mar* claim that the same things used to be revealed by means of Imbas Forosna, but that they were performed in a different manner, and that a different offering was made at each. Cormac complicates issues when he claims that Finn, when he put his thumb in his mouth, chanted teinm laida and instantly composed a song. Perhaps the term simply meant an oracle in verse, a poem that springs into awareness, revealing hidden lore by the simple act of bypassing the conscious mind. You can come to interesting results when you speak faster than you can think and record it. This is the basis of the art of the Welsh awenyddion and easy to learn. You can use it to write-simply take pen and paper and jot down everything, no matter how crazy, that comes into your mind.

Or you could give your oracle in a poetic way. Some poetic structures, especially those that require no rhymes, are easy to learn. Take a look at the gnomic poetry of the British bards (examples appear in the chapter on trees). To begin with, I have to explain that the gnomic poems of the British bards do rhyme. Generally, the triplet structure is employed, i.e. you have three lines which rhyme at the end. For magical purposes rhymes are not really needed. This is an exercise in spontaneity. Usually gnomic poetry begins with a set formula which is repeated in every verse. One long winded gnomic poem starts all stanzas using the set formula *Bright are the tops of...* Another one uses *Mountain snow...* or *The calends of winter....* This makes it easy to get going. Next, add two short or one long line listing other phenomena of nature and then top it off with a line of proverbial, possibly oracular advise. As this sounds rather complicated (luckily it isn't), here are three typical examples. You'll find more further on. The first begins with the set phrase '*bright are the tops*', freely develops some nature poetry and ends with a line of gnomic wisdom or a convenient proverb:

31. Bright the tops of the meadow sweet; and music
In the grove; bold the wind, the trees shake;
Interceding with the obdurate will not avail.
(RBoH 9)

The next two examples are from a poem that starts all stanzas with '*Mountain snow*'. Again, the same pattern is used to lead to a statement of wisdom. It may sound self

evident unless it is uttered at a time when this specific phrase happens to make a lot of sense to the listener. Proverbial advise has a long tradition in Celtic writing, the oldest samples occur on a fragment of Gaulish writing found at Lezoux. Only three lines of this text survive, in the translation of W. Meid they read:

> Praise by the worst (is) self damaging to the righteous. Now, my boy, do not yield to violence (?). One should go one's way by one's own judgement.

Such statements are simple to improvise and can make good oracles - do invent some of your own!

24. Mountain snow-noisy the roebuck;
The waves wash the margin of the strand;
Let the skilful conceal his design.

27. Mountain snow-bare the stalk-tops;
Bent the branches of trees; the fish are in the deep.
Where there is no learning there will be no natural gift. (RBoH 4)

Perhaps such lines remind you of Chinese and Japanese poetry. They are part of a tradition of nature poetry that has no equal in medieval Europe, and can only be found among the bards and filid of the Island Celts.

I suggest you practise with the verses in chapter 13, reading them aloud, until you are really familiar with the sort of thing you can expect from them. In each of them you find several lines suggesting the natural world and one final line of ethical nature. It might be thought that these proverbs are closely associated with the trees, plants and animals mentioned earlier in each verse, but this is not the case. Several long gnomic poems survive, and while much of them is highly original, the proverbs that end each verse tend to appear in other verses too, depending on the rhyme at the end of the line. This implies that the bards had a store of proverbs, and simply improvised some more or less suitable one at the end of each verse. If you practise this sort of poetry for a while you will find that the nature descriptions require awareness and perceptiveness. Call it heightened awareness if you like. But when we come to the end of the verse, it has been my experience, that a proverb or saying simply appears out of nothing and attaches itself to the verse. Anything coming as a surprise may be useful for divination. But it may also be good trance magick to practise gnomic poetry for the fun of it. Take a key-line, such as *Bright are the tops of...* and go for a walk in the country. How many plants do you see? Wonderful! Each of them has a bright top, so go ahead and improvise a verse for each of them. You may find that this induces a trance state: It may well be one of brightness and delight.

Cetnad

Another divination making use of song. It was made to discover theft, usually stolen cattle. The diviner sang it three times through the right fist on the track of the stolen animal, or on the track of the thief. If no track was available, the diviner sang through the fist and went to sleep. In the dreams, the thief was revealed. Another form of Cetnad was sung into the palm of

the hand. Then the singer rubbed the palm on the quarters of a horse, which was a sure way of protecting it and its rider from harm (see Hyde).

Toghairm

Dr. Armstrong's Gaelic Dictionary, quoted by Bonwick tells us that:

> The diviner was wrapped in the warm, smoking robe of a newly slain ox or cow, and laid at full length in the wild recess of some lonely waterfall. The question was then put to him, and the oracle was left in solitude to consider it. The answer was firmly believed to have been communicated by invisible beings.

Reading this, I wonder whether the answer came in the form of a vision or was imagined into the roaring and chanting voices of the thundering waterfall. Wrapping people in a cloak or hide is a common element in magic. I once read an Icelandic technique to conjure the devil. If I recall it properly, you had to go to a crossroads at midnight. At the center of the crossing, you had to lie down and wrap yourself up in a cow hide. You also had to have an axe in your hands, the cutting side poised straight at your face. In this awkward position you had to wait till the devil appeared. It says a lot about these rituals that you were lucky if indeed the devil, and not some human witness appeared. No doubt they made up for lack of finesse by adding a heady dose of fear of discovery.

Related to such fun activities is an Irish rite used to determine the king. Let me quote from *The Destruction of Da Derga's Hostel* (trans. Gantz):

> After that, the king, Eterscelae, died. The men of Eriu then assembled at the bull feast: a bull was killed, and one man ate his fill and drank its broth and slept, and an incantation of truth was chanted over him. Whoever this man saw in his sleep became king; if the man lied about what he saw in his sleep, he would die…The bull-feaster had in his sleep seen a naked man coming along the road to Temuir at daybreak and bearing a stone in his sling.

As the story goes, Conare happens to be riding his chariot when he sees a flock of unusual, white speckled birds flying past. He grabs his sling and gives chase, until the birds come to the ocean, where Conare overtakes them. All of a sudden, the birds take off their feather hoods and turn on him with spears and swords. One of them steps forward saying:

> I am Nemglan, king of your father's bird troop. You are forbidden to cast at birds, for, by reason of birth, every bird here is natural to you…Go to Temuir tonight, for that would be more fitting…There is a bull feast there, and it will make you king. The man who naked comes along the road to Temuir at daybreak with a stone in his sling, it is he who will be king.

Conare does so, and meets three Irish kings who are standing at the roadside with a load of garments for the naked king-to-be. Seeing that Conare is young and beardless, they exclaim that perhaps their bull-feast and incantation of truth have failed, but Conare assures them a young, generous king is no blemish, and that he is not corrupt.

Nice of him to say so. I leave it to the historians to argue whether Irish kings have ever been chosen in this fashion. Suffice it, that the filid believed in the validity of dreaming true. A Welsh parallel may be the *Dream of Rhonabwy*, you can find it in the *Mabinogi*. Here the protagonist and his companions perforce take shelter in a shabby hut where two crones and one bald fellow live a life of total filth and poverty. Two knights make do with the bed, and spend the night cursing armies of fleas infesting the mouldering straw. Rhonabwy gives a yellow calfskin a try, which he finds spread on a platform. As soon as he lies down, a vision comes to him. In his half-sleep, he meets King Arthur and the bold Knights of the Round Table, each of them a mighty giant, compared to the wretchedly small people who peopled medieval Britain.

In each of these samples, we had a cow skin associated with dream incubation. I find the incantation of truth the most important element - plain hypnotic suggestion will have done the job. Try this by all means! It's sound practise to ask the deep mind for interesting dreams before you go to bed, and for good recall in the morning. The cow hide has at least two functions. For one thing, it is obviously a sacred religious symbol. For another, it is in all likeliness a none too comfortable bed. Cow hides tend to get stiff and they are not famed for their padding either. I would guess that anyone sleeping on such a bed is likely to have a light and troubled sleep. This may be useful for recall - it's so much easier to recall a dream when you wake directly after it's over.

When I explored lucid dreaming, I used to set three alarm clocks to wake me several times during the night, the first one approximately 4½ hours after beginning to sleep. You end up knackered but you learn a lot, especially if you are wise and keep paper and pen at the bedside. The more attention you give to your dreams, the more dream information will remain in your memory.

South London's arch-sorcerer, Austin Spare, made an art of the trance states experienced between dreaming and waking, and drew quite a few pictures in this dazed realm. I wondered how he came to have so many detailed and easily remembered dreams until Gavin Semple showed me photos of Austin's quarters. The artist magician, living in abject poverty, used to sleep on two chairs. This sort of thing produces plenty of disturbed dreams, and a characteristic curve in the spine. In passing I would like to add that dream incubation was a favoured form of divination in the classical world. Ancient Greece had several temples where people could pray and fast for visions. Then they spent the night in a tiny cell, where they received their dream-oracle. If the dreams could not be recalled, the deity answered indirectly. Coming from the temple, the diviner listened to the very first words s/he heard, and took them as the answer.

It is a vague possibility that something similar took place at Lydney Park, where the Romano-Celtic population erected a temple associated with Nodens, god of the great deep, in the 3rd century. This site yielded a votive offerings in the shape an arm, so possibly it functioned as a temple of healing. Other deities appearing at the temple are a sea god in bronze relief, a sun god on a chariot, a dog, a statuette of a woman holding a horn of plenty and an inscription to Sylvanus, Roman god of the forest. Due to the votive arm, it has been hypothesized that the temple was dedicated to medicine. This is plain guesswork. We can only be sure that the temple was extremely wealthy, had a luxurious mosaic floor and was frequented by plenty of people. The ground plan of the temple revealed an unusual number of small cells. Accordingly, it has been speculated that there was a dream oracle attached to the healing temple. Though there is no proof for this assumption, it has a measure of possibility.

To end this chapter, I would like to mention a few other forms of divination. One text seems to imply that an Irish Druid made a prophecy by watching the clouds. Sadly, there is no comment on how this was done. One possibility, as far as we can guess, is that cloud gazing was combined with the lore of the winds. In old Ireland, there were twelve winds arranged around the compass, and each of them had a specific colour. There are at least two systems associating winds and colours. Take a look at them and keep in mind that colour itself tends to have great importance in symbolism and oracle. In the *Saltair Na Rann*, we learn that god created the four principal winds and the eight subwinds, each of them with a specific colour:

The white, the clear purple, the blue, the great green, the yellow, the red truly-bold, ...the black, the grey, the speckled (?), the dark (?), the dull-black, the dun-coloured.

The *Sanchas Mar* is more detailed:
The colour of each differs from the other, namely, the white and the crimson, the blue and the green, the yellow and the red, the black and the grey, the speckled and the dark, the ciar (dull black) and the grisly. From the east comes the crimson wind, from the south the white, from the north the black, from the west the dun. The red and yellow winds are produced between the white and the crimson, the green and the grey between the grisly and the white, the grey and the ciar between the grisly and jet-black, the dark and the mottled between the black and the crimson. (quoted after Hyde).

Though there is no evidence that these coloured winds were ever used for divination, it is certainly possible to do so. It is easy to attribute meaning to each colour and direction. It is also an option to make use of these colours in breathing exercises, much like the Chinese Taoists imagine and breathe coloured vapours in their rites of inner alchemy. A similar system may have been known among the British bards. At least we have a Taliesin enquiring how many winds there are, and asking when the breath is black. Breathing technique was used by the Druid Figal to stimulate the courage of the Tuatha De Dannan: each exhalation was to increase their valour and strength. Exhaling noxious druidic breaths is something that comes up in the myth of Mog Ruith, so we may well be on the track of a forgotten bit of elder magick here.

Another form of divination loosely alluded to in medieval Irish literature makes use of yew wands. These were used by a Druid, who cut ogham letters on them, to find the hiding place of Etain and Midir beneath their fairy mound. Maybe we come close to rune divination here, or to divination by casting lots with various symbols. Simple divination by lots was employed in medieval Britain and Ireland, especially in difficult judical cases. When the truth about a crime could not be detected, the probable culprit was granted the right of divine judgement. S/he had to draw a pebble from a bag or a seething cauldron. White was innocent, black was guilty and speckled was the sign of the trinity and meant 'have another go'. This sort of lottery was immensely popular and often associated with painful elements to cater to the taste of the audience. As in all public entertainment, the common denominator is the worst taste imaginable. You will forgive me for ignoring the various forms a divine judgement used to have. Much more interesting is how you can invent divinatory systems as good or even better than those dreamed up by bards and Druids. What have they overlooked? And what do you overlook now?

How can the world itself speak to you? How can intelligence multiply with intelligence?

Wake up. It's here, waiting for you.

Coins 22
top l: Dobunni,
Britain, tree with
fruit, evergreen?
Yew?
top r: Dobunni,
Britain, evergreen
tree!
center L. Belgic
coast, abstract
trees!
center r: Britain,
abstract trees!
bottom L: Britain,
abstract trees!
bottom r: Belgic
coast, proto-runes!

12. The Ever Hungry Cauldron

The tale of Taliesin begins with a cauldron of enchantment, it also ends with one. After shutting up the court-bards and scaring king Maelgwn into submission, Taliesin freed Prince Elphin from his silver chains. Let us take a look at the finale of the *Hanes Taliesin*:

Then he bade Elphin wager the king, that he had a horse both better and swifter than the king's horses. And this Elphin did, and the day, and the time, and the place were fixed, and the place was that which at this day is called Morva Rhiannedd; and thither the king went with all his people, and four and twenty of the swiftest horses he possessed. And after a long process the course was marked, and the horses were placed for running. Then came Taliesin with four and twenty twigs of holly, which he had burned black, and he caused the youth who was to ride his master's horse to place them in his belt, and he gave him orders to let all the king's horses get before him, and as he should overtake one horse after the other, to take one of the twigs and strike the horse with it over the crupper, and then let that twig fall; and after that to take another twig, and do in like manner to every one of the horses, as he should overtake them, enjoining the horseman strictly to watch when his own horse should stumble, and to throw down his cap on the spot. All these things did the youth fulfil, giving a blow to every one of the king's horses, and throwing down his cap on the spot where his horse stumbled. And to this spot Taliesin brought his master after his horse had won the race. And he caused Elphin to put workmen to dig a hole there; and when they had dug the ground deep enough, they found a large cauldron full of gold. And then said Taliesin, 'Elphin, behold a payment and reward unto thee, for having taken me out of the weir, and for having reared me from that time until now.' And on this spot stands a pool of water, which is

to this time called Pwllbair.

As life goes round the circuit, the cauldron initiated lad produces a cauldron of wealth for his patron. This gives us two cauldrons in one story, but if we look closely, we can discover a third one. What about the leather bag? Some may argue that a leather bag is miles away from a cauldron, and this is certainly true, as the bag is so much older. The leather bag goes all the way to the Paleolithic. Several so-called primitive cultures on this planet made use of leather bags to cook food in. This works because the leather is damp, if the temperature is just right, and the skin at the proper distance from the flame. Another version of this technique is to dig a small hole into which

the leather bag is inserted. The water is heated by dropping hot stones into the fluid. This method is not without danger, as some stones tend to explode on contact with the water. Nevertheless it was used by several old cultures, such as the reindeer hunters at Gönnersdorf, near the middle Rhine, around 12 500 BCE (Kuckenburg 2000). In all likeliness the leather bag is the earliest cauldron known to mankind, the very first vessel of transformation discovered by our ancestors. As Taliesin himself is placed in such a bag, it may be useful to consider whether he may represent the food offering or sacrifice itself. This leads to a couple of strange suspicions. For one thing, what exactly made the just-enlightened Gwion so thoroughly scared of

---

Sacred cauldrons
Top: fragment of a Celtic cauldron, found in Rynkeby, Denmark. Probably late La Tène period.
right: bronze cauldron, diameter 30 cm, Hallstatt, grave 671, Austria. The cow is fixed to rim and center of the vessel and served as a handle. Note that both cauldrons combine the ideas of cattle and the pit.

Ceridwen, and so certain of his own doom should she chance to catch him? Before she even returned to her cauldron he was already aware of her bloodthirsty intentions. Did he see himself as the last ingredient for her sorcerous elixir? Did the eldritch witch plan to slay him as a final act? While we cannot be certain of it, it appears glaringly obvious that Taliesin himself went through two cauldrons - Ceridwen's womb and the leather bag-before he came to be reborn as an enlightened seer. The cauldron of knowledge is also a cauldron of death and rebirth.

To understand the meaning of cauldrons in the pagan religions of ancient Europe, I shall now treat you to a couple of bizarre pieces of history. Our first piece of evidence comes from the late bronze age. Long before the Celts and Germans appear as linguistic and cultural groups, the people in Central Europe were happily burying their dead in mounds and celebrating whatever rituals it may have been. We have some archaeological evidence from these periods, but very little of it is of a religious nature. The Urnfield people, and most Bronze-age cultures before them were remarkably shy about making images of deities, people and

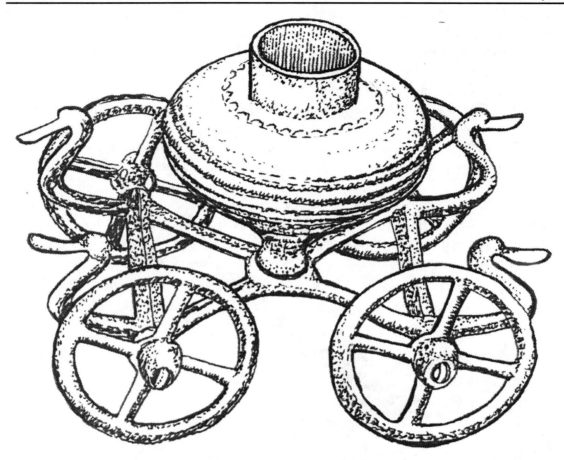

beasts, which makes it rather hard to guess about their magical and religious outlook. From the countless question marks emerge just one or two snippets that can enlighten us. One of them is the regular appearance of waterfowl images. Such image were popular across wide areas of Bronze age Europe. You can find waterbirds associated with chariots and ships from Scandinavia to the Balkans. Ducks, geese, swans and similar birds appear frequently on grave goods. They stand out as there are so few other animals in evidence. Now we could think of these birds in several ways. Maybe there used to be a thriving cult based on water-bird totems. Maybe it was basically a

cult of the dead. If you find images of waterfowl in tombs, this does not necessarily imply that such animals were worshipped by the living, it only proves that the dead were associated with them. Some middle European bronze age cultures enjoyed making clay-rattles in the shape of ducks or geese. A simple explanation is that such

Waterbirds of the Urnfield culture.
Above: cauldron/chariot with waterbirds, Acholshausen, Bavaria, bronze, height 12cm.
Opposite top: bronze ring with ducks, part of a chariot. Staudach, Upper Austria, height 7.1cm
Opposite bottom: horned duck. Bronze, lakeside settlement Hagnau-Burg, Baden-Wüttemberg, length 5.6cm.

rattles were merely musical instruments. On close examination, it appears that most of them were not made for simple festivity. The clay rattles contained small stones. If you shake such a rattle for a while, the stones erode the inside of the rattle. It can be measured how often such a rattle was used before it came to rest in a tomb. Well, most of them seem to have been made expressively for the burial, and played only once, presumably during the inhumation ceremony.

Water-birds say something about concepts of the otherworlds. Here we have creatures who can live in all three physical states, they can walk on land, swim in water and fly through the air. In a sense, all worlds are open to them. What does this tell you about the nature of the soul and its journey after death? Such rattles seem to have been popular with several sorts of bronze age cultures. They were also in use with the Urnfield people (considered by some as the ancestors of the Hallstatt Celts), and indeed, similar rattles, in the shape of waterfowl or little pigs are known from early Hallstatt time burials. Pigs are also otherworldly, just take a look at Island Celtic myths.

Another tradition that seems to have passed from the Urnfield people to the early Celts is small bronze models of chariots bearing a cauldron or a wide bowl. Several such items have been found. Historians are somewhat shy about attributing a meaning to such items. For one thing, they are valuable works of art, and certainly not children's toys. For another, chariots and cauldrons appear very prominently in Celtic and Germanic mythology. Several of these bronze wagons are adorned with more or less naturalistic images of waterfowl. In the Urnfield period, such items seem to have served a cultish purpose, though we cannot know what, it may well be possible that they were used in some dance, parade or ritual involving motion.

In the later Hallstatt period, the items are still popular, but the craftsmanship goes beyond the abstract rendering and reaches

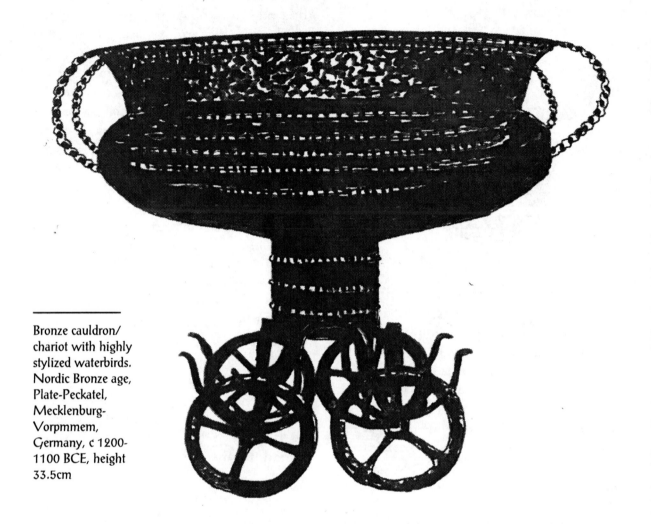

Bronze cauldron/
chariot with highly
stylized waterbirds.
Nordic Bronze age,
Plate-Peckatel,
Mecklenburg-
Vorpmmem,
Germany, c 1200-
1100 BCE, height
33.5cm

an amazing degree of artistic refinement in the chariot from Steiermark. Here we have a model of a cult-wagon with human figures, male and female, riders and deer. Better still, the center of the chariot is taken by a large female figure, much taller than the other figures, who bears a cauldron on her head. This may be one of the earliest renderings of a Celtic goddess. For all its abstraction - and the Hallstatt period was pretty shy and abstract when it came to rendering lifelike images of humans and beasts - this cult chariot is one of the most impressive items of early Celtic religion. In the Hallstatt period, cauldrons appear among the most popular grave goods of the so-called princely tombs. Often enough these vessels contained fluids, such as honey mead, but when we lack the ritual evidence, it becomes hard to guess whether we are dealing with luxury goods, ritual items or both. A household article can serve a religious purpose. Many of these vessels were expensive import goods crafted in Greece. The Hochdorf noble had a golden cauldron large enough to contain 500 litres of honey mead. It was topped by three golden lions. One of them seems to have broken off on some occasion. A Celtic goldsmith replace the missing beast with one that looks less like a lion than a puzzled rat. Such wealth was far exceeded by what is the largest vessel known from all antiquity. This crater was unearthed in the tomb of the 'Lady of Vix', Gaul, it has a height of 1,64 m, weighs 208 kg and could theoretically contain 1100 litres of fluid. The vessel is easily large enough to hold a human being. It was crafted in Greece and transported to Gaul in several parts, where they were finally welded together. It is one of those questions what the 'Lady of Vix' paid for such an amazing item. If you see the item in a museum, with its height, its frieze of Attic heroes and the huge Medusa heads that served as handles, their eyes bulging, fangs gleaming and tongues lolling, you may get the impression that this vessel has a sinister past indeed. There is something extremely sinister about the vessel, even when you know that the bronze walls are rather thin. Filled with fluids it would have burst apart.

Similar vessels abound in Celtic and Germanic myth. The Gundestrup cauldron is probably among the best known ones. It shows a number of unknown deities in a style that reminds me of the large Medusas of the vessel from Vix. Researchers are still quarreling whether the Gundestrup cauldron came from the Balkans or from Gaul. If from Gaul, it may have been influenced by the item from Vix. It would be too much to mention all cauldrons in this chapter, especially as I'm sure that once you've enjoyed the rites, you will explore the cauldron myths anyway. Some of these cauldrons are life giving, others have a bloody reputation. When the Romans encountered the huge migration of Cimbri, Teutons, Ambrones et al who came migrating southward in the late second century BCE, they recorded a cauldron divination (see Strabo for details). If we can trust the evidence, the Cimbri (a Celtic tribe according to modern research) used to employ a number of aging priestesses. They had grey hair, walked on bare feet, wore white robes, held by a brooch at the shoulder and by a belt of iron. Whenever a sign was needed, these charming grey haired ladies selected some suitable prisoners, crowned them with wreaths and led them up a ladder to a large ceremonial cauldron. Holding their victims over the rim, they cut their throats and read the future out of the crimson fountain spewing into the dark and crusty vessel. Others divined by slashing their victims open with a sword, carefully noting the involuntary twitches and cramps. Well, the entertainment industry wasn't too advanced in those days. We shouldn't criticize those priestesses too hard before we consider the stuff that appears on TV every day.

Cauldrons of the Fili

Cauldrons can also have a blessed countenance. Caitlin and John Matthews have unearthed a fascinating 15th century document entitled *The Three Cauldrons*, you can find it in their *Encyclopaedia of Celtic Wisdom*. If the interpretation is correct, a number of late medieval Irish poets believed that their bodies contain three cauldrons. In the head you can find the cauldron of knowledge (Coire Sois), in the chest the cauldron of vocation (Coire Ernmae) and in the belly the cauldron of heating (Coire Goiriath). The text is not without difficulties, as it seems to come from the pens of several poets, who do not entirely agree with each other. In one of them, attributed to the legendary Amairgen White-Knee of earliest Irish proto-history, you can find praise of the belly cauldron, which is associated with warmth and called the source of oral utterance and colourful verse. It also mentions the cauldron of knowledge, and praises its function to dispense the laws of each art. A poem attributed to Nede mac Adne emphasizes the function of the cauldron of vocation as a source of inspiration, eloquence, scholarship and poetic professionalism. It could be proposed that the cauldron of vocation resembles something like the True Will in Crowley's system, aligning the original self nature with the nature and evolution of the world. For poets, the True Will is obviously poetry, and so 'Nede' outlines the essentials of the poet's craft. It would have been interesting to read more of the function of this cauldron in people of different vocations. Together with these poems, we encounter a technical treatise on the nature and refinement of these cauldrons, and the consciousness states they relate to. It is an interesting fact that the three cauldrons have close parallels

in the human nervous system. The cauldron of knowledge obviously refers to the brain and the cauldron of vocation to the solar plexus. What is of comparatively recent date is the discovery of the enteral nervous system, the intelligence in the intestines. As it turned out, the digestive system has more nerve cells than the spine plus the entire peripheral nervous system. It produces and uses all the neurotransmitters that appear in the brain. Medical textbooks used to attribute the enteral to the parasympathetic nervous system. Systematic study revealed that this was a mistake. The intestines have a mind of their own. Though they do communicate with the brain, they are quite capable of doing their amazingly

---

The Gundestrup cauldron was found in a moor in Denmark. It consists of seven outside plates showing deities (an eighth one is missing), five inside plates showing mythological events and a bottom plate. All plates are made of silver plated with gold (nowadays rather worn). The cauldron is a Celtic work of art, but its age and place of origin are highly disputed. One theory favours the Balkan and points at Thracian and oriental elements in the design, such as the god holding two stags in the classical 'Lord of the Beasts' posture, and at the elephants. The other theory proposes Gaul and points out that the Celts of Gaul saw elephants when Hannibal crossed the Alps with Celtic help. May I mention that the costume and hairdress of the Medusa handles of the crater of Vix (a Greek vessel) show a lot of similarity to the goddesses shown on the Gundestrup cauldron? How the cauldron came to be offered as a sacrifcal gift on a Danish moor remains an open question. The item had been cut into its plates by the time.

Gundestrup cauldron. A goddess with birds (note small bird on her right hand) with what might be a seated priestess, a hair-plaiter, a carnivore and two beings, a dog/wolf and a one-armed man who are possibly dead, asleep or in trance.

complicated job in total independence, if need be in a laboratory tank. This led to the insight that the enteral nervous system is the third autonomous nervous system (see Gershon 1998).

Close parallels can be found in the textbooks of Taoist alchemy, where the three Irish cauldrons are mirrored by three alchemical ovens. Like the Chinese ovens, the Irish cauldrons are not a stable institution. Just like the Hindu chakras, the cauldrons are not simply there, you have to do something to purify, align and balance them. Everybody has the three in potential, but if you go for a walk through the city or make the mistake of watching TV for more than a minute, you may well realize that people are really good at abusing them. The cauldrons wholesome function can suffer from inertia, from ignorance, from mistreatment and misery. Only in the wisest of seers are all three cauldrons suspended

in an upright position. In most people, only the cauldron of heating (belly) is upright and confers a measure of health and vitality. The cauldron of vocation (heart) is often inverted or spins on its side, so that it permits a narrow focus on specific obsessions, but not a balanced and healthy life in accordance to one's true nature and will. Even worse is the state of the cauldron of knowledge and inspiration in our society. Most have shut theirs up so solidly that it takes a massive shock or overwhelming joy to re-align it. The head cauldron easily wobbles and inverts, you have to guard it carefully if you wish to keep it upright, and open to the influence of heaven. We are not talking of symbolism here but about an advanced form of yoga. The cauldrons may be metaphors, but the metaphors permit a certain amount of communication and interaction with the nervous systems. It is a task of subtlety to align all three cauldrons properly, and to stabilize them in an upright position. If you care to learn more about this useful topic, read, meditate, understand and use it.

Cauldron of the Underworld

That cauldrons may be found in strange locations is a theme that regularly appears in Norse and British myth. The prose and poetic *Edda* mention mysterious cauldrons, such as the collection guarded by the ancient giant Hymir, or Hel's well, called 'roaring cauldron', deep under the worm entangled roots of the world tree Yggdrassil.

In British myth, the second branch of the *Mabinogi* mentions an enchanted cauldron. We find the Irish king Mallolwch

and the British king Bran in polite conversation. The Irish regent accounts how one day, as he was hunting at a mound near the Lake of the Cauldron, he saw a strange couple emerge from the waves. The man was a huge, yellow haired, evil looking creature carrying a cauldron on his back. His name was Llassar Llaes Gyngwyd, his wife Kymidei Kymeinvoll was twice as large and ugly. When king Mallolwch invited the two to stay in his realm, he had hardly an idea what he could expect. The giantess gave birth to a fully armed huge warrior every couple of weeks, and her spawn grew fast and soon made itself a fearful nuisance molesting and killing the population. When Mallolwch learned of this, he thought long and hard. The fighting power of Kymidei's warriors was a boon, but the trouble they were causing made the lords of the realm clamour with complaints.

Finally, the council of aristocrats forced Mallolwch to take steps he dreaded: he invited the couple and their offspring to a feast within a chamber made entirely of iron. Once they were well sated with rich foods and strong liquors, the Irish left the chamber and bolted the doors from the outside. This done, they set to make a fierce fire flame around the iron hut, and soon the screams from within told that the dazed giants had recovered their senses. When the chamber became white hot, Llassar rushed at the wall and smashed a way to freedom with his shoulder. So the monstrous family escaped over land and sea and came to Britain. Here we have Bran

Gundestrup cauldron. A god with two men holding boars (warriors!), accompanied by a canine beast and a winged horse.

exclaiming that they came to his realm. Bran saw the great fighting strength of these rude beings. He granted them permission to dwell in his realm, and the huge man gave him the cauldron he was carrying as a gift. This cauldron, called the cauldron of rebirth, had the virtue: *Take a man who has been slain today and throw him into it, and tomorrow he will fight as well as ever, only he will not be able to speak.* Bran was mightily pleased with this enchanted gift, and saw to it that the children of the monstrous couple were always stationed separately, in distant districts, so they could cause no mischief. Later, Bran gave the cauldron as an apologetic offering to Mallolwch, who took it home and proceeded to use it in the subsequent war against the British. The cauldron was finally destroyed when the guilt ridden British warrior Evnissyen crept inside and stretched out so that it broke into four pieces, as did Evnissyen's heart.

As you noticed, we are dealing with a minimum of three cauldrons in this episode. The first is the lake of the Cauldron, the second the one carried by Llassar, and third, the iron chamber or hut in which Mallolwch attempted to incinerate his guests. As the *Mabinogi* informs us, Taliessin was present at these events, as he was in the last battle, when a poisoned spear hit Bran's foot or thigh from ambush. Only seven came home

to Harlech from this journey, and Bran's head, which spoke to them:

>...you will spend seven years feasting at Harddlech, with the birds of Rhiannon singing to you, and the head will be as good a companion as it ever was. After that you will spend eighty years at Gwales in Penvro, and as long as you do not open that door to the Bristol channel on the side facing Cornwall you may stay there and the head will not decay.

So the company crossed the sea, and when they came to Harlech a feast was ready for them, and three birds came flying, singing their tuneful enchantments, and right glad they became. They looked far over the glittering white crested sea to catch a glimpse of the birds, and though they were far, they were as easy to see as if they were close at hand. So they proceeded to Gwales, where they chanced upon a great royal hall facing the sea. They entered and found two open doors and one shut. The hall was set for a great feast, and so the seven survivors settled down to drink and sing and celebrate. For eighty years the company enjoyed bright laughter and happy revelry, they had forgotten all misery, all suffering and all the horrors of their futile war. Bran's head remained fresh and cheerful and spoke with them every day. Finally, one Heylin had to do the forbidden deed and opened the door. Instantly the spell shattered, the palace became a derelict hut, the head began to rot and the company recalled all forgotten tragedies and broke down sobbing pitifully.

What do you notice about this tale? I would like to direct your attention to the otherworldly qualities inherent in our tale. First, we have two ancient and terrifying creatures emerging from an otherworld beneath a cauldron - lake. These cause all sorts of unhappiness until they are handled properly, and according to their natural qualities. Next we have the cauldron of rebirth, fresh corpses stewing in the broth for a night return to life the next day. That they are mute can appear like a terrifying element - as if they were alive but not quite alive - but it can also be interpreted, as John Matthews proposed, that the cauldron born are mute about their experience on the other side. The cauldron acts as a representative for the otherworld itself in this episode: first, as a hungry mouth devouring the slain, then as a womb reshaping and bringing to birth at the dawning of the new day. Last, as soon as Bran is assassinated and his head cut off, the story leaves the realm of ordinary human affairs. With the head in their company, the seven survivors hardly interact with the known world any more. Coming to Britain, they learn that the throne was usurped by Caswallon mab Beli in their absence, but though their ears listen, their minds fail to grasp any significance. Instead, they become befuddled by the singing of real and / or imaginary birds flying very far very near, and eighty years of festivity go by without anyone having to set the table. The otherworld itself is present in this episode: the joyous bright realm, the land of innocence and pleasure. In the presence of the living/dead head, all participants are removed to the otherworld. As the company feasts and finds healing, the head remains whole: subjectively, for the company of the wondrous head, time has stopped. Keep this in mind: in Celtic otherworlds, time passes differently. Whoever composed or compiled the *Mabinogi* knew that the otherworld is not a place but a state of consciousness. This consciousness is often characterized by great clarity of awareness, wonderful colours, brightness, vivid detail, fascinating music, and strange distortions of time-perception. Like everything the mind does, it is a state of consciousness, or a trance state if you like. We'll get there yet. Suffice it to say that Bran became a Head of Annwvn in a very literal sense. He also made it into a number of early Grail legends, where he appears as a wounded or maimed king of the Grail castle in the wasteland, or as the brother of the Grail king. There are plenty of variations around two brothers called Bran and Beli hidden in this convoluted topic. You'll be delighted to hear that I spare you the details, life is complicated enough as it is.

The otherworlds of Island Celtic myth are not exactly realms where the souls of the dead go when they are done with living. These otherworlds are usually peopled by gods, giants, the fairy hosts and a number of inhuman entities. Humans may travel to this realm on occasion, or may be carried there by force, but in such cases the persons concerned do not die, they generally return to the world of mortals with a tale to tell. In this sense the otherworlds of the Island Celts had a highly shamanic function; they seem invisible to ordinary mortals, but visible and real to seers, shamans, dreamers, poets and lunatics. All spells, stories, songs, rituals and ceremonies are means by which the otherworlds (and otherworldly consciousness-forms) are influenced to change the world of everyday reality. By traveling to the otherworlds in a trance or dream state the reality of this side can be changed and life and consciousness transform. Countless shamans all over the globe have made such journeys, the Celtic and Germanic seers being no exception.

Arthur's Quest

A perplexingly similar theme echoes from one of the earlier Taliesin songs (c. 9th C.). From the few details that do make sense, we learn of an expedition of Arthur and company. For some unknown reason, the warrior king traveled to one or more otherworlds in his ship Prydwen. Taliesin was there and composed a song, and like the war in Ireland we just discussed, only seven survivors return to Britain with a sad tale. The song is occasionally entitled *The Spoils of Annwn* or *The Spoiling of Annwn*, though these titles do not appear in the original manuscript nor do they fit that much. Here it is:

Book of Taliessin 30
I will praise the sovereign, supreme king of the land,
Who hath extended his dominion over the shore of the world.
Complete was the prison of Gweir in Caer Sidi,
Through the spite of Pwyll and Pryderi.
No one before him went into it.
The heavy blue chain held the faithful youth,
And before the spoils of Annwvn woefully he sings,
And till doom shall continue a bard of prayer.

Thrice enough to fill Prydwen, we went into it;
Except seven, none returned from Caer Sidi.
Am I not a candidate for fame, if a song is heard?
In Caer Pedryvan, four its revolutions;
In the first word from the cauldron when spoken,
From the breath of nine maidens it was gently warmed.
Is it not the cauldron of the chief of Annwvn? What is its intention?
A ridge about its edge and pearls.
It will not boil the food of a coward, that has not been sworn,
A sword bright gleaming to him was raised,
And in the hand of Lleminawg it was left.
And before the door of the gate of Uffern the lamp was burning.
And when we went with Arthur, a splendid labour,
Except seven, none returned from Caer Vedwyd.

Am I not a candidate for fame with the listened song
In Caer Pedryvan, in the isle of the strong door?
The twilight and pitchy darkness were mixed together.
Bright wine their liquor before their retinue.
Thrice enough to fill Prydwen we went on the sea,
Except seven, none returned from Caer Rigor.

I shall not deserve much from the ruler of literature,
Beyond Caer Wydyr they saw not the prowess of Arthur.
Three score Canhwr stood on the wall,
Difficult was a conversation with its sentinel.
Thrice enough to fill Prydwen there went with Arthur,
Except seven, none returned from Caer Golud.
I shall not deserve much from those with long shields.
They know not what day, who the causer,
What hour in the serene day Cwy was born.
Who caused that he should not go to the dales of Devwy.
They know not the brindled ox, thick his head-band.
Seven score knobs in his collar.
And when we went with Arthur of anxious memory,
Except seven, none returned from Caer Vandwy.

I shall not deserve much from those of loose bias,
They know not what day the chief was caused.
What hour in the serene day the owner was born.
What animal they keep, silver its head.
When we went with Arthur of anxious contention,
Except seven, none returned from Caer Ochren.

Monks congregate like dogs in a kennel,
From contact with their superiors they acquire knowledge,
Is one the course of the wind, is one the water of the sea?
Is one the spark of the fire, of unrestrainable tumult?
Monks congregate like wolves,
From contact with their superiors they acquire knowledge.
They know not when the deep night and dawn divide.
Nor what is the course of the wind, or who agitates it,
In what place it dies away, on what land it

roars.

The grave of the saint is vanishing from the altar-tomb.

I will pray to the Lord, the great supreme, That I be not wretched. Christ be my portion.

Nine British Otherworlds

Before consulting the steaming fumes of the cauldron itself, let's take a look at the nature of the British otherworld. To begin with, the otherworld is not a single concept but a loose term that may refer to any of several strange realities outside of ordinary human consciousness. The British term **Annwn, Annwvn, Annwfn** is pretty mysterious, as several etymologies are possible. An- can mean *very*, *not* or *inside, inner*, the second part of the name possibly come from dwfn, meaning *deep* or *world*. Very-Deep, Very-World, Not-Deep, Not-World, Inside-Deep, Inner-World. What makes sense for you? Annwvn is a realm deep below the earth in some accounts, or an island in the world ocean far beyond all human lands, or an abstract place reached by Pwyll (*Mabinogi*) when he rode into a shady and desolate glen. In our poem, Arthur and friends reach this land after a journey over sea. Here they visit one or several distinct realms. For ease of understanding, here are some possible translations of the place-names.

Caer Sidi is the first place on our list, beyond the shore of the world it revolves in perfect harmony. Caer means fortress or castle, Sidi is usually translated as revolving. In all likeliness, the term Caer Sidi was used for the galaxy itself. It is a place out of time, in that pain and age are unknown there. It is also the place where Taliesin has his bardic seat and where the fruitful fountain pours forth its cascading elixirs, sweeter than white wine. These references come close to some of the otherworlds known to the Irish filid. The poets knew that the source of poetry is in the otherworldly realm, and they believed that poets are born in the otherworld, in the bright land, the beautiful realm, the land of many colours.

I come from the Land of the Living, Where neither death nor sin are known

Thus sang an otherworldly lady to the young hero Connla, beguiling him to come traveling with her, if we can trust the 8th C. manuscript.

Caer Pedryvan is the location of the cauldron, its name means Four-Cornered Castle. Remember the sinificance of the square enclosures in the La Téne period. These lines have some close parallels in the Grail legends. You find a four-cornered castle in our song, four times revolving. In the descriptions of the Grail castle, fourfold symmetries abound. Take the *Sone de Nansai*, a French poem, which speaks of a great tower surrounded by four smaller ones and a great hall with four pillars in the middle on an enchanted island where an immortal abbot and 12 ageless monks guard the Grail. This setting, appearing with some variation in several Grail romances, may well echo the most popular board game north of the Alps, called Gwyddbwyll, Tawlbwrdd, Tablut, Taefl etc. Its basic form has a single figure, the king, sitting on the central square, the 'navel' of the board, guarded by four, eight or twelve retainers arranged around his central seat of power. He is opposed by a numerous army of invaders appearing from the four sides of the board. These games are not simply a matter of amusement, as their order and rules reflects beliefs and traditions closely connected with myth and magick. The known world, the ordered world, the kingdom itself are constantly threatened by the unruly and catastrophic forces coming from without, be it marauding pirates, invading armies, the legions of the otherworlds or a spell of fatally bad weather. If Count Tolstoy's presentation is accurate, these games may well have been sacred games played on specific ceremonial occasions to restore order and harmony in the kingdom.

In this verse we also encounter the (or a?) cauldron of the otherworld. Nine maidens (priestesses, goddesses, muses?) breathe upon its fire, and a rim of pearls encapsulates the entirety of creation. It is a cauldron, but may well have been the earlier prototype for the holy grail.

I wouldn't dare to tell you what exactly is the nature and mystery of the cauldron, as the true knowledge of the cauldron comes from direct experience. You may speculate about it as much as you like, but unless you go there and find out, it'll remain a mystery to you. The metaphor of the cauldron is so valuable as it offers so many different interpretations on so many levels of understanding. This is what creative freedom is all about.

The head of the underworld may be of interest. Pen can mean head in the literal as well as the metaphorical sense. Are we dealing with a chief, like Annwvn's king Arawn and his friend Pwyll, Head of

Annwvn, or with a severed head, like Bran's? Heads often appear in company with the Grail, in the *Perlesvaus* (see Loomis) you even find one within the Grail, and a wealth of heads to accompany it. And heads - cauldrons of knowledge - were certainly popular in various Celtic cults, you stumble over them all the time. The cauldron of Annwvn, as you recall, will not boil the food of a coward or one forsworn. Closely related is the cauldron of Tyrnog, one of the fabled thirteen treasures of Britain, it: *does not boil the meat of a coward, but boils the meat of a brave man instantly.* Likewise, in the *Prose Lancelot* (early 13th C.) the Grail replenishes all tables with food, but leaves the unworthy unfed.

Uffern is a word that may be cautiously rendered as cold place. Uffern became a term for the Christian concept of hell, the fact that Uffern is called a cold place, a swamp, a morass, has a wide mouth and whirling trees makes it a likely option that we are dealing with a pagan idea (See BoT1).

Caer Vedwyd can be translated Castle of Revelry, sure sign of a lot of loose living in the Island Celtic otherworlds.

Caer Rigor could mean Royal Castle (Squire) or Castle of the Royal (Ri) Horn (Cor), as Loomis impressively proposes. Here we come to the Grail again. Popular belief has it that the Grail is a chalice containing the blood of Christ. This pious idea comes from the pen of Robert de Boron who ought to have known better. The earliest Grail legend, the *Conte del Graal* by Chretien de Troyes (c. 1175-1180) describes the sacred object as a (large) dish holding the sacramental wafer. As Loomis speculates, the wafer may be a mistranslation. Old French Cors (horn) was mistaken for the Cors, ie the corpus Christi by Chretien. The vision of the regal damsel carrying a dish large enough for a salmon or pike (so we read in Chretien) holding only a tiny wafer is a bit too incongruous, even if we ignore the fact that the church forbids women to carry or administer the sacrament. Looking at the thirteen treasures of Britain, we encounter the dysgl (dish) of Rhydderch Hael (The Generous) and the Horn of Bran, sources of as much food and drink as anyone could wish for, these may well be the sources that Chretien's Grail was composed of. It may well be that the Grail as a dish, saucer or disk connects several fruitful ideas, such as the round table of King Arthur, or the flying saucer.

Caer Wydyr means Castle of Glass. Possibly the glass-castle that appears in several folk tales of the dwellers round the North Sea, if not the amber castle, or Atlantis itself for that matter.

Caer Golud is Castle of Riches, or possibly Castle of Frustration. Most scholars favour the first translation on the grounds that the otherworlds ought to be realms of perfection, where everything is brighter, better and more beautiful than on earth. Though there is plenty of evidence for such otherworlds, especially in Irish myth, I find it unlikely that all otherworlds were sugar coated consumer's paradises. There is a dark side to Celtic and Germanic myth, and usually it is only a shadow's breadth away.

Caer Vandwy successfully defies translation. Matthews proposes that it was originally Caer (M) andwy, which could be a shortened form of Caer Manawydan. A castle of Manawydan is the fearsome bone-fortress of Oeth and Anoeth. Manawydan the Wise constructed it *in the shape of a bee-hive, entirely of human bones mortared together and divided into innumerable cells, forming a kind of labyrinth.* (Squire). Do you know where to find this place of horror and delight? I know my answers; legend has it that Oeth and Anoeth were on an island far out on the wide ocean. This fits much better with the Irish sea god Manannan than with the British half-god Manawydan, who has very little, if anything to do with the sea. Instead, he combats a host of fiendish otherworldlers appearing on the mound of Arberth in the shape of mice, i.e. beings from under-the-earth.

Caer Ochren is the ninth and last otherworldly location appearing in our song. Again, the word Ochren is elusive. Matthews proposes a misspelling of Achren, meaning forest. This would give us a castle of trees, and indeed, we find otherworldly forests in the myths of most Central and north European cultures. Some of these forests function as gates to the other side, or they enclose magical forces or entities, such as enchanted castles, witch-sisters, black men, beasts, brigands and other dangerous elements. The appearance of nine underworlds in this early poem is surely not coincidental, nor is the varied nature of these places. These beliefs show a range of possibilities. Ireland, situated on the western rim of Europe, had otherworlds which could be entered through the mounds of the Sidhe, several mysterious forests and, as a large body of literature reveals, by setting sail for the west. Where the sun descends, so the poets believed, are the lands of the blessed, the islands of eternal youth, realms of joy and perfection. The poets expressed great longing for this realm, where lies and sins and misdeeds are unknown, where beauty and innocence combine, where there is poetry in every word and a miraculous vision in every sight. Sometimes such otherworlds can be found under the very surface of the earth. An Irish myth has it that the last invaders of Ireland, the people of Mil, agreed to divide the Island equally between themselves and the former inhabitants, the Tuatha De Danann. The Sons of Mil were to have the surface of the land while the Tuatha De were to settle under the hollow hills as everything under the surface was theirs. This may be worth considering: Go for a walk and keep in mind that under each of your steps, divided by a narrow crust of soil, lies an entirely different and fascinating world.

Another Irish hypothesis is that the otherworlds are superimposed on the human world. The only difference between them being that humans are simply too dull, blind and sinful to see through the veil into the wider vision of joy and miracle, truth and beauty. The poets who sang about this otherworld knew that it is always present. Not as an obscure metaphor but as a sensible reality, a state of bliss and rapture that cannot be sensed by those who are shackled by their beliefs in sin, mortality and the inevitability of the world. The veil between this world and the other (a hedge of mist, a barrier of thorns, a crust of earth) is the egoistic mind, the concept of duality, stubborn convictions and a rigid sense of knowledge what is possible and what ain't. In fact, the more serious and earnest you become, the harder is it to sense the Land

of the Living. It's here if you wake up now.

Entirely different are a large number of otherworlds visited by pious Mael Duin on an extended boat journey. Some of his islands are simply places of joy and heady drinking, as might be desirable for simple minded folk. Others are so thoroughly bizarre that I wonder if Mael Duin saw them in human awareness at all. The otherworlds, as ever, are not just locations but states of mind. The Central European Celts understandably had less emphasis on mysterious islands, entrance to their otherworlds are usually darksome shady forests, narrow valleys, caves, lakes or wells. They had a rich lore of giants, gods, dwarves and eldritch beings living under the surface of the earth. To understand the nature of the otherworlds you could consider the nature of the gate and the nature of the world it connects with. We have space-gates, such as trees, forests, stones, mountains, caves, hills, mounds, hollows, wells, springs, pools, rivers, oceans, gates, doors, frontiers, stiles, hedges, bridges and cross-roads. Then there are the time-gates, such as dusk and dawn, midnight and noon, full and new moon, the solstices and the quarter days. Special time gates are related to local events. Or think of the weather-gates, such as storm, fog, snow,

---

Gundestrup cauldron. Goddess (with somewhat damaged face) between two gods. The nature of the two has raised a lot of speculation, including the question whether they are her two mates, or one mate and one son of hers. Both deities appear on other plates of the cauldron, the bearded one on an inside plate where he holds half of a wheel (possibly a symbol of the sky god or the thunderer), the clean shaved one, if we add horns, as the horned god amidst the beasts on an inside plate.

transforming the land we know into a vast and dangerous reality with its own rules. When you combine gates, strange things may happen. All of these gates lead to some part of Annwvn, the otherworlds, or, if you will, to another state of mind. Remember how you dreamed yourself into a mound earlier on? How many gates to the otherworld can you find in your neighbourhood? This knowledge is not simply romantic fairy tale stuff. It's there to

be used.

Books of Fferyllt

One of the first questions raised by the *Hanes Taliesin* is obviously where Lady Ceridwen had obtained the recipe for her miraculous cauldron of inspiration and science. The tale states that it came from the *Books of the Fferyllt*. Who or what is a fferyllt? On a simple level, the word means

chemist or metal-worker in modern Welsh. The song *The Battle of the Trees* (BoT8) ends with a reference to the fferyllt:

A golden gem in a golden jewel. I am splendid and shall be wanton from the oppression of the fferyllt.

Skene's version gives the word as metal workers. Nash comments:

Fferyllt is a worker in metals, a metallurgist, or artist in general, and as the subject here is a golden jewel, may very fairly be translated 'goldsmith'.

Yet it was certainly not a book on metallurgy that Ceridwen consulted for her sorceries. On a more abstract level, fferyllt could also mean a magician. Fferyllt is the Welsh version of the name Virgil. Here we encounter a fascinating mixture of historical fact and folksy legend. Virgil was a historical person. He was called Publius Vergilius Maro (70-19 BCE), a native of Mantua in Cisalpine Gaul, as the north of Italy was called at the time. His family owned land in the country, but as they noticed the talents of their son, they sent him to Rome for a proper education. In Rome, young Virgil became the friend of Octavius, who later assumed the name Augustus and became the first emperor. Little is known of Virgil's life. He seems to have been a quiet and shy person who preferred his studies to the excesses of social life and often suffered from weak health. Most of Virgil's life was spent in sunny Naples where he composed a number of important poetic works. Several short poems are attributed to him, but what made him famous are three longer pieces. The first of these was a collection of poems

on country life, known as *Bucolics* or *Eclogues*. The second, called *Georgics*, consisted of four volumes of poetry on farming and contains a number of practical instructions on keeping animals and bees, on crops, trees and vegetables.

The Aeneid

His final, and longest work is the well known epic poem, the *Aeneid*. This book begins at the end of the Trojan war. When the city of Troy went up in flames, the hero Aeneas and a number of like-minded associates fought their way to the harbour and managed to capture a ship. They escaped the wrath of the combined Greek forces and fled along an adventurous route across the Mediterranean. On their way, a storm brings them to Carthage, where Aeneas and Dido, Queen of Carthage, have an intense but short lived affair. Then the gods order Aeneas to set sail again, and while suffering Dido commits suicide, Aeneas and his faithful band of warriors land on the shores of Italy. There the Trojans have a number of battles with the locals until they win a kingdom and found what was to become the City of Rome.

While this story, like most epics, is basically a tale of warfare and bloodshed, it should in all fairness be remarked that Virgil attempted to introduce a moral background, and to make up for the cruelty of the action by praising the more peaceful and harmonious forms of behaviour. The resulting work, the *Aeneid*, became a bestseller. According to R. Hutton, Virgil was the most widely quoted classical author in the middle ages. This popularity was especially developed in Britain, as the British nobles believed that Aeneas was their own ancestor. According to a highly popular legend, Aeneas had a grandson called Brutus. With a number of enterprising Trojans, Brutus sailed out of the Mediterranean and then northwards. There he found those fabled islands which later received his name and became known as Britain. This enchanting tale was made popular by such authors as Geoffrey of Monmouth, whose works were read and devoutly believed by most of his contemporaries. While this sort of story was of great use in providing the British with some sort of ancient history (no matter how fantastic) it does not offer much in the way of magic.

Virgil died before he could complete the *Aeneid*, and apparently he was not very happy with this work, as he asked his friends to burn the manuscript. They didn't follow his request but published it, and soon after, Virgil was worshipped as a divinity. His reputation became so grandiose that even the Christians celebrated him as 'the prophet of the gentiles'.

Now while the *Aeneid* is a splendid piece of poetry, it is certainly not a magical cook-book. It does contain material, however, which portrayed thoroughly pagan beliefs. By reading it, the Christian population of Europe learned of a time when monotheism was inconceivable. Aeneas was a half god, his mother the goddess Venus, who appeared frequently during the tale to help her son achieve his destiny. Her divine scheming was opposed by the goddess Juno, wife of the supreme sky god Jupiter and a dedicated enemy of all Trojans. Jupiter again had some sympathies for the Trojans, and

with the help of the fates, aided Aeneas on his way to success. Juno recruited several deities to help her revenge on the Trojans, such as the wind-god Aeolus, who was bribed with a good-looking sea-nymph that later became his wife. Neptune, god of the oceans became angry when Aeolus dared to make storm-winds howl over his domain. Other deities soon became involved in the struggle, the result being a divine soap-opera of considerable complexity. Reading this book, the Christian audience was confronted with a world where several pagan deities were struggling for control. The human participants of the story were basically obedient servants of divine will and had very little choice about the matter.

Other items of the tale, which made it into medieval literature, were divination from the flight of birds, a protective mantle of mist, various sacrificial rites and ghosts of slain heroes appearing in dreams. There are numerous miraculous omina and signs, prophetic dreams, ritual dances, offerings of all descriptions, highly poetic prayers and invocations, a journey to the underworld and the frequent appearance of deities who tell their human favourites what actions are required. The astonished reader learned about the appearance, the symbols and attributes of most classical deities, not to mention sea-monsters, sacred trees (and their lore), holy forests or frenzied prophetesses. Shape-changing has its place in the story, and cursing, and fervent prayers uttered by the poet to the goddesses of song. Many of these items are given in detailed description, so detailed in fact, that it would be an easy matter to reconstruct (or invent) an entire religion out of the material.

As the *Aeneid* was such a popular work in the medieval period we can be sure that it was well-known to numerous bards and story-tellers. This produces problems when we wish to decide what particular items of medieval bardic lore were local pagan traditions and which have been lifted from the works of Virgil. The hedge of mists which appears in several medieval tales of Britain could be a local piece of enchantment, but it could also be a useful idea from the *Aeneid*. The same goes for most of the items listed above, many of which are frequently paraded as 'Celtic magic' in popular books even though there is next to no evidence that they were ever thought of by the Celts prior to the Roman occupation. This is an excellent opportunity to keep an open mind. Perhaps there were Druids or sorcerers who could conjure a protective cover of fog in the undocumented periods of early history and perhaps the medieval bards, who were not too well informed about prehistory, merely attributed it to them.

Virgil the Magician

While there is plenty of material in the *Aeneid* that can be used by ritual magicians there appears little evidence for the particular sorceries that Ceridwen performed. Nor would it seem likely that Virgil ever practised magic. Nevertheless, the readers of his books soon turned his reputation from that of an inspired poet to that of a magician. Dante (1265-1321), made Virgil an essential figure of his *Divine Comedy*. In this monumental work, Virgil leads the hero on the journey through hell and almost

to the top of the mountain of purification. This constitutes quite an achievement, if you consider that Virgil was not even a Christian. The books of Virgil were frequently used for divination, a process named Sortes Vergilianea (drawing lots from Virgil), which consisted of putting a finger at random into his pages. Such methods were usually performed using the *Bible*, their use with the writings of a pagan author says something about the esteem he enjoyed, and still enjoys.

By the twelfth century, a number of amazing legends had been connected with Virgil, who was clearly shown as a magician. Several books of the thirteenth century outline his amazing magical career, such as the *Otia Imperiala* by Gervasius of Tilbury and the *World-book* of Jansen Enenckel. Sadly, most of these tales are pretty standard material, and could have been told about any famous magician (see Petzold 1992). However, there is one among them which ought to be considered in relation to Ceridwen's cauldron and various international dismemberment rites. At the height of his powers, the sorcerer Virgil created an enchanted castle before the gates of Rome. This castle was surrounded by a deep moat and protected by a high wall which had only one gate. On each side of the gate stood twelve men who were continuously beating with iron flails, so no one could enter the gate unless he had the permission of the sorcerer. Having achieved this, Virgil thought that life would be a lot nicer if only he were young again. So he went to the emperor of Rome and asked permission to leave for a three-week holiday, but the emperor, who liked to have Virgil's company at all times, refused the request. This angered the enchanter, who went home and called for his most trusted servant. Together the two set out for the magical castle, and when they came to the gate, Virgil told the servant to go in. 'Lord', replied the servant, 'I cannot do this, the iron flails would beat me to death'. 'Do not worry' said Virgil, and showed the servant how to turn a certain screw at the side of the gate. Instantly the flails came to rest and the two could pass unharmed. Inside the castle, Virgil led the way down to the cellars. In the darkness of the deepest cell, he showed the servant a huge vat. 'As I trust you more than anyone else in this world' spoke the sorcerer, 'I shall ask you to perform a task for me. First of all you shall kill me. Then you shall hack my body to pieces, and split my head into four parts. You shall place my head on the bottom of the vat, and throw the parts of my body on top, so that the heart rests in the middle. You shall add salt and place a lamp above the vat, and for nine days you shall come and refill the lamp faithfully, every day, and the lamp will drip into the vat. After nine days you will find me renewed, a youth, healthy and long-lived, unless heaven forbids it.'

The servant shrank from this task, but Virgil, the mighty magician, threatened to punish and curse him, and finally the servant did all his master had asked. He killed and dismembered Virgil, he salted the flesh, he placed the lamp above the vat so it would drip into the barrel. And the servant left the castle and turned the screw, and the men at the gate resumed their incessant beating. Every day the servant duly returned to refill the lamp. The emperor, however, was angry that Virgil did not appear in court, and by the seventh day he had the servant arrested and brought before him. 'Where is your master?' demanded the emperor. 'I do not know, I have not seen him' answered the servant. Then the emperor forced the servant to open the gates of the enchanted castle, and he had the place searched from the highest turret to the deepest vault. Down in the cellar they discovered the vat, the dripping lamp and the salted corpse of Virgil. In a fit of rage the emperor beheaded the servant. As he collapsed on the ground, a tiny boy appeared before the emperor and his soldiers. The figure ran around the vat three times, screaming 'Accursed be the day and hour when you came!'. Then it disappeared and nothing remained save the dead sorcerer in his barrel. And this is the tale of the death of Virgil the magician.

A Rite of Rebirth

After reading about the slightly morbid world of Celto-Germanic cauldron sorcery, you may well wonder what it may be good for. What spell or enchantment could offer some new and exciting perspectives for your magick? Let me sum up a few points. The cauldron is a vessel which receives, transforms and provides. It is also a highly symbolic item with plenty of mythology and eldritch lore. Cauldrons feature prominently in the lore of countless shamanic cultures of Eurasia, and often enough, they are involved in the initiation rites of the shamans themselves. Here we are dealing with a very old level of religious beliefs. Bones and cauldrons - the two often come in company - are part of the religious equipment of many hunter cultures. To simplify things, in most north-Eurasian cosmologies the bones are the life. Numerous cultures believe that the essence of life dwells in the bone, or in the marrow. When they kill an animal, they dismember it carefully, without damage to the bones, as these contain the potential rebirth of the beast.

In a sense we are dealing with a matter of guilt here. A hunter who takes life owes something, and when you owe, you had better pay back. Many Siberian cultures believed that the bones were to be treated with great respect. The soul of the slain beast has to be placated, received apologies, gifts, offerings and prayer, to ensure that it will be reborn out there in the wide forest, and will allow itself to be taken once more. A good hunter is grateful and will never take life casually or carelessly. In the Baltic countries, rites for the placation of slain bears are well documented.

You might argue that the world of the early Celts was a long way from the hunter cultures of northern Eurasia. This may be the case, but we should consider that traces of such customs can be found in Europe. In the *Prose Edda*, thunder god Thor resurrects his dead goats by placing their bones on the hides. Then he waves his lightning hammer in the air and the goats come to life again. A similar theme appears in the tale of the juniper tree that the Grimm brothers collected. You find a boy who is killed and cooked by his mum, eaten by dad and whose soul is resurrected in a necromantic rite when his sister buries the bones under a juniper tree. Tough stuff to send kids to bed with. The pattern of killing/

dismemberment/cooking and resurrection from the bones appears in three Grimm tales altogether.

Burials in Several Phases

Possibly related to such bone rituals is the custom of giving the dead a sky-burial, for instance by placing corpses, skeletons or parts of these in trees or on platforms. This sort of thing goes back to the Paleolithic days, in more recent times, anthropologists have observed such rites among the Tartars, Evenks, Tungus, Mordwines, Jakuts, Golden and Finns. Often such rites are essential stages in what is commonly called a two-phase burial. This is a not uncommon phenomena, but certainly one that has been misunderstood. In two-phase burials, you do not take your corpse and put it in earth (or wherever) straight away, as is the modern custom. Instead, you prepare the corpse in some way and keep it for a certain amount of time before it goes to be covered by sod and stone. Some cultures meticulously cut all flesh from the bones of the deceased, others leave this job to beasts and birds. Then again there are cultures where bones are taken out of tombs from time to time for various reasons. Such forms of behaviour were common once and can often be observed in European prehistory, especially in megalith tombs.

In the early eighties, I spent many nights trancing on a mountain ridge in the Taunus, close to the site of the former Heidetränk-oppidum. High above the cauldron of the

---

Gundestrup cauldron. A god bearing two stags in the classical 'Lord of the Beasts' posture well known from the Balkan and the near east.

valley I shook and dreamt, and during these states a number of bizarre visions repeatedly appeared. One of them was a morbid scenario. Under the cold gleam of the moon, the pale rocks and boulders that litter the slope transformed into bones. In the rowans and beeches, half rotten skulls seemed to dangle, and between the nightblack twisted trees rose crude platforms where corpses decomposed. These visions reappeared with some regularity. I took them for subjective dream images evoked by the suggestive effects of stone, tree and moonlight. At the time, I only knew of such customs from far away cultures. The Celts, as far as I knew, used to bury the dead in mounds and consequently had nothing to do with these scenes. This turned out to be wrong. Over the last years, the amount of evidence for several phase burials has increased considerably. Several of the corpses of Hallstatt D appear as if they had been kept in storage before being inhumed in the great grave mounds. Especially in cases of mutual burials it is by no means clear if all participants died or went into the hollow

hills at once, or whether some were stored for a later date, when they could be inhumed with their spouses, friends or relations.

During the La Tène period, similar evidence appears. First of all the riddle of Manching, a large oppidum close to Ingolstadt, Bavaria. Manching was a thriving settlement and cultural centre till the middle of the first century BCE when the oppidum was abandoned with what seems to be some haste. It is not yet certain whether this happened after a violent defeat, but the evidence for destruction is certainly impressive. Consequently, excavations tend to unearth a lot of chaotic material. What surprised the archaeologists most is the amount of human bone material scattered carelessly amidst ceramic rubbish and animal bones all over the settlement. More than 5000 human bones were unearthed so far, they belong to at least 400 individuals. The first theory postulated that the bones came from a destruction of the settlement, possibly in 15 BCE, by the Roman legions. The flaw is that the bones were mainly skulls and long-bones, many of the latter lacking the end-joints. This state was soon explained as casual cannibalism, the sort where you eat a corpse and dump the garbage wherever you like. Recent studies have shown that a good many cases of so-called cannibalism may well belong to the group of several phase-burials. To scrape meat off a bone is, after all, no proof that it was actually eaten. To understand burial at Manching, you may recall that there is very little evidence for burials during the late La Tène period. We know that people used to live in settlements and cities housing thousands or ten-thousands of people, but

we have next to no insight how they disposed of their dead. The late La Tène offers hardly any burials, cemeteries or mounds. The dead simply disappear, and the nature of this disappearance has led to an amazing amount of colourful speculation. With regard to Manching, we can be certain that the dead did not decompose within the settlement. The bones show that the corpses were allowed to rot in the open, but as only a specific selection of bones (skulls and long-bones) appear within the oppidum, the place of decay must have been somewhere outside.

Imagine a secluded place where the dead could leisurely disintegrate into the elements, imagine screeching crows, buzzing flies and hungry scavengers. At some time, certain people (a priesthood?) went to the corpses and performed a macabre ritual. The extremities were chopped off, the bones extracted and a selection was taken to the settlement. What happened then is a fascinating question. Many bones show signs of animal teeth. One hypothesis postulates that the selected bones were ritually buried in the settlement, but that at a later time animals unearthed them and had a good bite. Another hypothesis proposes that the corpses were cut up into convenient portions at the place of decomposition, and left to animals who fed on them. At a certain time, a selection of bones was collected and carried to the settlement, where they were kept in buildings or buried (see H. Peter-Röcher 1998). In any case, it is likely that the people of Manching venerated these bones (a cult of the dead?) and that it was only after the oppidum was abandoned that they came to be scattered so carelessly. Of course it is still possible that a certain cannibalistic element appeared in these rites (remember Pliny's remark on cannibalistic Druids?), but then, it is just as possible that Roman travelers observed places where bones were exhibited and assumed the worst they could think of.

More evidence for a several phase burial was unearthed in the early nineties (see Metzler 2001). There used to be a thriving oppidum on the Titelberg in Luxembourg, where a branch of the Treveri had their seat. Beneath the mountain, a cemetery called Lamadelaine yielded an amazing 85 burials. These were not only unusual as they included at least a dozen graves containing several burials, but also as burials are so rare in the late La Tène anyway. To explain the high number of double or multiple burials, several theories were postulated. Among them was Caesar's questionable story of wives being burned with their husbands. Other interpretations proposed mass burials in times of war or pestilence and careless mixing of ashes when several corpses are burned at once. As it turned out they were all wrong. A careful analysis of partly burned bone fragments revealed that the dead had been allowed to decay in the open for an unspecified time. During this time, it was left to bacteria, birds and beasts to strip at least some of the flesh from the bones. Next, the bones were carefully gathered and burned on a huge pyre. This process involved sacrifices of animals (which were burned together with the dead), communal feasting and any amount of heavy drinking, as can be seen from shards of numerous amphora. After

this rite, the ashes were carefully collected and buried in properly made tombs. Presumably the mixture of human ashes and cinders was wrapped in cloth and placed within the grave, together with generous amounts of food and a small amount of personal goods, such as weapons, tools or ornaments. This triple ritual is well worth thinking about. The human being appears in three states. The corpse is reduced to bones, the bones are reduced to ashes and the ashes are buried in the deep.

Did the Treveri believe in a triple personality? Likewise, there are three means of transition involved. The first is what we may call otherworldly animals, such as pigs, dogs, crows, ravens, flies, wolves, vultures, buzzards and worms. Most of these appear with some regularity in Celtic myth. Maybe these beasts were believed to be of an otherworldly nature, maybe they were not even seen as beasts but as deities. In the shape of beasts, the gods fed on the corpse and took away its fleshly shape, its human personality. Next, the bones, representing a more endurable but also more anonymous self than the flesh, were given into the fire. During the second transformation, the bones turned into heat, light and smoke. Finally, the ashes went into the grave, into the dark rich earth, into the shady halls of the underworld. It could be proposed that the process turned a well known individual (flesh) into a more abstract self (bone) and eventually led to a total loss of the human form (ashes). This did not imply that the human being was forgotten or dissolved. Something continued. The ashes went into graves that had a human form and were accompanied by objects that had some use for the deceased. The whole rite may remind you, if you allow me to utter another crazy idea, of the OIV formula of the Welsh bards. The V relates to life-forms (animals, flesh), the I to elements and energies (fire) and the O to the earth, the world as a whole. Or maybe it makes you think of the square enclosure, the pillar and the pit. It is not only the cattle of Gournay or the slain of Ribemont who were allowed to decompose in the open. The same treatment seems to have been used for unusual or privileged individuals. It would be tempting to invent an entire after-death scenario on the foundation of these Treveri graves and a few other mutual burials of the same period. Sadly, whatever beliefs were reflected in these rites, they definitely did not reflect what happened after death in general. Most Treveri were not buried at all. Their rite of transition remains an unsolved riddle. The people in the Lamadelaine tombs are an exceptional minority. Recent excavation of the cult places of the Galatian Celts in Gordion, Turkey, brought up a number of incomplete skeletons. It is not yet settled how many of the dead were human sacrifices, executed criminals, mutilated enemies or several phase burials.

But let us return to our main topic. Bones and cauldrons often come together, and indeed the easiest way to clean the bones is to boil the corpse. This sort of thing is not just a matter of mythology, it was also widely practised in the medieval period when nobility happened to die in foreign countries. Around 1130, Sigurdr Njalsson, a native of Greenland, found a stranded Norwegian ship whose crew had died of hunger. Transport of the corpses would have been a difficult matter, so Sigurdr had the deceased boiled in cauldrons and took the bones to the bishop seat at Gardar for a decent burial. The same treatment was given to Ludwig of Bavaria when he died in Heidelberg in 1294. Ludwig IX died at Tunis in 1270, his body was boiled until the bones could be extracted. When Friedrich I (Barbarossa) and Pope Alexander III battled in Rome in 1167, the black plague turned out to be the winner. Into the cauldrons went Daniel I of Prague, the archbishop of Cologne, four bishops and plenty of worthies. Flesh and bone were carefully separated in flat cauldrons, the flesh being buried on location, the bones sewn into bags and sent home. Barbarossa himself died in 1190 while swimming and frolicking in the Mediterranean. His flesh was boiled and buried in Antioch, his carefully cleansed bones were temporarily kept in Tyrus, as it was intended to give them a last resting place in Jerusalem. Similar operations were performed on Ludwig III in 1190 and Ludwig IV in 1227. The custom was usually confined to members of high nobility, occasionally, our sources call it the 'Ritus Teutonicus'. That this rite had more than a practical purpose, and that in all likeliness some pagan elements were associated with it can be assumed as Pope Boniface VIII strictly prohibited it in 1300. To Boniface VIII, the practise was 'godless' and those treated in this fashion were to be denied a Christian burial. (see Uhsadel-Gülke, 1972)

Gundestrup cauldron. Goddess between elephants, probably some form of the horse- and riders goddess, Epona/Equona, as she is riding a chariot.

Rites of Dismemberment

You may recall that the slain warriors cast into the cauldron of rebirth returned to the battlefield the morning after, mute, but wonderfully restored. Greek myth has several parallel cases. In some cases the act of boiling a person took on an entirely demonic nature, in others, the rite of rejuvenation relied on it. Let me mention the myth of Pelops who was slain, cooked and offered to the gods by his father Tantalus. The gods, recognizing the nature of the meal, refused to partake of it, except for Demeter who had the munchies and absentmindedly ate a shoulder. Later Pelops was resurrected by boiling him a second time, and the missing piece of shoulder was replaced by a piece of ivory. Several versions of a legend recount how Lykaon served his grandson Arkas to Zeus as a light snack. The latter was so disgusted with the meal that he resurrected the child and subsequently granted him eternal life as a constellation. An even better example is the range of legends associated with Medea. Greek mythology has plenty of traditions regarding this witch, priestess and semi-goddess, many of them at odds with another. Some authors have Medea as a beautiful but tragic human heroine, others make her a sorceress who rides a dragon chariot through the air and collects enchanted herbs for a cauldron of rebirth, much like Ceridwen did, read it up in Ovid. In some cases, Medea is truly a sorceress, in others, her magic is based on trickery and delusion. In a poem by Eumelos, Medea kills and cooks her children as the goddess Hera had promised to revive them in immortal perfection. Sadly, Jason walks in and upsets the rite in the crucial moment. One tale has her cook Jason's aging father in her enchanted cauldron. This works fine, the elder arises as good as new. Pherekydes and Simonides claim that Medea rejuvenated Jason. Even the nurses of Dionysos are said to have gone through her cauldron rejuvenation. A more darksome mood colours the rejuvenation rite of King Pelias, the old enemy of Jason. Medea relates that she can rejuvenate and proves her skill by chopping up an old goat. Casting the pieces into her cauldron she mutters spells and adds forbidden herbs until a young he-goat jumps out of the broth. The old king is understandably excited and orders his guards (or even his daughters) to kill and chop him up. Medea lends a hand, but when it comes to his resurrection, she mounts her dragon chariot and disappears without a word. There is a lot of material which we will ignore in this place, but which you might like to read up leisurely at a future point. Give the story of Osiris and Set a try, and read up on the legend of Sati and Shiva.

Siberian Initiations

All of this should be enough evidence to show that rebirth from a cauldron was a well known topic in old European myth. A myth, however, is often more than just a lively tale. Hidden in this particular myth is a trance practise that comes up quite frequently in the initiation of Siberian shamans. In Siberian shamanism, as I detailed in *Seidways*, initiation was often conferred after a period of disease, misery, desolation or madness. The shaman-to-be is not elected by a human being but by the spirits, who see to it that the candidate is set apart, leaves human society and enters the otherworldly consciousness, a process which may easily take months or years. To the people of the community, the budding shaman is not yet a shaman but simply a lunatic. It is only when the spirits complete the initiation that the crucial difference appears. Usually, such initiations take place in the otherworld, be it out of doors in the forest or in the dream world of trance vision and lucid imagination. To understand this process you should remember that most of the spirits of Siberia are not nice. Each spirit represents a natural force, a specific place or even simpler, personifies a disease. These spirits assemble around the candidate. They take knifes and cleavers and chop her/him to pieces. Usually, the candidate watches the process in a strangely dissociated way, such as the initiate whose head was placed on a sideboard in the tent so he could get a good view. In most cases, the spirits cast the lumps of flesh and bone into a huge iron cauldron, where they leave them seething for a while. This can be a moment, a few hours or even the span of several years, time being as totally subjective as it is. Some shamans have to undergo this process a number of times, others do it once and feel quite content with it. Then the bones are fished dripping wet out of the churning fluids and placed on the floor to sort them. The spirits put the shaman's bones together and thereby resurrect him/her. Sometimes the bones are bound with cord or wire, sometimes glue is used, and finally the body receives a fresh coat of flesh and skin to make it functional again.

This stage is a bit risky in Siberian shamanism. When the spirits sort the bones,

it may well happen that one or several are missing. This is a dangerous situation, as without the missing bones, the new shaman will be handicapped. To make up for the lacking bones, the spirits take bones from the shaman's clan. For each missing bone, so the tradition had it, one relation of the shaman had to die. Other versions have it that the new flesh of the shaman must be taken from clan members. The more powerful shamans underwent this sort of rite several times in their lives, with all the drastic consequences. Other versions of the initiation have the spirits feed on the candidate. They devour the corpse or empty the cauldron, later they throw up the remnants and work their resurrection with a heap of half-digested flesh-pulp. Need I add that shamanism was not exactly a happy vocation in pre-communist Siberia?

The Chödpa Trance

A very similar event made its way into the ascetic practises of Tibetan Buddhism. Here the rite is called gChöd (related with the English word 'cut'). On the dramatic level, the chödpa enters a deep trance state and visualizes a number of spirits (many of them thoroughly malignant), dakinis, gurus and Buddhas. S/he offers her/his body as a sacrificial offering to these entities, who proceed with the happy routine of chopping, boiling, devouring and resurrecting. The whole rite is remarkable for its bloody and dramatic realism. In chöd rituals, much of the magic depends on getting the visions lifelike. For this purpose, the devotees of this rite studied human anatomy on the dead body. Chödpas were the very sort of person who got a job on the desolate sites where the Tibetans celebrated their air burials. It was often the task of the chödpas to cut the corpses into small fragments, bite sized for the flocks of vultures who came flapping out of the wide sky with a hungry gleam in their eyes. Chödpas were also well known for long solitary journeys. Unlike other pilgrims, the chödpas sought out the very places where they could expect danger, wild beasts, angry spirits and creeping disease. At such sites they settled down to meditate, and to offer themselves to the worst entities they could imagine. This was a task of liberation, as even the most hostile spirit is bound to gain some enlightenment when it devours a serene follower of the Buddha.

The rite of chöd is similar to the countless Eurasian rites of death and resurrection, but it is not the same. In Siberia, most shamans underwent such a process only once or twice. This was enough, as the spirits who ate of the shamans flesh automatically became her/his allies. Consequently it was in the best interest of each shaman to be devoured by as many spirits as possible. In Tibetan Buddhism, the rite is a work of compassion that aims at the enlightenment of all participants. It can be a rite to feed violent and stupid angry ghosts, but the gift offering of the entire being of the chödpa may well nourish other entities as well. In this sense it may be understandable that many experts stoutly deny that chöd has anything to do with shamanism. They point at the nun Machig Labdrön who supposedly invented the rite, and proudly insist that this is the only Tibetan rite which did not originate in India. This may be a moot point in my opinion, as similar rites have been popular all over northern Asia millennia before the first Buddhists came to Tibet, but I would agree that the ethical background of the act shows considerable divergence from the usual thing.

The Cauldron Rite

By now you have doubtlessly perceived the parallels between the bloody rites of cauldron resurrection and the spells woven by Ceridwen. Maybe you even want to work such a rite for your own refinement. Congratulations! Let me offer some bits of advice. Here is a simplified structure that ought to be developed and improved. May I count on your bardic creativity?

🜊 begin by choosing a quiet, peaceful place where you can trance for an hour or two without disturbance. Once you have gathered some experience, you can do it out of doors in some dramatically romantic site, but right now it's enough to practise at home. Make things easy for yourself!

🜊 lie down on the floor and relax thoroughly. Allow your attention to move over your body and loosen all those tight bits and tensed muscles. Take a few deep breaths, exhale, sigh and let go. If you find knotted or armoured muscles, tense them and relax, again and again, until they feel loose and warm and comfortable.

🜊 allow your mind to enter a gentle and

Gundestrup cauldron. Horned god, so called 'Cernunnos', holding a torque and a serpent, amidst various real and fantastic beasts.

pleasant trance state. There are plenty of ways to do so, such as watching breath, counting backwards, self-hypnosis, slowing down thoughts and so on. As I hope that you have read some of my earlier books I shall assume that you have a measure of experience. If not, it might be a good idea to master the basics before you set out to perform advanced rituals. The cauldron rites are not suited for most beginners.

🍲   when your body feels relaxed and comfy and your mind has calmed down, you may begin the ritual. It may be a good sign if your breathing has become soft and shallow. Yes, I know some people claim that in trance, breathing ought to be deep. However, much depends on the nature of the trance. Many people breathe very shallowly when they are visualizing, whereas deep feelings are often accompanied by deep belly breathing. If shallow breathing helps your imagination, by all means allow it.

🍲 a measure of dissociation may come in handy. How about astral projection? You can find a detailed treatment of this art in *Helrunar*. Here it ought to suffice that an astral journey is a journey in the imagination. It is inspired imagination, which is a long way from the everyday imagination or day-dreaming. Imagine that you can see yourself resting on the ground. Then imagine a doorway before you until it becomes vivid and clear. Talk with yourself if this helps to make the vision stronger. It may happen that your imagination is hazy and unconvincing at first. This is natural, it will improve as you practise. In every trance

there are phases when perception is not quite focused. If you fuss and get annoyed they will never improve, but if you simply persist and go ahead, your deep mind will soon imbue your vision with a life of its own. This also applies to the process itself. It may take several trances before you get things right. If you complain and wallow in disappointment, you will never get useful results. If you are patient however, and persist in doing your trance rite over days and weeks, you will be amazed to find that the world of imagination is a reality worthy of respect. Give yourself time! Now when the vision of the doorway is moderately clear, open it, pass through and close it from the other side. Explore the spaces you find. It may take a while to get anywhere useful. Each time you pass through a door or gate you get further from everyday reality and closer to pure imagination. It may be useful to go leisurely, and to enjoy the journey. Give your deep mind time to develop the dream worlds, don't expect them to be ready and waiting.

🍲 after a span, you will arrive in a good setting for the rite. Some mages work their rituals in self constructed astral temples, others seek a natural setting. Find a place that seems good and invoke the gods, spirits, ghosts, ancient ones or whoever. It's your choice who should feed on your body and mind.

🍲 leaving your body on the ground as a living sacrifice, assume the form of one of your deities. I usually chose one of the more drastically-minded, such as Kali, Helja or Hsi Wang Mu. If you want a Celtic setting, no doubt the Morrigan or Ceridwen may be a suitable option. Nemetona is a more abstract choice, but may well provide some surprises. Go into a god-form you already have some experience with, choose a darksome deity who has a liking for you.

At this point, you may introduce some several-phase burial elements into the rite. You could start by imagining your death. Looking down at your fleshly form, you can see it die and decompose. Take as long as you like.

🝳 as the god/dess, take a sharp tool and proceed to cut up this piece of carcass before you. Throw the lot into a cauldron. Heat and boil as much as you like.

🝳 invite the other gods, spirits etc. to participate. Let them add their energy to the seething. Then take pieces and joints out of the frothing fluids and offer them to the assembly.

🝳 have a good bite with the others. It is sound practise to eat the offering thoroughly and to leave nothing over.

🝳 When the former person is devoured and digested, you may be brought to life again. Lay out the bones on the ground. Align them properly.

🝳 now the bones have to be re-clothed with flesh. There are many choices. In one script the assembly vomits and throws up the bits and pieces. Excretion is another choice. Or you could be literally reborn out of the womb of some presiding goddess.

Maybe the ingredients of your new flesh appear from an entirely new source. You can recycle your old flesh if you like. You could also form a new body out of rainbow radiance, as happens in some versions of the chöd rite, or you could have all the gods and spirits embrace really close so that they become your new body. Think creatively! How else could you return to the world? Would you like to assemble out of the fruit of fruits, the fruit of the gods of the beginning, the primrose, flowers of the mounds, blossoms of tree and bush, crust of the earth, flowering nettles and waters of the ninth wave? Several lists of Celtic 'elements' appear in medieval myth. Which items seem meaningful for you?

🝳 Finally, shift your attention and awareness from the god/dess who worked the rite and re-enter your freshly reborn body. Go gently. How do you feel? It is a good sign if you find yourself wide-minded and silent at first. Enjoy it.

🝳 when you are done, give your thanks to all beings who participated and return the way you came.

It is often a good idea to do this rite not only once but regularly, say, once a day for the span of a week. By then the visions will have become very developed, the order of events will have attained a measure of elegance and you will vividly sense what is happening to you. Of course plenty of variations are possible. For some good Tibetan ones, see *Tibetan Yoga and Secret Doctrines* by Evans-Wentz, there is lovely stuff waiting for you. Others can be found in the myths of Siberian shamanism or the alchemical metaphors of Taoism. There are countless ways in which you can disintegrate your old form and reassemble in a better one. Before you do this rite, think it through properly. What happens to the corpse? What happens to the bones? Or try something different. Imagine yourself undergoing a complicated rite of refinement, such as the death cult of the Treveri. And what happens when you replace the cauldron with the pit? Solve et coagula is a useful formula in these trances. How can you die and how will you return? What are your ideas? And what do the gods propose? I bet they know much better what is good for you than anybody else. Finally, I would like to add that in my experience, such trances are excellent for health and peace of mind. It may seem that a vivid visualization of death and destruction could damage health, but on the contrary, I find it highly refreshing. Occasionally, such trances have helped me in restoring my health and in rejuvenating my outlook on life. What dies and resurrects is not life but simply belief, be it belief in the world or in the human personality. Whenever I get really stuck in the world of phenomena (a typical danger sign is taking things seriously) I know what is good for me and go straight for the cauldron. The crucial point is that the trance has to be thoroughly dramatic. If you make this a pale and superficial little thing, you shouldn't be surprised if very little happens. This is the time for drama. Remember how we explored your mind's working, and what you can do to make your visions, dreams and representation impressive. This is your mind, you are in charge, so do something useful for a change and do it now.

Cauldrons of Creativity

One of the greatest values in Celtic myth and bardic poetry is that it is so wonderfully creative. Not only that the tales and histories are full of amazing vividness and fresh experience, they also show a number of persons or demi-gods who act in a wonderfully creative fashion. If you know Celtic art, you will appreciate the artistic refinement of the culture, but culture is not only defined by its arts. It's too easy to conceive of cultures in terms of material objects. Behind the objects, the customs, the rituals, lies a wide field of dreamings. These inner visions are the forces that inspire human beings to transform their environment. This is creativity on a large scale. If you study Celtic art, you can see creativity not only in the delicate faces ornamenting a brooch but also in the way houses were built, settlements organized, society structured and so on. Think about it in this way. Creativity is not just a picture, a poem or a piece of music. It happens everywhere. This is one thing that amazes me about people, its how wonderfully creative they are, usually without ever noticing. It all starts really early. The child who learns to make sense of its world is creative. The adolescent who comes to terms with all sorts of hormonal eruptions is creative. Adults are living in a creative representation of what their reality is supposed to be. When two come together and mate, they blend realities; another highly creative act. We are all intensely creative in that we do not inhabit the real world (whatever that may be) but a uniquely subjective world of our very own making. Our creativity determined which parts of the world we chose to be aware of, what and how we think of it, and what we do to keep the trance going. Every consciousness state is the result of creative effort, creativity shaped it, routine maintains it and creativity gets us out of it again.

We find a lot about the way creativity functions when we think ourselves into the cauldron metaphor. The cauldron of knowledge is the head, so we may take the entire beginning of the *Hanes Taliesin* as an account of a yoga worked right in the mind. What do we need to come upon creative ideas?

Find a secluded hut and see to it that you are not disturbed and have enough to maintain your comfort. Clean the cauldron, so that you have an empty, open mind, put water in and add the ingredients. It is sound practise to put small items into the cauldron. For one thing, it takes ages to cook a mammoth unless you cut it up first, and for another, bite sized ideas are easier to handle.

Put plenty of stuff into the cauldron. One way to be creative is to combine a lot of really diverse ideas and to find out how they get along. If you add too many similar ideas, you may overlook something really amazing. Thinking the usual won't get you very far. For a creative broth, the mind needs plenty of variation and complete freedom to play around with it. Heat the cauldron over a steady fire, i.e. energize with emotion and power. Too much emotion and the broth comes surging over the rim, too little and your soup cools before its ready. Use a ladle to stir. This is what confusion tactics are good for - don't just put things (ideas) into your mind, give them a good stir so they get around and make

new friends. Random combinations can be really stimulating, this explains why divination can be so useful, no matter whether the results are obtained by chance or some more subtle means. Give the broth its proper good time to ripen. Patience is needed here, and perseverance and an optimistic attitude. When you know you can't accelerate things, do yourself a favour and enjoy the pause. To find out if you have cooked something edible, take out a ladle of the stuff. A small amount is easier to examine, move or ingest. The same goes for mind - how many ideas can you explore at the same time? Allow it to cool, and taste cautiously. Repeat the performance till satisfied. Or wait till it boils over and you get burned.

In the process of creativity, it can be useful to go through several personalities or points of view. Again, some of this appears in our legend. In Taliesin we have the visionary dreamer, seer, prophet and enchanter who has been everywhere and anything. In this context, Taliesin is your ability to imagine and invent with total freedom. Avagddu corresponds to the nightside of this dreaming, to total activity in realms of chaos and crazyness. Here we have nightmare and delirium. This is not what most people chose to dream, no matter how useful such dreams may be from time to time. The bright vision of Taliesin and the dark vision of Avagddu come together, so you may as well come to terms with them now. Well, after you have been in your visionary seer function you may want to put it into practice. This is essential, there are too many people in the world who dream of doing their will, but never get around to it.

Here we meet Gwion, who tends the fire and stirs the cauldron in steady, even sweeps. Day after day our lad is at work, and with the same patience we set out to effect what we have dreamed up. Observe that Gwion is no dreamer. He has a job to do, and when you ask him he knows everything about watchfulness, patient effort and how to bind the fuel into faggots so that the fire is easier to control. And Ceridwen. In our tale, she has a double function. In one identity, the benign goddess, she arranges for the cauldron, the fuel, the ingredients and keeps young Gwion well employed (if not celebrated). In another she is the malignant one who puts the work to test. This is a step in creative processes which is often mishandled. Testing must have good timing. If you test and criticize and argue about things in the visionary phase, you'll never get anywhere. If you do it in Gwion's phase, the job never gets completed. Once the vital transformation has occurred, the time for testing comes. Ceridwen tests Gwion's initiation by giving him a murderous chase through the elements. She is as fierce and ruthless as she can, and when she spots a flaw, she pounces on it. When she discovers Gwion as a grain of wheat she devours him instantly. Back into the cauldron for another nine months of gestation! Then, as he comes out, she first attempts to kill him - testing again. Being satisfied, she gives him a yet harder ordeal, and casts him into the cold dark waters of the bottomless sea.

In creative thinking, it is often useful to go from one state of mind to the other sequentially. First you hallucinate and imagine like mad. Then you find out what might possibly work, and put it into practise. Once you know it can be done, test it severely.

Creativity is not only stone circles and poesy, it is also brutal architecture and heaps of rubbish on the wayside. Humans creatively shape their environment, whatever they do. That so many streets have brain-damaging architecture may be accounted for when you consider that the architects were creative in cutting costs, not in shaping a life-worthy environment. Humans can be pretty horrible in their creativity unless someone speaks up and reminds us things can be different. So we have critical phases. We test and examine and compare, to estimate whether the new idea works. We also consider what happens if it works, what if too well, and under what circumstances we'd rather not have it working. The last part is really important for the fine tuning. A new idea may be really wonderful, but effect a number of unpleasant side effects. So you think 'What if it doesn't work?' and you also think 'What if it works?' And each time you find something about the idea that doesn't work, you can go round the loop, become the crazed artist again and invent something new.

People approach creativity in many ways. You find samples for many approaches in the Celtic myths. Some are only consciously creative when they feel miserable. Some people only write poems when they feel deeply depressed, others need to feel angry. One poet who was moved to creative song was A-Neirin, chanting the requiem for his slain companions after the battle of Catraeth. Even though no bard, the need, the misery and the tragedy moved him to song. Unhappy sentiments have motivated plenty of artists. Tough luck when misery is the only motivating force. I have met extremely gifted artists who could only be creative when they felt bad. As a result, they periodically wallowed in crisis or made themselves miserable to get their creativity going. This approach works but is very costly in terms of emotional damage. Mad Myrddin was moved to song by his need to communicate oracular visions, by loneliness, desolation, sorrow, misery and passionate remembrance of long bygone joys. The same goes for mad Suibhne, only that this Irish counterpart of Myrddin composed joyous poetry as well, alive with the joy of living a wild life in the wilds of nature.

Some are driven to creativity when they encounter obstacles, or find themselves in difficulties. Ceridwen's decision to boil the cauldron is one such idea born from need and desire, as are many of the fascinations and hugely creative enchantments wrought by the wizard Gwydyon. It is, of course in the songs of the Taliesins that we find the widest range of motivations. You find the bard imbued with wonder and wide-minded awe, praising nature, life and whatever comes his way. This is ecstatic art, fashioned out of joy, gladness and enlightened discovery. By contract the bard is moved to bitter admonishments when people follow erring ways. Sometimes there is a need to communicate, to educate, to stimulate and initiate, thereby passing the essence of the Awen to others in a continuous circuit. An obligation and an adjustment. And what of the songs that influence, that serve political functions, that move the hearts and minds of the multitude?

There are so many ways to be creative. You can start by being creative about when you are creative. When do you think you are most creative? And when the least? How could you put a lot of fresh and original let's have fun now and make it a tale worth telling creativity into those dreary parts of your life where you plod along like a grumpy robot?

If you read carefully, you will have noticed that there are lots of practises and experiences hidden in this book to make you more creative. Think about what it is like to be stuck. Sometimes people are stuck and they know it. If they find out how they achieve and maintain the stuckness, they can also do something different. They are the lucky ones. It's much worse when you are stuck but don't notice. So, just for the fun of it, can you think of three matters in your life that involve routine behaviour and dull repetition, where you could do with a creative boost and a surprise yourself attitude?

Every consciousness, including stuckness, requires some specific forms of behaviour, belief and thought. You have to do (or not to) something to keep it going. If you do anything else, the chances are good that your experience will change.

The Hedge of Mist

This brings us to disruption and confusion tactics, to overload, sense distortion, broken rhythms and other joys. You can see your day as a routine, or a rhythm. If you break the old rhythm, or introduce a new one, experience changes. If you introduced the sun and moon prayer into your daily routine, if you have celebrated seasonal festivities or rites of the times you will know what I'm talking about. Each new pattern produces re-reinterpretation of the world you believe in. This is intensely creative at first. If you make it an automatism however, the stimulating effect will be replaced by a confirming one. Then is the time to go back to the cauldron and fish out something new, or to do the new habit differently.

Or change the way you do something. Do it upside-down-inside-out-back-to-front and in reverse. Take a Taliesin poem. Read the lines starting at the end of the poem and work your way to the beginning. Strange, isn't it? Then read it to the end again. Is it the same poem you knew before? Or read each line as a separate unit. Or invent new punctuation, hell, the punctuation of Taliesin is lucky guesswork anyway. What happens when you deeply ponder each word on its own? Something similar happens when you take some difficult question, preferably an impossible one, and argue for different opinions. Forget about finding a 'right' answer or a 'true' meaning, the important thing is that your mind becomes more flexible. We did this with the Druids, what else can you do it with?

Riddles, enigmatic sayings, oracles and the like have a similar effect. In each case the data seems perplexingly obscure, but the more creative you are, the more sense can you make of it. I have no idea whether there are 'real' answers to the countless questions of the Taliesins, but I know for certain that reading and dreaming and wondering about them has been stimulating and inspiring for me. When data is

sufficiently confusing, the mind tends to invent meaning. It orders the data in convenient patterns. This is pure creativity. You find this approach in oracular prophecy and in the cascades of wildly ranted poetry uttered by foaming bards and feather-clad poets. Like the Nordic scalds, the bards and filid were obsessed by creating a world of dark and subtle poetry full of veiled allusions and secret meanings. The true secret meaning being the one that makes sense to you now, and the one that comes next.

Other ways to upset the usual ways of thinking and behaving present themselves in these pages. Loneliness, fasting, shock, exhaustion, extensive prayer, withdrawing from the world of men, going into the forest, seeking visions at the waters edge, lying in a dark cell, cloth around the head and a heavy stone on the belly come to mind. The bards sought creative vision in many ways, but what they have in common is that they leave the broad road of everyday humanity and enter introverted spaces off the map. The bard must be set apart, just like the witch, the shaman and the priest, to interact between the known world and the greater unknown beyond. On the large scale, this can mean that you ensure that you get at least an hour of being on your own each day, or that you have some time all to yourself from time to time…it's easier to be creative when you actually give yourself a chance to do so. It also means that you find out where you have routines and habits, and learn where these interfere with creativity in thought, experience, word and deed. Then you go out. Out of whatever constitutes normality to you. If you are reasonable, try being unreasonable, if you

Gundestrup cauldron. Bottom plate. The scene might be interpreted as the sacrifice of a bull in a pit, as was common practise in numerous square enclosures in northern Gaul. The bull rises from the bottom of the cauldron, its head used to be crowned by horns (now lost). There are three dogs in the pit (one engraved, the others in three-D) who may or may not be sacrifices. The greatest riddle is the figure with the sword. Her haircut and clothing is very much like that of several other figures on the vessel, but unlike them, she is definitely female. As she holds a sword, it may be that she performed the sacrifices, and as she holds a thumb to her mouth she is presumably some sort of initiate.

are logical, think by intuition, and vice versa. This creates confusion, a break, a gap, an interval, into which fresh inspiration may flow. Do this thoroughly. Make a list and define just what is normal in your life. Then experiment and play around, changing the patterns. You can also do this in your thinking. For some activities, such as decision making, I tend to see vivid movies and images in my mind, then I get an inner voice, speaking about or along, and finally a feeling comes up that settles things. This takes split seconds and may seem almost simultaneous, as the thought process is so well established through yearas of regular application. In most people, such processes take place entirely unconsciously. To make a good poem to encapsulate an atmosphere works much better when I start with a feeling, select images that suit and increase the emotion, and finally let the words flow free. Something similar may be useful to explore a new place or a fetish object. Start by sensing a feeling, then speak about it and watch visions arise before your mind's eye. There are so many variations available. Whatever it is you usually do, try other approaches and surprise yourself with new ways of thinking!

In creative thinking, a vital element is changes of perception. Math transformed Gwydyon and Gilfaethwy into beasts of the woodland in order to make them think differently. Taliesin assumed countless shapes and learned about the world from a million points of view. Here we encounter shape-shifting skills. The shaman who transforms into a spirit may do so in the astral, i.e. in the imagination. But if you want a more thorough change of perception,

a measure of physical enactment may be convenient. Mog Ruith donned his feather costume to arise into the air in shamanic battle. Myrddin ran on all fours and rode deer (Geoffrey), Suibhne wore deer antlers and grew feathers that allowed him to leap from mountain to mountain. Finn chewed his thumb. If you integrate body in your magick, and use it to behave and experience differently, you will get a lot further. Obsession magick, god-forms, invoking and evoking spirits, necromancy and all that are ways that shift perception into unusual channels. The same goes for visionary divination (Imbas Forosnai), for dream induction, astral journeys and the like. What did you learn when you went exploring the mounds of the dead in your imagination? Where else could you travel, what mystery is waiting for you?

Or try another personality. See the world through the eyes of a child, a traveling poet, a person from another age and culture or a visiting extra terrestrial. Use play-acting, assume the part, assume the posture, make use of body language and intonation and playacting to transform the as-if into the as-is. Find out how you breathe, move, hold yourself when you are happily creative. Compare it to your state when you are stuck, dull-minded or counter-productive. Body reflects mental activity, mind reflects body activity. When you know what your body does in each state, you have the choice. What I find especially useful is the eye accessing cues discovered by Bandler, Grinder and Dilts in the early years of NLP. It should suffice, in this place, that people

---

Foliage and flame. A tree of the otherworld.

tend to move their eyes systematically when they are thinking in different sensual representations. Your creativity comes with specific motions of your eyes, and the same happens when you find yourself uninspired or stuck. If you really want to learn something useful, observe how and where you tend to look when you are in various states. This is easier when a friend asks questions and observes your eye motions. Where do you look when you talk with yourself? Where is your gaze when you get access to feeling? Where do you find remembered pictures, and where constructed ones? You can deliberately look into specific directions to stimulate the way you think. And if you find that you don't like your state of mind, change it. If nothing helps, move your gaze in all sorts of directions randomly for a few minutes, you'll find that, whatever else may happen, you won't think the same way you used to.

What happens when you change descriptions? You can take a given event and make it a poem, a picture, a piece of music, a sculpture, a movie or a story. Take any event of today. Can you relate it as a tragedy, a satire, a praise-song, a news bulletin, a historical treatment, an ethnological study, a comedy? Go ahead and do it. What version did you like best? And coming to think of it, is your experience of the event the same it was before? The bards practised this sort of thing. What did they learn about the nature of reality?

Points of view may also be changed when we superimpose new meanings on the world. A rowan twig may be simply a bit of plant, but when you breathe a spell on it and wind it in a knot, it acquires an entirely new meaning and value and becomes a talisman. Superimposed new meanings appear extremely frequently in magical systems. You could call this paranoia in the original sense, all world-views and conceptions of reality are forms of paranoia (look it up, will you?). All models of the world, be they founded on the elements, the zodiac, stars, planets, hierarchies of spirits, assemblages of gods, letters, numbers, trees or whatever show that humans can attach a new significance to just about anything. For a bard, the answer to a given question may be stimulated by a passing bird, a tree at the wayside, a colourful blossom or the wind coming from a specific direction. All of these can make you think different and creativity depends on this. Or think of oracles and divination. If you have a problem, that may be tough enough, but with a bit of divination that problem may appear totally different, and be a challenge, a test, an ordeal, a chance or possibly the beginning of a really good thing. What about rituals, offerings, gestures, circum-ambulations and the like? In each of them, there are superimposed meanings behind forms, gestures, words etc. All of these constitute creative reinterpretation.

And there is communication. One of the best ways to receive useful new ideas is from the deep mind. The trick lies in establishing a channel of communication. Here again we come to diverse forms of divination. This is an active, but indirect approach. Better still, welcome to rites of communion with the spirits and a friendly chat with the muse. As you speak with the deep and carefully receive and consider the replies, you may find that self encounters self in an act of exchange and communion that transforms the mind and the world. The vehicle of this communion is imagination. But what of the roles? Too many only think of asking the deep for answers. They assume the role of the student who approaches an expert. It's not the only approach. Reverse the process, do it differently. What will you reply when the muse wants an answer? Perhaps you may find that you know a lot more than you were ever aware of when the gods, the spirits and the muses begin to question you. This may well be the beginning of a long and happy friendship.

13. Trees of Eternity

The Battle of the Trees

One of the most famous songs attributed to a Taliesin is entitled Cad Godeu, the Battle of the Trees. The song is an elaborate and complicated account involving several strands of meaning. One of them is a strange battle fought by all sorts of trees and shrubs against an unspecified opponent. Another is based on Christian chronology, and combines the proceedings with such Biblical events as the flood, the crucification and the final judgment. The first of these, the great catastrophes which almost extinguished human life on our planet, are a common topic in Celtic and Germanic myth. Here they appear in a Christian context, but are not necessarily a Christian invention. The Celts who proudly told Alexander the Great that they would fear nothing except that heaven might fall on them were not simply boasting; like many ancient culture they remembered a time when heaven did fall on earth, making mountains tremble, woods flame and oceans surge over the devastated land. Together

with these topic, the Battle of the Trees gives a catalogue of lives and consciousness-forms that Taliesin experienced, a glimpse of his creation out of nine qualities, and references to his activities as celebrated head of the bards of the west. The result is a complex and often confusing piece of poetry. Before we continue with it, let me quote the full text, so you may get an idea what we are talking about.

The Battle of Godeu

Book of Taliessin 8
I have been in a multitude of shapes,
Before I assumed a consistent form.
I have been a sword, narrow, variegated,
I will believe when it is apparent.
I have been a tear in the air,
I have been the dullest of stars.
I have been a word among letters,
I have been a book in the origin.
I have been the light of lanterns,
A year and a half.
I have been a continuing bridge,
Over three score Abers.

I have been a course, I have been an eagle.
I have been a coracle in the seas:
I have been compliant in the banquet.
I have been a drop in a shower;
I have been a sword in the grasp of the hand:
I have been a shield in battle.
I have been a string in a harp,
Disguised for nine years.
In water, in foam.
I have been a sponge in the fire,
I have been wood in the covert.
I am not he who would not sing of
A combat though small,
The conflict in the battle of Godeu of sprigs.
Against the Guledig of Prydain,
There passed central horses,
Fleets full of riches.
There passed an animal with wide jaws,
On it there were a hundred heads.
And a battle was contested
Under the root of his tongue;
And another battle there is
In his occiput.
A black sprawling toad,
With a hundred claws on it.
A snake speckled, crested.
A hundred souls through sin
Shall be tormented in its flesh.
I have been in Caer Vevenir,
Thither hastened grass and trees,
Minstrels were singing,
Warrior-bands were wondering,
At the exaltation of the Brython,
That Gwydyon effected.
There was calling on the Creator,
Upon Christ for causes,
Until when the Eternal
Should deliver those whom he had made.
The Lord answered them,
Through language and elements:
Take the forms of the principal trees,
Arranging yourself in battle array,
And restraining the public.
Inexperienced in battle hand to hand.

When the trees were enchanted,
In the expectation of not being trees,
The trees uttered their voices
From strings of harmony,
The dispute ceased.
Let us cut short heavy days,
A female restrained the din.
She came forth altogether lovely.
The head of the line, the head was a female.
The advantage of a sleepless cow
Would not make us give way.
The blood of men up to our thighs,
The greatest of importunate mental exertions
Sported in the world.
And one has ended
From considering the deluge,
And Christ crucified,
And the day of judgment near at hand.
The alder-trees, the head of the line,
Formed the van.
The willows and quicken-trees
Came late to the army.
Plum-trees, that are scarce,
Unlonged for of men.
The elaborate medlar-trees,
The objects of contention.
The prickly rose-bushes,
Against a host of giants,
The raspberry brake did
What is better failed
For the security of life.
Privet and woodbine
And ivy on its front,
Like furze to the combat
The cherry-tree was provoked.
The birch, notwithstanding his high mind,
Was late before he was arrayed.
Not because of his cowardice,
But on account of his greatness.
The laburnum held in mind,
That your wild nature was foreign.
Pine-trees in the porch,
The chair of disputation,
By me greatly exalted,

In the presence of kings.
The elm with his retinue,
Did not go aside a foot;
He would fight with the center,
And the flanks, and the rear.
Hazel-trees, it was judged
That ample was thy mental exertion.
The privet, happy his lot,
The bull of battle, the lord of the world.
Morawg and Morydd
Were made prosperous in pines.
Holly, it was tinted with green,
He was the hero.
The hawthorn, surrounded by prickles,
With pain at his hand.
The aspen-wood has been topped,
It was topped in battle.
The fern that was plundered.
The broom, in the van of the army,
In the trenches he was hurt.
The gorse did not do well,
Notwithstanding let it overspread.
The heath was victorious, keeping off on all
sides.
The common people were charmed,
During the proceeding of the men.
The oak, quickly moving,
Before him, tremble heaven and earth.
A valiant door-keeper against an enemy,
His name is considered.
The blue-bells combined,
And caused a consternation.
In rejecting, were rejected.
Others, that were perforated.
Pear-trees, the best intruders
In the conflict of the plain.
A very wrathful wood,
The chestnut is bashful,
The opponent of happiness,
The jet has become black,
The mountain has become crooked,
The woods have become a kiln,
Existing formerly in the great seas,
Since was heard the shout:-

The tops of the birch covered us with leaves,
And transformed us, and changed our faded
state.
The branches of the oak have ensnared us
From the Gwarchan of Maelderw.
Laughing on the side of the rock,
The Lord is not of an ardent nature.
Not of mother and father,
When I was made,
Did my Creator create me.
Of nine-formed faculties,
Of the fruit of fruits,
Of the fruit of the primordial God,
Of primroses and blossoms of the hill,
Of the flowers of trees and shrubs,
Of earth, of an earthly course,
When I was formed.
Of the flower of nettles,
Of the water of the ninth wave.
I was enchanted by Math,
Before I became immortal,
I was enchanted by Gwydyon
The great purifier of the Brython,
Of Eurwys, of Euron,
Of Euron, of Modron.
Of five battalions of scientific ones.
Teachers, children of Math.
When the removal occurred,
I was enchanted by the Guledig.
When he was half-burned,
I was enchanted by the sage
Of sages, in the primitive world.
When I had a being;
When the host of the world was in dignity,
The bard was accustomed to benefits.
To the song of praise I am inclined, which
the tongue recites.
I played in the twilight,
I slept in purple;
I was truly in the enchantment
With Dylan, the son of the wave.
In the circumference, in the middle,
Between the knees of kings,
Scattering spears not keen,

From heaven when came,
To the great deep, floods,
In the battle there will be
Four score hundreds,
That will divide according to their will.
They are neither older nor younger,
Than myself in their divisions.
A wonder, Canhwr are born, every one of
nine hundred.
He was with me also,
With my sword spotted with blood.
Honour was allotted to me
By the Lord, and protection (was) where he
was.
If I come to where the boar was killed,
He will compose, he will decompose,
He will form languages.
The strong-handed gleamer, his name,
With a gleam he rules his numbers.
They would spread out in a flame,
When I shall go on high.
I have been a speckled snake on the hill,
I have been a viper in the Llyn.
I have been a bill-hook crooked that cuts,
I have been a ferocious spear
With my chasuble and bowl
I will prophesy not badly,
Four score smokes
On every one what will bring.
Five battalions of arms
Will be caught by my knife.
Six steeds of yellow hue
A hundred times better is
My cream-coloured steed,
Swift as the sea-mew
Which will not pass
Between the sea and the shore.
Am I not pre-eminent in the field of blood?
Over it are a hundred chieftains.
Crimson (is) the gem of my belt,
Gold my shield border.
There has not been born, in the gap,
That has been visiting me,
Except Goronwy,

From the dales of Edrywy.
Long white my fingers,
It is long since I have been a herdsman.
I travelled in the earth,
Before I was proficient in learning.
I travelled, I made a circuit,
I slept in a hundred islands.
A hundred Caers have I dwelled in.
Ye intelligent Druids,
Declare to Arthur,
What is there more early
Than I that they sing of.
And one is come
From considering the deluge,
And Christ crucified,
And the day of future doom.
A golden gem in a golden jewel.
I am splendid
And shall be wanton
From the oppression of the metal workers.

There are several ways to make sense of these lines. We can read them like the inspired, but not necessarily well-structured poetry of a bard raving and shaking in the frenetic expression of the Awen. We could also play the Robert Graves game. This implies that our poem is a garbled mixture of several poems, and that we can wrest meaning out of the lines if only we cut them into pieces and rearrange them. Graves did so, in the hope of discovering his vision of the Irish ogham alphabet hidden in this piece of British poetry (the fact that the poets of these cultures spoke entirely different languages seems to have escaped him), and as he made use of Nash's not very accurate translation, which, judging from his correspondence, he did not even own but had to borrow whenever he wanted to comment on the material, the result turned out to be thoroughly fantastic. Now I should add that Graves did not intend to reconstruct anything practical. He wrote his best selling *White Goddess* in a few short weeks, without bothering to check his sources, as a poetic declaration of love for a goddess of poets which he had made up very much in his own mind. He knew that his approach was that of a poet and dreamer, and was surprised at the amount of eager but badly informed readers who gobbled up his fancies as if it were a historical study. Privately, he called the work a crazy book (see Hutton), but in public he never dared to disenchant the countless admirers who had fallen for his romantic delusions. After all, the *White Goddess* made a lot of money, which it wouldn't have if its author had been a bit more honest. That the work should become one of the pillars on which a wide range of neo-pagan faiths were erected was certainly not in his intention.

To continue with our poem, I very much doubt that we are dealing with a song that was deliberately garbled by a bunch of British bards who sought to hide the secret tree lore of their craft. Nor would I agree that the poem was compiled of several unrelated items by some monkish scribe - after all, the confused and ranting style of Taliesin poetry appears in plenty of songs, the *Cad* being no exception. Taliesin songs do rhyme and if we chop up lines and reintroduce them elsewhere it certainly ruins the poetic structure. No matter how we look at it, the song remains a mystery, and I for one enjoy this situation. There are, however, some small items of Celtic lore which might shed light into the dark. In the 13th century. Welsh Triads (trans. Bromwich) we find an item entitled:

Three futile battles of the Isle of Britain: One of them was the battle of Goddeu: it was brought about by the cause of a bitch, together with the roebuck and the plover; the second was the action at Ar(f)derydd, which was brought about by the cause of a lark's nest; and the third was the worst: that was Camlan, which was brought about because of a quarrel between Gwenhwyfar and Gwenn-hwy(f)ach. This is why those (battles) were called futile: because they were brought about by such a barren case as this.

While the deeds of these symbolic animals are anything but clear to understand, the three battles all appear prominently in Island Celtic lore. The first in the poem you have just read, the second is the incident when Myrddin saw his family and king slain and fled to the forest screaming with madness, the third is the final battle of old Arthur. A much younger reference appears in the *Myfyrian Archaiology*, a compendium of bardic lore compiled by various enthusiasts in the early 19th century. Here we read:

These are the englyns that were sung at the Cad Goddeu, or as others call it, the battle of Achren (trees), which was on account of a white roebuck, and a whelp; and they came from Annwn, and Amatheon ap Don brought them. And therefore Amatheon ap Don, and Arawn, king of Annwn, fought. And there was a man in that battle, who unless his name were known could not be overcome, and there was on the other side a woman

called Achren, and unless her name were known her party could not be overcome. And Gwydion ap Don guessed the name of the man, and sang the two englyns following:

Sure footed my steed, impelled by the spur;
The high sprigs of alder are on thy shield;
Bran are thou called, of the glittering
branches.
Sure-hoofed my steed, in the day of battle:
The high sprigs of alder are in thy hand;
Bran thou art, by the branch thou bearest-
Amatheon the good has prevailed.

If we assume that this is a reliable fragment of bardic lore, we are dealing with a myth that is nowhere else recorded. Some figures of the *Mabinogi* appear. Amatheon son of Don is a brother of Gwydion and Govannon, he is an elusive figure who seems to be some divine ploughman. If we can trust this text, Amatheon somehow went to the other or underworld Annwn.

Arawn (Silver Tongue?) was one of the regents of Annwfn, as you read in the first branch of the *Mabinogi*, a friend of the human chieftain Pwyll and the person responsible for the existence of such otherworldly creatures like pigs on this merry earth. Pwyll, as you recall, received his pigs as a gift, whereas Amatheon seems to have acquired his white roebuck and whelp without Arawn's consent. The colour white, by the way, is typical for otherworldly beasts in Island Celtic myth. We may assume that Gwydyon and Achren (trees) fought

---

The gorge.

on the side of Amatheon, and that Bran and Arawn were their opponents. Bran is not quite a ruler of the otherworld, his royal seat being at Harlech in North Wales, but in a strange way he does connect with the unearthly realm. After his ill-fated war with the Irish, a poisoned missile caught the gigantic monarch in his leg or thigh. Knowing that he would soon die, he had his brother Manawyddan decapitate him, and asked that his head be borne to Britain. Grievously Manawyddan performed the offensive task. To his surprise, Bran's wonderous head remained alive, and when they returned to their homeland, they were amazed that it did not rot but spoke with the company every day. Bran, though dead, was still alive in the merrymaking of his friends, who feasted in the company of the wonderous head for eighty years. Then a forbidden door was opened, the spell broke and the head began to rot. It was buried so that it might protect Britain from all invasions, but as legend has it, Arthur unearthed it again, as he did not want his people to rely on the protective virtues of a skull. Bran the Blessed, however, found his way into the myths of the continental troubadours, where he appears prominently as the wounded fisher king who guides the holy grail, or as the brother of some such regent. As the grail castle is an otherworldly location, we can at least assume why Bran appears in company with Arawn. The gloss from the *Myfyrian Archaiology* identifies Bran with the alder, in the second branch of the *Mabinogi* it is Bran's nephew, the unlucky Gwern, whose name means alder. That Bran bears an alder branch may or may not connect him with various branch bearers of

Island Celtic myth, and perhaps with the Irish poets who traveled under branches made of precious metals. It may be worth considering that the bards and poets are so frequently associated with trees, bushes and flowering plants. Taliesin has several references to this topic, and when you look at the nine qualities that went into his creation, you can see that kinship with plants is more important to the ancient singer than kinship with humanity.

A place of complete benefit,
And bards and blossoms.
And gloomy bushes,
And primroses and small herbs,
And the points of the tree-shrubs. (*BoT 13*)

The list of nine qualities is such an important item that I strongly suggest you spend some time contemplating its meaning. Several magical elements appear in it. The fruit of fruits, for instance, is possibly an abstract essence and appears on the list before the fruit of the primordial god (s). The primrose -a loose term that may refer to several plants of the primula family - could be a reference to the primula veris, the cowslip, which appears in several folk tales as the key-flower which can open the gates to the deep. The primula are all springtime plants and among the first to greet the new year. Is it flowers of the hills we see in the next line, or flowers growing on the mounds? Who or what is represented by the flowering trees and bushes? Trees for aristocracy and bushes for peasants? Or trees for the gods and shrubs for humans? Earth of an earthly course could be the circuit made by bards or kings each year, a sacred journey around frontiers and boundaries, or possibly refer to the ancient belief that it is but a thin crust of earth that divides the world of mortals from the subterranean underworld. For those who know, the veil is very thin. The nettle-provided we are talking about the stinging nettle - is a plant well suited to symbolize the bardic power to admonish or destroy by means of black satire. The waters of the ninth wave are at the very limit of the known world, any further and we leave the foam sparkling sea and disappear into the wider and unknown waters of space. If you recall that we are often dealing with abstractions, not with the things used to symbolize them, we may learn a bit about Taliesin's secret nature. A somewhat similar list appears in poem 6 of the *Black Book*:

It was with seven faculties that I was thus blessed,
With seven created beings I was placed for purification;
I was gleaming fire when I was caused to exist;
I was dust of the earth, and grief could not reach me;
I was a high wind, being less evil than good;
I was a mist on a mountain seeking supplies of stags;
I was blossoms of trees on the face of the earth.

What is going on at the battle of the trees and what shall we make of it? Plenty of solutions have been offered to this questions, none of them fully satisfactory. One possible explanation might be that the trees refer to clans or tribes who once participated in some war. Some families derived their names from trees: Mac Cuill (Son of Hazel), Mac Cuilinn (Son of Holly), Mac Ibar (Son of Yew), Guidgen (Son of Wood), Guerngen (Son of Alder) and Dergen, from Dervo-genos (Son of Oak), see Ann Ross.

Maybe the enduring custom of Scottish plant badges is related to this idea. Most clans had one or several plants or trees that could be used as a symbol of their kinship-line. Among the most widely popular trees are oak (Anderson, Macanderson, Buchanan, Cameron, Kennedy, Macfie, Stewart), pine (Ferguson, Fletcher, Grant, Macalpine, Macaulay, Macfie, Macgregor, Mackinnon, Macnab, Macquarrie, Rob Roy), holly (Drummond, Macinnes, Mackenzie, Macmillan), boxwood (Macbain, Macduff, Macgillivray, Macpherson, Macqueen), mountain ash (Maccallum, Maclachlan, Malcolm, Menzies), juniper (Gunn of Kilernan, Macleod, Murray, Ross), heather (Macalister, Maccoll, Macdonald, Macdonell, Macintyre, Macnab). Less widely used are bramble (Macnab), fern (Chisholm), hazel (Colquhon), Scots fir (Farquharson), Poplar (Ferguson), broom (Forbes, Matheson), yew (Frazer of Lovat), ivy (Gordon), mistletoe (Hay), hawthorn (Johnston, Ogilvie), crab apple (Lamont), lime (Lindsay), furze (Logan), cypress (Macdougall), bracken (Robertson), whin (Sinclair). Not all clans made use of trees for symbolism, you also encounter fir club moss, deer-grass, bulrush, bog-myrtle, cranberry, red whortleberry and other plants (See R. Bain 1968). I leave it to the historians to work out which symbolic associations started the fashion and which trees or plants were introduced later, when more and more clans came into being.

Has there ever been a battle of trees? I was greatly delighted when I chanced to read in Livy (59 BCE-14CE) that a Celtic tribe, the Boii, fought the Roman legions with trees. This is how the story went. Sometime after the year 215 BCE, Lucius Postumius, potential consul, led two legions and a large voluntary army, altogether 25 000 armed men, through the forest of Litana into the land of unruly Gaulish tribes. As they passed through a densely wooded ravine, the forest came falling on them, mighty trees shattering on the ground, scattering the cavalcade, demolishing wagons, crushing men and beasts. After the trees followed volleys of arrows, and before long not a single Roman soldier remained alive. Livy tells us that the cunning Boii had almost cut through the tree-trunks of the entire forest, so that even a light touch would send the trees toppling. When they knew the Romans had entered the ravine, they immediately cut down the outer trees of the forest. These toppled inwards, the wide crowns and massive stems crashing into the next row of trees, and before long the forest itself went surging like a green flood. The Boii were thorough. They caught Lucius at the end of the ravine, as he was trying to reach a bridge, and he died fighting. The Boii took his head and his armour to the holiest of their temples in triumph, *and when they had cleaned the skull as is their custom, they inlaid the skull with gold and it served as a sacred vessel, which they used to offer libations and as a cup for the priests and the overseer of the temple...*

Here we have, though the account is doubtlessly a bit exaggerated, a semi-historical account of trees destroying an army. The Romans recorded their version of the event, how did the Boii and their friends preserve their version? Is it possible that oral history has transmitted some vague and distorted shadow of the original battle to the medieval bards of Britain? Though we cannot be sure of the answer, we do know that oral history sometimes can reach a surprising age. Tacitus tells us that the Gaulish Celts, when they rose in armed revolt against the Roman conquerors in the year 69, roused their fighting spirit by recalling how Celtic warriors had sacked Rome under the command of Brennius (Bran) in 387 BCE. Story tellers had kept that event in living memory for more than 400 years.

Ogham Trees.

To the Irish filid, there were two sorts of wood. One is the natural wood, as it grows in the forest, the other is the artificial wood. The Irish word fidh means both an alphabetical letter and a tree, or sort of wood. In Gaelic, just as in the German language, the letters were intimately connected with the trees. Principal wood was vowels, cross-wood diphthongs, side woods are consonants. For the sake of the metaphor, the Irish poets may well have thought of themselves as experts in wood-work. A similar strand of thought appears among the Welsh bards, who liked to describe themselves as *Carpenters of Song* and who taunted imitators to seek the forest and to cut their own wood. Here we come to a knotty subject that can do with a bit of exploration. The Gaelic Celts of Ireland and Scotland had an alphabet of 20, later of 25 letters which was perfectly adapted for carving bold strokes into a memorial stone or a wooden rod. Such inscriptions can be found on memorial stones in Ireland, Scotland and in Wales, mainly on the side facing Ireland. This should not suggest that the British wrote in ogham, there are no ogham inscriptions in their language. It simply points at the uneasy period in the time of the 4th-6th centuries. when much of coastal Wales was occupied by Irish settlers.

The memorial stones amount to some 300 inscriptions, some of them in Gaelic and Latin. Usually these texts consist only of tribal or personal names. Medieval lore tells us of ogham inscriptions on wood. Cu Chulain for example used to write challenges in riddle form on hoops and forks of wood, and left them, with the odd head or three, to be read by his countless enemies. Others used ogham to pass secret messages. The filid themselves handled ogham as a secret language. While the ordinary form of the letters is easy to write and read, they invented dozens of more or less complicated codes, sign language and the like to keep the alphabet exclusive to themselves. The structure of the letters is wonderfully simple. You start out from a central line. In a stone, this was usually the ridge. Using a chisel,

Top: the common ogham alphabet.
Center: two methods to encode the letters.
Bottom: Two mysterious signs given on a page of the Ogham text without explanation. The square shape is called Fionn's Window, the round one Wheel Ogham of Roigne Roscadach, *Book of Ballymote.* Are we dealing with magical amulets, meditation mandalas or diagrams to encipher writing!

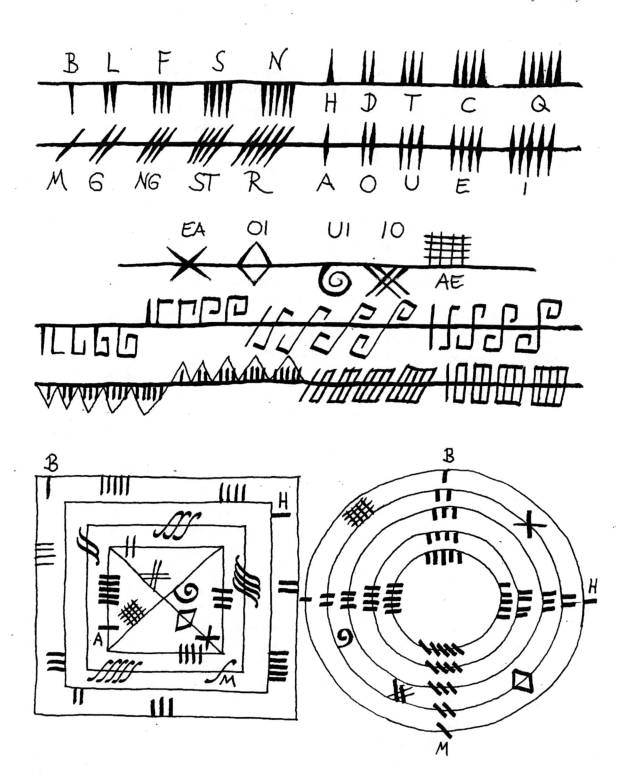

the letters were carved below the edge (B-group), above the edge (H-group), slanted across the edge (M-group) and straight across the edge (A-group). The letters of each group resemble numbers in that they consist of one to five lines grouped closely together. As this works on all sorts of ridges, the poets could make do of many items to signal their secret messages across the noisy and tumultuous halls of the lords. One method is to use the shin as a ridge and the fingers for letters (to the right of the shin for group b, to the left for group h, athwart for group m and straight across for group a, this was called *foot ogham*), another used the nose, or the central axis of the body itself. By placing up to five fingers to the right or left, slanted or across the ridge, a letter could be communicated. I doubt that whole phrases were communicated thus, as spelling them out takes time and close observation, but in many cases we can expect that a single word, or even a single letter could signal an important idea with no outsider recognizing what was going on.

According to medieval legend, it was the Irish god Ogma mac Elathan, called Sun-face, who invented the alphabet and fought at the side of the Tuatha De Danann against the monstrous Fomors. Some researchers identify him with the earlier Gaulish god Ogmios who is an old man in a lion fur, wielding a club and looking remarkably like Hercules. He is a miracle of eloquence, and leads his audience by chains that run from his tongue to their ears, or so Lukian tells us. A lead curse-tablet found in Vorarlberg names Ogmios together with two typical deities of the underworld. Maybe he also pulled his audience to the netherworld with his finely crafted chains.

Most modern Celtic enthusiasts are aware of ogham as a 'tree alphabet' and many are familiar with the peculiar version invented by Robert Graves. What few seem to be aware of is that there is not one, but several ogham alphabets, and that these are not only concerned with trees but with a wide range of subjects. To begin with, the ogham is an alphabet. Now some of the tree names are more or less identical with the names of the letters. One or more trees are associated with each letter. The choice of trees depends upon the arbitrary relation of sound, not upon any occult principle or secret cosmology, unless one believes that Gaelic is the perfect language (as the filid did). Let me explain.

The ogham begins with the letters b,l,f, and these are associated with beithe, the birch, luis, elm or rowan, and farn, alder. The reason behind the association is similarity of the letters and the words. If you wished to make an English tree alphabet, you might begin apple, birch, chestnut, dog-rose, elder, fern, gorse, hawthorn...this order is based on sound and alphabetical syntax, it does not have a secret reason why apple came first, birch second and so on. Mind you, there might be occult reasons to prefer apple to alder or ash, there being several choices for the letter a. This also happened in Gaelic, so there are occasionally several trees and plants under the heading of a single letter. With other letters, scant choice is possible and you have to be happy to find a tree at all. This is the background to the idea that ogham is a tree alphabet.

Some ogham letters have several trees associated to them, others include miscellaneous items. Better still, the filid made up ogham alphabets for a lot of subjects, such as castles, rivers, kings, crafts and trades, birds, colours, so it is by no means certain whether the ogham started as a tree alphabet, or whether the trees were assigned later. Again, these alphabets went by letter. B stood for beithe (birch), ban (white) and besan (pheasant), King Bran, the church of Bangor, castle Bruden, river Barrow, St. Brennain and so on. Now birch and white suit each other admirably. What

they have in common with the pheasant is less obvious, let alone with kings, saints and fortresses. It takes a bit of really creative qabalistic thinking to make sense out of this connection. To modern minds, such relations may seem arbitrary. To a poet who believes that there is a divine and blessed element to the Gaelic language, the connection of birch, white and pheasant was by no means coincidental. Given enough creative thought, you can find or invent a connection between these

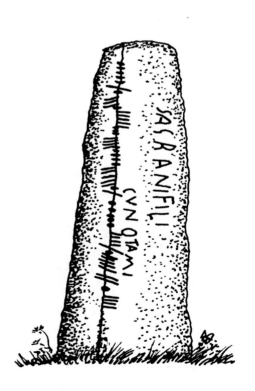

Ogham stone with Latin and Gaelic inscription.

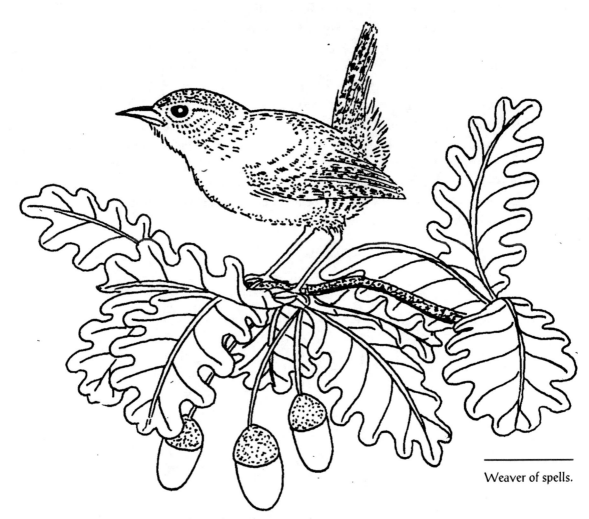

Weaver of spells.

seemingly unrelated phenomena. This is what qabalistic models are good for: they widen the mind and produce creative interpretations. If you expect a secret connection, you will be sure to find one.

Let us now look at several ogham alphabets. The first entry, marked (BWAnE) refers to a brief list of trees given in the *Auraicept-Na N-Eces*, the *Scholar's Primer*, named the *Book of Woods*. A second, even shorter list appearing in the *Primer* is marked (TFAnE), for *Trees in the Forest*. A simple (AnE) refers to miscellaneous short entries

scattered here and there throughout the text. The third list is entitled *Word Ogham of Morann Mac Main* (MMM), the fourth *Word Ogham of Mac Ind Oic* (MIO). These come from the *Ogham Tract* of the *Book of Ballymote* and the *Yellow Book of Lecan*. To simplify the grammatical structure, which is full of repetitions, I have slightly shortened and rearranged George Calder's excellent translation. As you will see, the lists are neither complete nor always in agreement with each other. At the end of each section you can find the associations of *bird ogham*, *colour ogham* and *art ogham*. Similar lists naming kings, churches, saints, rivers, agricultural tools etc. were omitted - you can look them up in Calder's translation of the *Primer*. Even a *herb ogham* and a *food ogham* used to exist, sadly, the *Ogham Tract* offers no details. All of these lists are based on the earlier twenty letter ogham.

B-Group

B, Beithe, on the birch was written the first ogham inscription that was brought to Ireland, to wit, seven birches were brought to Lugh son of Ethleann, to wit, thy wife will be taken from thee…unless thou watch her. It is on that account B is still written at the beginning of the ogham alphabet. (BWAnE)
B, Beithe, first letter on the path of the ogham alphabet. (TFAnE)
B, birch, faded trunk and fair hair. (MMM)
B, birch, most silvery of skin. (MIO)
Besan (pheasant?), ban (white), bethumnacht (livelihood).

L, Luis, the mountain-ash, delight of eye is mountain-ash, i.e. rowan, on account of the beauty of its berries. (BWAnE)
L, Luis, elm in the forest. (TFAnE)
L, Luis, quicken tree, delight of eye, a flame. (MMM)
L, Luis, elm, quicken tree, friend of cattle, dear to cattle is the elm for its bloom and for down. (MIO)

Lachu (duck), liath (grey), luamnacht (pilotage).
 F, Fern, alder, the van of the warrior bands, alder, for thereof are the shields. (BWAnE)
 F, Fern, alder in the forest. (TFAnE)
F, Fern, alder, shield of warrior bands, owing to the redness in the same respect, the material of the shield. (MMM)
F, alder, guarding of milk, for of it are made the vessels containing the milk. (MIO)
Faelin (gull), flann (red), filideacht (poetry).
        (F reads V in the inscriptions)

S, Sail, willow, the colour of a lifeless one, i.e. it has no colour, i.e. owing to a resemblance of its hue to a dead person. (BWAnE)
S, Sail, willow in the forest. (TFAnE)
S, Sail, willow, hue of the lifeless, hue of the dead. (MMM)
S, willow, activity of bees, willow for its bloom and for its catkin. (MIO)
Seg (hawk), sodath (fine-coloured), sairsi (handicraft).

N, Nin, ash, of it are made the spear-shafts by which the peace is broken, or, a check on peace, a maw of a weaver's beam which is made of ash, in time of peace weaver's beams are raised. (BWAnE)
N, Nin, maw of spear or nettles in the woods. (TFAnE)

N, Nin, ash, checking of peace, the maw of a weaver's beam, a sign of peace. (MMM)
N, ash, fight of women, maw of a weaver's beam. (MIO)
Naescu (snipe), necht (clear), notaireacht (notary work).

H-Group

H, Huath, white-thorn, a meet of hounds, it is formidable owing to its thorns. (BWAnE)
H, Uath, test tree or white-thorn, on account of its thorniness. (TFAnE)
H, Uath, thorn, pack of wolves for a terror to any one is a pack of wolves. They are a thorn, and in the same way. (MMM)
H, Huath, blanching of face, fear, blanched is a man's face when he is encompassed with fear or terror. (MIO)
Hadaig (night raven?), huath (terrible), h-airchetul (trisyllabic poetry).
(The letter H does not occur in any surviving inscriptions. In speech, it was usually used to denote that the letter preceding it should be deleted. Thus, the word Ogham is pronounced Oam, the word Sidhe is Shee. Combined with b, h produces a p, a letter that does not occur in Gaelic but was needed to write foreign names. H in itself was never pronounced, except as a mark of aspiration. Calder refers to G. Atkinson, who pointed out that the letters of the h-group may be named after the five Gaelic numerals haon, do, tri, ceathar, cuig.)

D, Duir, oak, higher than bushes is an oak. (BWAnE)

D, Dur, oak in the forest. (TFAnE)
D, Dur, oak, highest of bushes. (MMM)

D, oak, carpenter's work. (MIO)
Droen (wren), dub (black), druidheacht (wizardry).

T, Tinne, holly, a third of a wheel is holly because holly is one of the three timbers of the chariot wheel. (BWAnE)
T, Tinne, holly or elderberry in the forest. (TFAnE)
T, Trian, another thing the meaning of that to-day. (MMM)
T, Tinne, holly, fires of coal. (MIO)
Truith (starling), temen (dark grey), tornoracht (turning).

C, Coll, hazel, fair wood, every one is eating of its nuts. (BWAnE)
C, Coll, hazel in the forest. (TFAnE)
C, hazel, fairest of trees, owing to its beauty in woods. (MMM)
C, Coll, hazel, friend of cracking. (MIO)
(no bird recorded), cron (brown), cruitireacht (harping).

Q, Queirt, apple tree, shelter, a wild hind. (BWAnE)

Q, Quert, quicken tree or aspen. (TFAnE)

Q, Quert, apple-tree, shelter of a hind, i.e. a fold: to wit, boscell, lunatic, that is bas-ceall, death sense, it is then that his sense comes to him when he goes to his death. Boscell, that is, hinds, to wit, they are light. Lunatics or hinds. (MMM)

Q, Queirt, apple tree, force of the man. (MIO)

Querc (hen), quiar (mouse-coloured), quislenacht (fluting).

M-Group

M, Muin, vine-tree, highest of beauty, because it grows aloft. (BWAnE)

M, Muin, vine, mead (from it). (TFAnE)

M, Muin, vine, strongest of effort, owing to identity of name with muin, back of man or ox, for it is they that are the strongest in existence as regards effort. (MMM)

M, a man's back, condition of slaughter. (MIO)

Mintan (titmouse), mbracht (variegated), milaideacht (soldiering).

G, Gort, ivy, greener than pastures is ivy. (BWAnE)

G, Gort, cornfield, fir. (TFAnE)

G. Gort, ivy, cornfield. Sweeter than grasses. (MMM)

G, ivy. (MIO)

Geis (swan), gorm (blue), gaibneacht (smithwork).

NG, Ngetal, broom or fern, a physician's strength is broom or fern. (BWAnE)

NG, Getal, broom. (TFAnE)

NG, Getal, broom, a physician's strength, there is an affinity between cath, panacea (?), and getal, broom. (MMM lists this letter twice)

NG, (missing in MIO)

Ngeigh (goose), nglas (green), ngibae (modelling).

ST, Straiph, black-thorn, the hedge of a stream is blackthorn. (BWAnE)

STR, Straif, willowbrake in the forest. (TFAnE)

STR, Straif, sloe, strongest of red, in the sloe red for dyeing the things is stronger, for it is it that makes the pale silver become azure, making it genuine (?) silver. It is it which is boiled through the urine into the white gold so as to make it red. (MMM)

STR, sloe, increasing of secrets. (MIO)

Stmolach (thrush), sorcha (bright), sreghuindeacht (deer-stalking).

(No authenticated inscriptions bear this letter)

R, Ruis, elder, the redness of shame. (BWAnE)

R, (missing in TFAnE)

R, Ruis, elderberry, intensest

of blushes, from the reddening or shame according to fact, it is a reddening that grows in a man's face through the juice of the herb being rubbed under it. An ingot of a blush. (MMM)

R, Ruis, elder, redness of faces, sap of the rose, so that blushing is in them. (MIO)
Rocnat (small rook?), ruadh (red), ronnaireacht (dispensing).

A-Group

A, Ailm, fir-tree, pine-tree. (BWAnE)
A, (missing in TFAnE)
A, eldest of letters and noblest among vowels. The first expression of all living and the last sigh of all deceased. (AnE)
A, Ailm, fir-tree, loudest of groanings, wondering, for it is A a man says while groaning in disease, or wondering, that is, marvelling at whatever circumstance. (MMM)
A, Ailm, beginning of an answer, the first expression of every human being after birth. (MIO)
Aidhircleog (lapwing), alad (piebald), airigeacht (sovereignity).

O, Onn, furze. (BWAnE)
O, Onn, furze or ash. (TFAnE)
O, Onn, furze, helper of horses, the wheels of the chariot. Whin, equally wounding. (MMM)
O, Onn, stone, smoothest of work. (MIO)
Odoroscrach (scrat?), odhar (dun), ogmoracht (harvesting).

U, Ur, heath. (BWAnE)
U, Ur, thorn. (TFAnE)
U, Ur, heath, fresh, cold dwellings; Uir, mould of the earth. (MMM)
U, Ur, heath, growing of plants; Uir, soil of the earth. (MIO). Uiseog (lark), usgdha (resinous), umaideacht (brasswork).

E, Ebhadh, aspen, test-tree, horrible grief. (BWAnE)
E, Edad, yew. (TFAnE)

E, Edad, aspen, trembling tree, distinguished wood. (MMM)
E, aspen, synonym for a friend. (MIO)
Ela (swan), erc (red), enaireacht (fowling).

I, Ido, yew. (BWAnE)
I, Ida, service tree. (TFAnE)
I, Idad, yew, service tree, oldest of woods. (MMM)
I, Idad, yew, most withered of wood, or sword, service tree. (MIO)
Illait (eaglet?), irfind (very white), iascaireacht no ibroracht (fishing or yew wood work).

Diphthong-Group

EA, Ebhadh, aspen. (BWAnE)
EA, Ebad, elecampane. (TFAnE)
EA, Ebad, aspen, most buoyant of wood, fair swimming is this wood, a name for the great raven, for salmon, for stag, for ousel. (MMM)
EA, Ebad, aspen, woodbine, corrective of a sick man. (MIO)

OI, Oir, spindle tree or ivy. (BWAnE)
OI, Oir, spindle tree. (TFAnE)
Oi, Oir, spindle tree, most venerable of structures. (MMM)
OI, heath, beauty of form. (MIO)

UI, Uilleant, honeysuckle. (BWAnE)
UI, Uilleann, ivy.
UI, Ui, woodbine, honeysuckle. (MMM)
UI, woodbine, great equal length. (MIO)

IO, Iphin, gooseberry or thorn. (BWAnE)
IO, Pin, pine, gooseberry.
IO, Ifin, gooseberry, sweetest of woods. (MMM)

IO, Pin, Ifin, gooseberry, most wonderful of taste. (MIO)

AE, (letter is missing in BWAnE)
AE, Emancoll, witch hazel. (TFAnE)
AE, Emancoll, expression of a weary one, alas (Ach! Uch!), though it may be taken for something else. (MMM)
AE, (letter is missing in MIO)

(The dipthongs may be pronounced as their vowels indicate, or they may stand for long vowels. AE was occasionally used for X when required to introduce a word from Latin. Likewise, IO was occasionally used for the P sound missing in Gaelic)

To complicate things further, the four groups (b, h, m, a) are associated with a wealth of other phenomena. In *water ogham* you have rivulets for group b, weirs for group h, rivers for group m and wells for group a, i.e. four wells equals the letter e. Then there was *women ogham*, group b featuring heroines, group h nuns, group m maidens and group a girls. Thus, a poet speaking or chanting of two heroines could well be referring to the letter l and whatever was associated with it - a subtle code that only made sense to fellow poets. *Dog ogham* supplied watch dogs for group b, greyhounds for group h, herd's dogs for group m and lap dogs for group a. *Cattle* being of such importance, group b could be represented by bulls and milch cows, group h by oxen and strippers, group m by bullocks

First green
in the
beech
forest.

and three year old heifers, group a by steers and yearling heifers. *Human being ogham* had men for group b, nobles, women and clerics for group h, youths for group m and lads for group a.

Origins of Ogham

As you see, the ogham alphabets are not identical. To begin with, while we usually have one or more trees for each letter, for some obscure reasons the tree association is occasionally absent. Did the ogham start out as a tree alphabet? The *Scholar's Primer* proposes several answers. According to the filid's version of the *Tower of Babel* story, the letters were named after the 25 noble poets who studied with Fenius Farsaidh, you may recall him from the chapter on the Irish filid, he practically invented Gaelic by assembling all that was best in the languages of the world. As an alternative theory, the filid proposed that the letters come from trees:

> Others, however, say that it is not from men at all that the Ogham vowels are named in Gaelic but from trees, though some of those trees are not known today. For there are four classes of trees, to wit, chieftain trees, peasant trees, herb trees and shrub trees; and it is from these four that the Ogham vowels are named.

Chieftain trees are oak, hazel, holly, apple, ash, yew, fir.
Peasant trees: alder, willow, birch, elm, white-thorn, aspen, mountain ash.
Shrub trees: black-thorn, elder, spindle tree, test-tree, honeysuckle, bird-cherry, white hazel.
Herb trees: furze, heather, broom, bog-myrtle, lecla, rushes, etc.
To make things more difficult, the *Scholar's Primer*, as usual, contradicts itself by offering a second version of this list:
Eight chieftain trees: alder, oak, hazel, vine, ivy, sloe, furze, heath.
Eight peasant trees: birch, quicken tree, willow, ash, white-thorn, whin, apple tree. All other shrubs are peasant trees.

This list does not clear up the problems in working out the origin of the ogham, as it does not fully fit any of the known ogham alphabets. Please keep in mind that to the filid, ogham itself was something of a mystery. Its origin was unknown, and if the ogham lists included trees which were unknown to the poets of medieval Ireland, the wonderful question comes up just where the oghams originally came from. This is a really tricky question. No matter what some simple minded enthusiasts claim, ogham is not 'the ancient Celtic alphabet' as it was only used by the Gaelic Celts. Its earliest appearance is on memorial stones of 3rd century. southern Ireland. The letters are miles away from the Gaulish alphabets, the Alpine and north Italian alphabets or the curious script favoured by the Ibero-Celts. For some mysterious reason, the letters written by the Continental Celts before the Roman occupation have more in common with runes and the late medieval coelbren alphabet (used by the British bards) than with the stark simplicity of the ogham script. Most ancient alphabets of Europe had letters which had evolved out of signs and symbols. By contrast, ogham is based on numbers.

Who evolved the ogham scripts? You can answer this question any way you like. There were even some serious scholars in 19th century Ireland who proposed that ogham, pronounced Oam, is cognate with the sacred word of Hindus and Buddhists, and proves that Druidry came from India.

There are many more questions regarding ogham. You already noticed that the ogham letters come in five groups of five letters. In the original inscriptions surviving on memorial stones, the last group of five diphthongs is completely absent. It may be assumed that these letters were introduced much later, and that the filid got so confused about attributing trees and creepers to them as they were not originally part of their alphabet. Calder notes that the vowels in the dipthongs were usually pronounced separately. Robert Graves, doing horrible things to the ogham alphabet, reconstructed what he fancied to be its original form. This involved moving some sounds around (he never bothered to consider that his alphabet cannot be used to read old inscriptions) and inventing a calendrical system, the so-called Celtic tree calendar, an entirely artificial and modern hybrid. In his work, Graves wished to redefine an ancient and poetical language and accidentally invented a modern one. I very much agree with the subjective and personal approach, but believe that in all honesty, we should consider it not as a reconstruction but as an innovation. If you wish to bring a tree alphabet to life, it should be one suited to your will and nature. It should fit the trees you know and love, and the time you live in. It should be honestly subjective, it shouldn't hide its origin behind a mask of ancient authority

and venerable tradition. As you saw earlier, reconstructing the 'original' or 'true' ogham alphabet is impossible, even the medieval filid failed at the job. They were already mightily confused and we are more so. Who knows if a single tree alphabet ever existed, or whether there were several such systems from the start? So I suggest we forget about the genuine old thing and replace it with genuine new insight. What sort of tree alphabet would you chose for yourself?

Tree Magic

In the first twilight, Mogh Ruith and his son Buan left the house of the Druidess Banbhuana where they had received a prophecy and stayed for the night. Buan had had a vision and Mogh Ruith was explaining it. As they returned, messengers from High King Cormac arrived, asking Mogh Ruith to come to an agreement. Angrily, the old blind Druid refused, and the messengers left to inform Cormac of the failure of their mission. One of Cormac's Druids, Cith Rua, spoke up and declared their final stategem. 'There is nothing we can do for our troops' he announced, 'except to make a Druidic fire!' 'How is it made?' inquired Cormac.

'Send your troops into the forest to cut rowan wood, for in the circumstances it is the best we can use. Fires shall be lit by each party and when the fires turn southward, it will be well to pursue the men of Munster. Should they turn to the north, however, it is our own troops that will be defeated.'

While Cormac's troops set out to gather as much rowan as they could carry, the Munstermen observed their efforts and came running to inform Mogh Ruith about it. The old Druid instantly understood the enemies intentions. He ordered the Munstermen to go south to the wood of Leathaird, were they were to collect an armful of firewood each. All except for Fiacha, who was to *bring a load on his shoulders of a hard tree where the birds of spring rest (?) from a mountainside where the three shelters meet - shelter from the March wind, from the wind from the sea, from the wind of flame (?), so that once kindled, it will become an inferno.'* Soon they returned to the camp and erected a mighty pyre in its center. Mogh Ruith then ordered Ceann Mor to build up the firewood. He did so, forming it *like a churn but having three sides and three corners and seven doors, while the northern fire only had three doors. Moreover, it was not properly sited or arranged.* When all was ready, the old Druid got out his flint. Scowling at the terrified Munster warriors, he ordered them to cut shavings from their spears. He made a bundle of them and recited a spell, invoking a powerful fire, an angry flame, fast and furious, that will rush to heaven, incinerate the forests and subdue the hosts of King Cormac. As the pyre erupted in flame he sang another song, invoking the *god of Druids,* his *god above every god,* to make the wind blow, to burn young and old vegetation,

A quick burning of the old,
A quick burning of the new
Sharp smoke of the rowan-tree,
Gentle smoke of the rowan-tree,
I practise druidic arts,
I subdue Cormac's power...

Hastily, he ordered his own ox drawn chariot to be made ready, and that all warriors be prepared for the moment when the fires turn northward. Then Mogh Ruith exhaled a Druidic breath *into the air and the firmament so that an obscuring thicket and a dark cloud arose* over the men of Cormac and drenched them with a rain of blood. As the Druidic fires roared over the land, they devoured all the plants and trees on the central plain of Munster and ascended to the heavens where they attacked each other like two lions. At this point, Mogh Ruith asked for the hide of a hornless brown bull. Wrapping himself up in it, he *donned his speckled bird-mask with its billowing wings... He proceeded to fly up into the sky and the firmament along with the fire, and he continued to turn and beat the fire towards the north as he chanted a rhetoric. 'I fashion Druid's arrows....'* Soon Mogh Ruith had overcome the spells and fire of Cith Rua. Descending from the sky he got into his ornamental chariot with its raging oxen and ordered the army of Munster to march against the panicking troops of Cormac. On the way, he overtook Cormac's three chief Druids, Ceacht, Crotha and Cith Rua. As his gods had promised to petrify the three, Mogh Ruith merely had to exhale a Druidic breath at each of them, and the wise men turned into rocks. This put an end to High King Cormac's efforts to extract unjust taxes from Munster.

With this account ends our story of Mogh Ruith. It is so valuable that I propose you get yourself Sean O Duinn's translation and read it up in full. Here you have the lot: spellcraft, enchantment, astral projection, breath-magic, all in a setting that will remind

---

Dazzled by dancing leaves.

readers of Velikovsky or the countless end-of-the-world myths you can find all over this planet, most of them involving fierce floods, blood rain, fires in the sky and a devastated land. What other cultures attributed to divine wrath or fighting deities, the Irish filid blamed their Druids for.

In actual spell craft, plenty of plants were used by the Gaels. In Skye, mistletoe, club moss, watercress, ivy, bramble, figwort, St. John's wort and bog violet were magical plants, and used for enchantment and folk spells. In southern Scotland, herbs to banish witches were ivy, bindwood and fern. Plants favoured by witches were hemlock, nightshade and foxglove. Witches were known to hate rowan, yew, elder, witch-elm and holly. Instead, they much prefered to ride on broom, thorn and ragweed. It s no coincidence that the white wand of Bride was generally made by peeling birch, broom, bramble or white willow. Carmichael collected a strange rhyme called the *Choice of Timber*. I very much doubt that it refers to firewood and leave it to you to decide just what the timber was chosen for:

Choose the willow of the streams,
Choose the hazel of the rocks,
Choose the alder of the marshes,
Choose the birch of the waterfalls,
Choose the ash of the shade,
Choose the yew of resilience,
Choose the elm of the brae,
Choose the oak of the sun.

Closely connected may be the tradition of the sacred trees. You may recall the La Tène Celts with what seems to be trees or poles set in the dark hollow of cult shafts deep below the surface. Perhaps their builders thought in terms of a sexual symbolism, but just as well they may have made a tree for the underworld. That the other- (not necessarily under-) world has a special tree appears from the *Mabinogi*. In the tale of *Peredur*, our hero comes to a bizarre otherworldly place. Here he sees two flocks of sheep, grazing on both sides of a river. One flock is black, the other white, Ever so often, when a white sheep bleated a black sheep would cross the river and turn white, and when a black sheep bleated, a white sheep came over and turned black. Could this be an allegory for people dying and being reborn?

On the bank of the river he saw a tall tree: from roots to crown one half was aflame and the other green with leaves. (Trans. Gantz) Few images are as fascinating as this dual tree, thriving and flourishing, but all the time being devoured by hungry fire. It is a tree that embodies life and death, or spring and autumn, the bright and the dark half of the year. We know of the Goloring, a large circular La Tène earthwork with a massive timber post in its center. Trees were important to the Celto-Germanic people of central Europe, many of whom believed in a pillar, a tree or a column connecting heaven, earth and underworld.

In ancient Ireland, a number of sacred trees are on record. According to the Rennes Dindsenchas, translated by W. Stokes, quoted by Ann Ross, there were :

The tree of Ross and the tree of Mugna and the ancient tree of Dath-i and the branching tree of Uisnech and the ancient tree of Tortu - five trees are those. The tree of Ross is a yew...a king's wheel, a prince's right...a straight firm tree, a firm strong god. Now the branchy tree of Belach Dath-i is an ash...Now the tree of Mugna is an oak (Anne Ross notes the Eo means yew, not oak)...three crops it bore every year i.e. apples, goodly, marvellous, and nuts, round, blood-red, and acorns, brown, ridgy. The tree of Tortu was an ash...Due northwards fell the Ash of Uisnech.

So we have three ash trees and two yews. No oaks n spite of Pliny's tale. Sacred trees can be observed in several Indo-European cultures. To this day planting and worshipping a tree is part of the Indian Navaratri festivals. In earlier times, this ritual was more elaborate. The king used to invade a neighbouring realm, to cut down the tree worshipped by the locals and to plant his own. Nowadays the rite is softer and shorter, the kings have been abolished and small-scale warfare between provinces is frowned upon in a democracy. Nevertheless, the sacred tree of a district counts as its religious focus. The same presumably went for the five Irish provinces with their sacred trees. Occasionally the king was praised as a mighty tree towering over the land. Warriors were regularly compared with strong trees in bardic poetry, as they were supposed to stand firmly rooted on the battlefield. People identified with trees, but not arbitrarily. Each tree had a number of qualities, real or metaphorical, and these were something people could identify with. Last, there were the two great lovers of Irish romance, the Ulster chieftain Baile mac Buain and Ailinn, princess of Leinster. Like so many romantic lovers, they received false tidings regarding the

death of the other and immediately died of grief. From Baile's grave, a yew grew, while Ailinn's grave was graced by an apple. Only seven years later, both trees had reached full height, the crown of each having a resemblance to the person buried underneath. The filid cut them down and made a tablet of wood from each of them. On these tablets, they recorded the visions, espousals and courtships of Ulster and Leinster. When 150 years later the tablets were brought together, they flew towards each other and stuck so that they could not be separated. Thus they were kept, so legend has it, in the treasury of Tara till the palace was burned in 241 CE, so some scribes recorded in 1511.

A Tree Companion

I am a depository of song; I am a literary man;
I love the high trees, that afford a protection above, (BoT3)

What we observe in the ogham alphabet can also be see in the bardic tradition of Britain: a deep flowing stream of love, respect and veneration for the trees that formed the face of the land. Tree worship, healing lore and spellcraft are all intimately connected, and form a blend of knowledge and myth that was vital for the lore of our ancestors. In their love and veneration for trees, the so called Celtic and Germanic people are very much alike. The *Edda* proposed that the first humans were created by Odin, who shaped the men out of ash and the women out of elm or alder (the translation is not without difficulties). Tacitus, in his *Germania*, referred to the sacred groves in which his 'Germans' keep their idols and 'certain signs' and adored their deities. According to Tacitus, they found it unfitting to confine their gods in walls or to picture them in human shape. The same was reported regarding the inhabitants of Gaul and Britain, if we can trust the accounts of Druidic open air worship in secluded forest dales and sacred groves. This is not quite true, as some tribes evidently had small temple buildings or shrines, and the odd wooden idol, sometimes humanoid, sometimes abstract, has appeared from the confines of the swamps that conserved them. With and without idols and buildings, the sacred, dedicated forest appears prominently in Central European religions. The 'Germans' in his works are not necessarily Germans, however, as the term is completely artificial and loosely applied on anyone living in the Roman provinces of Germania inferior and superior, including plenty of Celtic speaking tribes.

Similar groves, if we can trust our sources, were the hallowed sites of Druid ritual and sacrifice in Gaul and Britain. Even the early church buildings seem to have picked up some of this belief, as their pillars and roofs were often adorned with symbolic branches and leafs. Be that as it may, trees and their lore were essential to survival. The cultures were so intimately connected with the forest, and the knowledge of tree medicine, tree properties and tree magic was in their very life blood. To these early cultures, the distinctions between magic and medicine were anything but defined. The forest contained blessings and dangers of many shapes, and no doubt a lot of tribes developed their very own tree lore, depending on whether they preferred to dwell in windy hill country, swampland or in the tangled forest at the riverside.

In this chapter I shall cite a number of folklore traditions regarding trees. The bards and poets, as custodians of the knowledge of their culture, were wise in the myths and legends of the green world. If we set out to recover their knowledge in this age, we encounter the problem that so very little reliable old lore has survived. Tree lore still exists, usually in the shape of countless folk customs, but it is next to impossible to identify specific 'Celtic' or 'Germanic' elements. I shall now treat you to a small dictionary of tree knowledge, compiled from a number of Central and West European sources. It is in all likeliness not exactly what the British bards or the Irish filid believed about trees. Even between these traditions a lot of divergences appear, let alone on the Continent where cultural confusion and churchly repression of pagan lore were so much more thorough. Early sources on the topic are rare, and occasionally tainted by the legends given by the Greek and Roman authors, with whom many medieval scholars were more familiar than with the beliefs entertained by the peasants of their own country. Nevertheless what emerges is a picture of a wide spectrum of tree beliefs. Take it as an example and make use of it to define and distill your own tree alphabet, your own range of sacred and enchanted tree spirits. This is not just innovative syncretism, it may be the best way to make the forest-myths come to life for you, and as such closer to the direct inspiration of the bards. Regarding sources,

I have to add that regretably, most of the earlier legends (and we are talking about medieval legends, not about the countless myths enjoyed by pre-historic cultures and since then long distorted or forgotten) are woefully incomplete when it comes to their origin, time and place. Few medieval writers bothered to give their sources with any degree of accuracy, and when we come to folk customs recorded in the last centuries, many researchers were just as sloppy as the earlier authors. For simplicities sake, the trees are listed in the modern alphabetical order, not in one of the ogham alphabets. Several plants were included as the ogham alphabets class them as trees.

S = Scots folklore
I = Irish folklore
B = British folklore
G = German speaking countries
BoT = Book of Taliesin
RBoH = Red Book of Hergest (trans Skene)
BBoC = Black book of Carmarthen (trans Skene)
BoA = Book of Aneirin (trans Skene)
SG = Attributed to the seer Suibne Geilt, Translation:
Murphy

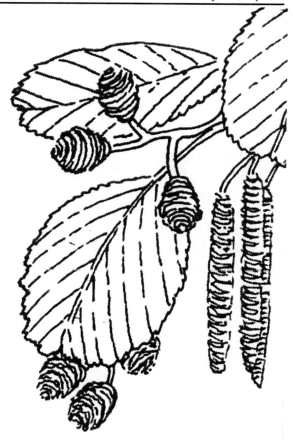

Alder.
(Alnus glutinosa, Alnus incana)
The alder-trees, the head of the line,
Formed the van. (BoT 8)
When is of purplish hue the alder. (BoT 7)

Alder, you are not hostile; beautiful do you gleam;
You are not...prickly (?) in the gap in which you are. (SG)

As a tree of swamp and stream, the alder survives more water than any other European variety. This is due to a symbiosis between the tree and a fungus that waterproofs the roots and allows the tree to survive extended springtime floods. Alder wood bleeds red sap when it is cut. It is not very durable in its dry state, but in contact with water it lasts longer than other timbers. Troughs, buckets and water funnels were made of alder. Much of Venice was built on alder poles. (G): Mythologically, alders grew in uncanny swampland where all sorts of witches, fairies and malignant spirits could be expected. In folklore, the alder (German:

Erle) appears as a Lady Arle, Irle or Else. The later, known as the Rough Else, was a formidable apparition whose tale was told in the *Wolfdietrichsage* in the 13th century. Wolfdietrich is sitting at the campfire when Rough Else appears, her skin rough like bark, her hair tangled, her eyes gleaming madly. When she asks him to marry her, the poor fool says no. So she puts him under a spell, and as he strains to escape her embrace, he goes insane and runs through the nightside swamp forest like a crazed beast. When he wakes the next day, covered in leaves and mud, she is already there and waiting for him. Again she appeals for his love. Again he refuses, and this time she curses him. A sleep spell knocks him out, and once he lies helpless, she cuts two locks from his hair and two nails from his hands. This makes him her prisoner. For half a year he errs through tangled growth and twisted roots, for half a year he sleeps on the ground, feeds on grasses and herbs. Then an angel appeals to the sorceress to take the curse from him. Lady Else eventually does so, and asks a third time for his hand. Obviously still beside himself, he gives in and marries her. Then she takes him to the harbour, where a great ship is waiting for them. The ship traverses the wide foaming sea and finally the young couple arrive in a strange country where Rough Elsie is greeted as the queen. She smilingly acknowledges the orations, then goes for a bath in the fountain of youth and reappears with wonderfully restored beauty and a much happier outlook on life.

What lies behind the tale of the swampland apparition is not only the archetypal story of the bright and dark lady, but also a curious belief in swamp demons. The swamp is the darksome simmering cauldron of many strange fevers and afflictions, and those who unwarily dwell there, may well be plagued by worse creatures than Rough Else. Folk medicine often seeks the cure where the disease originates. Alder bark was used in tea to reduce fever. The inner bark was soaked with vinegar and rubbed on the skin to make it unattractive for vermin.

Apple. (Malus sylvestris, Malus domestica)

12. Bright the tops of the apple-tree; circumspect is
Every prudent one, a chider of another;
And after loving, indiscretion leaving it.
13. Bright the tops of the apple-tree, circumspect is
Every prudent one, in the long day a stagnant pool is malarious;
Thick is the veil on the light of the blind prisoner. (RBoH 9)

Sweet appletree of delightful branches,
Budding luxuriantly, and shooting forth renowned scions...
Sweet appletree, a green tree of luxurious growth,
How large are its branches, and beautiful its form...
Sweet appletree, and a yellow tree,
Grow at Tal Ardd, without a garden surrounding it...
Sweet appletree that luxuriantly grows!
Food I used to take at its base to please a fair maid,
When, with my shield on my shoulder, and my sword on my thigh,
I slept all alone in the woods of Celyddon...

Sweet appletree that grows in the glade!
Their vehemence will conceal it from the
lords of Rhydderch...
Sweet appletree of delicate bloom,
That grows in concealment in the woods!...
Sweet appletree, which grows at the
riverside!
With respect to it, the keeper will not thrive
on its splendid fruit.
While my reason was not aberrant, I used to
be about its stem
With a fair sportive maid, a paragon of
slender form.
Ten years and fourty, as the toy of lawless
ones,
Have I been wandering in gloom and among
spirits...
Sweet appletree of delicate blossoms,

Which grows in the soil amid the trees!
The Sibyl foretells a tale that will come to
pass-
A golden rod of great value, will, for bravery,
Be given to glorious chiefs before the
dragons...
Sweet appletree, and tree of crimson hue,
Which grows in concealment in the wood of
Celyddon;
Though sought for their fruit, it will be in
vain...(BBoC 17, attributed to Myrddin)

Apple-tree, apple-treelike one, strongly do all
men shake you; (SG)
Lots of apple-trees appear in European
myth. In general, they were believed to
carry the blessing of heaven. In Norse myth,
you find the goddess Idun (related to the
Island Celtic Dana or Don?) whose special
gift are the apples of immortality. Each of
the gods has to eat an apple a year, otherwise
the aging process sets in very swiftly. In
folklore, apples are often love-gifts, traces
of this custom appear in the *Edda*, where
Skirnir offers apples as a love gift to the
unwilling giantess Gerda. (G): In Germany,
Christian myth did not favour apples that
much, as the apple was held to be the fruit
of the tree of the knowledge of good and
evil, forbidden to man by Godalmighty
personally. Eve and Adam couldn't resist a
bite, and suffered from shame, mortality
and having to go to work. To hint at the
evils of carnal lust and the wages of sin, a
common medieval symbolism combines
apples with skulls.

In prehistoric Europe, the wild apple
from the forest was one of the few varieties
of fruit available. They could be stored over
the vitamin hungry winter. Wild apples are
much smaller, harder and more sour than

the modern varieties, most of which were introduced during the Roman occupation or the Christian conquest, courtesy of 'Saxonbutcher' Charlemagne. The oldest preserved apple comes from a Neolithic settlement near Heilbronn and is almost 6000 years old. It is possible that the cultivation of wild apples began in this early period. It didn't progress very far, to the Romans the German apples were something of a joke, as were the folks who ate them.

In many rural districts the last apples on the tree, usually the ones hanging from the highest branches, were left on the tree as a gift for the heavenly forces. This echoes an important tradition: if you collect plants or fruit, go gently and leave some. Pseudo-Christian folklore has it that on Xmas night, the apples in the forest flower suddenly. Those who spend this night under an apple tree can see heaven open above them, and catch a glimpse of God and the angels. Traditionally, for each boy an apple tree was planted, and a pear or hazel for every girl. These trees were closely connected to the humans they represented, to hew them down could be a fatal deed. Apples were always stored far from the rooms where people sleep as they can cause headaches. The ethylen emitted by the apple can make other fruit ripen more rapidly, but it can also cause them to grow in odd shapes and rot more speedily. Folk medicine used raw scraped apple against diarrhea, backed apple against constipation, tea made from dried apple slices as a fever reducing remedy and apple-blossom water to improve the skin.

(B): In Island Celtic tradition, the apples were associated with paradise, and with the enchanted land of Avalon, a word meaning apple-dale. The apple was an otherworldly fruit. (I): Here the association with the otherworld is just as strong. An apple is the gift that young Connla receives from the otherworldly immortal lady who came from the western paradise. He immediately fell in love with her, and in the weeks to come subsided entirely on a diet of this one apple, which luckily renewed itself. A branch of an apple tree was carried by the fairy woman who came to visit Bran, it had twigs of white silver and crystal fringes with flowers.

Ash. (Fraxinus excelsior)

The extensive booty of the ashen shaft is my fair Awen. (BoT 37)

A hundred received his attack on the earth,
Like the roaring of the wind against the
ashen spears. (BoT 46)
1. Bright are the ash-tops; tall and white will
they be
When they grow in the upper part of the
dingle;
The languid heart, longing is her complaint.
(RBoH 9)

30. Mountain snow-the hart on the slope;
The wind whistles over the ash-tops.
A third foot for the aged is his stick. (RBoH
4)

1. Entangling is the snare, clustered is the
ash;
The ducks are in the pond; white breaks the
wave;
More powerful than a hundred is the counsel
of the heart. (RBoH 8)

Ash-tree, baleful one, weapon for a
warrior's hand. (SG)

An English rhyme goes:
With a four-leafed clover,
a double-leafed ash, and green-topped seave
(rush),
You may go before the queen's daughter
without asking leave.

Double leafed ashes are a rarity, the twigs
usually terminating in a single leaf, so if you
are lucky enough to find a double-leafed
one, that luck is bound to last. Some
inhabitants of the British isles also had the
belief that ash trees keep serpents away.

Many superficial researchers call the ash
the primal world tree of the Germanic
people. More cautious researchers point at
the fact that this myth comes from Iceland,
where the ash doesn't grow, but the rowan,
or mountain ash does. Rowans are not
related to ash trees, but they look so much
like smaller cousins that old literature
invariably believed them related. So the
ash, or the mountain ash appears as the
world tree of the Nordic cultures. In this
function it has three aspects: as Yggdrassil
it is the shamanic horse ridden by Odin
(Yggr) between height and depth. As
Mimameith it is the mysterious tree of the
giants, of unknown origin and unknown
destiny. As Laerad (Giver of Peace) the tree
provides food and nourishment for all living
beings (see *Helrunar*). Medieval medicine
made use of boiled bark, roots and leaves to
produce snake bite medicine. The leaves
were frequently fed to cattle and horses as
a welcome change of diet. They were also
brewed as a tea against arthritis and
rheumatism. The bark of young branches
yielded a tea against fever, otherwise the
fresh bark was used to bind wounds. Ash
wood is tough and elastic, making it
excellent for spears and hunting weapons.

Aspen. (Populus tremula) and Poplar (Populus alba, Populus nigra)

The aspen-wood has been topped,
It was topped in battle. (BoT 8)
The poplar by its trembling is heard by me in
due course;
It's quickly moving leaves remind me of a
foray. (SG)

(G): A medieval belief had it that the cross
was made of aspen, and that this ill deed
makes the leaves of every aspen shake to
this very day. Aspen is the loudest of all
poplars, as its leaves catch the slightest

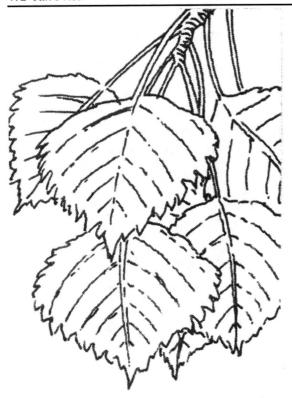

This may be related with a special type of ogham script that was used to record the ill deeds of kings and great male and female personages - in code, so things didn't become too widely known. The aspen rod may well have been used for curses.

Beech. (Fagus sylvatica)

The most common tree of the central European forest, the beech is a tree that throws so much shadow that underneath, no other trees can grow. Consequently, the primal beech/oak forest of the prehistoric Celts and Germans had little undergrowth. Like massive pillars, the beeches towered over wide and shady halls. Beeches occasionally grow in twisted and

breeze and tremble. The trembling made the tree a synonym for a coward.

(S):In Scotland the fable assumed such proportions that aspen were cursed and sweared at, as the tree was considered haughty. In their myths, the aspen had not bent its head when Jesus passed on his way to his execution. Witnessing this, the Roman soldiers made the cross from aspen. Pious highlanders used to throw stones at the tree, and never used it for farming gear (Carmichael).

(I) *Cormac's Glossary*, trans. Stokes, states: *Fe, then, is a wand of aspen, and gloomy the thing which served with the Gaels for measuring bodies and graves, and this wand was always in the cemeteries of the heathen, and it was horrible to every one to take it in his hand, and everything that*

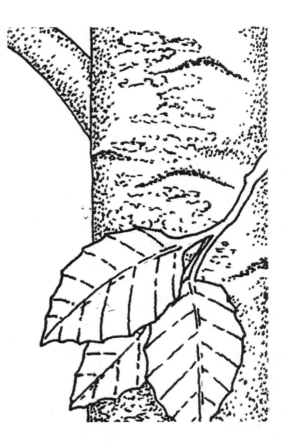

wonderfully distorted forms. When the branches grow apart and later join again, a natural hole appears. Such 'needle-eye' trees, just like the oaks, were popular sites to find a cure. One such tree in northern Germany was used for rejuvenation. You have to approach the tree in the night before May. A bath in a nearby spring cleans the body, a prayer the soul. Then you have to climb through the hole in silence, each repetition makes you younger by one year. One person overdid it, the next morning the locals found a screaming child under the tree.

A tradition from the south claims that cutting beeches at night raises the wrath of the wild hunt. A splinter cut at Halloween shows what winter will be like: is it wet, so will be the season. Likewise, plenty of beechnuts are said to predict a cold winter. Beeches are closely connected with writing and divination: the word Buchstabe, i.e. staff of beech means alphabetical letter in German. The smooth skin of the tree is ideal for writing and scratching, and for this reason, spells and messages were recorded on it. In common belief, a beech was the best shelter in thunderstorms (common sense disagrees). Beech-ash was a popular remedy against toothache, it was also used for soap. To make beech-lye, the ash was steeped in warm water for six hours or more. According to Pliny, the Gaulish Celts made a shampoo out of beech, goat fat and bramble juice (for a reddish tinge). Shampoo was unknown to the Romans, they soon began to import great quantities, as fluid and in balls, from Hessen. Beech-ash mixed with St. John's wort appears in medieval medicine as a disinfecting paste. The leaves, whole or crushed, were used to cool infected wounds or swollen eyes. Beechnuts were vital for the mast of the great squealing pig herds that were driven into the beech forest each autumn. The nuts are rich in oil (up to 25, some say to 40%) and people used to eat them as a snack. This is not recommended as the nuts (unlike the oil) contain hydrocyanic acid. Leaves, bark and husks contain fagine, a slightly narcotic chemical which can produce vertigo in men and beasts when large amounts are ingested. The wood of beeches was always highly valued fuel as it burns very hot.

Birch. (Betula pendula, Betula pubescens)

The birch, notwithstanding his high mind,
Was late before he was arrayed.
Not because of his cowardice,
But on account of his greatness...
The tops of the birch covered us with leaves,
And transformed us, and changed our faded
state. (BoT 8)

3. The calends of winter, the stags are lean,
Yellow, the tops of birch, deserted the
summer dwelling;
Woe to him who for a trifle deserves
disgrace. (RBH 7)
4. The saplings of the green-topped birch
Will extricate my foot from the shackle;
Disclose not thy secret to a youth. (RBH 8)

Blessed is the birch in the valley of the Gwy,
Whose branches will fall off one by one,
two by two,
It will remain when there will be a battle in
Ardudwy...
Blessed is the birch in Pumlumon,
Which will see when the front of the stag
shall be exalted...
Blessed is the birch in the heights of
Dinwythwy,
Which will know when there shall be a
battle in Ardudwy...(BBoC 16)

Smooth blessed birch, musical and proud,
beautiful is every entangled branch high up
on your top. (SG)

(G) A popular tree symbolizing
springtime, fresh green and innocence. The
green twigs appear in countless May-time
festivals, when the village population went
out into the forest to cut twigs or even
young trees to bring 'the May' into the
settlement. Being touched with such a
branch confers health and blessings. Doors
of houses and stables were decorated with
birch twigs. When the leaves had dried up
they were powdered and fed to farmyard
animals, to protect them from evil and
disease for a year. Burning such leaves as
incense banishes evil spirits. On the first of
May, many a lass found a fresh birch branch
or even a young tree in front of her door,
left as a token of affection by her sweetheart.
To keep the fey folk from your farm during
dangerous Walpurgisnacht (Beltane), place
a branch across your doorstep, or even
better, set up a whole young tree. Any witch
desiring to come in is forced to count all
leaves, which hopefully takes till sunrise.

Birches were also used as may trees in
some districts, though spruce and fir seem
to have been more popular. To combat the
last surviving pagan rites, in 1225 a certain
minister called Johannes boldly cut down
the may tree in Aachen, while the population
was happily dancing under the wreaths
hanging from its leafy crown. The resulting
tumult soon became a political problem,
ending eventually in the grudging
permission that may festivities were
henceforth officially allowed. An oracle of
three birch rods: peel one, peel another
partly and leave the third as it is. Place them
under your pillow on the 22nd of June. The
next morning, pull one out without looking.
The lot you draw shows the financial state
of your future spouse: peeled equals poor,
bark equals wealth, the third is middlish.
Brooms are often made of birch, the ones
made during the 12 nights between the
winter solstice and the 6th of January, when
the wild hunt roars across the snow laden
skies, are said to last longest. A birch broom
placed across the doorstep is a sure method

to ward off evil, the same goes for one placed upright behind the door.

Brooms can also be used to sweep diseases from pigs, no doubt the method works wonders on people as well. In the Alps, when thunderstorms threatened, a birch-twig thrown into the hearth-fire could ensure safety from lightning stroke. An amulet of birch worn next to the skin, prevents cramp. The 77 spirits of arthritis can be banished into a birch tree if you know the right spell, the disease is transferred and when the tree recovers from it, so do you. Birch leaves were also added to food, drunk as tea for a springtime cure (it stimulates the bladder) or the bark was slashed open so the sap could be collected ('forest water'), a practise I cannot recommend, as the tree suffers badly. A strong glue was made out of birch pitch (Pliny mentions that the Celts of Gaul use it) and the bright bark was used to form waterproof containers, hats or manuscripts. A German saying has it that 'the birch arms late'; meaning that the branches take a while to become firm. Something similar may have been on the mind of the Taliesin who wrote the *Cad.*

(B) The Welsh bard Gruffydd ab Addaf ap Dafydd, c. 1340-1370, composed a lengthy ode to a birch entitled *To a Birch Tree Cut Down, and Set Up in Llanidloes for a Maypole.* In no uncertain terms the bard complains that the tree, when it used to grow in the wild was *a majestic sceptre of the wood... a green veil.* Now, he protests, it had been violated, crudely cut and carried by brutal force to the town center where it stands mean and miserable. In the forest, the bard had enjoyed many a May night

underneath the tree with his beloved, on the market place its leaves are withering and no birds sing from its wretched, tangled twigs. (see K. Jackson, 1971)

Blueberry. (Vaccinium myrtillus)

(G) Those who collect berries can expect to run into trouble. Earth spirits, forest spirits, the berry-folk and even the wild hunt itself can be hungry for the collected berries, so the children or adults on the job have to take extra precautions to avoid theft, ill-health or a sprained foot. In some districts, there are bells which can be heard ringing deep underground. As they sound a black

dog appears, and when it's gone again, so are the berries. In Bavaria, the berry-man was placated by an offering of berries, bread and fruit, placed in three orderly heaps on a convenient stone. In Bohemia, all berries that fell to the ground were a gift to Mary, to pick them up again was to invite an accident. A handful of berries had to be offered by throwing them into a hollow tree in wide parts of middle and southern Germany, in Bendahl there was an oak that received the offering. Each collector had to take the first three berries and crush them on the tree trunk, which eventually turned totally black. Otherwise the first three berries could be tossed over the head or the left shoulder. On the 2nd of July, berry collecting was especially dangerous. The virgin Mary was said to be in the berries on that date, combing her hair or riding a white horse, and for some unchristian reason she used to steal children. To dream of the berries was bad luck. Astonishingly, the medical use of the berries and leaves to cure diarrhea was next to unknown in medieval literature. The plant supplied a strong colour valued by painters.

Bramble. (Rubus fruticosus, Rubus caesius)

7. The saplings of the bramble have berries on them;
The thrush is on her nest;
And the liar will never be silent. (RBoH 8)

(S) Occasionally, bramble was combined with rowan and ivy to form an amulet of protection. In such cases, it replaced the more popular woodbine (MacNeill).

(G)From all the thorns, bramble is perhaps the most persistent in taking hold, tearing coats and drawing blood. The slender tendrils of the plant can produce fantastic thickets. When such a branch reaches out far enough, it can grow into the ground again. This forms a natural arch. If you crawl underneath, the thorns take hold of your diseases, especially of skin troubles, and release you cured. A child that fails to walk can be made to crawl silently under such an arch on Friday morning before sunrise. Three repetitions are said to cure the affliction. In northern Germany, a wreath of bramble roots is worn under the hat on the way to church, it makes witches visible, who seem to carry small barrels on their heads. Barrels? What about cauldrons?

In folk medicine, bramble leaves are fermented to produce a good tasting tea which was occasionally prescribed to soothe a nervous stomach or to reduce menstrual bleeding. The leaves contain mild astringents. Boiled in ash-lye, bramble leaves could produce a dark hair-colour, while the juice of the berries was used to make wines more colourful. Bramble berries were also crushed to make a delicious hot drink against colds and bronchitis.

Broom, Gorse. (Sarothamnus scoparius)

The broom, in the van of the army,

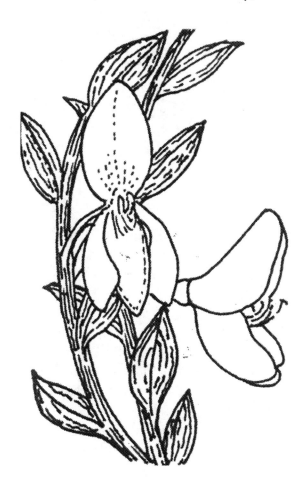

In the trenches he was hurt.
The gorse did not do well,
Notwithstanding let it overspread. (BoT 8)

11. Bright the tops of the broom; let the lover make assignations;
Very yellow are the clustered branches;
Shallow ford; the contended is apt to enjoy sleep. (RBoH 9)

Gwydyon and Math took the flowers of oak, meadowsweet and broom and by their magic arts created the most beautiful woman in the world out of them. She was called Blodeuedd, from blodeu=flowers, and married young Lleu, who had been sworn never to have a mortal wife. Who, or shall we ask, what was Lleu's'wife? One hypothesis points at the varieties of broom containing psychoactive substances (see Rätsch). In bardic poetry, the brightly yellow broom symbolizes springtime celebration, May-time madness and gentle lovemaking in the woodland glades.

Cherry. (Prunus avium, Prunus cerasus)

The cherry-tree was provoked. (BoT 8)
Walking staffs of bird cherry were favoured by the people of Torridon, Scotland, as they were certain to keep their owners from being lost in the mist. They were also known to break fairy enchantments.

The wild cherry is a tree that was cultivated, to a small degree, in neolithic Europe. Later the Romans introduced the ordinary cherry (a product of Persia). The cherry was occasionally a symbol for making love. In some parts of rural Germany, a 'girl who became a cherry tree' is one who got

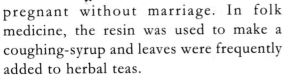

pregnant without marriage. In folk medicine, the resin was used to make a coughing-syrup and leaves were frequently added to herbal teas.

Chestnut. (Aesculus hippocastanum)

A very wrathful wood,
The chestnut is bashful,
The opponent of happiness (BoT 8)
The chestnut has little folklore, probably as it was introduced into central Europe in the late medieval period and became really popular in the sixteenth century. Folk medicine occasionally made use of its astringents, but not very often, as the proper dosages is a real problem.

Cornfield.

Pleasant, berries in the time of harvest;
Also pleasant, wheat upon the stalk...
Also pleasant, the charlock in the springing corn.(BoT 4)

When the dew is undisturbed,
And the wheat is reaped, (BoT 13)
Though cornfields are not exactly forests in the botanical sense, the Irish poets included them in their tree lists. This is sound subjectivity. A cornfield in summer is a world to itself. Mice are climbing through

the stalks, roe deer rest in its secluded center, hares are finding shelter and the odd nibble under the swaying grains and above it all, the falcons are poised in steady balance, the lark is chanting, singer and shaman of the upper air, as it ascends the heavens, shaking mightily. As humans cannot pass through the grains without leaving a trail of destruction, the field was a forbidden world to itself. Countless rural kids were scared with the demon spirits of the grains, the crooked corn woman with her sickle, the corn wolf, and plenty of similar place guardians waiting for unwary intruders in the dazzling air of the midday

sun. When molested, the corn spirit easily took offence. This made the harvest a time of danger, and produced a host of bizarre little ceremonies in which the farmers could give vent to their unreleased emotions. Have you been in the country during the last days before harvest? Many farmer is tense, excited, and yet patient in an angry, brooding way. The toil and survival of the whole year depends on taking the harvest in time. When at last the weather promises stability, the cutting begins, a long term effort that takes place under great psychological strain. What if it rains too early, or too much? The survival of the whole farmstead depends on getting the harvest cut in time.

In medieval times, the farmers were often obliged to harvest the grain of aristocracy and church before they were allowed to look after their own interests. This certainly did not improve the mood. It was a risk when to start harvesting, as any unforeseen thunderstorm might ruin the labour of months, and a great relief when the sheaves where bound and gathered. Then follow festivities. To begin with, the last sheaf of corn is usually cut with a special ceremony, as it holds the grain spirit itself. Often enough, it is bound, dressed in colourful rags, and taken home as the 'corn king'. There the grains are given a place of honour and receive of food and drink while the feast goes on. This placates, and cheers its spirit, so the next year will be another fruitful one.

Regarding species of plant, the old European cultures planted many grains which are rare today, as they do not produce enough seeds to compete with the more economical types. The old Celts knew more than a dozen grains, their modern descendants considerably less. Call it progress if you like. In the late La Tène time the north Italian countryside, cultivated by various Celtic people, was an agricultural paradise and the envy of Rome. In Gaul we have evidence for the first harvesting machines. These were donkey-powered carts which cut and collected the tops of the grains while leaving the stalks standing.

Straw was used by the famed witch Isabel Gowdie of Auldearn to ride to the sabbath in the mid of the 17th century, as she confessed under torture. Straw figures, often woven or knotted into beautiful ornaments, featured prominently in many harvest rituals, and several magnificent and elaborate crosses are associated with the Irish Bride or Brigid.

Eugene O'Curry (1873) tells us that some Irish Druids of antiquity used to pronounce a charm on a wisp of straw, grass or hay, called the Dlui Fulla (fluttering wisp).

They threw it into the face of a person, turning her/him into a lunatic or restless vagabond. A jealous Druid hurled such a bundle into the face of prince Comgan, as he fancied that Comgan had been in bed with the Druid's wife, and Comgan, innocent or guilty, was immediately struck with blisters and boils, lost his speech, his mind and his hair and spent the remainder of his life roving the country in the company of idiots. Another Druid, the old, blind enchanter Dill, kept an enchanted wisp of straw in his shoe. He planned to use it in the destruction of the Decies of Munster, but while he slept, the wisp was stolen, carried to his enemies, and the whole project failed miserably.

Dog-rose. (Rosa canina)

The prickly rose-bushes,
Against a host of giants, (BoT 8)

When are red the hips, (BoT 7)

There are three fountains
In the mountain of roses,
There is a Caer of defence
Under the ocean's wave. (BoT 1)

Bright the tops of the dogrose; hardship has no formality;
Let every one preserve his purity of life.
The greatest blemish is ill-manners. (RBoH 9)

Briar, ridgy one, you do not grant fair terms:
You cease not to tear me till you are full of blood. (SG)

Another plant closely connected with love and desire. For the Romans, rose leaves were a fashionable extra for stylish festivity. Nero had such a massive layer of rose petals on the floor that some of the celebrants, doubtlessy drunk beyond hope, chanced to suffocate in them. The first Christians were wary of a plant so thoroughly associated with lust, love and merrymaking. It took them a while to interpret the five leaves as the five wounds of Christ, thus making the joyous rose a symbol for just martyrdom. Gifts of roses were popular love-tokens in medieval times, but they could also symbolized devotion and purity. Usually the virgin Mary was associated with them, earlier deities are not recorded. Several legends have her walking through barren, wintery thorns which miraculously begin to flower. Rose wood was a favourite material

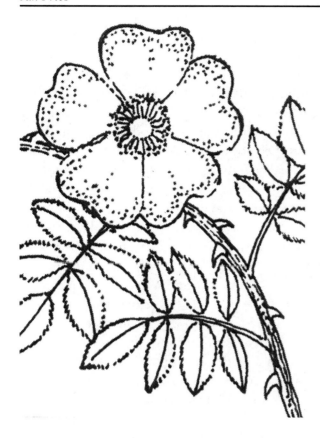

for her statues. Enchanted rose-gardens appear in several myths, sometimes as gardens of joy and plenty, and sometimes as a metaphor for a bloody battlefield. Flowering rose bushes appear as signs of God's grace, sometimes they indicate locations where a chapel ought to be erected. A rose was also a symbol for privacy: what was revealed *sub rosa* was to remain secret.

An unusual sight is a rose-king. This is a rose with a flower out of which another one or two flowers grow, an omen that a happy marriage will soon occur. When you pour blood on a rose, and give it to another, that person is said to fall in love with you. The galls growing on the dog rose are called sleep-apples and are kept in a pillow to

ensure a good night's sleep. Rose hips are one of the essentials in folk-medicine. They are exceptionally rich in vitamin C and appear prominently in many household remedies. The essential oil (it takes 4000 kg rose leaves to produce a litre of oil) was a valued but expensive ingredient of many cosmetic concoctions. Rose blossoms were often used to heal swollen eyes or infected wounds. The wild, or dog-rose has its name from the popular delusion that bites of rabid dogs could be cured with it.

Elder. (Sambucus niger)

I have been a circumference, I have been a head.
A goat on an elder-tree. (BoT 25)

32. Bright the tops of the elder-trees; bold is the solitary songster;
Accustomed is the violent to oppress;
Woe to him who takes a reward from the hand. (RBoH 9)

(S) In Scotland, elder was a valued defense against witches. An eldercross protects stables and farmhouses, a twig in the buttonhole does the same job when you are out and about. People standing under an elder near a fairy mound on Samhain can see the Good Neighbours dancing and feasting. Even a few drops of green elder-sap on the eyelids, so legend has it, grants the power to foresee.

(G) This graceful tree was often planted close to houses, as it was sure to house a helpful and beneficial spirit. In many rural districts, the bush was so sacred that it could only be cut after receiving profound apologies. One such custom, recorded in 17th C. Schlesien, is to take off the hat, get down on one knee and humbly promise: '*Lady Ellhorn, give me of your wood, and I will give mine to you when it grows in the forest.*' This connects the tree firmly with death, and indeed the German names Holunder and Holler contain the name of Helja, darksome goddess of winter and the underworld. As Hel she appears in the *Eddas*, terrifying goddess of nine hells, half black and half white.

In Germany, she is a kinder figure, but has terrifying teeth. Her hidden realm can be found beneath the lake, on desolate mountaintops and deep down in nightblack

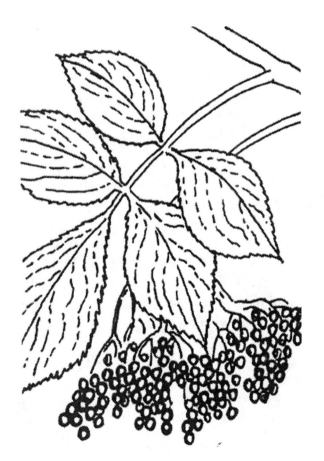

caves. An entry in Hessian court records dealing with a witches trial states: *Lady Holle was from in front a nice woman-person, but from behind like a hollow tree with rough bark.* In the English, the El - refers to her, while -der means tree. In Nordic myth, her equivalent, the forest goddess Huldra lives in the root of an elder tree. She, the mother of all elfs, dwarves and changelings is totally hollow, and likewise the branches of the elder tree have a hollow core, making it a favourite tree for those who make flutes. It is said that the wood, if burned, brings ill luck, sadness and disease to humans and beasts. Similar traditions have it that those who sleep under an elder tree may not awake for several days. The tree is said to protect from lightning. In the Rhineland, a cross of elder was placed on the coffin, or stuck into the freshly covered grave (Southern Germany). If it grows roots and sprouts branches, as elder easily does, the deceased is said to be free of sin and ascends to heaven. Often enough, the grave was measured with an elder rod, another rod of the tree was used to drive the funeral chariot. If you take the pith and soak it in oil, it can be lit. Such a light, floating on water on Xmas eve, is said to reveal all witches and evil sprites.

Elder supplied several sorts of medicine. The juice of the dark reddish berries was often prescribed to induce sweating, a tea of the flowers had a similar effect and was a popular curative for fever and colds. Even the seeds were used to make oil. Elderberry-juice was a well known drink conferring immortality, it was also used to improve the colour of wine. While juice and medicine could be used to combat fever, folk sorceries approached the tree directly. A twig broken by the feverish patient was believed to hold the fever. It was stuck in the ground silently, and as it grew roots and branches, the disease disappeared - surely a slow process indeed. The same was done to get rid of arthritis. If you wished to recover stolen property you could bend down a branch, muttering a spell that the thief would be likewise inconvenienced till s/he returned the stolen goods.

Elm. (Ulmus glabra, Ulmus minor)

The elm with his retinue,
Did not go aside a foot;
He would fight with the center,

And the flanks, and the rear. (BoT 8)

Not a tree with much mythology, apart from the Icelandic *Edda*, which tells us that Odin and company created the first woman out of an elm. The issue is not certain however, the word could also mean alder. (I): a medical MS of 1509 tells us that it is possible to cure impotence, provided it has been caused by charms, by writing the name of the patient in ogham letters on a wand of elm and striking him with it. Nowadays you can rarely see a healthy elm. A fungus has killed or badly infected 90% of the central European and British elms. Folk medicine used elm bark as a calming tea for the stomach and as a remedy against diarrhea. The soft fibres beneath the bark, boiled in water, were applied to cuts and bruises, while the fluids were used to treat cough. This is an old method of therapy, the Greek healer Dioskurides recorded it in the 1st century.

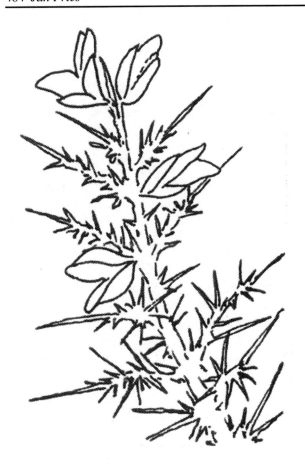

Furze. (Ulex europaeus)

4. Bright are the tops of the furze; have confidence
In the wise; and to the unwise be repulsive;
Except God, there is none that divines. (RBoH 9)

Falling from the tops of withered branches; going through furze (a deed truly done); shunning mankind; keeping company with wolves;
Racing a red stag across a moor. (SG)

Hawthorn, White-thorn. (Crataegus monogyna, Crataegus laevigata)

The hawthorn, surrounded by prickles,
With pain at his hand. (BoT 8)

When a thorn is so sharp.
Knowest thou which is best?
Its base or its point, (BoT 9)

27. Bright the tops of the hawthorn;
confident is the sight of the steed;
It is usual for the lover to be a pursuer;
May the diligent messenger do good. (RBoH 9)

Usual is wind from the east, usual for a man with swelling breast to be
Proud; usual for the thrush to be among thorns;
Usual against oppression is an outcry;
Usual for crows to find flesh in a nook. (RBoH 6)

The brightly flowering hedge of spring shows few signs of the witches and spirits who lurk deep in the shadow between branches and thorns. Hawthorn has a strange reputation. According to Robert de Boron's novel of Merlin (c.1180), the old wizard was spell bound by the young witch Viviane (whose name means 'I'll do none of these' in the Chaldean tongue, as Robert tells us, and whose father Dyonas was a close friend of the goddess Diana) underneath a flowering hawthorn tree. She kissed the old wizard to sleep and drew a circle around him and the bush with her veil, all the while uttering strange things. When Merlin awoke, he found himself lying in a high tower. There he remained, invisible and immortal, and only Viviane knew how

witches, on the other hand, when witches travel to their sabbath, they are known to have a rest in the hawthorn hedge. The German word Hexe (witch) is a shortened form of Hagazussa (hedge-sitter), symbolizing that the witch is a person in-between realities, a traveler between the known world and the dangerous world out there. Hedges of hawthorn were often used to protect farmsteads and villages. According to Squire, the name of the monster giant Yspaddaden means Hawthorne. He appears in the Romance of Culhwch in the *Mabinogi*. The use of hawthorn tea (leaves and blossoms) to regulate heart disorders and blood pressure seems to be a relatively recent discovery, medieval literature seems ignorant of this therapy, possibly as the medicine has to be taken over several months before the effects become obvious.

to visit him, which she did almost every day. Or think of the wonder working hawthorn growing on Glastonbury hill. Legend has it that Jesus' cross and crown were made of a hawthorn tree. As the tree was innocent, or so it said, you can hear it sighing with bitter regret. When Charlemagne slaughtered unbelievers on the battlefield of Roncevalle, his troops were shocked to find that they could not tell the difference between slain Christians and Pagans. The next morning, however, a white flower had sprung up next to every Christian corpse, while a hawthorn had grown through the corpse of every pagan. A thorny twig of hawthorn is said to banish

Hazel. (Corylus avellana, Colyrus colurna)

Hazel-trees, it was judged
That ample was thy mental exertion. (BoT 8)

He would not breed nuts without trees, (BoT 3)

14. Bright the hazel-trees by the hill of Digoll;
Unafflicted will be every squabby one;
It is an act of the mighty to keep a treaty. (RBoH 9)

Little hazel, branchy one, coffer for hazel-nuts. (SG)

(S) Hazel nuts are closely linked with Samhain. The green nuts contain a fluid, called hazel-milk, providing good luck. Lucky autumn children got drops of hazel-milk as their first drink, (and presumably a dram of whisky as their second). During the Imbolc festivity, Bride was adorned with a white wand, preferably of hazel.

(G) A happy shrub like tree with slender rods and nourishing nuts, the hazel was a popular plant in many a rural garden. In the forest it often prefers damp ground and undersurface waterlines. Hazel is a favourite wood for magic wands, it is also popular for dowsing rods. To find water underground, dowsers used to cut their V shaped rods, often muttering a little spell in the process:

I cut you, dearest rods, that you shall tell, what I will ask, and shall not move, till you feel truth. Folk-lore associates hazel trees with sexual pleasure. For this reason, St. Hildegard frothed: *The hazel is a symbol of carnal lust, for medicine it is hardly useful.* Nevertheless she prescribed a remedy against impotence making use of hazel, pepper and the flesh of an adolescent goat and a pig.

A common myth associates hazel and serpents. Either you read that hazel is the perfect plant to scare snakes witless or it is the white king of all serpents who is said to live under an ancient hazel tree. Wearing a hazel twig on the hat was said to protect from lightning. Cracking a nut is a common German idiom for solving a riddle or a problem. The same idea may be found in the tale of the Irish salmons of wisdom. These ancient fish used to come swimming up the rivers Boyne (or up the well of Connla) where an enchanted Hazel grew. It had the virtue that its leaves, blossoms and fruit all appeared, shining in a rich purple, in the same hour. When they all fell into the spring of the well, the salmon were ready and waiting to feed on the nuts, and from these they derived their fabled wisdom. In the Fennian myth cycle you can read how Finn chanced to catch one of these enchanted beasties. As he cooked it over the fire, three drops came flying and burned his thumb. Sucking the wound, he was surprised to find all the wisdom of the deep surging into his mind. As mentioned in chapter 2, hazel leaves and nuts were used in a cult shaft to pad a cluster of urns. An Austrian tale sounds very similar: underneath a hazel crowned by mistletoe dwells a worm who eats tiny round holes into the foliage. This hazel worm, who is imagined to be a young woman in disguise, can be caught. Whoever eats or carries her is certain to become a mighty enchanter.

Heather. (Calluna vulgaris)

The heath was victorious, keeping off on all sides. (BoT 8)

leasant, the heath when it is green; (BoT 4)

Like seeking for ants in the heath. (BoT 3)

17. Bright the tops of the heath; usual is miscarriage
To the timid; water will be intrusive in front of the shore;
Usual with the faithful, an unbroken word. (RBoH 9)

24. At All-Saints it is habitual for the heath tops to be dun;
High-foaming is the sea-wave;
Short the day:-Druid, your advice! (BBoC 30)

Heather, especially white heather, was a popular charm in Scotland. It was thought to banish witches and to bring good luck. It was used in folk medicine against infections of the mouth, skin and bladder.

Holly. (Ilex aquifolium)

Holly, it was tinted with green,
He was the hero. (BoT 8)

When the holly is green (BoT 7)

24. Bright the tops of the hard holly, and others, let gold be distributed;
When all fall asleep on the rampart,
God will not sleep when he gives deliverance. (RBoH 9)

The gold of the heroes, the crowd of holly lances covered it with gore. (BoA 5)

Holly, sheltering one, barrier against the wind; (SG)

It is a possibility that the word holly is related to holy. The evergreen tree with its shining spiky foliage and its brightly glowing scarlet berries scares evil spirits and protects houses from lightning. The Romans had holly garlands during their midwinter saturnalia. The Christian church picked the plant up by the bold claim that Christ's thorny crown was made of holly. In the 2nd century, the Christian author Tertullian raged against Christians who decorated their doors with ivy and holly, a custom he rightly considered pagan (i.e. Roman). The combination of these two plants remained popular, however, and continued till recent time in outdoor - Xmas decoration. In Britain, the plant was often used as a decoration in wintertime, especially during the twelve nights. A ghostly holly tree is said to dance on a road near Loch Fyne, where it scares the locals and produces frightful traffic jams. In Austria, holly has a reputation of scaring evil spirits if it is hung above the door.

Hornbeam. (Carpinus betulus)

Often mistaken for a smallish beech, the hornbeam is a tree that returned late after the ice ages to northern Europe. Unlike beeches, the hornbeam is relatively small and its leaves have jagged edges. Hornbeams occasionally grow in strangely twisted form. As they seem to recover from any wound, they were selected as an ideal tree for hedges, boundaries and fortification. Hornbeam grows very easily, and yields a wood that is heavy and exceedingly tough. Hornbeam fortifications were popular in the medieval period up to the 17th century. Much earlier, Caesar had his problems when encountering these fortifications during the conquest of

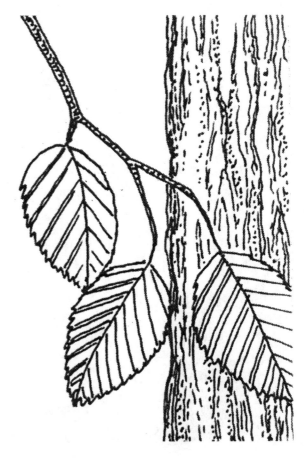

Gaul (*Bellum Gallicum*, 2.17) You take a small hornbeam shoot and bend it. Then you put its end into the earth and cut some slits into the top of the arch. From these, new shoots grow which can also be bent, knotted or woven. If you persist in doing this to a couple of rows of hornbeam, you get a densely grown wall of living trees. Brambles planted between the tree rows do the rest: as a barrier, walls of hornbeam were used to fortify settlements and castles. This worked wonders provided the villagers cared for their line of defence and resisted the temptation of cutting shortcuts through the tangle. With the invention of heavy field artillery, the end of these walls of trees and thorns had come. In the 30 years war (1618-1648), the last remaining hornbeam walls were shot to pieces.

Ivy. (Hedera helix)

And ivy on its front, (BoT 8)

I have been dead, I have been alive.
A branch there was to me of ivy,
I have been a convoy,
Before God I have been poor. (BoT 7)

Have I not listened to the cuckoo on the ivied tree?
Did not my shield hang down?
What I loved is but vexation; what I loved is no more. (RBoH 10)

Ivy, O ivied one, you are frequent in a dark wood. (SG)

(S) a useful amulet to protect milk and flocks. Adventurous Scotch lasses pinned three ivy leaves to their nightshirts to dream

of their future husbands on quarter days. An amulet against witches and evil spirits was made out of rowan, woodbine and ivy (MacNeill).

Ivy plucked with the left hand puts milk into udders (Carmichael)

Juniper. (Juniperus communis)

(S) called the 'mountain yew' in the Highlands, branches of the bristly tree were burned in houses and stables to cleanse and purify them on New Year's morn. The tree had to be pulled out by its roots, a tough labour, to make it fully efficacious. Four bundles of branches were held between the five fingers, and a spell did the trick: *I will pull the bounteous yew, through the five bent ribs of Christ, In the name of the Father, the Son and Holy Ghost, against drowning, danger and confusion.* The fumigation was otherwise held to work against diseases, ill-fortune, fatigue, hardness, pain and so on.

Not a tree of the forest, the juniper enjoys to grow under the wide sky of the heath. The evergreen tree was a common symbol of life. To begin with, everybody knew that the smoke of the branches banishes evil spirits. This observation is founded on the fact that the smoke has a strong disinfecting quality. After diseases and especially in times of plague and pestilence, juniper smoke was one of the few remedies that helped. To exorcise evil spirits, and as it is said to induce trance states, smoking juniper branches were used in several Eurasian shamanic traditions. In a tale recorded by the Grimm brothers, the bones of an innocently murdered child, placed beneath a juniper, evoke an astonishing vision. The tree opens up, a glowing mist shines through the branches while deeper inside a flickering fire dances. Out of smoke and flame the soul of the child appears as a cheerful songbird who flies from house to house chanting how its mother slaughtered, its father ate, and the little sister placed the bone under the tree, in what looks like one of the oldest rites of hunting communities: the resurrection of the dead from their bones. The mist rising from the juniper may be its thick pollen, people collected the fine dust and kept it in capsules as a talisman. In Norse tales, the tree sometimes seems to smoke or burn. At

night, voices can be heard deep inside, laughter, dancers and dwarves who count their money. Sleeping in the shade of a juniper is sure to restore health and vitality. A twig, worn in the cap, is said to triple physical strength. In Austria, juniper branches were cut in the name of the trinity. They were used to give unknown or absent thieves a thorough bashing, until the telepathic punishment made them return the stolen goods. The berries were popular medicine to increase urine flow and detoxify the body, nowadays this is not very popular any more, as regular use tends to damage the kidneys.

Larch. (Larix decidua)

Not a tree with much folk lore, except for the Alps, where it is common and reaches amazing heights. The name of the tree is thought to come from a Celtic root. The only European needlewood that sheds its foliage is closely connected to benevolent forest nymphs. In Tyrol, the forest maidens and the Säligen (blessed ladies) used to congregate beneath this tree. They used to help pregnant women and blessed well raised children, if ever they could find any. Larch trees could grant children to barren couples. The resin was used to make turpentine, small amounts of it were added to salves against arthritis and lung diseases.

Lime, Linden. (Tilia platyphylos, Tilia cordata)

(G) This majestic tree with its large, heart shaped leaves was popular as a symbol of love and peace. Limes were once dedicated to the love goddess Fria, Freya, and as Frouwa to women in general. After the Christianization, the missionaries dedicated these trees to their only feminine divinity, the virgin Mary. Countless Maria-limes show the popularity of the cult. In the song of the leaves, the voice of the deity was heard. The lime is a lighthearted and cheerful tree. It was often planted in the center of rural communities or at places used for festivity and dance. Some limes grew so large that

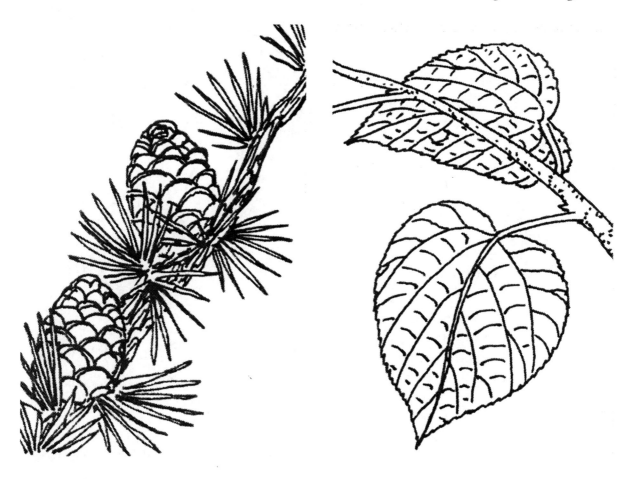

the wide ranging branches had to be suppoerted with up to a hundred pillars. As a tree of the love goddess, the lime was regularly involved in love spells. Many a lad spoke a spell to the tree, asking it to make his amorous dreams come true. If it didn't work, the tree was blamed and threatend that it would have to carry its share of the misery.

Troubadour Walther von der Vogelweide rhymed verses praising a bed under a lime tree, crushed grasses and blossoms, and above us sings the nightingale...while Dietrich von Bern and company were led to rest under a lime by a dwarf, there they espied the strange games of countless animals and birds. When Siegfried took his bath in dragon blood and became invulnerable, a falling lime leaf dropped on his shoulders and ensured his mortality. Later, love problems brought about his treacherous assassination, which happened to take place at a fresh spring underneath a lime. Solitary limes were also popular as rural courts. Condemned criminals could sometimes appeal to show their innocence by planting a young lime upside down. When, after a year or two, the branches took root and fresh green appeared between the roots, the deity had spoken and the criminal was considered innocent.

cold and dry. All through the medieval period, the crushed leaves were laid on feverish brows or inflamed bruises to cool them. By drilling a hole into the trunk in spring, up to one litre of sugary sap could be collected a day. The sap was boiled into a syrup, it takes approximately 100 l sap to crystallize 1 kg of sugar.

Maple. (the Acer family)

Though several European varieties grow in the countryside, in forests and on mountains, folklore has strangely ignored this tree. There are next to no myths or surviving traditions. St. Hildegard calls it

Oak. (Quercus robur, Quercus petrae)

The oak, quickly moving,
Before him, tremble heaven and earth.
A valiant door-keeper against an enemy,
His name is considered...
The branches of the oak have ensnared us
From the Gwarchan of Maelderw. (BoT 8)

The praise of Gogyrwen is an oblation,
which has satisfied
Them, with milk, and dew, and acorns. (BoT 14)

The nature of the oak and thorns
In song will harmonize. (BoT 10)

I saw the ruler of Catraeth beyond the plains
Be my oak (i.e. prince) the gleaming spirit
(i.e. lightning) of the Cymry.(BoT 37)

9. Bright the tops of the oak; bitter the ash branches;
Sweet the cow-parsnip, the wave keeps laughing;
The cheek will not conceal the anguish of the heart. (RBoH 9)

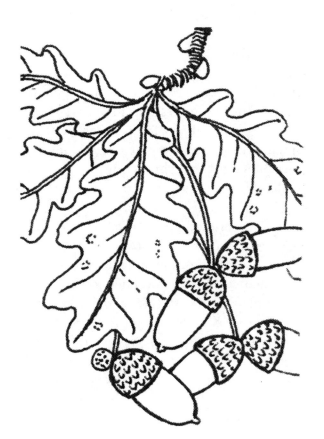

21. Bright the tops of the oak, incessant is the tempest;
The bees are high; brittle the dry brushwood;
Usual for the wanton to laugh excessively. (RBoH 9)

22. Bright the tops of the grove; constantly the trees
And the oak-leaves are falling;
Happy is he who sees the one he loves. (RBoH 9)

23. Bright the tops of the oaks; coldly purls the stream;
Let the cattle be fetched to the birch enclosed area;
Abruptly goes the arrow of the haughty to give pain. (RBoH 9)

High above the merry oak,
I have listened to the songs of birds.
The loud cuckoo - every one remembers what he loves. (RBoH 10)
6. Usual an eagle's nest in the top of the oak,
And in the congress-house, men of renown;
The eye of the fond one is on whom he loves. (RBoH 6)

5. The saplings of the oak in the grove
Will extricate my foot from the chain;
Disclose no secret to a maid.

6. The saplings of the leafy oaks
will extricate my foot from the prison;
Divulge no secret to a babbler. (RBoH 8)

20. The delicate white corpse will be covered to-day,
Amidst earth and oak:
Woe my hand, that my cousin is slain. (RBoH 12)

Sigh of wintery wind; sound of storm beneath an oak tree:

Cold sheeted ice roars, breaking up at the cry of the garb. (SG)

Bushy, leafy oak, you are high above every tree; (SG)

What most I hate in woods (I conceal it not from all)
Is an infertile (?) leafy oak swaying evermore. (SG)

(S) Just like the Druids of Gaul cutting their mistletoe from oaks with golden sickles, a Scots family tradition of the Hays of Errol makes use of mistletoe. To obtain an unequaled amulet, certain to dispel glamours and evil bewitchment, a sprig of oak-mistletoe had to be cut on Samhain with a new dirk, after walking solemnly around the tree three times, muttering a spell. Placed within the cradle, it protected the infant from fairy hands. (MacNeill).

(G) In times of pestilence or suffering, many rural communities used to light need-fires. First, all fires of the village had to be extinguished, as they were considered evil and corrupt. Then, with an elaborate ceremony, a new fire was made, using a variety of up to nine sorts of wood and a drill or saw made from dry oak wood. The new fire (need-fire) carried the blessings of heaven and was born to every hearth of the community. Oak and beech occasionally grow in unusual shapes, so that you can find two branches spreading and then growing together again. Such holes were frequently used to cure diseases. Especially those afflicted with lame limbs, weak bones and stiff joints were wont to crawl through them, with the firm conviction that the tree holds on to the disease, leaving the patient

as good as new. Usually there was a ritual connected with the custom. One version has it that you have to crawl through the hole Friday morning before sunrise. You have to pray first, and wash in a nearby spring, and then perform the climbing without uttering a word. A full cure may require three repetitions, in extreme cases up to twelve. One such tree in Northern Germany used to be highly popular in spite of the fact that the hole was fairly high up, making it difficult to reach (especially for those who walked with crutches). When steps were fixed to the stem, the healing power was greatly reduced; this says a lot about belief in complications.

In some cases, oak branches were carefully split. Then a child suffering from hernia was passed through the gap. The branch was bound with twine from the linden tree, and as it healed and grew together again, so did the groin of the child (Bavaria). Fever, toothache and general exhaustion can be transferred to an oak by drilling a small hole, placing hair or fingernails inside and plugging it shut. The same goes for evil spirits and the spirit of bad luck, and woe to the fool who dared to take such a plug out again.

Oaks generally had lots of symbolic meaning. Around 723, St. Boniface made a name for himself by cutting down the great oaks dedicated to the thunder god Donar in the land of the Chatti (Hessen). His mission was favoured by pope Gregor II and by the local ruler, one Karl Martell, who supplied the man of god with an armed escort under orders to kill any pagan who dared to oppose them. Other venerable oaks were simply de-paganized by carving images of Mary or the saints into their wood. Charlemagne passed a law stating that anyone caught making vows or sacrificing at springs, trees or in groves, or who would eat food in honour of spirits, would have to pay a substantial penalty or immediately become a servant (slave?) of the church.

Memories of sacred groves lingered on for a while in spite of all persecution. In the 11th century, a monk from Regensburg deplored that there are still some peasants who deem it sinful to cut trees in a grove where pagan priests used to consult their oracles. Solitary oaks appear as places for sacrifice and prayer, in many Indo-European traditions they are sacred to the gods of the sky, the lightning wielders, such as Donar, Thunor, Zeus and Iuppiter. Consequently, they were also used as sites for rural courts, and plenty of criminals came to dangle from their branches. In this function oaks often had a shady reputation, and were said to be haunted by ghosts, the devil, black dogs, three legged hares and the like. The galls were used to predict the weather in the coming winter; some galls yielded a useful ink. The wood was favoured for building as it is so strong and enduring, and the barks and leaves with their powerful astringents (up to 20% tannin in the bark) were useful to tan leather and to draw wounds together.

Acorns were baked into bread in times of need, mind you, to eat them you have to water them, preferably in a fresh stream, for several days. They are usually horribly bitter, very rarely oaks can be found that produce acorns that taste almost sweet. In Gaul, so Pliny recorded, oaks nurtured the growth of the all-healing mistletoe recommended by the Druids. Mistletoe growing on other trees, so he recorded, wouldn't do. Late additions to the work of Lucan claim that the Druids used to chew acorns before working prophecy.

Pear. (Pyrus pyraster, Pyrus communis)

Pear-trees, the best intruders
In the conflict of the plain. (BoT 8)

Pleasant, the blossoms on the tops of the pear-trees; (BoT 4)

Like the apple, the pear comes in a wild and a cultivated form. We owe the latter to the Greeks and Romans, the former is a much

smaller fruit with a pretty sour taste. Its mythology is not that overwhelming. Pears and apples were considered a complimentary pair in the middle ages, Albertus Magnus, for example, states that the pear symbolizes the male element. In folksy love oracles, the lads appealed to the apple and the lasses to the pear. During the twelve nights in midwinter, the lasses used to throw their shoes into the bare branches of a pear tree. If a branch caught a shoe, the girl could expect marriage within a year, and possibly cold feet on the way home.

In later centuries the symbolism reversed and pears became female symbols. Wild pears, growing in the forest, are known to house witches and potential stomach cramps. The seeds were a valuable source of oil, 12 kg of seeds yielding up to 1.5 litres. Medieval doctors were cautious in prescribing fresh pear as it can be hard to digest, some even thought pears poisonous. Boiled pears or juice are easier to deal with, and were regularly prescribed to cure folk suffering from bad digestion, high blood pressure or an infected bladder. A good old healing spell against miscellaneous afflictions goes as follows:

Pear tree I appeal to thee, three worms are plaguing me, one is grey, one is blue, one is red, I wish all three were dead.

While the spell looks like a worm spell in modern eyes, it should be remarked that in the medieval period worms were blamed for all sorts of diseases. Some were visible worms in our sense of the word, but many were invisible, lurking under tree bark or among tangled roots, always ready to infect the unwary. Worm diseases were tuberculosis, headaches, toothache and digestion problems. This spell, and others pretty much like them, were certain to kill them.

Pine, Scotch Pine. (Pinus sylvestris)

Pine-trees in the porch,
The chair of disputation,
By me greatly exalted,
In the presence of kings...
Morawg and Morydd
Were made prosperous in pines. (BoT 8)

It is one of those questions what happened to the pines reputation. When the last ice age ended and the glaciers slowly retreated

across the flattened land, birches were the first trees to grow. Next followed pines, and characteristic birch-pine forests developed. Then it got colder again, the birches growing smaller and most pines disappearing. After a cold span they came back again. Now the birch was and is one of the top trees in ancient myth. What happened to the pines? In those early birch and pine dominated forests our Mesolithic ancestors gathered and hunted. The tree must have been of immense importance to them. What happened to the myths? In the leafy forests of central Europe, much of the knowledge simply disappeared. Some cultures in Bosnia and Herzegovina have retained the belief that pine wood can banish evil spirits.

Pines were rarely planted next to middle European churches. I know of one singular case in Usamaturze. The pilgrims used to pray and offer alms in the church. Then a few pine twigs were broken and taken home. The twigs were boiled in water, which was subsequently used to bathe retarded children. If they died in the process, so the legend goes, they were changelings left by the fairies, if they survived and recovered this proved their essential humanity. Folk medicine used pines much like spruce or larch: the resin and the essential oils were used to combat lung diseases and chronic bronchitis.

Reeds and Rushes.

When the reed is white,
When it is a moonlight night. (BoT 9)

6. Bright the tops of reed grass; furious is the jealous,

And he can hardly be satisfied;
It is an act of the wise to love with sincerity.
(RBoH 9)

15. Bright the tops of reeds; it is usual for the sluggish
To be heavy, and the young to be a learner;
None but the foolish will break the faith.
(RBoH 9)

18. Bright the tops of rushes; cows are profitable,
Running are my tears this day;
Comfort for the miserable there is not.
(RBoH 9)

26. Bright the tops of rushes; prickly will they be
When spread under the pillow;

The wanton mind will be haughty. (RBoH 9)

11. Rain without, the ocean is drenched;
The wind whistles over the tops of the reeds;
After every feat, still without the genius.
(RBoH 8)

Reeds and rushes are of importance when it came to making pre-historical and medieval houses comfy. Think of the reed thatched roof. Its not only beautiful but also watertight, at least for a few years, and with a bit of luck it didn't go up in flames. Especially in those days when houses had no chimneys (a Roman import) and got fresh ait through holes in the ceiling and crude openings called wind-eyes (hence windows). But comfort wasn't confined to the roof. People also used to cover the floor with a thick layer of reeds and rushes. They sat on rushes, stuffed pillows with rushes, slept on rushes and generally froze stiff overnight, as Gerald of Wales so touchingly recounts. It must be one hell of a romantic life when you wake four times a night as it's simply too damned cold. Not exactly what I'd call restful, but useful if you want to remember lots of troubled dreams and have a nice bone weary day being ill-mooded and quarrelsome. Reeds are also important for poets and musicians as so many instruments depended on them.

Rowan, Quicken or Mountain-Ash.
(Sorbus acuparia)
The willows and quicken-trees
Came late to the army. (BoT 8)
Rowan-tree, berried one, your blossom is lovely. (SG)

(S) In Scots belief, a necklace of dried rowan berries strung on red thread was a reliable amulet. A cross of two rowan rods, also bound with red thread, protected the beasts in the stables:

Rowan tree and red threid
Gar the witches tyne their speed.

Planted close to the front door, the tree made witches flinch and flee. On the quarter days of the Gaelic year, a rowan wand was kept in the pocket, another was kept above the lintel of houses. It provided a much needed defence against the creatures roaming freely on the uncanny nights between seasons. MacNeill also tells of

festival cakes baked over a fire of rowan faggots.

(I) In Irish myth, the Tuatha de Danann *had for food… crimson nuts and arbutus apples and scarlet quicken berries, which they had brought from the land of promise. These fruits were gifted with many secret virtues; and the Dedannans were careful that neither apple nor nut nor berry should touch the soil of Erin.* (Joyce 1879). One of the berries fell to the ground and as a result a towering and thoroughly sacred rowan grew in the wood of Dooros. Its fruit tasted of honey, improved the spirits and rejuvenated so immensely, that the Tuatha De Danann immediately appointed a Fomorian giant to guard the berries from abuse. This was Sharvan the Surly, huge, cruel, ugly, with a flaming eye in the middle of his dark brow. His magic was so strong that he could be killed only by giving him three blows from his own club. You can find his tale in the Finn cycle (*The Pursuit of Dermat and Grania*), as well as a tale relating how Finn and company were held prisoner in an enchanted *Palace of Quicken Trees.* When invited to come in, they thought to enter a magnificent hall with seven doors, rich furniture, beautiful paneling and great otherworldly wealth, but as soon as their host had departed, the whole thing became an ill constructed shabby hut with a single door, facing to the north, and they couldn't get it open at all, as the ground held them fast. Another strange rowan appears in the eight century romance of Froech, who was sent swimming across a dark pool in the mountains to collect a branch of rowan by the ill-wishing Ailill, who well knew that there was an aquatic monster hiding in the deep.

(B) In British folklore, the rowan has an important role. Its wood could banish witches and evil spirits. A slender rowan twig, bound into a knot was easily hidden above a door or gate to make sure no evil could come in.

(N) In *Eddic* mythology, the world-tree is an ash tree. In Iceland, where the *Eddic* tales were recorded, the ash does not grow. Instead, there is the rowan, or mountain ash, which, though unrelated to the bigger ash, appears much like a smaller cousin. It is a moot point whether Snorri was thinking of an ash or a rowan when he compiled the myths. The words 'Rowan' and 'Rune' may well be related.

(G) In Continental folklore, the rowan is not very prominent. The shining red berries were often used to bait bird traps. Birds appear prominently in the life process of the rowan, as the seeds grow best when they have gone through the digestive tract. In consequence, many rowans grow in inaccessible sites, having dropped from heaven. A rowan growing on another tree, i.e. a rowan that has never touched the ground was thought to be especially magical. In folk medicine, they are occasionally prescribed to stimulate the digestion (raw) or to soothe it (dried). Hieronymus Boch (16th C.) notes that *they are of a strangely unhappy taste, so if one eats too much, they make unwilling.* They are rich in vitamin C, but taste so sour that few seem to like them. A variety found in Czech tastes much sweeter. The leaves seem to have gone into herbal beers, as a tea they were applied as a mildly constipating substance against nervous stomach and diarrhea. The flowers were drunk as tea to cure cough, bronchitis and diseases of the lungs. Farmers used to heal sick goats by feeding them rowan foliage, they also gave a tap with a rowan twig to their cattle on the 1ˢᵗ of May to protect the livestock from diseases for a year. It was also known as a quicken, you can observe the word quick, meaning alive. The quicken supplied rods of life, which were used on Easter, New Year or Xmas, by children who went from door to door, hit people and asked for gifts. This was believed to constitute a blessing.

Service-tree. (Sorbus domestica)

20. Bright the tops of the service-tree;
accustomed to care,
Is the aged one, and bees to the wilds;
Except God, there is no avenger. (RBoH 9)

Sloe or Blackthorn. (Prunus spinosa)

Blackthorn, thorny one, dark bearer of sloes;
(SG)

This thorny bush bears large blue berries which were cherished by most early cultures. Dried berries have been found in prehistoric settlements, be it in the lakeside dwellings of southern Germany and Switzerland, be it in the food offerings found in Celtic tombs. Even the glacier man from the Ötztal had a dried sloe in his bag. Sloes look attractive but are so full of astringents that they numb the mouth and tongue. To eat them you have to wait till the first frost has made them sweet (freezing them can also do the trick). In mythology Continental myth,

blackthorn is a tree associated with giants
(but so are many other thorns).

Spruce and Fir. (Picea abies, Abies alba)

21. Mountain snow-red the top of the fir;
Wrathful the push of many spears.
Alas, for longing, my brethren! (RBoH 4)

(S) At their gatherings, Scotch witches
used to carry fir torches in their left hands
(MacNeill). If they circumambulated
widdershins, as tradition demands, this
placed the torch hand in the middle of each
individual circle.

(G): We shall treat these trees together,
as folklore makes little difference between
them and most people can't tell them apart
anyway. Can you? The modern Christmas
tree has only a few centuries of history, but
as a May - and midsummer tree, you can
find these towering evergreens popular in
most countries north of the Alps. Such
trees were usually put up by the village
community for the 1st of May, Whitsunday
or the summer solstice, a custom that can
be traced to the 13th century. Usually, a
group of villagers went out into the forest
to 'seek the May' They cut a large spruce or
fir and stripped it of most branches and
bark, so that no witches can hide in it,
occasionally the tree was painted. Then the
bushy crown was decorated. The custom of
tying ribbons and flags to the crown remains,
in medieval times, various local customs
necessitated that the signs of the professions
and any amount of edibles were used for
decoration. The May dances were celebrated
around these trees, occasionally villages
made a sport of stealing the tree of their
neighbours overnight. Small May trees -
spruce, fir and sometimes birch, were used
to decorate farmsteads and rooms. Branches
tied to the roof invited the Holy Ghost.
Cattle was brushed with such branches
before the 1st of May to keep them from
plague for a year, sometimes the branches
were used to sprinkle holy water over the
bovine population of the village. In folk
medicine, the evergreens were used to cure
scurvy. Especially in wintertime the needles
are rich in vitamin C, which was extracted
by seething them in water. Hunters used to
chew on little pellets of spruce resin to
ward off the common cold, professional

singers did the same to protect their voices. Spruce resin is full of aromatic essences which have highly disinfecting qualities. It was often included in salves against rheumatism and arthritis. In Britain, spruce beer was a classical beverage.

Wine

I have drunk liquor of wine and bragett,
from a brother departed. (BoT 45)

Usual for a prince to provide a feast;
Usual after drinking is derangement of the
senses. (RBoH 6)

69. From the banquet of wine and mead
They went to the strife...
70. From the banquet of wine and mead they
hastened,
Men renowned in difficulty, careless of their
lives; (BoA 1)

Called 'the blood of the earth' by Pliny, wine has inspired plenty of Greek and Roman literati. Already in Hallstatt times, large amounts of Mediterranean wine found their way north of the Alps. It was in all likeliness not only an expensive but also religious beverage. The many masks, weird creatures and bizarre symbols gracing Hallstatt jugs and bottles probably had an apotropaic function. A drink that changes consciousness obviously needs to be guarded against the influence of evil spirits. Or think of those vessels showing trefoil symbols.

Wine cultivation was introduced centuries later thanks to the Roman occupation, Mark Aurel being one of its promoters. With wine cultivation came a curious vegetation spirit, the green man. This spirit, often considered a Celtic or Germanic deity by the uninformed, appeared in its earliest shape with a face full of wine leaves. In the wake of wine cultivation it spread over Europe and finally, in the high medieval period, came to grace many a church. As a later derivation, a green woman was invented, and finally, other sorts of leaves came to adorn the bizarre faces of these benign creatures. Legend mentions all sorts of curious varieties of wine, some grapes sporting beards, having leaves of pure gold or with their wood growing in the shape of Jesus on the cross. Wine cultivation can be a difficult art, as wine does not tolerate a number of plants in its neighbourhood. Cutting and planting followed the moon using a variety of complicated and occasionally contradicting rules. Wearing a wreath of ivy was said to make the wine-harvest especially successful. Folk medicine incorporated wine in plenty of remedies, be it for its intoxicating quality, be it as a basic fluid into which other plants could be mixed.

Willow (Salix alba, Salix caprea, Salix fragilis etc.)

The willows and quicken-trees
Came late to the army. (BoT 8)

3. Bright are the willow-tops; playful the fish
In the lake; the wind whistles over the tops
of the branches;
Nature is superior to learning. (RBoH 9)

25. Bright the tops of the willow; inherently bold
Will the war-horse be in the long day, when leaves are abounding;
Those that have mutual friendship will not despise one another. (RBoH 9)

Bending their graceful branches over sparkling waters, the willow family feels at home near brooks and rivers, pools and swamps. By day, the fresh green shines in playful beauty, at night, when mists rise from the waters and the pale moonlight silvers the haze, the willows are the meeting-place of water spirits, witches, demons and ghosts. New year's night and in the night of the summer solstice, willows can come to walk and dance. A tradition from north

Germany has it that witches are initiated under willows. Under the swaying branches, the novice cursed the Christian god and sealed a pact with a signature in blood.

Willows were also popular with suicides, as the slender twigs make tough nooses, and with people who believe in rough justice, such as the secret Feme-courts of medieval Germany.

Folk spells relied on willow to clean up skin diseases (a piece of skin was transferred to the tree and left under the bark), otherwise the cold fever and arthritis were bound into the tree when three twigs were knotted. Willows were also used to make pipes and overtone-flutes, an especial blessing being attributed to willows that

had never heard a stream or a cock crowing. Otherwise, willow rods were immensely popular as so many useful items can be woven out of them. Baskets of willow were regularly used by Hallstatt time Celts to carry heavy loads and many a child was raised in a cradle of woven willow twigs.

Folk medicine made use of leaves and bark, with their high content of salicylic-acid, to treat headaches, rheumatism and to reduce fever. A willow wand appears in a strange Scottish tale. A cunning man from Stratherrick carried such a wand on a tour through the nine most fertile glens of Scotland. At each of them he bound the wealth of the soil in his rod. Thus he returned to his home, carrying all the stolen power in his staff, but when he chanced to come to his last stop, in Killin, he happened to encounter another sorcerer, who knew what game was going on. The two had a fierce battle that came to end when the staff was cut with an enchanted knife. Instantly all the pent-up power escaped from the wand and surged into the soil of Killin, which had been fertile before, and now became eight times more so

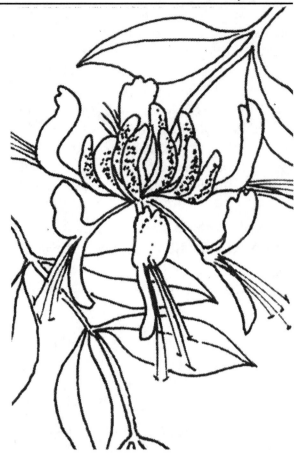

Woodbine (Lonicera caprifolium)

When the march-moon was waxing, the inhabitants of Moray used to cut woodbine, which they twisted and bent into wreaths. The wreaths were carefully preserved. Children suffering from fever and consumption were passed through the hoops three times in order to take the affliction from them (MacNeill).

Yew (Taxus baccata)

Yew-tree, yewlike one, you are evident in churchyards; (SG)

Cormac has it that the most lasting things in the world are grass, copper and yew. As you may recall, two of the five districts of Ireland had sacred yew trees.

These dark evergreens acquired a shady reputation early in history. For the classical authors, the sombre yew was a tree of death. Ovid recorded that yews grow along the path to the underworld, in his time the twigs were a sign of sorrow. Another legend has it that those who sleep under the shadow of a yew will never wake up again. Virgil warns that yews should never be planted next to bee hives. A legendary Gaulish tradition was to serve wine in cups of yew wood, which was supposed to kill the drinker.

Behind this belief lies the fact that the yew is one of the most poisonous trees of Europe. Needles, bark and seeds are thoroughly toxic, relatively small amounts can make the heart race and kill in an hour or two. Caesar informs us that the ruler of the Eburoni, one Catunolcus, used Yew poison for suicide, as he felt too old to fight or flee his enemies (*Bellum Gallicum* 6.31)

Nordic myth, Yews were sacred to the god Ullr, patron of hunters. This was sound thinking, as the very best hunting weapons, be it spears, bows or crossbows were made of yew. The yew grows very slowly, producing a wood that is strong, elastic and endures great tension. The Neanderthal people made mammoth spears of it, our stone age ancestors used it for hunting bows, and so did the outlaws of Sherwood forest and the Welsh archers. Medieval warfare almost drove the tree into extinction. As it grows so slowly, the popular demand was much greater than the natural supply. Nowadays only a handful of free growing yews remain. As the tree is a popular evergreen in the cemetery it survived. Though yews grow slowly, they endure longer than most other trees. Some yews have been known to reach 2000 years, this makes them a fitting symbol for great age. In Germany, yew twigs, as they were of such a darksome nature, were an efficient barrier against evil spirits, if placed properly across the road or doorstep. An amulet of yew wood, worn underneath the clothes, protected against spirits, diseases, and as the proverb goes 'Before yews, no enchantment can endure.' Somewhat unusually, St. Hildegard of Bingen proposed that yews are a symbol of joyousness and that a walking stick of yew was good to fortify health. Medically, yews were rarely used, as their toxins were too strong.

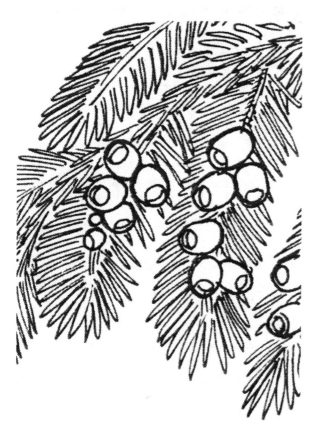

A Hand Full of Forests

What is the imagination of trees. (BoT 7)

In the previous pages, you read how trees and parts of them were used in folk magic. Generally, some trees were used for the passage-effect. By crawling or climbing through them, one could get rid of diseases or ill luck and appear rejuvenated on the other side. Trees could hold and heal diseases. Their wood was used for talismans, the leaves and blossoms for spells of enchantment or protection. There are other uses of trees in bardic sorcery. Of all the forms of Irish divination mastered by the filid, only dichetal do chenaib was permitted by St. Patrick: *The practise of dichetal do chennaib he alone allowed, since it was not necessary to make offerings to spirits, for the revelation comes straight away from the ends of the poets fingers.* (*Cormac's Glossary*).

This sounds mysterious and stimulating. How can we interpret these words? Robert Graves, aware that the Irish poets used to communicate with their fingers in a secret sign language, proposed that the digits of the fingers may be associated with the letters of the alphabet and hence with the trees of the ogham alphabet. Accordingly he mapped out the hands to find space for 25 trees. This brilliant idea was thoroughly marred when he added his personal 'reconstruction' of the ogham alphabet and his totally fictional tree calendar.

If we overlook these major flaws, we still retain an excellent model that combines finger digits with trees, and consequently their spirits. In ritual Taoism, the digits of the fingers are employed in a similar way. One system projects the signs of the *pa kua*, the eight trigrams, into nine digits (one is in the center), or the nine chambered square of Yü. Another assigns the twelve digits of the four fingers to the twelve animal signs of the Chinese zodiac. By pressing the appropriate digit, visualizing a specific spirit, intoning its secret names (in the mind) and swallowing saliva, the Taoist sorcerers worked their rites of evocation. Usually this was done with great secrecy, the digit pressing happening on the left hand, hidden deep within the sleeve of the ritual robe, while the right hand was busy waving a sword in obscure and complicated sigil-patterns (see *Living Midnight*).

Now you might ask just what is so special about pressing some part of a finger. In spite of all acupuncture theories, the Taoist priests were well aware that the spirits, energies or signs do not exist within the digits unless they are settled there properly. Any part of the human anatomy can house a spirit, the trick lies in getting it there. To work this magick you need a strong association, preferably one with vivid experience and emotion. Would you like to learn this art? Would you settle and nourish a series of forests in your fingers? To begin with, you should work out which trees should make up your enchanted forest.

The Matrix of Nemetona

Think of the sacred groves of the Druids, the nemeton (sacred forest or sacred space) of the La Téne Celts whose personification and place guardian is the goddess Nemetona. She appears in the sanctuary, outwardly in the trees, flowers, animals, stones and springs that constitute her body, inwardly in the shape you dream, fed by the love for all that is holy to you. What is a sacred grove for you? When I ask you to imagine one, what comes into your mind and what moves you? It is important that you suit you selection to the environment you are inhabiting. It's no use when you include wonderfully Druidic trees if they are so rare in your world that you have to travel to an arboretum to see one. More useful are the trees of your neighbourhood, the trees you meet on nature walks, the trees that have been prominent in your life. Think of the trees that mean a lot to you. And think of those you'd love to know better. If the sacred trees of your homeland happen to be olive, bamboo or baobab, you should by all means include them. These are your trees, they are the material to form a magick universe from. As I developed this system, I decided to make use of twelve trees. Graves assigned 25 spots on the fingers to ogham letters. To do this he not only used three digits on the inside of each finger, but also one at the fingertip and one below the root of each finger. I excluded the fingertips, as these get too much pressure in daily life to make the association reliable. The same went for the locations below the base of each finger, as they are a bit inconvenient to press. This leaves a total of twelve trees, or tree-families, on four fingers, or 15 if we include the thumb. If you want more trees, you could assign several similar or related ones to each digit. In this fashion, one digit might contains all members of the willow family, another one might have all sorts of thorn trees, or fruit bearing trees, or trees with nuts. If you want more available spaces, you could also use the fingernails and the second digit of each finger on the outside of the hand, as these can still be reached by the thumb. Think about it and chose a solution that suits you. To begin with, I decided to class them in four groups. The index finger for air and trees of the mountaintops, the middle finger for fiery trees and those of the high forest, the ring finger for trees of watery nature and the little finger for earth, field and garden trees. The thumb has the job of pressing the digits. Of course it is possible to group trees in several ways. You could go by environment, by preference, by medical use, by the time of their flowering each spring, by alphabetical order, invent a calendar, go for directions of the compass, assign them to seasons, durability of wood, shape of leaves or whatever strikes your fancy. It does not matter much what you invent, the main thing is that you invent an order that pleases you and includes a variety of different trees that can symbolize many interesting ideas.

Or go by function - do you know which trees spell mystery, love, joy, dreaming, enchantment, protection, resistance, adaptability, danger, death and rebirth to you? A good spectrum of trees, a well harmonized enchanted forest contains blessings of all sorts. A language of tree signs should be able to communicate just about everything, this is the main criterion for the efficiency of any magickal model of the world. Make a map of the trees that mean a lot for you. You don't have to include all species, just a range of typical ones. It may be useful to consider that in a sense, you are grouping trees and types of forest. In another, the trees themselves are convenient symbols for energies, moods, awareness and intelligences. A tree can be a tree, it can also be a tree-formed symbol for something entirely abstract. If you see trees only as trees, you are missing a lot. Often, the sentience behind a tree is more important for your magick than the simple plant growing in the forest.

Assign a tree, or family of trees, to each digit of your fingers. If its a good one, it should not only show your favourite magickal trees in a meaningful order, it should also be possible to make a journey from digit to digit and finger to finger. This means that your model should include a meaningful walk through varied environments. In other words, try to arrange the trees in a sequence natural to the forest.

Once you have made a map of the order of trees on your digits, you can bring it to life. We could call this phase imprinting, but as I do not believe in permanent imprints and unchangeable belief structures, I would much prefer to speak of vivid association here. The best thing you can do is read up on the symbology and meaning of the trees. Then select three to evoke on your first journey.

For example birch. Go and find a group of impressive birches. Not weak and polluted birches withering at the street-side but strong and rugged specimens with a mind and a force of their own. Spend some time there. Look at them from all sides. Touch their bright skin. Listen to the wind in the branches. Sense them as intently as you can. Speak to them. Invoke their spirit with an open heart, free flowing prose and gentle laughter. Go into the mood of the trees. If you can do it, trance a while and transform into a tree.

Calm down. Slow down. Trees have lots of time. They don't have many choices but they do their job very thoroughly. Go silent and dreamy.

Stand with your feet closely together. Relax. Imagine your feet grow roots, and how those roots are reaching firmly deep deep down into the dark soil. There are big roots and they are so strong that you can rely on them and there are finer roots deep down and they draw nourishment. Some of your roots go to the secret flow of water below ground, others touch stones that have been resting and dreaming for ages.

Sense the darkness as you stand there, and as your roots draw energy from the deep, and feel how your body sways as the wind is gently moving through your branches. You stand there, swaying gently, breath flowing easily, and the silence surrounds you, like the bright bark, and your leaves are fluttering and the birds are singing and you can sense the trees next to you. When you sense them really strongly, and experience them more intensely than you have ever sensed that tree before, press the birch-digit of your hand and take the experience in. Do this whole-heartedly, with all your being, all the lust and awareness of your senses. The stronger your experience, the stronger will your association be. If you wish to amplify it by some ritual, an offering, extended prayer, a trance state or a bit of story telling, by all means do so. Make the experience strong, press your thumb against the digit, and form a link that makes the birch awareness available as soon as you press the digit again.

The important thing is that your experience is intense. The pressure on your digit does not have to be strong, you should take care to keep the sensation in the pleasant range. A few minutes light pressure with strong imagination and emotion is worth much more than several hours with cramp and creeping boredom. If you associate the tree experiences with pain you won't be inclined to appreciate them much. Then relax, take in something else from your surroundings. Go back to the birch, go into the birch consciousness, and press the digit again. Repeat as long as it's fun, stop before it becomes a routine chore. Then take a few leaves or a piece of wood, place them on your altar or under your pillow when you come home. Find some other birches, young and old. Go into birch awareness and 'anchor' (an NLP term for intense associations triggered by a signal) them to the birch digit.

Do so until you have several intense birch experiences associated with a specific pressure on the digit. Do the same with another type of tree, and perhaps a third species. That's quite enough for a day. Three species a day is a very good score if you look for quality, especially if you find several different trees individuals for each species. Remember to give your mind resting periods in between states of intense perception, this way your attention remains fresh for longer. If you find yourself a bit dull-minded or unfocussed on occasion this is quite natural: the brain needs its little pauses of fluffy mindedness to recreate itself. Enjoy them, they are an interesting consciousness state.

If you go for several walks over a few weeks, you will build up a range of memories and vivid associations in each finger digit.

Pressing the digit will make the memories and feelings come to your awareness again, provided you use the association to go into the experience. This is an active deed of imagination and remembrance, you shouldn't expect to be stunned by hundreds of birch memories just because you accidentally pressed the digit as you were walking to the bus. The trees are all there, waiting for you. Your attention is the key.

Now the next step is to turn the association to the inner world of dreaming and imagination. At home, find some rest and silence. Relax, allow your muscles to become loose, let your breath flow gently, slow down, close your eyes and allow attention to go inward. If you want to induce a good trance first, do so, but if not, you may find a nice trance developing naturally while you visualize your trees. Press a digit and allow that forest to come to life for you. Go walking between your memories and visions. Explore what lies hidden round the wayside, find the secrets in secluded glades, in shady groves, in tangled undergrowth. Meet Nemetona in the secret forests of your mind. You may recall what you discovered earlier regarding impressive visualizations. Make your inner pictures large, vivid, colourful, bring them close to you, wrap them around you and go exploring in their midst. Do as you did to make the association convincing in the outer world: see the trees in the imagination, hear them, feel them, smell them, experience them as fully as you can.

Here you will leave the world of memory and find that your visions become creative. Each group of enchanted trees may be a gateway to unexpected realities. In folk tales, the great and uncultivated forest always appears like a place of promise and danger, a wild place with its own creatures and dream-cells. The forest is a living entity, and so are the dream forests you create in your mind. When you find yourself dreaming in unexpected directions, when you encounter beings in your mind's woods, when you discover hidden treasures and forbidden dangers, you can be sure the astral forests have woken and that you are no longer in the realm you cultivated by your forest walks. The deep has come to life and you are there to deal with it. How are the forests of your mind? What are the secrets that they hold? What tunes will they respond to?

This sort of trance journey should be developed for a while. For one thing, you won't know your forests unless you have been with them in all seasons and all times of day. As you explore them, you may find that each journey is different. Sometimes a given group of trees is full of strange insights, another time it may just be a couple of trees swaying in the breeze, and a third time you could get into a dreaming of such intensity that you entirely forget the cluster of trees you started out with. All of this is exploration. You are not only creating dream-places, you are also opening channels that allow the deep mind to communicate unexpected ideas to you. In the events that happen, in the figures you did not make up, in the surprises you never expected, the deep is responding to you. As you go walking inner and outer forests, the bardic circuit becomes initiation.

This leads to the subject of divination. Occasionally I like to ask myself 'what sort of energy/awareness would do me good now?' and allow my thumb to wander aimlessly over the finger digits. After a while, I get a jolt (usually in my spine) and the thumb sticks to a digit. The sensation is very developed, its the same sensation I get when I grasp a rune sign in a bag or a tarot card. What signals that a card or rune is right to you? Do you hear something, is it a feeling or a vision? Whatever it is, it will be functional for you. Use it if you like or invent another signal and ask your deep mind to use it. Or ask the deep mind for a signal it would like to use, and watch out in all sensory channels. With a bit of help from your deep mind you can set up one or several signals, or fine tune them so they work really elegantly. When I get the signal I keep pressure on the digit, go into the vision, and find out what happens. Sometimes I learn something on the way, at other times I simple find myself delighting in a specific forest atmosphere, and when I return to mundane consciousness, find myself refreshed and restored. I suspect that animal spirits connect with the excitable sympathetic nervous system, and that the seeming passivity of trees might relate them with the parasympathetic system (the vagus) and its calming and restoring effect. This is not always the case, as trees in some moods are anything but soothing.

As you explore your dream forests, you may learn how the worlds within and without reflect and influence each other. You can also use the divination to find answers to other questions. Keep each question simple and short. Repeat it in a regular rhythm as your thumb wanders over the digits. Keep your mind open, you are divining to learn something new, not to confirm what you knew anyway. Then, when you find the forest of your answer, go in and explore. Who knows what waits for you behind the next turn of the crooked path? What else can you do with your hand full of forests? What spells can you work in leafy glades and gnarled undergrowth? How about evocation? You could ask which particular tree embodies a consciousness/energy you could use now. Your answer appears on one or more digits. It looks like trees, it feels like trees, it sounds like trees but behind it are myriads of subtle processes going on. The thing is not the same as the idea it represents. Magick often works with symbols: as you walk amidst the trees, you are changing yourself and your world. The harp of the woods sings sweet melodies. What is the next enchantment on your way? Find it and go for it.

Horned one

14. Coda: The bed of Taliesin

Beyond Tre Taliesin near Aberystwth, a road leads up the slope of Moel y Garn. Between grasses and weeds a peaceful sight awaits the visitor. A large, flat table stone is resting on the ground. A few boulders support this heavy roof. Underneath a space, empty, hollow, narrow, dark. The wind blows and the grasses whisper. In the distance, the cries of gulls echo the moaning of the waves. The grave on the extended slope, under fleeting clouds and howling winds, who used to rest in it? Here we can say goodbye to scholarly caution, to precise research and studious plodding. The salt bearing gale carries dreams in its gusts, the sea is awash with visions. Wave of Iwerdon, wave of Manau, wave of the north and wave of Prydain, hosts comely in fours, singing the death song of a forgotten age. For an instant, time seems to stop. Who moved the stones, who dug the hole, who set up the edifice and who, if any, went to rest in it? Local tradition calls it the Bedd Taliesin, the grave of Taliesin. Between the heather and gorse, under a mindwide sky, the stones contain a cell of dreams and hopes.

To those who named the Bedd Taliesin, the origin of the monument was a riddle. They called it a tomb, knowing well enough that every grave is but site of transformation and transcendence. A bed it is, a temporary resting place, a womb, tomb, chamber to rest the limbs and heal the soul. Those bards who named it after Taliesin knew all too well that the poet can sleep and trance, but never die. The seeds of consciousness, the bright red rowan berries, the traveling heads, with milk and dew and acorns they come to life again. Who knows this gate, who has been coming through again and again? Who knows how to die, to return, to learn anew, to remember what has always been?

And how did the Taliesins think about their own death? *The Primary Address of Taliesin*, BoT.1 , ends with the triumphant lines:

And before I desire the end of existence,
And before the broken foam shall come

upon my lips,
And before I become connected with
wooden boards,
May there be festivals to my soul!
Book-learning scarcely tells me
Of severe afflictions after death bed;
And such as have read my bardic books
They shall obtain the region of heaven, the
best of all abodes.

The term heaven is quite literal in this context. The otherworld is essentially extraterrestrial, and Taliesin is an extraterrestrial consciousness, like all of us who care to remember and understand. Cauldron of the deep, breath of inspiration, song of the Awen flowing from dark cells of song, revealing the unknown, reforming the world. The traveling heads go a long way. They are like berries. They must go through the surface to come back again. They go through the surface of the worlds to be with their fellows. Some of those who came, arrived in a disk of burning gold. They sought to make their homes on earth, but were driven away. So they went into the dark and hid beneath the hollow hills, under the waves, beneath the crust of the world. This is their dwelling place. Sometimes they come out and inhabit the hill of the body, incarnate in living flesh, behind a triple veil of forgetfulness. The stars are not out there. They are here, and earth is floating like a tiny jewel in their midst. If only we remember.

I have been in an uneasy chair
Above Caer Sidin,
And the whirling round without motion
Between three elements.
        (Hanes Taliesin, translated by Nash)

Taliesin's chair above Caer Sidin is above the galaxy itself, on the very border to the infinities beyond. Around and below him the whole universe revolves. As a guess, may I propose that Taliesin's seat is at the north star, the one motionless place in space, surrounded by the spinning whirls and eddies of the stellar wheel? This is the region of the summer stars, the land of the cherubim, the ancestral home of the bard. Other Taliesins referred to reincarnation. The *Hanes Taliesin* contains the line :

Three times have I been born, I know by meditation;

Only three times? Have three times ever been enough? How many initiations do we need to return to the simplicity and wonder of our very self?

Did the bards believe the Bedd Taliesin to be a grave or an initiation chamber, a dark cell where the burning intensity of the Awen could unhinge reason and unlock the word hoard of the initiate? As the legends have it, a person who spends a night at the Bedd Taliesin will be dead, insane or an inspired poet in the morning. It's something of a choice. To go down under stone. Into a tiny and dark cell. To rest on cold earth and under solid rock, the mind wide open to the inspiration burning visions in flaming glory across the blackness of the darknight solitude.

A very similar tale comes from one of Wales most beautiful mountains. Cader Idris, waterfalls cascading down its tree rimmed and meadow green flanks, crowned by a majestic pinnacle of greyish rock and purple heather, used to be the chair of the giant Idris, who ascended to the mountain top solitude with its refreshing gales to gaze into the infinity beyond our narrow world, and to study the dancing movement of the stars. Again, a cheerful folk-tradition claims that a night on the giant's seat will turn you into a corpse, a loony or a brilliant poet. Here we come upon a stimulating idea. In one case, the place of magical transformation is a dark and stony hole under the surface of the earth. In the other, high and exposed on a mountain under the sparkling canopy of heaven. These two orientations, to the height and depth, vaguely echo the primary direction of sacrifice in the earlier times, the Urn-field and Hallstatt people sacrificing to the gods of the height from windy rock pinnacles and stony mountain cliffs, and the La Tène Celts with their devotion to wells, pits, caves and cult shafts reaching deep into the sod. In our case, the poet is the sacrificer, but also the offering, and ultimately the receiver of the offering. Like Odin atop the wind swept tree, sacrificing *myself to myself*, s/he goes into the care of the greater spirits, intelligences and deities and emerges the next dawn severely damaged or highly inspired. Sometimes its hard to tell the difference.

Yet what are the damages actually about? The first option is death. In a literal sense, this is the end of incarnate existence. In a magical way, all initiation involves a certain death. This is not the death of the body, vehicle of consciousness, but the death of the earlier personality. The thief and beggar Gwion had to die before he could handle the impact of the Awen. Totally nameless, he had to drift on the waters of the great

sparkling sea, 40 years (this could explain the interval between Arthur's time, when Ceridwen set the cauldron cooking, and Maelgwn's time), or 40 weeks, the approximate length of a pregnancy. After refinement in the great deep, far beyond the glistening girdle of salty water and out in the darker fluids of stellar space, the ageless child returns ripe and perceptive to the world of men, to assume a name, a form, a destiny. This pattern is fundamental to most initiations. Death is one way to think of it. The metaphor is nice and dramatic. Another is simply a suspension of personality so that the new knowledge can pour into the cauldron of inspiration, right up there in your head.

There are many ways of inducing new insight, vision and illumination in a receptive a mind. Creativity and inspiration are always present. For those with a solid personality, who are well settled in their ways, dying is one way to go beyond the everyday human mind. Another approach is confusion, shock and overload. This leads to a state of temporary insanity, from which a new formation of habits, personality and belief emerge. Death in its ordinary, physical sense means that the initiation has failed, in its magical sense it is a sign of spiritual evolution. Insanity in its ordinary sense is blind and destructive. In the magical sense, all true art involves a measure of insanity, in that the artist explores the senses in an unusual way, and communicates this new experience to the audience. If art is any good, it takes you beyond what you perceived earlier. Death happens to the mind structures that define personality (the phantasm of I and its phantom counterpart,

All-otherness) and time-experience (past-present-future), madness happens to the models and belief we have regarding the world we be-live.

A true bard goes beyond both, like a hedge sitting witch crawling cautiously through labyrinths of thorns and blossoms to reach the otherworlds beyond. Viewed in this way, death and insanity are not accidents nor do they abort the initiatory process. They are merely side effects of a communion of self and sentience which shatters the human personality to rebuild a better vehicle for joy and genius. Bards are not always concerned with the bright side of nature. The dance of visions begins and ends in the twilight realm between form and absence, between life and death, in the place where two cataracts of wind fall and the bard's bones turn to mist.

The three choices are three paths leading wherever you will. Dead refers to solid states, insane to fluid perception, inspired to gaseous states of being and awareness. The same trinity, solid, fluid and gaseous runs like a red thread through the tangled byways of Island Celtic lore. In beast form, Gwion is chased over land, through water and finally air. The Awen combines knowledge, memory, habit for solid states; thinking, dreaming, experiment for fluid awareness and unites them in inspiration, art, illumination, the gaseous realm of experience. Awareness of the world around you tends to appear solid, experience of the inner worlds of dreaming and thinking more fluid, beyond both is reality, be it as total awareness or total lack of consciousness, in dreamless sleep. When going about your circuit, you dwell between sobriety, intoxication and pure perception, and daily life involves regular work, celebration and doing your true will. All of these, and more, are yours to enjoy. And before your tired flesh goes to rest under the mounds that the rains wet and the sun warms, and before your self goes voyaging along Gwydyon's stellar pathway through the spirals of infinity, high above Caer Sidin, let there be celebrations to your soul.

Beneath the hollow hills. Entrance at Cader Idris.

The boar knot.

Appendix

A rough time table regarding events mentioned in this book.

1200-800 BCE(?) Central European Urnfield culture, one of the possible ancestors of the Celtic culture.

800-450 BCE (?) Early Celtic Hallstatt culture.

450 to Roman occupation (?) Celtic La Tène culture.

600 BCE (?) The Greek Phokaii found a trading colony in the land of the Celtic Salluvi (Marseilles).

570-500 BCE Pythagoras of Samos, philosopher, mathematician, teacher of reincarnation.

387 BCE Celts under Brennus plunder Rome.

279 BCE Celts under Brennos plunder Greece and Macedonia.

278 BCE The Celtic Tolistobagi, Trokmeri and Tektosagi move into Asia Minor and blend to become the Galateans.

231 BCE the Celtic Insubres and Boii of northern Italy unite to fight Rome.

225 BCE total defeat of Insubres and Boii at Telamon. Last use of Celtic war-chariots on the Continent.

218 BCE Hannibal crosses the Alps with the help of the Celtic Allobroges to fight Rome.

197 and 196 BCE defeat of Hannibal and his Celtic allies.

121 BCE Rome occupies land north of the Alps and creates the province Gallia Narbonensis.

120 BCE (?) A huge horde of Teutones, Cimbri, Ambrones and a number of Celto-Germanic tribes move en masse from the north, center and south of Germany to find new living space in Gaul or elsewhere. Overpopulation and colder weather cause the migration.

113 BCE These tribes encounter the Romans north of the Alps, leading to various bloody battles. After some internal disputes, the tribes divide into two groups.

105 BCE The Teutones, Cimbri, Ambrones etc. defeat the Roman army at Orange.

102 BCE Teutones and Ambrones are destroyed by the Romans under Gaius Marius.

101 BCE The Cimbri are destroyed by Marius at Vercelli, Piemont.

70-19 BCE life of Vergilius Maro (Virgil), poet and author of the *Aeneid*.

58 BCE The Celtic tribe of the Helvetii (formerly inhabitants of southern Germany, later of Switzerland) under Orgetorix attempts to leave their territory in Switzerland to move to southern France. This provides Gaius Julius Caesar with an excuse for warfare outside of his legitimate domain.

59-49 BCE Julius Caesar conquers Gaul and pays a brief visit to Germany and Britain.

54 BCE Cassivellaunus leads the British against Iulius Caesar. His name appears as Caswallan fab Beli Mawr in bardic lore, but his tale is completely unhistorical.

15 BCE Celtic southern Germany is occupied by the Roman army.

-41 (?) Gaulish Druidry is forbidden for all Roman citizens (Suetonius)

40-50 (?) Pomponius Mela records that the rites of the Druids are no longer practised in Gaul.

41-51 Reign of emperor Claudius. Druidry is thoroughly suppressed.

43 Roman invasion of Britain.

60 Suetonius Paulinus raids the Druidic stronghold on Mona (Anglesey) and puts a stop to Druidry in Britain (Tacitus)

61 Uprising of queen Boudicca and the Iceni against the Romans ends in failure.

77 (?) Pliny records Druidic rites involving mistletoe, vervain, selago, samolus, cannibalism and the serpent egg. He states that the cult has been stopped.

83 The Limes (548 km of frontier-wall between Rhine and Danube) is begun under the reign of Domitian.

Late 2nd century Coligny calendar (used to be dated in the 1st century by early researchers)

3rd century (?) Reign of the semi-legendary Irish king Cormac Mac Airt

3rd century earliest ogham inscriptions in Ireland

235 Alexander Severus meets a Druidess in Gaul who prophecies doom for him.

258 The Alemanni, a union of Germanic-Celtic tribes breaks through the Limes, thereby ending the Roman occupation of central and southern Germany.

Late 3rd century Picts and Celtic tribes attempt to break through Hadrians Wall.

4th -6th century British settlers move across the channel and form Brittany, mainly to escape the Anglo-Saxon invasion.

312 Roman emperor Constantine becomes Christian

331 Start of persecution of pagan cults in the Roman empire.

337 Pagan sacrifices are officially outlawed in the Roman empire.

357 Pagan temples are closed in the Roman empire.

361 Emperor Julian abolishes Christianity and reintroduces paganism.

363 Julian dies, Christianity is reestablished but pagan religions are tolerated.

383 Magnus Maximus is declared emperor by his troops in Britain. He leaves Britain, taking along its last legions, and manages to conquer Gaul and Spain before being

defeated. His departure for the Continent leaves Britain defenseless so that the invasion of Anglo-Saxons resumes.

391 Emperor Eugenius usurps the western part of the empire and reestablishes paganism.

394 Emperor Theodosis disposes of Eugenius and enforces Christianity, prohibiting all pagan temples and sacrifices.

5th century Irish settlers occupy parts of northern Scotland.

5th century (?) Cunedda and his sons move from Scotland to Wales, where they successfully fight the Irish invaders and establish a royal house.

5th -6th century The British language develops into Cymric, Cornish, Bretonic and Kumbric.

5th century St. Patrick (Padraig, earlier Cothraig) converts the Irish and fights Druidry.

518 (?) Saxons defeated by Arthur at Mount Badon (*Annales Cambriae*).

539 (?) Arthur and Medrawd die after the futile battle of Camlan (*Annales Cambriae*).

540 (?) Gildas writes *The Ruin of Britain* and rages against the godless ways of the kings of Britain, especially against Maelgwn Gwyned, whom he seems to know personally.

560 (?) King Ida dies. Roughly contemporary with him are the leading lights of British poetry, the Cynfeirdd (early bards) namely Taliesin, Bluchbard, Talhaiarn Cataguen, Cian, Neirin, according to Nennius.

565 Death of Diarmait Mac Cerbail, last semi pagan king of Ireland.

573 Battle of Arfderydd. Gwenddoleu, last-semi pagan king of Britain dies and Myrddin goes mad and flees to the forest where he lives as a wild man, a shadow among shades.

590 At the uprising of Drumketta, the filid lose much of their power, their number is reduced.

597 Colum Cille (St. Columba) dies after converting the Picts of Scotland

600 (?) *Y Gododdin*. Battle of Catraeth. Neirin composes an elegy for the slain.

634 Cadwallawn defeats King Edwin and the Angles.

Late 7th century Cadwaladr fab Cadwallawn reigns over Gwynedd. In spite of Taliesin's predictions he does not unite the Island Celts against the Anglo-Saxons.

679 Cenn Faelad, first author of the *Auraicept Na N Eces* dies.

9th century (?) First version of the *Colloquy of the Two Sages* detailing the dispute of the two filid Ferchertne and Nede over the office of the highest ollam of Ireland.

830 (?) An anonymous author composes the *Historia Brittonum*. This influential work is later ascribed to Nennius.

850 (?) King Kenneth Mac Alpin unites the Picts (called Prydyn by the Welsh, Cruithin by the Irish) and the Scoti (Scottish Irish).

900 (?) Cormac Mac Cuilennain, bishop and king of Munster writes *Sanas Chormaic*, a glossary attempting to explain old and obscure words and names.

930 (?) A Taliesin composes the *Armes Prydein*, the greater Prophecy of Britain, which predicts a massive defeat of the Anglo-Saxons by the combined hosts of all Celtic lands plus the Vikings of Dublin.

11th century Virgil widely known as a powerful enchanter in popular folklore.

11th century Anonymous author invents or records the *Pedeir Ceinc Y Mabinogi, The Four Branches of the Mabinogi.*

1100 (?) *Lebor Gabala Erenn*, the *Book of Invasions* details the prehistory of Ireland. *Lebor Na Huidre (Book of the Dun Cow)*, earliest Irish collection of manuscripts, includes material from the mythological cycle, such as the history of shape-changing Tuan Mac Cairell who experienced most of Ireland's history in animal form, and *CuChullain's Sickbed or The Only Jealousy of Emer.*

1160 (?) *Lebor Laignech (Book of Leinster)*, manuscript containing versions of the *Tain Bo Cuailnge*, the *Dindsenchas* and several tales of the Ulster cycle.

1155 Death of Geoffrey of Monmouth, author of *The History of the Kings of Britain* and *The Life of Merlin.*

1160-1190 Chretien de Troyes writes his romances, including the unfinished *Perceval*. He introduces the figure of Lancelot.

1190 (?) Giraldus Cambrensis (Gerald of Wales 1146-1223) visits the wild west and writes a description of the country.

1191 Monks from Glastonbury pretend to discover the grave of Arthur and Guinevere.

1200 (?) Wolfram von Eschenbach rhymes his major work, the voluminous *Parzival* which combines old French and British sources with his own heretical vision of the Grail and its knights.

13th-17th century *Trioedd Ynys Prydein, The Welsh Triads*, a collection of triads of British mythology and pseudo-history. Probably these triads formed a list that was used by the bards as an aid in memorization.

13th century *Llyfr Du Caerfyrddin (Black Book of Carmarthen)* collection of heroic and religious poems and songs, mainly anonymous but occasionally ascribed to Llywarch Hen and the historical Myrddin (Merlin), both of whom lived in the 6th century.

early 14th century *Llyfr Taliessin (Book of Taliesin)*, incomplete collection of songs ascribed to one or more bards called Taliesin. Includes history, heroic praise poetry, prophecy, religious and Biblical matters, cosmology, mythological material. A few of the heroic eulogies come from the 6th century , the majority from the gogynfeirdd period century 11th -14th century.

14th century *Llyfr Gwyn Rhydderch (White Book of Rhydderch)* collection of ten tales (later published as the *Mabinogi*), religious texts, apocryphal items, hagiographies and Welsh translations of Latin texts.

14th century *Book of Ballymote, Yellow Book of Lecan* include the *Forbhais Droma Damhghaire*, i.e. the legend of the Druid Mog Ruith.

1400 (?) *Llyfr Coch Hergest (Red Book of Hergest)* extensive collection of eleven tales (later published as the *Mabinogi*), poetry, proverbs, treatises on medicine, grammar etc.

1450-1470 sitting in prison, Sir Thomas Malory retells a number of French romances in his voluminous *Morte D'Arthur*, an influential work on Arthur which did much to produce the myth of fantastic chivalry.

1626-1697 John Aubrey, author and scholar, inventor of the misleading theory that the megalithic monuments are of Druidic origin.

1687-1765 William Stukeley, doctor of medicine and scholar, identifies Stonehenge and Avebury as Druidic temples and starts a popular fashion.

1747-1826 Edward Williams (Iolo Morgannwg), stonesmith, collector, scholar, forger and enthusiastic visionary, founder of the Bardic Order of the Isle of Britain (1792).

1760-1765 James Macpherson publishes his forgeries as the works of the legendary poet Ossian which influence the romantic idea of Celtic mythology.

1792 Beginning of the bardic revival.

1838-1849 Lady Charlotte Guest (1812-1895) publishes her translation of the *Mabinogi* containing tales from the *Red Book of Hergest* and the *Hanes Taliesin* from the manuscripts of Elis Gruffydd (c1490-1552) and Llewelyn Sion.

1858 First semi-reliable translation of Taliesin by Nash.

1862 *Barddas* published, MS. by E. Williams, edited by W. ab Ithel

1868 William Skene (1809-1892) publishes the first reliable translation of *The four ancient Books of Wales*.

1948 Poet Robert Graves publishes *The White Goddess*, an inspiring but thoroughly unreliable and misleading study on a triple moon goddess of his own invention. The book has an immense influence on popular Neo-Celticistic dogma and modern pagan religion.

Appendix 2. Language and Sources

British before the 5th or 6th century (rare inscriptions and names in Latin texts).

Early Cymric 6th -8th century (inscriptions).

Old Cymric 8th -12th century (Names, glosses in Latin and Anglo-Saxon texts, very few manuscripts).

Middle Cymric 12th -14th century (numerous Manuscripts).

New Cymric after 14th century.

Early Irish before the 8th century (ogham inscriptions).

Old Irish 8th-9th century (glosses in Latin texts).

Middle Irish 9th- 13th century (numerous manuscripts, generally recorded after the 11th century).

Early new Irish 14th -16th century.

New Irish 17th century.

Bibliography

Derek **Allen**, *The Coins of the Ancient Celts*, Edinburgh University Press, 1980

The American Heritage Dictionary of the English Language, Appendix Indo-European Roots, Houghton Mifflin, Boston, 1981

Ancient Irish Tales, trans. & edited T. **Cross** & C. **Slover**, Barnes & Noble, New York 1996

William **Anderson**, *Green Man*, Harpercollins, London 1990

Aneirin, *The Gododdin*, trans. Steve Short, Llanerch Publishers, Felinfach, 1994

Archäologische Ausgrabungen in Baden-Württemberg, Theiss Verlag, Stuttgart 1981

Robert **Bain**, *The Clans and Tartans of Scotland*, Collins, Glasgow & London 1968

Richard **Bandler**, *Using your Brain for a Change*, Real People Press, Moab 1985

Richard **Bandler**, *Time for a Change*, Meta Publications, Cupertino, Cal, 1993

Richard **Bandler** & John **Grinder**, *Trance-formations*, Real People Press, Moab, 1981

Richard **Bandler** & John **Grinder**, *Patterns of the Hypnotic Techniques of Milton H. Erickson, M.D.*, Vol 1, Meta Publications, Cupertino, Cal. 1975

Bede, *Ecclesiastical History of the English People*, Penguin, London, 1990

Michael **Bertiaux**, *The Voudon Gnostic Workbook*, Magickal Childe, NY, 1988

Helmut **Bode**, *Frankfurter Sagenschatz*, Kramer Verlag, Frankfurt, 1978

James **Bonwick**, *Irish Druids and Old Irish Religions*, Dorset Press, 1986, (1894)

Robert de **Boron**, *Merlin-Künder des Grals*, trans. Sandkühler, Ogham Verlag, Stuttgart, 1980

Andrew **Breeze**, *Sion Cent, The Oldest Animals and the Day of Man's Life*, Bulletin of the

Board of Celtic Studies, Univ. of Wales Press, vol. 34, 1987

Katharine **Briggs**, *An Encyclopedia of Fairies*, Pantheon, New York, 1976

Jean-Louis **Brunaux**, *Les Gaulois, Sanctuaires et Rites*, Edition Errance, Paris 1986

Jean-Louis **Brunaux**, *Die keltischen Heiligtümer Nordfrankreichs*, Heiligtümer und Opferkulte der Kelten, Theiss Verlag, Stuttgart 1995

Gaius Iulius **Caesar**, *Der Gallische Krieg*, Reclam, Stuttgart, 1980

John **Carey**, *A Tuath De Miscellany*, Bulletin of the Board of Celtic Studies, Univ. of Wales Press, vol. 39, 1992

Alexander **Carmichael**, *Carmina Gadelica*, Floris Books, Edinburgh, 1992 (1899)

Jon B. **Coe** & Simon **Young**, *The Celtic Sources for Arthurian Legend*, Llanerch Publishers, Felinfach, 1995

Das Rätsel der Kelten vom Glauberg, catalogue, Theiss, Stuttgart, 2002.

Thomas **Costain**, *The Pageant of England 1135-1216*, Tandem, London, 1973

John **Davies**, *A History of Wales*, Penguin, London, 1994

Jonathan **Davies**, *Folk-Lore of West and Mid-Wales*, Llanerch Publishers, Felinfach, 1992 (1911)

Die Keltenfürsten vom Glauberg, F. **Herrmann**, O. **Frey**, Archäologische Denkmäler in Hessen, Wiesbaden 1996

Myles **Dillon**, *Early Irish Literature*, Four Courts Press, Blackrock, 1994 (1948)

Hans Ferdinant **Döbler**, *Die Germanen*, Prisma Verlag 1975

Eactra An Madra Maoil, The Story of the Crop-Eared Dog, Eactra Macaoim-An-Iolair, The Story of Eagle Boy, trans. R. Stewart **Macalister**, Irish Texts Society, London, 1908

Edda, transl. **Simrock**, Phaidon, Essen, 1987 (1876)

Jérome **Edou**, *Machig Labdrön and the Foundations of Chöd*, Snow Lion Publications, Ithaca, N.Y. 1996

Ein frühkeltischer Fürstengrabhügel am Glauberg im Wetteraukreis, Hessen, F. **Herrmann**, O. **Frey**, A. **Bartel**, A. **Kreuz**, M. **Rösch**, Archäologische Gesellschaft in Hessen, Wiesbaden, 1998

Milton H. **Erickson**, E. & S. **Rossi**, *Hypnotic Realities*, Irvington Publishers, NY, 1976

Milton H. **Erickson**, E. **Rossi**, *Hypnotherapy, An Exploratory Casebook*, Irvington Publishers, NY,

1979

Alvaro **Estrada**, *Maria Sabina*, Trikont Verlag, München, 1981

Ludwig **Ettmüller**, *Altnordischer Sagenschatz*, (Saxo G.), Magnus, Stuttgart, no year

Eugen **Fehrle**, *Zauber und Segen*, Eugen Diederichs Verlag, Jena 1926

S. **Fischer-Fabian**, *Die ersten Deutschen*, Droemersche Verlagsanstalt, München, 1975

Forbhais Droma Damhghaire, The Siege of Knocklong, trans. Sean **O'Duinn**, Mercier Press, Dublin, 1992

Sir J. G. **Frazer**, *The Golden Bough*, Macmillan Press, London, abridged edition, 1978

Jan **Fries**, *Visual Magick*, Mandrake of Oxford, 1992

Jan **Fries**, *Helrunar*, Mandrake of Oxford, 1993,

Jan **Fries**, *Seidways*, Mandrake of Oxford, 1996

Jan **Fries**, *Living Midnight*, Mandrake of Oxford, 1998

Jeffrey **Gantz**, *Early Irish Myths and Sagas*, Penguin, London, 1981

Gerald of Wales, *The Journey Through Wales, The Description of Wales*, trans. L. **Thorpe**, Penguin, London, 1978

Gerald of Wales, *The History and Topography of Ireland*, trans. J. **O'Meara**, Penguin, London, 1982

Michael **Gershon**, *The Second Brain*, HarperCollins, N.Y. 1998

Gold der Helvetier, Catalogue, Schweizerisches Landesmuseum, Zürich, 1991

Wolfgang **Golther**, *Handbuch der germanischen Mythologie*, Magnus, Kettwig, 1987 (1908)

Robert **Graves**, *The White Goddess*, 1948, 1976, German trans. Rowohlt, Hamburg, 1985

Miranda **Green**, *Celtic Art*, Calmann & King, London, 1996

Toby **Griffen**, *Names from the Dawn of British Legend*, Llanerch Publishers, Felinfach,1994

Jakob & Wilhelm **Grimm**, *Deutsche Sagen*, Insel Verlag, Frankfurt 1981 (1818)

Jakob & Wilhelm **Grimm**, *Die wahren Märchen der Brüder Grimm*, (ed. Rölleke), Fischer Verlag, Frankfurt 1989 (early tales, 1810, 1812, 1856)

Robert **Gurney**, *Bardic Heritage*, Chatto & Windus, London, 1969

Alfred **Haffner**, *Allgemeine Übersicht*, Heiligtümer und Opferkulte der Kelten, Theiss Verlag, Stuttgart 1995

Jay **Haley**, *Conversations with Milton H. Erickson, M.D., Vol 2*, Triangle Press, NY & London, 1985

Joan **Halifax**, *Shamanic Voices*, Penguin, London, 1979

Herodot, *Historien*, Kröner Verlag, Stuttgart, 1971

Wolfram von **Eschenbach**, *Parzival*, Langen Müller, 1993

Harald **Haarmann**, *Universalgeschichte der Schrift*, Campus, Frankfurt 1991

Herkunftswörterbuch Etymologie, Duden #7, Duden Verlag, Mannheim 1989

F. **Herrmann**, *Die Vorgeschichte Hessens*, Theiss, Stuttgart, 1990

Hessische Sagen, ed. Ulf **Diederichs**, Diederichs Verlag, Köln, 1978

Peter **Hunter-Blair**, *Roman Britain and Early England*, Sphere, London, 1969 (1963)

Peter **Hunter-Blair**, *An Introduction to Anglo-Saxon England*, Cambridge Univ. Press, 1977

Ronald **Hutton**, *The Pagan Religions of the Ancient British Isles*, Blackwell Publishers, Oxford 1993

Ronald **Hutton**, *The Stations of the Sun*, Oxford University Press, 1996

Ronald **Hutton**, *The Triumph of the Moon*, Oxford University Press, 1999

Douglas **Hyde**, *A Literary History of Ireland*, Benn, London, 1967 (1899)

Irische Volksmärchen, Diederichs Verlag, München, 1962

Kenneth **Jackson**, *Studies in Early Celtic Nature Poetry*, Llanerch Publishers, Felinfach, 1995 (1935)

W. **Joyce**, *Old Celtic Romances*, Talbot Press, Dublin, 1961 (1879)

T. **Kendrick**, *The Druids*, Methuen, London, 1927

Rolf **Ködderitzsch**, *Die grosse Felsinschrift von Penalba de Villastar*, in Sprachwissenschaftliche Forschungen, Festschrift für Johann Knobloch, Innsbruck 1985

M. **König**, *Am Anfang der Kultur*, Ullstein Verlag, Frankfurt, 1981

Martin **Kuckenburg**, *Vom Steinzeitlager zur Keltenstadt*, Theiss, Stuttgart, 2000

Raymond **Lamont-Brown**, *Chambers Scottish Superstitions*, Edinburgh, 1990

Doris **Laudert**, *Mythos Baum*, BLV, München, 1999

Thierry **Lejars**, *Archeologie Aujourd'hui, Gournay III, Les Fourreaux D'epee*, Edition Errance, Paris 1994

Lancelot **Lengyel**, *Das geheime Wissen der Kelten*, Bauer Verlag, Freiburg, 1976

Brigitte **Lescure**, *Das kelto-ligurische Heiligtum von Roquepertuse*, Heiligtümer und Opferkulte der Kelten, Theiss Verlag, Stuttgart 1995

Carl **Lofmark**, *Bards and Heroes,* Llanerch Publishers, Felinfach, 1989

Roger **Loomis**, *Celtic Myth and Arthurian Romance*, Constable, London, 1993 (1926)

Roger **Loomis**, *The Grail*, Constable, London, 1992 (1963)

Herbert **Lorenz**, *Bemerkungen zum Totenbrauchtum*, in: Die Kelten in Mitteleuropa, Catalogue, Keltenmuseum Hallein, Salzburg 1980

Lucan, *The Civil War / Pharsalia*, tran. Rowe, Everyman, London, 1998 (1719)

Märchen aus Schottland, ed. H. **Aitken**, Diederichs, München, 1965

Bernhard **Maier**, *Lexikon der keltischen Religion und Kultur*, Kröner Verlag, Stuttgart 1994

Ferdinand **Maier**, *Das Heidetränk - Oppidum*, Theiss, Stuttgart, 1985

Caitlin and John **Matthews**, *The Encyclopaedia of Celtic Wisdom*, Element, Shaftesbury, 1994

John **Matthews**, *Taliesin*, Aquarian Press, London, 1991

John **Matthews** (editor), *A Celtic Reader*, Thorsons, London, 1995

F. Marian **McNeill**, *The Silver Bough*, Vol. I, Maclellan, Glasgow, 1957

Sir Thomas **Malory**, *Morte D'Artur*, Insel Verlag, Leipzig, 1973

R. & V. **Megaw**, *Celtic Art*, Thames and Hudson, London, 1990

Wolfgang **Meid**, *Gaulish inscriptions*, Archaeolingua, Budapest 1992

Wolfgang **Meid**, *Celtiberian Inscriptions*, Archaeolingua, Budapest 1994

Wolfgang **Meid**, *Die keltische Sprache und Literaturen*, Archaeolingua, Budapest 1997

Otto **Milfait**, *Verehrung von Quelle und Baum im Mühlviertel*, Verlag Denkmayr, Gallneukirchen 1990

Geoffrey of **Monmouth**, *Vita Merlini*, trans. Inge Vielhauer, Castrum Peregrini Presse, Amsterdam, 1964

Geoffrey of **Monmouth**, *The History of the Kings of Britain*, trans. L. Thorpe, Penguin, 1966

Daphne **Nash**, *Coinage in the Celtic World*, Seaby, London, 1987

D. W. **Nash**, *Taliesin or the Bards and Druids of Britain*, J. Russel Smith, 1858

Nema, *Maat Magick*, Weiser, NY 1995

Nema, *The Way of Mystery. Magick, Mysticism & Self* - Transcendence, Llewellyn, St. Paul, 2003

Birgit **Neuwald**, *Germanen und Germanien in römischen Quellen*, Phaidon, Kettwig, 1991

Elias **Owen**, *Welsh Folk-Lore*, Llanerch Publishers, Felinfach, 1976 (1887)

Eugene **O'Curry**, *On the Manners and Customs of the Ancient Irish*, Williams and Norgate 1873, in Matthews 1995

Ludwig **Pauli**, *Keltischer Volksglaube*, C.H.Beck'sche Verlagsbuchhandlung, München 1975

Ludwig Pauli, *Die Herkunft der Kelten, Das keltische Mitteleuropa, Der Dürrnberg und die keltische Welt*, in: Die Kelten in Mitteleuropa, Catalogue, Keltenmuseum Hallein, Salzburg 1980

Leander **Petzold**, *Sagen*, Diederichs, München, 1992

Heidi Peter - Röcher, Mythos Menschenfresser, Beck, München, 1998

H. **Pleticha** & O. **Schönberger**, *Die Römer*, Gondrom, Bindlach 1992

Pliny the Elder, *Natural History*, Penguin, London, 1991

Plutarch, *Große Griechen und Römer*, Propyläen Verlag, Berlin, no year

J. **Pokorny**, *Altkeltische Dichtungen*, Bern 1944

Jane **Pugh**, *Welsh Witches and Warlocks*, Gwasg Carreg Gwalch, Llanrwst 1987

Qu Yuan, *The Songs of the South*, trans. David Hawkes, Penguin, London1985

Christian **Rätsch**, *Lexikon der Zauberpflanzen*, VMA Verlag, Wiesbaden, 1988

A. & B. **Rees**, *Celtic Heritage*, Thames and Hudson, London, 1961

S. Rieckhoff, J. Biel, Die Kelten in Deutschland, Theiss, Stuttgart, 2001

T. W. **Rolleston**, *Myths and Legends of the Celtic Race*, Lemma Publishing, NY 1974 (1934)

Ann **Ross**, *Pagan Celtic Britain*, Constable, London, 1992

E. I. **Rowlands**, *Bardic Lore and Education*, Bulletin of the Board of Celtic Studies, Univ. of

Wales Press, vol. 32, 1985

Denny **Sargent**, *Global Ritualism*, Llewellyn, St. Paul, 1994

Karl H. **Schmidt**, *Zur keltiberischen Inschrift von Botorrita*, Bulletin of the Board of Celtic Studies, Univ. of Wales Press, vol. 26, 1976

Karl H. **Schmidt**, *The Gaulish Inscription of Chamalieres*, Bulletin of the Board of Celtic Studies, Univ. of Wales Press, vol. 29, 1981

R. **Schultes** & A. **Hofman**, *Plants of the Gods*, MacGraw-Hill, Maidenhead 1979

Arthur **Scott**, *The Saxon Age*, Scott & Finlay, London, 1979

Gavin W. **Semple**, *Zos-Kia. An Introductory Essay on the Art and Sorcery of Austin Osman Spare*, Fulgur, London 1995

Francisco Marco **Simon**, *Die Religion im keltischen Hispanien*, Archaeolingua, Budapest 1998

William **Skene**, *The Four Ancient Books of Wales*, Edmonston and Douglas, Edinburgh, 1868

Lewis **Spence**, *Celtic Britain*, Parragon, Bristol, 1998 (1929)

Konrad **Spindler**, *Die frühen Kelten*, Reclam, Stuttgart, 1983

Charles **Squire**, *Celtic Myth and Legend*, Newcastle Publishing, Van Nuys, Cal. 1975 (1905)

Ian M. **Stead**, *Die Schatzfunde von Snettisham*, Heiligtümer und Opferkulte der Kelten, Theiss Verlag, Stuttgart 1995

Alfred **Stolz**, *Schamanen: Ekstase und Jenseitssymbolik*, Du mont, Köln, 1988

Cornelius **Tacitus**, *Sämtliche erhaltenen Werke*, trans. Bötticher & Schaefer, Phaidon, Essen

Taliesin, in *The Shrine of Wisdom*, vol. 12, No. 48, London 1931

Taliesin Poems, trans. Meirion **Pennar**, Llanerch Publishers, Felinfach, 1988

The Black Book of Carmarthen, trans. Meirion **Pennar**, Llanerch Publishers, Felinfach, 1989

The Book of Kells, Sir Edward **Sullivan**, Studio Editions, London, 1986

The Tain, trans. Thomas **Kinsella**, Oxford University Press, 1970

Rudolf **Thurneysen**, *Keltische Sagen*, Insel Verlag, Frankfurt/M, 1991

Nikolai **Tolstoy**, *The Coming of the King*, Corgi, London, 1989

Nikolai **Tolstoy**, *The Quest for Merlin*, Hamilton, London 1985

Henri De La **Tours**, *Atlas de Monnaies Gauloises*, Revue Archeologique Sites, Avignon 1982

Trioedd Ynys Prydein, The Welsh Triads, trans. Rachel **Bromwich**, Univ. of Wales Press, Cardiff, 1961

Christina **Uhsadel-Gülke**, *Knochen und Kessel*, Beiträge zur klassischen Philologie 43, Verlag Anton Hain, Meisenheim 1972

August **Verleger**, *Taunus Sagen*, Hirschgraben Verlag, Frankfurt, 1960

Virgil, *The Aeneid*, trans. Jackson **Knight**, Penguin, London, 1958

Günther **Wieland**, *Die spätkeltischen Viereckschanzen in Süddeutschland-Kultanlagen oder Rechteckhöfe?* Heiligtümer und Opferkulte der Kelten, Theiss Verlag, Stuttgart 1995

Christoph **Willms**, *Der Keltenfürst von Frankfurt*, catalogue, Museum für Vor- und Frühgeschichte, Frankfurt, 2002

Hans - Jürgen **Wolf**, *Hexenwahn*, Gondrom, Bindlach, 1994

Juliette **Wood**, *The Folklore Background of the Gwion Bach Section of the Hanes Taliesin*, Bulletin of the Board of Celtic Studies, Univ. of Wales Press, vol. 29, 1982

Juliette **Wood**, *Versions of Hanes Taliesin by Owen John and Lewis Morris*, Bulletin of the Board of Celtic Studies, Univ. of Wales Press, vol. 29, 1981

Ifor **Williams**, *The Poems of Taliesin*, Dublin Institute of Advanced Studies, 1968

W. B. **Yeats** (editor), *Fairy and Folk Tales of Ireland*, Colin Smythe, Gerrards Cross, 1973 (1888, 1892)

Index

CPSIA information can be obtained
at www.ICGtesting.com
Printed in the USA
FFOW02n1924230115
10476FF